KU-094-810

Lerwick

Kirkwall

Wick

YORKSHIRE AND THE HUMBER REGION
Pages 380–413

NORTHUMBRIA
Pages 414–429

LANCASHIRE AND THE LAKES
Pages 354–379

erland

LONDON
Pages 70–155

THE HEART OF ENGLAND
Pages 306–329

EAST MIDLANDS
Pages 330–343

rk

Kingston upon Hull

field

ANDS

Nottingham

cester

ntry

Cambridge

Northampton

Ipswich

Luton

rd

LONDON

UTHEAST ENGLAND   Dover

ampton

rtsmouth   Brighton

THE DOWNS AND CHANNEL COAST
Pages 164–189

THAMES VALLEY
Pages 216–237

EAST ANGLIA
Pages 190–215

EYEWITNESS TRAVEL

Portrait of
Britain

EYEWITNESS TRAVEL

Portrait of
Britain

MAIN CONTRIBUTOR: MICHAEL LEAPMAN

LONDON, NEW YORK, MELBOURNE, MUNICH AND DELHI
www.dk.com

ART EDITOR Stephen Bere
PROJECT EDITOR Marian Broderick
EDITORS Carey Combe, Sara Harper, Elaine Harries,
Kim Inglis, Ella Milroy, Andrew Szudek, Nia Williams
DESIGNERS Susan Blackburn, Elly King,
Colin Loughrey, Andy Wilkinson

CONTRIBUTORS
Josie Barnard, Christopher Catling,
Juliet Clough, Lindsay Hunt, Polly Phillimore,
Martin Symington, Roger Thomas

MAPS
Jane Hanson, Phil Rose, Jennifer Skelley (Lovell Johns Ltd)
Gary Bowes (Era-Maptec Ltd)

PHOTOGRAPHERS
Joe Cornish, Paul Harris, Rob Reichenfeld, Kim Sayer

ILLUSTRATORS
Gary Cross, Richard Draper, Jared Gilby (Kevin Jones Assocs),
Paul Guest, Roger Hutchins, Chris Orr & Assocs,
Maltings Partnership, Ann Winterbotham, John Woodcock

Reproduced by Colourscan (Singapore)
Printed and bound by South China Printing Co. Ltd., China

First published in Great Britain in 2010
by Dorling Kindersley Limited
80 Strand, London WC2R 0RL

Copyright 1995, 2010 © Dorling Kindersley Limited, London
A Penguin Company

THIS BOOK IS AN ABBREVIATED EDITION OF
DK EYEWITNESS TRAVEL GUIDE: GREAT BRITAIN, PUBLISHED IN 2010.

A CIP catalogue record is available from the British Library.

ISBN 978 1 4053 6116 3

This edition produced for The Book People Ltd,
Hall Wood Avenue, Haydock, St Helens, WA11 9UL

Floors are referred to throughout in accordance with British
usage; ie, the "first floor" is above ground level.

Front cover main image: Sunset at Hadrian's Wall, Northumberland.

MIX
Paper from
responsible sources
FSC
www.fsc.org   FSC™ C018179

CONTENTS

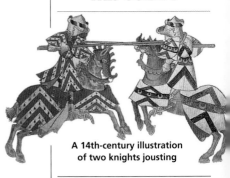

**A 14th-century illustration
of two knights jousting**

INTRODUCING GREAT BRITAIN

Beefeater at the Tower of London

LONDON

Eilean Donan Castle on Loch Duich in the Scottish Highlands

Jacobean "Old House" in Hereford

Cliffs of the Pembrokeshire Coast National Park

Renaissance roundel from Stirling Castle

HOW TO USE THIS GUIDE

This book is a visual celebration of the very best of Britain's cities, landscapes and rich cultural heritage. It provides both detailed practical information and expert recommendations for visitors and armchair traveller alike. The chapter entitled *Introducing Great Britain* maps the country and sets it in its historical and cultural context. The six regional chapters, plus *London*, profile all the major places of interest using maps, cutaway artworks and photographs. Features cover topics from famous houses and gardens to culinary delights and sporting heritage.

LONDON

The centre of London has been divided into four sightseeing areas. Each has its own chapter, which opens with a list of the sights described. The last section, *Further Afield*, covers the most attractive suburbs. All sights are numbered and plotted on an area map. The information for each sight follows the map's numerical order, making sights easy to locate within the chapter.

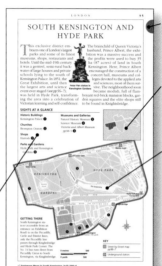

Sights at a Glance lists the chapter's sights by category: Historic Streets and Buildings; Museums and Galleries; Churches and Cathedrals; Shops; Parks and Gardens.

All pages relating to London have red thumb tabs.

A locator map shows where you are in relation to other areas of the city centre.

1 Area Map
For easy reference, the sights are numbered and located on a map. Sights in the city centre are also marked on the Street Finder *on pages 127–47.*

2 Street-by-Street Map
This gives a bird's-eye view of the key areas in each chapter.

Stars indicate the sights that no visitor should miss.

A suggested route for a walk is shown in red.

3 Detailed information
The sights in London are described individually. Addresses, telephone numbers, opening hours, admission charges, tours and wheelchair access are also provided, as well as public transport links.

1 Introduction
The landscape, history and character of each region is outlined here, showing how the area has developed over the centuries and what it has to offer the visitor today.

GREAT BRITAIN AREA BY AREA
Apart from London, Great Britain has been divided into 14 regions, each of which has a separate chapter. The most interesting towns and places to visit have been numbered on a *Regional Map*.

Each area of Great Britain can be identified quickly by its colour coding, shown on the inside front cover.

2 Regional Map
This shows the main road network and gives an illustrated overview of the whole region. All entries are numbered and there are also useful tips on getting around the region by car, train and other forms of transport.

3 Detailed information
All the important sights, towns and other places to visit are described individually. They are listed in order, following the numbering on the Regional Map. Within each entry, there is detailed information on important buildings and other sights.

Story boxes explore related topics.

For all the top sights, a Visitors' Checklist provides the practical information you need to plan your visit.

4 The top sights
These are given one or more full pages. Three-dimensional illustrations reveal the interiors of historic buildings. Interesting town and city centres are given street-by-street maps, featuring individual sights.

INTRODUCING GREAT BRITAIN

DISCOVERING GREAT BRITAIN

Each one of Great Britain's counties, that have grown out of kingdoms, principalities, shires, fiefs, boroughs, and parishes, has its own special flavour. This derives from Britain's landscape, its resources and its history, all of which have shaped its peoples, too.

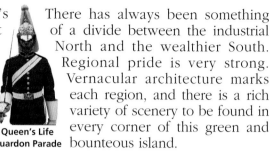
Queen's Life Guardon Parade

There has always been something of a divide between the industrial North and the wealthier South. Regional pride is very strong. Vernacular architecture marks each region, and there is a rich variety of scenery to be found in every corner of this green and bounteous island.

A view of Big Ben and the London Eye

LONDON

- **A ride on the London Eye**
- **Majestic parks**
- **World-class museums**

Britain's capital can be enjoyed in all weathers. So many buildings, from **Big Ben** *(see p77)* to the **Tower of London** *(see pp118–19)*, are emblematic of the city. To get an overview take a bus riverboat or the **London Eye** *(see p81)*; visit the West End for the most exciting shops, or stroll through its lovely parks. The **National Gallery** *(see p82–3)* is one of the finest art museums in the world, the **British Museum** *(see pp106–7)* and **Victoria and Albert Museum** *(see pp98–9)* are storehouses of treasures while **Tate Modern** *(see 121)* has set a standard for contemporary art.

THE DOWNS AND CHANNEL COAST

- **Great days out from London**
- **Fairytale castles**
- **Brighton's brilliant sea front**

This is "The Garden of England", green and rural, with rolling Downs. Many places in this corner of the country are accessible on a day trip from London; **Hampton Court** *(see p173)* and **Leeds Castle** *(see p189)* are favourite excursions. Many estates have connections with great figures from history: Winston Churchill's **Chartwell** *(see p188)*, Queen Victoria's **Osborne** *(see p168)* on the Isle of Wight and J.M.W. Turner's **Petworth** *(see p172)*, an antiques-hunters' paradise. Ancient cathedrals rise from **Chichester** *(see pp171)*, **Winchester** *(see pp170–1)* and **Canterbury** *(see pp186–7)*, which has many tales to tell. Breezy resorts dot the coast. The liveliest is **Brighton** *(see pp174–9)*, known as "London-on-Sea", with its famous Lanes, Palace Pier and seafront promenade.

Punting on the River Cam past King's College Chapel, Cambridge

EAST ANGLIA

- **A punt in Cambridge**
- **Magnificent Ely Cathedral**
- **A day at the races**

This part of the country grew wealthy on the wool trade and its merchants built fabulous half-timbered houses and pretty towns such as **Lavenham** *(see p206)*. In the charming university town of Cambridge *(see p210–15)* try

The promenade and Palace Pier, Brighton, Sussex

◁ *Salisbury Cathedral: from the meadows* by John Constable (1776–1837)

punting on the Backs with the students or, for a less vigourous outing, admire **King's College Chapel** *(see p212–13)*. For another cultural high, visit **Ely Cathedral** *(see pp194–5)*. Spend a day at the races at **Newmarket** *(see p207)*, or visit **Aldeburgh** *(see pp202–203)* during its prestigious annual music festival. The ports on the lovely coast provide seafood for your table.

THAMES VALLEY

- **Attractive riverside pubs**
- **Oxford's dreaming spires**
- **Imposing Blenheim Palace**

The River Thames has long been a pleasure ground. The riverside, from London's outer suburbs to **Windsor** *(see pp235–7)*, **Oxford** *(see pp222–7)* and beyond, has many appealing waterside pubs and restaurants located in attractive towns. Boats can be hired, and the annual rowing regatta at **Henley-on-Thames** *(see p63 and p66)* is the height of the summer season. No wonder that the song of Britain's most exclusive private school, Eton *(see p235)*, which is located by the river, is *The Eton Boating Song*. **Windsor Castle** *(see pp236–7)* is undoubtedly a main draw, easily reached in a day trip from London, as are the beautiful colleges of **Oxford University** *(see pp226–7)*. Not far away are other historic places to visit, including the Churchill family home at **Blenheim Palace** *(see*

Stonehenge, Wiltshire, Great Britain's famous prehistoric monument

pp228–9), the Duke of Bedford's **Woburn Abbey** *(see p230)* and **Stowe** *(see p230)*, which has one of the most magnificent gardens in England.

WESSEX

- **Mysterious Stonehenge**
- **Cheddar cheese and Taunton Cider**
- **Fine architecture in Bath and Salisbury**

The former kingdom of the West Saxons echoes with history and legends. Here are some of the most important Neolithic sites in the country, including the mysterious and magnificent **Stonehenge** *(see pp262–3)*. This is the country of good living, with Cheddar cheese from around the Cheddar Gorge, and Somerset cider. The Georgian spa town of **Bath** *(see pp258–61)* makes an excellent centre to explore the region. There are two coasts – in the north on the Bristol Channel and in the south on the English channel where **Poole** *(see pp270–1)* is a great yachting centre. Bath, **Wells** *(see pp252–3)* and **Salisbury** *(see pp264–5)* all have outstanding cathedrals. There are wild animals at **Longleat** *(see p266)*, wild landscapes on **Exmoor National Park** *(see pp250–1)*, while the **Glastonbury** *(see pp253)* music festival attracts fans in their thousands.

A view of Blenheim Palace, Woodstock, Oxfordshire

DEVON AND CORNWALL

- **Surfing fit for champions**
- **Seafood and cream teas**
- **Fabulous gardens**

Britain's best beaches are in the West Country, some of which have high cliffs and waves worthy of champion surfers. Its fishing villages have long attracted artists, in particular St Ives, where the **Tate St Ives** gallery *(see p277)* can be visited. Seafood is plentiful, and rich pasture-lands brings dairy ice-cream and cream teas. Seafaring is a way of life, as the **National Maritime Museum Cornwall** *(see pp280–1)* in Falmouth attests. **Bodmin Moor** *(see pp284–5)* and **Dartmoor** *(see p81)* present an untamed wilderness but some fine gardens are here, too, including the **Eden Project** *(see pp282–3)*.

Eden Project, Cornwall, a garden for the 21st century

THE HEART OF ENGLAND

- Shakespeare's birthplace
- Typically English Cotswold villages
- Half-timbered border towns

There is a great mix of attractions in this region where the Industrial Revolution began *(see pp314–15)*. The most popular sites are **Warwick Castle** *(see pp322–3)* and Shakespeare's birthplace in **Stratford-upon-Avon** *(see pp324–5)*. Cotswold villages built of golden limestone are quintessentially English. Other lovely rural spots include the Malvern Hills and the Wye Vallley. Attractive architecture distinguishes the half-timbered Welsh border towns including the city of **Chester** *(see pp310–11)*.

Anne Hathaway's cottage, Stratford-upon-Avon, Warwickshire

EAST MIDLANDS

- Chatsworth, a fine country house
- Great walking in the Peak District
- Buxton spa and opera house

One of the most impressive country houses, **Chatsworth** *(see pp334–5)*, is a high spot of this region. It sits at the edge of the **Peak District** *(see pp338–9)*, a popular area for walking. There are several attractive towns such as **Buxton** *(see p334)*, a spa town with an opera house while **Lincoln** *(see pp340–1)* has medieval buildings and a fine cathedral.

Mist on Rydal Water, Lake District, Cumbria

LANCASHIRE AND THE LAKES

- England at its most picturesque
- Liverpool, maritime city of Empire
- Manchester, capital of the North

The **Lake District** *(see pp352–68)* is where walking as an activity rather than a chore began, and you will see why when you encounter the stunning scenery of fells and lakes. Serious walkers put on their waterproofs and boots, while Sunday strollers hire row boats, or look in at Dove Cottage, where the poets William and Dorothy Wordsworth lived. To the south is **Liverpool** *(see pp354–5)*, a Unesco World Heritage city, with wonderful architecture and great art galleries. **Blackpool** *(see p371)* is the main resort, known for its illuminations. Inland is **Manchester** *(see pp372–5)* England's second largest city.

YORKSHIRE AND THE HUMBER REGION

- Haunting abbey ruins
- The Brontë sisters' dramatic moors
- The ancient city of York

Yorkshire is known for its striking moors, which the literary Brontë sisters of **Haworth** *(see p412)* knew so well. It is also known for its great abbeys, such as **Fountains** *(see pp390–1)*, **Rievaulx** *(see p393)* and **Whitby** *(see p396)*, which were reduced to haunting ruins after the English church broke from Rome. **York Minster** *(see pp406–407)* remains the most important church in the north and the ancient town is worth exploring. Sculptures by Henry Moore grace **Yorkshire Sculpture Park** *(see p413)*.

Whitby harbour and St Mary's Church, Yorkshire

NORTHUMBRIA

- The trail of Celtic Christianity
- Life as it was lived, in Beamish Open Air Museum
- Hadrian's Wall from coast to coast

A boat trip to the **Farne Islands** *(see p418)* off Lindisfarne is the starting point to unravelling early Celtic Christianity, a journey that can be followed as far as **Durham Cathedral** *(see pp428–9).* The **Beamish Open Air Museum** *(see pp424–5),* which re-creates life in the northeast in the 19th century, makes a great family day out. Castles on Northumberland's coast were built to withstand Viking attack, but it is **Hadrian's Wall** *(see pp422–3),* erected by the Romans to keep out the Scots, that is particularly impressive.

NORTH WALES

- **Wild Snowdonia National Park**
- **Narrow-gauge railways**
- **Stunning medieval castles**

This is the part of Wales, where Welsh is commonly spoken, and the annual Eisteddfod literary festival is held. Its wildness is captured around Snowdon, the highest mountain in England and Wales. The centre for exploring **Snowdonia National Park** *(see pp450–1)* is Llanberis from where a narrow-gauge railway runs to the top. Another former slate-quarry railway takes passengers up from the coast at Porthmadog near **Portmeirion** *(see p454–5).* Medieval castles keep watch at **Harlech** *(see p454),* **Caernarfon** *(see p444)* and **Conwy** *(see p438 and p447).*

SOUTH AND MID WALES

- **Pony trekking in the hills**
- **Scenic coastal walks**
- **Hay-on-Wye literary festival**

This is a region to tour by car, to go walking or pony trekking, across mountains like the **Brecon Beacons** *(see pp468–9).* The roads are emptier than England's and the valleys are green and lush. The coast has some delightful ports and long-established resorts. The most attractive are around the **Gower Peninsula** *(see p466)*

Cliffs of the Pembrokeshire Coast National Park, South Wales

and in Pembrokeshire in the south west where there is the diminutive **St David's Cathedral** *(see pp464–5).* Wales is known for its male voice choirs – as well as its men of letters – **Hay-on-Wye** *(see p461)* hosts an annual literary festival.

SCOTTISH LOWLANDS

- **Glasgow, dynamic city of art**
- **Medieval Edinburgh and its Georgian New Town**
- **Magnificent abbeys and castles**

The capital **Edinburgh** *(see pp504–11)* and **Glasgow** *(see pp516–21)* are Scotland's dazzling cities, both full of interest and worth several

days' exploration. Charles Rennie Mackintosh left his Art Nouveau mark on Glasgow, while thousands of hopeful performers attempt to find fame in Edinburgh each August at the famous festival. The capital's high points are **Edinburgh Castle** *(see pp506–7),* keeper of the Scottish Crown jewels and the **Palace of Holyroodhouse** *(see p510),* the Queen's official Scottish residence. Castles abound in the Lowlands, notably the Renaissance gem **Stirling** *(see pp497–8).*

SCOTTISH HIGHLANDS AND ISLANDS

- **Mountain climbing and skiing**
- **The castles of Royal Deeside**
- **Remote, idyllic hills**

This is as wild as Britain gets: mountainous, heather-clad and dramatically remote, drifting into offshore islands. You may well see eagles and stags, while on the west coast seals swoop in on the beautiful shores. **Aberdeen** *(see pp538–40)* is the starting point for a tour of the castles of **Royal Deeside** *(see p540–1).* Climb mountains, go skiing in Aviemore in the **Cairngorms** *(see pp544–5),* follow the whisky trails and take a ferry to the Western Isles.

A view of Edinburgh Castle, Scotland

Putting Great Britain on the Map

Lying in northwestern Europe, Great Britain is bounded by the Atlantic Ocean, the North Sea and the English Channel. The island's landscape and climate are varied, and it is this variety that even today affects the pattern of settlement. The remote shores of the West Country peninsula and the inhospitable mountains of Scotland and Wales are less populated than the relatively flat and fertile Midlands and Southeast, where the vast majority of the country's 61 million people live. Due to this population density, the south is today the most built-up part of the country.

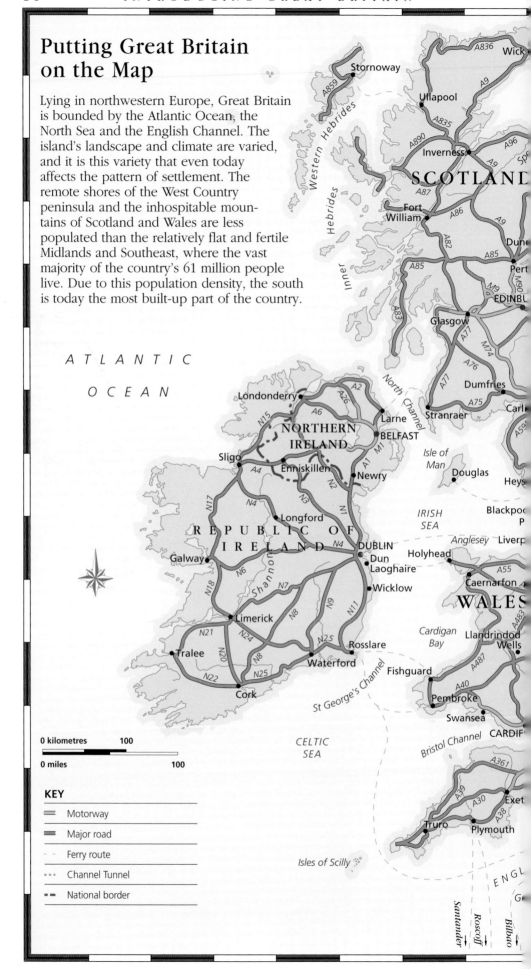

KEY

Motorway
Major road
Ferry route
Channel Tunnel
National border

Unst

Shetland Islands

Yell

Mainland

Foula

Lerwick

Europe
Great Britain is situated in the northwest corner of Europe. Its nearest neighbours are Ireland to the west, and the Netherlands, Belgium and France across the Channel. Denmark, Norway and Sweden are also easily accessible.

Fair Isle

Westray

Sanday

Mainland

Stronsay

Stromness

Kirkwall   *Orkney Islands*

Hoy

A836

Wick

A9

Aberdeen

EUROPE

NORWAY   FINLAND

SWEDEN   ESTONIA

RUSSIAN FED.

LATVIA

DENMARK   LITHUANIA

RUSSIAN FED.

BELORUSSIA

NETHERLANDS   POLAND

London

BELGIUM   GERMANY

LUXEMBOURG   CZECH REPUBLIC   SLOVAKIA   UKRAINE

FRANCE   AUSTRIA   HUNGARY

SWITZERLAND   SLOVENIA   CROATIA   ROMANIA

ITALY   BOSNIA AND HERZEGOVINA   SERBIA AND MONTENEGRO   BULGARIA

KOSOVO

SPAIN   MACEDONIA

ALBANIA   GREECE

PORTUGAL

ALGERIA   TUNISIA

Shetland and Orkney Islands
These islands form the northernmost part of Great Britain, with the Shetlands lying six degrees south of the Arctic Circle. There are transport links to the mainland.

Tyne

Sunderland

N O R T H

S E A

vale

A1(M)

York   A165

Leeds

M62

Kingston upon Hull

Huddersfield

M1

M180

Grimsby

nchester

Sheffield   A16

A6

rent

E N G L A N D

erby   Nottingham

A1

Peterborough   A47   Norwich

A11

ngham   A1(M)   A14   A12

Northampton   A12

Cambridge

M11

Stratford-upon-Avon   M1(M)   Ipswich   Felixstowe

ucester   Harlow   Harwich

Oxford   A12

Windsor   M3

LONDON   M2   Ramsgate

Salisbury   M25   Canterbury   Dover

M23   Folkestone   Dover

mpton   Brighton   Strait of Dover

mouth   Portsmouth   Newhaven   Calais

Isle of Wight   Boulogne   A25

NNEL

erbourg   Dieppe   Amiens

Le   N15   N27   A28   D901

Havre   Rouen   N1

F R A N C E

St Malo   N13   N175   A13   Caen   N138   N14

N158   **PARIS**

Göteborg
Esbjerg
Hamburg

Groningen   A7

A31   A7   A28

N37

N E T H E R L A N D S

AMSTERDAM   A6   Zwolle

A4   A1

The Hague   Utrecht   A50   A31

A15   A12   Arnhem

Rotterdam   A57   A3

A58   A59   Duisburg

Eindhoven   A67   Essen

Zeebrugge   A1   A61

Ostend   N9   A14   Antwerp

Dunkirk   BRUSSELS   A2

A14   A10   Cologne

B E L G I U M   Liege   Aachen

Lille   A3   A4

A26   A2   **G E R M A N Y**

A1   A15   A4

A2

A26   A1

L U X E M B O U R G

N51   A4

LUXEMBOURG   A31   A1

Reims   A4   Metz

Regional Great Britain: London, the South, the Midlands and Wales

Great Britain has airline connections with most cities in the world. London is the main transport hub with three major international airports, including Heathrow, the world's busiest. Southern England, Britain's most populous area, is divided, within this book, into four regions – Southeast England, the West Country, Wales and the Midlands – with a separate chapter for London. Road and rail links to the North and Scotland (*see pp18–19*) are plentiful, as are links between all main towns.

KEY TO COLOUR-CODING

- London

Southeast England

- The Downs and Channel Coast
- East Anglia
- Thames Valley

The West Country

- Wessex
- Devon and Cornwall

Wales

- North Wales
- South and Mid-Wales

The Midlands

- The Heart of England
- East Midlands

KEY TO MAP

- Ferry port
- Airport
- Motorway
- Major road
- Railway line
- Channel Tunnel

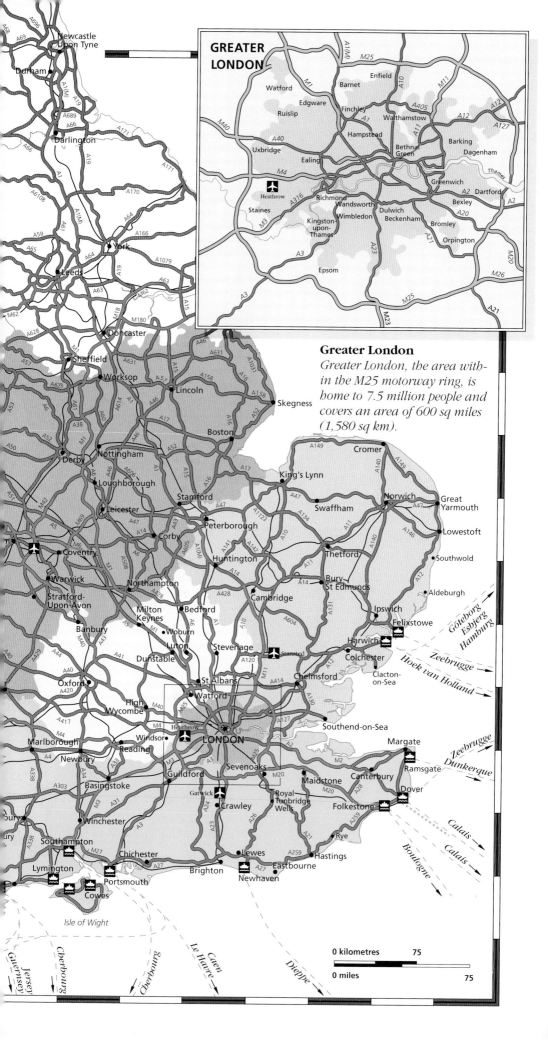

GREATER LONDON

Greater London

Greater London, the area within the M25 motorway ring, is home to 7.5 million people and covers an area of 600 sq miles (1,580 sq km).

Regional Great Britain: The North and Scotland

This part of Great Britain is divided into two sections in this book. Although it is far less populated than the southern sector of the country, there are good road and rail connections, and ferry services link the islands with the mainland.

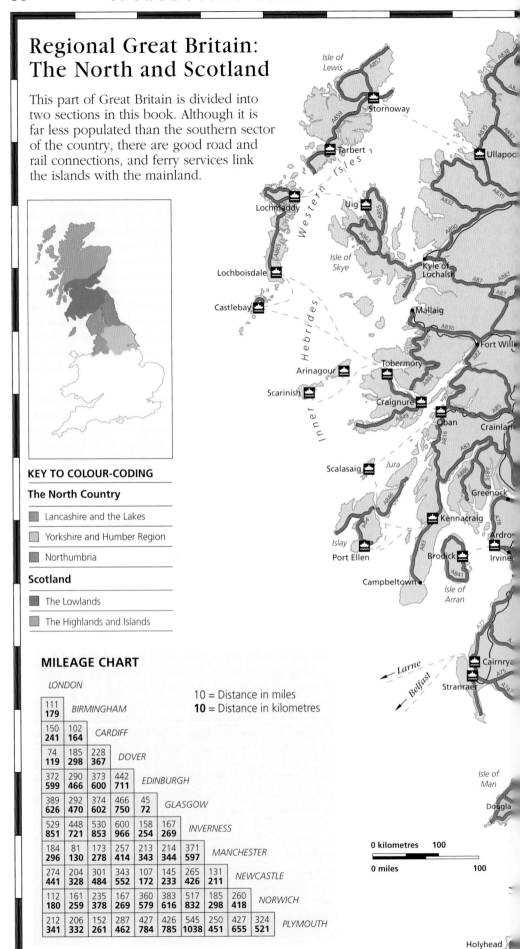

KEY TO COLOUR-CODING

The North Country

- Lancashire and the Lakes
- Yorkshire and Humber Region
- Northumbria

Scotland

- The Lowlands
- The Highlands and Islands

MILEAGE CHART

10 = Distance in miles
10 = Distance in kilometres

LONDON										
111 **179**	BIRMINGHAM									
150 **241**	102 **164**	CARDIFF								
74 **119**	185 **298**	228 **367**	DOVER							
372 **599**	290 **466**	373 **600**	442 **711**	EDINBURGH						
389 **626**	292 **470**	374 **602**	466 **750**	45 **72**	GLASGOW					
529 **851**	448 **721**	530 **853**	600 **966**	158 **254**	167 **269**	INVERNESS				
184 **296**	81 **130**	173 **278**	257 **414**	213 **343**	214 **344**	371 **597**	MANCHESTER			
274 **441**	204 **328**	301 **484**	343 **552**	107 **172**	145 **233**	265 **426**	211 **211**	NEWCASTLE		
112 **180**	161 **259**	235 **378**	167 **269**	360 **579**	383 **616**	517 **832**	185 **298**	260 **418**	NORWICH	
212 **341**	206 **332**	152 **261**	287 **462**	427 **784**	426 **785**	545 **1038**	250 **451**	427 **655**	324 **521**	PLYMOUTH

Map labels: Isle of Lewis, Stornoway, Tarbert, Ullapoc, Lochmaddy, Uig, Western Isles, Isle of Skye, Kyle of Lochalsh, Lochboisdale, Mallaig, Castlebay, Fort Willi, Hebrides, Tobermory, Arinagour, Scarinish, Craignure, Oban, Crainlari, Scalasaig, Jura, Greenock, Inner, Kennacraig, Ardros, Islay, Port Ellen, Brodick, Irvine, Campbeltown, Isle of Arran, Larne, Belfast, Cairnrya, Stranraer, Isle of Man, Dougla, 0 kilometres 100, 0 miles 100, Holyhead

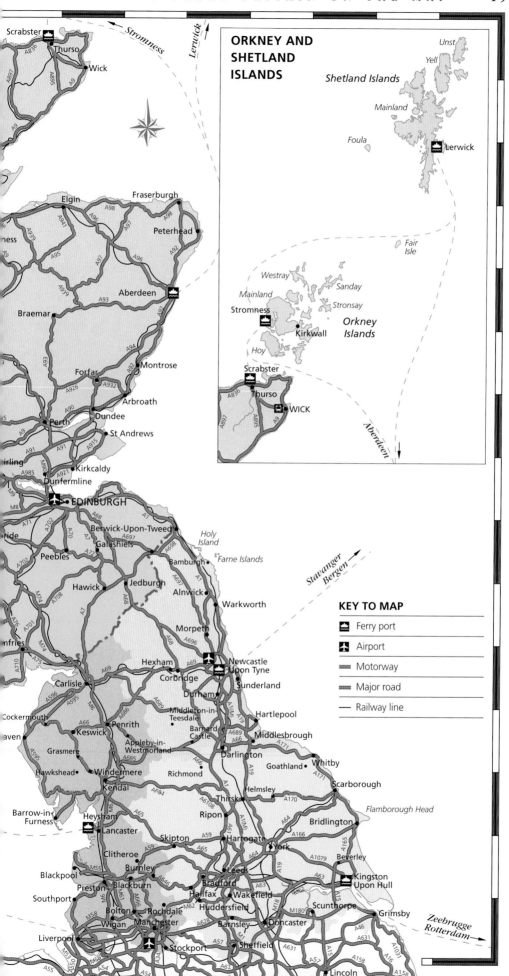

ORKNEY AND SHETLAND ISLANDS

Shetland Islands

Unst

Yell

Mainland

Foula

Lerwick

Fair Isle

Westray

Mainland

Stromness

Sanday

Stronsay

Kirkwall

Orkney Islands

Hoy

Scrabster

Thurso

WICK

Scrabster

Thurso

Wick

Stromness

Lerwick

Elgin

Fraserburgh

Peterhead

Aberdeen

Braemar

Forfar

Montrose

Arbroath

Perth

Dundee

St Andrews

Kirkcaldy

Dunfermline

EDINBURGH

Berwick-Upon-Tweed

Galashiels

Peebles

Holy Island

Bamburgh

Farne Islands

Hawick

Jedburgh

Alnwick

Warkworth

Morpeth

Hexham

Corbridge

Newcastle Upon Tyne

Sunderland

Durham

Carlisle

Cockermouth

Penrith

Middleton-in-Teesdale

Hartlepool

Keswick

Barnard Castle

Middlesbrough

Grasmere

Appleby-in-Westmorland

Darlington

Hawkshead

Windermere

Richmond

Goathland

Whitby

Kendal

Helmsley

Scarborough

Barrow-in-Furness

Heysham

Thirsk

Flamborough Head

Lancaster

Ripon

Bridlington

Blackpool

Skipton

Harrogate

York

Beverley

Clitheroe

Preston

Burnley

Blackburn

Leeds

Kingston Upon Hull

Southport

Halifax

Bradford

Wakefield

Bolton

Rochdale

Huddersfield

Scunthorpe

Grimsby

Wigan

Manchester

Barnsley

Doncaster

Liverpool

Stockport

Sheffield

Chester

Lincoln

Stromness

Lerwick

Stavanger Bergen

Aberdeen

Zeebrugge Rotterdam

KEY TO MAP

Ferry port

Airport

Motorway

Major road

Railway line

A PORTRAIT OF GREAT BRITAIN

Britain has been assiduous in preserving its traditions, but offers the visitor much more than stately castles and pretty villages. A diversity of landscape, culture, literature, art and architecture, as well as its unique heritage, results in a nation balancing the needs of the present with those of its past.

Britain's character has been shaped by its geographical position as an island. Never successfully invaded since 1066, its people have developed their own distinctive traditions. The Roman invasion of AD 43 lasted 350 years but Roman culture and language were quickly overlain with those of the northern European settlers who followed. Ties with Europe were loosened further in the 16th century when the Catholic church was replaced by a less dogmatic established church.

Although today a member of the European Union, Britain continues to delight in its non-conformity, even in superficial ways such as driving on the left-hand side of the road instead of the right. The opening of the rail tunnel to France is a topographical adjustment that does not necessarily mark a change in national attitude.

The British heritage is seen in its ancient castles, cathedrals and stately homes with their gardens and Classical parklands. Age-old customs are renewed each year, from royal ceremonies to Morris dancers performing on village greens.

For a small island, Great Britain encompasses a surprising variety in its regions, whose inhabitants maintain distinct identities. Scotland and Wales are separate countries from England with their own legislative assemblies.

Tudor rose

Walking along the east bank of the River Avon, Bath

◁ **Punting, a popular pastime on the River Cam, Cambridge**

Widecombe-in-the-Moor, a Devon village clustered round a church and set in hills

They have different customs, traditions, and, in the case of Scotland, different legal and educational systems. The Welsh and Scots Gaelic languages survive and are sustained by their own radio and television networks. In northern and West Country areas, English itself is spoken in a rich variety of dialects and accents, and these areas maintain their own regional arts, crafts, architecture and food.

The landscape is varied, too, from the craggy mountains of Wales, Scotland and the north, through the flat expanses of the Midlands and eastern England to the soft, rolling hills of the south and west. The long, broad beaches of East Anglia contrast with the picturesque rocky inlets along much of the west coast.

Scottish coat of arms at Edinburgh Castle

Despite the spread of towns and cities over the last two centuries, rural Britain still flourishes. Nearly three-quarters of Britain's land is used for agriculture. The main commercial crops are wheat, barley, sugar beet and potatoes, though what catches the eye in early summer are the fields of bright yellow rape or slate-blue flax.

The countryside is dotted with farms and charming villages, with picturesque cottages and lovingly tended gardens – a British passion. A typical village is built around an ancient church and a small, friendly pub. Here the pace of life slows. To drink a pint of ale in a cosy, village inn and relax before a fire is a time-honoured British custom. Strangers will be welcomed cordially, though perhaps with caution; for even if strict formality is a thing of the past, the British have a tendency to be reserved.

In the 19th and early 20th centuries, trade with the extensive British Empire, fuelled by abundant coal supplies, spurred manufacturing and created wealth. Thousands of people moved from the countryside to towns and cities near mines, mills and factories. By 1850 Britain was the world's strongest industrial nation. Now many

Lake and gardens at Petworth House, Sussex

of these old industrial centres have declined, and today manufacturing employs only 22 per cent of the labour force, while 66 per cent work in the growing service sector. These service industries are located mainly in the southeast, close to London, where modern office buildings bear witness to comparative prosperity.

Crowds at Petticoat Lane market in London's East End

SOCIETY AND POLITICS

British cities are melting-pots for people not just from different parts of the country but also from overseas. Irish immigration has long ensured a flow of labour into the country, and since the 1950s hundreds of thousands have come from former colonies in Africa, Asia and the Caribbean, many of which are now members of the Commonwealth. Nearly six per cent of Britain's 60 million inhabitants are from non-white ethnic groups – and about half of these were born in Britain. The result

is a multi-cultural society that can boast a wide range of music, art, food and religions. However, prejudice does exist and in some inner-city areas where poorer members of different communities live, racial tensions can occasionally arise. Even though discrimination in housing and employment on the grounds of race is against the law, it does occur in places.

Britain's class structure still intrigues and bewilders many visitors, based as it is on a subtle mixture of heredity and wealth. Even though many of the great inherited fortunes no longer exist, some old landed families still live on their

Bosses in Norwich Cathedral cloisters

large estates, and many now open them to the public. Class divisions are further entrenched by the education system. While more than 90 per cent of children are educated free by the state, richer parents often opt for private schooling, and the products of these private schools are disproportionately represented in the higher echelons of government and business.

The monarchy's position highlights the dilemma of a people seeking to preserve its most potent symbol of national unity in an age that is suspicious of inherited privilege. Without real political power, though still head of the Church of England, the Queen and her family are subject to increasing public scrutiny. Following a spate of personal scandals, some citizens advocate the abolition of the monarchy.

Democracy has deep foundations in Britain: there was even a parliament of sorts in London in the 13th century.

Priest in the Close at Winchester Cathedral

Yet with the exception of the 17th-century Civil War, power has passed gradually from the Crown to the people's elected representatives. A series of Reform Acts between 1832 and 1884 gave the vote to all male citizens, though women were not enfranchised on an equal basis until 1928. Margaret Thatcher – Britain's first woman Prime Minister – held office for 12 years from 1979. During the 20th

Afternoon tea on the back lawn at the Thornbury Castle Hotel, Avon

century, the Labour (left wing) and Conservative (right wing) parties have, during their periods in office, favoured a mix of public and private ownership for industry and ample funding for the state health and welfare systems.

The position of Ireland has been an intractable political issue since the 17th century. Part of the United Kingdom for 800 years, but divided in 1921, it has seen conflict between Catholics and Protestants for many years. The Good Friday Peace Agreement of 1998 was a huge step forward and the path to lasting peace now seems possible.

CULTURE AND THE ARTS

Britain has a famous theatrical tradition stretching back to the 16th century and William Shakespeare. His plays

The House of Lords, in Parliament

have been performed on stage almost continuously since he wrote them and the works of 17th- and 18th-century writers are also frequently revived. Contemporary British playwrights such as Tom Stoppard, Alan Ayckbourn and David Hare draw on this long tradition with their vivid language and by using comedy to illustrate serious themes. British actors such as Helen Mirren, Ian McKellen, Ralph Fiennes and Anthony Hopkins have international reputations.

While London is the focal point of British theatre, fine drama is to be seen in many other parts of the country. The Edinburgh Festival and its Fringe are the high point of Great Britain's cultural calendar with theatre and music to suit all tastes. Other music festivals are held across the country, chiefly in summer, while there are annual

Schoolboys at Eton, t[h]e famous public schoo[l]

festivals of literature at Hay-on-Wye and Cheltenham. Poetry has had an enthusiastic following since Chaucer wrote the *Canterbury Tales* in the 14th century: poems from all eras can even be read on the London Underground, where they are interspersed with the advertisements in the carriages and on the station platforms.

In the visual arts, Britain has a strong tradition in portraiture, caricature, landscape and watercolour. In modern times David Hockney and Lucian Freud, and sculptors Henry Moore and Barbara Hepworth, have enjoyed worldwide recognition. Architects including

Christopher Wren, Inigo Jones, John Nash and Robert Adam all created styles that define British cities; and today, Norman Foster and Richard Rogers carry the standard for Post-Modernism. Britain is becoming famous for its

Reading the newspaper in Kensington Gardens

innovative fashion designers, many of whom now show their spring and autumn collections in Paris.

The British are avid newspaper readers. There are 11 national newspapers published from London on weekdays: the standard of the serious newspapers is very high; for example, *The Times* is read the world over because of its reputation for strong intentional reporting. Most popular, however, are the tabloids packed with gossip, crime and sport, which account for some 80 per cent of the total.

Naomi Campbell, a British supermodel

The indigenous film industry has produced international hits such as *The Queen*; though blockbusters such as the Harry Potter films are often backed by the US. British television is famous for the quality of its news, current affairs and drama programmes. The publicly funded British Broadcasting Corporation (BBC), which controls five national radio networks and two terrestrial television channels, as well as additional radio stations and television channels via digital technology, is widely admired.

The British are great sports fans, and soccer, rugby, cricket and golf are popular. An instantly recognizable English image is that of the cricket match on a village green. Nationwide, fishing is the most popular sporting pastime, and the British make good use of their national parks as keen walkers.

British food used to be derided for a lack of imagination. The cuisine relied on a limited range of quality ingredients, plainly prepared. But recent influences from abroad have introduced a wider range of ingredients and more adventurous techniques. Typical English food – plain home cooking and regional dishes – has also enjoyed a revival in recent years.

In this, as in other respects, the British are doing what they have done for centuries: accommodating their own traditions to influences from other cultures, while leaving the essential elements of their national life and character intact.

Whitby harbour and St Mary's Church, Yorkshire

Gardens Through the Ages

Styles of gardening in Britain have expanded alongside architecture and other evolving fashions. The Elizabethan knot garden became more elaborate and formal in Jacobean times, when the range of plants greatly increased. The 18th century brought a taste for large-scale "natural" landscapes with lakes, woods and pastures, creating the most distinctively English style to have emerged. In the 19th century, fierce debate raged between supporters of natural and formal gardens, developing into the eclecticism of the 20th century when "garden rooms" in differing styles became popular.

Monumental column

A grotto and cascade brought romance and mystery.

Capability Brown (1715–83) *was Britain's most influential garden designer, favouring the move away from formal gardens to man-made pastoral settings.*

Blackthorn

Classical temples were a much appreciated feature in 18th-century gardens and were often exact replicas of buildings that the designers had seen in Greece.

Elaborate parterres *were a feature of aristocratic gardens of the 17th century, when the fashion spread from Europe. This is the Privy Garden at Hampton Court Palace, restored in 1995 to its design under William III.*

IDEAL LANDSCAPE GARDEN

Classical Greece and Rome inspired the grand gardens of the early 18th century, such as Stourhead and Stowe. Informal clumps of trees played a critical part in the serene, manicured landscapes.

Maple

Winding paths were carefully planned to allow changing vistas to open out as visitors strolled around the garden.

DESIGN AND FORMALITY

A flower garden is a work of artifice, an attempt to tame nature rather than to copy it. Growing plants in rows or regular patterns, interspersed with statues and ornaments, imposes a sense of order. Designs change to reflect the fashion of the time and the introduction of new plants.

Medieval gardens usually had a herber (a turfed sitting area) and a vine arbour. A good reconstruction is Queen Eleanor's Garden, Winchester.

Tudor gardens featured edged borders and sometimes mazes. T Tudor House Garden, Southamp also has beehives and heraldic sta

Herbaceous borders, *full of lush plants, are the glory of the summer garden. Gertrude Jekyll (1843–1932), was high priestess of the mixed border, with her eye for seductive colour combinations.*

Cedar of Lebanon

Yew

Rhododendron

The Palladian bridge was a favourite feature, often decorative rather than practical.

Knot Gardens *were in vogue in the 1500s. Intersecting lines of lavender or box were filled with flowers, herbs or vegetables, as in this restoration at Pitmedden in Scotland.*

VISITORS' CHECKLIST

The "yellow book", Gardens of England and Wales, *the annual guide to the National Gardens Scheme, lists gardens open to the public.*

DEVELOPMENT OF THE MODERN PANSY

All garden plants derive from wild flowers, bred over the years to produce qualities that appeal to gardeners. The story of the pansy, one of our most popular flowers, is typical.

The wild pansy (Viola tricolor) native to Britain is commonly known as heartsease. It is a small-flowered annual which can vary considerably in colour.

The mountain pansy (Viola lutea) is a perennial. The first cultivated varieties resulted from crossing it with heartsease in the early 19th century.

The Show Pansy was bred by florists after the blotch appeared as a chance seedling in 1840. It was round in form with a small, symmetrical blotch.

The Fancy Pansy, developed in the 1860s, was much larger. The blotch covered all three lower petals save for a thin margin of colour.

Modern hybrids of pansies, violas and violettas, developed by selective breeding, are varied and versatile in a wide range of vibrant new colours.

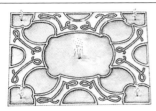

17th-century gardening was more elaborate. Water gardens like those at Blenheim were often combined with parterres of exotic foreign plants.

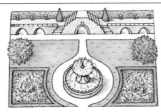

Victorian gardens, their formal beds a mass of colour, were a reaction to the landscapes of Capability Brown. Alton Towers has a good example.

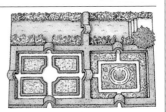

20th-century gardens mix historic and modern styles, as at Hidcote Manor, Gloucestershire. Growing wild flowers is becoming a popular choice.

Stately Homes

Adam sketch (c.1760) for ornate panel

The grand country house reached its zenith in the 18th and 19th centuries, when the old landed families and the new captains of industry enjoyed their wealth, looked after by a retinue of servants. The earliest stately homes date from the 14th century, when defence was paramount. By the 16th century, when the opulent taste of the European Renaissance spread to England, houses became centres of pleasure and showplaces for fine art *(see pp302–03)*. The Georgians favoured chaste Classical architecture with rich interiors, the Victorians flamboyant Gothic. Due to 20th-century social change many stately homes have been opened to the public, some administered by the National Trust.

The saloon, a domed rotunda based on the Pantheon in Rome, was designed to display the Curzon family's Classical sculpture collection to 18th-century society.

The Drawing Room, the main room for entertaining, contains the most important pictures and some exquisite plasterwork.

The Marble Hall *is where balls and other social functions took place among Corinthian columns of pink alabaster.*

The Family Wing is a self-contained "pavilion" of private living quarters; the servants lived in rooms above the kitchen. The Curzon family still live here.

The Music Room is decorated w musical them Music was the main entertainm on social occasi

TIMELINE OF ARCHITECTS

1650				1750

Colen Campbell (1676–1729) designed Burlington House *(see p81)*

William Kent (1685–1748) built Holkham Hall *(see p197)* in the Palladian style

Robert Adam (1728–92), who often worked with his brother James (1730–94) was as famous for decorative details as for buildings

Henry Holland (1745–1806) designed the Neo-Classical sout range of Woburn Abb *(see p230)*

Sir John Vanbrugh *(see p398)* was helped by **Nicholas Hawksmoor** (1661–1736) on Blenheim Palace *(see pp228–29)*

John Carr (1723–1807) designed the Palladian Harewood House *(see p410)*

Castle Howard (1702) by Sir John Vanbrugh

Adam fireplace, Kedleston Hall, adorned with Classical motifs

NATIONAL TRUST

At the end of the 19th century, there were real fears that burgeoning factories, mines, roads and houses would obliterate much of Britain's historic landscape and finest buildings. In 1895 a group that included the social reformer Octavia Hill formed the National Trust, to preserve the nation's valuable heritage. The first building acquired by the

National Trust oak leaf design

trust was the medieval Clergy House at Alfriston in Sussex, in 1896 *(see p180)*. Today the National Trust is a charity that runs many historic houses and gardens, and vast stretches of countryside and coastline. It is supported by more than two million members nationwide.

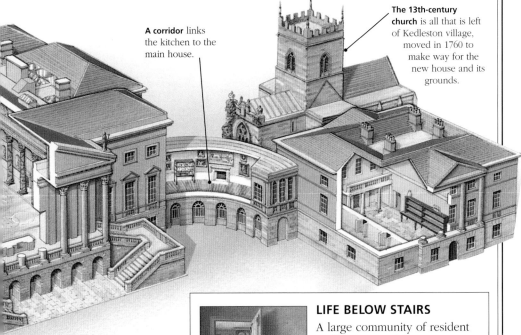

A corridor links the kitchen to the main house.

The 13th-century church is all that is left of Kedleston village, moved in 1760 to make way for the new house and its grounds.

KEDLESTON HALL

This Derbyshire mansion *(see p336)* is an early work of the influential Georgian architect Robert Adam, who was a pioneer of the Neo-Classical style derived from ancient Greece and Rome. It was built for the Curzon family in the 1760s.

Life Below Stairs by Charles Hunt (c.1890)

LIFE BELOW STAIRS

A large community of resident staff was essential to run a country house smoothly. The butler was in overall charge, ensuring that meals were served on time. The housekeeper supervised uniformed maids who made sure the place was clean. The cook ran the kitchen, using fresh produce from the estate. Ladies' maids and valets acted as personal servants.

1800	1850	

Philip Webb (1831–1915) was a leading architect of the influential Arts and Crafts movement *(see p328)*, whose buildings favoured the simpler forms of an "Old English" style, instead of flamboyant Victorian Gothic

Sir Edwin Lutyens (1869–1944) designed the elaborate Castle Drogo in Devon *(see p295)*, one of the last grand country houses

Dining Room, Cragside, Northumberland

Norman Shaw (1831–1912) was an exponent of Victorian Gothic, as in Cragside (above), and a pioneer of the Arts and Crafts movement *(see p328)*

Standen, West Sussex (1891–94) by Philip Webb

Heraldry and the Aristocracy

Order of the Garter medal

The British aristocracy has evolved over 900 years from the feudal obligations of noblemen to the Norman kings, who conferred privileges of rank and land in return for armed support. Subsequent monarchs bestowed titles and property on their supporters, establishing new aristocratic dynasties. The title of "earl" dates from the 11th century; that of "duke" from the 14th century. Soon the nobility began to choose their own symbols, partly to identify a knight concealed by his armour: these were often painted on the knight's coat (hence the term "coat of arms") and also copied onto his shield.

The College of Arms, London: housing records of all coats of arms and devising new ones

ROYAL COAT OF ARMS

The most familiar British coat of arms is the sovereign's. It appears on the royal standard, or flag, as well as on official documents and on shops that enjoy royal patronage. Over nearly 900 years, various monarchs have made modifications. The quartered shield in the middle displays the arms of England (twice), Scotland and Ireland. Surrounding it are other traditional images including the lion and unicorn, topped by the crown and the royal helm (helmet).

Edward III *(1327–77) was the founder of the chivalric Order of the Garter. The garter, bearing the motto,* Honi soit qui mal y pense *(evil be to him who thinks of evil), goes round the central shield.*

The lion is the most common beast in heraldry.

The red lion is the symbol of Scotland.

The unicorn is a mythical beast, generally regarded as a Scottish royal beast in heraldry.

Henry II *(1154–89) formalized his coat of arms to include three lions. This was developed by his son Richard I to become the "Gules three lions passant guardant or" seen on today's arms.*

The royal helm with gold protective bars was introduced to the arms by Elizabeth I (1558–1603).

Dieu et mon droit (God and my right) has been the royal motto since the reign of Henry V (1413–22).

Henry VII *(1485–1509) devised the Tudor rose, joining the white and red roses of York and Lancaster.*

ADMIRAL LORD NELSON

When people are ennobled they may choose their own coat of arms if they do not already have one. Britain's naval hero (1758–1805) was made Baron Nelson of the Nile in 1798 and a viscount in 1801. His arms relate to his life and career at sea; but some symbols were added after his death.

A seaman supports the shield.

The motto means "Let him wear the palm (or laurel) who deserves it".

A tropical scene shows the Battle of the Nile (1798).

The San Joseph was a Spanish man o'war that Nelson daringly captured.

TRACING YOUR ANCESTRY

For records of births, deaths and marriages in England and Wales since 1837, contact the **General Register Office** (0845 603 7788; www.gro.gov.uk), and in Scotland **New Register House**, 3 West Register St, Edinburgh EH1 3YT (0131 334 0380; www.gro-scotland. gov.uk). For help in tracing family history, consult the **Society of Genealogists**, 14 Charterhouse Bldgs, London EC1 (020 7251 8799).

Inherited titles *usually pass to the eldest son or the closest male relative, but some titles may go to women if there is no male heir.*

The Duke of Edinburgh (born 1921), husband of the Queen, is one of several dukes who are members of the Royal Family.

The Marquess of Salisbury (1830–1903), Prime Minister three times between 1885 and 1902, was descended from the Elizabethan statesman Robert Cecil.

Earl Mountbatten of Burma (1900–79) was ennobled in 1947 for diplomatic and military services.

Viscount Montgomery (1887–1976) was raised to the peerage for his military leadership in World War II.

Lord Byron (1788–1824), the Romantic poet, was the 6th Baron Byron: the 1st Baron was an MP ennobled by Charles I in 1625.

PEERS OF THE REALM

There are nearly 1,200 peers of the realm. In 1999 the process began to abolish the hereditary system in favour of life peerages that expire on the death of the recipient *(see left and below)*. Ninety-two hereditary peers are entitled to sit in the House of Lords, including the Lords Spiritual – archbishops and senior bishops of the Church of England – and the Law Lords. In 1958 the Queen expanded the list of life peerages to honour people who had performed notable public service. From 1999 the system of "peoples peerages" began to replace inherited honours.

KEY TO THE PEERS

☐	25 dukes
☐	35 marquesses
☐	175 earls and countesses
☐	98 viscounts
☐	800+ barons and baronesses

THE QUEEN'S HONOURS LIST

Twice a year several hundred men and women nominated by the Prime Minister and political leaders for outstanding public service receive honours from the Queen. Some are made dames or knights, a few receive the prestigious OM (Order of Merit), but far more receive lesser honours such as OBEs or MBEs (Orders or Members of the British Empire).

Mother Theresa *received the OM in 1983 for her work in India.*

Terence Conran, *founder of Habitat, was knighted for services to industry.*

The Beatles *were given MBEs in 1965. Paul McCartney was knighted in 1997.*

Rural Architecture

For many, the essence of British life is found in villages. Their scale and serenity nurture a way of life envied by those who live in towns and cities. The pattern of British villages dates back some 1,500 years, when the Saxons cleared forests and established settlements, usually centred around a green or pond. Most of today's English villages existed at the time of the *Domesday Book* in 1086, though few actual buildings survive from then. The settlements evolved organically around a church or manor; the cottages and gardens were created from local materials. Today, a typical village will contain structures of various dates, from the Middle Ages onward. The church is usually the oldest, followed perhaps by a tithe barn, manor house and cottages.

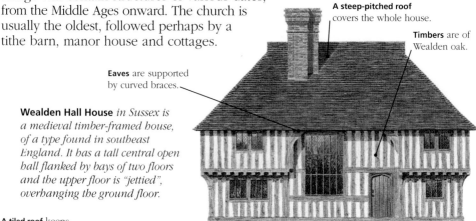

Abbotsbury, in Dorset – a typical village built up around a church

A steep-pitched roof covers the whole house.

Timbers are of Wealden oak.

Eaves are supported by curved braces.

Wealden Hall House *in Sussex is a medieval timber-framed house, of a type found in southeast England. It has a tall central open hall flanked by bays of two floors and the upper floor is "jettied", overhanging the ground floor.*

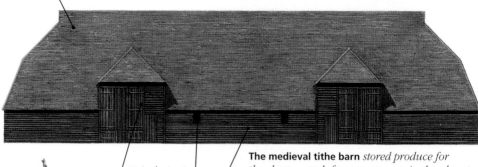

A tiled roof keeps the grain dry.

The entrance is big enough for ox-wagons.

Holes let in air – and birds.

Walls and doors are weatherboarded.

The medieval tithe barn *stored produce for the clergy – each farmer was required to donate one tenth (tithe) of his annual harvest. The enormous roofs may be supported by crucks, large curved timbers extending from the low walls.*

THE PARISH CHURCH

The church is the focal point of the village and, traditionally, of village life. Its tall spire could be seen – and its bells heard – by travellers from a distance. The church is also a chronicle of local history: a large church in a tiny village indicates a once-prosperous settlement. A typical church contains architectural features from many centuries, occasionally as far back as Saxon times. These may include medieval brasses, wall paintings, misericords *(see p341)*, and Tudor and Stuart carvings. Many sell informative guide books inside.

Slender spire from the Georgian era

West elevation

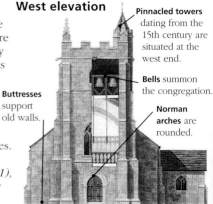

Pinnacled towers dating from the 15th century are situated at the west end.

Bells summon the congregation.

Buttresses support old walls.

Norman arches are rounded.

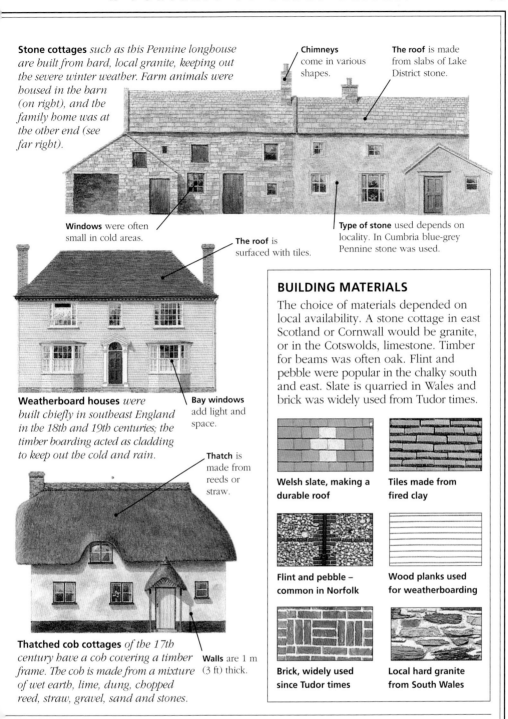

Stone cottages *such as this Pennine longhouse are built from hard, local granite, keeping out the severe winter weather. Farm animals were housed in the barn (on right), and the family home was at the other end (see far right).*

Chimneys come in various shapes.

The roof is made from slabs of Lake District stone.

Windows were often small in cold areas.

The roof is surfaced with tiles.

Type of stone used depends on locality. In Cumbria blue-grey Pennine stone was used.

Weatherboard houses *were built chiefly in southeast England in the 18th and 19th centuries; the timber boarding acted as cladding to keep out the cold and rain.*

Bay windows add light and space.

Thatch is made from reeds or straw.

Thatched cob cottages *of the 17th century have a cob covering a timber frame. The cob is made from a mixture of wet earth, lime, dung, chopped reed, straw, gravel, sand and stones.*

Walls are 1 m (3 ft) thick.

BUILDING MATERIALS

The choice of materials depended on local availability. A stone cottage in east Scotland or Cornwall would be granite, or in the Cotswolds, limestone. Timber for beams was often oak. Flint and pebble were popular in the chalky south and east. Slate is quarried in Wales and brick was widely used from Tudor times.

Welsh slate, making a durable roof

Tiles made from fired clay

Flint and pebble – common in Norfolk

Wood planks used for weatherboarding

Brick, widely used since Tudor times

Local hard granite from South Wales

South elevation

The nave is often the oldest part of the building, with extensions added in later centuries.

Towers are often later additions, due to their tendency to collapse.

Ropes used by bell-ringers.

The font, where babies are baptized, is often a church's oldest feature.

Pointed arches date from the 13th century.

Many pulpits are Jacobean.

A screen separates nave from chancel.

The chancel houses the choir and altar.

The Countryside

Common Blue butterfly

For its size, Britain contains an unusual variety of geological and climatic conditions that have shaped diverse landscapes, from treeless windswept moorland to boggy marshes and small hedged cattle pastures. Each terrain nurtures its typical wildlife and displays its own charm through the seasons. With the reduction in farming and the creation of footpaths and nature reserves, the countryside is becoming more of a leisure resource.

INDIGENOUS ANIMALS AND BIRDS

There are no large or dangerous wild animals in Britain but a wealth of small mammals, rodents and insects inhabit the countryside, and the rivers and streams are home to many varieties of fish. For bird-watchers there is a great range of songbirds, birds of prey and seabirds.

Livestock graze on low pastures.

Trees provide shelter and protection for wildlife.

Higher land is uncultivated.

Bushes and trees grow between rocks.

Streams flow over a stony bed from mountain springs.

The highest ground is often covered in snow until spring.

WOODED DOWNLAND

Chalk downland, seen here at Ditchling Beacon on the Downs (see p181), has soil of low fertility and is grazed by sheep. However crops are sometimes grown on the lower slopes. Distinctive wild flowers and butterflies thrive here, while beech and yew predominate in the woods.

Spear thistle *has pink heads in summer that attract several species of butterfly.*

The dog rose *is one of Britain's best-loved wild flowers; its pink single flower is widely seen in hedgerows.*

Hogweed *has robust stems and leaves with large clusters of white flowers.*

WILD HILLSIDE

Large tracts of Britain's uplands remain wild terrain, unsuitable for crops or forestry. Purple heather is tough enough to survive in moorland, the haunt of deer and game birds. The highest craggy uplands, such as the Cairngorms (see p544–45) in Scotland, pictured here, are the habitat of birds of prey, such as the golden eagle.

Ling, *a low-growing heather with tiny pink bell-flowers, adds splashes of colour to peaty moors and uplands.*

Meadow cranesbill *is a wild geranium with distinctive purple flowers.*

Tormentil *has small yellow flowers. It prefers moist, acid so and is found near water on heaths and moors in summer.*

Swallows, *swifts and house martins are all summer visitors.*

Kestrels *are small falcons that prey on mammals such as voles.*

Rabbits *are often spotted feeding at the edge of fields or near woods.*

Robins, *common in gardens and hedgerows, have distinctive red breast feathers.*

Foxes, *little bigger than domestic cats, live in hideaways in woods, near farmland.*

Cereal crops ripen in small fields.

Hedgerows provide refuge for wildlife.

Small mixed woods break up the field pattern.

Sheep graze on salty marshes.

Culverts drain water from the field.

Reed beds edge the water.

TRADITIONAL FIELDS

The patchwork fields here in the Cotswolds *(see p304)* reflect generations of small-scale farming. A typical farm would produce silage, hay and cereal crops, and keep a few dairy cows and sheep in enclosed pastures. The tree-dotted hedgerows mark boundaries that may be centuries old.

MARSHLAND

Flat and low-lying wetlands, criss-crossed with dykes and drainage canals, provide the scenery of Romney Marsh *(see also p182)* as well as much of East Anglia. Some areas have rich, peaty soil for crops, or salty marshland for sheep, but there are extensive uncultivated sections, where reed beds shelter wildlife.

The oxeye daisy *is a larger relative of the common white daisy, found in grassland from spring to late summer.*

Orchids *are among the rarer wild flowers. This species is the Common Spotted Orchid.*

Cowslips *belong to the primrose family. In spring they are often found in the grass on open meadowlands.*

Sea lavender *is a saltmarsh plant that is tolerant of saline soils. It flowers in late summer.*

Poppies *glow brilliant red in cornfields.*

Buttercups *are among the most common wild flowers. They brighten meadows in summer.*

Walkers' Britain

Walkers of all levels of ability and enthusiasm are well served in Britain. There is an unrivalled network of long-distance paths through some spectacular scenery, which can be tackled in stages with overnight stays en route, or dipped into for a single day's walking. For shorter walks, Britain is dotted with signposts showing public footpaths across common or private land. You will find books of walk routes in local shops and a large map will keep you on track. Choose river routes for easy walking or take to the hills for a greater challenge.

Walker resting on Scafell Pike, Lake District

The West Highland Way is an arduous 95 mile (153 km) route from Milngavie, near Glasgow, to north of Fort William, across mountainous terrain with fine lochs and moorland scenery (*see p494*).

Fort William

The Pennine Way *was Britain's first designated long-distance path. The 268 mile (431 km) route from Edale in Derbyshire to Kirk Yetholm on the Scottish border is a challenging upland hike, with long, lonely stretches of moorland. It is only for experienced hill walkers.*

Glasgow

St Bees Hea

Offa's Dyke Footpath *follows the boundary between Wales and England. The 168 mile (270 km) path goes through the beautiful Wye Valley (see p461) in the Welsh borders.*

Dales Way runs from Ilkley in West Yorkshire to Bowness-on-Windermere in the Lake District, 81 miles (130 km) of delightful flat riverside walking and valley scenery.

Pres

Pembrokeshire Coastal path *is 186 miles (299 km) of rugged cliff-top walking from Amroth on Carmarthen Bay to the west tip of Wales at Cardigan.*

St Dogmaels

Amroth

ORDNANCE SURVEY MAPS

The best maps for walkers are published by the Ordnance Survey, the official mapping agency (08456 050505). Out of a wide range of maps the most useful are the *Explorer* series, which include the more popular regions and cover a large area, on a scale of 1:25,000, and the *Landranger* series, on a scale of 1:50;000.

Mineh

The Southwest Coastal Path offers varied scenery from Minehead on the north Somerset coast to Poole in Dorset, via Devon and Cornwall – in all a marathon 630 mile (1,014 km) round trip.

SIGNPOSTS

Long-distance paths are well signposted, some of them with an acorn symbol (or with a thistle in Scotland). Many shorter routes are marked with coloured arrows by local authorities or hiking groups. Local councils generally mark public footpaths with yellow arrows. Public bridleways, marked by blue arrows, are paths that can be used by both walkers and horse riders – remember, horses churn up mud. Signs appear on posts, trees and stiles.

TIPS FOR WALKERS

Be prepared: The weather can change very quickly: dress for the worst. Always take a compass, a proper walking map and get local advice before undertaking any ambitious walking. Pack some food and drink if the map does not show a pub en route.
On the walk: Always keep to the footpath and close gates behind you. Never feed or upset farm animals, leave litter, pick flowers or damage plants.
Where to stay: The International Youth Hostel Federation has a network of hostels which cater particularly for walkers. Bed-and-breakfast accommodation is also available near most routes.
Further information: The Ramblers' Association (020–7339 8500; www.ramblers.org.uk) is a national organization for walkers, with a guide to accommodation.

The Coast to Coast Walk *crosses the Lake District, Yorkshire Dales and North York Moors, on a 190 mile (306 km) route. This demanding walk covers a spectacular range of North Country landscapes. All cross-country routes are best walked from west to east to take advantage of the prevailing wind.*

etholm

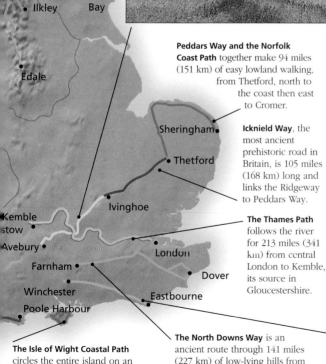

The Ridgeway *is a fairly easy path that follows an ancient track once used by cattle drovers. Starting near Avebury (see p263) it covers 85 miles (137 km) to Ivinghoe Beacon.*

rmere

Robin
Hood's
Bay

Ilkley

Edale

Peddars Way and the Norfolk Coast Path together make 94 miles (151 km) of easy lowland walking, from Thetford, north to the coast then east to Cromer.

Sheringham

Icknield Way, the most ancient prehistoric road in Britain, is 105 miles (168 km) long and links the Ridgeway to Peddars Way.

Thetford

Ivinghoe

Kemble
stow

Avebury

Farnham

Winchester

Poole Harbour

London

Dover

Eastbourne

The Thames Path follows the river for 213 miles (341 km) from central London to Kemble, its source in Gloucestershire.

The South Downs Way *is a 101 mile (162 km) walk from Eastbourne on the south coast to Winchester (see p170–71). It can be completed in a week.*

The Isle of Wight Coastal Path circles the entire island on an easy 65 mile (105 km) footpath.

The North Downs Way is an ancient route through 141 miles (227 km) of low-lying hills from Farnham in Surrey to Dover or Folkestone in Kent.

THE HISTORY OF GREAT BRITAIN

Britain began to assume a cohesive character as early as the 7th century, with the Anglo-Saxon tribes absorbing Celtic and Roman influences and finally achieving supremacy. They suffered repeated Viking incursions and were overcome by the Normans at the Battle of Hastings in 1066. Over centuries, the disparate cultures of the Normans and Anglo-Saxons combined to form the English nation, a process nurtured by Britain's position as an island. The next 400 years saw English kings involved in military expeditions to Europe, but their control over these areas was gradually wrested from them. As a result they extended their domain over Scotland and Wales. The Tudor monarchs consolidated this control and laid the foundations for Britain's future commercial success. Henry VIII recognized the vital importance of sea power and under his daughter, Elizabeth I, English sailors ranged far across the world, often coming into conflict with the Spanish. The total defeat of the Spanish Armada in 1588 confirmed Britain's position as a major maritime power. The Stuart period saw a number of internal struggles, most importantly the Civil War in 1641. But by the time of the Act of the Union in 1707 the whole island was united and the foundations for representative government had been laid. The combination of this internal security with continuing maritime strength allowed Britain to seek wealth overseas. By the end of the Napoleonic Wars in 1815, Britain was the leading trading nation in the world. The opportunities offered by industrialization were seized, and by the late 19th century, a colossal empire had been established across the globe. Challenged by Europe and the rise of the US, and drained by its leading role in two world wars, Britain's influence waned after 1945. By the 1970s almost all the colonies had become independent Commonwealth nations.

Medieval knights, masters of the arts of war

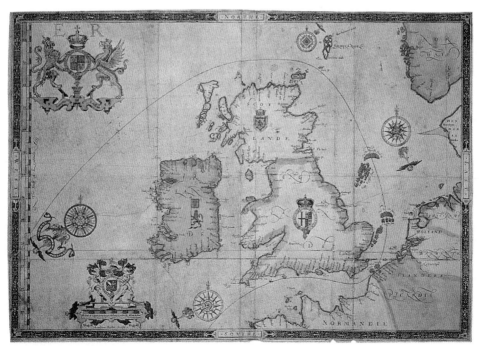

Contemporary map showing the defeat of the Armada (1588), making Britain into a world power

◁ **Henry VIII, founder of the British navy, seen here with his son, Edward, and wife Jane Seymour**

Kings and Queens

All English monarchs since the Norman Conquest in 1066 have been descendants of William the Conqueror. Scottish rulers, until James VI and the Union of Crowns in 1603 *(see pp482–3)*, have been more diverse. When the Crown passes to someone other than the monarch's eldest son, the name of the ruling family usually changes. The rules of succession have been precisely laid down and strongly favour men over women, but Britain has still had six queens since 1553. In Norman times the monarchy enjoyed absolute power, but today the position is largely symbolic.

1066–87 William the Conqueror

1087–1100 William II

1100–35 Henry I

1135–54 Stephen

1327–77 Edward III

1413–22 Henry V

1399–1413 Henry IV

1509–47 Henry VIII

1485–1509 Henry VII

1483–5 Richard III

1050	1100	1150	1200	1250	1300	1350	1400	1450	150
NORMAN		PLANTAGENET					LANCASTER	YORK	TUD
1050	1100	1150	1200	1250	1300	1350	1400	1450	150

1154–89 Henry II

1189–99 Richard I

1199–1216 John

1216–72 Henry III

1307–27 Edward II

1272–1307 Edward I

1422–61 and 1470–1 Henry VI

1461–70 and 1471–83 Edward IV

1377–99 Richard II

Matthew Paris's 13th-century chronicle showing clockwise from top left, Richard I, Henry II, John and Henry III

1483 Edward V

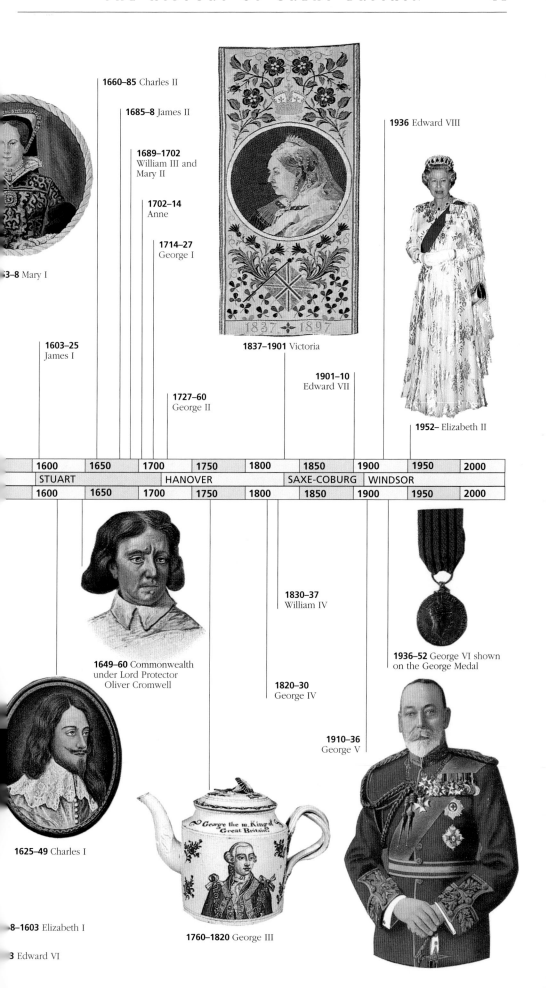

1660–85 Charles II

1685–8 James II

1689–1702
William III and
Mary II

1702–14
Anne

1714–27
George I

3–8 Mary I

1936 Edward VIII

1603–25
James I

1837–1901 Victoria

1901–10
Edward VII

1727–60
George II

1952– Elizabeth II

1600	1650	1700	1750	1800	1850	1900	1950	2000
STUART		HANOVER			SAXE-COBURG	WINDSOR		
1600	1650	1700	1750	1800	1850	1900	1950	2000

1830–37
William IV

1936–52 George VI shown
on the George Medal

1649–60 Commonwealth
under Lord Protector
Oliver Cromwell

1820–30
George IV

1910–36
George V

1625–49 Charles I

8–1603 Elizabeth I

1760–1820 George III

3 Edward VI

Prehistoric Britain

Britain was part of the European landmass until the end of the last Ice Age, around 6000 BC, when the English Channel was formed by melting ice. The earliest inhabitants lived in limestone caves: settlements and farming skills developed gradually through the Stone Age. The magnificent wooden and stone henges and circles are masterworks from around 3000 BC, but their significance is a mystery. Flint mines and ancient pathways are evidence of early trading and many burial mounds (barrows) survive from the Stone and Bronze Ages.

Axe Heads
Stone axes, like this one found at Stonehenge, were used by Neolithic men.

Cup and ring marks were carved on standing stones, such as this one at Ballymeanoch.

MAPPING THE PAST

Monuments from the Neolithic (New Stone), Bronze and Iron Ages, together with artifacts found from these periods, provide a wealth of information about Britain's early settlers, before written history began with the Romans.

Neolithic Tools
Antlers and bones were made into Neolithic leather-working tools. These were found at Avebury (see p263).

Pottery Beaker
The Beaker People, who came from Europe in the early Bronze Age, take their name from these drinking cups often found in their graves.

Gold Breast Plate
Made by Wessex goldsmiths, its spectacular pattern suggests it belonged to an important chieftain.

Pentre Ifan, an impressive Neolithic burial chamber in South Wales, was once covered with a huge earth mound.

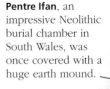

Mold Cape
Gold was mined in Wales and Cornwall in the Bronze Age. This intricately worked warrior's cape was buried in a grave at Mold, Clwyd.

This gold cup, found in a Cornish barrow, is evidence of the wealth of Bronze Age tribes.

TIMELINE

6000–5000 As the Ice Age comes to an end, sea levels rise, submerging the land-link between Britain and the Continent

Neolithic flint axes

6000 BC	5500 BC	5000 BC	4500 BC	4000 BC

A gold pendant and button (1700 BC), found in Bronze Age graves

3500 Neolithic Age begins. Long barrows and stone circles built around Britain

Skara Brae is a Neolithic village of about 2500 BC *(see p529)*.

Maiden Castle
An impressive Iron Age hill fort in Dorset, its concentric lines of ramparts and ditches follow the contours of the hill top (see p269).

Iron Age Brochs, round towers with thick stone walls, are found only in Scotland.

Iron Age Axe
The technique of smelting iron came to Britain around 700 BC, brought from Europe by the Celts.

Castlerigg Stone Circle is one of Britain's earliest Neolithic monuments *(see p361)*.

Uffington White Horse
Thought to be 3,000 years old, the shape has to be "scoured" to keep grass at bay (see p221).

A chalk figure, thought to be a fertility goddess, was found at Grimes Graves *(see p194)*.

This bronze Celtic helmet (50 BC) was found in the River Thames, London.

Stonehenge was begun around 3,500 years ago *(see pp262–63)*.

WHERE TO SEE PREHISTORIC BRITAIN
Wiltshire, with Stonehenge *(p262)* and Avebury *(p263)*, has the best group of Neolithic monuments, and the Uffington White Horse is nearby *(p221)*. The Scottish islands have many early sites and the British Museum *(pp106–7)* houses a huge collection of artefacts.

A circular bank *with over 180 stones encloses the Neolithic site at Avebury (see p263).*

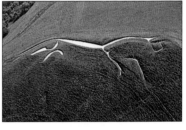

Snettisham Torc
A torc was a neck ring worn by Celtic men. This one, found in Norfolk, dates from 50 BC and is made from silver and gold.

3C	2500 BC	2000 BC	1500 BC	1000 BC	500 BC
500 Temples, or henges, are built of wood or stone	**1650–1200** Wessex is at the hub of trading routes between Europe and the mines of Cornwall, Wales and Ireland		**1000** First farmsteads are settled	**550–350** Migration of Celtic people from southern Europe	**500** Iron Age begins. Hill forts are built
2100–1650 The Bronze Age reaches Britain. Immigration of the Beaker People, who make bronze implements and build ritual temples		*Chieftain's bronze sceptre (1700 BC)*	**1200** Small, self-sufficient villages start to appear		**150** Tribes from Gaul begin to migrate to Britain

Roman Britain

Roman jasper seal

Throughout the 350-year Roman occupation, Britain was ruled as a colony. After the defeat of rebellious local tribes, such as Boadicea's Iceni, the Romans remained an unassimilated occupying power. Their legacy is in military and civil construction: forts, walls, towns and public buildings. Their long, straight roads, built for easy movement of troops, are still a feature of the landscape.

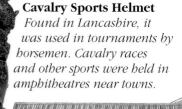

Cavalry Sports Helmet
Found in Lancashire, it was used in tournaments by horsemen. Cavalry races and other sports were held in amphitheatres near towns.

Silver Jug
This 3rd-century jug, the earliest known silver item with Christian symbols, was excavated near Peterborough.

Exercise corridor

Main baths

Fishbourne Palace was built at the site of a natural harbour and ships could moor here.

Entrance hall

Mithras
This head of the god Mithras was found on the London site of a temple devoted to the cult of Mithras. The sect demanded of its Roman followers loyalty and discipline.

Hadrian's Wall
Started in 120 as a defence against the Scots; it marked the northern frontier of the Roman Empire and was guarded by 17 forts housing over 18,500 foot-soldiers and cavalry.

TIMELINE

54 BC Julius Caesar lands in Britain but withdraws

Julius Caesar (c.102–44 BC)

AD 61 Boadicea rebels against Romans and burns their towns, including St Albans and Colchester, but is defeated *(see p195)*

AD 70 Romans conquer Wales and the North

Boadicea (1st century), Queen of the Iceni

140–143 Romans occupy southern Scotland and build Antonine Wall to mark the frontier

| 55 BC | AD 1 | AD 50 | | 150 |

AD 43 Claudius invades; Britain becomes part of the Roman Empire

AD 78–84 Agricola advances into Scotland, then retreats

120 Emperor Hadrian builds a wall on the border with Scotland

Flavian Mosaic
Roman floors of the 1st century used patterns in black and white stone. More mosaics survive at Fishbourne than at any other British site.

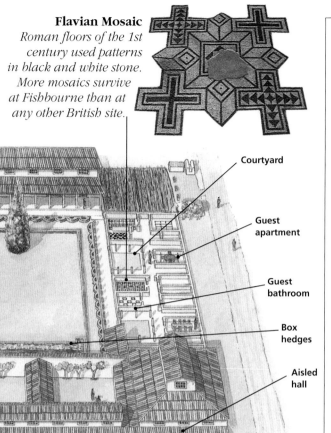

Courtyard

Guest apartment

Guest bathroom

Box hedges

Aisled hall

WHERE TO SEE ROMAN BRITAIN

Many of Britain's main towns and cities were established by the Romans and have Roman remains, including York *(see pp404–09)*, Chester *(see pp310–11)*, St Albans *(see p232)*, Colchester *(see p205)*, Bath *(see pp258–61)*, Lincoln *(see pp340–41)* and London *(see pp70–155)*. Several Roman villas were built in southern England, favoured for its mild climate and proximity to Europe.

The Roman baths in Bath
(see pp258–61), known as Aquae Sulis, were built between the 1st and 4th centuries around a natural hot spring.

FISHBOURNE PALACE

Built during the 1st century for Togidubnus, a pro-Roman governor, the palace (here reconstructed) had sophisticated functions such as under-floor heating and indoor plumbing for baths *(see p171)*.

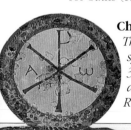

Chi-Rho Symbol
This early Christian symbol is from a 3rd-century fresco at Lullingstone Roman villa in Kent.

Battersea Shield
Found in the Thames near Battersea, the shield bears Celtic symbols and was probably made at about the time of the first Roman invasion. Archaeologists suspect it may have been lost by a warrior while crossing the river, or offered as a sacrifice to one of the many river gods. It is now at the British Museum (see pp106–7).

206 Tribes from northern Scotland attack Hadrian's Wall

254 St Alban is beheaded, and becomes Britain's first Christian martyr

Aberlemno Pictish stone in Scotland

410 Romans withdraw from Britain

250   300   350   400

306 Roman troops in York declare Constantine emperor

350–69 Border raids by Picts and Scots

440–450 Invasions of Angles, Saxons and Jutes

209 Septimius Severus arrives from Rome with reinforcements

Anglo-Saxon Kingdoms

King Canute (1016–35)

By the mid-5th century, Angles and Saxons from Germany had started to raid the eastern shores of Britain. Increasingly they decided to settle, and within 100 years Saxon kingdoms, including Wessex, Mercia and Northumbria, were established over the entire country. Viking raids throughout the 8th and 9th centuries were largely contained, but in 1066, the last invasion of England saw William the Conqueror from Normandy defeat the Anglo-Saxon King Harold at the Battle of Hastings. William then went on to assume control of the whole country.

Viking Axe
The principal weapons of the Viking warriors were spear, axe and sword. They were skilled metal-workers with an eye for decoration, as seen in this axe-head from a Copenhagen museum.

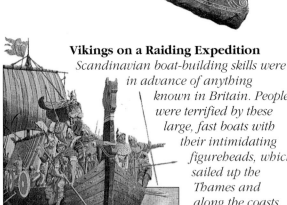

Vikings on a Raiding Expedition
Scandinavian boat-building skills were in advance of anything known in Britain. People were terrified by these large, fast boats with their intimidating figureheads, which sailed up the Thames and along the coasts.

ANGLO-SAXON CALENDAR

These scenes from a chronicle of seasons, made just before the Norma invasion, show life in late Anglo-Saxon Britain. At first people lived small farming communities, but by t 7th century towns began to spring and trade increased. Saxon kings we supported by nobles but most of the population were free peasants

TIMELINE

St Augustine (d.604)

450	500	550	600	650	700

c.470–495 Saxons and Angles settle in Essex, Sussex and East Anglia

c.556 Saxons move across Britain and set up seven kingdoms

635 St Aidan establishes a monastery on Lindisfarne

730–821 Supremacy of Mercia, whose king, Offa (d.796), builds a dyke along the Mercia–Wales border

450 Saxons first settle in Kent

563 St Columba lands on Iona

617–85 Supremacy of Northumbrian kingdom

597 St Augustine sent by Rome to convert English to Christianity

Mercian coin which bears the name of King Offa

Ox-drawn plough for tilling

Minstrels entertaining at a feast

Hawks, used to kill game

Alfred Jewel
This 9th-century gold ornament in the Ashmolean Museum (see p224) has the inscription: "Alfred ordered me made". This may refer to the Saxon King Alfred.

Edward the Confessor
In 1042, Edward – known as "the Confessor" because of his piety – became king. He died in 1066 and William of Normandy claimed the throne.

Harold's Death
This 14th-century illustration depicts the victorious William of Normandy after King Harold was killed with an arrow in his eye. The Battle of Hastings (see p181) was the last invasion of Britain.

WHERE TO SEE ANGLO-SAXON BRITAIN

The best collection of Saxon artefacts is from a burial ship unearthed at Sutton Hoo in Suffolk in 1938 and now on display at the British Museum *(see pp106–7)*. There are fine Saxon churches at Bradwell in Essex and Bosham in Sussex *(see p171)*. In York the Viking town of Jorvik has been excavated *(see p408)* and actual relics are shown alongside models of people and dwellings.

The Saxon church *of St Laurence (see p255) was built in the late 8th century.*

Legend of King Arthur
Arthur is thought to have been a chieftain who fought the Saxons in the early 6th century. Legends of his knights' exploits appeared in 1155 (see p285).

An invading Norman ship

802–839 After the death of Cenwulf (821), Wessex gains control over most of England

867 Northumbria falls to the Vikings

878 King Alfred defeats Vikings but allows them to settle in eastern England

1016 Danish King Canute *(see p171)* seizes English crown

| 800 | 850 | 900 | 950 | 1000 | 1050 | 1100 |

843 Kenneth McAlpin becomes king of all Scotland

793 Lindisfarne sacked by ‹Vi›king invaders; first Viking raid ‹o›‹n› Scotland about a year later

926 Eastern England, the Danelaw, is reconquered by the Saxons

1042 The Anglo-Saxon Edward the Confessor becomes king (d.1066)

1066 William of Normandy claims the throne, and defeats Harold at the Battle of Hastings. He is crowned at Westminster

The Middle Ages

Noblemen stag hunting

Remains of Norman castles on English hill tops bear testimony to the military might used by the invaders to sustain their conquest – although Wales and Scotland resisted for centuries. The Normans operated a feudal system, creating an aristocracy that treated native Anglo-Saxons as serfs. The ruling class spoke French until the 13th century, when it mixed with the Old English used by the peasants. The medieval church's power is shown in the cathedrals that grace British cities today.

Magna Carta

To protect themselves and the church from arbitrary taxation, the powerful English barons compelled King John to sign a "great charter" in 1215 (see p235). This laid the foundations for an independent legal system.

Becket is received into heaven.

Craft Skills

An illustration from a 14th-century manuscript depicts a weaver and a copper-beater – two of the trades that created a wealthy class of artisans.

Henry II's knights murder Becket in Canterbury Cathedral.

MURDER OF THOMAS BECKET

The struggle between church and king for ultimate control of the country was brought to a head by the murder of Becket, the Archbishop of Canterbury. After Becket's canonization in 1173, Canterbury became a major centre of pilgrimage.

Ecclesiastical Art

Nearly all medieval art had religious themes, such as this window at Canterbury Cathedral (see pp186–7) depicting Jeroboam.

Black Death

A plague swept Britain and Europe several times in the 14th century, killing millions of people. This illustration, in a religious tract, produced around 100 years later, represents death taking its heavy toll.

TIMELINE

1071 Hereward the Wake, leader of the Anglo-Saxon resistance, defeated at Ely

1154 Henry II, the first Plantagenet king, demolishes castles, and exacts money from barons instead of military service

1170 Archbishop of Canterbury, Thomas à Becket, is murdered by four knights after quarrelling with Henry II

1100 **1150** **1200** **12**

1086 The *Domesday Book*, a survey of every manor in England, is compiled for tax purposes

Domesday Book

1215 Barons compel King John to sign the *Magna Carta*

1256 Parliame inc ord citi

Battle of Agincourt
In 1415, Henry V took an army to France to claim its throne. This 15th-century chronicle depicts Henry beating the French army at Agincourt.

This casket (1190), in a private collection, is said to have contained Becket's remains.

Becket takes his place in Heaven after his canonization.

Two clergymen look on in horror at Becket's murder.

Richard III
Richard, shown in this 16th-century painting, became king during the Wars of the Roses: a bitter struggle for power between two factions of the royal family – the houses of York and Lancaster.

John Wycliffe *(1329–84)*

This painting by Ford Madox Brown (1821–93) shows Wycliffe with the Bible he translated into English to make it accessible to everyone.

WHERE TO SEE MEDIEVAL BRITAIN
The university cities of Oxford *(pp222–27)* and Cambridge *(pp210–15)* contain the largest concentrations of Gothic buildings. Magnificent cathedrals rise high above many historic cities, among them Lincoln *(pp340–41)* and York *(pp404–09)*. Both cities still retain at least part of their ancient street pattern. Military architecture is best seen in Wales *(pp438–9)* with the formidable border castles of Edward I.

All Souls College *in Oxford (see p226), which only takes graduates, is a superb blend of medieval and later architecture.*

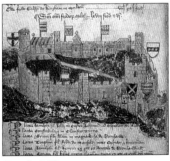

Castle Life
Every section of a castle was allotted to a baron whose soldiers helped defend it. This 14th-century illustration shows the coats of arms (see p30) of the barons for each area.

1314 Scots defeat English at the Battle of Bannockburn *(see p482)*

1387 Chaucer starts writing the *Canterbury Tales (see p186)*

1485 Battle of Bosworth ends Wars of the Roses

82–3 ward I nquers ales

1348 Europe's population halved by Black Death

Geoffrey Chaucer (c.1345–1400)

| 1300 | 1350 | 1400 | 1450 |

1296 Edward I invades Scotland but Scots resist stoutly

1381 Peasants' revolt after the imposition of a poll tax on everyone in the country over 14

Edward I (1239–1307)

1415 English victory at Agincourt

1453 End of Hundred Years' War against France

Tudor Renaissance

After years of debilitating civil war, the Tudor monarchs established peace and national self-confidence, reflected in the split from the church of Rome – due to Henry VIII's divorce from Catherine of Aragon – and the consequent closure of the monasteries.

Hawking, a popular pastime

Henry's daughter, Mary I, tried to reestablish Catholicism but under her half-sister, Elizabeth I, the Protestant church secured its position. Overseas exploration began, provoking clashes with other European powers seeking to exploit the New World. The Renaissance in arts and learning spread from Europe to Britain, with playwright William Shakespeare adding his own unique contribution.

Curtains behind the queen are open to reveal scenes of the great English victory over the Spanish Armada in 1588.

Sea Power
Henry VIII laid the foundations of the powerful English navy. In 1545, his flagship, the Mary Rose *(see p169), sank before his eyes in Portsmouth harbour on its way to do battle with the French.*

Theatre
Some of Shakespeare's plays were first seen in purpose-built theatres such as the Globe *(see p120) in south London.*

The globe signifies that the queen reigns supreme far and wide.

Monasteries
With Henry VIII's split from Rome, England's religious houses, like Fountains Abbey (see pp390–91), were dissolved. Henry stole their riches and used them to finance his foreign policy.

TIMELINE

1497 John Colet denounces the corruption of the clergy, supported by Erasmus and Sir Thomas More

1533–4 Henry VIII divorces Catherine of Aragon and is excommunicated by the Pope. He forms the Church of England

1542–1567 Mary, Queen of Scots rules Scotland

1490

1510

1530

1497 John Cabot *(see p256)* makes his first voyage to North America

1513 English defeat Scots at Flodden *(see p482)*

1535 Act of Union with Wales

1536–40 Dissolution of the Monasteries

1549 First Boo Common Pr introd

Henry VIII (1491–1547)

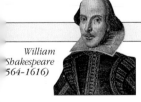

Mary, Queen of Scots
As great-granddaughter of Henry VII, she laid claim to the English throne in 1559. But in 1567, Elizabeth I had her imprisoned for 20 years until her execution for treason in 1587.

Jewels symbolize triumph.

WHERE TO SEE TUDOR BRITAIN

Hampton Court Palace *(p173)* has been altered over the centuries but remains a Tudor showpiece. Part of Elizabeth I's former home at Hatfield *(p231)* still survives. In Kent, Leeds Castle, Knole *(pp188–9)* and Hever Castle *(p189)* all have connections with Tudor royalty. Burghley House *(pp342–3)* and Hardwick Hall *(p302)*, both Midlands mansions, retain their 16th-century character.

This astronomical clock *at Hampton Court (see p173), with its intriguing zodiac symbols, was installed in 1540 by Henry VIII.*

DEFEAT OF THE ARMADA

Spain was England's main rival for supremacy on the seas, and in 1588 Philip II sent 100 powerfully armed galleons towards England, bent on invasion. The English fleet – under Lord Howard, Francis Drake, John Hawkins and Martin Frobisher – sailed from Plymouth and destroyed the Spanish navy in a famous victory. This commemorative portrait of Elizabeth I by George Gower (d.1596) celebrates the triumph.

Protestant Martyrs
Catholic Mary I reigned from 1553 to 1558. Protestants who opposed her rule were burned, such as these six churchmen at Canterbury in 1555.

William Shakespeare 1564–1616)

1570 Sir Francis Drake's first voyage to the West Indies

1584 Sir Walter Raleigh tries to colonize Virginia after Drake's first unsuccessful attempt

1591 First play by Shakespeare performed

1600 East India Company founded, beginning British involvement on the Indian continent

1570

1590

53 Death of ward VI; one passes the Catholic ry I

1559 Mary, Queen of Scots lays claim to English throne

1558 Elizabeth I ascends the throne

1587 Execution of Mary, Queen of Scots on the orders of Elizabeth I

1588 Defeat of the Spanish Armada

Sir Walter Raleigh (1552–1618)

1603 Union of Crowns. James VI of Scotland becomes I of England

Stuart Britain

The end of Elizabeth I's reign signalled the start of internal turmoil. The throne passed to James I, whose belief that kings ruled by divine right provoked clashes with Parliament. Under his son, Charles I, the conflict escalated into Civil War that ended with his execution. In 1660 Charles II regained the throne, but after his death James II was ousted for Catholic leanings. Protestantism was reaffirmed with the reign of William and Mary, who suppressed the Catholic Jacobites (see p483).

A 17th-century barber's bowl

Oliver Cromwell

A strict Protestant and a passionate champion of the rights of Parliament, he led the victorious Parliamentary forces in the Civil War. He became Lord Protector of the Commonwealth from 1653 to 1658.

On the way to his death, the king wore two shirts for warmth, so onlookers should not think he was shivering with fright.

Science

Sir Isaac Newton (1642–1727) invented this reflecting telescope, laying the foundation for a greater understanding of the universe, including the law of gravity.

Charles I stayed silent at his trial.

Theatre

After the Restoration in 1660, when Parliament restored the monarchy, theatre thrived. Plays were performed on temporary outdoor stages.

EXECUTION OF CHARLES I

Cromwell was convinced there would be no peace until the king was dead. At his trial for treason, Charles refused to recognize the authority of the court and offered no defence. He faced his death with dignity on 30 January 1649, the only English king to be executed. His death was followed by a republic known as the Commonwealth.

TIMELINE

1605 "Gunpowder Plot" to blow up Parliament thwarted	**1614** "Addled Parliament" refuses to vote money for James I	**1620** Pilgrim Fathers sail in the *Mayflower* to New England	**1642** Civil War breaks out	**1653–8** Cromwell rules as Lord Protector	
	1625		**1650**		
James I (1566–1625)	**1611** New translation of Bible published, known as King James Version	**1638** Scots sign National Covenant, opposing Charles I's Catholic leanings	**1649** Charles I executed outside Banqueting House and Commonwealth declared by Parliament	**1660** Restorati of the monarc under Charle	

Restoration of the Monarchy

This silk embroidery celebrates the fact that Charles II escaped his father's fate by hiding in an oak tree. There was joy at his return from exile in France.

WHERE TO SEE STUART BRITAIN

The best work of the two leading architects of the time, Inigo Jones and Christopher Wren, is in London, and includes St Paul's Cathedral (pp114–15). In the southeast two classic Jacobean mansions are Audley End (p208) and Hatfield House (p231). The Palace of Holyrood (p510), in Edinburgh, is another example.

The headless body kneels by the block.

The axeman holds the severed head of Charles I.

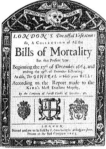

Plague

Bills of mortality showed the weekly deaths as bubonic plague swept London in 1665. Up to 100,000 Londoners died.

Hatfield House (p231) *is a splendid Jacobean mansion.*

Onlookers soaked up the king's blood with their handkerchiefs to have a memento.

Anatomy

By dissecting corpses, physicians began to gain an understanding of the working of the human body – a crucial step towards modern surgery and medicine.

Pilgrim Fathers

In 1620 a group of Puritans sailed to America. They forged good relations with the native Indians; here they are shown being visited by the chief of the Pokanokets.

5–6 at Plague

The Great Fire of London

1707 Act of Union with Scotland

666 Great Fire London

1688 The Glorious Revolution: Catholic James II deposed by Parliament

1675

1700

1690 Battle of the Boyne: William's English/Dutch army defeats James II's Irish/French army

1692 Glencoe Massacre of Jacobites (Stuart supporters) by William III's forces

William III (1689–1702)

Georgian Britain

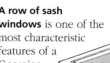

The 18th century saw Britain, now recovered from the trauma of its Civil War, develop as a commercial and industrial powerhouse. London became a centre of banking, and a mercantile and professional class grew up. Continuing supremacy at sea laid the foundations of an empire; steam engines, canals and railways heralded the Industrial Revolution. Growing confidence was reflected in stately architecture and elegant fashions but, as cities became more crowded, conditions for the underclass grew worse.

Actress Sarah Siddons (1785), Gainsborough

Slate became the preferred tile for Georgian buildings. Roofs became less steep to achieve an Italian look.

A row of sash windows is one of the most characteristic features of a Georgian house.

Battle of Bunker Hill

In 1775 American colonists rebelled against British rule. The British won this early battle in Massachusetts, but in 1783 Britain recognized the United States of America.

Oak was used in the best dwellings for doors and stairs, but pine was standard in most houses.

The saloon was covered in wallpaper, a cheaper alternative to hanging walls with tapestries or fabrics.

The drawing room was richly ornamented and used for entertaining visitors.

The dining room was used for all family meals.

Watt's Steam Engine

The Scottish engineer James Watt (1736–1819) patented his engine in 1769 and then developed it for locomotion.

Lord Horatio Nelson

Nelson (see p31) became a hero after his death at the Battle of Trafalgar fighting the French.

Steps led to the servants' entrance in the basement.

TIMELINE

1714 George, Elector of Hanover, succeeds Queen Anne, ending the Stuart dynasty and giving Britain a German-speaking monarch

George I (1660–1727)

1720 "South Sea Bubble" bursts: many speculators ruined in securities fraud

1721 Robert Walpole (1646–1745) becomes the first Prime Minister

Satirical engraving about the South Sea Bubble, 1720

1746 Bonnie Prince Charlie *(see p535)*, Jacobite claimant to throne, defeated at the Battle of Culloden

1757 Britain's first canal completed

1715	1730	1745	1760

Canal Barge *(1827)*
Canals were a cheap way to carry the new industrial goods but were gradually superseded by railways during the 19th century.

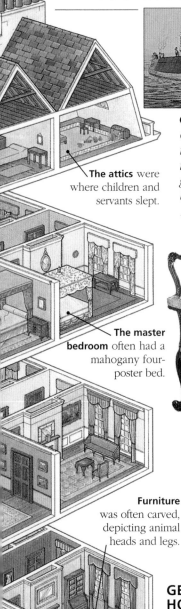

The attics were where children and servants slept.

The master bedroom often had a mahogany four-poster bed.

Furniture was often carved, depicting animal heads and legs.

Chippendale Armchair *(1760)*
Thomas Chippendale (1718–79) designed elegant furniture in a style still popular today.

WHERE TO SEE GEORGIAN BRITAIN

Bath *(see pp258–61)* and Edinburgh *(see pp504–11)* are two of Britain's best-preserved Georgian towns. The Building of Bath Museum in Bath *(see p261)* has a real Georgian flavour and Brighton's Royal Pavilion *(see pp178–9)* is a Regency extravaganza by John Nash.

Charlotte Square (see p504) *in Edinburgh has fine examples of Georgian architecture.*

GEORGIAN TOWN HOUSE

Tall, terraced dwellings were built to house wealthy families. The main architects of the time were Robert Adam *(see p28)* and John Nash *(see p105).*

The servants lived and worked in the basement during the day.

Kitchen

Hogarth's Gin Lane
Conditions in London's slums shocked William Hogarth (1697–1764), who made prints like this to urge social reform.

1788 First convict ships are sent to Australia

1811–17 Riots against growing unemployment

1776 American Declaration of Independence

1805 The British, led by Lord Nelson, beat Napoleon's French fleet at Battle of Trafalgar

1815 Duke of Wellington beats Napoleon at Waterloo

Caricature of Wellington (1769–1852)

75	1790	1805	1820

1783 Steam-powered cotton mill invented by Sir Richard Arkwright (1732–92)

1807 Abolition of slave trade

1811 Prince of Wales made Regent during George III's madness

1825 Stockton to Darlington railway opens

1829 Catholic Emancipation Act passed

Silver tureen, 1774

Victorian Britain

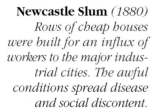

When Victoria became Queen in 1837, she was only 18. Britain was in the throes of its transformation from an agricultural country to the world's most powerful industrial nation. The growth of the Empire fuelled the country's confidence and opened up markets for Britain's manufactured goods. The accelerating growth of cities created problems of health and housing and a powerful Labour movement began to emerge. But by the end of Victoria's long and popular reign in 1901, conditions had begun to improve as more people got the vote and universal education was introduced.

Victoria and Disraeli, 1887

Florence Nightingale *(1820–1910) Known as the Lady with the Lamp, she nursed soldiers in the Crimean War and pioneered many improvements in army medical care.*

Glass walls and ceiling

Prefabricated girders

Newcastle Slum *(1880) Rows of cheap houses were built for an influx of workers to the major industrial cities. The awful conditions spread disease and social discontent.*

UNITED SOCIETY OF BOILERMAKERS AND IRON AND STEEL SHIPBUILDERS ESTD 1834

UNITY IS STRENGTH

LONDON DISTRICT COMMITTEE

Union Banner *Trade unions were set up to protect industrial workers against unscrupulous employers.*

As well as silk textiles exhibits included carriages, engines, jewels, glass, plants, cutlery and sculptures.

Ophelia by Sir John Everett Millais *(1829–96) The Pre-Raphaelite painters chose Romantic themes, reflecting a desire to escape industrial Britain.*

TIMELINE

1832 Great Reform Bill extends the vote to all male property owners

1841 London to Brighton railway makes resort accessible

Vase made for the Great Exhibition

1851 Great Exhibition

1867 Second Reform gives the vote to all m householders in to

1830	1840	1850	1860

1834 Tolpuddle Martyrs transported to Australia for forming a union

1833 Factory Act forbids employment of children for more than 48 hours per week

1854–6 Britain victorious against Russia in Crimean War

1863 Opening of the London Underground

Triumph of Steam and Electricity
This picture from the Illustrated London News (1897) sums up the feeling of optimism engendered by industrial advances.

Elm trees were incorporated into the building along with sparrows, and sparrow hawks to control them.

WHERE TO SEE VICTORIAN BRITAIN

The industrial cities of the Midlands and the North are built around grandiose civic, commercial and industrial buildings. Notable Victorian monuments include the Manchester Museum of Science and Industry *(see p374)* and, in London, the Victoria and Albert Museum *(see pp98–9)* and St Pancras train station.

The Rotunda, Manchester *is a stately Victorian building.*

GREAT EXHIBITION OF 1851

The brainchild of Prince Albert, Victoria's consort, the exhibition celebrated industry, technology and the expanding British Empire. It was the biggest of its kind held up until then. Between May and October, six million people visited Joseph Paxton's lavish crystal palace, in London's Hyde Park. Nearly 14,000 exhibitors brought 100,000 exhibits from all over the world. In 1852 it was moved to south London where it burned down in 1936.

Cycling Craze
The bicycle, invented in 1865, became immensely popular with young people, as illustrated by this photograph of 1898.

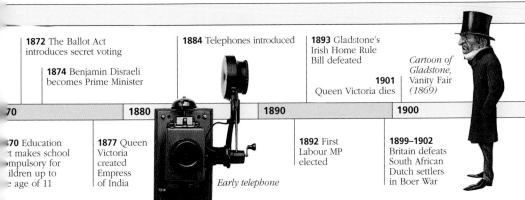

1872 The Ballot Act introduces secret voting

1874 Benjamin Disraeli becomes Prime Minister

1884 Telephones introduced

1893 Gladstone's Irish Home Rule Bill defeated

1901 Queen Victoria dies

Cartoon of Gladstone, Vanity Fair (1869)

70   1880   1890   1900

70 Education t makes school mpulsory for ildren up to e age of 11

1877 Queen Victoria created Empress of India

Early telephone

1892 First Labour MP elected

1899–1902 Britain defeats South African Dutch settlers in Boer War

Britain from 1900 to 1950

When Queen Victoria's reign ended in 1901, British society threw off many of its 19th-century inhibitions, and an era of gaiety and excitement began. This was interrupted by World War I. The economic troubles that ensued, which culminated in the Depression of the 1930s, brought misery to millions. In 1939 the ambitions of Germany provoked World War II. After emerging victorious from this conflict, Britain embarked on an ambitious programme of social, educational and health reform.

Playwright Noel Coward

Welwyn Garden City was based on the Utopian idea of Sir Ebenezer Howard (1850–1928), founder of the garden city movement.

The Roaring Twenties
Young flappers discarded the rigid social codes of their parents and instead discovered jazz, cocktails and the Charleston.

Suffragettes
Women marched and chained themselves to railings in their effort to get the vote; many went to prison. Women over 30 won the vote in 1919.

NEW TOWNS

A string of new towns was created on the outskirts of London, planned to give residents greenery and fresh air. Welwyn Garden City was originally founded in 1919 as a self-contained community, but fast rail links turned it into a base for London commuters.

World War I
British troops in Europe dug into deep trenches protected by barbed wire and machine guns, only metres from the enemy, in a war of attrition that cost the lives of 17 million.

Wireless
Invented by Guglielmo Marconi, radios brought news and entertainment into homes for the first time.

TIMELINE

1903 Suffragette movement founded

1911 MPs are given a salary for the first time, allowing working men to be elected

1914–18 World War I

1924 La government

| 1905 | 1910 | 1915 | 1920 |

Henry Asquith (1852–1928), Prime Minister

1908 Asquith's Liberal government introduces old age pensions

1918 Vote given to all women over 30

1922 First national radio service begins

Marching for Jobs

These men were among thousands who marched for their jobs after being put out of work in the 1920s. The stock market crash of 1929 and the ensuing Depression caused even more unemployment.

World War II

German night-time air raids targeted transport, military and industrial sites and cities, such as Sheffield, in what was known as the "Blitz".

Modern Homes

Labour-saving devices, such as the vacuum cleaner, invented by William Hoover in 1908, were very popular. This was due to the virtual disappearance of domestic servants, as women took jobs outside the home.

rden cities had trees, nds and en spaces.

Cheap housing and the promise of a cleaner environment attracted many people to these new cities.

Family Motoring

By the middle of the century, more families could afford to buy mass-produced automobiles, like the 1950s Hillman Minx pictured in this advertisement.

26 General Strike	1936 Abdication of Edward VIII	1944 Education Act: school leaving age raised to 15; grants provided for university students	1948 National Health Service introduced
Edward VIII (1894–1972) and Wallis Simpson (1896–1986)			1947 Independence for India and Pakistan
1930	**1935**	**1940**	**1945**
1929 Stock market crashes	1936 First scheduled television service begins	1939–45 Winston Churchill leads Britain to victory in World War II	1945 Majority Labour government; nationalization of railways, road haulage, civil aviation, Bank of England, gas, electricity and steel
1928 Votes for all men and women over 21		*Food ration book*	

Britain Today

With the deprivations of war receding, Britain entered the Swinging Sixties, an explosion of youth culture characterized by the mini-skirt and the emergence of pop groups. The Age of Empire came to an end as most colonies gained independence by the 1970s – although Britain went to war again in 1982 when Argentina sought to annexe the tiny Falkland Islands.

Designer Vivienne Westwood and Naomi Campbell

People were on the move; immigration from the former colonies enriched British culture – though it also gave rise to social problems – and increasing prosperity allowed millions of people to travel abroad. Britain joined the European Community in 1973, and forged a more tangible link when the Channel Tunnel opened in 1994.

1982 British troops set sail to drive the Argentinians from the British-owned Falkland Islands

1970s The outlandish clothes, hair and make-up of Punk Rockers shock the country

1960s The miniskirt takes British fashion to new heights of daring – and Flower Power arrives from California

1951 Winston Churchill comes back as Prime Minister as Conservatives win general election

1965 Death penalty is abolished

1976 Supersonic Concorde makes first commercial flight

1950	1960	1970	1980

1950	1960	1970	1980

1953 Elizabeth II crowned in first televised Coronation

1975 Drilling begins for North Sea oil

1981 Charle Prince Wales ries La Diana Spenc in "fa" wedd. St Pau Cathe

1963 The Beatles pop group from Liverpool captures the spirit of the age with numerous chart-topping hits

1951 Festival of Britain lifts postwar spirits

1959 First motorway, the M1, built from London to the Midlands

1979 The "Iron Lady" Margaret Thatcher becomes Britain's first woman Prime Minister; her right-wing Conservative Government privatizes several state-owned industries

1957 First immigrants arrive from the Caribbean by boat

VOTE!

...GET BRITAIN OUT

1973 After years of negotiation, Britain joins the European Community

1984 Year-long miners' strike fails to stop pit closures and heralds decline in trade union power

2005 The Prince of Wales marries Camilla Parker-Bowles at the Guildhall in Windsor

1991 Britain's tallest building, Canada Tower *(see p125)*, erected as part of the huge Docklands development – London's new financial centre

2004 One of London's most distinctive buildings, 30 St Mary Axe, also known as "the Gherkin", opens

1992 Conservative Government elected for fourth term – a record for this century

1997 New Labour ends 18 years of Conservative government

2005 London's transport system hit by four bombs in a terrorist attack

2012 Britain is set to host the 2012 Olympic Games

1990	2000	2010

1990	2000	2010

2007 Gordon Brown takes office as Prime Minister after Tony Blair's resignation

2005 The Labour party is elected for a record third term under Tony Blair

1990 Mrs Thatcher forced to resign by Conservative MPs; replaced by John Major

2003 Britain joins the US-led coalition in the Iraq war and thousands take to the streets to protest against the imminent invasion

1999 Formation of Scottish Parliament and Welsh Assembly

1985 Concern for famine in Africa gives rise to giant Live Aid pop concert to raise money for the starving

1994 Channel Tunnel opens to give direct rail link between Britain and Continental Europe

GREAT BRITAIN THROUGH THE YEAR

Film festival sign

Every British season has its particular charms. Most major sights are open all year round, but many secondary attractions may be closed in winter. The weather is changeable in all seasons and the visitor is as likely to experience a crisp, sunny February day as to be caught in a cold, heavy shower in July. Long periods of adverse weather and extremes of temperature are rare. Spring is characterized by daffodils and bluebells, summer by roses and autumn by the vivid colours of changing leaves. In wintertime, country vistas are visible through the bare branches of the trees. Annual events and ceremonies, many stemming from age-old traditions, reflect the attributes of the seasons.

Bluebells in spring in Angrove woodland, Wiltshire

SPRING

As the days get longer and warmer, the countryside starts to come alive. At Easter many stately homes and gardens open their gates to visitors for the first time, and during the week before Whit Sunday, or Whitsun (the seventh Sunday after Easter), the Chelsea Flower Show takes place. This is the focal point of the gardening year and spurs on the nation's gardeners to prepare their summer displays. Outside the capital, many music and arts festivals mark the middle months of the year.

MARCH

Ideal Home Exhibition (*second week*), Earl's Court, London. New products and ideas for the home.
Crufts Dog Show, National Exhibition Centre, Birmingham.
International Book Fair (*third week*), Olympia, London.
St Patrick's Day (*17 March*). Musical events in major cities celebrate the feast day of Ireland's patron saint.

APRIL

Maundy Thursday (Thursday before Easter), the Queen gives money to pensioners.
St George's Day (*23 April*), English patron saint's day.
Antiques for Everyone (*last week*), National Exhibition Centre, Birmingham.

Water garden exhibited at the Chelsea Flower Show

MAY

Furry Dancing Festival (*8 May*), Helston, Cornwall. Spring celebration (*see p280*).
Well-dressing festivals (*Ascension Day*), Tissington, Derbyshire (*see p337*).
Chelsea Flower Show (*May*), Royal Hospital, London.
Brighton Festival (*last three weeks*). Performing arts.
Glyndebourne Festival Opera Season (*mid-May– end Aug*), near Lewes, East Sussex. Opera productions.
International Highland Games (*last weekend*), Blair Atholl, Scotland.

Yeomen of the Guard conducting the Maundy money ceremony

SUMMER

Life moves outdoors in the summer months. Cafés and restaurants place tables on the pavements and pub customers take their drinks outside. The Queen holds garden parties for privileged guests at Buckingham Palace while, more modestly, village fêtes – which include traditional games and local stalls – are organized. Beaches and swimming pools become crowded and office workers picnic in city parks at lunch. The rose, England's national flower, bursts into bloom in millions of gardens. Cultural treats include open-air theatre performances, outdoor concerts, the Proms in London, the National Eisteddfod in Wales, Glyndebourne's opera festival, and Edinburgh's festival of the performing arts.

Glastonbury music festival, a major event attracting thousands of people

Deck chair at Brighton

JUNE

Royal Academy Summer Exhibitions *(Jun–Aug)*. Large and varied London show of new work by many artists.
Bath International Festival *(late May–early Jun)*, various venues. Arts events.
Beaumaris Festival *(27 May–4 Jun)*, various venues. Concerts, craft fairs plus fringe activities.
Trooping the Colour *(Sat closest to 10 Jun)*, Whitehall,

Assessment of sheep at the Royal Welsh Show, Builth Wells

London. The Queen's official birthday parade.
Glastonbury Festival *(late June)*, Somerset.
    Aldeburgh Festival *(second and third weeks)*, Suffolk. Arts festival with concerts and opera.
    Royal Highland Show *(third week)*, Ingliston, near Edinburgh. Scotland's agricultural show.
    Leeds Castle *(last week)*. Open-air concerts.
Glasgow International Jazz Festival *(last weekend)*. Various venues.

JULY

Royal Show *(first week)*, near Kenilworth, Warwickshire. National agricultural show.
International Eisteddfod *(first week)*, Llangollen, North Wales. International music and dance competition *(see p450)*.
Hampton Court Flower Show *(early July)*, Hampton Court Palace, Surrey.
Summer Music Festival *(third weekend)*, Stourhead, Wiltshire.
International Henley Royal Regatta *(first week)*, Henley-on-Thames. Rowing regatta on the Thames.
Cambridge Folk Festival *(last weekend)*. Music festival with top international artists.
Royal Welsh Show *(last weekend)*, Builth Wells, Wales. Agricultural show.
International Festival of Folk Arts *(late Jul–early Aug)*, Sidmouth, Devon *(see p289)*.

AUGUST

Royal National Eisteddfod *(early in month)*. Traditional arts competitions, in Welsh *(see p435)*. Various locations.

Reveller in bright costume at the Notting Hill Carnival

Henry Wood Promenade Concerts *(mid-Jul–mid-Sep)*, Royal Albert Hall, London. Famous concert series popularly known as the Proms.
Edinburgh International Festival *(mid-Aug–mid-Sep)*. The largest festival of theatre, dance and music in the world *(see p481)*.
Edinburgh Festival Fringe. Alongside the festival, there are 400 shows a day.
Brecon Jazz *(mtd-Aug)*, jazz festival in Brecon, Wales.
Beatles Festival *(last weekend)*, Liverpool. Music and entertainment related to the Fab Four *(see p377)*.
Notting Hill Carnival *(last weekend)*, London. West Indian street carnival with floats, bands and stalls.

Boxes of apples from the autumn harvest

AUTUMN

After the heady escapism of summer, the start of the new season is marked by the various party political conferences held in October and the royal opening of Parliament. All over the country on 5 November, bonfires are lit and fireworks let off to celebrate the foiling of an attempt to blow up the Houses of Parliament by Guy Fawkes and his co-conspirators in 1605. Cornfields become golden, trees turn fiery yellow through to russet and orchards

Fireworks over Edinburgh on Guy Fawkes Night

are heavy with apples and other autumn fruits. In churches throughout the country, thanksgiving festivals mark the harvest. The shops stock up for the run-up to Christmas, their busiest time of the year.

SEPTEMBER

Blackpool Illuminations *(beg Sep–end Oct)*. A 5 mile (8 km) spectacle of lighting along Blackpool's seafront.
Royal Highland Gathering *(first Sat)*, Braemar, Scotland. Kilted clansmen from all over the country toss cabers, shot putt, dance and play the bagpipes. The royal family usually attends.
International Sheepdog Trials *(14–16 Sep)*, all over Britain, with venues changing from year to year.

Shot putting at Braemar

Great Autumn Flower Show *(third weekend)*, Harrogate, N Yorks. Displays by nurserymen and national flower organizations.
Oyster Festival *(Sat at beginning of oyster season)*, Colchester. Lunch hosted by the mayor to celebrate the beginning of the much awaited oyster season.

OCTOBER

Harvest Festivals *(whole month)*, all over Britain especially in farming areas.
Horse of the Year Show *(6–10 Oct)*, NEC, Birmingham.
Nottingham Goose Fair *(second weekend)*. One of Britain's oldest traditional fairs now has a funfair.
Canterbury Festival *(second and third weeks)*. Music, drama and the arts.
Aldeburgh Britten Festival *(third weekend)*. Concerts with music by Britten *(see p201)* and other composers.

Procession leading to the state opening of Parliament

NOVEMBER

Opening of Parliament *(Oct or Nov)*. The Queen goes from Buckingham Palace to Westminster in a state coach, to open the new parliamentary session.
London Film Festival *(end Oct–beg Nov)*. Forum for new films, various venues.
Lord Mayor's Procession and Show *(second Sat)*. Parade in the City, London.
Remembrance Day *(second Sun)*. Services and parades at the Cenotaph in Whitehall, London, and all over Britain.
RAC London to Brighton Veteran Car Rally *(first Sun)*. A 7am start from Hyde Park, London to Brighton, East Sussex.
Guy Fawkes Night *(5 Nov)*, fireworks and bonfires all over the country.
Regent Street Christmas Lights *(mid-Nov)*, London.

Winter landscape in the Scottish Highlands, near Glencoe

WINTER

Brightly coloured fairy lights and Christmas trees decorate Britain's principal shopping streets as shoppers rush to buy their seasonal gifts. Carol services are held in churches across the country, and pantomime, a traditional entertainment for children deriving from the Victorian music hall, fills theatres in major towns.

Brightly lit Christmas tree at the centre of Trafalgar Square

Many offices close between Christmas and the New Year. Shops reopen for the January sales on 27 December – a paradise for bargain-hunters.

DECEMBER

Christmas Tree *(first Thu)*, Trafalgar Square, London. The tree is donated by the people of Norway and is lit by the Mayor of Oslo; this is followed by carol singing.
Carol concerts *(whole month)*, all over Britain.
Grand Christmas Parade *(beg Dec)*, London. Parade with floats to celebrate myth of Santa Claus.
Midnight Mass *(24 Dec)*, in churches everywhere around Britain.
Allendale Tarbaal Festival *(31 Dec)*, Northumberland. Parade by villagers with burning tar barrels on their heads to celebrate the New Year.

Sprig of holly

JANUARY

Hogmanay and **New Year** *(31 Dec, 1 Jan)*, Scottish celebrations. **Burns Night** *(25 Jan)*. Scots everywhere celebrate poet Robert Burns' birth with poetry, feasting and drinking.

FEBRUARY

Chinese New Year *(late Jan or early Feb)*. Lion dances, firecrackers and processions in Chinatown, London.

PUBLIC HOLIDAYS

New Year's Day (1 Jan).
2 Jan (Scotland only).
Easter weekend (March or April). In England it begins on **Good Friday** and ends on **Easter Monday**; in Scotland there is no Easter Monday holiday.
May Day (usually first Mon in May).
Late Spring Bank Holiday (last Mon in May).
Bank Holiday (first Mon in August, Scotland only).
August Bank Holiday (last Mon in August, except Scotland).
Christmas and Boxing Day (25– 26 December).

Morris dancing on May Day in Midhurst, Sussex

The Sporting Year

Many of the world's major competitive sports, including soccer, cricket and tennis, were invented in Britain. Originally devised as recreation for the wealthy, they have since entered the arena of mass entertainment. Some, however, such as the Royal Ascot race meeting and Wimbledon tennis tournament, are still valued as much for their social prestige as for the sport itself. Other delightful sporting events in Britain take place at a local level: village cricket, point-to-point racing and the Highland Games are all popular amateur events.

Kelly Holmes

Royal Ascot *is the fou day social highlight of t horse racing year. The hi class of the thoroughbre is matched by the hi style of the fashions, w royalty attendin*

Oxford and Cambridge Boat Race, *first held in 1829 at Henley, has become a national event, with the two university eights now battling it out between Putney and Mortlake on the Thames.*

The FA Cup Final *is the apex of the football season.*

Derby Day horse races, Epsom

January	February	March	April	May	June

Cheltenham Gold Cup steeplechase *(see p328)*

Grand National steeple-chase, Aintree *(see p376),* **Liverpool**

Rugby League Cup Final, Wembley

Embassy World Snooker Championships, Sheffield

Wimbledon Lawn Tennis Tournment *is the world's most prestigious lawn tennis championship.*

Six Nations Rugby Union *is an annual contest between England, France, Italy, Ireland (left), Scotland (right) and Wales. This league-based competition runs through winter ending in March.*

London Marathon *attracts thousands of long-distance runners, from the world's best to fancy-dressed fund raisers.*

Henley Royal Regatta *(see p234) is an international rowing event on the Thames (first held in 1839). It is also a glamorous social occasion.*

British Grand Prix, *held at Silverstone, is Britain's round of the Formula One World Championship.*

TICKETS AND TOUTS

For many big sporting events, the only official source of tickets is the club concerned. Booking agencies may offer hard-to-get tickets – though often at high prices. Unauthorized touts may lurk at popular events but their expensive tickets are not always valid. Check carefully.

Tickets for the Grand Prix

British Open Golf Championship, *a major golf event, is held at one of several British courses. Here, Nick Faldo putts.*

The Cheltenham and Gloucester Trophy *is the final of a season of competition to find the year's county cricket champions. It takes place at Lord's (see p155).*

Cowes week *(see p168)*, a yachting festival, covers all classes of racing.

Horse of the Year Show brings together top show-jumpers to compete on a tough indoor course *(see p64).*

Oxford versus Cambridge rugby union, Twickenham

August	September	October	November	December

European Show jumping Championships at Hickstead

Braemar High-land Games *(see p64)*

British Figure Skating and Ice Dance Champion-ships *are a feast of elegance on ice (various venues).*

Winmau World Masters Darts Champion-ships

Gold Cup Humber powerboat race, Hull

KEY TO SPORT SEASONS

▬	Cricket
▬	River fishing
▬	Football (soccer)
▬	Hunting and shooting
	Rugby (union and league)
▬	Flat racing
▬	Jump racing
▬	Athletics – track and field
▬	Road running and cross-country
▬	Polo

Cartier International Polo, *at the Guards Club, Windsor (see p235), is one of the main events for this peculiarly British game, played mainly by royalty and army officers.*

The Climate of Great Britain

Britain has a temperate climate. No region is far from the sea, which exerts a moderating influence on temperatures. Seldom are winter nights colder than -15°C, even in the far north, or summer days warmer than 30°C in the south and west: a much narrower range than in most European countries. Despite Britain's reputation, the average annual rainfall is quite low – 108 cm (42 inches) – and heavy rain is rare. The Atlantic coast is warmed by the Gulf Stream, making the west slightly warmer, though wetter, than the east.

Inverness

The Highlands and Islands

EDINBU
Glasgow

The Lowlan

Lancash
and
the Lak

Liver

North Wales
Caernarfo

South and
Mid-Wales

CARDIF

West Co

Exeter
Devon and
Cornwall

LANCASHIRE AND THE LAKES

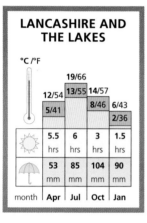

°C /°F

month	Apr	Jul	Oct	Jan
	12/54	13/55 19/66	14/57	6/43
	5/41		8/46	2/36
sunshine	5.5 hrs	6 hrs	3 hrs	1.5 hrs
rainfall	53 mm	85 mm	104 mm	90 mm

THE HEART OF ENGLAND

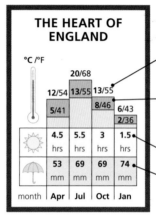
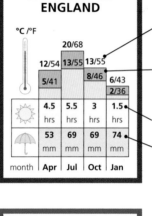

°C /°F

month	Apr	Jul	Oct	Jan
	12/54	13/55 20/68	13/55	6/43
	5/41		8/46	2/36
sunshine	4.5 hrs	5.5 hrs	3 hrs	1.5 hrs
rainfall	53 mm	69 mm	69 mm	74 mm

Average monthly maximum temperature

Average monthly minimum temperature

Average daily hours of sunshine

Average monthly rainfall

SOUTH AND MID-WALES

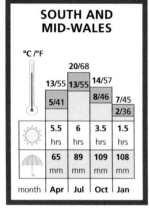

°C /°F

month	Apr	Jul	Oct	Jan
	13/55	13/55 20/68	14/57	7/45
	5/41		8/46	2/36
sunshine	5.5 hrs	6 hrs	3.5 hrs	1.5 hrs
rainfall	65 mm	89 mm	109 mm	108 mm

NORTH WALES

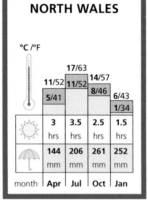

°C /°F

month	Apr	Jul	Oct	Jan
	11/52	11/52 17/63	14/57	6/43
	5/41		8/46	1/34
sunshine	3 hrs	3.5 hrs	2.5 hrs	1.5 hrs
rainfall	144 mm	206 mm	261 mm	252 mm

DEVON AND CORNWALL

°C /°F

month	Apr	Jul	Oct	Jan
	13/55	13/55 19/66	15/59 9/48	8/46
	6/43			4/39
sunshine	6 hrs	6.5 hrs	3.5 hrs	2 hrs
rainfall	53 mm	70 mm	91 mm	99 mm

WEST COUNTRY

°C /°F

month	Apr	Jul	Oct	Jan
	14/57	14/57 21/70	15/59 9/48	7/45
	6/43			2/36
sunshine	5.5 hrs	6.5 hrs	3.5 hrs	2 hrs
rainfall	49 mm	65 mm	85 mm	74 mm

THAMES VALLEY

°C /°F

month	Apr	Jul	Oct	Jan
	14/57	13/55 22/72	15/59	7/45
	5/41		7/45	1/34
sunshine	5.5 hrs	6 hrs	3 hrs	1.5 hrs
rainfall	41 mm	55 mm	64 mm	61 mm

THE HIGHLANDS AND ISLANDS

°C /°F

	17/63		
11/52	10/50	13/55	
3/37		7/45	7/45
			1/34

	4.5 hrs	3.5 hrs	2 hrs	1 hrs
	111 mm	137 mm	215 mm	200 mm
month	Apr	Jul	Oct	Jan

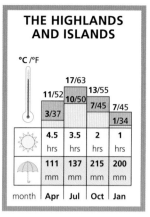

THE LOWLANDS

°C /°F

	19/66		
11/52	11/52	14/57	
4/39		7/45	6/43
			1/34

	5 hrs	5.5 hrs	3 hrs	1.5 hrs
	38 mm	69 mm	56 mm	47 mm
month	Apr	Jul	Oct	Jan

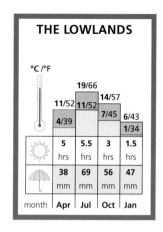

NORTHUMBRIA

°C /°F

	18/64		
11/52	13/55	13/55	
5/41		8/46	6/43
			2/36

	5 hrs	5.5 hrs	3 hrs	1.5 hrs
	38 mm	64 mm	61 mm	62 mm
month	Apr	Jul	Oct	Jan

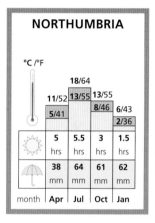

YORKSHIRE

°C /°F

	21/70		
13/55	12/54	14/57	
5/41		7/45	6/43
			1/34

	5 hrs	5.5 hrs	3 hrs	1.5 hrs
	41 mm	62 mm	56 mm	59 mm
month	Apr	Jul	Oct	Jan

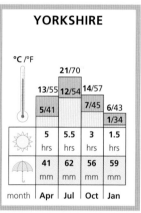

EAST MIDLANDS

°C /°F

	21/70		
13/55	12/54	14/57	
4/39		6/43	6/43
			0/32

	5 hrs	5.5 hrs	3 hrs	1.5 hrs
	38 mm	58 mm	56 mm	56 mm
month	Apr	Jul	Oct	Jan

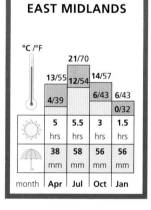

rthumbria

wcastle
on Tyne

orkshire

York

hester

East Midlands

mingham

Norwich

rt of
and

Cambridge

East
Anglia

Thames Valley

Oxford

London

Downs and
Channel Coast

Dover

Portsmouth

THE DOWNS AND CHANNEL COAST

°C /°F

	22/72		
14/57	12/54	14/57	
4/39		6/43	6/43
			0/32

	5.8 hrs	7.3 hrs	4 hrs	2 hrs
	38 mm	58 mm	56 mm	56 mm
month	Apr	Jul	Oct	Jan

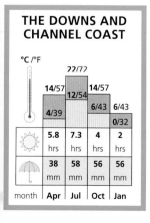

LONDON

°C /°F

	22/72		
13/55	15/59	16/61	
7/45		10/50	8/46
			4/39

	5 hrs	6 hrs	3.5 hrs	1.5 hrs
	39 mm	45 mm	50 mm	44 mm
month	Apr	Jul	Oct	Jan

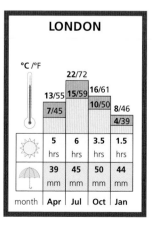

EAST ANGLIA

°C /°F

	22/72		
14/57	12/54	15/59	
4/39		6/43	7/45
			1/34

	5 hrs	6 hrs	3.5 hrs	2 hrs
	37 mm	58 mm	51 mm	49 mm
month	Apr	Jul	Oct	Jan

LONDON

🎐 London at a Glance

The largest city in Europe, London is home to over seven million people and covers 625 sq miles (1,600 sq km). The capital was founded by the Romans in the first century AD as a convenient administrative and communications centre and a port for trade with Continental Europe. For a thousand years it has been the principal residence of British monarchs as well as the centre of business and government, and it is rich in historic buildings and treasures from all periods. In addition to its diverse range of museums, galleries and churches, London is an exciting contemporary city, packed with a vast array of entertainments and shops. The attractions on offer are virtually endless but this map highlights the most important of those described in detail on the following pages.

Buckingham Palace (pp86–7) *is London home and office to the monarchy. The Changing of the Guard takes place on the palace forecourt.*

REGENT'S PARK AND BLOOMSBUI
(see pp102–1(

WEST AN WESTMI *(see pp7*

SOUTH KENSINGTON AND HYDE PARK
(see pp94–101)

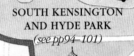

Hyde Park (p75), *the largest central London park, boasts numerous sports facilities, restaurants, an art gallery and Speakers' Corner. The highlight is the Serpentine Lake.*

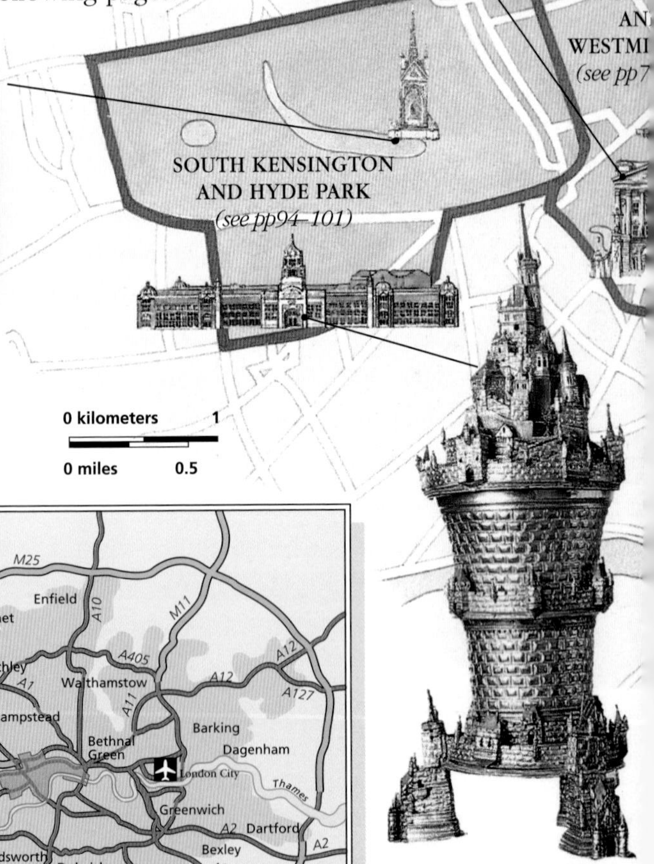

0 kilometers   1

0 miles   0.5

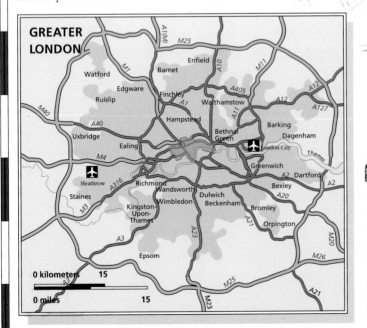

GREATER LONDON

The Victoria and Albert Museum (pp98–99) *is the world's largest museum of decorative arts. This German cup is 15th century*

KEY

▨ Main sightseeing area

The British Museum's (pp106–7) *vast collection of antiquities from all over the world includes this Portland Vase from the 1st century BC.*

The National Gallery's (pp82–3) *world-famous collection of paintings includes works such as* Christ Mocked *(c.1495) by Hieronymus Bosch.*

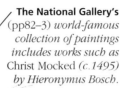

THE CITY AND SOUTHWARK *(see pp108–121)*

THAMES

St Paul's (pp114–15) *huge dome is the cathedral's most distinctive feature. Three galleries around the dome give spectacular views of London.*

Westminster Abbey (pp92–3) *has glorious medieval architecture and is crammed with impressive tombs and monuments to some of Britain's greatest public figures.*

The Tower of London (pp118–19) *is most famous as the prison where enemies of the Crown were executed. The Tower houses the Crown Jewels, including the Imperial State Crown.*

Tate Britain (p91) *displays an outstanding collection of British art ranging from stylized Elizabethan portraiture, such as* The Cholmondeley Ladies, *to cutting edge installation and film.*

London's Parks and Gardens

Camellia japonica

London has one of the world's greenest city centres, full of tree-filled squares and large expanses of grass, some of which have been public land since medieval times. From the elegant terraces of Regent's Park to the Royal Botanic Gardens at Kew, every London park and garden has its own charm and character. Some are ancient crown or public land, while others were created from the grounds of private houses or disused land. Londoners make the most of these open spaces: for exercise, listening to music, or simply escaping the bustle of the city.

Holland Park (see pp122–23) *offers acres of peaceful woodland, an open-air theatre* (see p153) *and a café.*

Kew Gardens
(see p126) *are the world's premiere botanic gardens. An amazing variety of plants from all over the world is complemented by an array of temples, monuments and a landscaped lake.*

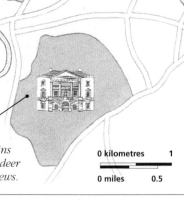

Richmond Park (see p126), *London's largest Royal Park, remains unspoiled with roaming deer and magnificent river views.*

0 kilometres   1

0 miles   0.5

SEASONAL BEST

As winter draws to a close, spectacular drifts of crocuses, daffodils and tulips are to be found peeping above the ground in Green Park and Kew. Easter weekend marks the start of outdoor events with funfairs on many commons and parks. During the summer months the parks are packed with picnickers and sunbathers and you can often catch a free open-air concert in St James's or Regent's parks. The energetic can play tennis in most parks, swim in Hyde Park's Serpentine or the ponds on Hampstead Heath, or take rowing boats out on the lakes in Regent's and Battersea parks. Autumn brings a different atmosphere, and on 5 November firework displays and bonfires celebrate Guy Fawkes Night *(see p64).* Winter is a good time to visit the tropical glasshouses and the colourful outdoor winter garden at Kew. If the weather gets really cold, the Round Pond in Kensington Gardens may be fit for ice-skating.

Winter in Kensington Gardens, adjoining Hyde Park

Hampstead Heath *(see p124)* is a breezy open space embracing a variety of landscapes.

Regent's Park (see p103) *has a large boating lake, an open-air theatre (see p153) and London Zoo. Surrounded by Nash's graceful buildings, it is one of London's most civilized retreats.*

St James's Park, *in the heart of the city, is a popular escape for office workers. It is also a reserve for wildfowl.*

THAMES

Green Park, *with its shady trees and benches, offers a cool, restful spot in the heart of London.*

Battersea Park is a pleasant riverside site with a man-made boating lake.

Greenwich Park (see p125) *is dominated by the National Maritime Museum. There are fine views from the Old Royal Observatory on the hill top.*

Hyde Park and Kensington Gardens (see p101) *are both popular London retreats. There are sporting facilities, a lake and art gallery in Hyde Park. This plaque is from the ornate Italian Garden in Kensington Gardens.*

HISTORIC CEMETERIES

In the late 1830s, a ring of private cemeteries was established around London to ease the pressure on the monstrously overcrowded and unhealthy burial grounds of the inner city. Today the cemeteries, notably **Highgate** *(see p124)* and **Kensal Green**, are well worth visiting for their flamboyant Victorian monuments.

Kensal Green cemetery on the Harrow Road

WEST END AND WESTMINSTER

The West End is the city's social and cultural centre and the London home of the royal family. Stretching from the edge of Hyde Park to Covent Garden, the district bustles all day and late into the night. Whether you're looking for art, history, street- or café-life, it is the most rewarding area in which to begin an exploration of the city.

Horse Guard on Whitehall

Westminster has been at the centre of political and religious power for a thousand years. In the 11th century, King Canute founded Westminster Palace and Edward the Confessor built Westminster Abbey, where all English monarchs have been crowned since 1066. As modern government developed, the great offices of state were established in the area.

SIGHTS AT A GLANCE

Historic Streets and Buildings
Banqueting House **18**
Buckingham Palace pp86–7 **13**
Cabinet War Rooms and Churchill Museum **16**
Downing Street **17**
Houses of Parliament pp90–91 **19**
Piccadilly Circus **8**
Ritz Hotel **10**
Royal Mews **15**
Royal Opera House **3**
The Mall **12**
The Piazza and Central Market **1**

Museums and Galleries
London's Transport Museum **2**
National Gallery pp82–3 **6**
National Portrait Gallery **7**
Royal Academy **9**
Somerset House **4**
Tate Britain **21**
The Queen's Gallery **14**

Churches
Queen's Chapel **11**
Westminster Abbey pp92–3 **20**

Attractions
London Eye **5**

KEY

▨	Street-by-Street map *pp78–9*
▨	Street-by-Street map *pp84–5*
▨	Street-by-Street map *pp88–9*
⊖	Underground station
⇄	Railway station
⚓	River boat pier

GETTING THERE
This area is the hub of the city's public transport system, served by virtually all tube lines and scores of buses. The most convenient tube and railway station is Charing Cross.

0 metres   500
0 yards   500

◁ **Big Ben and the Houses of Parliament**

Street-by-Street: Covent Garden

Until 1973, Covent Garden was an area of decaying streets and warehouses, which only came alive after dark when the fruit and vegetable market traders packed up for the day. Since then the Victorian market and elegant buildings nearby have been converted into stylish shops, restaurants, bars and cafés, creating an animated district which attracts a lively young crowd, night and day.

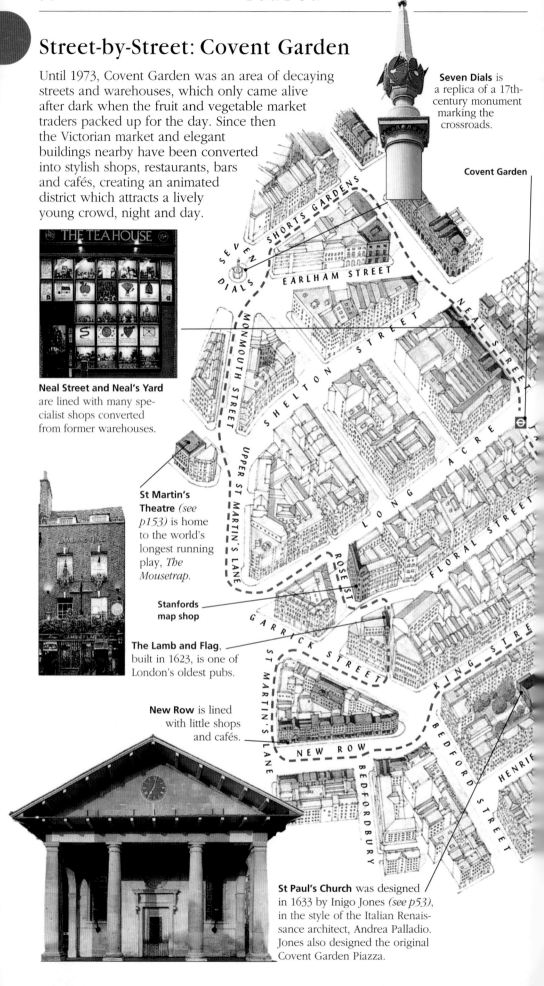

Seven Dials is a replica of a 17th-century monument marking the crossroads.

Covent Garden

Neal Street and Neal's Yard are lined with many specialist shops converted from former warehouses.

St Martin's Theatre *(see p153)* is home to the world's longest running play, *The Mousetrap*.

Stanfords map shop

The Lamb and Flag, built in 1623, is one of London's oldest pubs.

New Row is lined with little shops and cafés.

St Paul's Church was designed in 1633 by Inigo Jones *(see p53)*, in the style of the Italian Renaissance architect, Andrea Palladio. Jones also designed the original Covent Garden Piazza.

Royal Opera House
Some of the world's greatest opera singers and ballet dancers have performed at the Royal Opera House ❸

REGENT'S PARK & BLOOMSBURY

THE CITY & SOUTHWARK

SOUTH KENSINGTON & HYDE PARK

WEST END & WESTMINSTER

THAMES

LOCATOR MAP
See Street Finder map 11

KEY

– – – Suggested route

0 meters 100

0 yards 100

London's Transport Museum
This museum's intriguing collection brings to life the history of the city's tubes, buses and trains. It also displays examples of 20th-century commercial art ❷

BOW STREET

RUSSELL ST

COVENT GARDEN

SOUTHAMPTON ST

N LANE

Jubllee Market

★ Piazza and Central Market
Shops and cafés fill the piazza and market ❶

STAR SIGHTS

★ Piazza and Central Market

The Piazza and Central Market ❶

Covent Garden WC2. **Map** 11 C2.
🚇 *Covent Garden.* ♿ *cobbled streets.* **Street performers in Piazza:** *10am–dusk daily.*

The 17th-century architect Inigo Jones *(see p53)* planned the Piazza in Covent Garden as an elegant residential square, modelled on the piazza in the Tuscan town of Livorno, which he had seen under construction during his travels in Italy. For a brief period, the Piazza became one of the most fashionable addresses in London, but it was superseded by the even grander St James's Square *(see p85)* which lies to the southwest.

Decline accelerated when a fruit and vegetable market developed. By the mid-18th century, the Piazza had become a haunt of prostitutes and most of its houses had turned into seedy lodgings, gambling dens, brothels and taverns.

A mid-18th-century view of Covent Garden's Piazza

Meanwhile the wholesale produce market became the largest in the country and in 1828 a market hall was erected to ease congestion. The market, however, soon outgrew its new home and despite the construction of new buildings, such as Floral and Jubilee halls, the congestion grew worse. In 1973 the market moved to a new site in south London, and over the next two decades Covent Garden was redeveloped. Today only St Paul's Church remains of Inigo Jones's buildings, and Covent Garden, with its many small shops, cafés, restaurants, market stalls and street entertainers, is one of central London's liveliest districts.

London's Transport Museum ❷

The Piazza, Covent Garden WC2.
Map 11 C2. **Tel** *020 7379 6344.*
🄴 *Covent Garden.* ⬤ *10am–6pm
Sat–Thu, 11am–9pm Fri.* 📶 🔵 📷
phone in advance. ⬜ ⬜
www.ltmuseum.co.uk

This collection of buses, trams and underground trains ranges from the earliest horse-drawn omnibuses to a present-day Hoppa bus. Housed in the Victorian Flower Market of Covent Garden built in 1872, the museum is particularly good for children, who can sit in the driver's seat of a bus or an underground train, operate signals and chat to an actor playing a 19th-century tube-tunnel miner.

London's bus and train companies have long been prolific patrons of artists, and the museum holds a fine collection of 19th- and 20th-century commercial art. Copies of some of the best posters and works by distinguished artists, such as Paul Nash and Graham Sutherland, are on sale at the museum shop.

Poster by Michael Reilly (1929), London Transport Museum

Royal Opera House ❸

Covent Garden WC2. **Map** 11 C2.
Tel *020 7304 4000.* 🄴 *Covent
Garden.* ⬤ *for performances and
guided tours (phone to check).* 🍴
www.roh.org.uk

The first theatre on this site was built in 1732, and staged plays as well as concerts. However, the building was destroyed by fire in 1808 and again in 1856. The present

structure was designed in 1858 by E M Barry. John Flaxman's portico frieze, depicting tragedy and comedy, survived from the previous building of 1809.

The Opera House is home to the Royal Opera and Royal Ballet companies. After two years of renovation the building reopened in the new millennium, complete with a second auditorium and new rehearsal rooms. Backstage tours are available, and once a month visitors can watch the Royal Ballet rehearse.

Somerset House ❹

Strand WC2. **Map** 11 C2. **Tel** *020
7845 4600.* 🄴 *Temple.* ⬤ *10am–6pm
daily (last adm: 5.15pm).* ⬤ *1 Jan,
24–26 Dec.* **Ice rink** ⬤ *two months in
winter.* 📶 ⬜ **Courtauld Institute of
Art Gallery.** ⬜ ⬜ 🔵 **Admiralty
Restaurant. Tel** *020 7845 4646.*
www.somerset-house.org.uk

Designed in 1770 by William Chambers, Somerset House presents two great collections of art, the **Courtauld Institute of Art Gallery** and the

Somerset House: Strand façade

Embankment Galleries.

The courtyard forms an attractive piazza (which becomes an ice rink in winter), and the riverside terrace has a café. The Admiralty Restaurant is also highly regarded. Located in Somerset House but famous in its own right is the Courtauld Institute of Art Gallery, which includes important Impressionist and Post-Impressionist works by artists such as Manet, Renoir and Cezanne. In spring 2008 the new riverside Embankment Galleries were launched. Occupying 750 square metres of exhibition space on the two

---

SOHO AND CHINATOWN

Soho has been renowned for pleasures of the table, the flesh and the intellect ever since it was first developed in the late 17th century. At first a fashionable residential area, it declined when high society shifted west to Mayfair and immigrants from Europe moved into its narrow streets. Furniture-makers and tailors set up shop here and were joined in the late 19th century by pubs, nightclubs, restaurants and brothels. In the 1960s, Hong Kong Chinese moved into the area around Gerrard and Lisle streets and they created an aromatic Chinatown, packed with many restaurants and food shops. Soho's raffish reputation has long attracted artists and writers, ranging from the 18th-century essayist Thomas de Quincey to poet Dylan Thomas and painter Francis Bacon. Although strip joints and peep shows remain, Soho has enjoyed something of a renaissance, and today is full of stylish and lively bars and restaurants.

Lion dancer in February's Chinese New Year celebrations

The opulent Palm Court of the Ritz Hotel

lower floors, the changing programme covers a broad range of contemporary arts, including photography, design, fashion and architecture.

London Eye ❺

Jubilee Gardens, South Bank, SE1. **Map** 12 D2. **Tel** 0870 5000 600 (information and 24-hr advance booking – recommended as tickets sell out days in advance). ⊖ Waterloo, Westminster. 🚌 11, 24, 211. ◯ Oct–May: 10am–8pm daily; Jun–Sept: 10am–9pm daily (Jul & Aug: to 9:30pm). ● 25 Dec & early Jan (for maintenance). 🎟 Pick up tickets at County Hall (adjacent to Eye) at least 30 mins before boarding time. 💻 📱 ♿ www.londoneye.com

The London Eye is a 135-m (443-ft) observation wheel that was installed on the South Bank to mark the Millennium. Its enclosed passenger capsules offer a gentle, 30-minute ride as the wheel makes a full turn, with breathtaking views over London and for up to 42 km (26 miles) around. Towering over one of the world's most familiar riverscapes, it has understandably captured the hearts of Londoners and visitors alike, and is one of the city's most popular attractions. "Flights" on the wheel are on the hour and half-hour.

National Gallery ❻

See pp82–3.

National Portrait Gallery ❼

2 St Martin's Place WC2. **Map** 11 B3. **Tel** 020 7312 2463. ⊖ Charing Cross, Leicester Sq. ◯ 10am–6pm Sat–Wed, 10am–9pm Thu & Fri. ● 24–26 Dec. ♿ 🎫 🍴 📱 📷 www.npg.org.uk

This museum celebrates Britain's history through portraits, photographs and sculptures; subjects range from Elizabeth I to David Beckham. The 20th-century section contains paintings and photographs of the royal family, politicians, rock stars, designers, artists and writers.

Piccadilly Circus ❽

W1. **Map** 11 A3. ⊖ Piccadilly Circus.

Dominated by garish neon advertising hoardings, Piccadilly Circus is a hectic traffic junction surrounded by shopping malls. It began as an early 19th-century crossroads between Piccadilly and John Nash's (see p105) Regent Street. It was briefly an elegant space, edged by curving stucco façades, but by 1910 the first electric advertisements had been installed. For years people have congregated at its centre, beneath the delicately poised figure of Eros, erected in 1892.

The Statue of Eros

Royal Academy ❾

Burlington House, Piccadilly W1. **Map** 10 F3. **Tel** 020 7300 8000. ⊖ Piccadilly Circus, Green Park. ◯ 10am–6pm Sat–Thu, 10am–10pm Fri. ● 24–25 Dec, Good Fri. 🎟 ♿ 🎫 by appointment. 🍴 💻 📱 📷 www.royalacademy.org.uk

Founded in 1768, the Royal Academy is best known for its summer exhibition, which has been an annual event for over 200 years and comprises a rewarding mix of around 1,200 new works by established and unknown painters, sculptors and architects. During the rest of the year, the gallery shows prestigious touring exhibitions from around the world, and the courtyard in front of Burlington House, one of the West End's few surviving mansions from the early 18th century, is often filled with people waiting to get in. Quite apart from its aesthetic delights, the Royal Academy provides the weary traveller with a little lacuna of tranquillity. Its interior decoration inspires calm, and seems to be cut off from the stresses and strains of modern city life.

Ritz Hotel ❿

Piccadilly W1. **Map** 10 F3. **Tel** 020 7493 8181. ⊖ Green Park. ♿ See **Where to Stay** p540. www.theritzlondon.com

Cesar Ritz, the Swiss hotelier who inspired the word "ritzy", had virtually settled down to a quiet retirement by 1906 when this hotel was built and named after him. The colonnaded front of the château-style building was erected in 1906 to suggest just the merest whiff of Paris, where the grandest hotels were to be found at the turn of the century. It still maintains its Edwardian air of fin de siècle opulence and sophisticated grandeur, and is a popular venue for afternoon tea (reservations are required). A touch of soigné danger may be found in the casino.

National Gallery **⑥**

The National Gallery is London's leading art museum, with over 2,300 paintings, most on permanent display. It has flourished since 1824, when the House of Commons agreed to purchase 38 major paintings. These became the core of a national collection of European art that now ranges from Cimabue in the 13th century to 19th-century Impressionists. The gallery's particular strengths are in Dutch, Italian Renaissance and 17th-century Spanish painting. To the left of the main gallery lies the Sainsbury Wing, financed by the grocery family and completed in 1991. It houses the Early Renaissance collection.

The Adoration of the Kings *(1564)*
This realistic work is by Flemish artist Pieter Bruegel the Elder (c.1525–69).

Education Centre entrance ♿

Stairs to lower floor

The Ambassadors
The strange shape in the foreground of this Hans Holbein portrait (1533) is a distorted skull, a symbol of mortality.

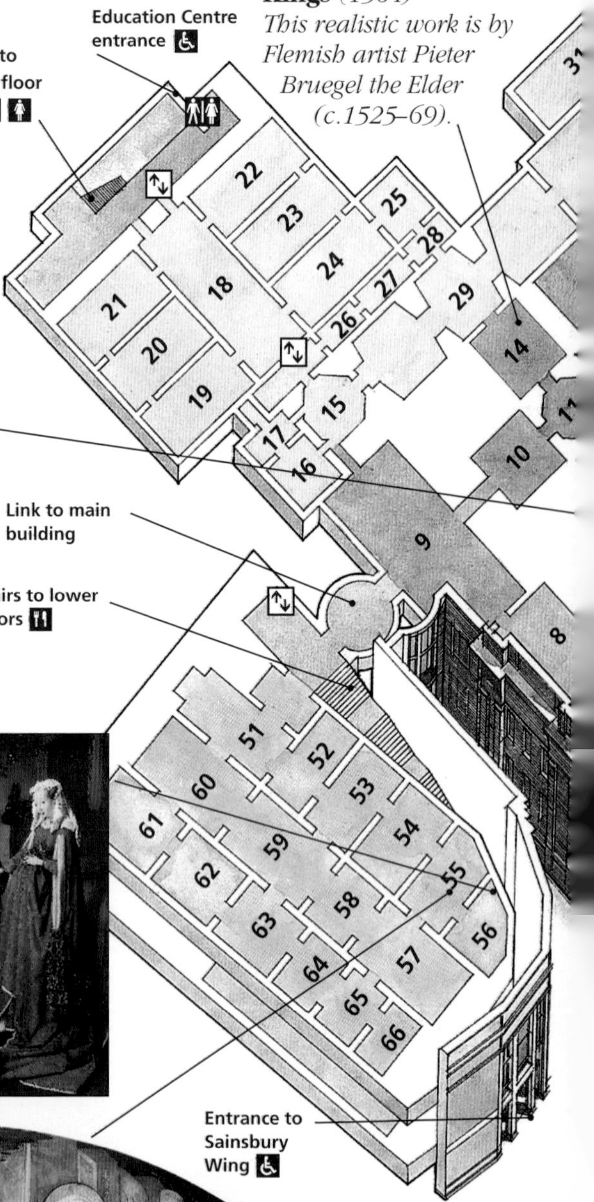

Link to main building

Stairs to lower floors

KEY TO FLOORPLAN

▢	Painting 1250–1500
▦	Painting 1500–1600
▢	Painting 1600–1700
▢	Painting 1700–1900
▦	Special exhibitions
▢	Non-exhibition space

Arnolfini Portrait
Jan van Eyck (c.1385–1441), one of the pioneers of oil painting, shows his mastery of colour, texture, and minute detail in this portrait of 1434.

Entrance to Sainsbury Wing ♿

The Annunciation
This refined work of the early 1450s, by Fra Filippo Lippi, forms part of the gallery's exceptional Italian Renaissance collection.

★ **'The Rokeby Venus'**
This is Velázquez's only surviving female nude (1647–51).

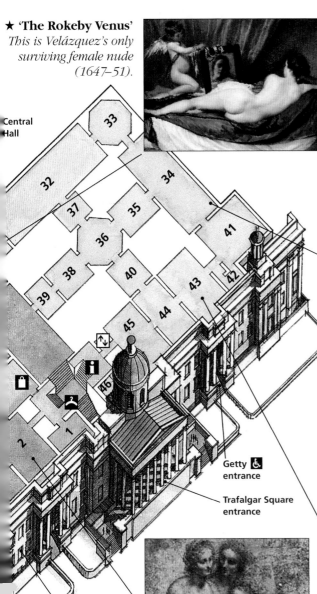

Central Hall

33
32 34
37 35
36 41
38 40 43 42
39 44 45 46
2 1

VISITORS' CHECKLIST

Trafalgar Sq WC2. **Map** 11 B3.
Tel 020 7747 2885.
⊖ *Charing Cross, Leicester Sq, Piccadilly Circus.* 🚌 *3, 6, 9, 11, 12, 13, 15, 23, 24, 29, 53, 77A, 88, 91, 139, 159, 176, 453.*
🚆 *Charing Cross.*
◯ *10am–6pm daily (9pm Fri).*
● *1 Jan, 24–26 Dec.* ♿ *via Sainsbury Wing and Getty entrances.* 📷 🍴 🖥 🛍
www.nationalgallery.org.uk

Getty ♿ **entrance**

Trafalgar Square entrance

★ **The Hay Wain** *(1821)*
The great age of 19th-century land-scape painting is represented by Constable and Turner (see p91). This picture shows how Constable caught changing light and shadow.

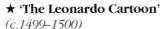

The Neo-Classical façade is made of Portland stone.

GALLERY GUIDE

Most of the collection is housed on one floor. The paintings hang chronologically, with the earliest works, 1250–1500, in the Sainsbury Wing. Lesser paintings of all periods are dis-played on the lower floor of the main building. There is a restaurant on the first floor in the Sainsbury Wing.

★ **'The Leonardo Cartoon'**
(c.1499–1500)
The genius of Leonardo da Vinci glows through this picture of the Virgin and Child, St Anne and St John the Baptist.

STAR PAINTINGS

★ 'The Leonardo Cartoon' by Leonardo da Vinci

★ 'The Rokeby Venus' by Diego Velázquez

★ The Hay Wain by John Constable

At the Theatre *(1876–7)*
Renoir was one of the greatest painters of the Impressionist movement. The theatre was a popular subject among artists of the time.

Street-by-Street: Piccadilly and St James's

As soon as Henry VIII built St James's Palace in the 1530s, the surrounding area became the centre of fashionable court life. Today Piccadilly forms a contrast between the bustling commercial district full of shopping arcades, eateries and cinemas, with St James's, to the south, which is still the domain of the wealthy and the influential.

St James's Church was designed by Sir Christopher Wren in 1684.

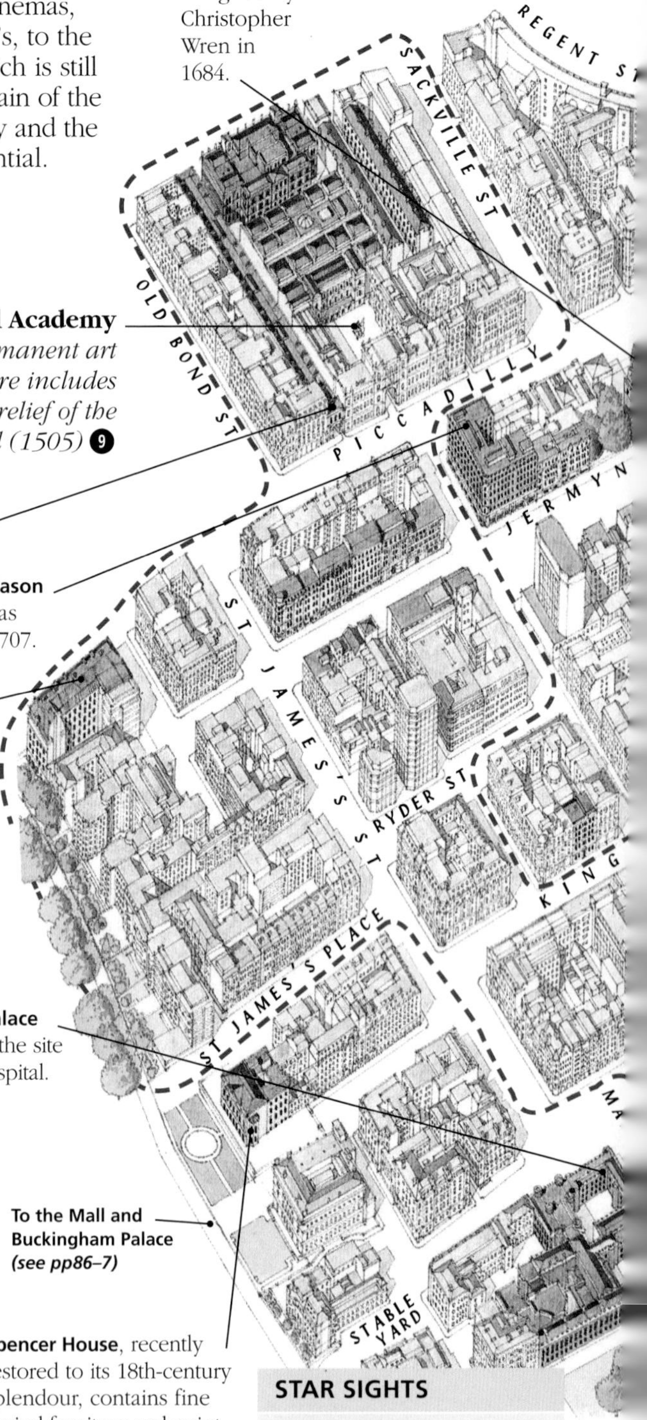

★ Royal Academy
The permanent art collection here includes this Michelangelo relief of the Madonna and Child (1505) **9**

Fortnum & Mason *(see p148)* was founded in 1707.

The Ritz *César Ritz founded one of London's most famous hotels in 1906* **10**

Burlington Arcade, an opulent covered walk, has fine shops and beadles on patrol.

St James's Palace was built on the site of a leper hospital.

To the Mall and Buckingham Palace *(see pp86–7)*

Spencer House, recently restored to its 18th-century splendour, contains fine period furniture and paintings. This Palladian palace was completed in 1766 for the 1st Earl Spencer, an ancestor of the late Princess of Wales.

STAR SIGHTS

★ Piccadilly Circus

★ Royal Academy

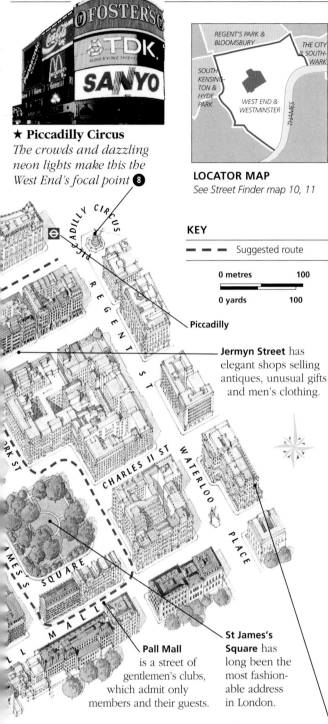

★ **Piccadilly Circus**
The crowds and dazzling neon lights make this the West End's focal point **8**

LOCATOR MAP
See Street Finder map 10, 11

KEY

– – – Suggested route

0 metres	100
0 yards	100

Piccadilly

Jermyn Street has elegant shops selling antiques, unusual gifts and men's clothing.

St James's Square has long been the most fashionable address in London.

Pall Mall is a street of gentlemen's clubs, which admit only members and their guests.

Queen's Chapel
This was the first Classical church in England **11**

Royal Opera Arcade is lined with quality shops. Designed by John Nash, it was completed in 1818.

Queen's Chapel **11**

Marlborough Rd SW1. **Map** 11 A4. **Tel** 020-7930 4832. Green Park. to the public Sun services (Easter–end Jul) and major Saints' Days only.

The sumptuous Queen's Chapel was designed by Inigo Jones for the Infanta of Spain, the intended bride of Charles I *(see pp52–3)*. Work started in 1623 but ceased when the marriage negotiations were shelved. The chapel was finally completed in 1627 for Charles's eventual queen, Henrietta Maria. It was the first church in England to be built in a Classical style, with a coffered ceiling based on a reconstruction by Palladio of an ancient Roman temple.

Interior of Queen's Chapel

The Mall **12**

SW1. **Map** 11 A4. Charing Cross, Green Park.

This broad triumphal approach from Trafalgar Square to Buckingham Palace was created by Aston Webb when he redesigned the front of the palace and the Victoria Monument in 1911. The spacious tree-lined avenue follows the course of an old path at the edge of St James's Park. The path was laid out in the reign of Charles II, when it became London's most fashionable and cosmopolitan promenade. The Mall is used for royal processions on special occasions. Flagpoles down both sides fly the national flags of foreign heads of state during official visits. The Mall is closed to traffic on Sundays.

Buckingham Palace ⓭

Queen Elizabeth II

Opened to visitors for the first time in 1993 to raise money for repairing fire damage to Windsor Castle *(see pp236–7)*, the Queen's official London home and office is an extremely popular attraction in August and September. John Nash *(see p105)* began converting the 18th-century Buckingham House into a palace for George IV in 1826 but was taken off the job in 1831 for overspending his budget. The first monarch to occupy the palace was Queen Victoria, just after she came to the throne in 1837. The tour takes visitors up the grand staircase and through the splendour of the State Rooms, but not into the royal family's private apartments.

Music Room
State guests are presented and royal babies christened in this room.

White Drawing Room

Green Drawing Room

Grand Staircase

Blue Drawing Room

State Dining Room

The Queen's Gallery
Masterpieces from the Royal Collection, such as Vermeer's The Music Lesson *(c.1660), are displayed here in a series of changing exhibitions.*

Throne Room
The Queen carries out many formal ceremonial duties here, under the richly gilded ceiling.

View over the Mall
On special occasions the Royal Family wave to crowds from the balcony.

The Royal Standard flies while the Queen is in residence.

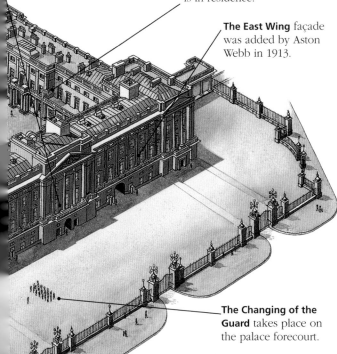

The East Wing façade was added by Aston Webb in 1913.

The Changing of the Guard takes place on the palace forecourt.

The Queen's Gallery ⑭

Buckingham Palace Rd SW1. **Map** 10 F5. *Tel 020 7766 7301.* ⊖ *St James's Park, Victoria.* ◯ *10am–5:30pm daily (last admission for exhibitions: 4:30pm).* ● *25, 26 Dec. Call for more details.* 📷 📷 www.royalcollection.org.uk

The Queen's art collection is one of the finest and most valuable in the world, rich in the works of old masters such as Rembrandt and Leonardo. The gallery hosts a rotating programme of exhibitions, enabling the year-round display of many masterpieces, drawings and decorative arts from the Queen's collection.

Detail: **The Gold State Coach (1762), Royal Mews**

Royal Mews ⑮

Buckingham Palace Rd SW1. **Map** 10 E5. *Tel 020 7766 7302.* ⊖ *Victoria.* ◯ *Apr–Oct: 11am–4pm Sat–Thu (advisable to check opening times on day of visit). Extended opening hrs may operate Aug–Sep.* 📷 *open 9:30am–5pm daily all year (closed 25, 26 Dec).* 📷 ♿ www.royalcollection.org.uk

Lovers of horses and royal pomp should not miss this working stable and coach house. Designed by John Nash in 1825, it houses horses and state coaches used on official occasions. Among them is the glass coach used for royal weddings and foreign ambassadors. The star exhibit is the ornate gold state coach, built for George III in 1762, which was used by the Queen during the Golden Jubilee celebrations in 2002. The shop sells interesting merchandise.

THE CHANGING OF THE GUARD

Dressed in brilliant scarlet tunics and tall furry hats called bearskins, the palace guards stand in sentry boxes outside the Palace. Crowds gather to watch the colourful and musical military ceremony as the guards march from Wellington Barracks to Buckingham Palace, parading for half an hour while the palace keys are handed by the old guard to the new.

Street-by-Street: Whitehall and Westminster

The broad avenues of Whitehall and Westminster are lined with imposing buildings that serve the historic seat of both government and the established church. On weekdays the streets are crowded with civil servants whose work is based here, while at weekends the area takes on a diffe-rent atmosphere with a steady flow of tourists.

Downing Street
Sir Robert Walpole was the first Prime Minister to live here in 1732 **17**

Cabinet War Rooms and Churchill Museum
Now open to the public, these were Winston Churchill's World War II headquarters **16**

St Margaret's Church is a favourite venue for political and society weddings.

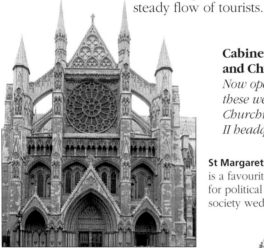

★ Westminster Abbey
The abbey is London's oldest and most important church **20**

Central Hall (1911) is a florid example of the Beaux Arts style.

Richard I's Statue is an 1860 depiction of the king, killed in battle in 1199.

Dean's Yard is a secluded grassy square surrounded by picturesque buildings from different periods, many used by Westminster School.

The Burghers of Calais is a cast of Auguste Rodin's 1886 original in France.

To Trafalgar Square

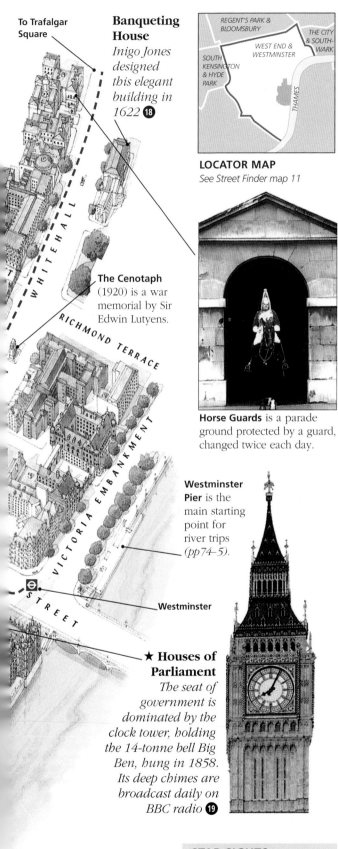

Banqueting House

Inigo Jones designed this elegant building in 1622 **18**

LOCATOR MAP
See Street Finder map 11

REGENT'S PARK & BLOOMSBURY

THE CITY & SOUTHWARK

WEST END & WESTMINSTER

SOUTH KENSINGTON & HYDE PARK

THAMES

Horse Guards is a parade ground protected by a guard, changed twice each day.

The Cenotaph (1920) is a war memorial by Sir Edwin Lutyens.

WHITEHALL

RICHMOND TERRACE

VICTORIA EMBANKMENT

STREET

Westminster Pier is the main starting point for river trips *(pp74–5).*

Westminster

★ **Houses of Parliament**
The seat of government is dominated by the clock tower, holding the 14-tonne bell Big Ben, hung in 1858. Its deep chimes are broadcast daily on BBC radio **19**

KEY

- - - Suggested route

0 metres   100

0 yards   100

STAR SIGHTS

★ Westminster Abbey

★ Houses of Parliament

Cabinet War Rooms and Churchill Museum **16**

Clive Steps, King Charles St SW1.
Map 11 B5. **Tel** *020 7930 6961.*
⊖ *Westminster.* ◯ *9:30am–6pm daily (last adm: 5pm).* ● *24–26 Dec.*
♨ ♿ 🖥 📷 www.iwm.org.uk

This warren of cellars below a government office building is where the War Cabinet – first under Neville Chamberlain, then Winston Churchill from 1940 – met during World War II when German bombs were falling on London. The rooms include living quarters for ministers and military leaders and a Cabinet Room, where strategic decisions were taken. They are laid out as they were when the war ended, complete with Churchill's desk, communications equipment, and maps for plotting battles and strategies. The Churchill Museum records and illustrates Churchill's life and career.

Telephones in the Map Room, Cabinet War Rooms

Downing Street **17**

SW1. **Map** 11 B4. ⊖ *Westminster.*
● *to the public.*

Number 10 Downing Street has been the official residence of the British Prime Minister since 1732. It contains a Cabinet Room in which government policy is decided, an impressive State Dining Room and a private apartment; outside is a well-protected garden.

Next door at No. 11 is the official residence of the Chancellor of the Exchequer, who is in charge of the nation's financial affairs. In 1989, iron gates were erected at the Whitehall end of Downing Street for security purposes.

Banqueting House ⑱

Whitehall SW1. **Map** 11 B4. *Tel 020 3166 6151.* ⊖ *Charing Cross.* ◯ *10am–5pm Mon–Sat.* ● *pub hols & for functions. Always call before your visit.* 🅿 🏷 ♿ www.hrp.org.uk

Completed by Inigo Jones *(see p53)* in 1622, this was the first building in central London to embody the Palladian style of Renaissance Italy. In 1629 Charles I commissioned Rubens to paint the ceiling with scenes exalting the reign of his father, James I. They symbolize the divine right of kings, disputed by the Parliamentarians, who executed Charles I outside the building in 1649 *(see pp52–3).*

Panels from the Rubens ceiling (1629–34), Banqueting House

Houses of Parliament ⑲

SW1. **Map** 11 C5. *Tel 020 7219 3000.* ⊖ *Westminster.* **Visitors' Galleries** ◯ *2:30–10:30pm Mon & Tue; 11:30am–7:30pm Wed; 11:30am–6:30pm Thu; 9:30am–3pm sitting Fri. Queue or UK residents may apply in advance to local MP.* ● *frequently for parliamentary recesses.* ♿ 🎫 *call 0870 906 3773 or go to* www.keithprowse.com *to book tickets for tours.* 🅿 www.parliament.uk

There has been a Palace of Westminster here since the 11th century, though only Westminster Hall remains from that time. The present Neo-Gothic structure by Sir Charles Barry was built after the old palace was destroyed by fire in 1834. Since the 16th century it has housed the two Houses of Parliament, the Lords and the Commons. The House of Commons consists of elected Members of Parliament (MPs).

The party with most MPs forms the Government, and its leader becomes Prime Minister. The House of Lords comprises peers, law lords, bishops and archbishops.

Westminster Abbey ⑳

See pp92–3.

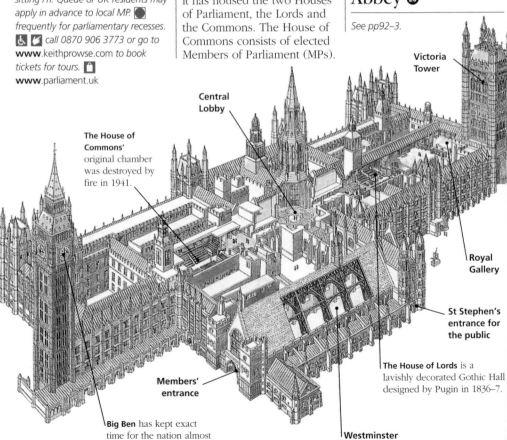

Victoria Tower

Central Lobby

The House of Commons' original chamber was destroyed by fire in 1941.

Royal Gallery

St Stephen's entrance for the public

The House of Lords is a lavishly decorated Gothic Hall designed by Pugin in 1836–7.

Members' entrance

Big Ben has kept exact time for the nation almost continuously since 1859.

Westminster Hall

Portico of Tate Britain

Tate Britain ㉑

Millbank SW1. **Map** *19 B2.* **Tel** *020 7887 8888.* ⊖ *Pimlico.* 🚌 *77a, 88, C10.* 🚆 *Victoria, Vauxhall.* 🚤 *to Tate Modern every 40 mins.* 🕙 ○ *10am–5:50pm daily.* ● *24–26 Dec.* 💷 *for major exhibitions.* ♿ *Atterbury St.* 📷 🍴 💻 🛍 www.*tate.org.uk*

Formerly the Tate Gallery, Tate Britain is the national gallery of British art, and includes works from the 16th to the 21st century. Displays draw on the enormous Tate Collection, which also includes the international modern art seen at Tate Modern *(p121)*. A river boat, *Tate to Tate*, takes visitors between the two galleries. Located in the Clore Galleries are works from the Turner Bequest *(see box)*.

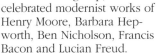

Recumbent Figure (1938) by Henry Moore

The size of the collection necessitates some rotation of displays. Major themes change on a yearly basis, solo artists' rooms and smaller themed rooms more frequently. Loan exhibitions are installed in the ground floor galleries and part of the main floor.

The section on the years 1500–1800 covers a period of dramatic change in British history, from the Tudors and Stuarts through to the age of Thomas Gainsborough. The section concludes with a series of changing displays about the poet and artist William Blake.

The years 1800 to 1900 saw dramatic expansion and change in the arts in Britain. This section shows the new themes that began to emerge. Included are the "Victorian Narrative" painters such as William Powell Frith, and the work of the Pre-Raphaelites, such as John Everett Millais and Dante Gabriel Rossetti. The period 1900–1960 includes the work of Jacob Epstein, that of Wyndham Lewis and his Vorticist group, and the celebrated modernist works of Henry Moore, Barbara Hepworth, Ben Nicholson, Francis Bacon and Lucian Freud.

The Tate collection of British art from 1960 to the present is outstanding, and the displays in this section are changed on a regular basis. From the 1960s, Tate's funding for the purchase of works began to increase substantially, while artistic activity continued to pick up speed, encouraged by public spending. As a result, Tate Britain's collection is particularly rich in this period. Works range from the 1960s Pop artists

The First Marriage (A Marriage of Styles I) (1962) by David Hockney

David Hockney, Richard Hamilton and Peter Blake, through the works of Gilbert and George and the landscape artist Richard Long, to the 1980s paintings of Howard Hodgkin and R B Kitaj. The so-called Young British Artists (YBAs) of the 1990s are well represented by leading figures Damian Hirst, Tracey Emin and Sarah Lucas. A small space called Art Now is dedicated to contemporary artists.

Captain Thomas Lee (1594) by Marcus Gheeraerts II

THE TURNER BEQUEST

The Turner Bequest comprises some 300 oil paintings and 20,000 watercolours and drawings, received by the nation from the great landscape painter J M W Turner some years after his death in 1851. Turner's will had specified that a gallery be built to house his pictures and this was finally done in 1987 with the opening of the Clore Galleries. Most of the oils are on view in the main galleries, and the watercolours are the subject of changing displays.

Shipping at the Mouth of the Thames (c.1806–7)

Westminster Abbey ⑳

Westminster Abbey has been the burial place of
Britain's monarchs since the 11th century and the
setting for many coronations and royal weddings. It
is one of the most beautiful buildings in London, with
an exceptionally diverse array of architectural styles,
ranging from the austere French Gothic of the nave to
the astonishing complexity of Henry VII's chapel. Half
national church, half national museum, the abbey aisles
and transepts are crammed with an extraordinary collection of tombs and monuments honouring some of Britain's
greatest public figures, ranging from politicians to poets.

North Entrance
*The mock-medieval
stonework is
Victorian.*

**Statesmen's
Aisle**

Flying buttresses help
redistribute the great
weight of the roof.

★ Nave
*At a height of 31 m
(102 ft), the nave is
the highest in England.
The ratio of height to
width is 3:1.*

CORONATION
The coronation ceremony
is over 1,000 years old
and since 1066, with the
crowning of William the
Conqueror on Christmas
Day, the abbey has been
its sumptuous setting.
The coronation of Queen
Elizabeth II, in 1953, was
the first to be televised.

Cloisters
*Built mainly in the 13th and
14th centuries, the cloisters
link the Abbey church with
the other buildings.*

STAR FEATURES

★ Nave

★ Henry VII Chapel

★ Chapter House

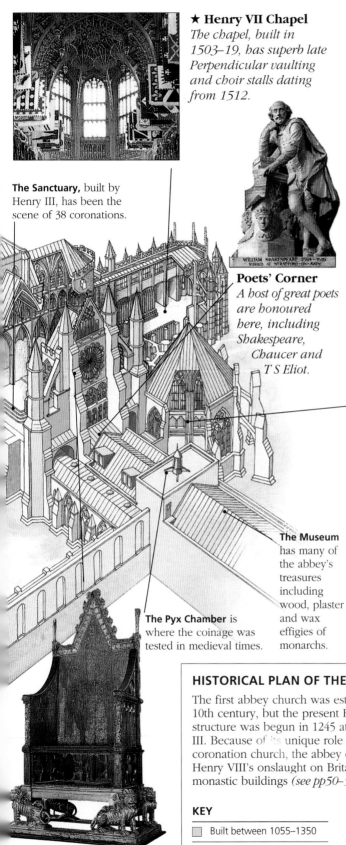

★ Henry VII Chapel
The chapel, built in 1503–19, has superb late Perpendicular vaulting and choir stalls dating from 1512.

The Sanctuary, built by Henry III, has been the scene of 38 coronations.

Poets' Corner
A host of great poets are honoured here, including Shakespeare, Chaucer and T S Eliot.

The Pyx Chamber is where the coinage was tested in medieval times.

The Museum has many of the abbey's treasures including wood, plaster and wax effigies of monarchs.

St Edward's Chapel
The shrine of Edward the Confessor is housed here, along with the tombs of many medieval monarchs.

★ Chapter House
A beautiful octagonal room, remarkable for its 13th-century tile floor. It is lit by six huge stained glass windows showing scenes from the abbey's history.

VISITORS' CHECKLIST

Broad Sanctuary SW1.**Map** 11 B5. **Tel** 020 7222 5152. ⊖ Westminster. 🚌 3, 11, 12, 24, 29, 53, 70, 77, 77a, 88, 109, 159, 170. 🚊 Victoria. 🚢 Westminster Pier. **Cloisters** ◯ 9am–5:30pm daily. **Abbey (Royal Chapels, Poets' Corner, Choir, Statesmen's Aisle, Nave)** ◯ 9:30am–3:45pm Mon–Fri (to 6pm Wed), 9:30am–1:30pm Sat (last adm: 12:45pm). ♿ **Chapter House, Pyx Chamber & Museum** ◯ 10:30am–4pm daily. ♿ **College Garden** ◯ Apr–Sep: 10am–6pm Tue–Thu; Oct–Mar: 10am–4pm Tue–Thu. **Evensong** 5pm Mon–Fri (evening prayers Wed), 3pm Sat, Sun. **Concerts.** 📷 🚻 www.westminster-abbey.org

HISTORICAL PLAN OF THE ABBEY

The first abbey church was established as early as the 10th century, but the present French-influenced Gothic structure was begun in 1245 at the behest of Henry III. Because of its unique role as the coronation church, the abbey escaped Henry VIII's onslaught on Britain's monastic buildings *(see pp50–51).*

KEY

▨	Built between 1055–1350
▦	Added from 1350–1420
▨	Built between 1500–1512
☐	Towers completed 1745
☐	Restored after 1850

SOUTH KENSINGTON AND HYDE PARK

This exclusive district embraces one of London's largest parks and some of its finest museums, shops, restaurants and hotels. Until the mid-19th century it was a genteel, semi-rural backwater of large houses and private schools lying to the south of Kensington Palace. In 1851, the Great Exhibition, until then the largest arts and science event ever staged (*see pp56–7*), was held in Hyde Park, transforming the area into a celebration of Victorian learning and self-confidence.

Peter Pan statue in Kensington Gardens

The brainchild of Queen Victoria's husband, Prince Albert, the exhibition was a massive success and the profits were used to buy 35 ha (87 acres) of land in South Kensington. Here, Prince Albert encouraged the construction of a concert hall, museums and colleges devoted to the applied arts and sciences; most of them survive. The neighbourhood soon became modish, full of flamboyant red-brick mansion blocks, garden squares and the elite shops still to be found in Knightsbridge.

SIGHTS AT A GLANCE

Historic Buildings
Kensington Palace **7**

Churches
Brompton Oratory **2**

Shops
Harrods **1**

Parks and Gardens
Hyde Park and Kensington Gardens **6**

Museums and Galleries
Natural History Museum **5**
Science Museum **4**
Victoria and Albert Museum pp98–9 **3**

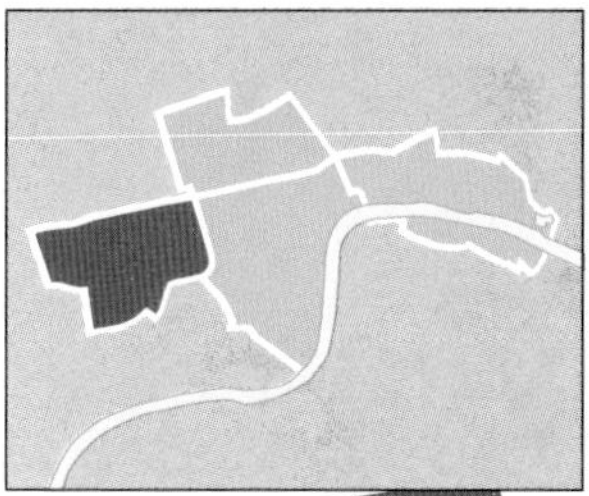

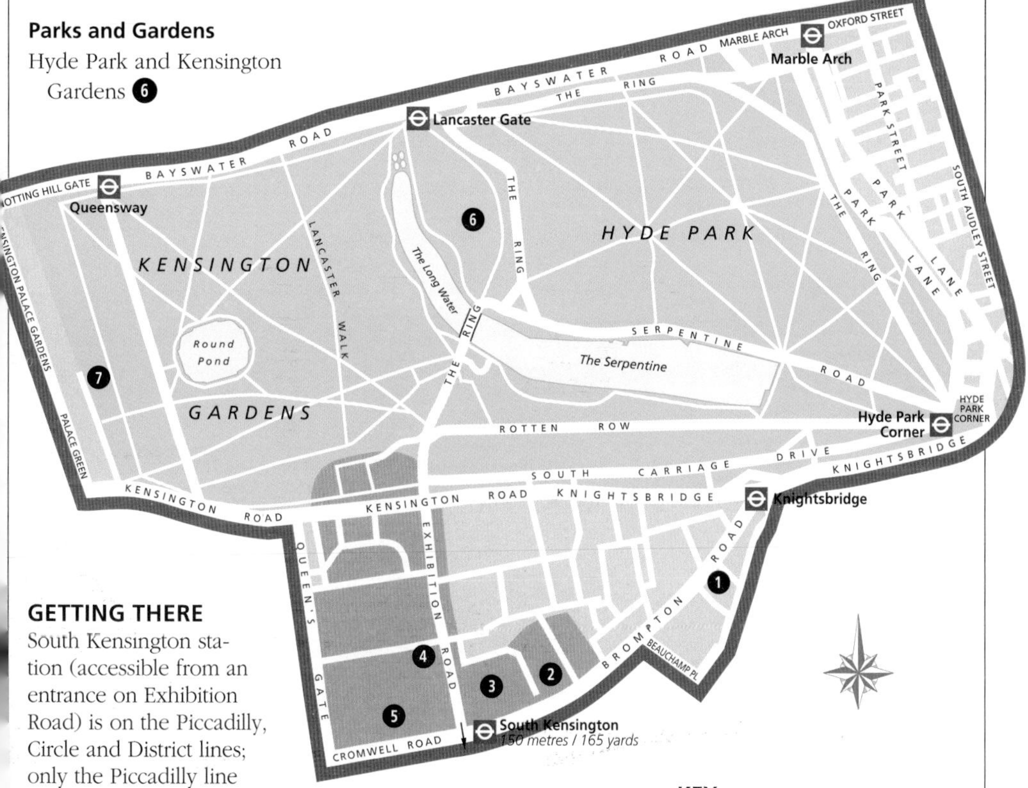

GETTING THERE

South Kensington station (accessible from an entrance on Exhibition Road) is on the Piccadilly, Circle and District lines; only the Piccadilly line passes through Knightsbridge and Hyde Park Corner. The No. 14 bus runs direct from Piccadilly Circus to South Kensington, via Knightsbridge.

KEY

Street-by-Street map *pp96–7*

Underground station

0 metres 500
0 yards 500

◁ **Ennismore Mews in South Kensington, built 1843–6**

Street-by-Street: South Kensington

The numerous museums and colleges created in the wake of the Great Exhibition of 1851 *(see pp56–7)* continue to give this neighbourhood an air of leisured culture. Visited as much by Londoners as tourists, the museum area is liveliest on Sundays and on summer evenings during the Royal Albert Hall's famous season of classical "Prom" concerts *(see p154).*

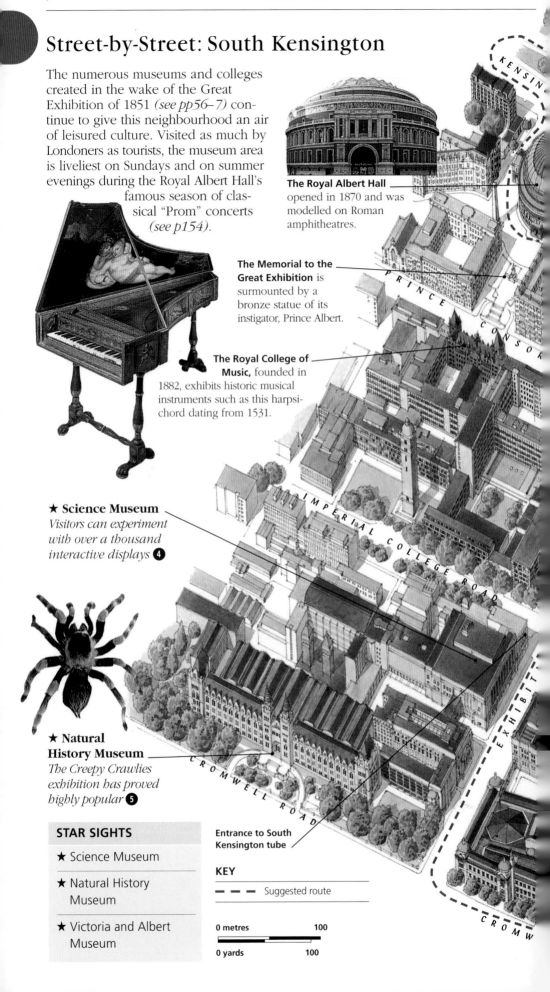

The Royal Albert Hall opened in 1870 and was modelled on Roman amphitheatres.

The Memorial to the Great Exhibition is surmounted by a bronze statue of its instigator, Prince Albert.

The Royal College of Music, founded in 1882, exhibits historic musical instruments such as this harpsichord dating from 1531.

★ **Science Museum**
Visitors can experiment with over a thousand interactive displays ❹

★ **Natural History Museum**
The Creepy Crawlies exhibition has proved highly popular ❺

Entrance to South Kensington tube

STAR SIGHTS

- ★ Science Museum
- ★ Natural History Museum
- ★ Victoria and Albert Museum

KEY

– – – Suggested route

| 0 metres | 100 |
| 0 yards | 100 |

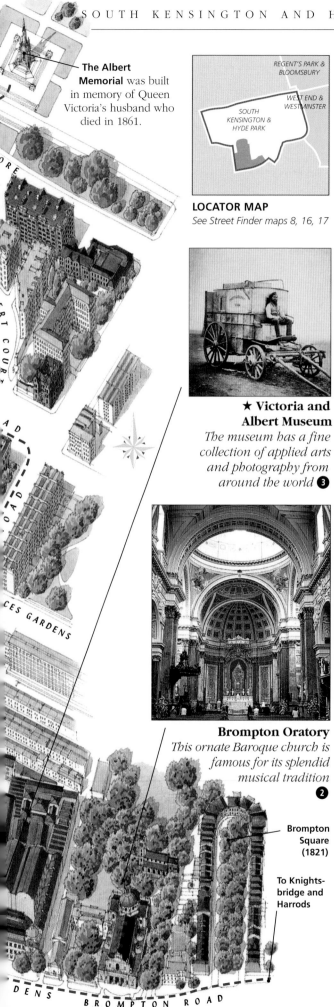

The Albert Memorial was built in memory of Queen Victoria's husband who died in 1861.

LOCATOR MAP
See Street Finder maps 8, 16, 17

★ **Victoria and Albert Museum**
The museum has a fine collection of applied arts and photography from around the world ❸

Brompton Oratory
This ornate Baroque church is famous for its splendid musical tradition ❷

Brompton Square (1821)

To Knightsbridge and Harrods

Harrods Food Hall

Harrods ❶

Knightsbridge SW1. **Map** 9 B5. **Tel** 020 7730 1234. ⊖ *Knightsbridge.* ◯ *10am–8pm Mon–Sat, noon–6pm Sun.* 🚾 🍴 🛍 *See* **Shops and Markets** *pp120–21.* **www**.harrods.com

In 1849 Henry Charles Harrod opened a small grocery shop on Brompton Road, which soon became famous for its impeccable service and quality. The store moved into these extravagant premises in Knightsbridge in 1905.

Brompton Oratory ❷

Brompton Rd SW7. **Map** 17 B1. **Tel** 020 7808 0900. ⊖ *South Kensington.* ◯ *6:30am–8pm daily.* 🚾 🛍 **www**.bromptonoratory.com

The Italianate Oratory is a lavish monument to the 19th-century English Catholic revival. It was established as a base for a community of priests by John Henry Newman (later Cardinal Newman), who introduced the Oratorian movement to England in 1848. The church was opened in 1884, and the dome and façade added in the 1890s.

The sumptuous interior holds many fine monuments. The 12 huge 17th-century statues of the apostles are from Siena Cathedral, the elaborate Baroque Lady Altar (1693) is from the Dominican church at Brescia, and the 18th-century altar in St Wilfred's Chapel is from Rochefort in Belgium.

Victoria and Albert Museum ❸

The Glass gallery, room 131

The Victoria and Albert Museum (the V&A) contains one of the world's widest collections of art and design, ranging from early Christian devotional objects and the mystical art of southeast Asia to cutting-edge furniture design. Originally founded in 1852 as the Museum of Manufactures to inspire students of design, it was renamed by Queen Victoria in 1899 in memory of Prince Albert. The museum has undergone a dramatic redisplay of its collection, including work on the Ceramics galleries, Sackler Education Centre and Medieval and Renaissance galleries, which span three levels. The Gilbert Collection also opened here in 2009.

Silver galleries
Radiant pieces such as the Burgess Cup (Britain, 1863) fill these stunning galleries.

★ British Galleries
The Great Bed of Ware has been a tourist attraction since 1601, when Shakespeare sparked interest in it by making reference to it in Twelfth Night.

KEY TO FLOORPLAN

▦	Level 0
▦	Level 1
▦	Level 2
□	Level 3
▦	Level 4
▦	Level 6
▦	Henry Cole Wing
▦	Non-exhibition space

STAR EXHIBITS

★ British Galleries

★ Fashion gallery

★ Medieval and Renaissance galleries

★ Islamic Middle East gallery

★ Fashion gallery
In this gallery, European clothing from the mid-1500s to the present day is displayed, such as these famous Vivienne Westwood shoes.

Exhibition Road entrance

GALLERY GUIDE

The V&A has a 7-mile (11-km) layout spread over six levels. Level 1, houses the China, Japan and South Asia galleries, as well as the Fashion gallery and the Cast Courts. The British Galleries are on levels 2 and 4. Level 3 contains the 20th Century galleries and displays of silver, jewellery, ironwork, paintings and works of 20th-century design. The glass display is also on upper level 4. The Ceramics galleries are on level 6. The Henry Cole Wing houses the Sackler Education Centre, RIBA Architecture Study Rooms and the Prints and Drawings Study Rooms.

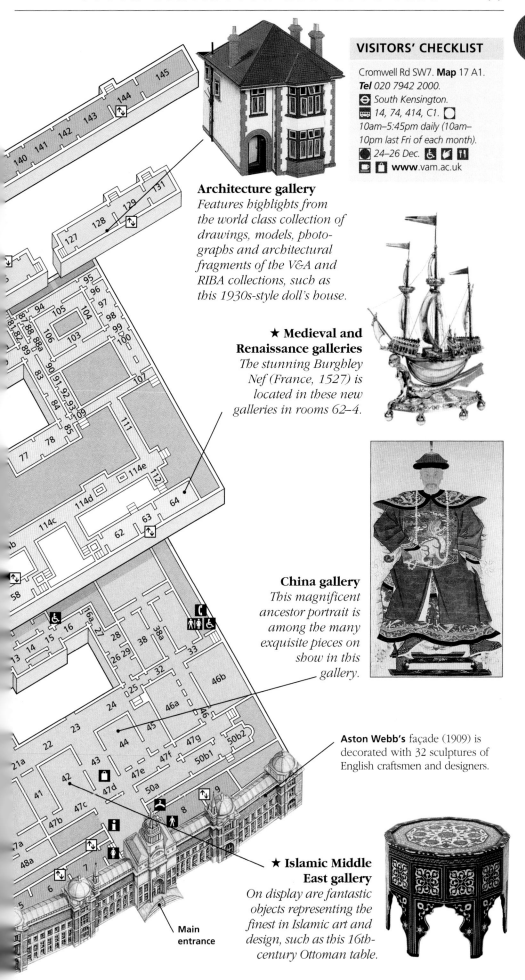

VISITORS' CHECKLIST

Cromwell Rd SW7. **Map** 17 A1.
Tel 020 7942 2000.
South Kensington.
14, 74, 414, C1.
10am–5:45pm daily (10am–
10pm last Fri of each month).
24–26 Dec.
www.vam.ac.uk

Architecture gallery

*Features highlights from
the world class collection of
drawings, models, photo-
graphs and architectural
fragments of the V&A and
RIBA collections, such as
this 1930s-style doll's house.*

★ Medieval and Renaissance galleries

*The stunning Burghley
Nef (France, 1527) is
located in these new
galleries in rooms 62–4.*

China gallery

*This magnificent
ancestor portrait is
among the many
exquisite pieces on
show in this
gallery.*

Aston Webb's façade (1909) is
decorated with 32 sculptures of
English craftsmen and designers.

★ Islamic Middle East gallery

*On display are fantastic
objects representing the
finest in Islamic art and
design, such as this 16th-
century Ottoman table.*

**Main
entrance**

Science Museum ❹

Exhibition Rd SW7. **Map** 16 F1. **Tel** 0870 870 4868. 🚇 South Kensington. 🕐 10am–6pm daily. ⬤ 24–26 Dec. 📷 for IMAX, special exhibitions and simulators only. ♿ 🎞 📷 📱 🏛
www.sciencemuseum.org.uk

Centuries of continuing scientific and technological development lie at the heart of the Science Museum's massive collections. The hardware displayed is magnificent: from steam engines to aeroengines; spacecraft to the very first mechanical computers. Equally important is the social

Newcomen's Steam Engine (1712), Science Museum

context of science – what discoveries and inventions mean for day-to-day life – and the process of discovery itself. There are many interactive and hands-on displays which are very popular with children.

The museum is spread over seven floors and includes the high-tech Wellcome Wing at the west end of the museum. The basement features the excellent hands-on galleries for children, including The Garden. The Energy Hall dominates the ground floor, and is dedicated to steam power, with the still-operational Harle Syke Mill Engine of 1903. Here too are Space and Making the Modern World, a highlight of which is the display of the scarred Apollo 10 spacecraft, which carried three astronauts to the moon and back in May 1969. In Challenge of Materials, located on the first floor, our

expectations of materials are confounded with exhibits such as a bridge made of glass and a steel wedding dress.

The Flight gallery on the third floor is packed with early flying contraptions, fighter planes, aeroplanes and the Launchpad. The fourth and fifth floors house the medical science galleries, where Science and the Art of Medicine has a 17th-century Italian vase for storing snake bite treatment.

The high-tech Wellcome Wing offers four floors of interactive technology, including 'Who Am I?', a fascinating exhibition exploring the science of you. With an IMAX 3D Cinema and the SimEx simulator ride, it is a breathtaking addition to the museum. The museum cafés and shop are particularly good.

Natural History Museum ❺

Cromwell Rd SW7. **Map** 16 F1. **Tel** 020 7942 5000. 🚇 South Kensington. 🕐 10am–5:50pm daily. ⬤ 24–26 Dec. 🏛 ♿ 🎞 📱
www.nhm.ac.uk

This cathedral-like building's richly sculpted stonework conceals an iron and steel frame; this construction technique was revolutionary when the museum opened in 1881. The imaginative displays tackle fundamental issues such as the ecology and evolution of the planet, the origin of species and the development of human beings – all explained through a dynamic combination of the latest technology, interactive techniques and traditional displays. The museum is divided

Relief from a decorative panel in the Natural History Museum

into four sections: the Blue Zone, Green Zone, Red Zone and the Orange Zone. In the Blue Zone, the Ecology exhibition explores the complex web of the natural world through a replica of a moonlit rainforest buzzing with the sounds of insects. One of the most popular exhibits is the Dinosaur Gallery, which includes life-like animatronic models of dinosaurs. The Vault, located in the Green Zone, contains a dazzling collection of the finest gems, crystals, metals and meteorites from around the world. The Darwin Centre, which opened in 2009, is the largest curved structure in Europe. The eight-storey-high cocoon houses the museum's vast collection of insects and plants.

The Tuojiangasaurus skeleton (about 150 million years old), Natural History Museum

Statue of the young Queen Victoria outside Kensington Palace, sculpted by her daughter, Princess Louise

Hyde Park and Kensington Gardens ❻

W2. **Map** 9 B3. *Tel* 020 7298 2000.
Hyde Park ⊖ Hyde Park Corner,
Knightsbridge, Lancaster Gate, Marble
Arch. ◯ dawn–midnight daily. ♿
Kensington Gardens. Tel 020 7298
2000. ⊖ Queensway, Lancaster Gate.
◯ dawn–dusk daily. ♿ ▢ See also
pp74–5. **Diana, Princess of Wales
Memorial Playground** ⊖ Queensway, Bayswater. ◯ 10am–dusk daily.
♿ ▢ www.royalparks.org.uk

The ancient manor of Hyde
was part of the lands of
Westminster Abbey seized by
Henry VIII at the Dissolution
of the Monasteries in 1536
(see pp50–51). James I opened
the park to the public in the
early 17th century, and it was
soon one of the city's most
fashionable public spaces.
Unfortunately it also
became popular
with duellists and
highwaymen,
and conse-
quently

William III had 300 lights
hung along Rotten Row,
the first street in England to
be lit up at night. In 1730,
the Westbourne River was
dammed by Queen Caroline
in order to create the
Serpentine, an artificial lake
that is today used for boating
and swimming, and Rotten
Row for horse riding. The
park is also a rallying point
for political demonstrations,
while at Speaker's Corner, in
the northeast, anyone has
had the right to address the
public since 1872. Sundays
are particularly lively, with
many budding orators
and a number of
eccentrics revealing
their plans for the
betterment of
mankind.
   Adjoining Hyde
Park is Kensington
Gardens, the
former grounds
of Kensington
Palace. Three
great attractions
for children are
the innovative
Diana, Princess of Wales
Memorial Playground, the
bronze statue of J M Barrie's
fictional Peter Pan (1912), by
George Frampton, and the
Round Pond where people
sail model boats. Also worth-
seeing is the dignified
Orangery (1704),
once used by
Queen Anne as
a "summer supper house"
and now a summer café.

**Detail of the Coalbrookdale
Gate, Kensington Gardens**

Kensington Palace ❼

Kensington Palace Gdns W8. **Map** 8
D4. *Tel* 0844 482 7777. ⊖ High St
Ken, Queensway. ◯ Nov–Feb: 10am–
5pm daily; Mar–Oct: 10am–6pm daily
(last adm: 1 hr before close). ◐ 1 Jan,
24–26 Dec. 🔒 📷 ♿ ground floor.
▢ www.hrp.org.uk

Kensington Palace was the
principal residence of the
royal family from the 1690s
until 1760, when George III
moved to Buckingham
Palace. Over the years it
has seen a number of
important royal events.
In 1714 Queen Anne
died here from a fit of
apoplexy brought on
by over-eating and, in
June 1837, Princess
Victoria of Kent was
woken to be told
that her uncle
William IV had
died and she
was now queen
– the beginning
of her 64-year
reign. Half of the palace still
holds royal apartments, but the
other half is open to the public. Among the highlights are
the 18th-century state rooms
with ceilings and murals by
William Kent *(see p28)*. After
the death of Princess Diana
in 1997, the palace became a
focal point for mourners who
gathered in their thousands at
its gates and turned the area
into a field of bouquets.

REGENT'S PARK AND BLOOMSBURY

Cream stuccoed terraces built by John Nash (*see p105*) fringe the southern edge of Regent's Park in London's highest concentration of quality Georgian housing. The park, named for the Prince Regent, was also designed by Nash, as the culmination of a triumphal route from the Prince's house in St James's (*see pp84–5*). Today it is the busiest of the royal parks and boasts a zoo, an open air theatre, boating lake, rose garden, cafés and London's largest mosque. To the northeast is Camden Town (*see p124*) with its popular market, shops and cafés, reached by walking, or taking a boat, along the picturesque Regent's Canal.

Ancient Greek vase, British Museum

Bloomsbury, an enclave of attractive garden squares and Georgian brick terraces, was one of the most fashionable areas of the city until the mid-19th century, when the arrival of large hospitals and railway stations persuaded many of the wealthier residents to move west to Mayfair, Knightsbridge and Kensington. Home to the British Museum since 1753 and the University of London since 1828, Bloomsbury has long been the domain of artists, writers and intellectuals, including the Bloomsbury Group (*see p163*), George Bernard Shaw, Charles Dickens and Karl Marx. Traditionally a centre for the book trade, it remains a good place for literary browsing.

SIGHTS AT A GLANCE

Historic Streets
Bloomsbury ❺

Museums and Galleries
British Museum pp106–7 ❹

Madame Tussaud's ❶
Sherlock Holmes Museum ❷
Wallace Collection ❸

GETTING THERE
For most of Regent's Park, the nearest tube stations are Regent's Park, Great Portland Street and Baker Street. Buses 13, 139 and 159 run from Trafalgar Square to near Baker Street. The closest station to the zoo is Camden Town. Russell Square tube station is in the heart of Bloomsbury.

KEY

❷ Underground station

0 metres 500
0 yards 500

Madame Tussaud's ❶

Marylebone Rd NW1. **Map** 2 D5.
📱 *0870 400 3000*. 🚇 *Baker St.*
🕐 *9:30am–5:30pm Mon–Fri, 9am–
6pm Sat–Sun.* ⬛ *25 Dec.* ⬛
📷 ♿ *phone first.* 🅿️
www.madame-tussauds.com

Madame Tussaud began her
wax-modelling career making
death masks of victims of the
French Revolution. She
moved to
England and in 1835
set up an exhib-ition
of her work in
Baker Street, near
the present site.
Traditional tech-
niques are still
used to create
figures of royal-
ty, politicians,
actors, pop stars
and
sporting
heroes. The
main sec-
tions of the
exhi-bition are:
Blush, where
visitors get to
feel what it is like to be at a
celebrity A-list party; Première
Night, devoted to the giants of
the entertainment world; and
the World Stage, a collection
of various royalty, statesmen,
world leaders, writers and
artists.

**Wax figure of
Elizabeth II**

The Chamber of Horrors is
the most renowned part of
Madame Tussaud's for its
recreations of murders and
executions. In the Spirit of
London finale, visitors travel
in stylized taxi-cabs through

**Conan Doyle's fictional detective
Sherlock Holmes**

the city's history to "witness"
events, from the Great Fire of
1666 to the Swinging 1960s.
Ticket prices also include
entry to temporary exhibitions
featuring media icons of the
moment. Educational tours
are also available for groups.

Sherlock Holmes Museum ❷

221b Baker St NW1. **Map** 1 C4.
Tel *020-7935 1127.* 🚇 *Baker St.* 🕐
9:30am–6pm daily. ⬛ *25 Dec.* 📷 ⬛
www.sherlock-holmes.co.uk

Sir Arthur Conan Doyle's
fictional detective was
supposed to live at 221b
Baker Street, which did not
exist. The museum, labelled
221b, actually stands between
Nos. 237 and 239, and is the
only surviving Victorian lodging house in the street. There
is a reconstruction of Holmes's
front room, and memorabilia
from the stories decorate
every room. Visitors can buy
plaques, Holmes hats, Toby
jugs and meerschaum pipes.

Wallace Collection ❸

Hertford House, Manchester Sq W1.
Map 10 D1. 📱 *020-7563 9500.*
🚇 *Bond St, Baker St.* 🕐
10am–5pm daily. ⬛ *24–26 Dec, 1
Jan, Good Fri.* ♿ *phone first.* 🍴 ⬛
www.wallacecollection.org

One of the world's finest
private collections of European
art, it has remained intact
since 1897. The product of

passionate collecting by four
generations of the Seymour-
Conway family who were
Marquesses of Hertford, it
was bequeathed to the state
on the condition that it would
go on permanent public display with nothing added or
taken away. Hertford House
still retains the atmosphere of
a grand 19th-century house,
and the recent Centenary
Project has created more
gallery space and a stunning
high-level glass roof for the
central courtyard, which now
contains a sculpture garden
and an elegant restaurant.

The 3rd Marquess (1777–
1842), a flamboyant London
figure, used his Italian wife's
fortune to buy works by
Titian and Canaletto, along
with numerous 17th-century
Dutch paintings including
works by Van Dyck. The collection's particular strength is
18th-century French painting,
sculpture and decorative arts,
acquired by the 4th Marquess
(1800–70) and his natural son,
Sir Richard Wallace (1818–90).

**A 16th-century Italian majolica
dish from the Wallace Collection**

The Marquess had a taste for
lush romanticism, and notable
among his acquisitions are
Watteau's *Champs Elysées*
(1716–17), Fragonard's *The
Swing* (1766) and Boucher's
*The Rising and Setting of the
Sun* (1753).

Other highlights at the
Wallace Collection include
Rembrandt's *Titus, the Artist's
Son* (1650s), Titian's *Perseus
and Andromeda* (1554–6)
and Hals's famous *Laughing
Cavalier* (1624). There is also
an important collection of
Renaissance armour, and
superb examples of Sèvres
porcelain and Italian majolica.

**Wax model of Luciano Pavarotti
(1990), Madame Tussaud's**

John Nash's Regency London

John Nash, the son of a Lambeth millwright, was designing houses from the 1780s. However, it was not until the 1820s that he also became known as an inspired town planner, when his "royal route" was completed. This took George IV from his Pall Mall palace, through Piccadilly Circus and up the elegant sweep of Regent Street to Regent's Park, which Nash bordered with rows of beautiful

Statue of John Nash (1752–1835)

Neo-Classical villas, such as Park Crescent and Cumberland Terrace. Though many of his plans were never completed, this map of 1851, which unusually places the south at the top, shows Nash's overall architectural impact on London. His other work included the revamping of Buckingham Palace *(see pp86–7),* and the building of several theatres and churches.

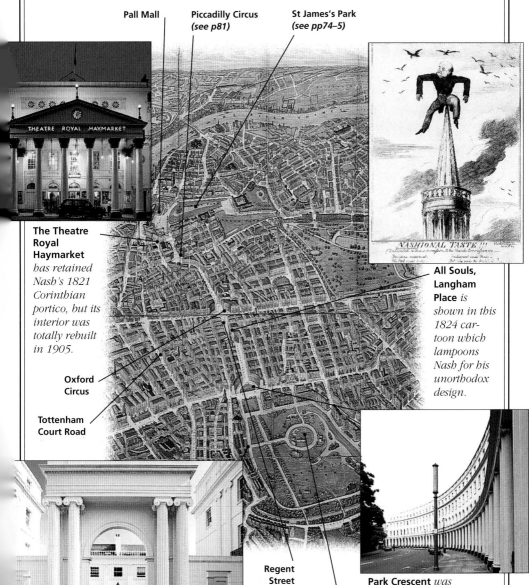

Pall Mall

Piccadilly Circus (see p81)

St James's Park (see pp74–5)

The Theatre Royal Haymarket *has retained Nash's 1821 Corinthian portico, but its interior was totally rebuilt in 1905.*

Oxford Circus

Tottenham Court Road

All Souls, Langham Place *is shown in this 1824 cartoon which lampoons Nash for his unorthodox design.*

Cumberland Terrace, *the longest and most ornate of the stuccoed terraces surrounding Regent's Park, was intended to face a royal palace, which was never built.*

Regent Street

Regent's Park (see p103)

Park Crescent *was designed by Nash to be the southern half of a circle, but the northern half was never built. The interiors were refurbished in the 1960s but the dramatic façade was kept intact.*

British Museum ❹

Helmet from Sutton Hoo ship burial

The oldest public museum in the world, the British Museum was established in 1753 to house the collections of the physician Sir Hans Sloane (1660–1753). Sloane's collection has been added to by gifts and purchases from all over the world, and the museum now contains objects spanning thousands of years. The main part of the building (1823–50) is by architect Robert Smirke, but the architectural highlight is the modern Great Court, with the Reading Room at its centre.

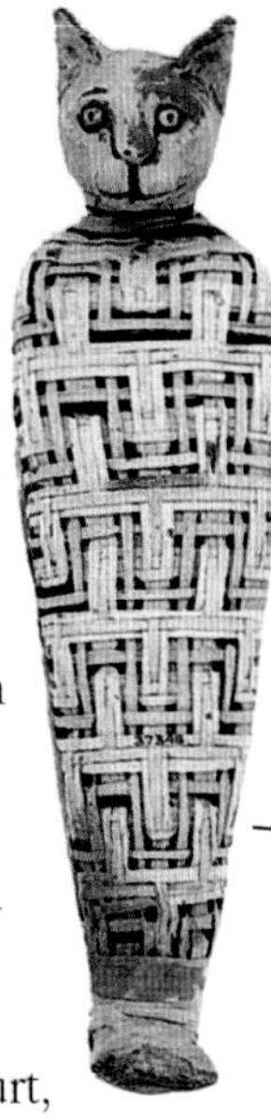

★ Egyptian Mummies
Animals such as this cat (30 BC) were preserved alongside humans by the ancient Egyptians.

Bronze Figure Shiva Nataraja
This statue of the Hindu God Shiva Nataraja (c.1100) from South India forms part of the fine collection of Oriental art.

The Egyptian Gallery on the main floor houses the Rosetta Stone, the inscription that enabled 19th-century scholars to decipher Egyptian hieroglyphs.

GALLERY GUIDE

The Greek and Roman, and Middle Eastern collections are found on all three levels of the museum, predominantly on the west side. The African collection is located on the lower floor, while Asian exhibits are found on the main and upper floors on the north side of the museum. The Americas collection is located in the northeast corner off the main floor. Egyptian artifacts are found in the large gallery to the west of the Great Court and on the first floor.

★ Parthenon Sculptures
These reliefs from the Parthenon in Athens were brought to London by Lord Elgin around 1802 and are housed in a special gallery.

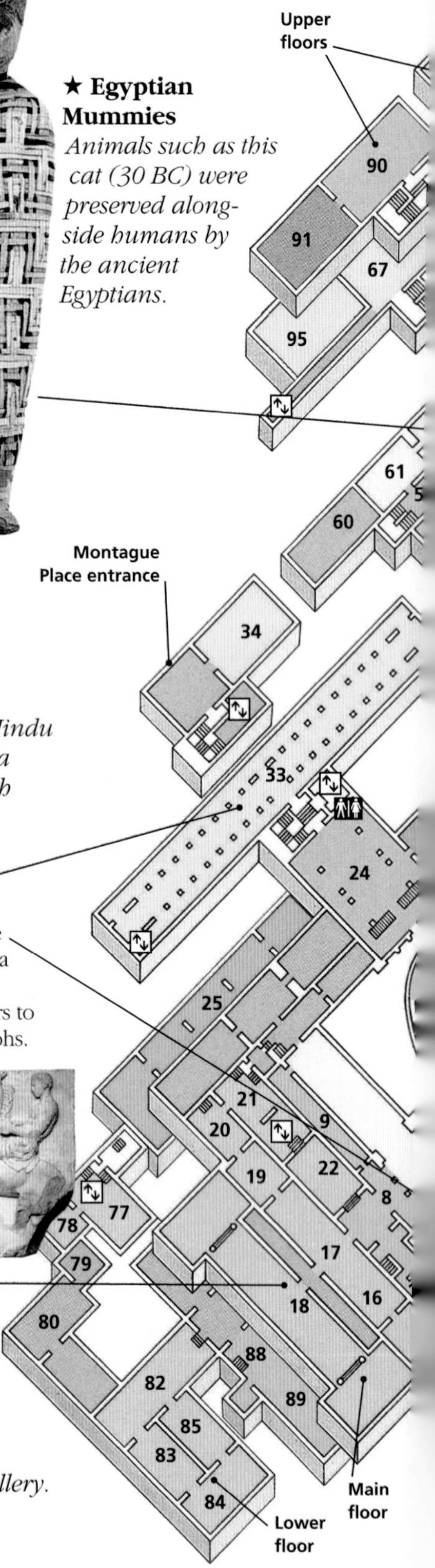

Upper floors

Montague Place entrance

Main floor

Lower floor

STAR EXHIBITS

★ Egyptian Mummies

★ Parthenon Sculptures

★ Lindow Man

KEY TO FLOORPLAN

☐ Asian collection	☐ Middle Eastern collection
◼ Enlightenment	☐ Europe collection
☐ Coins and medals	☐ Temporary exhibitions
◼ Greek and Roman collections	◼ Non-exhibition space
☐ Egyptian collection	◻ World collection

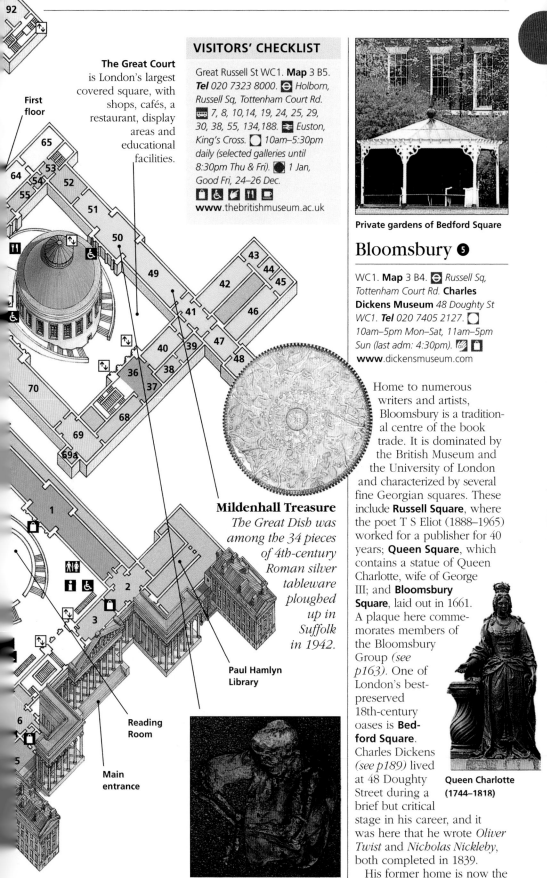

First floor

The Great Court is London's largest covered square, with shops, cafés, a restaurant, display areas and educational facilities.

92

65
64 **54** **53** **52**
55
51
50
49 **43** **44** **45**
42 **46**
41 **47**
40 **39** **48**
36 **38** **37**
70
68
69
69a
1
2
3
6
5

Paul Hamlyn Library

Reading Room

Main entrance

VISITORS' CHECKLIST

Great Russell St WC1. **Map** 3 B5. **Tel** *020 7323 8000.* ⊖ *Holborn, Russell Sq, Tottenham Court Rd.* 🚌 *7, 8, 10,14, 19, 24, 25, 29, 30, 38, 55, 134,188.* 🚆 *Euston, King's Cross.* ◯ *10am–5:30pm daily (selected galleries until 8:30pm Thu & Fri).* ● *1 Jan, Good Fri, 24–26 Dec.*
www.thebritishmuseum.ac.uk

Mildenhall Treasure
The Great Dish was among the 34 pieces of 4th-century Roman silver tableware ploughed up in Suffolk in 1942.

★ Lindow Man
The skin on this 2,000-year-old human body was preserved by the acids of a peat-bog in Cheshire. He was probably killed in an elaborate ritual.

Private gardens of Bedford Square

Bloomsbury ⑤

WC1. **Map** 3 B4. ⊖ *Russell Sq, Tottenham Court Rd.* **Charles Dickens Museum** *48 Doughty St WC1.* **Tel** *020 7405 2127.* ◯ *10am–5pm Mon–Sat, 11am–5pm Sun (last adm: 4:30pm).* www.dickensmuseum.com

Home to numerous writers and artists, Bloomsbury is a traditional centre of the book trade. It is dominated by the British Museum and the University of London and characterized by several fine Georgian squares. These include **Russell Square**, where the poet T S Eliot (1888–1965) worked for a publisher for 40 years; **Queen Square**, which contains a statue of Queen Charlotte, wife of George III; and **Bloomsbury Square**, laid out in 1661. A plaque here commemorates members of the Bloomsbury Group *(see p163)*. One of London's best-preserved 18th-century oases is **Bedford Square**. Charles Dickens *(see p189)* lived at 48 Doughty Street during a brief but critical stage in his career, and it was here that he wrote *Oliver Twist* and *Nicholas Nickleby*, both completed in 1839.

His former home is now the **Charles Dickens Museum**, which has rooms laid out as they were in Dickens's time, with objects taken from his other London homes and first editions of many of his works.

Queen Charlotte (1744–1818)

THE CITY AND SOUTHWARK

Dominated today by glossy office blocks, the City is the oldest part of the capital. The Great Fire of 1666 obliterated four-fifths of its buildings. Sir Christopher Wren rebuilt much of it and many of his churches survived World War II (*see pp58–9*). Commerce has always been the City's lifeblood, and the power of its merchants and bankers secured it a degree of autonomy from state control. Humming with activity in business hours, it empties at night.

In the Middle Ages Southwark, on the south bank of the Thames, was a

Old bank sign on Lombard Street

refuge for pleasure-seekers, prostitutes, gamblers and criminals. Even after 1550, when the area fell under the jurisdiction of the City, its brothels and taverns thrived. There were also several bear-baiting arenas in which plays were staged until the building of theatres such as the Globe (1598), where many of Shakespeare's works were first performed. Relics of old Southwark are mostly on the waterfront, which has been imaginatively redeveloped and provided with a pleasant walkway.

SIGHTS AT A GLANCE

Historic Sights and Buildings
HMS Belfast ⓬
Lloyd's Building ❼
Monument ❽
The Old Operating Theatre ⓮
Temple ❸
Tower Bridge ❿
Tower of London pp118–19 ❾

Pubs
George Inn ⓯

Museums and Galleries
Design Museum ⓫
London Dungeon ⓭
Museum of London ❻
Shakespeare's Globe ⓲
Sir John Soane's Museum ❹
Tate Modern ⓳

Markets
Borough Market ⓰

Churches and Cathedrals
St Bartholomew-the-Great ❺
St Paul's Cathedral pp114–15 ❷
St Stephen Walbrook ❶
Southwark Cathedral ⓱

GETTING THERE
The City is served by the Circle, Central, District, Northern and Metropolitan lines and by a number of buses. London Bridge is the main station for Southwark – served by the Northern and Jubilee lines and by trains running from Charing Cross, Cannon Street and Waterloo.

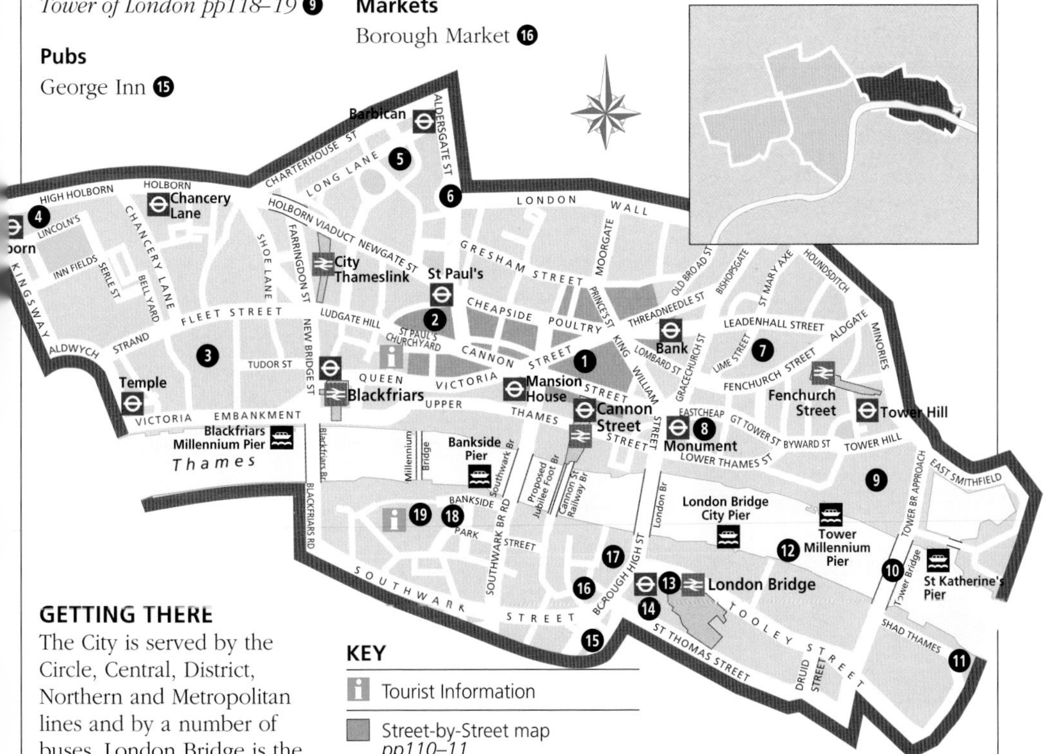

KEY
🛈 Tourist Information

▨ Street-by-Street map *pp110–11*

Ⓔ Underground station

⇌ Railway station

⇌ River boat pier

0 metres   500

0 yards   500

◁ St Paul's Cathedral in the heart of the City, with the NatWest Tower (1980) to the left

Street-by-Street: The City

This is the financial heart of London and has been ever since the Romans set up a trading post here 2,000 years ago. For years it was London's main residential area but today very few people live here. The City was severely bombed in World War II and the main clues to its past are streets named after vanished inns and markets.

Detail: St Paul's Cathedral

Its numerous churches, many built after the Great Fire of 1666 by the architect Sir Christopher Wren *(see p114),* are now dwarfed by lavish banks and post-modern developments.

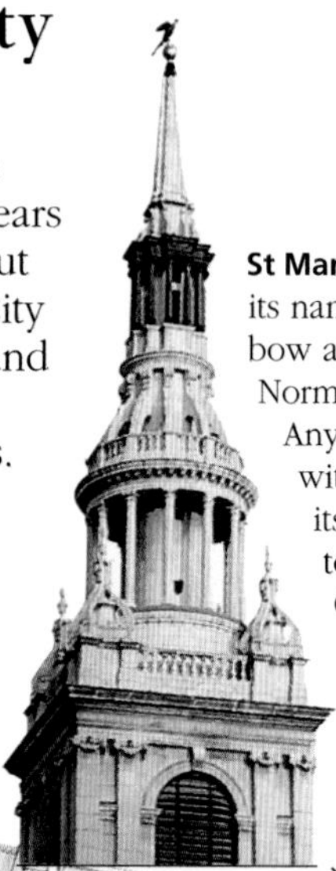

St Mary-le-Bow takes its name from the bow arches in the Norman crypt. Anyone born within earshot of its bells is said to be a true Cockney.

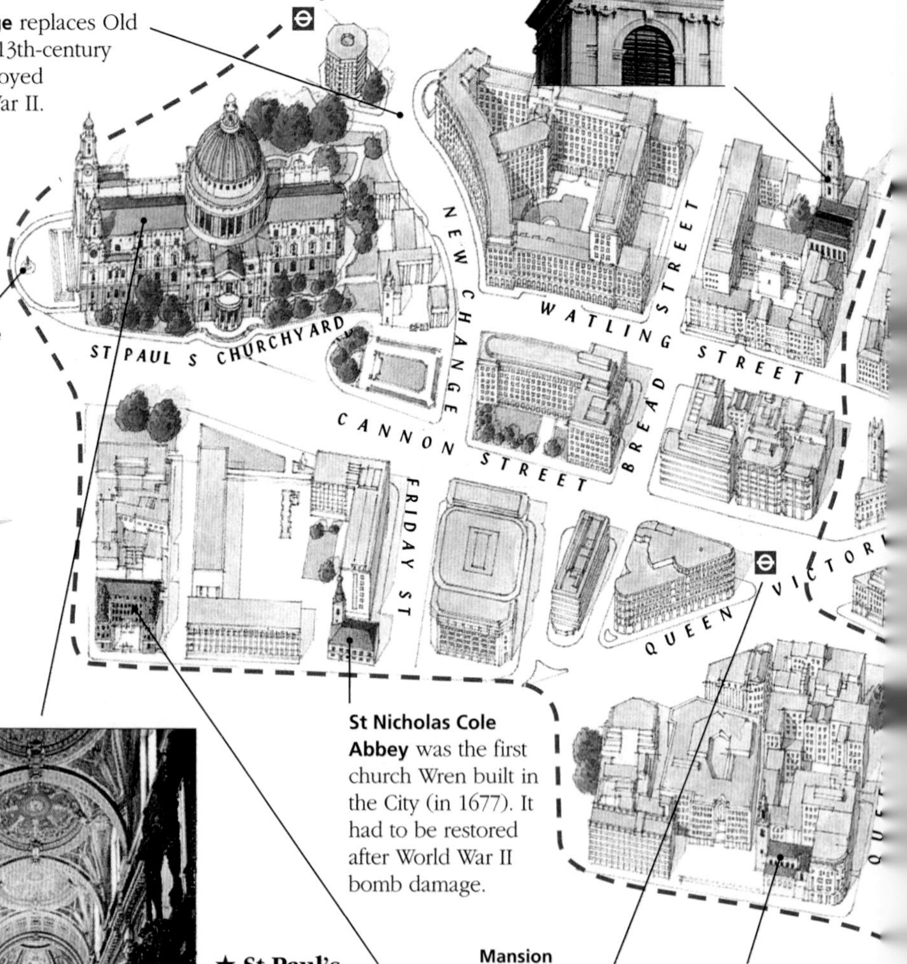

New Change replaces Old Change, a 13th-century street destroyed in World War II.

St Paul's station

Statue of Queen Anne

ST PAUL'S CHURCHYARD

NEW CHANGE

WATLING STREET

BREAD STREET

CANNON STREET

FRIDAY ST

QUEEN VICTOR

St Nicholas Cole Abbey was the first church Wren built in the City (in 1677). It had to be restored after World War II bomb damage.

★ **St Paul's Cathedral**
Built after the Great Fire of 1666, Wren's masterpiece was funded by a tax on coal ❷

Mansion House station

St James Garlickhythe contains unusual sword rests and hat stands, beneath Wren's elegant spire of 1717.

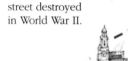

STAR SIGHTS

★ St Paul's Cathedral

★ St Stephen Walbrook

COLLEGE · OF · ARMS

The College of Arms is the official repository of the coats of arms and pedigrees of British families *(see p30).* It was rebuilt here, on its former site, in the 1670s after the Great Fire.

Mansion House (1753), designed by George Dance the Elder, is the official home of the Lord Mayor. The Palladian façade is a familiar City landmark.

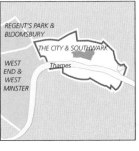

LOCATOR MAP
See Street Finder map 13

Bank of England Museum

The Royal Exchange was founded in 1565 by Sir Thomas Gresham as a centre for commerce. The current building dates from 1844.

Bank station

Lombard Street, named after bankers who came here from Lombardy in the 13th century, retains its traditional banking signs.

KEY

— — — Suggested route

St Mary Abchurch owes its unusually spacious feel to Wren's large dome. The altar carving is by Grinling Gibbons.

★ St Stephen Walbrook
This fine Wren church contains a striking white stone altar by Henry Moore ❶

0 metres 100
0 yards 100

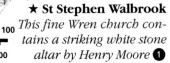

Skinners' Hall is an 18th-century Italianate building constructed for the ancient guild that controlled trade in fur and leather.

St Stephen Walbrook ❶

39 Walbrook EC4. **Map** 13 B2. **Tel** 020 7626 9000. 🚇 *Bank, Cannon St.* ⬜ *10am–4pm Mon–Thu, 10am–3pm Fri.* ● *public hols.* ✝ *12:45am Thu.* **http://**ststephenwalbrook.net

The Lord Mayor's parish church was built by Sir Christopher Wren in the 1670s and is among the finest of all his City churches. The bright, airy interior is flooded with light by a huge dome that appears to float above the eight columns and arches that support it. The dome, deep and coffered with ornate plasterwork, was a forerunner of St Paul's. Original fittings, such as the highly decorative font cover and pulpit canopy, contrast with the stark simplicity of Henry Moore's massive white stone altar (1987). The best time to see the church is during one of its free organ recitals from 12.30 to 1.30pm on Fridays.

St Paul's ❷

See pp116–17.

Effigies in Temple Church

Temple ❸

Inner Temple, King's Bench Walk EC4. **Tel** 020 7797 8250. **Map** 12 E2. 🚇 *Temple.* ⬜ *12:30–3pm Mon–Fri (grounds only).* 🚻 **Middle Temple Hall**, *Middle Temple Ln EC4.* **Tel** 020 7427 4800. ⬜ *10–11:30am, 3–4pm Mon–Fri.* 🚻 **Temple Church.** **Tel** 020 7353 8559. ⬜ *Wed–Fri; call for times and services.* 📷 *book ahead.*

A cluster of atmospheric squares form the Inner and Middle Temples, two of London's four Inns of Court, where law students are trained. The name Temple derives from the medieval Knights Templar, a religious order which protected pilgrims to the Holy Land and was based here until 1312. Marble effigies of knights lie on the floor of the circular Temple Church, part of which dates from the 12th century. Middle Temple Hall has a fine Elizabethan interior.

St Bartholomew-the-Great ❺

West Smithfield EC1. **Map** 12 F1. **Tel** 020 7606 5171. 🚇 *Barbican, St Paul's.* ⬜ *8:30am–5pm (4pm in winter) Mon–Fri, 10:30am–4pm Sat, 8:30am–8pm Sun.* ● *1 Jan, 25, 26 Dec.* 📷 🚻 📷 *by appt.* **Concerts.** **www**.greatstbarts.com

The historic area of Smithfield has witnessed a number of bloody events over the years, among them the execution of rebel peasant leader Wat Tyler in 1381, and, in the reign of Mary I (1553–58), the burning of scores of Protestant martyrs.

Sir John Soane's Museum ❹

13 Lincoln's Inn Fields WC2. **Map** 12 D1. **Tel** 020 7405 2107. 🚇 *Holborn.* ⬜ *10am–5pm Tue–Sat, 6–9pm 1st Tue of month.* ● *public hols, 24 Dec.* 🚻 *ground floor only.* 📷 *Sat 2:30pm.* **www**.soane.org

One of the most eccentric museums in London, this house was left to the nation by Sir John Soane in 1837, with a stipulation that nothing should be changed. The son of a bricklayer, Soane became one of Britain's leading late Georgian architects developing a restrained Neo-Classical style of his own. After marrying the niece of a wealthy builder, whose fortune he inherited, he bought and reconstructed No. 12 Lincoln's Inn Fields. In 1813 he and his wife moved into No. 13 and in 1824 he rebuilt No. 14, adding a picture gallery and the mock medieval Monk's Parlour. Today, true to Soane's wishes, the collections are much as he left them – an eclectic gathering of beautiful, instructional and often simply peculiar artifacts. There are casts, bronzes, vases, antique fragments, paintings and a selection of bizarre trivia which ranges from a giant fungus from Sumatra to a scold-bridle, a device designed to silence nagging wives. Highlights include the sarcophagus of Seti I, Soanes's own designs, including those for the Bank of England, models by leading Neo-Classical sculptors and the *Rake's Progress* series of paintings (1734) by William Hogarth, which Mrs Soane bought for £520.

The building itself is full of architectural surprises and illusions. In the main ground floor room, cunningly placed mirrors play tricks with light and space, while an atrium stretching from the basement to the glass-domed roof allows light on to every floor.

A glass dome lets light on to all the floors.

A vast sarcophagus (1300 BC) stands on the floor of the crypt.

Hidden in a quiet corner behind Smithfield meat market (central London's only surviving wholesale food market), this is one of London's oldest churches. It once formed part of a priory founded in 1123 by a monk, Rahere, whose tomb is here. He was Henry I's court jester until he dreamed that St Bartholomew had saved him from a winged monster.

The 13th-century arch, now topped by a Tudor gatehouse, used to be the entrance to the church until the old nave was pulled down during the Dissolution of the Monasteries (see pp50–51). The painter William Hogarth was baptized here in 1697. The church featured in the films *Four Weddings and a Funeral* and *Shakespeare in Love*.

St Bartholomew's gatehouse

Museum of London ⑥

London Wall EC2. **Map** 13 A1.
Tel 0870 444 3855. ⊖ Barbican, St Paul's. ◻ 10am–6pm daily. ◉ 24–26 Dec. ♿🖥📷
www.museumoflondon.org.uk

This museum traces life in London from prehistoric times to the outbreak of World War I. Displays of archaeological finds and domestic objects alternate with reconstructed street scenes and interiors.

Delft plate made in London 1600, Museum of London

There is also a working model of the Great Fire of 1666 in the London's Burning section. The Roman London gallery has a brightly coloured 2nd-century fresco from a Southwark bath house.

The museum has spent over £20 million redeveloping its lower galleries, retelling London's history from 1666 to the present day with over 4,000 objects and interactive exhibits. The galleries are due to open in the spring of 2010, and visitors will be able to discover the city's many incarnations in the London before London, Roman London and Medieval London galleries.

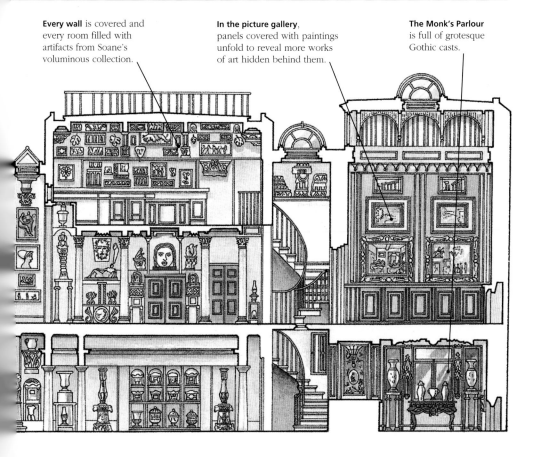

Every wall is covered and every room filled with artifacts from Soane's voluminous collection.

In the picture gallery, panels covered with paintings unfold to reveal more works of art hidden behind them.

The Monk's Parlour is full of grotesque Gothic casts.

St Paul's Cathedral ❷

The Great Fire of London in 1666 left
the medieval cathedral of St Paul's in
ruins. Wren was commissioned to rebuild
it, but his design for a church on a Greek
Cross plan (where all four arms are equal)
met with considerable resistance. The
authorities insisted on a conventional
Latin cross, with a long nave and short
transepts, which was believed to focus
the congregation's attention on the altar.
Despite the compromises, Wren created
a magnificent Baroque cathedral, which
was built between 1675 and 1710 and
has since formed the lavish setting for
many state
ceremonies.

★ Dome
*At 111 m (360
ft), the elabo-
rate dome
is one of the
highest in
the world.*

The balustrade
along the top was
added in 1718
against Wren's
wishes.

**★ West Front
and Towers**
*Inspired by the Italian
Baroque architect,
Borromini, the towers were
added by Wren in 1707.*

The West Portico
consists of two storeys of
coupled Corinthian columns,
topped by a pediment carved
with reliefs showing the
Conversion of St Paul.

The Nave
*An imposing succession of massive arches
and saucer domes open out into the vast
space below the cathedral's main dome.*

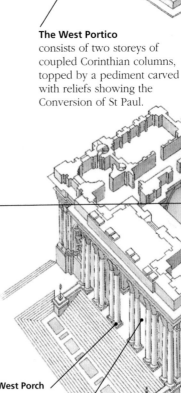

West Porch

Main entrance
approached from
Ludgate Hill

CHRISTOPHER WREN

Trained as a scientist,
Sir Christopher Wren
(1632–1723) began his
impressive architectural
career at the age of 31. He
became a leading figure in
the rebuilding of London
after the Great Fire of 1666,
building a total of 52 new churches.
Although Wren never visited Italy, his
work was influenced by Roman, Baroque
and Renaissance architecture, as is appar-
ent in his masterpiece, St Paul's Cathedral.

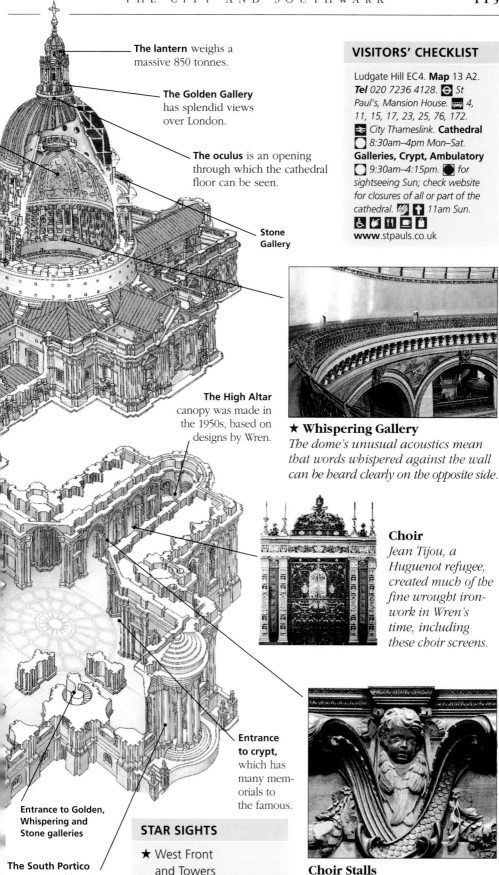

The lantern weighs a massive 850 tonnes.

The Golden Gallery has splendid views over London.

The oculus is an opening through which the cathedral floor can be seen.

Stone Gallery

VISITORS' CHECKLIST

Ludgate Hill EC4. **Map** 13 A2. **Tel** 020 7236 4128. 🚇 St Paul's, Mansion House. 🚌 4, 11, 15, 17, 23, 25, 76, 172. 🚆 City Thameslink. **Cathedral** ⏰ 8:30am–4pm Mon–Sat. **Galleries, Crypt, Ambulatory** ⏰ 9:30am–4:15pm. 🌑 for sightseeing Sun; check website for closures of all or part of the cathedral. 📷 ✝ 11am Sun. ♿ 🚻 🏪 📷 📖 www.stpauls.co.uk

The High Altar canopy was made in the 1950s, based on designs by Wren.

★ **Whispering Gallery**
The dome's unusual acoustics mean that words whispered against the wall can be heard clearly on the opposite side.

Choir
Jean Tijou, a Huguenot refugee, created much of the fine wrought iron-work in Wren's time, including these choir screens.

Entrance to crypt, which has many memorials to the famous.

Entrance to Golden, Whispering and Stone galleries

STAR SIGHTS

★ West Front and Towers

★ Dome

★ Whispering Gallery

The South Portico was inspired by the porch of Santa Maria della Pace in Rome. Wren absorbed the detail by studying a friend's collection of architectural engravings.

Choir Stalls
The 17th-century choir stalls and organ case were made by Grinling Gibbons (1648–1721), a wood-carver from Rotterdam. He and his team of craftsmen worked on these intricate carvings for two years.

Richard Rogers's Lloyd's building

Lloyd's Building ❼

1 Lime St EC3. **Map** 13 C2. **Tel** *020 7327 6586.* ⊖ *Monument, Bank, Aldgate.* ● *to the public.*

Lloyd's was founded in the late 17th century and soon became the world's main insurers, issuing policies on everything from oil tankers to Betty Grable's legs. The present building, designed by Richard Rogers, dates from 1986 and is one of the most interesting modern buildings in London. Its exaggerated stainless-steel external piping and high-tech ducts echo Rogers' forceful Pompidou Centre in Paris. Lloyd's is well worth seeing floodlit at night.

Monument ❽

Monument St EC3. **Map** 13 C2. **Tel** *020 7626 2717.* ⊖ *Monument.* ○ *9:30am–5pm daily.* ● *1 Jan, 24–26 Dec.* ✉ **www**.towerbridge.org.uk

This doric column, designed by Wren to commemorate the Great Fire of London that devastated the original walled city in September 1666, was, in 1681, the tallest isolated stone column in the world. Topped with a bronze flame, the Monument is 62 m (205 ft) high; the exact distance west to Pudding Lane, where the fire is believed to have started. Reliefs around the column's base show Charles II restoring the city after the tragedy.

The now restored column has 311 tightly spiralled steps that lead to a tiny viewing platform. (In 1842, it was enclosed with an iron cage to prevent suicides.) The steep climb is well worth the effort as the views from the top are spectacular and visitors are rewarded with a certificate.

Tower of London ❾

See pp118–19.

Tower Bridge ❿

SE1. **Map** 14 D3. **Tel** *020 7403 3761.* ⊖ *Tower Hill.* **The Tower Bridge Exhibition** ○ *Apr–Sep: 10am–5:30pm daily; Oct–Mar: 9:30am–5pm daily (last adm: 4pm).* ● *24–26 Dec.* ✉ ♿ *access lift.* ⚑ **www**.towerbridge.org.uk

This flamboyant piece of Victorian engineering, designed by Sir Horace Jones, was completed in 1894 and soon became a symbol of London. Its two Gothic towers contain the mechanism for raising the roadway to permit large ships to pass through. The towers are made of a supporting steel framework clad in stone, and are linked by two high-level walkways which were closed between 1909 and 1982 due to their popularity with suicides and prostitutes. The bridge now houses The Tower Bridge Exhibition, with interactive displays bringing the bridge's history to life. There are fine river views from the walkways, and a look at the steam engine room that powered the lifting machinery until 1976, when the system was electrified.

Walkways, open to the public, give panoramic views over the Thames and London.

The roadway, when raised, creates a space 40 m (135 ft) high and 60 m (200 ft) wide, big enough for large cargo ships.

Engine room

South Bank

Lifts and 300 steps lead to the top of the towers.

The Victorian winding machinery was originally powered by steam.

Entrance

North Bank

Design Museum ⓫

Butlers Wharf, Shad Thames SE1.
Map 14 E4. **Tel** 0870 909 9009.
🚇 Tower Hill, London Bridge.
🕐 10am–5:45pm daily (last adm:
5:15pm). ⬤ 25 & 26 Dec. 🅰 ♿
🍴 **Blueprint Café** 020 7940 8785
for reservations. ♿ 💻 📷
www.designmuseum.org

This museum was the first
in the world to be devoted
solely to modern and contemporary design when it was
founded in 1989. A frequently
changing programme of
exhibitions explores landmarks in modern design
history and the most exciting
innovations in contemporary
design set against the context
of social, cultural, economic
and technological changes.
The Design Museum embraces
every area of design, from
furniture and fashion, to
household products, cars,
graphics, websites and architecture in exhibitions and
new design commissions.
Each spring the museum
hosts Designer of the Year, a
national design prize, with an
exhibition at which the public
can vote for the winner.
    The museum is arranged
over three floors, with major
exhibitions on the first floor.
There is a choice of smaller
displays on the second,
which also houses an
Interaction Space, where
visitors can play vintage video
games and learn about the
designers featured in the
museum in the Design at
the Design Museum online
research archive. The shop
and café are on the ground
floor. On the first floor is the
Blueprint Café restaurant,
which has stunning views of
the Thames (booking ahead
recommended).

Exterior of the Design Museum

**The now familiar sight of the naval
gunship HMS Belfast on the Thames**

HMS Belfast ⓬

Morgan's Lane, Tooley St SE1.
Map 13 C3. 🛈 020 7940 6300.
🚇 London Bridge, Tower Hill. 🕐
Mar–Oct: 10am–6pm daily; Nov–Feb:
10am–5pm daily (last adm: 45 mins
before closing). ⬤ 24–26 Dec. 🅰
♿ limited. 💻 📷 www.iwm.org.uk

Originally launched in 1938
to serve in World War II,
the 11,500-ton battle ship
HMS *Belfast* was instrumental
in the destruction of the
German battle cruiser
Scharnhorst in the battle of
North Cape, and also played
an important role in the
Normandy Landings.
    After the war, the battle
cruiser, designed for offensive
action and for supporting
amphibious operations, was
sent to work for the United
Nations in Korea. The ship
remained in service with the
British navy until 1965.
    Since 1971, the cruiser has
been used as a floating naval
museum. Part of it has been
atmospherically recreated
to show what the ship was
like in 1943, when it partici-
pated in sinking the German
battle cruiser. Other displays
portray life on board during
World War II, and there are
also general exhibits which
relate to the history of the
Royal Navy.
    As well as being a great
family day out, it is also
possible for children to
take part in the educational
activity weekends that take
place on board the ship.

London Dungeon ⓭

Tooley St SE1. **Map** 13 C3. 🛈 0871
360 2049. 🚇 London Bridge. 🕐 Jul–
Aug 9:30am–6pm; Easter–Jun, Sep &
Oct 10am–5:30pm; Nov–Easter
10:30am–5pm; daily. ⬤ 25 Dec. 🅰
book in advance to avoid queues. ♿
💻 📷 www.thedungeons.com

In effect a much expanded
version of the chamber of
horrors at Madame Tussaud's
(*see p104*), this museum is
a great hit with children. It
illustrates the most bloodthirsty events in British history.
It is played strictly for terror,
and screams abound as Druids
perform a human sacrifice at
Stonehenge, Henry VIII's wife
Anne Boleyn is beheaded,
and a room full of people die
in agony during the Great
Plague. Other displays include
torture, murder and witchcraft.

19th-century surgical tools

The Old Operating Theatre ⓮

9a St Thomas St SE1. **Map** 13 B4. **Tel**
020 7188 2679. 🚇 London Bridge.
🕐 10:30am–5pm daily. ⬤ 15 Dec–
5 Jan. 🅰 📷 www.thegarret.org.uk

St Thomas's Hospital stood
here from its foundation in
the 12th century until it was
moved west in 1862. At this
time most of its buildings
were demolished to make
way for the railway. The
women's operating theatre
(The Old Operating Theatre
Museum and Herb Garret)
survived only because it was
located away from the main
buildings, in a garret over the
hospital church. It lay, bricked
up and forgotten, until the
1950s. Britain's oldest operating theatre, dating back to
1822, it has now been fitted
out as it would have been in
the early 19th century.

Tower of London ❾

Soon after William the Conqueror became king in 1066, he built a fortress here to guard the entrance to London from the Thames Estuary. In 1097 the White Tower was completed in sturdy stone; other fine buildings have been added over the centuries. The tower has served as a royal residence, armoury, treasury and, most famously, as a prison. Some were tortured here and among those who met their death were the "Princes in the Tower", the sons and heirs of Edward IV. Today the tower is a popular attraction, housing the Crown Jewels and other exhibits, such as the displays about the Peasants' Revolt of 1381, the only time the Tower's walls were breached. The most celebrated residents are the ravens; legend has it that the kingdom will fall if they desert the tower. Some guided tours are led by the colourful Beefeaters.

Beauchamp Tower
Many high-ranking prisoners were held here, often with their own retinues of servants. The tower was built by Edward I around 1281.

"Beefeaters"
Thirty-five Yeomen Warders guard the Tower and live here. Their uniforms hark back to Tudor times.

Two 13th-century curtain walls protect the tower.

Tower Green was the execution site for favoured prisoners, away from crowds on Tower Hill, where many had to submit to public execution. Seven people died here, including two of Henry VIII's six wives, Anne Boleyn and Catherine Howard.

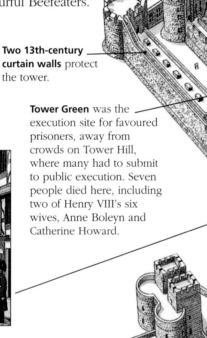

Queen's House
This Tudor building is the sovereign's official residence at the Tower.

Main entrance from Tower Hill

THE CROWN JEWELS

The world's best-known collection of precious objects, now displayed in a splendid exhibition room, includes the gorgeous regalia of crowns, sceptres, orbs and swords used at coronations and other state occasions. Most date from 1661, when Charles II commissioned replacements for regalia destroyed by Parliament after the execution of Charles I *(see pp52–3)*. Only a few older pieces survived, hidden by royalist clergymen until the Restoration – notably, Edward the Confessor's sapphire ring, now incorporated into the Imperial State Crown *(see p73)*. The crown was made for Queen Victoria in 1837 and has been used at every coronation since.

The Sovereign's Ring (1831)

The Sovereign's Orb (1661), a hollow gold sphere encrusted with jewels

★ Jewel House

Among the magnificent Crown Jewels is the Sceptre with the Cross (1660), which now contains the world's biggest diamond.

★ White Tower

When the tower was finished in 1097, it was the tallest building in London at 27 m (90 ft) high.

VISITORS' CHECKLIST

Tower Hill EC3. **Map** 14 D3. **Tel** 0844 482 7799 for advance booking. ⊖ Tower Hill; Tower Gateway (DLR). 🚌 RV1, 15, X15, 25, 42, 78, 100, D1, D9, D11. 🚆 Fenchurch Street. ◯ Mar–Oct: 9am–6pm (from 10am Sun, Mon); Nov–Feb: 9am–5pm (from 10am Sun, Mon) daily. (Last adm: 1 hr before closing.) ● 1 Jan, 24–26 Dec. 🈺 ♿ limited, except Jewel House. 🚻 🎁 **Ceremony of the Keys:** 9:30pm daily (book in advance). **www.hrp.org.uk**

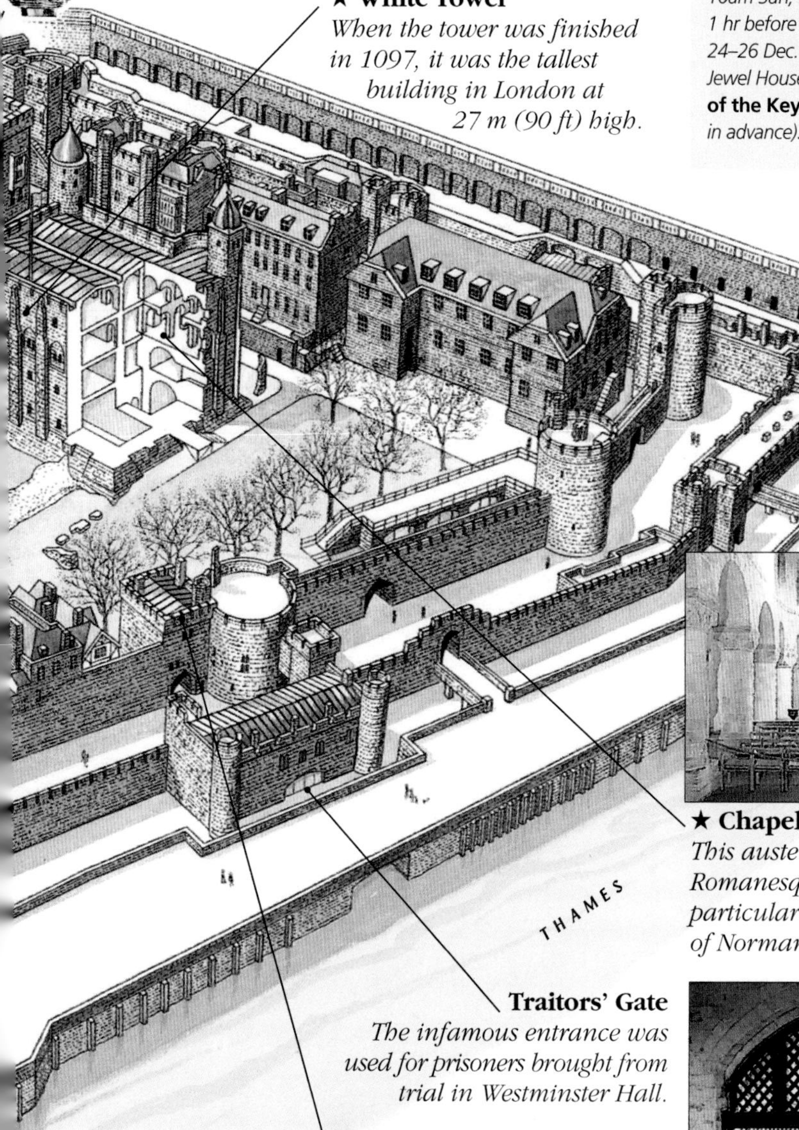

★ Chapel of St John

This austerely beautiful Romanesque chapel is a particularly fine example of Norman architecture.

THAMES

Traitors' Gate

The infamous entrance was used for prisoners brought from trial in Westminster Hall.

Bloody Tower

A new permanent display explores the mysterious disappearance of Edward V's two sons, who were put ere by their uncle, Richard f Gloucester (later Richard III), after their father died n 1483. The princes disappeared and Richard was crowned later that year. In 1674 the skeletons of two hildren were found nearby.

STAR SIGHTS

★ Jewel House

★ White Tower

★ Chapel of St John

The George Inn, now owned by the National Trust

George Inn ⑮

(NT) 77 Borough High St SE1.
Map 13 B4. **Tel** 020 7407 2056.
ⓔ *London Bridge, Borough.*
◯ *11am–11pm Mon–Sat, noon–10:30pm Sun.* 🍴

Dating from the 17th century, this building is the only traditional galleried coaching inn left in London and is mentioned in Dickens's *Little Dorrit*. It was rebuilt after the Southwark fire of 1676 in a style that dates back to the Middle Ages. There were originally three wings around a courtyard, where plays were staged in the 17th century. In 1889 the north and east wings were demolished, so there is only one wing remaining.

The inn is still a popular pub with a well-worn, comfortable atmosphere, perfect on a cold, damp day. In the summer, the yard fills with picnic tables, and patrons are occasionally entertained by actors and morris dancers. The house bitter is highly recommended.

Borough Market ⑯

8 Southwark St SE1. **Map** 13 B4.
ⓔ *London Bridge.* **Retail market**
◯ *11am–5pm Thu, noon–6pm Fri, 9am–4pm Sat.*

Borough Market was until recently a wholesale fruit and vegetable market, which had its origins in medieval times, and moved to its current position beneath the railway tracks in 1756. This hugely popular fine-food market has now become well established, selling gourmet foods from Britain and abroad, as well as quality fruit and vegetables, to locals and tourists alike.

Shakespeare window (1954),
Southwark Cathedral

Southwark Cathedral ⑰

Montague Close SE1.
Map 13 B3. **Tel** 020 7367 6700.
ⓔ *London Bridge.* ◯ *8am–6pm daily.* 🖥 📷 **www.**southwark.
anglican.org/cathedral

Although some parts of this building date back to the 12th century, it was not until 1905 that it became a cathedral. Many original medieval features remain, notably the tomb of the poet John Gower (c.1325–1408), a contemporary of Chaucer *(see p172)*. There is a monument to Shakespeare, carved in 1912, and a memorial window *(above)* installed in 1954.

Shakespeare's Globe ⑱

New Globe Walk SE1. **Map** 13 A3.
Tel *020 7902 1400. Box office: 020 7401 9919.* ⓔ *Southwark, London Bridge.* **Exhibition** ◯ *Late Apr–early Oct: 9am–12:30pm, 1–5pm Mon–Sat, 9–11:30am & noon–5pm Sun; early Oct–late Apr: 10am–5pm daily.* ●
24, 25 Dec. 🎦 ♿ 🎁 *every 30 mins. (Rose Theatre tours for groups of 15 or more by appt only).* **Performances** *late Apr–early Oct.* ♿ *limited.* 🍴 🖥
📷 **www.**shakespeares-globe.org

Opened in 1997, this circular building is a faithful reproduction of an Elizabethan theatre, close to the site of the original Globe where many of Shakespeare's plays were first performed. It was built using handmade bricks and oak laths, fastened with wooden pegs rather than metal screws, and has the first thatched roof allowed in London since the Great Fire of 1666. The theatre was erected thanks to a heroic campaign by the American actor and director Sam Wanamaker. Open to the elements (although the seats are protected), it operates only in the summer, and seeing a play here can be a thrilling experience, with top-quality acting under the artistic direction of Mark Rylance among others.

Beneath the theatre, Shakespeare's Globe Exhibition is open all year and covers many aspects of Shakespeare's work and times. Groups of 15 or more may book to see the foundations of the nearby Rose Theatre.

Shakespeare's *Henry IV* (performed at the Globe Theatre around 1600)

Tate Modern ⓲

Holland St, SE1. **Map** 13 A3. *Tel 020 7887 8888.* ⊖ *Blackfriars, Southwark.* 🚢 *to Tate Britain every 40 mins.* 📷 *Blackfriars.* ⏲ *10am–6pm Sun–Thu, 10am–10pm Fri & Sat.* ⚫ *24–26 Dec.* 📷 *major exhibitions.* ♿ 🍴 💻 📷 **www**.tate.org.uk/modern

Looming over the southern bank of the Thames, Tate Modern occupies the converted Bankside power station, a dynamic space for one of the world's premier collections of contemporary art. Tate Modern draws its main displays from the expansive Tate Collection, also shown at the other Tate galleries: Tate St Ives *(p277),* Tate Liverpool *(p377)* and Tate Britain *(p91).* A river boat, *Tate to Tate,* transports visitors between Tate Modern and Tate Britain. Tate Modern completed a major re-hang of its collection in 2006, and displays on level 5 also underwent changes in 2009.

Inverno from ***Quattro Stagioni*** **(1993–4) by Cy Twombly**

The gallery's west entrance leads straight into the massive Turbine Hall. Each year an artist is commissioned to install in this space. Louise Bourgeois was the first to do so, creating three giant towers and a gargantuan spider, *Maman* (2000). In 2008, Dominique Gonzalez-Foerster's *TH 2058* filled the Turbine Hall with 200 yellow and blue bunk beds.

An escalator whisks visitors from the Turbine Hall, up to level 3 where the main galleries are located. In a break with convention, Tate Modern organizes its displays by theme rather than chronology or school – a practice that cuts across movements and mixes up media. Four themes based on traditional genres reveal how traditions have been confronted, extended or rejected by artists throughout the 20th and into the 21st centuries.

Tate Modern's displays are arranged into two thematic wings on level 3 and the displays continue on level 5. The collection focuses on key periods of modern art: Cubism, Futurism and Vorticism; Surrealism and Surrealist tendencies; Abstract Expressionism and European Informal Art; and Minimalism. At the centre of each of the four exhibitions is a focal display, from which all the other displays rotate.

Spatial Concept "Waiting" **(1960) by Lucio Fontana**

Soft Drainpipe – Blue (Cool) (1967) by Claes Oldenburg

Over 40 per cent of the work on display since the major re-hang in 2006 has never been on display at Tate Modern before. The collection includes works such as the iconic paintings *Whaam!* by Roy Lichtenstein, *Spatial Concept "Waiting"* by Lucio Fontana and *Quattro Stagioni* by Cy Twombly as well as other important pieces by the likes of Francis Picabia and Anish Kapoor. To complement its permanent collection, Tate Modern presents a dynamic programme of temporary exhibitions, including three large-scale shows per year. Major live events are staged each year, taking their inspiration from the Collection.

BANKSIDE POWER STATION

This forbidding fortress was designed in 1947 by Sir Giles Gilbert Scott, the architect of Battersea Power Station, Waterloo Bridge and London's famous red telephone boxes. The power station is of a steel framed brick skin construction, comprising over 4.2 million bricks. The Turbine Hall was designed to accommodate huge oil-burning generators and three vast oil tanks are still in situ, buried under the ground just south of the building. The tanks are to be employed in a future stage of Tate Modern development. The power station itself was converted by Swiss architects Herzog and de Meuron who designed the two-storey glass box, or lightbeam, which runs the length of the building. This serves to flood the upper galleries with light and also provides wonderful views of London.

The façade, chimney and light beam of Tate Modern

FURTHER AFIELD

Over the centuries London has steadily expanded to embrace the scores of villages that surrounded it, leaving the City as a reminder of London's original boundaries. Although now linked in an almost unbroken urban sprawl, many of these areas have maintained their old village atmosphere and character. Hampstead and Highgate are still distinct enclaves, as are artistic Chelsea and literary Islington. Greenwich, Chiswick and Richmond have retained features that hark back to the days when the Thames was an important artery for transport and commerce, while just to the east of the City the wide expanses of the former docks have, in the last 20 years, been imaginatively rebuilt as new commercial and residential areas.

SIGHTS AT A GLANCE

Camden and Islington **7**
Chelsea **1**
Chiswick **10**
East End and Docklands **8**

Greenwich **9**
Hampstead **4**
Hampstead Heath **5**
Highgate **6**

Holland Park **2**
Notting Hill and
  Portobello Road **3**
Richmond and Kew **11**

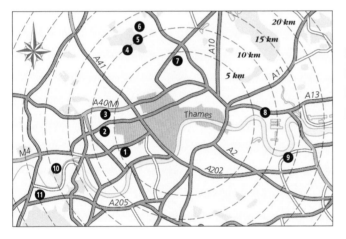

KEY

Main sightseeing areas

Greater London

Parks

Motorway

Major road

Minor road

10 miles = 15 km

Chelsea **1**

SW3. ⊖ *Sloane Square*. **Map** 17 B2.

Riverside Chelsea has been fashionable since Tudor times when Sir Thomas More, Henry VIII's Lord Chancellor

**Statue of Sir Thomas More
(1478–1535), Cheyne Walk**

(see p50), lived here. The river views attracted artists and the arrival of the historian Thomas Carlyle and essayist Leigh Hunt in the 1830s began a literary connection. Blue plaques on the houses of **Cheyne Walk** celebrate former residents such as J M W Turner *(see p91)* and writers George Eliot, Henry James and T S Eliot.

Chelsea's artistic tradition is maintained by its galleries and antique shops, many of them scattered among the clothes boutiques on **King's Road**. This begins at **Sloane Square**, named after the physician Sir Hans Sloane, who bought the manor of Chelsea in 1712. Sloane expanded the **Chelsea Physic Garden** (1673) along Swan Walk to cultivate plants and herbs.

Wren's **Royal Hospital**, on Royal Hospital Road was built in 1692 as a retirement home for old soldiers and still houses 400 Chelsea Pensioners.

Arab Hall, Leighton House (1866)

Holland Park **2**

W8, W14. ⊖ *Holland Park*. **Map** 7 B5.

This park is more intimate than the large royal parks such as Hyde Park *(see p101)*. It was opened in 1952 on the grounds of **Holland House**, a centre of social and political intrigue in its 19th-century heyday.

Around the park are some magnificent late Victorian houses. **Linley Sambourne**

House was built about 1870 and has received a much-needed facelift, though it remains much as Sambourne furnished it, in the Victorian manner, with china ornaments and heavy velvet drapes. He was a political cartoonist for the satirical magazine *Punch* and drawings cram the walls.

Leighton House, built for the Neo-Classical painter Lord Leighton in 1866, has been preserved as an extraordinary monument to the Victorian Aesthetic movement. The highlight is the Arab Hall, which was added in 1879 to house Leighton's stupendous collection of 13th- to 17th-century Islamic tiles. The best paintings include some by Leighton himself and by his contemporaries Edward Burne-Jones and John Millais.

🏛 Linley Sambourne House
18 Stafford Terrace W8. *Tel 020 7602 3316 (020 7938 1295 Sat, Sun).* ⊖ *High St Ken.* ○ *Mar–Dec: tours only, Mon–Fri by appt, Sat & Sun every hr till 3:30pm.* 🖼 🎦 🛈

🏛 Leighton House
12 Holland Park Rd W14. *Tel 020 7602 3316.* ⊖ *High St Ken.* ○ *11am–5:30pm Wed–Mon.* ◑ *public hols.* 🖼 🎦 *Wed & Thu.* 🛈

Notting Hill and Portobello Road ❸

W11. ⊖ *Notting Hill Gate.* **Map** 7 B2.

In the 1950s and 60s, Notting Hill became a centre for the Caribbean community and today it is a vibrant cosmo-politan part of London. It is also home to Europe's largest street carnival *(see p63)* which began in 1965 and takes over the entire area on the August bank holiday weekend, when costumed parades flood through the crowded streets.

Nearby, Portobello Road market *(see pp148–9)* has a bustling atmosphere with hundreds of stalls and shops selling a variety of collectables.

Hampstead ❹

NW3, N6. ⊖ *Hampstead.* ⊒ *Hampstead Heath.*

On a high ridge north of the metropolis, Hampstead is essentially a Georgian village with many perfectly maintained mansions and houses. It is one of London's most desirable residential areas, home to a community of artists and writers since Georgian times.

Situated in a quiet Hampstead street, **Keats House** (1816) is an evocative tribute to the life and work of the poet John Keats (1795–1821). Keats lived here for two years before his tragic death from consumption at the age of 25, and it was

Georgian house, Hampstead

under a plum tree in the garden that he wrote his celebrated *Ode to a Nightingale*. Mementoes of Keats and of Fanny Brawne, the neighbour

to whom he was engaged, are on show. Renovated in 2009, Keats House now benefits from more extensive displays.

The **Freud Museum**, which opened in 1986, is dedicated to the dramatic life of Sigmund Freud (1856–1939), the founder of psychoanalysis. At the age of 82, Freud fled from Nazi persecution in Vienna to this Hampstead house where he lived and worked for the last year of his life. His daughter Anna, pioneer of child psychoanalysis, continued to live here until her death in 1982. Inside, Freud's rich Viennese-style consulting rooms remain unaltered, and 1930s home movies show moments of Freud's life, including scenes of the Nazi attack on his home in Vienna.

🏛 Keats House
Keats Grove NW3. 📠 *020 7435 2062.* ⊖ *Hampstead, Belsize Pk.* ○ *1–5pm Tue–Sun (am by appt).* 🛈 **www**.cityoflondon.gov.uk/keats

🏛 Freud Museum
20 Maresfield Gdns NW3. *Tel 020 7435 2002.* ⊖ *Finchley Rd.* ○ *noon–5pm Wed–Sun.* 🖼 ⚅ *limited.* 🛈 **www**.freud.org.uk

Antique shop on Portobello Road

View east across Hampstead Heath to Highgate

Hampstead Heath ❺

N6. 🚇 *Hampstead, Highgate.* 🚉 *Hampstead Heath.*

Separating the hill-top villages of Hampstead and Highgate, the open spaces of Hampstead Heath are a precious retreat from the city. There are meadows, lakes and ponds for bathing and fishing, and fine views over the capital from **Parliament Hill**, to the east.

Situated in landscaped grounds high on the edge of the Heath is the magnificent **Kenwood House**, where classical concerts *(see p154)* are held by the lake in summer. The house was remodelled by Robert Adam *(see p28)* in 1764 and most of his interiors have survived, the highlight of which is the library. The mansion is filled with Old Master paintings, such as works by Van Dyck, Vermeer, Turner *(see p91)* and Romney; the star attraction is Rembrandt's self-portrait of 1663.

🏛 **Kenwood House**
Hampstead Lane NW3. **Tel** 020 8348 1286. ◯ *daily.* ♿ 🖥 📷
www.english-heritage.org.uk

Handmade crafts and antiques, Camden Lock indoor market

Highgate ❻

N6. 🚇 *Highgate, Archway.*

A settlement since the Middle Ages, Highgate, like Hampstead, became a fashionable aristocratic retreat in the 16th century. Today, it still has an exclusive rural feel, aloof from the urban sprawl below, with a Georgian high street and many expensive houses.

Highgate Cemetery *(see p75)*, with its monuments and hidden overgrown corners, has an extraordinary, magical atmosphere. Tour guides (daily in summer, weekends in winter) tell of the many tales of intrigue, mystery and vandalism connected with the cemetery since it opened in 1839. In the eastern section is the tomb of Victorian novelist George Eliot (1819–80) and of the cemetery's most famous incumbent, Karl Marx (1818–83).

🏛 **Highgate Cemetery**
Swains Lane N6. **Tel** 020 8340 1834. 🚇 *Archway, Highgate.* ◯ *daily.* ● *during burials, 25–26 Dec.* 📷 🎥 www.highgate-cemetery.org

Camden and Islington ❼

NW1, N1. **Camden** 🚇 *Camden Town, Chalk Farm.* **Islington** 🚇 *Angel, Highbury & Islington.*

Camden is a lively area packed with restaurants, shops and a busy **market** *(see p148-9).* Thousands of people come here each weekend to browse among the wide variety of stalls or simply to soak up the atmosphere of the lively cobbled area around the canal, which is enhanced by the buskers and street performers.

Neighbouring Islington was once a fashionable spa but the rich moved out in the late 18th century and the area deteriorated rapidly. In the 20th century, writers such as Evelyn Waugh, George Orwell and Joe Orton lived here. In recent decades, Islington has been rediscovered and is again fashionable as one of the first areas in London to become "gentrified", with many professionals buying the old houses.

East End and Docklands ❽

E1, E2, E14. **East End** 🚇 *Aldgate East, Liverpool St, Bethnal Green.* **Docklands** 🚇 *Canary Wharf.*

In the Middle Ages the East End was full of craftsmen practising noxious trades such as brewing, bleaching and vinegar-making, which were banned within the City. The area has also been home to numerous immigrant communities since the 17th century, when French Huguenots, escaping religious persecution moved into Spitalfields, and made it a silk-weaving centre. Even after the decline of the silk industry, textiles and clothing continued to dominate, with Jewish tailors and furriers setting up workshops in the 1880s, and Bengali machinists sewing in cramped premises from the 1950s.

A good way to get a taste of the East End is to explore its Sunday street markets *(see p149)*, and sample freshly baked bagels and spicy Indian food. By way of contrast, anyone interested in contemporary architecture should visit the **Docklands**, an ambitious redevelopment of disused docks, dominated by the Canada Tower; at 250 m (800 ft) it is London's tallest building. Other attractions include the **V&A Museum of Childhood**, a delightful toy museum with lots of activities, and **Dennis Severs' House**, in which you are taken on a historic journey from the 17th to the 19th centuries.

Royal Naval College framing the Queen's House, Greenwich

🏛 **V&A Museum of Childhood**

Cambridge Heath Rd E2. *Tel 020 8983 5200.* ⬜ *10am–5.45pm daily.* ⬤ *1 Jan, 25–26 Dec.* ♿ 📷 🚻 **www.museumofchildhood.org.uk**

🏚 **Dennis Severs' House**

18 Folgate St E1. *Tel 020 7247 4013.* ⬜ *noon–2pm Mon after 1st & 3rd Sun of month, Mon eve (by candlelight), noon–4pm Sun.* 📷 🎫 **www.dennissevershouse.co.uk**

Greenwich ❾

SE10. 🚆 *Greenwich, Maze Hill.* 🚇 *Cutty Sark (DLR).*

The world's time has been measured from the **Royal Observatory Greenwich** (now housing a museum) since 1884. The area is full of maritime and royal history, with Neo-Classical mansions, a park, many antique and book shops and various markets *(see pp148–9)*.

The **Queen's House**, designed by Inigo Jones for James I's wife, was completed in 1637 for Henrietta Maria, the queen of Charles I. The Queen's House has now been restored to its original state, and

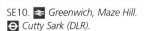

Canada Tower, Canary Wharf

its highlights include the perfectly cubic main hall and the unusual spiral "tulip staircase".

The adjoining **National Maritime Museum** has exhibits that range from primitive canoes, through Elizabethan galleons, to modern ships. Anyone interested in naval history should visit the **Old Royal Naval College**, which was designed by Christopher Wren *(see p114)* in two halves

An 18th-century compass, National Maritime Museum

so that the Queen's House kept its river view. It began as a royal palace, became a hospital in 1692, and in 1873 the Old Royal Naval College moved here. The Rococo chapel and the 18th-century *trompe l'oeil* Painted Hall are open to the public.

🏛 **Royal Observatory Greenwich**

Greenwich Park SE10. *Tel 020 8312 6565.* ⬜ *10am–5pm daily (last Planetarium show: 4pm).* ⬤ *24–26 Dec.* 🚻 **www.rog.nmm.ac.uk**

🏛 **Queen's House and National Maritime Museum**

Romney Rd SE10. *Tel 020 8312 6565.* ⬜ *daily.* ⬤ *24–26 Dec.* 📷 ♿ *limited.* 🚻 🚻 **www.nmm.ac.uk**

🏚 **Old Royal Naval College**

King William Walk, Greenwich SE10. *Tel 020 8269 4747.* ⬜ *10am–5pm daily.* ⬤ *public hols.*

Chiswick ❿

W4. ⊖ *Chiswick.*

Chiswick is a pleasant sub-urb of London, with pubs, cottages and a variety of birdlife, such as herons, along the picturesque riverside. One of the main reasons for a visit is **Chiswick House**, a magnificent country villa inspired by the Renaissance architect Andrea Palladio. It was designed in the early 18th century by the 3rd Earl of Burlington as an annexe to his larger house (demol-ished in 1758), so that he could display his art collec-tion and entertain friends. The gardens are now fully restored.

Heron

🏛 **Chiswick House**
Burlington Lane W4. *Tel 020 8995 0508.* ◻ *Apr–Oct: Sun–Wed & bank hols.* ▧ ♿ *call ahead.* ▯
www.english-heritage.org.uk

Richmond and Kew ⓫

SW15. ⊖ ⇌ *Richmond.*

The attractive village of Richmond took its name from a palace built by Henry VII (the former Earl of Richmond in Yorkshire) in 1500, the remains of which can be seen off the green. Nearby is the expansive **Richmond Park**, which was once Charles I's royal hunting ground. In summer, boats

sail down the Thames from Westminster Millennium Pier, making a pleasant day's excursion from central London.

The nobility continued to favour Richmond after royalty had left, and some of their mansions have survived. The Palladian villa, **Marble Hill House**, was built in 1724–9 for the mistress of George II and has been restored to its original appearance. On the opposite side of the Thames, the brooding **Ham House**, built in 1610, had its heyday later that century when it became the home of the Lauderdales. The Countess of Lauderdale inherited the house from her father, who had been Charles I's "whip-ping boy" – meaning that he was punished whenever the future king misbehaved. He was rewarded as an adult by being given a peerage and the lease of Ham estate.

A little further north along the Thames, **Syon House** has been inhabited by the Dukes and Earls of Northumberland for over 400 years. Numerous attractions here include a but-terfly house, a museum of historic cars and a spectacular conservatory built in 1830. The lavish Neo-Classical inter-iors of the house, created by Robert Adam in the 1760s *(see p28)*, remain the highlight.

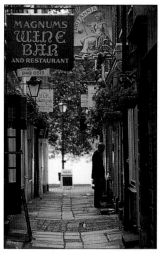
Brewers Lane, Richmond

On the riverbank to the south, **Kew Gardens**, the world's most complete botanic gardens, fea-ture examples of nearly every plant that can be grown in Brit-ain. There are also conserva-tories displaying thousands of exotic tropical blooms.

🏛 **Marble Hill House**
(EH) Richmond Rd, Twickenham. *Tel 020 8892 5115.* ◻ *Apr–Oct: Sat, Sun, pub hols.* ♿ *limited.* ▯▯ ▯ ▯

🏛 **Ham House**
(NT) Ham St, Richmond. *Tel 020 8940 1950.* ◻ *Apr–Oct: Sat–Wed.* ▧ ♿

🏛 **Syon House**
London Rd, Brentford. *Tel 020 8560 0881.* **House** ◻ *mid-Mar–Oct: Wed, Thu, Sun & pub hols.* **Gardens** ◻ *daily.* ● *Nov–mid-Mar.* ▧ ▯ ♿ *gardens only.* ▯ ▯ www.syonpark.co.uk

♣ **Kew Gardens**
Royal Botanic Gdns, Kew Green, Richmond. *Tel 020 8332 5655.* ◻ *daily.* ● *1 Jan, 24–25 Dec.* ▧ ♿ ▧ ▯▯ ▯ ▯ www.kew.org

Chiswick House

LONDON STREET FINDER

The map references given with the sights, hotels, restaurants, shops and entertainment venues based in central London refer to the following four maps. All the main places of interest within the central area are marked on the maps in addition to useful practical information, such as tube, railway and coach stations. The key map below shows the area of London that is covered by the Street Finder. The four main city-centre areas (colour-coded in pink) are shown in more detail on the inside back cover.

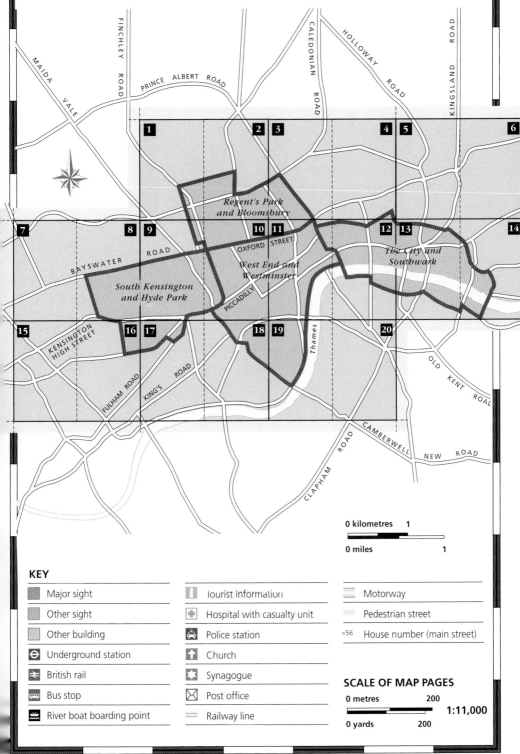

KEY

Major sight	Tourist Information	Motorway
Other sight	Hospital with casualty unit	Pedestrian street
Other building	Police station	«56 House number (main street)
Underground station	Church	
British rail	Synagogue	**SCALE OF MAP PAGES**
Bus stop	Post office	0 metres 200
River boat boarding point	Railway line	0 yards 200 **1:11,000**

0 kilometres   1

0 miles   1

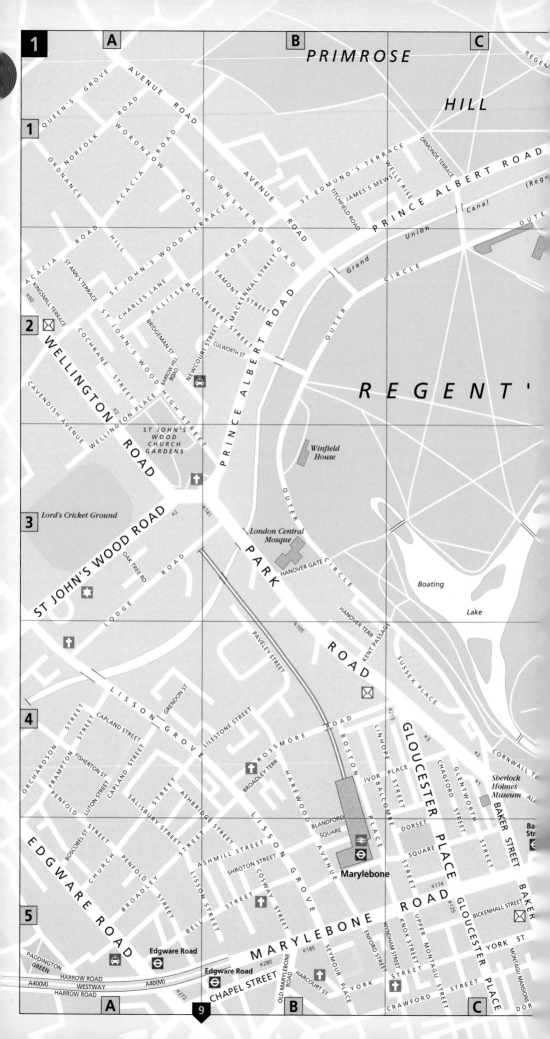

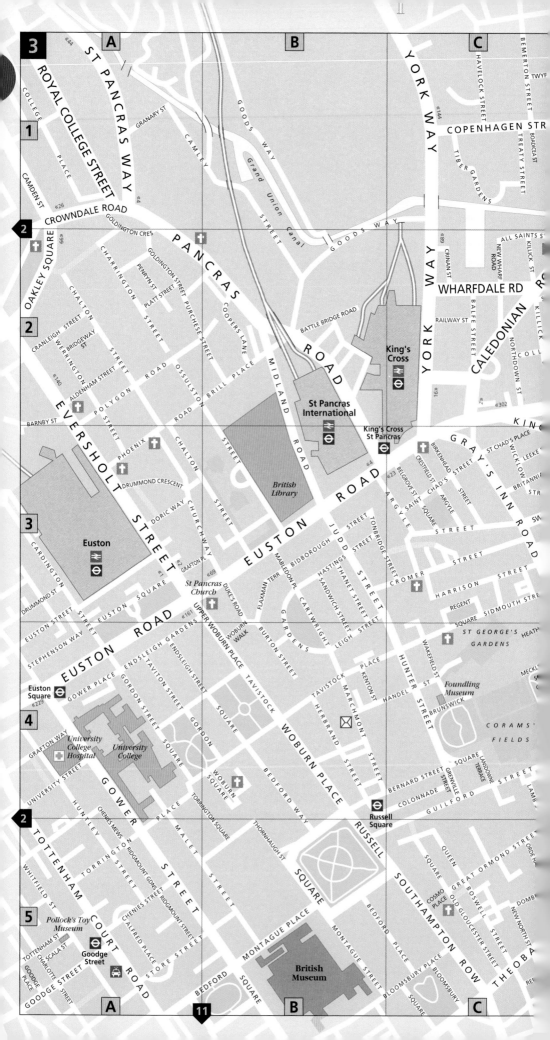

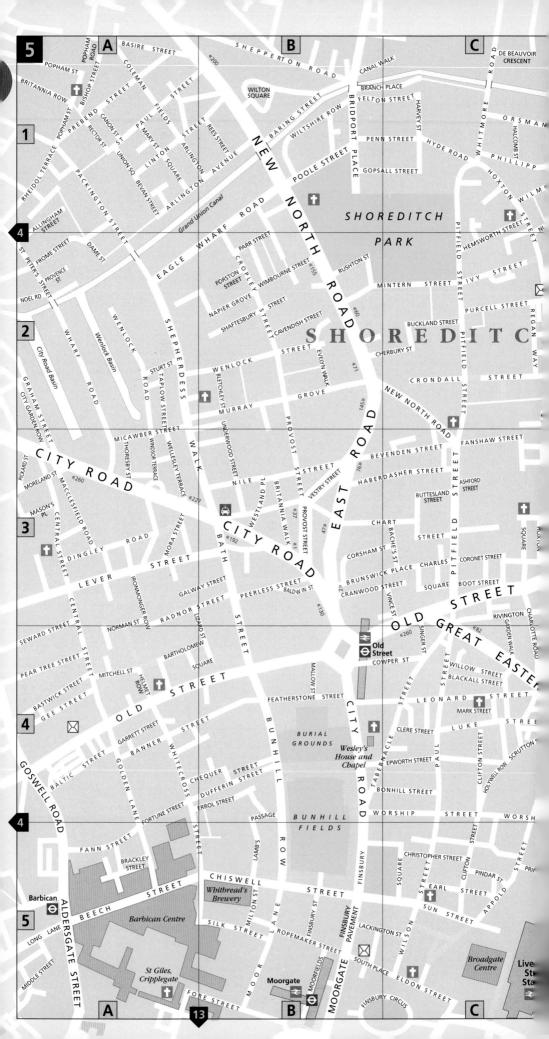

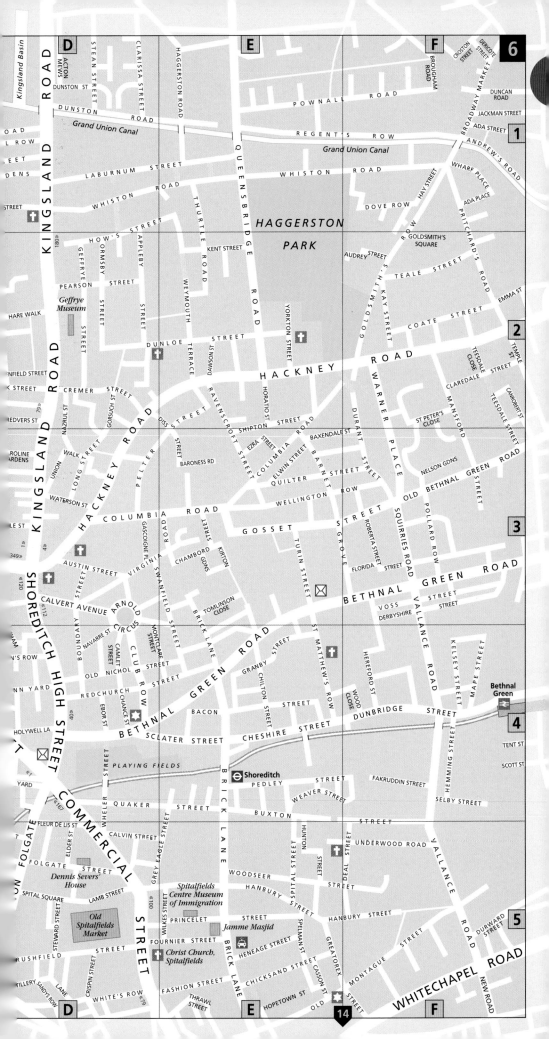

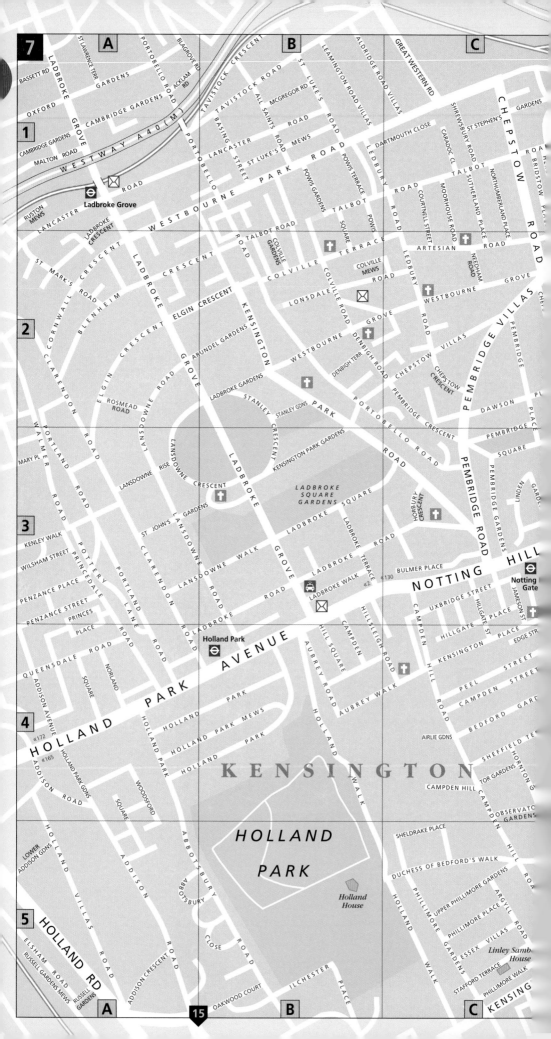

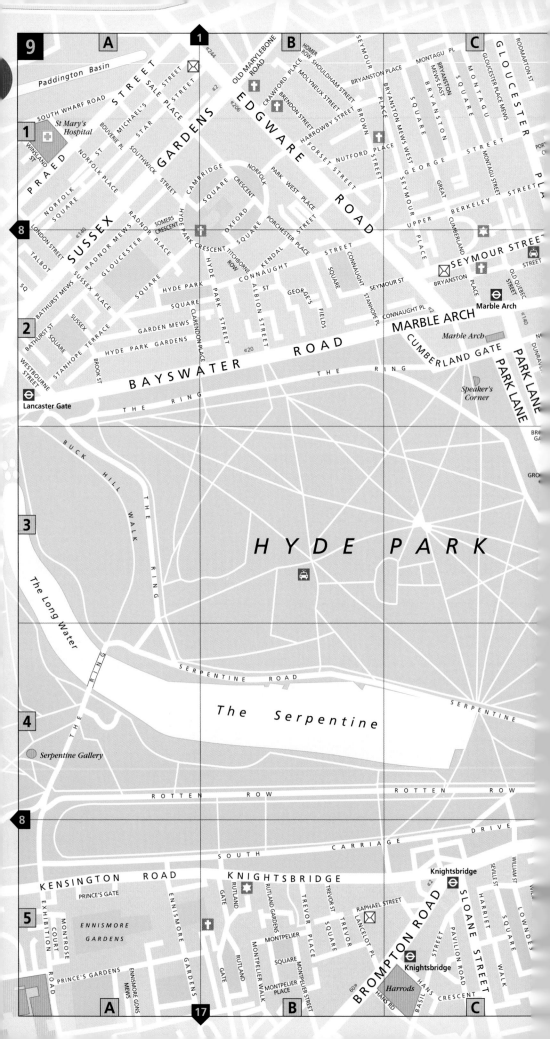

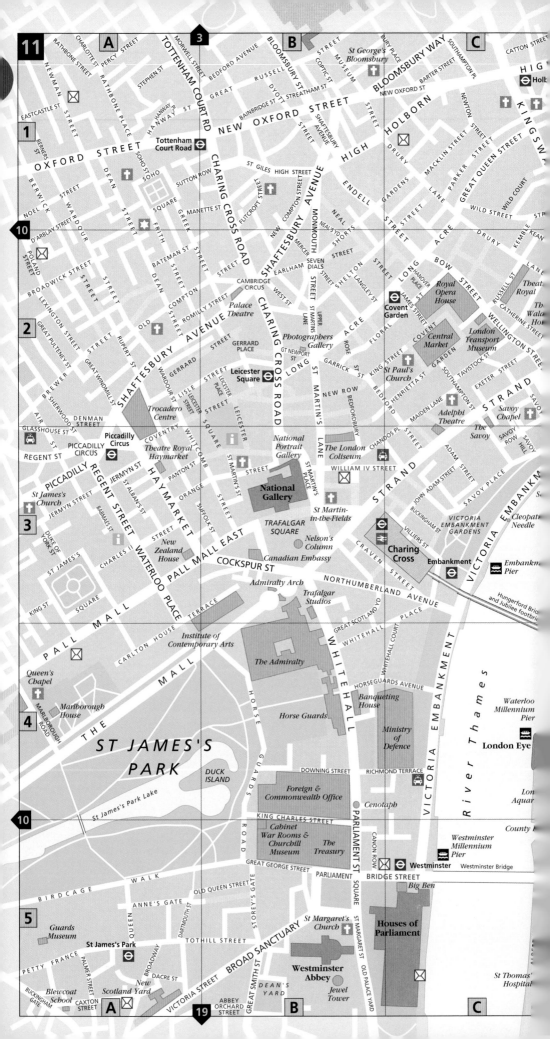

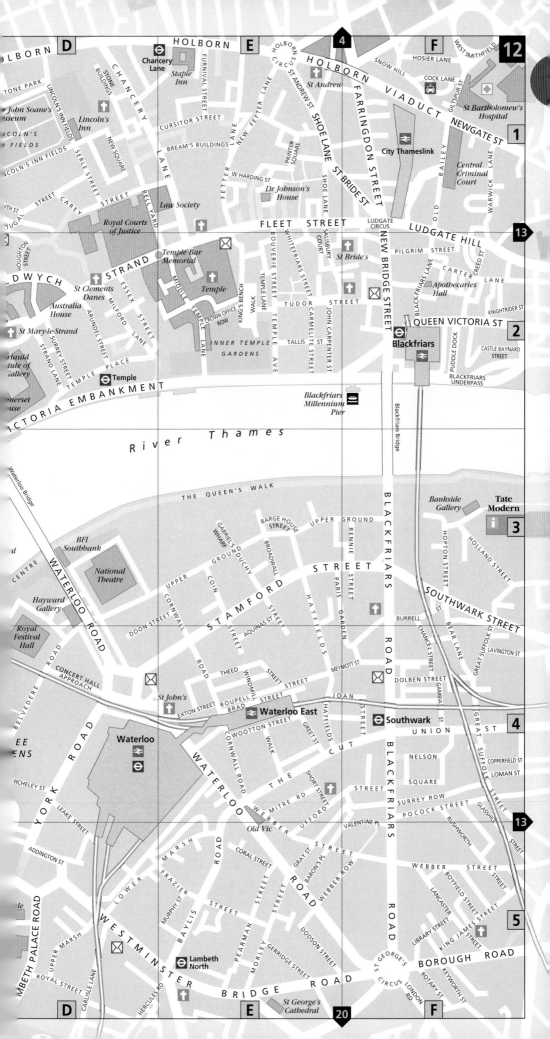

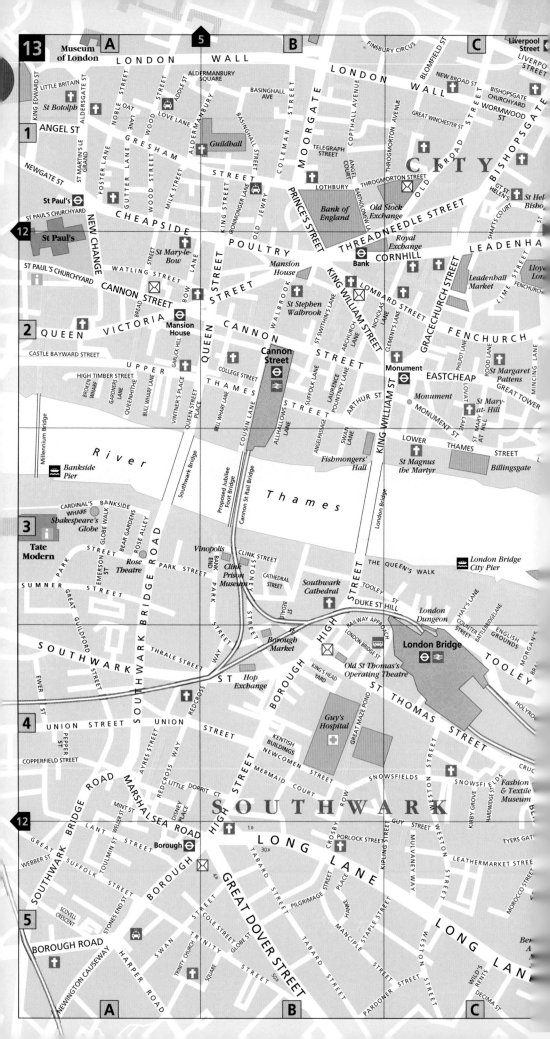

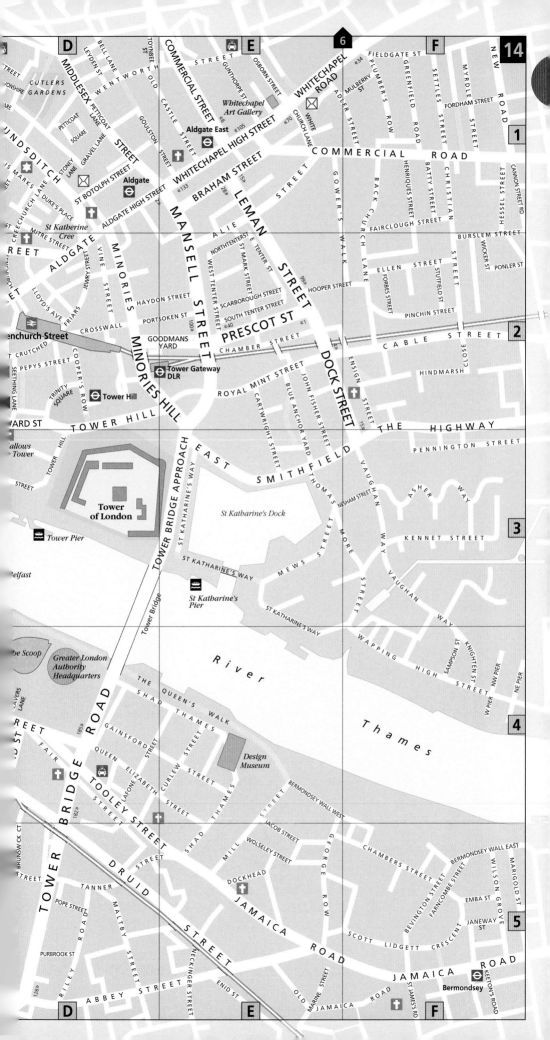

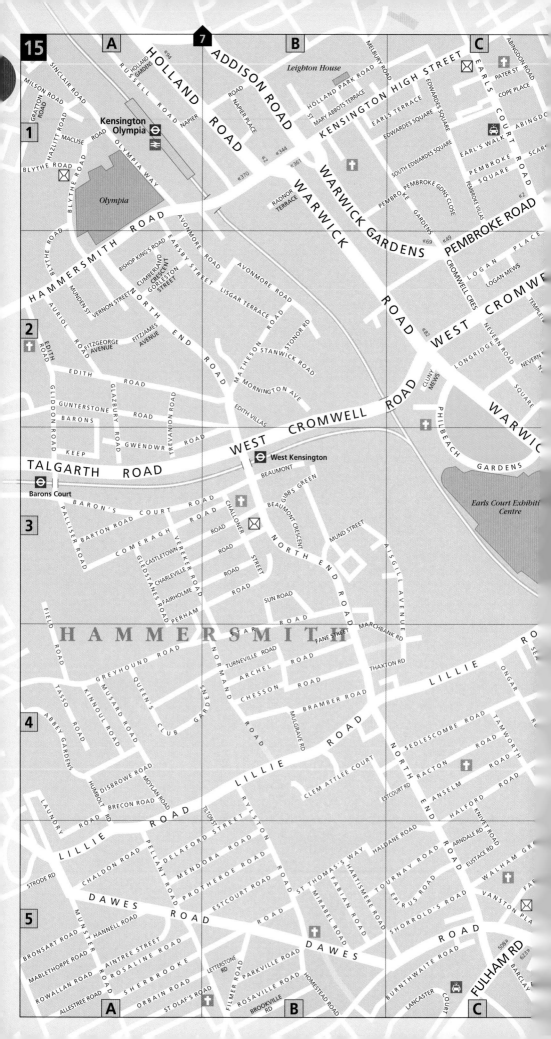

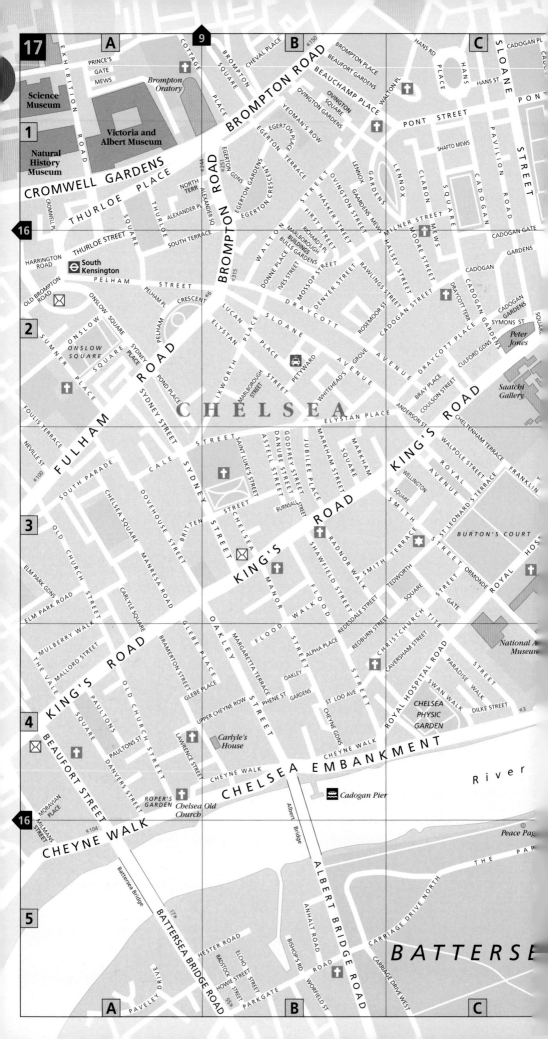

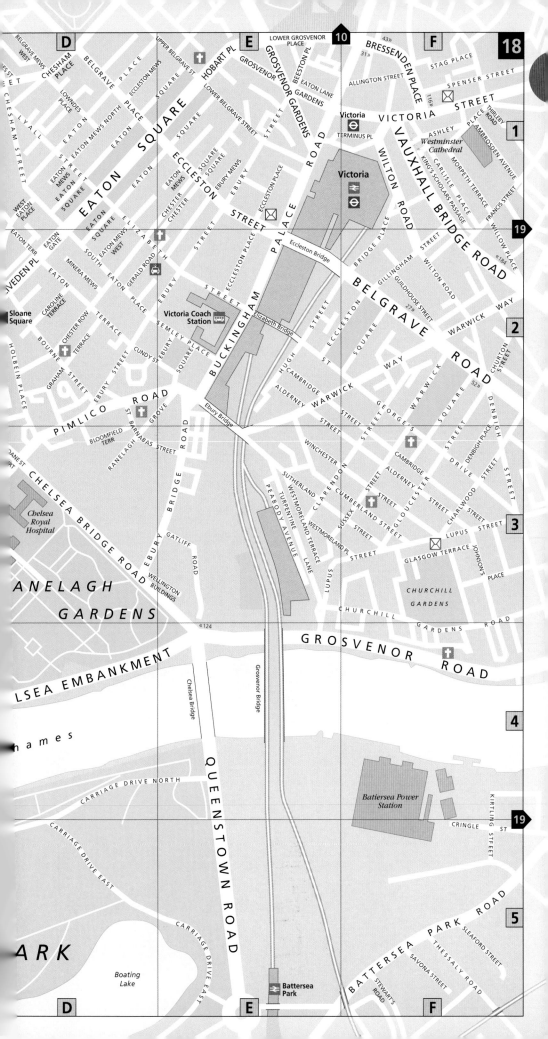

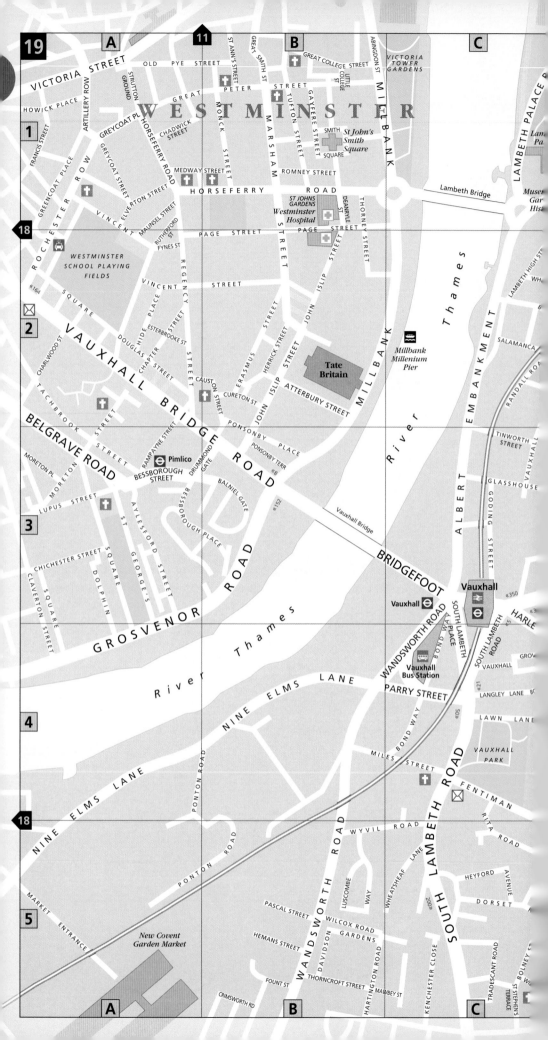

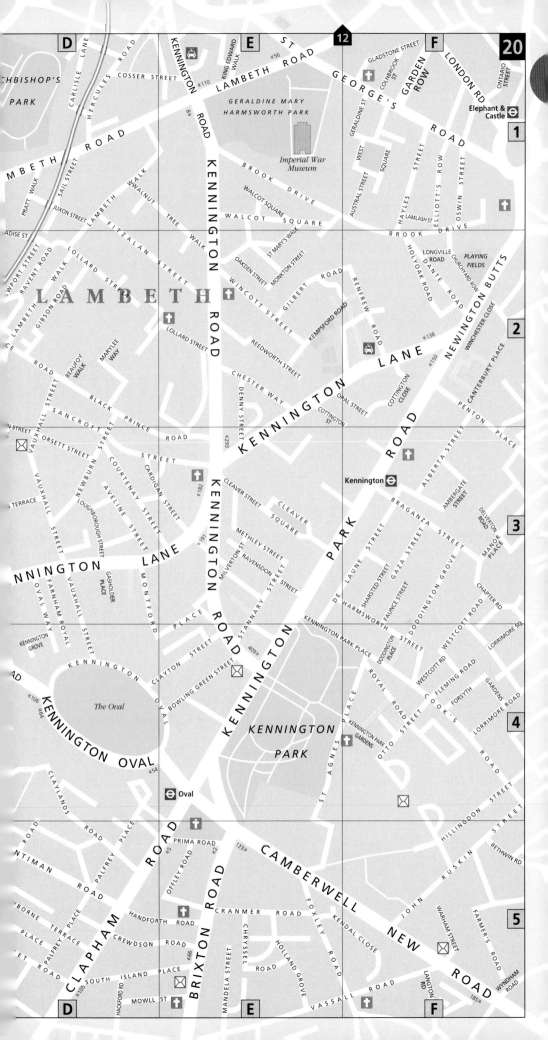

SHOPS AND MARKETS

Bags from two famous London department stores

London is one of the great shopping cities of Europe, with bustling, lively street markets, world-famous department stores and a wide variety of eclectic shops selling clothes, antiques, crafts and much more. The best shopping areas range from up-market districts such as Knightsbridge and Bond Street, which sell expensive designer clothes, to the busy, chaotic stretch of Oxford Street. The vibrant markets of Covent Garden, Berwick Street and Brick Lane are also popular. The city is best known, however, for its huge range of clothes shops selling everything from traditional tweeds to the latest zany designs of the ever-changing high-street fashion trends.

WHEN TO SHOP

In central London, most shops stay open from 10am to about 5.30–6pm Monday to Saturday. Many department stores, however, have longer hours. The "late night" shopping until 7 or 8pm is on Thursday and Friday in Oxford Street and the rest of West End; and on Wednesday in Knightsbridge and Chelsea. Some shops in tourist areas, such as Covent Garden and the Trocadero, are open until 7pm or later every day, including Sunday. Some street markets and a number of other shops are usually open on Sundays as well.

TWICE-YEARLY SALES

The traditional sale season is from January to February and from June to July, when shops slash prices and sell off left-over stock. The department stores have some of the best reductions – queues for the famous Harrods sale start to form long before it opens.

SHOPPING AREAS

London's best shopping areas range from the up-market Knightsbridge, where porcelain, jewellery and couture come at the highest prices, to colourful markets, where getting the cheapest bargains is what it's all about.

The city beckons specialist shoppers with its treasures and collectibles crammed into inviting antiques shops, and streets full of antiquarian booksellers and art galleries.

BEST OF THE DEPARTMENT STORES

Harrods is the king of the city's department stores with over 300 departments and a staff of 5,000. The spectacular food hall with Edwardian tiles displays fish, cheese, fruit and vegetables. Other specialities include fashion, china and glass, kitchenware and electronics. Londoners also often head for the nearby **Harvey Nichols**, which stocks the best of everything. The clothing department is particularly strong, with an emphasis on talented British, European and American names. The food hall, opened in 1992, is one of London's most stylish.

Selfridges, on Oxford Street, has expanded its range in recent years. It has arguably the widest choice of labels, a great lingerie department and a section devoted to emerging designers. It also has a food hall that features delicacies from all over the world.

Originally a drapery, **John Lewis**, to this date, has a good selection of fabrics and haberdashery. Its china, glass and household items make this store and its Sloane Square partner, **Peter Jones**, equally popular with Londoners.

Liberty, near Carnaby Street, has been famous ever since 1875 for its beautiful silks and other Oriental goods. Don't forget to check out the famous scarf department.

Fortnum and Mason's is best known for its ground-floor food department. It has everything from Fortnum's tins of biscuits and tea to cured meats and lovely wicker hampers. In fact, these exquisite delicacies are so engrossing that the upper floors filled with classic fashion and luxury items often remain free of crowds.

Harrods at night, illuminated by 11,500 lights

MARKETS

Whatever you're looking for, it's definitely worth visiting one of London's colourful markets. Many of them mix English traditions with those of more recent immigrants, creating an exotic atmosphere and a truly fascinating array of merchandise. At some, the seasoned hawkers have honed their sales patter to an entertaining art, which reaches fever pitch just before closing, when the plummeting prices at the end of the day are announced. Keep your wits about you, your hand on your purse and join in the fun.

Among the best of the West End markets are **Grays Antiques** and **Jubilee and Apple** markets in Covent Garden. Although it is somewhat touristy, **Piccadilly Crafts** is also very popular. In Soho, the spirited costermongers of **Berwick Street** peddle some of the cheapest and freshest fruit and vegetables in the area.

In the East End, **Petticoat Lane** is probably the most famous of London's street markets. Those in search of the latest street fashions make a beeline for **Old Spitalfields**, while **Brick Lane** is massively popular due

Bustling Petticoat Lane market, officially known as Middlesex Street

to its trendy location. Here you can find everything from shellfish to trainers. Nearby, **Columbia Road** is perfect for greenery and blossoms.

South of the river, **East Street** also has a flower market, but the majority of its traders sell clothes. **Bermondsey Market** is a gathering point for London's antiques traders. Collectors set off early to scrutinize the fine paintings and old jewellery. **Borough** (*see p120*) caters to the restaurant trade with it's fine food and farmer's market. **Brixton Market** stocks a superb

assortment of Afro-Caribbean foods, often to the pounding beat of reggae music.

In north London, **Camden Lock Market** offers a vibrant atmosphere and stalls selling everything from vintage clothes to lovely crafts. In nearby Islington, **Camden Passage** is a quiet cobbled street where charming cafés nestle among quaint antiques shops.

In Notting Hill, **Portobello Road** is actually a bunch of markets rolled into one, and an entire afternoon can be spent browsing there.

DIRECTORY

DEPARTMENT STORES

Fortnum & Mason
181 Piccadilly W1. **Map 11** A3. **Tel** 020 7734 8040.

Harrods
87–135 Brompton Rd SW1. **Map** 9 C5. **Tel** 020 7730 1234.

Harvey Nichols
109–125 Knightsbridge SW1. **Map** 9 C5. **Tel** 020 7235 5000.

John Lewis
278–306 Oxford St W1. **Map** 10 E1. **Tel** 020 7629 7711.

Liberty
210–20 Regent St W1. **Map** 10 F2. **Tel** 020 7734 1234.

Peter Jones
Sloane Sq, SW1. **Map** 18 D2. **Tel** 020 7730 3434.

Selfridges
400 Oxford St W1. **Map** 10 D2. **Tel** 0800 123 400.

MARKETS

Bermondsey Market
Long Lane & Bermondsey St SE1. **Map** 13 C5.
⬜ 5am–2pm Fri.

Berwick Street
Berwick St W1.
Map 11 A2.
⬜ 9am–6pm Mon–Sat.

Borough
8 Southwark St SE1.
Map 13 B4. ⬜ 11am–5pm Thu, noon–6pm Fri, 9am–4pm Sat.

Brick Lane
Brick Lane E1. **Map** 6 E5.
⬜ dawn–1pm Sun.

Brixton Market
Electric Ave SW9.
⬜ 8.30am–5.30pm daily.

Camden Lock Market
Chalk Farm Rd NW1.
🚇 Camden Town, Chalk Farm.
⬜ 9:30am–5:30pm daily.

Camden Passage
Camden Passage N1.
Map 4 F1.
⬜ 10am–2pm Wed, 10am–5pm Sat.

Columbia Road
Columbia Rd E2.
Map 6 D3.
🚇 Shoreditch, Old St.
⬜ 8am–2pm Sun.

East Street
East St SE17. 🚇 Elephant & Castle. ⬜ 8am–5pm daily (to 2pm Thu & Sun).

Grays Antiques
58 Davies St, Mayfair.
Map 10 E2.
⬜ 10am–6pm Mon–Fri.

Greenwich
College Approach SE10.
⬜ 11am–6pm Wed, 10am–5:30pm Thu & Fri, 9am–6pm Sat & Sun.

Jubilee and Apple
Covent Gdn Piazza WC2.
Map 11 C2. ⬜ 9am–5pm daily.

Old Spitalfields
Commercial St E1. 🚇 Liverpool St. **Map** 6 D1.
⬜ 9:30am–5:30pm daily.

Petticoat Lane
Middlesex St E1. **Map** 14 E2. ⬜ 9am–2pm Sun.

Piccadilly Crafts
St James's Church, Piccadilly W1. **Map** 11 A3.
⬜ 9am–6pm Wed–Sat.

Portobello Road
Portobello Rd W10.
Map 7 C3. ⬜ daily (main market Sat).

Exclusive designer clothes on sale at Harrods, Knightsbridge

CLOTHES

British tailoring and fabrics are world renowned for their high quality. **Henry Poole & Co, H Huntsman & Sons** and **Gieves & Hawkes** are among the most highly respected tailors on Savile Row.

The past decade has seen the advent of a new generation of trend conscious tailors who specialize in modern cuts and fabrics. The line-up includes **Richard James** and **Ozwald Boateng**. Several stalwarts of classic British style have also recently reinvented themselves as fashion labels. **Burberry** is the best example, although it still does a brisk trade in its famous trenchcoats, and distinctive accessories. Designers **Margaret Howell** and **Nicole Farhi** create trend-setting versions of British country garments for men as well as women.

London designers are known for their eclectic, irreverent style. *Grande dames* of fashion, **Zandra Rhodes** and **Vivienne Westwood** have been on the scene since the 1970s. Many other British designers of international stature also have their flagship stores in the capital, including the popular **Stella McCartney, Alexander McQueen, Paul Smith** and **Matthew Williamson**. Designer clothes, however, are not just the preserve of the rich. If you want to flaunt a bit of British design, but can't afford the high prices, it's worth

visiting **Debenhams**, which has harnessed the talents of numerous leading designers. Cheaper versions of all the latest styles appear in the shops almost as soon as they have been sashayed down the catwalk. **Topshop** and **Oasis** have both won celebrity fans for their up-to-the-minute ensembles of hip and youthful fashions for women; young professionals head to **French Connection**. The up-market chains **Jigsaw** and **Whistles** are more expensive, with their emphasis on beautiful fabrics and shapes. Fashion-conscious young men can turn to **Reiss** and **Ted Baker** for trendy clothing.

SHOES

Some of the most famous names in the footwear industry are based in Britain. If you can spare a few thousand pounds, you can have a pair custom-made by the Royal Family's shoemaker, **John Lobb**. Ready-made, traditional brogues and Oxfords are the mainstay of **Church's Shoes**. **Oliver Sweeney** gives classics a contemporary edge. **The British Boot Company** in Camden has the widest range of funky Dr Martens, appropriated by rock'n'rollers and the grunge set. **Jimmy Choo** and **Manolo Blahnik** are two all-time favourites of most fashionable women all over the world. Less expensive, yet good quality designs can be found in **Hobbs** or **Pied à Terre**, while **Faith** and **Office** turn out young, voguish styles.

GIFTS AND SOUVENIRS

Contemporary Applied Arts and the market in Covent Garden Piazza stock uniquely British pottery, knitwear and other crafts. To buy all your gifts under one roof, visit Liberty *(see p148),* where all kinds of exquisite items can be found in every department.

Leading museums such as the Victoria and Albert *(see pp98–9),* Natural History and Science Museums *(see p100)* sell unusual mementos as well. Alternatively, try **Hamley's** for gifts and toys.

BOOKS AND MAGAZINES

The bookshops in London rank among its most illustrious specialities. Charing Cross Road is a treasure trove for those hunting for antiquarian, second-hand as well as new volumes. It is the home of **Foyles**, famous for its massive stock. Large branches of chains such as **Waterstone's** co-exist with many specialist stores in this highly learned street.

Hatchards in Piccadilly is the city's oldest bookshop, and also one of its best, offering an extensive choice of titles.

Vintage Magazines in Soho, as its name suggests, stocks publications dating back to the early 1900s – collectors of back issues will be delighted.

Well-stocked bookshop on the legendary Charing Cross Road

ART AND ANTIQUES

Art and antiques shops abound in London, and you are sure to find something of beauty and value within your means.

Cork Street is the centre of Britain's contemporary art world. **Waddington Galleries** is the best known, while **Redfern Art Gallery** and **Flowers** exhibit unusual modern art.

Visit **Roger's Antiques Galleries** and Grays Antiques *(see p148)* for striking vintage jewellery and objets d'art.

The East End is a growing area for contemporary art. The cutting-edge **White Cube Gallery** is there, as is the internationally renowned **Whitechapel Art Gallery**.

For photography, visit the **Photographers' Gallery**, which has the largest collection of originals for sale in Britain. **Hamiltons Gallery** also hosts interesting exhibitions.

DIRECTORY

CLOTHES

Alexander McQueen
4–5 Old Bond St W1.
Map 10 F3.
Tel 020 7355 0088.

Burberry
21–23 New Bond St W1.
Map 10 F2.
Tel 020 7930 3343.
One of several branches.

Debenhams
334–348 Oxford St W1.
Map 10 E2.
Tel 08445 616 161.

French Connection
249–251 Regent St W1.
Map 10 F2.
Tel 020 7493 3124.
One of several branches.

Gieves & Hawkes
1 Savile Row W1. **Map** 10
F3. *Tel 020 7434 2001.*

H Huntsman & Sons
11 Savile Row W1. **Map**
10 F3. *Tel 020 7734 7441.*

Henry Poole & Co
15 Savile Row W1. **Map**
10 F3. *Tel 020 7734 5985.*

Jigsaw
6 Duke of York Sq, Kings
Rd SW3. **Map** 17 C2.
Tel 020 7730 4404.

Margaret Howell
34 Wigmore St W1. **Map**
10 E1. *Tel 020 7009 9009.*

Matthew Williamson
28 Bruton St W1.
Map 10 E3.
Tel 020 7629 6200.

Nicole Farhi
158 New Bond St W1.
Map 10 E2.
Tel 020 7499 8368.

Oasis
12–14 Argyll St W1.
Map 10 F2.
Tel 020 7434 1799.

Ozwald Boateng
30 Savile Row &
9 Vigo St W1. **Map** 10 F3.
Tel 020 7437 0620.

Paul Smith
Westbourne House
120 & 122 Kensington
Park Rd W11. **Map** 7 B2.
Tel 020 7727 3553.

Reiss
Kent House, 14–17
Market Place W1.
Map 10 F1.
Tel 020 7637 9112.
One of several branches.

Richard James
29 Savile Row W1.
Map 10 F2.
Tel 020 7434 0605.

Stella McCartney
30 Bruton St W1.
Map 10 E3.
Tel 020 7518 3100.

Ted Baker
9–10 Floral St WC2.
Map 11 C2.
Tel 020 7836 7808.
One of several branches.

Topshop
Oxford Circus W1.
Map 10 F1.
Tel 08448 487 487.
One of several branches.

Vivienne Westwood
6 Davies St W1.
Map 10 E2.
Tel 020 7629 3757.

Whistles
303 Brompton Rd SW3.
Map 17 B2.
Tel 020 7823 9134.

Zandra Rhodes
79 Bermondsey St, SE1.
Map 11 C5.
Tel 020 7403 5333.

SHOES

The British Boot Company
5 Kentish Town Rd NW1.
Map 2 F1.
Tel 020 7485 8505.

Church's Shoes
201 Regent St W1.
Map 10 F2.
Tel 020 7734 2438.

Faith
192–194 Oxford St W1.
Map 10 F1.
Tel 020 7580 9561.

Hobbs
47–48 South Molton St
W1. **Map** 10 E2.
Tel 020 7629 0750.
One of several branches.

Jimmy Choo
27 New Bond St W1.
Map 10 F2.
Tel 020 7493 5858.

John Lobb
9 St James's St SW1.
Map 10 F4.
Tel 020 7930 3664.

Manolo Blahnik
49–51 Old Church St,
Kings Road SW3. **Map** 17
A4. *Tel 020 7352 8622.*

Office
57 Neal St WC2.
Map 11 B1.
Tel 020 7379 1896.
One of several branches.

Oliver Sweeney
66 New Bond St W1.
Map 10 E2.
Tel 020 7355 0387.

Pied à Terre
179 South Molton St W1.
Map 10 E2.
Tel 020 7629 1362.

GIFTS AND SOUVENIRS

Contemporary Applied Arts
2 Percy St WC1.
Map 11 A1.
Tel 020 7436 2344.

Hamley's
2 Fouberts Place W1.
Map 10 F2.
Tel 0870 333 2450.

BOOKS AND MAGAZINES

Blackwell's
100 Charing Cross Rd
WC2. **Map** 11 B2.
Tel 020 7292 5100.
One of several branches.

Foyles
113–119 Charing Cross Rd
WC2. **Map** 11 B1.
Tel 020 7437 5660.

Hatchards
187 Piccadilly W1.
Map 10 F3.
Tel 020 7439 9921.

Vintage Magazines
39–43 Brewer St W1.
Map 11 A2.
Tel 020 7439 8525.

Waterstone's
203–205 Piccadilly W1.
Map 11 A3.
Tel 020 7851 2400.
One of several branches.

ART AND ANTIQUES

Flowers
21 Cork St W1.
Map 10 F3.
Tel 020 7439 7766.

Hamiltons Gallery
13 Carlos Place W1.
Map 10 E3.
Tel 020 7499 9493.

Photographers' Gallery
16–18 Ramillies St W1.
Map 10 F2.
Tel 0845 262 1618.

Redfern Art Gallery
20 Cork St W1.
Map 10 F3.
Tel 020 7734 1732.

Roger's Antiques Galleries
65 Portobello Road W11.
Map 7 A1.
Tel 020 7467 5787.

Waddington Galleries
11, 12 Cork St W1.
Map 10 F3.
Tel 020 7851 2200.

White Cube Gallery
48 Hoxton Square N1.
Map 5 C3.
Tel 020 7930 5373.

Whitechapel Art Gallery
80–82 Whitechapel
High St E1.
Map 14 E1.
Tel 020 7522 7888.

ENTERTAINMENT IN LONDON

Many London cafés have free live music

London has the enormous variety of entertainment that only the great cities of the world can provide. The historical backdrop and the lively bustling atmosphere add to the excitement. Whether dancing the night away at a famous disco or making the most of London's varied arts scene, the visitor has a bewildering choice. A trip to London is not complete without a visit to the theatre which ranges from glamorous West End musicals to experimental Fringe plays. There is world-class ballet and opera in fabled venues such as Sadler's Wells and the Royal Opera House. The musical menu covers everything from classical, jazz and rock to rhythm and blues performed in atmospheric basement clubs, old converted cinemas and outdoor venues such as Wembley. Movie buffs can choose from hundreds of films each night. Sports fans can watch cricket at Lord's or participate in a host of activities from water sports to ice skating.

Time Out, published every Tuesday, is the most comprehensive guide to what is on in London, with detailed weekly listings and reviews. *The Evening Standard, The Guardian* (Saturday) and *The Independent* also have reviews and information on events. If you buy tickets from booking agencies rather than direct from box offices, do compare prices – and only buy from ticket touts if you are desperate.

WEST END AND NATIONAL THEATRES

Palace Theatre poster (1898)

The glamorous, glittering world of West End theatreland, emblazoned with the names of world-famous performers, offers an extraordinary range of entertainment.

West End theatres (see Directory for individual theatres) survive on their profits and rely on financial backers, known as "angels". Consequently, they tend to stage commercial productions with mass appeal: musicals, classics, comedies and plays by bankable contemporary playwrights.

The state-subsidized **National Theatre** is based in the Southbank Centre *(see p154)*. It has three auditoriums – the large, open-staged Olivier, the proscenium-arched Lyttelton, and the small studio space of the Cottesloe.

The **Royal Shakespeare Company** (RSC) regularly stages Shakespeare plays, but its repertoire includes Greek tragedies, Restoration comedies and modern works. Based at Stratford-upon-Avon *(see pp325–27)*, its major productions perform at London West End theatres. The RSC ticket hotline has information. **The Old Vic** has been rejuvenated recently under the artistic directorship of Kevin Spacey, whose exciting programme of drama attracts wide audiences.

Theatre tickets generally cost from £5 to £50 (for a top price West End show) and can be bought direct from box offices, by telephone or post. The "tkts" discount theatre ticket booth in Leicester Square sells tickets for a wide range of shows on the day of performance. It is open Monday to Saturday (10am–7pm) for matinees and evening shows, and Sundays (noon–3pm) for matinees only.

OFF-WEST END AND FRINGE THEATRES

Off-West End theatre is a middle category bridging the gap between West End and Fringe theatre. It includes venues that, regardless of location, have a permanent management team and often provide the opportunity for established directors and actors to turn their hands to more adventurous works in a smaller, more intimate, environment. Fringe theatres, on the other hand, are normally venues hired out to visiting companies. Both offer a vast array of innovative productions, serving as an outlet for new, often experimental writing.

Venues (too numerous to list – see newspaper listings),

The Old Vic, the first home of the National Theatre from 1963

Open-air theatre at Regent's Park

range from tiny theatres or rooms above pubs such as the Gate, which produces neglected European classics, to theatres such as the Donmar Warehouse, which attracts major directors and actors.

OPEN-AIR THEATRE

In summer, a performance of one of Shakespeare's airier creations such as *A Midsummer Night's Dream*, takes on an atmosphere of enchantment among the green vistas of Regent's Park (0870-060 1811). Lavish summer opera productions are staged at Holland Park (020-7602 7856). Shakespeare's Globe *(see p120)* offers open-air theatrical performances in a beautifully recreated Elizabethan theatre.

CINEMAS

The West End abounds with multiplex cinema chains (MGM, Odeon, UCI) which show big budget Hollywood films, usually in advance of the rest of the country, although release dates tend to lag well behind the US and many other European countries.

The Odeon Marble Arch has the largest commercial screen in Europe, while the Odeon Leicester Square boasts London's biggest auditorium with almost 2,000 seats.

Londoners are well-informed cinema-goers and even the larger cinema chains include some low-budget and foreign films in their repertoire. The majority of foreign films are subtitled, rather than dubbed. A number of independent cinemas, such as the Renoir and Prince Charles in central London, and the Curzon in Mayfair, show foreign-language and art films.

The largest concentration of cinemas is in and around Leicester Square although there are local cinemas in most areas. Just off Leicester Square, the Prince Charles is the West End's cheapest cinema. Elsewhere in the area you can expect to pay as much as £10 for an evening screening – almost twice the price of the local cinemas. Monday and afternoon performances in the West End are often cheaper.

The BFI Southbank, at the Southbank Centre, is London's flagship repertory cinema. Subsidized by the British Film Institute, it screens a wide range of films, old and new, from all around the world. Nearby at Waterloo is the BFI IMAX, with one of the world's largest screens.

BFI IMAX Cinema, at Waterloo

DIRECTORY

Adelphi
Strand. **Map** 11 C3.
Tel 0870 403 0303.

Aldwych
Aldwych. **Map** 11 C2.
Tel 0870 400 0805.

Apollo
Shaftesbury Ave.
Map 11 B2.
Tel 020 7834 6318.

Cambridge
Earlham St. **Map** 11 B2.
Tel 0870 264 3333.

Comedy
Panton St. **Map** 11 A3.
Tel 0870 060 6637.

Criterion
Piccadilly Circus. **Map**
11 A3. *Tel 0870 847 1778.*

Dominion
Tottenham Court Rd. **Map**
11 A1. *Tel 0870 607 7400.*

Duchess
Catherine St. **Map** 11 C2.
Tel 020 7632 9600.

Duke of York's
St Martin's Lane. **Map** 11
B2. *Tel 0870 060 6623.*

Fortune
Russell St. **Map** 11 C2.
Tel 0870 060 6626.

Garrick
Charing Cross Rd. **Map**
11 B2. *Tel 0870 040 0083.*

Gielgud
Shaftesbury Ave. **Map**
11 B2. *Tel 0844 482 5130.*

Her Majesty's
Haymarket. **Map** 11 A3.
Tel 0844 412 2707.

Lyceum
Wellington St. **Map** 11
C2. *Tel 0870 243 9000.*

Lyric
Shaftesbury Ave. **Map** 11
B2. *Tel 0870 890 1107.*

National
South Bank. **Map** 12 D3.
Tel 020 7452 3000.

New London
Drury Lane. **Map** 11 C1.
Tel 0870 890 0141.

Noel Coward
St Martin's Lane. **Map** 11
B2. *Tel 0844 482 5120.*

Novello Theatre
Aldwych. **Map** 12 D2.
Tel 0844 482 5120.

The Old Vic
Waterloo Rd SE1.
Map 12 E4.
Tel 0870 060 6628.

Palace
Cambridge Circus W1. **Map**
11 B2. *Tel 0870 890 0142.*

Phoenix
Charing Cross Rd. **Map** 11
B2. *Tel 0870 060 6629.*

Piccadilly
Denman St. **Map** 11 A2.
Tel 0870 060 0123.

Prince Edward
Old Compton St. **Map** 11
D5. *Tel 0844 482 5151.*

Prince of Wales
Coventry St. **Map** 11 A3.
Tel 0844 482 5115.

Queen's
Shaftesbury Ave. **Map**
11 B2. *Tel 0844 482 5160.*
RSC *Tel 01789 403 444.*

Shaftesbury
Shaftesbury Ave. **Map**
11 B2. *Tel 0844 482 5160.*

St Martin's
West St. **Map** 11 B2.
Tel 0844 499 1515.

**Theatre Royal:
Drury Lane**
Catherine St. **Map** 11 C2.
Tel 020 7087 7500.

**Theatre Royal:
Haymarket**
Haymarket. **Map** 11 A3.
Tel 0870 844 2353.

Vaudeville
Strand. **Map** 11 C3.
Tel 020 7836 9987.

Wyndham's
Charing Cross Rd. **Map**
11 B2. *Tel 0844 482 5120.*

Royal Festival Hall, South Bank Centre

CLASSICAL MUSIC, OPERA AND DANCE

London is one of the world's great centres for classical music, with five symphony orchestras, internationally renowned chamber groups such as the Academy of St-Martin-in-the-Fields and the English Chamber Orchestra, as well as a number of contemporary groups. There are performances virtually every week by major international orchestras and artists, reaching a peak during the summer Proms season at the **Royal Albert Hall** *(see p63)*. The newly restored **Wigmore Hall** has excellent acoustics and is a fine setting for chamber music, as is the converted Baroque church (1728) of **St John's, Smith Square**.

Although televised and outdoor performances by major stars have greatly increased the popularity of opera, prices at the **Royal Opera House** *(see p80)* are still aimed at corporate entertainment but the policy now is to keep a few cheaper seats. The refurbished building is elaborate and productions are often extremely lavish. English National Opera, based at the **London Coliseum**, has more adventurous productions, appealing to a younger audience (nearly all operas are sung in English). Tickets range from £5 to £200 and it is advisable to book in advance.

The Royal Opera House is also home to the Royal Ballet, and the London Coliseum to the English National Ballet, the two leading classical ballet companies in Britain. Visiting ballets also perform in both. There are numerous young contemporary dance companies, and **The Place** is a dedicated contemporary dance theatre where many companies perform. Other major dance venues are **Sadler's Wells**, the **ICA**, the **Peacock Theatre** and the **Chisenhale Dance Space**.

The **Barbican Concert Hall** and **Southbank Centre** (comprising the Royal Festival Hall, Queen Elizabeth Hall and Purcell Room) host an impressive variety of events ranging from touring opera and classical music performances to free foyer concerts.

Elsewhere in London many outdoor musical events take place in summer *(see pp62–3)* at venues such as **Kenwood House**. Events to look out for are: the London Opera Festival (June) with singers from all over the world; the City of London Festival (July) which hosts a range of varied musical events; and contemporary dance festivals Spring Loaded (February–April) and Dance Umbrella (October) – see *Time Out* and newspaper listings.

Kenwood House on Hampstead Heath *(see p124)*

DIRECTORY

CLASSICAL MUSIC, OPERA AND DANCE

Barbican Concert Hall
Silk St EC2. **Map** 5 A5.
Tel 020 7638 4141.
www.barbican.org.uk

Chisenhale Dance Space
64–84 Chisenhale Rd E3.
⊖ *Bethnal Green, Mile End.* **Tel** *020 8981 6617.*
www.chisenhaledance
space.co.uk

ICA
The Mall SW1. **Map** 11 A4. **Tel** *020 7930 3647.*
www.ica.org.uk

Kenwood House
(EH) Hampstead Lane NW3. **Tel** *020 8348 1286.*

London Coliseum
St Martin's Lane WC2.
Map 11 B3. **Tel** *0870 145 0200.* www.eno.org

Peacock Theatre
Portugal St WC2. **Map** 12 D1. **Tel** *0844 412 4322.*

The Place
17 Duke's Rd WC1. **Map** 3 B3. **Tel** *020 7121 1100.*
www.theplace.org.uk

Royal Albert Hall
Kensington Gore SW7.
Map 8 F5. **Tel** *020 7589 8212.* www.royal
alberthall.com

Royal Opera House
Floral St WC2. **Map** 11 C2. **Tel** *020 7304 4000.*
www.roh.org.uk

Sadler's Wells
Rosebery Ave EC1.
Tel *0844 412 4300.*
www.sadlerswells.com

St John's, Smith Sq
Smith Sq SW1. **Map** 19 B1. **Tel** *020 7222 1061.*
www.sjss.org.uk

Southbank Centre
SE1. **Map** 12 D3. **Tel** *0871 663 2500.* www.
southbankcentre.co.uk

Wigmore Hall
Wigmore St W1. **Map** 10 D1. **Tel** *020 7935 2141.*
www.wigmore-hall.org.uk

ROCK, POP, JAZZ AND CLUBS

100 Club
100 Oxford St W1. **Map** 10 F1. **Tel** *020 7636 0933.*
www.the100club.co.uk

333
333 Old St EC1.
Tel 020 7739 1800.

Brixton Academy
211 Stockwell Rd SW9.
⊖ *Brixton.* **Tel** *0870 771 2000.* www.brixton-
academy.co.uk

Café de Paris
3 Coventry St W1. **Map** 4 D5. **Tel** *020 7734 7700.*

The Hippodrome, Leicester Square

ROCK, POP, JAZZ AND CLUBS

An ordinary week night in London features scores of concerts, ranging from rock and pop, to jazz, Latin, world, folk and reggae. Artists guaranteed to fill thousands of seats play large venues such as **Wembley Arena** or the **Royal Albert Hall**. However, many major bands prefer to play the **Brixton Academy** and the **Forum**, both former cinemas.

There are a number of live jazz venues. Best of the old crop is **Ronnie Scott's**, although the **100 Club**, **Jazz Café** and **Pizza on the Park** have good reputations.

London's club scene is one of the most innovative in Europe. It is dominated by big-name DJs, who host different nights in different clubs, and some of the best clubs are one-nighters (see *Time Out* and newspaper listings). The West End discos **Ruby Blue** and the **Café de Paris** are glitzy, expensive and very much on the tourist circuit. The **Hippodrome** was a popular club for more than 20 years. Originally built for circus and variety performances, the building reopened as a performing arts venue in 2008. In contrast, the New York-style **Ministry of Sound**, the camp cabaret of **Madame Jojo's**, the trendy Shoreditch clubs **333** and **Cargo**, and a host of other venues ensure that you will never be short of choice. Alternatives are the excellent laser and light shows at **Heaven**, the glamorous super-club **Pacha London**, or the live music venue **Koko** in Camden, which also hosts a variety of club nights. **Heaven** and the **Fridge** are among the most popular of London's gay clubs.

Opening times are usually 10pm–3am, but on weekends many clubs open until 6am.

SPORTS

An impressive variety of public sports facilities are to be found in London and they are generally inexpensive to use. Swimming pools, squash courts, gyms and sports centres, with an assortment of keep-fit classes, can be found in most districts, and tennis courts hired in most parks. Water sports, ice skating and golf are among the variety of activities on offer. Spectator sports range from football and rugby at various club grounds to cricket at **Lord's** or the **Oval**, and tennis at the **All England Lawn Tennis Club**, Wimbledon. Tickets for the most popular matches can often be hard to come by *(see p67)*. More traditional sports include polo at **Guards**, croquet at **Hurlingham** (private members only) and medieval tennis at **Queen's Club Real Tennis**.

Ticket agency, Shaftesbury Avenue

Cargo
83 Rivington St EC2. 🚇
Old St. **Tel** 020 7749 7844.

Forum
9–17 Highgate Rd NW5.
🚇 *Kentish Town.*
Tel 020 7428 4099.

Fridge
Town Hall Parade, Brixton
Hill SW2. 🚇 *Brixton.*
Tel 020 7326 5100.

Heaven
Under the Arches, Villiers
St WC2. **Map** 11 C3.
Tel 020 7930 2020.

Jazz Café
3–5 Parkway NW1.
🚇 *Camden Town.*
Tel 020 7485 6834.

Koko
1A Camden High St NW1.
🚇 *Mornington Crescent*
Tel 0870 432 5527.

Madame Jojo's
8–10 Brewer St W1. **Map**
11 A2. **Tel** 020 7734 3040.

Ministry of Sound
103 Gaunt St SE1.
🚇 *Elephant & Castle.*
Tel 0870 060 0010.

Pacha London
Terminus Place, SW1. **Map**
18 F1. **Tel** 0845 371 4489.
www.pachalondon.com

Pizza on the Park
11 Knightsbridge SW1.
Map 10 D5. **Tel** 020
7235 7825.

Ronnie Scott's
47 Frith St W1.
Map 11 A2.
Tel 020 7439 0747.
www.ronniescotts.co.uk

Ruby Blue
Leicester Sq WC2. **Map**
4 E5. **Tel** 0871 223 0869.

SPORTS

All England Lawn Tennis Club
Church Rd, Wimbledon
SW19. 🚇 *Southfields.*
Tel 020 8946 2244.

Guards Polo Club
Windsor Great Park,
Englefield Green, Egham.
🚇 *Egham.*
Tel 01784 434212.

Hurlingham Club
Ranelagh Gdns SW6.
Map 18 D3. **Tel** 020
7736 8411.

Lord's Cricket Ground
St John's Wood NW8.
🚇 *St John's Wood.*
Tel 020 7289 1611.

Oval Cricket Ground
The Oval, Kennington
SE11. 🚇 *Oval.*
Tel 020 7820 5700.

Queen's Club Real Tennis
Palliser Rd W14.
🚇 *Barons Court.*
Tel 020 7385 3421.

SOUTHEAST ENGLAND

Southeast England at a Glance

The old Saxon kingdoms covered the areas surrounding London, and today, while their accessibility to the capital makes them a magnet for commuters, each region retains a character and history of its own. The attractions include England's oldest universities, royal palaces, castles, stately homes and cathedrals, many of which played critical roles in the nation's early history. The landscape is soft, with the green and rounded hills of the south country levelling out to the flat fertile plains and fens of East Anglia, fringed by broad, sandy beaches.

Blenheim Palace (see pp228–9) *is a Baroque masterpiece. The Mermaid Fountain (1892) is part of the spectacular gardens.*

Bedfordshire

Hertfor...

Buckinghamshire

THAMES VALLEY
(see pp216–37)

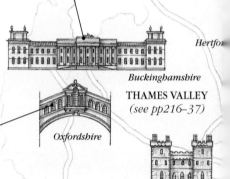

Oxfordshire

Oxford University's *buildings (see pp222–7) amount to a textbook of English architecture from the Middle Ages to the present. Christ Church College (1525) is the largest in the university.*

Surre...

Hampshire

West Suss...

Windsor Castle (see pp236–7) *is Britain's oldest royal residence. The Round Tower was built in the 11th century when the palace guarded the western approaches to London.*

Winchester Cathedral (see pp170–1) *was begun in 1097 on the ruins of a Saxon church. The city has been an important centre of Christianity since the 7th century. The cathedral's northwest door is built in a characteristic medieval style.*

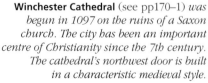

◁ **The white cliffs of Dover, Kent**

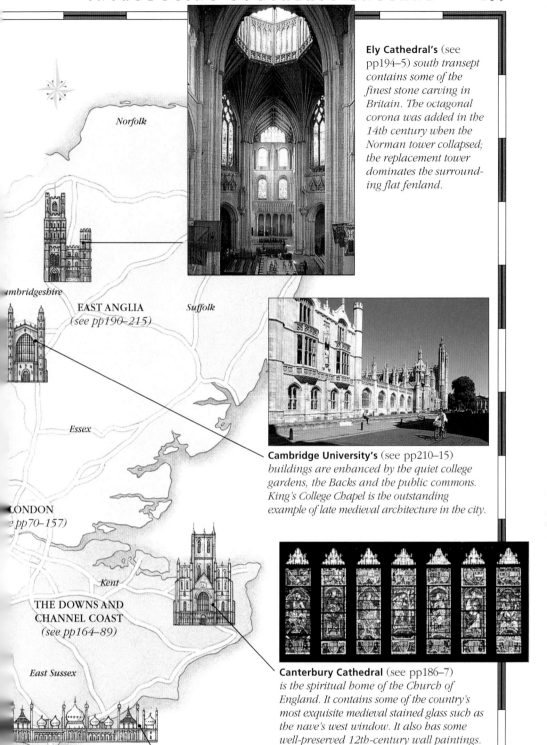

Ely Cathedral's (see pp194–5) *south transept contains some of the finest stone carving in Britain. The octagonal corona was added in the 14th century when the Norman tower collapsed; the replacement tower dominates the surrounding flat fenland.*

Norfolk

Cambridgeshire

EAST ANGLIA
(see pp190–215)

Suffolk

Essex

LONDON
(see pp70–157)

Kent

THE DOWNS AND CHANNEL COAST
(see pp164–89)

East Sussex

Cambridge University's (see pp210–15) *buildings are enhanced by the quiet college gardens, the Backs and the public commons. King's College Chapel is the outstanding example of late medieval architecture in the city.*

Canterbury Cathedral (see pp186–7) *is the spiritual home of the Church of England. It contains some of the country's most exquisite medieval stained glass such as the nave's west window. It also has some well-preserved 12th-century wall paintings.*

Brighton's Royal Pavilion (see pp178–9) *was built for the Prince Regent and is one of the most lavish buildings in the land. Its design by John Nash (see p107) is based on Oriental themes and it has recently been restored to its original splendour.*

0 kilometres 25

0 miles 25

The Garden of England

With its fertile soil, mild climate and regular rainfall, the Kentish countryside has flourished as a fruit-growing region ever since its first orchards were planted by the Romans. There has been a recent boom in wine-making, as the vine-covered hillsides around Lamberhurst show, and several vineyards may be visited. The orchards are dazzling in the blossom season, and in the autumn the branches sag with ripening fruit – a familiar sight which inspired William Cobbett (1762–1835) to describe the area as "the very finest as to fertility and diminutive beauty in the whole world". Near Faversham, the fruit research station of Brogdale is open to the public, offering orchard walks, tastings and informative displays.

White wine from the southeast

HOPS AND HOPPING

Hop-picking, a family affair

Oast houses, topped with distinctive angled cowls, are a common feature of the Kentish landscape and many have now been turned into houses. They were originall[y]

SEASONAL FRUIT

This timeline shows the major crops in each month of the farming year. The first blossoms may appear when the fields are still dusted with snow. As the petals fall, fruit appears among the leaves. After ripening in the summer sun, the fruit is harvested in the autumn.

Peach blossom *is usually to be found on south-facing walls, as its fruit requires warm conditions.*

Orchards *are used to grow plums, pears and apples. The latter (blossoming above) remain Kent's most important orchard crop.*

Raspberries *are a luscious soft fruit. Many growers allow you to pick your ow[n] from the fields, an[d] then pay by weig[ht.]*

MARCH	APRIL	MAY	JUNE	JU[LY]

Sour cherry blossom *is the earliest flower. Its fruit is used for cooking.*

Pear blossom *has creamy white flowers which appear two or three weeks before apple blossom.*

Cherry plum blossom *is one of the most beautiful blossoms; the plum is grown more for its flowers than its fruit.*

Srawberries *are Britain's favourite and earliest soft fru[it.] New strains allow them to be picked all summer.*

Gooseberries *are not always sweet enough to eat raw, though all types are superb in pies and other desserts.*

ilt to dry hops, an ingredient
brewing beer. Many are still
ed for that, for although
ports have reduced domestic
p-growing, more than four
llion tonnes are produced in
tain annually, mostly in
nt.

In summer, the fruiting plants
i be seen climbing the rect-
gular wire frames in fields by
roadside. Until the middle of
20th century thousands of
iilies from London's East End
uld move to the Kentish hop
ds every autumn for working
idays harvesting the crop and
nping in barns. That tradition
faded, because now the
os are picked by machine.

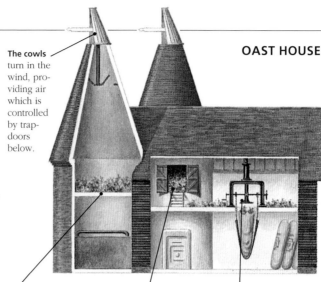

OAST HOUSE

The cowls turn in the wind, providing air which is controlled by trapdoors below.

Hops are dried above a fan which blows hot air from the underlying radiators.

After drying, the hops are cooled and stored.

A press packs the hops into bags, ready for the breweries.

Plums *are often served stewed, in pies, or dried into prunes. The Victoria plum (left) is the classic English dessert plum and is eaten raw. The Purple plum is also popular.*

Greengages *are green plums. They have a distinctive taste and can be made into jam.*

Cherries *are the sweetest of Kent's fruit: two popular varieties are Stella (top) and Duke.*

Bramley Seedling *is one of the best cooking apples, but it is not sweet enough to eat raw.*

Pears, *such as the William (left), should be eaten at the height of ripeness. The Conference keeps better.*

AUGUST	SEPTEMBER	OCTOBER	NOVEMBER

...ants *are ...ng the most assertively ...oured fruit and are ...d in desserts and jams.*

...eaches, *grown in China 4,000 years ago, came to ...land in the 19th century.*

Dessert apples, *such as Cox's Orange Pippin (right), are some of England's best-loved fruits. The newer Discovery is easier to grow.*

The Kentish cob, *a variety of hazelnut, is undergoing a revival, having been eclipsed by European imports. Unlike many nuts, it is best picked fresh from the tree.*

Vineyards *are now a familiar sight in Kent (as well as Sussex and Hampshire). Most of the wine produced, such as Lamberhurst, is white.*

Houses of Historical Figures

Visiting the homes of artists, writers, politicians and royalty is a rewarding way of gaining an insight into their private lives. Southeast England, near London, boasts many historic houses that have been preserved as they were when their illustrious occupants were alive. All these houses, from large mansions such as Lord Mountbatten's Broadlands to the more modest dwellings, like Jane Austen's House, contain exhibits relating to the life of the famous people who lived there.

Florence Nightingale
(1820–1910), the "Lady with the Lamp", was a nurse during the Crimean War (see p56). She stayed at Claydon with her sister, Lady Verney.

Nancy Astor *(1879–1964) was the first woman to sit in Parliament in 1919. She lived at Cliveden until her death and made it famous for political hospitality.*

Claydon House, Winslow, nr Milton Keynes

The Duke of Wellington *(1769–1852) was given this house by the nation in 1817, in gratitude for leading the British to victory at Waterloo (see p55).*

THAMES VALLEY
(see pp216–17)

Cliveden House, nr Maidenhead

Stratfield Saye, Basingstoke, nr Windsor

Jane Austen *(1775–1817) wrote three of her novels, including* Emma, *and revised the others at this house where she lived for eight years until shortly before her death (see p172).*

Jane Austen's House, Chawton, nr Winchester

Broadlands, nr Southampton

Lord Mountbatten (1900–79), a British naval commander and statesman, was the last Viceroy of India in 1947. He lived here all his married life and remodelled the original house considerably.

Osborne House, Isle of Wight

Queen Victoria (1819–1901) and her husband, Prince Albert, built Osborne House *(see p168)* in 1855 as a seaside retreat for their family because they never truly warmed to the Royal Pavilion in Brighton.

BLOOMSBURY GROUP

A circle of avant-garde artists, designers and writers, many of them friends as students, began to meet at a house in Bloomsbury, London, in 1904 and soon gained a reputation for their Bohemian lifestyle. When Duncan Grant and Vanessa Bell moved to Charleston in 1916 *(see p180)*, it became a Sussex outpost of the celebrated group. Many of the prominent figures associated with the circle, such as Virginia Woolf, EM Forster, Vita Sackville-West and JM Keynes paid visits here. The Bloomsbury Group was also known for the Omega Workshops, which made innovative ceramics, furniture and textiles.

Vanessa Bell at Charleston by Duncan Grant (1885–1978)

**Gainsborough's House,
Sudbury, nr Ipswich**

EAST ANGLIA
(see pp190–215)

Thomas Gainsborough *(1727–88), one of Britain's greatest painters, was born in this house* (see p194). *He was best known for his portraits, such as this one of* Mr and Mrs Andrews.

Charles Darwin *(1809–82), who developed the theory that man and apes have a common ancestor, wrote his most famous book,* On the Origin of Species, *at the house where he lived.*

**Down House, Downe,
nr Sevenoaks**

**THE DOWNS AND
CHANNEL COAST**
(see pp164–89)

**Bleak House,
Broadstairs,
nr Margate**

Charles Dickens (1812–70), the prolific and popular Victorian novelist *(see p189),* had many connections with Kent. He took holidays at Bleak House, later named after his famous novel.

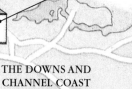

**Chartwell,
Westerham,
nr Sevenoaks**

**Batemans, Burwash,
nr Hastings**

Winston Churchill
(1874–1965), Britain's inspirational Prime Minister in World War II *(see p189),* lived here for 40 years until his death. He relaxed by rebuilding parts of the house.

**Charleston,
Lewes**

Vanessa Bell (1879–1961), artist and member of the Bloomsbury Group, lived here until her death in 1961. The 18th-century farmhouse reflects her decorative ideas and is filled with murals, paintings and painted furniture *(see p180).*

Rudyard Kipling
(1865–1936), the poet and novelist, was born in India, but lived here for 34 years until his death. His most famous works include Kim, *the two* Jungle Books *and the* Just So Stories.

THE DOWNS AND CHANNEL COAST

HAMPSHIRE · SURREY · EAST SUSSEX · WEST SUSSEX · KENT

When settlers, invaders and missionaries came from Europe, the southeast coast was their first landfall. The wooded chalk ridges and lower-lying weald beyond them made an ideal base for settlement and proved to be productive farmland.

The Romans were the first to build major fortifications along the Channel Coast to discourage potential attackers from the European mainland. The remains of many of these can be seen today, and some, like Portchester Castle just outside Portsmouth, were incorporated into more substantial defences in later centuries. There also exists substantial evidence of Roman domestic buildings, such as Fishbourne Palace, in coastal areas and further inland.

The magnificence of cathedrals such as Canterbury and Winchester bear witness to their role as important bases of the medieval church, then nearly as powerful as the state. Many Kent and Sussex ports grew prosperous on trade with the Continent – as did the hundreds of smugglers who operated from them. From Tudor times on, monarchs, noblemen and courtiers acquired estates and built manor houses in the countryside between London and the coast, appreciating the area's moderate climate and proximity to the capital. Many of these survive and are popular attractions for visitors. Today the southeast corner of England is its most prosperous and populous region. Parts of Surrey and Kent, up to 20 miles (32 km) from the capital, are known as the Stockbroker Belt: the area has many large, luxurious villas belonging to wealthy people prominent in business and the professions, attracted by the same virtues that appealed to the Tudor gentry.

The fertile area of Kent has long been known as the Garden of England, and despite the incursion of bricks and mortar, it is still a leading area for growing fruit *(see pp160–1)*, being in a prime position for the metropolitan market nearby.

Aerial view of the medieval and moated Leeds Castle

◁ A lush covering of bluebells in the deciduous woodlands of Kent

Exploring the Downs and Channel Coast

The North and South Downs, separated by the lower-lying Weald are ideal walking country as well as being the site of many stately homes. From Tudor times, wealthy, London-based merchants and courtiers built their country residences in Kent, a day's ride from the capital, and many are open to the public. On the coast are the remains of sturdy castles put up to deter invaders from across the Channel. Today, though, the seashore is largely devoted to pleasure. Some of Britain's earliest beach resorts were developed along this coast, and sea bathing is said to have been invented in Brighton.

View of Brighton Pier from the promenade

Oast houses at Chiddingstone near Royal Tunbridge Wells

0 kilometres 20

0 miles 10

GETTING AROUND

The area is well served, with a network of motorways and A roads from London to the major towns. The A259 is a scenic coast road which offers fine views over the English Channel. Bus and rail transport is also good, with a number of coach companies providing regular tours to the major sites. An InterCity train service runs to all the major towns.

SIGHTS AT A GLANCE

Arundel **8**
Beaulieu **2**
Bodiam Castle **18**
Brighton pp174–9 **13**
Canterbury pp186–7 **23**
Chichester **7**
Dover **21**
The Downs **16**
Eastbourne **15**
Guildford **10**
Hampton Court p173 **11**
Hastings **17**
Hever Castle **27**
Isle of Wight **1**

Knole **26**
Leeds Castle **24**
Lewes **14**
Margate **22**
Rochester **25**
New Forest **3**
Petworth House **9**
Portsmouth **5**
Romney Marsh **20**
Royal Tunbridge Wells **28**
Rye pp184–5 **19**
Southampton **4**
Steyning **12**
Winchester pp170–71 **6**

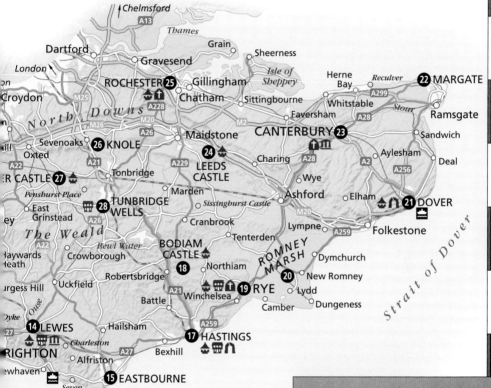

KEY

— Motorway

— Major road

— Secondary road

— Minor road

— Scenic route

— Main railway

— Minor railway

▲ Summit

Canterbury Cathedral's spire, dominating the skyline

The Victorian Osborne House, Isle of Wight

Isle of Wight ❶

Isle of Wight. 🏛 138,000.
🚢 from Lymington, Southampton,
Portsmouth. ℹ Western Esplanade,
Brading Road, Ryde (01983 813813).
www.islandbreaks.co.uk

A visit to **Osborne House**,
the favoured seaside retreat
of Queen Victoria and Prince
Albert *(see p160),* is alone
worth the ferry ride from the
mainland. Furnished much
as they left it, the house
provides a marvellous insight
into royal life and is dotted
with family mementoes.

The **Swiss Cottage** was
built for the royal children to
play in. It is now a museum
attached to Osborne House.
Adjacent to it you can see the
bathing machine used by the
queen to preserve her modesty
while taking her to the edge
of the sea *(see p369).*

The other main sight on the
island is **Carisbrooke Castle**,
built in the 11th century. A
walk on its outer wall and the
climb to the top of its keep
provides spectacular views. It
was here that Charles I *(see
pp52–3)* was held prisoner in
1647; an attempt to escape
was foiled when he got stuck
between the bars of a window.

The island is a base for
ocean sailing, especially during
Cowes Week *(see p67).* The
scenic highlight is the
Needles – three towers of
rock jutting out of the sea at
the island's western end. This
is only a short walk from

Alum Bay, famous for its
multi-coloured cliffs and sand.

🏛 **Osborne House**
(EH) East Cowes. **Tel** 01983 200022.
◯ daily (Nov–Mar: Wed–Sun for 🎫
only, phone for details). 🎫 ♿
limited. 🍴 📷 (also 📷 in Swiss
Cottage Apr–Oct only). 🎁

♟ **Carisbrooke Castle**
Newport. **Tel** 01983 522107.
◯ daily. ● 1 Jan, 24–26 Dec. 🎫
♿ limited. 🎫 📷 in summer. 🎁

Beaulieu ❷

Brockenhurst, Hampshire. **Tel** 01590
612345. 🚆 Brockenhurst then taxi.
◯ daily. ● 25 Dec. 🎁 🎫 ♿ 🎫
by appt. 📷 **www**.beaulieu.co.uk

Palace House, once the gatehouse of Beaulieu Abbey,
has been the home of Lord
Montagu's family since 1538. It
now contains the finest collection of vintage cars in the
country at the **National Motor
Museum**, along with boats
used in the James Bond films.

There is also an exhibition
of monastic life in the ruined
ancient **abbey**, founded in

1204 by King John *(see p48)*
for Cistercian monks. The
original refectory now serves
as the parish church.

Environs: Just south is the
maritime museum at **Buckler's
Hard**, telling the story of shipbuilding in the 18th century.
The yard employed 4,000
men at its peak but declined
when steel began to be used.
Boat trips are available.

🏛 **Buckler's Hard**
Beaulieu. **Tel** 01590 614645. ◯
daily. ● 25 Dec. 🎫 ♿ ltd. 📷 🎁

New Forest ❸

Hampshire. 🚆 Brockenhurst.
Lymington then bus. ℹ main car
park, Lyndhurst (023 8028 2269).
◯ 10am–5pm daily. ● 1 Jan, 24–
26 Dec. **www**.thenewforest.co.uk

This unique expanse of heath
and woodland is, at 145 sq
miles (375 sq km), the largest
area of unenclosed land in
southern Britain.

Despite its name, this is
one of the few primeval oak
woods in England. It was the
popular hunting ground of
Norman kings, and in 1100
William II was fatally wounded here in a hunting accident.

Today it is enjoyed by up to
seven million visitors a year,
who share it with the New Forest ponies, unique to the area,
and over 1,500 fallow deer.

Southampton ❹

Hampshire. 🏛 220,000. ✈ 🚆 🚌
🚢 ℹ 9 Civic Centre Road (023 8083
3333). **www**.visit-southampton.co.uk

For centuries this has been
a flourishing port. The
Mayflower sailed from here
to America in 1620 with the

A 1909 Rolls-Royce Silver Ghost at Beaulieu's National Motor Museum

Pilgrim Fathers, as did the *Titanic* on its maiden and ultimately tragic voyage in 1912.

The **Maritime Museum** has exhibits about both these ships, along with displays on the huge romantic liners that sailed from the port in the first half of the 20th century.

There is a walk around the remains of the medieval city wall. At the head of the High Street stands the old city gate, **Bargate**, the most elaborate gate to survive in England. It still has its 13th-century drum towers and is decorated with intricate, 17th-century armorial carvings. **God's**

The luxurious liner the *Titanic*, which sank in 1912

House Tower Museum of Archaeology consists of a 13th-century gatehouse and 15th-century gallery and tower, and includes displays from the Roman to medieval periods.

🏛 **Maritime Museum**
Town Quay Rd. **Tel** 023 8022 3941.
◯ 10am–4pm Tue–Sat, 1–4pm Sun. ● 1 Jan, 25, 26 Dec, some public hols. ♿ limited. 📷 ⬜

🏛 **God's House Tower Museum**
Winkle St. **Tel** 023 8063 5904.
◯ 10am–4pm Tue–Sat, 1–4pm Sun. ♿ foyer & shop only. ⬜

Portsmouth ❺

Hampshire. 👥 190,000. ✈ 🚉 ℹ
The Hard (023 9282 6722). ⛴ Thu–Sat. **www**.visitportsmouth.co.uk

Once a vital naval port, Portsmouth is today a quiet town but fascinating for those interested in English naval history.

Under the banner of **Portsmouth Historic Dockyard**, the city's historic dockyard is the hub of Portsmouth's most important sights. Among these is the hull of the **Mary Rose**, the favourite of Henry VIII *(see p50)*, which capsized on its maiden voyage as it left to fight the French in 1545. It was recovered from the sea bed in 1982 along with thousands of 16th-century objects now on display nearby, giving an absorbing insight into life at sea in Tudor times.

Alongside it is **HMS Victory**, the English flagship on which Admiral Nelson was killed at Trafalgar *(see p31)* and now restored to its former glory. You can also visit the **Royal Naval Museum** which deals with naval history from the 16th century to the Falklands War, the 19th-century **HMS Warrior,** and galleries telling the story of Nelson.

Portsmouth's other military memorial is the **D-Day Museum**. This is centred on the *Overlord Embroidery*, a masterpiece of needlework commissioned in 1968 from the Royal School of Needlework, depicting the World War II Allied landing in Normandy in 1944.

The figurehead on the bow of HMS *Victory* at Portsmouth

Portchester Castle, on the north edge of the harbour, was fortified in the third century and is the best example of Roman sea defences in northern Europe. The Normans later used the Roman walls to enclose a castle – only the keep survives – and a church. Henry V used the castle as a garrison before the Battle of Agincourt *(see p49)*. In the 18th–19th centuries it was a prisoner-of-war camp.

Among less warlike attractions is the **Charles Dickens Museum** *(see p189)*, the house where the author was born in 1812.

The striking **Spinnaker Tower** adds an innovative touch to Portsmouth's skyline. Rising to 170 m (558 ft), the views over the harbour and beyond are quite magnificent.

🏛 **Portsmouth Historic Dockyard**
The Hard. **Tel** 023 9272 8060.
◯ daily (last adm: 4pm). ● 24–26 Dec. 📷 ♿ 🍴 ⬜

🏛 **D-Day Museum**
Museum Rd. **Tel** 023 9282 7261.
◯ daily. ● 24–26 Dec. 📷 ♿ ⬜ ⬜

🏰 **Portchester Castle**
Castle St, Porchester. **Tel** 023 9237 8291. ◯ daily. ● 1 Jan, 24–26 Dec. 📷 📷 🏰

🏛 **Charles Dickens Museum**
393 Old Commercial Rd. **Tel** 023 9282 7261. ◯ May–Sep: daily; 7 Feb (Dickens's birthday). 📷 ⬜ 🍴

🌿 **Spinnaker Tower**
Gunwharf Quays. **Tel** 023 9285 7520. ◯ daily. 📷 ⬜ ⬜

A wild pony and her foal roaming freely in the New Forest

Winchester ❻

Hampshire. 36,000.
Guildhall, High St (01962 840500). Wed–Sat.
www.visitwinchester.co.uk

Capital of the ancient kingdom of Wessex, the city of Winchester was also the headquarters of the Anglo-Saxon kings until the Norman Conquest *(see p47)*.

William the Conqueror built one of his first English castles here. The only surviving part of the castle is the **Great Hall**, erected in 1235 to replace the original. It is now home to the legendary Round Table. The story behind the table is a mix of history and myth. King Arthur *(see p285)* had it shaped so no knight could claim precedence. It was said to have been built by the wizard Merlin but was actually made in the 13th century.

The 13th-century Round Table, Great Hall, Winchester

The **Westgate Museum** is one of the two surviving 12th-century gatehouses in the city wall. The room (once a prison) above the gate has a 16th-century painted ceiling. It was moved here from Winchester College, England's oldest fee-paying, or "public" school. Winchester has been an ecclesiastical centre for many centuries. **Wolvesey Castle** (built around 1110) was the home of the **cathedral's** bishops after the Conquest. The **Hospital of St Cross** is an almshouse built in 1446.

STUDY TO BE QUIET

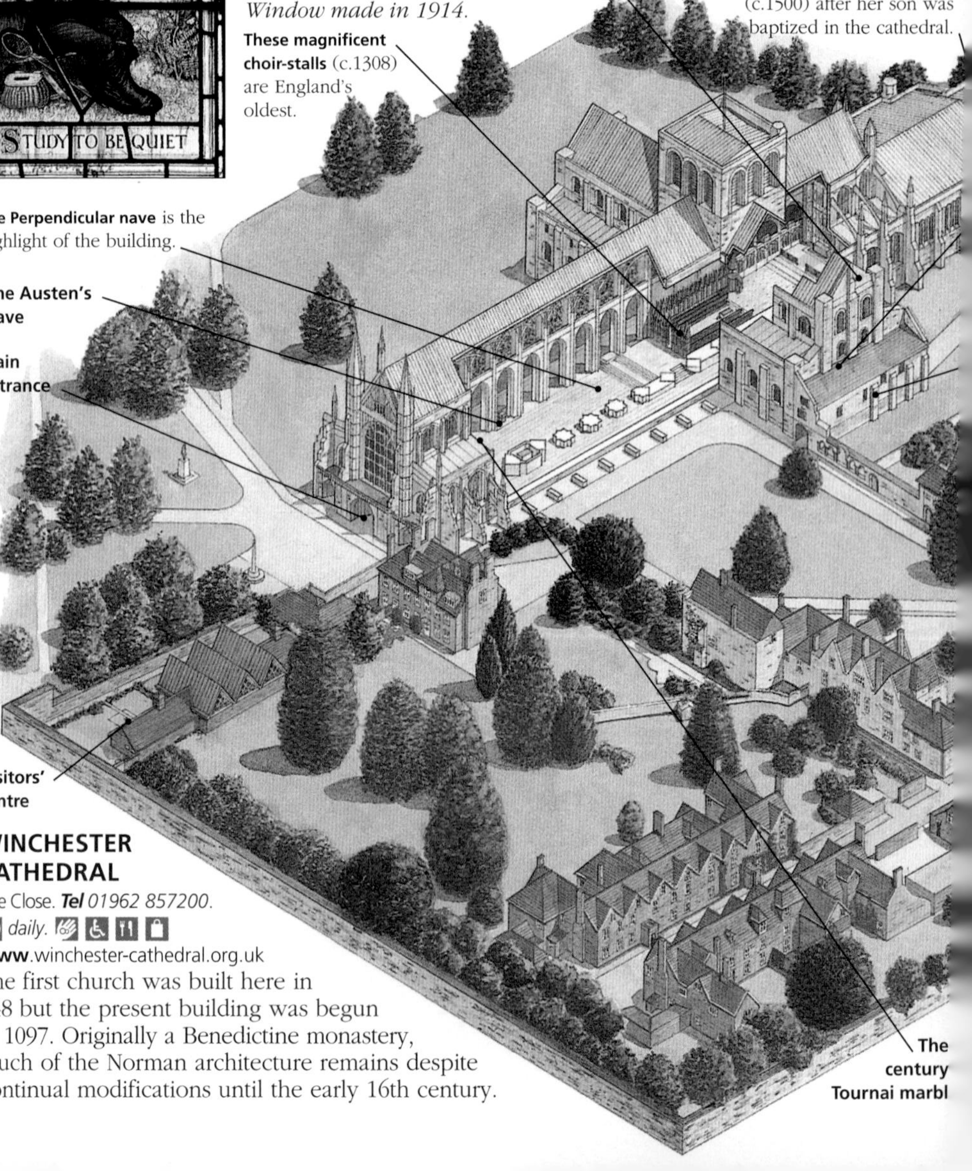
Author Izaac Walton *(1593–1683) is depicted in the stained glass Anglers' Window made in 1914.*
These magnificent choir-stalls (c.1308) are England's oldest.
The Lady Chapel was rebuilt by Elizabeth of York (c.1500) after her son was baptized in the cathedral.
The Perpendicular nave is the highlight of the building.
Jane Austen's grave
Main entrance
Visitors' centre
The century Tournai marbl

WINCHESTER CATHEDRAL

The Close. ***Tel*** *01962 857200.*
daily.
www.winchester-cathedral.org.uk

The first church was built here in 648 but the present building was begun in 1097. Originally a Benedictine monastery, much of the Norman architecture remains despite continual modifications until the early 16th century.

Weary strangers may claim the "Wayfarer's Dole" a horn (cup) of ale and bread, given out since medieval times.

Great Hall & Visitor Centre
Castle Ave. **Tel** 01962 846476.
☐ daily. ● 25, 26 Dec. ♿

Westgate Museum
High St. **Tel** 01962 869864.
☐ Feb, Mar: Tue–Sun; Apr–Oct: Mon–Sun. ☐

Hospital of St Cross
St Cross Rd. **Tel** 01962 851375.
☐ Mon–Sat. ● Good Fri, 25 Dec.
♿ www.stcrosshospital.co.uk

The Library
has over 4,000 books. This "B" from Psalm 1 is found in the Winchester Bible, an exquisite work of 12th-century illumination.

The Norman chapter house ceased to be used in 1580. Only the Norman arches survive.

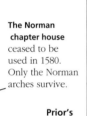

Prior's Hall

The Close originally contained the domestic buildings for the monks of the Priory of St Swithun – the name before it became Winchester Cathedral. Most of the buildings, such as the refectory and cloisters, were destroyed during the Dissolution of the Monasteries (*see p50*).

Chichester 7

West Sussex. 🏘 26,000. ⇄ 🚌 ℹ
29A South St (01243 775888). ⛴
Wed, Sat. **www**.visitchichester.org

This wonderfully preserved market town, with an elaborate early 16th-century market cross at its centre, is dominated by its **cathedral**, consecrated in 1108. The exterior is a lovely mix of greenish limestone and Caen stone and its graceful spire, said to be the only English cathedral spire visible from the sea, dominates the town. The cathedral still contains much of interest, including a unique detached bell tower dating from 1436.

There are two carved stone panels in the choir, dating from 1140. Modern works include paintings by Graham Sutherland (1903–80), and a stained-glass window by Marc Chagall (1887–1985).

Environs: Just west at Bosham is the Saxon **Holy Trinity Church**, thought to have been used by King Canute (*see p46*). Myth has it that this was where Canute failed to stop the incoming tide and so proved to his courtiers that his powers had limits. The church appears in the *Bayeux Tapestry*, held in France, because Harold heard mass here in 1064 before he was shipwrecked off Normandy and then rescued by William the Conqueror (*see p47*).

The refurbished **Fishbourne Roman Palace** (*see p45*), between Bosham and Chichester, is the largest Roman villa in Britain. It covers 3 ha (7 acres) and was discovered in 1960 by a workman. Constructed from AD 75, it

Chagall's stained-glass window (1978), Chichester Cathedral

was destroyed by fire in 285. The north wing has some of the finest mosaics in Britain, including one of Cupid.

To the north is the 18th-century **Goodwood House**. Its magnificent art collection features works by Canaletto (1697–1768) and Stubbs (1724–1806). This impressive house, home to the Earl of March, has a racecourse on the Downs.

🛈 Chichester Cathedral
West St. **Tel** 01243 782595. ☐
daily. ● for Mass. ♿ 🎧 🛍 📷

🏛 Fishbourne Roman Palace
Fishbourne. **Tel** 01243 785859. ☐
Feb–mid-Dec: daily; mid-Dec–Jan (café closed): Sat, Sun. ♿
📷 www.sussexpast.co.uk

Goodwood House
Goodwood. **Tel** 01243 755048. ℹ
01243 755040. ☐ Apr–Sep: Sun–Mon (pm); Aug: Sun–Thu (pm). ●
special events, last-minute closures.
Always call ahead. ♿ 🛍 📷

WILLIAM WALKER

At the beginning of the 20th century, the cathedral's east end seemed certain to collapse unless its foundations were underpinned. But because the water table lies only just below the surface, the work had to be done under water. From 1906 to 1911, Walker, a deep-sea diver, worked six hours a day laying sacks of cement beneath the unsteady walls until the building was safe.

William Walker in his diving suit

The dominating position of Arundel Castle, West Sussex

Arundel Castle ❽

Arundel, West Sussex. *Tel* 01903 882173. ⚡ Arundel. ◯ Apr–Oct: 10am–4pm Tue–Sun. ● public hols. 🖼 🎫 by arrangement. 🍴 💻 📷 www.arundelcastle.org

Dominating the small river-side town below, this vast, grey hill-top castle, surrounded by castellated walls, was first built by the Normans.

During the 16th century it was acquired by the powerful Dukes of Norfolk, the country's senior Roman Catholic family, whose descendants still live here. They rebuilt it after the original was virtually destroyed by Parliamentarians in 1643 *(see p52)*, and restored it again in the 19th century.

In the castle grounds is the parish church of **St Nicholas**. The small Catholic Fitzalan chapel (c.1380) was built into its east end by the castle's first owners, the Fitzalans, and can only be entered from the grounds.

Petworth House ❾

(NT) Petworth, West Sussex. *Tel* 01798 343929. ⚡ Pulborough then bus. **House** ◯ Mar–Nov: Sat–Wed. Call for Christmas opening times. **Park** ◯ daily. 🖼 🅰 limited. 🍴 📷 www.nationaltrust.org.uk/petworth

This late 17th-century house was immortalized in a series of famous views by the painter J M W Turner *(see p91)*. Some of his best paintings are on display here and are part of Petworth's outstanding art

collection, which also includes works by Titian (1488–1576), Van Dyck (1599–1641) and Gainsborough *(see p163)*. Also extremely well represented is ancient Roman and Greek sculpture, such as the 4th-century BC *Leconfield Aphrodite*, widely thought to be by Praxiteles.

The Carved Room is decorated with intricately carved wood panels of birds, flowers and musical instruments, by Grinling Gibbons (1648–1721).

The large deer park includes some of the earliest work of Capability Brown *(see p26)*.

The Restoration clock on the Tudor Guildhall, Guildford

Guildford ❿

Surrey. 🏠 63,000. ⚡ 🚌 ℹ 14 Tunsgate (01483 444333). 🛒 Fri, Sat. www.visitguildford.com

The county town of Surrey, settled since Saxon times, incorporates the remains of a small refurbished Norman

castle. The high street is lined with Tudor buildings, such as the impressive **Guildhall**, and the huge modern red-brick cathedral, completed in 1954, dominates the town's skyline.

Environs: Guildford stands on the end of the North Downs, a range of chalk hills that are popular for walking *(see p37)*. The area also has two famous beauty spots: **Leith Hill** – the highest point in southeast England – and **Box Hill**. The view from the latter is well worth the short, gentle climb from West Humble.

To the north of Guildford is **Wisley** with 97 hectares (240 acres) of beautiful gardens. To the south of the town is **Clandon Park**, an 18th-century house with a sumptuous interior. Its Marble Hall boasts an intricate Baroque ceiling.

Southwest is Chawton, where **Jane Austen's House** *(see p162)* is located. This red-brick house is where Austen wrote most of her witty novels, such as *Emma*. Celebratory events until July 2010 will mark the 200th anniversary of Austen's arrival at the house.

🏛 **Wisley**
(RHS) Off A3. *Tel* 0845 260 9000. ◯ daily. 🖼 🅰 💻 🍴 📷

🏛 **Clandon Park**
(NT) West Clandon, Surrey. *Tel* 01483 222482. ◯ Mar–Oct: Tue–Thu, Sun; public hols. 🖼 🅰 limited. 🍴 📷

🏛 **Jane Austen's House**
Alton, Hants. *Tel* 01420 83262. ◯ Jan–Feb: Sat & Sun; Mar–Dec: daily. ● 25 & 26 Dec. 🖼 🅰 limited. 📷

Hampton Court ⓫

East Molesey, Surrey. 📞 0844 482 7777. 🚃 *Hampton Court.* ◯ *daily.* ⬤ *24–26 Dec.* 🎫 ♿ 📷 🍴 🏪
www.hrp.org.uk

The powerful chief minister and Archbishop of York to Henry VIII *(see pp50–51)*, Cardinal Wolsey, leased a small manor house in 1514 and transformed it into a magnificent country residence. In 1528, to retain royal favour, Wolsey gave it to the king. After the royal takeover, Hampton Court was extended twice, first by Henry himself and in the 1690s by William and Mary, who used Christopher Wren *(see p114)* as the architect. From the outside the palace is a harmonious blend of Tudor and English Baroque; inside there is a striking contrast between Wren's Classical royal rooms,

Ceiling decoration, Hampton Court

which include the King's Apartments, and Tudor architecture, such as the Great Hall. Many of the state apartments are decorated with paintings and furnishings from the Royal Collection. The Baroque gardens, with their radiating avenues of majestic limes, collections of rare plants and formal plant beds, have been painstakingly restored.

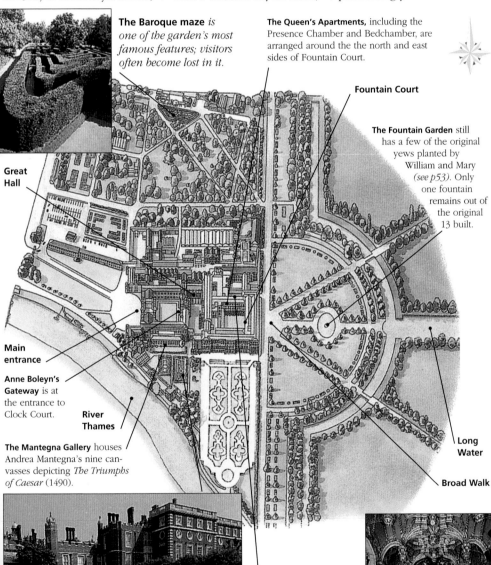

The Baroque maze *is one of the garden's most famous features; visitors often become lost in it.*

The Queen's Apartments, including the Presence Chamber and Bedchamber, are arranged around the the north and east sides of Fountain Court.

Fountain Court

The Fountain Garden still has a few of the original yews planted by William and Mary *(see p53).* Only one fountain remains out of the original 13 built.

Great Hall

Main entrance

Anne Boleyn's Gateway is at the entrance to Clock Court.

River Thames

The Mantegna Gallery houses Andrea Mantegna's nine canvasses depicting *The Triumphs of Caesar* (1490).

Long Water

Broad Walk

The Pond Garden, *a sunken water garden, was part of Henry VIII's elaborate designs. The small pond in the middle contains a single-jet fountain.*

The Tudor Chapel Royal *was completed by Henry VIII. But the superb woodwork, including the massive reredos by Grinling Gibbons, all date from a major refurbishment by Queen Anne (c.1711).*

Steyning ⓬

West Sussex. *5,000* *9 The Causeway, Horsham (01403 211661).*

This lovely little town in the lee of the Downs is packed with timber-framed houses from the Tudor period and earlier, with some built of flint and others in sandstone.

In Saxon times, Steyning was an important port and shipbuilding centre on the River Adur: King Ethelwulf, father of King Alfred *(see p47)*, was buried here in 858; his body was later moved to Winchester. The *Domesday Book (see p48)* records that Steyning had 123 houses, making it one of the largest towns in the south. The 12th-century church is spacious and splendid, evidence of the area's ancient prosperity; the tower, of chequered stone and flint, was added around 1600.

In the 14th century the river silted up and changed course away from the town, putting an end to its days as a port. Later it became an important coaching stop on the south coast road: the **Chequer Inn** recalls this prosperous period, with its unusual 18th-century flint and stone façade.

Environs: The remains of a **Norman castle** can be visited at Bramber, east of Steyning. This small, pretty village also contains the timber-framed **St Mary's House** (1470). It has fine panelled rooms, including the Elizabethan Painted Room, and one of the oldest trees in the country, a *Ginkgo biloba*.

Chanctonbury Ring and **Cissbury Ring**, on the hills west of Steyning, were Iron Age forts and the latter has the remains of a Neolithic flint mine. Worthing is the resort where Oscar Wilde (1854–1900) wrote *The Importance of Being Earnest*.

St Mary's House
Bramber. ***Tel*** *01903 816205.*
May–Sep: Sun, Thu (pm), public hols.

Street-by-Street: Brighton ⓭

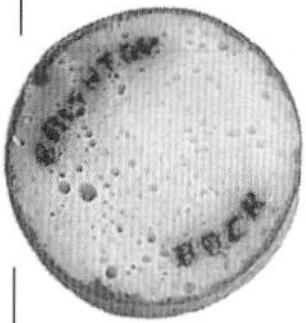

A stick of Brighton rock

As the nearest south coast resort to London, Brighton is perennially popular, but has always been more refined than its boisterous neighbours further east, such as Margate *(see p183)* and Southend. The spirit of the Prince Regent *(see p179)* lives on, not only in the magnificence of his Royal Pavilion, but in the city's reputation as a venue for adulterous weekends in discreet hotels. Brighton has always attracted actors and artists – Laurence Olivier made his final home here.

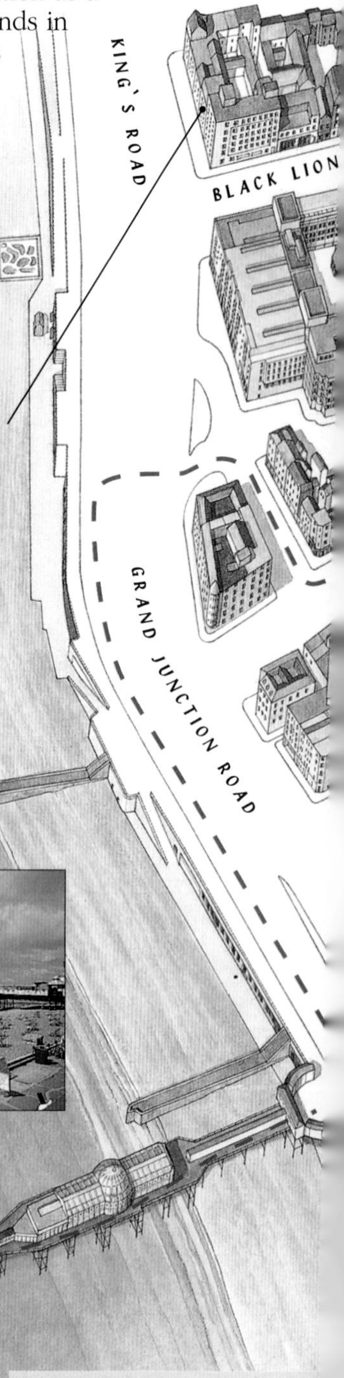
KING'S ROAD
BLACK LION
GRAND JUNCTION ROAD

Old Ship Hotel
Built in 1559, it was later bought by Nicholas Tettersells, with the money given to him by Charles II as a reward for taking him to France during the Civil War (see p52).

★ Brighton Pier
Built in 1899, this typical late-Victorian pier now caters for today's visitors with amusement arcades.

KEY

— — — Suggested route

STAR SIGHTS

★ Brighton Pier

★ Royal Pavilion

★ Royal Pavilion
The Prince Regent's fantastic Oriental palace helped turn Brighton into a fashionable resort, and is today its principal attraction.

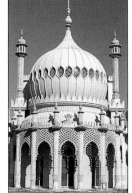

VISITORS' CHECKLIST

East Sussex. 249,000. Brighton Central. Pool Valley. Royal Pavilion shop (0906 7112255). Mon–Sat. International Arts Festival: May.

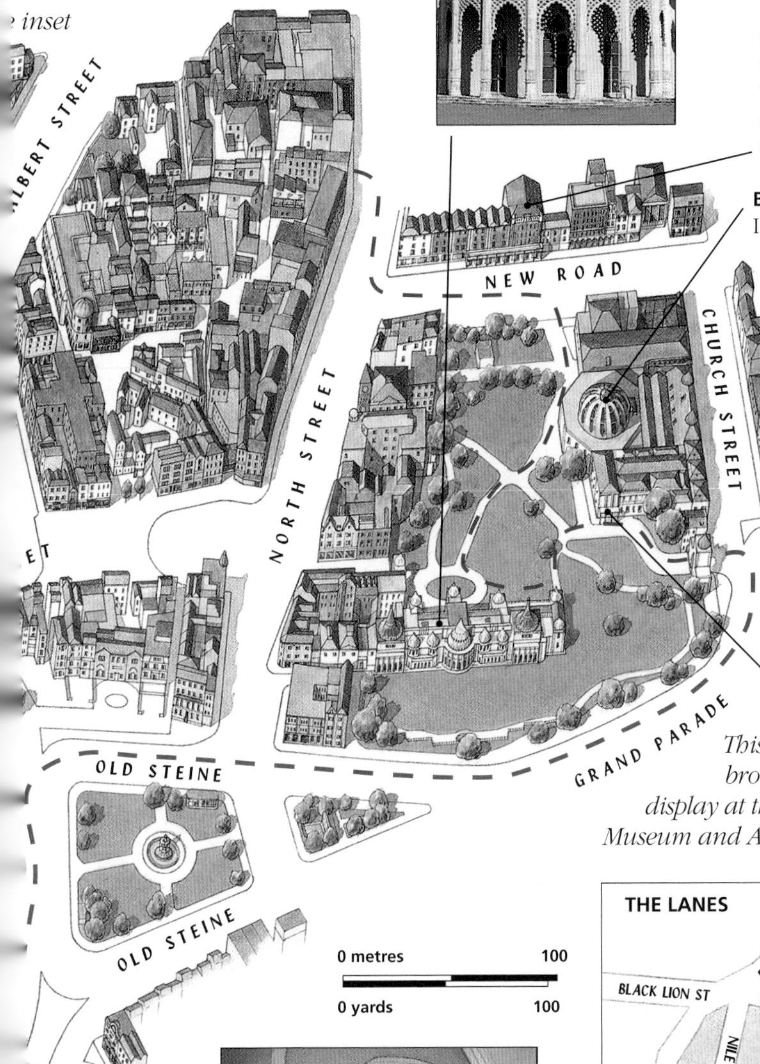

Many new plays are first staged in the charming Theatre Royal, established in 1807, before they move to the West End of London.

Brighton Dome, an Indian-style building opposite the Royal Pavilion and once George IV's stables, is now a major arts venue.

NEW ROAD

ALBERT STREET

NORTH STREET

CHURCH STREET

Art Deco
This 1920s Art Deco bronze lamp is on display at the Brighton Museum and Art Gallery.

GRAND PARADE

OLD STEINE

OLD STEINE

0 metres 100

0 yards 100

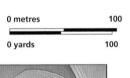

THE LANES

PRINCE ALBERT ST

BLACK LION ST

NILE ST

UNION ST

MEETING HOUSE LA

MEETING HOUSE LA

MEETING HOUSE LA

BRIGHTON PL

MARKET ST

BARTHOLOMEWS

REGENT ARCADE

NORTH ST

EAST ST

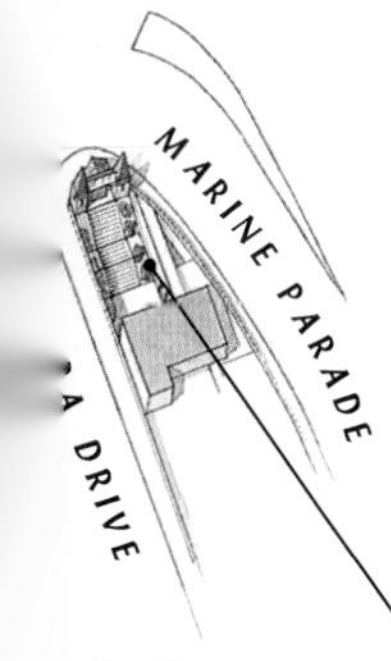

MARINE PARADE

A DRIVE

Eastbourne

Sea Life Centre
Built in 1872 as a menagerie, it became an aquarium in 1929. Don't miss the sharks and other British marine life.

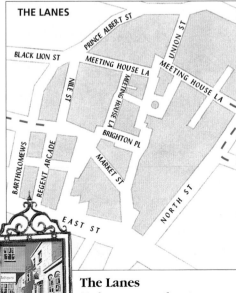

The Lanes
Today a maze of antique and independent shops, the Lanes were the original streets of the village of Brighthelmstone.

THE LANES

Brighton: Royal Pavilion

As sea bathing became fashionable in the mid-18th century, Brighton was transformed into England's first seaside resort. Its gaiety soon appealed to the rakish Prince of Wales, who became George IV in 1820. When, in 1785, he secretly married Mrs Fitzherbert, it was here that they conducted their liaison. He moved to a farmhouse near the shore and had it enlarged by Henry Holland *(see p28)*. As his parties grew more lavish, George needed a suitably extravagant setting for them, and in 1815 he employed John Nash *(see p105)* to transform the house into a lavish Oriental palace. Completed in 1823, the exterior has remained largely unaltered. Queen Victoria sold the Pavilion to the town of Brighton in 1850.

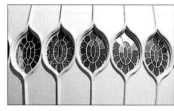

Central Dome
Nash adopted what he called the Hindu Style, as in this delicate tracery on one of the imposing turban domes.

★ Banqueting Room
Fiery dragons feature in many of the interior schemes. This colourful one dominates the centre of the Banqueting Room's extraordinary ceiling, and has a huge crystal chandelier suspended from it.

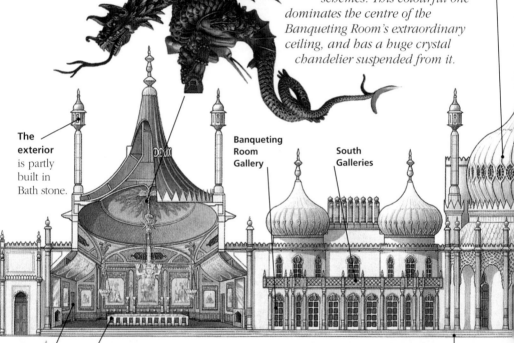

The exterior is partly built in Bath stone.

Banqueting Room Gallery

South Galleries

The banqueting table, which seats 24 people, is laid as for a splendid feast.

The eastern façade of the Pavilion

Standard Lamps
More dragons, along with dolphins and lotus flowers, figure on the Banqueting Room's eight original standard lamps, made of porcelain, ormolu and gilded wood.

STAR SIGHTS

★ Banqueting Room

★ Great Kitchen

★ Great Kitchen
The Prince's epic banquets required a kitchen of huge proportions. The vast ranges and long shelves of gleaming copper pans were used by famous chefs of the day.

◁ **Front façade of George IV's extravagant Royal Pavilion, Brighton**

Saloon

The gilded wall decorations were designed on Indian themes, but the Chinese wallpaper harks back to an earlier decorative scheme. The long couch mimics an Egyptian river boat.

VISITORS' CHECKLIST

Old Steine, Brighton. **Tel** 01273 290900. ⬤ Apr–Sep: 9:30am–5:45pm; Oct–Mar: 10am–5:15pm (last adm: 45 mins before closing); daily. ⬤ 25, 26 Dec. ♿ & limited. 🅿 🔊 📷 💻 🛍
www.royalpavilion.org.uk

Long Gallery

Mandarin figures, which can nod their heads, line the pink and blue walls of this 49 m (162 ft) gallery.

Queen Victoria's Bedroom

This reproduction four-poster is on display in the upper floor apartments that were used by Queen Victoria (see pp56–7).

The Music Room, with its crimson and gold murals, was where a 70-piece orchestra played to the Prince's guests.

The domes are made of cast iron.

Music Room Gallery

Yellow Bow Rooms

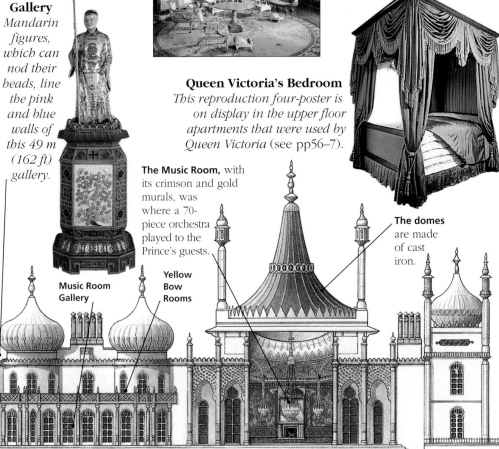

Exit   Entrance

Octagon Hall

Stairs to upper floor

King's Apartments

Shop

eat tchen

Banqueting Room

Banqueting Room Gallery

Saloon

Long Gallery

Music Room Gallery

Music Room

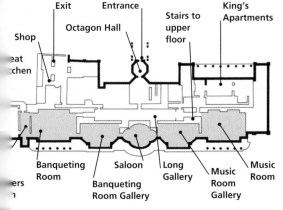

PLAN OF THE ROYAL PAVILION

Both Holland and Nash made additions and changes to the original farmhouse. The upper floor contains bedrooms, such as the Yellow Bow Rooms, which George's brothers used. The shaded areas represent the artwork above.

PRINCE OF WALES AND MRS FITZHERBERT

The Prince of Wales was only 23 years old when he fell in love with Maria Fitzherbert, a 29-year-old Catholic widow, and secretly married her. They lived in the farmhouse together and were the toast of Brighton society until George's official marriage took place to Caroline of Brunswick in 1795. Mrs Fitzherbert moved into a small house nearby.

Upstairs interior of Anne of Cleves House, Lewes

Lewes ⑭

East Sussex. 🏠 *16,000.* 🚂
ℹ️ *187 High St (01273 483448).*
www.lewes.gov.uk

The ancient county town of
Sussex was a vital strategic site
for the Saxons, because of its
high vantage point looking
out over the coastline. William
the Conqueror built a wooden
castle here in 1067 but this
was soon replaced by a large
stone structure whose remains
can be visited today.

In 1264 it was the site of a
critical battle in which Simon
de Montfort and his barons
defeated Henry III, enabling
them to establish the first
English Parliament.

The Tudor **Anne of Cleves
House** is a museum of local
history, although Anne of
Cleves, Henry VIII's fourth
wife, never actually lived here.

On Guy Fawkes Night *(see
p64)* lighted tar barrels are
rolled to the river and various
effigies, including of the Pope
and Guy Fawkes, are burned.
This commemorates the town's
17 Protestant martyrs burnt at
the stake by Mary I *(see p51).*

Environs: Nearby are the 16th-
century **Glynde Place**, a fine
courtyard house, and the charming **Charleston**, home to the
Bloomsbury Group *(see p163).*

🏛 **Anne of Cleves House**
Lewes. **Tel** *01273 474610.* ⭕ *Sun–
Thu (Nov–Feb: Sat, Sun; school half
term: daily).* ● *24–26 Dec.* 🏷 🅿️

🏯 **Glynde Place**
Lewes. **Tel** *01273 858224.* ⭕ *May–
Aug: Wed, Sun, pub hols.* 🏷 🅿️ 🅿️

🏯 **Charleston**
Lewes. **Tel** *01323 811265.* ⭕ *Apr–
Oct: Wed–Sun, Bank Hol Mon.* 🏷
🗂 🅿️ 🅿️ **www**.charleston.org.uk

Eastbourne ⑮

East Sussex. 🏠 *93,000.* 🚂 🚌 ℹ️
Cornfield Rd (0871 663 0031). ⚓
Tue, Sat. **www**.visiteastbourne.com

This Victorian seaside resort
is a popular place for
retirement, as well as a first-
rate centre for touring the
Downs. The South Downs
Way *(see p37)* begins at
Beachy Head, the spectacular
163 m (536 ft) chalk cliff just
on the outskirts of the town.
From here it is a bracing walk
to the cliff top at Birling Gap,
with views to the **Seven
Sisters**, the chalk hills that end
abruptly as they meet the sea.

Environs: To the west of Eastbourne is **Seven Sisters Country
Park**, a 285 ha (700 acre) area
of chalk cliffs and Downland
marsh that is open all year.
The **Park Visitor's Centre** contains information on the local
area, history and geology.

Just north is the pretty
village of **Alfriston**, with an
ancient market cross and a
15th-century inn, **The Star**, in
its quaint main street. Near
the church is the 14th-century
Clergy House that, in 1896,
became the first National
Trust property *(see p29)*. To
the east is the huge prehistoric
chalk carving, the **Long Man
of Wilmington** *(see p221)*.

ℹ️ **Park Visitor's Centre**
Exceat, Seaford. **Tel** *01323 870280.*
⭕ *Apr–Oct: daily; Nov–Mar: Sat,
Sun.* ● *25 Dec.* 🅿️ ♿ 🍴

🏯 **Clergy House**
(NT) Alfriston. **Tel** *01323 870001.*
⭕ *Sat–Mon, Wed, Thu.*
● *Jan.* 🏷 🅿️

The lighthouse (1902) at the foot of Beachy Head, Eastbourne

The meandering River Cuckmere flowing through the South Downs to the beach at Cuckmere Haven

The Downs 🔟

East Sussex. 🚆 🚌 *Eastbourne.* ℹ️ *Cornfield Rd, Eastbourne (0871 663 0031).* **www**.visiteastbourne.com

The North and South Downs are parallel chalk ridges that run from east to west all the way across Kent, Sussex and Surrey, separated by the lower-lying and fertile Kent and Sussex Weald.

The smooth Downland hills are covered with springy turf, kept short by grazing sheep, making an ideal surface for walkers. The hill above the precipitous **Devil's Dyke,** just north of Brighton, offers spectacular views for miles across the Downs. The legend is that the Devil cut the gorge to let in the sea and flood the countryside, but was foiled by divine intervention. The River Cuckmere runs through one of the most picturesque parts of the South Downs.

Located at the highest point of the Downs is **Uppark House.** This neat square building has been meticulously restored to its mid-18th-century appearance after a fire in 1989.

🏛 Uppark House **(NT)** *Petersfield, West Sussex.* **Tel** *01730 825857.* ⬜ *Apr–Oct: Sun–Thu (pm).* 🖼 ♿ 🍴 🛍

Hastings 🔢

East Sussex. 🏘 *83,000.* 🚆 🚌 ℹ️ *Priory Meadow, Queens Square (0845 2741001).* **www**.visithastings.com

This fascinating seaside town was one of the first Cinque Ports *(see p182)* and is still a thriving fishing port. The town is characterized by the unique tall wooden "net shops" on the beach, where for hundreds of years fishermen have stored their nets.

In the 19th century, the area to the west of the Old Town was built up as a seaside resort, which left the narrow, characterful streets of the old

The wooden net shops, on Hastings' shingle beach

fishermen's quarter intact. There are two cliff railways and smugglers' caves displaying where contraband used to be stored *(see p280)*.

Environs: Seven miles (11 km) from Hastings is Battle. The centre square of this small town is dominated by the gatehouse of **Battle Abbey.** William the Conqueror built this on the site of his great victory, reputedly placing the high altar where Harold fell, but the abbey was destroyed in the Dissolution *(see p50)*. There is an evocative walk around the actual battlefield.

🏰 Battle Abbey **(EH)** *High St, Battle.* **Tel** *01424 775705.* ⬜ *daily: Easter–Sep: 10am–6pm; Oct–Easter: 10am–4pm.* ⬛ *1 Jan, 24–26 Dec.* 🖼 ♿ 🛍

BATTLE OF HASTINGS

In 1066, William the Conqueror's *(see p47)* invading army from Normandy landed on the south coast, aiming to take Winchester and London. Hearing that King Harold and his army were camped just inland from Hastings, William confronted them. He won the battle after Harold was mortally wounded by an arrow in his eye. This last successful invasion of England is depicted on the *Bayeux Tapestry* in Normandy, France.

King Harold's death, Bayeux Tapestry

The fairy-tale 14th-century Bodiam Castle surrounded by its moat

Bodiam Castle ⓲

(NT) Nr Robertsbridge, E Sussex. **Tel** 01580 830196. ⇌ Robertsbridge then taxi. ◯ mid-Feb–Oct: daily; Nov–23 Dec: Wed–Sun; 27 Dec–mid-Feb: Sat, Sun. ● 24–26 Dec. ▨ ♿ ltd. ▢ ▯

Surrounded by its wide, glistening moat, this late 14th-century castle is one of the most romantic in England.

It was previously thought to have been built as a defence against French invasion, but is now believed to have been intended as a home for a Sussex knight. The castle saw action during the Civil War *(see p52)*, when it was damaged in an assault by Parliamentary soldiers. They removed the roof to reduce its use as a base for Charles I's troops.

It has been uninhabited since, but its grey stone has proved indestructible. With the exception of the roof, it was restored in 1919 by Lord Curzon who gave it to the nation.

Environs: To the east is **Great Dixter**, a 15th-century manor house restored by Sir Edwin Lutyens in 1910. The late Christopher Lloyd created a magnificent garden with a blend of terraces and borders, and a great nursery, too.

> 🏰 **Great Dixter**
> Northiam, Rye. **Tel** 01797 252878.
> ◯ Apr–Oct: 2–5:30pm Tue–Sun &
> public hols. ▨ ▯
> **www**.greatdixter.co.uk

Rye ⓳

See pp184–5.

Romney Marsh ⓴

Kent. ⇌ Ashford. ✈ Ashford, Hythe. 🛈 Dymchurch Rd, New Romney (01797 369487). ◯ Feb–Dec.

Until Roman times Romney Marsh and its southern neighbour Walland Marsh were entirely covered by the sea at high tide. The Romans drained the Romney section, and Walland Marsh was gradually reclaimed during the Middle Ages. Together they formed a large area of fertile land, particularly suitable for the bulky Romney Marsh sheep bred for the quality and quantity of their wool.

Dungeness, a desolate and lonely spot at the southeastern tip of the area, is dominated by a lighthouse and two nuclear power stations that

COASTAL DEFENCE AND THE CINQUE PORTS

Before the Norman Conquest *(see pp46–7)*, national government was weak and, with threats from Europe, it was important for Saxon kings to keep on good terms with the Channel ports. So, in return for keeping the royal fleet supplied with ships and men, five ports – Hastings, Romney, Hythe, Sandwich and Dover – were granted the right to levy taxes; others were added later. "Cinque" came from the old French word for five. The privileges were revoked during the 17th century. In 1803, in response to the growing threat from France, 74 fixed defences were built along the coast. Only 24 of these Martello towers still exist.

The cliff-top position of Dover Castle

A Martello tower, built as part of the Channel's defences

break up the skyline. It is also the southern terminus of the popular **Romney, Hythe and Dymchurch Light Railway** which was opened in 1927. During the summer this takes passengers 14 miles (23 km) up the coast to Hythe on trains a third the conventional size.

The northern edge of the marsh is crossed by the Royal Military Canal, built to serve both as a defence and supply line in 1804, when it was feared Napoleon was planning an invasion *(see p55)*.

Dover ㉑

Kent. 🏛 *30,000.* ⇄ 🚌 ⛴
🛈 *Old Town Gaol, Biggin St (01304 205108).* 🛍 *Sat.*
www.whitecliffscountry.org.uk

Its proximity to the European mainland makes Dover, with its neighbour Folkestone (the terminal for the Channel Tunnel), the leading port for cross-Channel travel. Its famous white cliffs exert a strong pull on returning travellers.

Dover's strategic position and large natural harbour mean the town has always had an important role to play in the nation's defences.

Built on the original site of an ancient Saxon fortification, **Dover Castle**, superbly positioned on top of the high cliffs, has helped defend the town from 1198, when Henry II first built the keep, right up to World War II, when it was used as the command post for the Dunkirk evacuation. Exhibits in the castle and in the labyrinth of tunnels beneath made by prisoners in the Napoleonic Wars *(see p55)* cover all these periods.

Environs: One of the most significant sites in England's early history is the ruin of **Richborough Roman Fort**. Now a large grassy site two miles (3 km) inland, this was where, in AD 43, Claudius's Roman invaders *(see p44)* made their first landing. For hundreds of years afterwards, Rutupiae, as it was known, was one of the most important ports of entry and military bases in the country.

⛫ **Dover Castle**
(EH) Castle Hill. *Tel 01304 211067.* 🕐 *daily (Nov–Jan: Thu–Mon).* ● *1 Jan, 24–26 Dec.* 🌐
🎫 *of the tunnels, by appt.* 🔲 🏠

♜ **Richborough Roman Fort**
(EH) Richborough. *Tel 01304 612 013.* 🕐 *Apr–Sep: daily.* 🌐 🛗 🏠

Margate ㉒

Kent. 🏛 *40,000.* ⇄ 🚌
🛈 *12–13 The Parade (0870 2646111).* **www**.visitthanet.co.uk

A boisterous seaside resort on the Isle of Thanet, Margate has been a popular destination for a long time. Nowadays **The Turner Centre** is the big draw, both architecturally and for its varied contemporary exhibitons.

Environs: Just south is a 19th-century gentleman's residence, **Quex House**, which has two unusual towers in its grounds. The adjoining museum has a fine collection of African and Oriental art, as well as unique dioramas of tropical wildlife. To the west is a Saxon church, built within the remains of the

Visitors relaxing on Margate's popular sandy beach

bleak Roman coastal fort of **Reculver**. Dramatic twin towers, known as the Two Sisters, were added to the church in the 12th century. The church now stands at the centre of a very pleasant, if rather windy, 37 ha (91 acre) camp site.

🏛 **The Turner Centre**
17–18 The Parade. *Tel 01843 294 208.* 🕐 *phone for details.* 🌐 🔲
🏠 **www**.turnercontemporary.org

⛪ **Quex House**
Birchington. *Tel 01843 842168.* 🕐 *Easter–Oct: Sun–Thu.* **House** 🕐 *pm only.* 🌐 🛗 🎫 *for groups.* 🍴 🏠

♜ **Reculver Fort**
(EH) Reculver. *Tel 01227 361911 (Herne Bay Tourist Information).* 🕐 *daily (exterior only).*

A drainage dyke running through the fertile plains of Romney Marsh

Street-by-Street: Rye ⑲

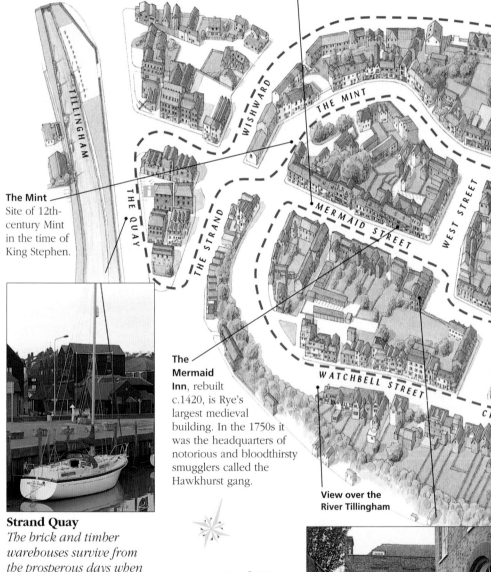

The Mermaid Inn sign

This ancient and charming fortified town was added to the original Cinque ports (see p182) in the 12th–13th century. A huge storm in 1287 diverted the River Rother so that it met the sea at Rye, and for more than 300 years it was one of the most important Channel ports. However, in the 16th century the harbour began to silt up and the town is now 2 miles (3 km) inland. Rye was frequently attacked by the French, culminating in 1377 when it was burnt to the ground.

★ **Mermaid Street**
This delightful cobbled street, its huddled houses jutting out at unlikely angles, has hardly altered since it was rebuilt in the 14th century.

The Mint
Site of 12th-century Mint in the time of King Stephen.

The Mermaid Inn, rebuilt c.1420, is Rye's largest medieval building. In the 1750s it was the headquarters of notorious and bloodthirsty smugglers called the Hawkhurst gang.

View over the River Tillingham

Strand Quay
The brick and timber warehouses survive from the prosperous days when Rye was a thriving port.

STAR SIGHTS

★ Mermaid Street

★ Ypres Tower

Lamb House
This fine Georgian house was built in 1722. George I stayed here when stranded in a storm, and author Henry James (1843–1916) lived here.

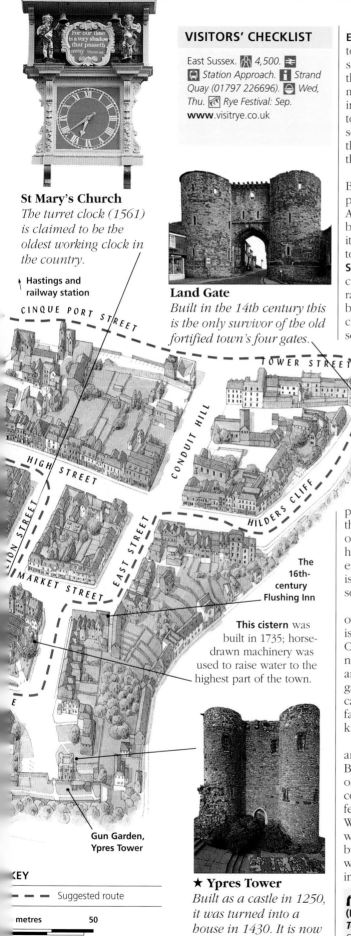

St Mary's Church
*The turret clock (1561)
is claimed to be the
oldest working clock in
the country.*

↑ **Hastings and
railway station**

CINQUE PORT STREET

HIGH STREET

MARKET STREET

EAST STREET

TOWER STREET

CONDUIT HILL

HILDERS CLIFF

**Gun Garden,
Ypres Tower**

VISITORS' CHECKLIST

East Sussex. 4,500.
Station Approach. Strand
Quay (01797 226696). Wed,
Thu. Rye Festival: Sep.
www.visitrye.co.uk

Land Gate
*Built in the 14th century this
is the only survivor of the old
fortified town's four gates.*

The
16th-
century
Flushing Inn

This cistern was
built in 1735; horse-
drawn machinery was
used to raise water to the
highest part of the town.

★ Ypres Tower
*Built as a castle in 1250,
it was turned into a
house in 1430. It is now
used as the museum.*

Environs: Just 2 miles (3 km)
to the south of Rye is the
small town of **Winchelsea**. At
the behest of Edward I, it was
moved to its present position
in 1288, when most of the old
town on lower land to the
southeast, was drowned by
the same storm that diverted
the River Rother in 1287.

Winchelsea is probably
Britain's first coherently
planned medieval town.
Although not all of it was
built as originally planned,
its rectangular grid survives
today, as does the **Church of
St Thomas Becket** (begun
c.1300) at its centre. Several
raids during the 14th century
by the French damaged the
church and burned down
scores of houses. The church
has three tombs, and
there are also two
well-preserved medie-
val tombs in the
chantry. The three
windows (1928–33)
in the Lady Chapel
were designed by
Douglas Strachan as
a memorial to those
who died in World War I.
Just beyond the edges of
present-day Winchelsea are
the remains of three of the
original gates – showing just
how big a town was first
envisaged. The beach below
is one of the finest on the
southeast coast.

Camber Sands, to the east
of the mouth of the Rother,
is another excellent beach.
Once used by fishermen, it is
now popular with swimmers
and edged with seaside bun-
galows and a bustling holiday
camp. Camber Sands is also a
favourite spot in the UK for
kite- and windsurfing.

The ruins of **Camber Castle**
are west of the sands, near
Brede Lock, Rye. This was one
of the forts built along this
coast by Henry VIII when he
feared an attack by the French.
When the castle was built it
was on the edge of the sea
but it was abandoned in 1642
when it became stranded
inland as the river silted up.

♖ Camber Castle
(EH) Camber, Rye.
Tel 01797 223862. ◯ Jul–Sep:
Sat, Sun pm for ▨ only.

KEY
– – – Suggested route

metres   50
yards   50

Jesus on Christ Church Gate, Canterbury Cathedral

Canterbury ㉓

Kent. 🚶 50,000. 🚆 🚌 ℹ️ Sun St, Buttermarket (01227 378100). 🚢 Wed, Fri. **www**.canterbury.co.uk

Its position on the London to Dover route meant Canterbury was an important Roman town even before the arrival of St Augustine in 597, sent by the pope to convert the Anglo-Saxons to Christianity. The town rose in importance, soon becoming the centre of the Christian Church in England.

With the building of the **cathedral** and the martyrdom of Thomas Becket (see p48), Canterbury's future as a religious centre was assured.

Adjacent to the ruins of **St Augustine's Abbey**, destroyed in the Dissolution (see p50), is **St Martin's Church**, the oldest in England. This was where St Augustine first worshipped and it has impressive Norman and Saxon work.

West Gate Museum, with its round towers, is an imposing medieval gatehouse. It was built in 1381 and contains a display of arms and armoury.

The Poor Priests' Hospital, founded in the 12th century, now houses the **Museum of Canterbury**.

🏛 **West Gate Museum**
St Peter's St. **Tel** 01227 789576.
⬜ Mon–Sat. ⬤ 1 Jan, Good Fri, 24–28 Dec. 📷 🚻

🏛 **Museum of Canterbury**
Stour St. **Tel** 01227 475202. ⬜ Jun–Sep: daily; Oct–May: Mon–Sat. 📷 🚻
www.canterbury-museums.co.uk

Canterbury Cathedral

To match Canterbury's growing ecclesiastical rank as a major centre of Christianity, the first Norman archbishop, Lanfranc, ordered a new cathedral to be built on the ruins of the Anglo-Saxon cathedral in 1070. It was enlarged and rebuilt many times and as a result embraces examples of all styles of medieval architecture. The most poignant moment in its history came in 1170 when Thomas Becket was murdered here (see p48). Four years after his death a fire devastated the cathedral and the Trinity Chapel was built to house Becket's remains. The shrine quickly became an important religious site and until the Dissolution (see p50) the cathedral was one of Christendom's chief places of pilgrimage.

The nave at 60 m (188 ft) makes Canterbury one of the longest medieval churches.

The South West Porch (1426) may have been built to commemorate the victory at Agincourt (see p49).

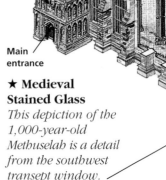

Main entrance

★ **Medieval Stained Glass**
This depiction of the 1,000-year-old Methuselah is a detail from the southwest transept window.

GEOFFREY CHAUCER

Considered to be the first great English poet, Geoffrey Chaucer (c.1345–1400), a customs official by profession, wrote a rumbustious and witty account of a group of pilgrims travelling from London to Becket's shrine in 1387 in the *Canterbury Tales*. The pilgrims represent a cross-section of 14th-century English society and the tales remain one of the greatest and most entertaining works of early English literature.

Wife of Bath, *Canterbury Tales*

Bell Harry Tower

The central tower, dominating the skyline, was built in 1498 to house a bell donated by Henry of Eastry 100 years before. The fan vaulting is a superb example of the late Perpendicular style.

VISITORS' CHECKLIST

11 The Precincts, Canterbury. **Tel** 01227 762862. ◯ 9am–4:30pm Mon–Sat (Jun–Sep: to 5pm; also 12:30–2pm Sun). Contact advised. ◐ for services & concerts; Good Friday, 24 & 25 Dec. 🎫 ✝ 8am daily; 5:30pm Mon–Fri; 3:15pm Sat, Sun; 11am Sun. ♿ 📷 **www**.canterbury-cathedral.org

★ Site of the Shrine of St Thomas Becket

This Victorian illustration (anon) portrays Becket's canonization. The Trinity Chapel was built to house his tomb which stood here until it was destroyed in 1538. The spot is now marked by a lighted candle.

Great Cloister

Chapter House

The Great South Window has four stained glass panels (1958) by Erwin Bossanyi.

★ Black Prince's Tomb

This copper effigy is on the tomb of Edward III's son, who died in 1376.

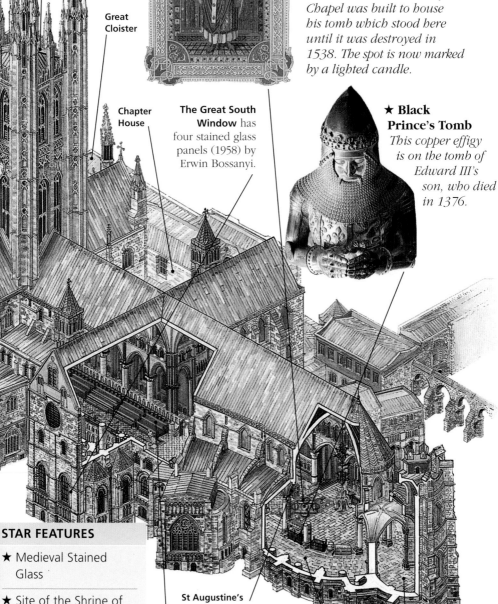

STAR FEATURES

★ Medieval Stained Glass

★ Site of the Shrine of St Thomas Becket

★ Black Prince's Tomb

St Augustine's Chair

The quire (choir), completed in 1184, is one of the longest in England.

Trinity Chapel

The circular Corona Chapel

The keep of Rochester Castle, dominating Rochester and the Medway Valley

Leeds Castle ㉔

Maidstone, Kent. *Tel* *01622 765400.*
🚆 *Bearsted then bus.* ⃝ *10am–5pm
daily.* ⬤ *for concerts & 25 Dec.* 🎫 ♿
🍴 ⬛ 📷 www.leeds-castle.com

Surrounded by a lake that
reflects the warm buff stone
of its crenellated turrets, Leeds
is often considered to be
the most beautiful castle in
England. Begun in the early
12th century, it has been
continuously inhabited and its
present appearance is a result
of centuries of rebuilding and
extensions, most recently in
the 1930s. Leeds has royal connections going back to 1278,
when it was given to Edward I
by a courtier seeking favour.
  Henry VIII loved the castle
and visited it often, escaping
from the plague in London.
It contains a life-sized bust of
Henry from the late 16th century. Leeds passed out of royal
ownership when Edward VI
gave it to Sir Anthony St Leger
in 1552 as a reward for helping to pacify the Irish.

Rochester ㉕

Kent. 🏛 *145,000.* 🚆 🚌
ℹ *95 High Street (01634 843666).*

Clustered at the mouth of
the River Medway are the
towns of Rochester, Chatham
and Gillingham, all rich in
naval history, but none more
so than Rochester, which

occupied a strategic site on
the London to Dover road.
  England's tallest Norman
keep is at **Rochester Castle**,
worth climbing for the views
over the Medway. The town's
medieval history is still visible,
with the original city walls –
which followed the lines of the
Roman fortifications – on view
in the High Street, and some
well-preserved wall paintings
in the **cathedral**, built in 1088.

Environs: In Chatham, the
Historic Dockyard is now a
museum of shipbuilding and
nautical crafts. **Fort Amherst**
nearby was built in 1756 to
protect the dockyard and river
entrance from attack, and has
1,800 m (5,570 ft) of tunnels
to explore that were hewn by
Napoleonic prisoners of war.

🏰 **Rochester Castle**
Castle Hill. *Tel* *01634 402276.* ⃝
*10am–4pm (5pm Apr–Sep) daily (last
adm: 45 mins before close).* ⬤ *1 Jan,
24–26 Dec.* 🎫 ♿ *grounds only.* 📷

A gladiator,
Knole

🏛 **Historic Dockyard**
Dock Rd, Chatham. *Tel* *01634
823807.* ⃝ *mid-Feb–Oct: daily;
Nov: Sat, Sun.* 🎫 ♿ 🍴 ⬛ 📷
⛩ **Fort Amherst**
Dock Rd, Chatham. *Tel* *01634
847747.* ⃝ *call for details.* 🎫 ⬛
www.fortamherst.com

Knole ㉖

(NT) Sevenoaks, Kent. *Tel* *01732
450608.* 🚆 *Sevenoaks then taxi.*
House ⃝ *Mar–Jul: Wed–Sun (pm);
Aug: Tue–Sun; Sep–Oct: Wed–Sun
(pm), Good Fri & pub hols.* **Park** ⃝
daily. 🎫 ♿ *ltd.* 📷 *by appt.* ⬛ 📷

This huge Tudor mansion
was built in the late 15th
century, and was seized by
Henry VIII from the Arch-
bishop of Canterbury at the
Dissolution *(see p50)*. In 1566
Queen Elizabeth I gave it to
her cousin Thomas Sackville.
His descendants have lived
here ever since, including the
writer Vita Sackville-West,
(1892–1962). The house is
well known for its
17th-century furni-
ture, such as the
elaborate bed
made for James II.
The 405-ha (1,000-acre) park
has deer and lovely walks.

Environs: A small manor
house, **Ightham Mote**, east
of Knole, is one of the finest
examples of English medieval
architecture. Its 14th-century
timber-and-stone building

encloses a central court and is encircled by a moat.

At **Sissinghurst Castle Garden** are gardens created by Vita Sackville-West and her husband Harold Nicolson in the 1930s.

🏰 **Ightham Mote**
(NT) Ivy Hatch, Sevenoaks.
Tel *01732 810378.* ⬤ *mid-Mar–Oct: Wed–Fri, Sun, Mon & public hols.* 🎫 ♿ 🍴 📷

🍁 **Sissinghurst Castle Garden**
(NT) Cranbrook. **Tel** *01580 710701.*
⬤ *mid-Mar–Oct: 11am–6:30pm Fri–Tue.* 🎫 ♿ *limited.* 🍴 📺 📷

The façade of Chartwell, Winston Churchill's home

Hever Castle ㉗

Edenbridge, Kent. **Tel** *01732 865224.*
🚃 *Edenbridge Town.* ⬤ *Apr–Oct: daily (Thu–Sun Nov, Dec, Mar).* **Gardens** *11am–6pm;* **Castle** *noon–6pm.* 🎫 ♿ *limited.* 🍴 🛍 *groups by arrangement.* 📷 www.hever-castle.co.uk

This small, moated castle is famous as the 16th-century home of Anne Boleyn, the doomed wife of Henry VIII, executed for adultery. She lived here as a young woman and the king often visited her while staying at Leeds Castle. In 1903 Hever was bought by William Waldorf Astor, who undertook a restoration programme, building a Neo-Tudor village alongside it to accommodate guests and servants. The moat and gatehouse date from around 1270.

Environs: To the northwest of Hever is **Chartwell**, the family home of Sir Winston Churchill *(see p59).* It remains furnished as it was when he lived here. Some 140 of his paintings are on display.

🏰 **Chartwell**
(NT) Westerham, Kent. 📠 *01732 868381.* ⬤ *mid-Mar–Jun, Sep–Nov: 11am–5pm Wed–Sun & public hols; Jul–Aug: 11am–5pm Tue–Sun & public hols.* 🎫 ♿ *limited.* 🍴 📷

CHARLES DICKENS

Charles Dickens (1812–70), a popular writer in his own time, is still widely read today. He was born in Portsmouth but moved to Chatham aged five. As an adult, Dickens lived in London but kept up his Kent connections, taking holidays in Broadstairs, just south of Margate – where he wrote *David Copperfield* – and spending his last years at Gad's Hill, near Rochester. The town celebrates the famous connection with an annual Dickens festival.

Royal Tunbridge Wells ㉘

Kent. 🏘 *55,000.* 🚃 🚌
ℹ *Old Fish Market, The Pantiles (01892 515 675).* 🏪 *Sat.*
www.visittunbridgewells.com

Helped by royal patronage, the town became a popular spa in the 17th and 18th centuries after mineral springs were discovered in 1606. The Pantiles – the colonnaded and paved promenade – was laid out in the 1700s.

Environs: Nearby is a superb manor house, **Penshurst Place**. Built in the 1340s, it has an 18-m- (60-ft-) high Great Hall.

🏰 **Penshurst Place**
Tonbridge, Kent. **Tel** *01892 870307.*
⬤ *Apr–Oct: daily; Mar: Sat, Sun:* **House** *noon–4pm;* **Gardens** *10:30am–6pm;* **Toy Museum** *noon–5pm.* 🎫 ♿ *limited.* 🍴 📺 📷

An early 18th-century astrolabe to measure the stars, Hever Castle garden

EAST ANGLIA

NORFOLK · SUFFOLK · ESSEX · CAMBRIDGESHIRE

The bulge of land between the Thames Estuary and the Wash, flat but far from featureless, sits aside from the main north – south axis through Britain, and for that reason it has succeeded in maintaining and preserving its distinctive architecture, traditions and rural character in both cities and countryside.

East Anglia's name derives from the Angles, the people from northern Germany who settled here during the 5th and 6th centuries. East Anglians have long been a breed of plain-spoken and independent people. Two prominent East Anglians – Queen Boadicea in the 1st century and Oliver Cromwell in the 17th century – were famous for their stubbornness and their refusal to bow to constituted authority. During the Civil War, East Anglia was Cromwell's most reliable source of support. The hardy people who made a difficult living hunting and fishing in the swampy fens, which were drained in the 17th century, were called the Fen Tigers. After draining, the peaty soil proved ideal for arable farming, and today East Anglia grows about a third of Britain's vegetables. The rotation of crops, heralding Britain's agricultural revolution, was perfected in Norfolk in the 18th century. Many of the region's towns and cities grew prosperous on the agricultural wealth, including Norwich. The sea also plays a prominent role in East Anglian life. Coastal towns and villages support the many fishermen who use the North Sea, rich in herring in former days but now known mainly for flat fish.

In modern times, the area has become a centre of recreational sailing, both off the coast and on the inland waterway system known as the Norfolk Broads. East Anglia is also home to one of Britain's top universities: Cambridge.

Lavender fields in full bloom in July, Heacham, Norfolk

◁ Cley windmill overlooking the sea marshes on the north Norfolk coast

Exploring East Anglia

As you move away from London, you soon reach the countryside immortalized by the painter Constable *(see p204)*, scattered with churches, windmills and medieval agricultural barns. Nature lovers will find it fruitful territory, especially North Norfolk with its bird reserves and seal colonies. Boating enthusiasts, too, are well catered for in this, Britain's driest and sunniest region. The local architecture ranges from a mix of medieval to modern. The distinctive pink-washed cottages in Suffolk, flint cottages in Norfolk and thatched roofs everywhere, are also much in evidence.

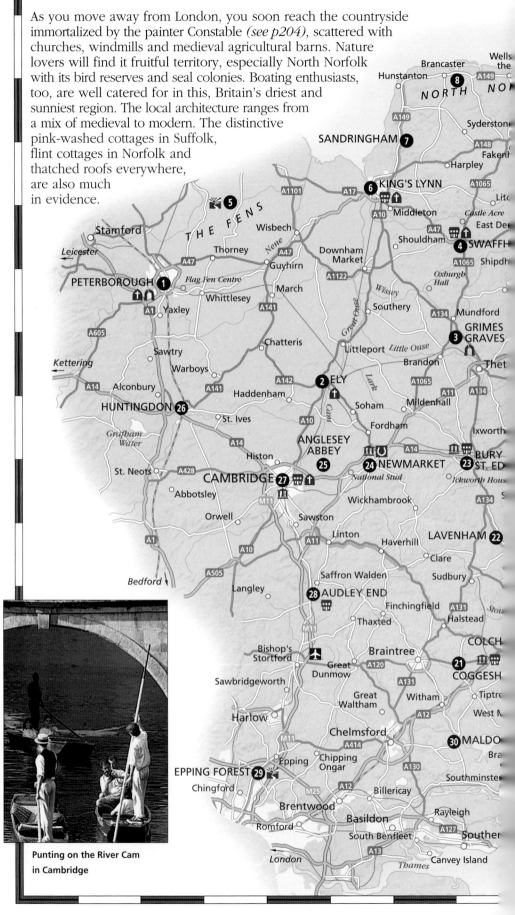

Punting on the River Cam
in Cambridge

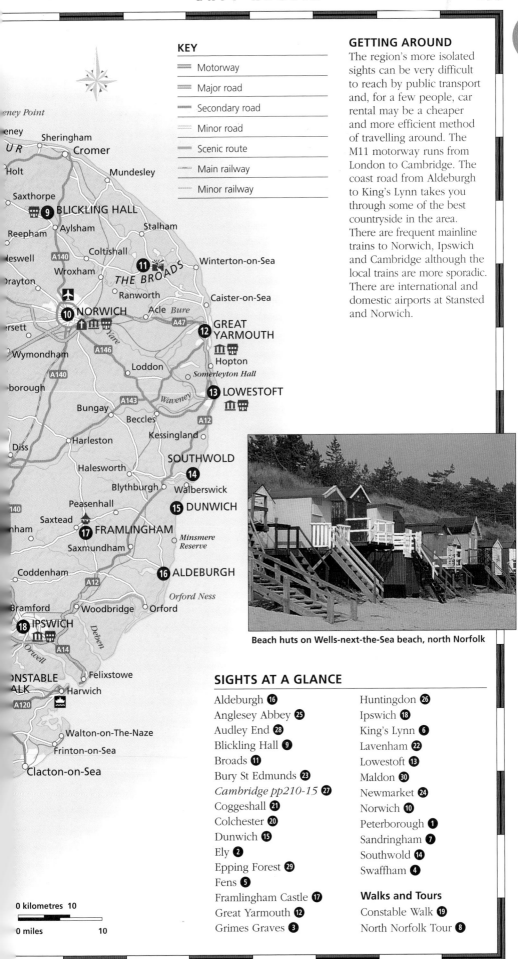

KEY

▬▬	Motorway
▬▬	Major road
▬▬	Secondary road
▭▭	Minor road
▬▬	Scenic route
▬▬	Main railway
▭▭	Minor railway

GETTING AROUND

The region's more isolated sights can be very difficult to reach by public transport and, for a few people, car rental may be a cheaper and more efficient method of travelling around. The M11 motorway runs from London to Cambridge. The coast road from Aldeburgh to King's Lynn takes you through some of the best countryside in the area. There are frequent mainline trains to Norwich, Ipswich and Cambridge although the local trains are more sporadic. There are international and domestic airports at Stansted and Norwich.

Beach huts on Wells-next-the-Sea beach, north Norfolk

SIGHTS AT A GLANCE

Aldeburgh ⑯	Huntingdon ㉖
Anglesey Abbey ㉕	Ipswich ⑱
Audley End ㉘	King's Lynn ⑥
Blickling Hall ⑨	Lavenham ㉒
Broads ⑪	Lowestoft ⑬
Bury St Edmunds ㉓	Maldon ㉚
Cambridge pp210-15 ㉗	Newmarket ㉔
Coggeshall ㉑	Norwich ⑩
Colchester ⑳	Peterborough ①
Dunwich ⑮	Sandringham ⑦
Ely ②	Southwold ⑭
Epping Forest ㉙	Swaffham ④
Fens ⑤	
Framlingham Castle ⑰	**Walks and Tours**
Great Yarmouth ⑫	Constable Walk ⑲
Grimes Graves ③	North Norfolk Tour ⑧

0 kilometres 10

0 miles 10

Peterborough ❶

Cambridgeshire. 🚶 156,000.
🚊 🚌 ℹ️ 3–5 Minster Precinct
(01733 452336). 🅿️ Tue–Sat.
www.visitpeterborough.com

Although one of the oldest
settlements in Britain, Peterborough was designated a
New Town in 1967, and is
now a mixture of ancient
and modern.

The city centre is dominated
by the 12th-century **St Peter's
Cathedral** which gave the city
its name. The interior of this
classic Norman building, with
its vast yet simple nave, was
badly damaged by Cromwell's
troops (see p52), but its unique
painted wooden ceiling (1220)
has survived intact. Catherine
of Aragon, the first wife of

Peterborough's coat of arms with
a Latin inscription: Upon this Rock

Henry VIII, is buried here,
although Cromwell's troops
also destroyed her tomb.

Environs: The oldest wheel in
Britain (1,300 BC) was found
preserved in peat at **Flag Fen
Bronze Age Centre**. The site
provides a fascinating glimpse
into prehistory.

🏛 **Flag Fen Bronze Age Centre**
The Droveway, Northey Rd.
Tel 0844 414 0646. ⭕ Mar–Oct:
Tue–Sun, public hols. ♿🅿️🅣🖼️🖥️
www.flagfen.com

Grimes Graves ❸

(EH) Lynford, Norfolk. **Tel** 01842
810656. 🚊 Brandon then taxi.
⭕ Apr–Sep: daily; Oct, Mar:
Thu–Mon. 🖼️🅣♿

One of the most important
Neolithic sites in England,
this was once an extensive
complex of flint mines – 433
shafts have been located –
dating from before 2000 BC.

Using antlers as pickaxes,
Stone Age miners hacked
through the soft chalk to
extract the hard flint below
to make weapons and tools.
The flint may have been transported long distances around
England on the prehistoric
network of paths. You can
descend 9 m (30 ft) by ladder
into one of the shafts and see

Ely ❷

Cambridgeshire. 🚶 14,000. 🚊
ℹ️ 29 St Mary's St (01353 662062).
⭕ Mon. 🅿️ Thu (general), Sat
(craft & antiques). **http://**visitely.
eastcambs.gov.uk

Built on a chalk hill, this
small city is thought to be
named after the eels in the
nearby River Ouse. The hill
was once an inaccessible
island in the then marshy and
treacherous Fens (see p196).
It was also the last stronghold
of Anglo-Saxon resistance,
under Hereward the Wake
(see p48), who hid in the
cathedral until the Normans
crossed the Fens in 1071.

Today this small prosperous
city, totally dominated by the
huge **cathedral**, is the market
centre for the rich agricultural
area surrounding it.

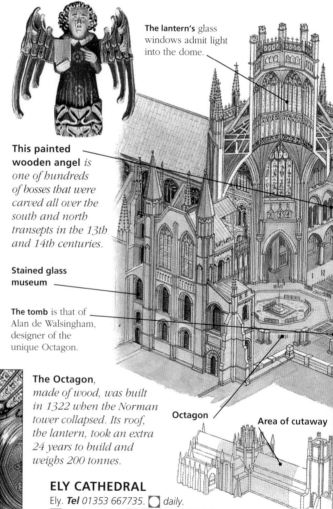

The lantern's glass
windows admit light
into the dome.

**This painted
wooden angel** is
one of hundreds
of bosses that were
carved all over the
south and north
transepts in the 13th
and 14th centuries.

**Stained glass
museum**

The tomb is that of
Alan de Walsingham,
designer of the
unique Octagon.

The Octagon,
made of wood, was built
in 1322 when the Norman
tower collapsed. Its roof,
the lantern, took an extra
24 years to build and
weighs 200 tonnes.

Octagon

Area of cutaway

ELY CATHEDRAL
Ely. **Tel** 01353 667735. ⭕ daily.
⭕ special events. 🖼️♿🅣🍴🖥️🅟
Begun in 1083, the cathedral took 268 years to
complete. It survived the Dissolution (see p50)
but was closed for 17 years by Cromwell (see
p52) who lived in Ely for a time.

the galleries where the flint was mined. During excavations, unusual chalk models of a fertility goddess *(see p43)* and a phallus were discovered.

Environs: Nearby, at the centre of the once fertile plain known as the Breckland, is the small market town of **Thetford**.

Once a prosperous trading town, its fortunes dipped in the 16th century, when its priory was destroyed *(see p50)* and the surrounding land deteriorated due to excessive sheep grazing. The area was later planted with pine trees. A mound in the city marks the site of a pre-Norman castle.

The revolutionary writer and philosopher Tom Paine, author of *The Rights of Man*, was born here in 1737.

The huge cathedral dominates the flat Fens countryside surrounding Ely.

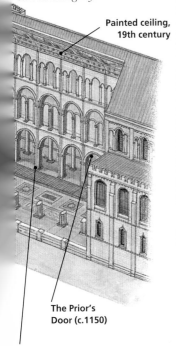

Painted ceiling, 19th century

The Prior's Door (c.1150)

The south aisle has 12 classic Norman arches at its foot, with pointed Early English windows above.

Oxburgh Hall surrounded by its medieval moat

Swaffham ④

Norfolk. 🚶 *6,700.* 🚉 ℹ️
Market Place (01760 722255).
🕐 *Apr–mid-Oct.* 🛒 *Sat.*
www.aroundswaffham.co.uk

The best-preserved Georgian town in East Anglia and a fashionable resort during the Regency period, Swaffham is at its liveliest on Saturdays when a market is held in the square around the market cross of 1783. In the centre of the town is the 15th-century **Church of St Peter and St Paul**, with a small spire added in the 19th century. It has a magnificent Tudor north aisle, said to have been paid for by John Chapman, the Pedlar of Swaffham. He is depicted on the two-sided town sign near the market place. Myth has it that he went to London and met a stranger who told him of hidden treasure at Swaffham. He returned, dug it up and used it to embellish the church, where he is shown in a window.

Environs: Castle Acre, north of the town, has the remains of a massive Cluniac **priory**. Founded in 1090, its stunning Norman front still stands.

A short drive south is **Oxburgh Hall and Garden**, built by Sir Edmund Bedingfeld in 1482. The hall, entered through a huge 24 m (80 ft) fortified gatehouse, displays the velvet Oxburgh Hangings, embroidered by Mary, Queen of Scots *(see p511)*.

🏰 **Castle Acre Priory**
(EH) Castle Acre.
Tel 01760 755394.
🕐 daily (Oct–Mar: Thu–Mon.
1 Jan, 24–26 Dec. 🚫 ♿ ltd. 🅿️

🏛️ **Oxburgh Hall & Garden**
(NT) Oxborough. *Tel 01366 328258.* 🕐 *Mar–Oct: Sat–Wed (Aug: daily).* **Garden** 🕐 Dec: Sat, Sun. 🚫 ♿ ltd. 🍴 🅿️

Swaffham town sign

BOADICEA AND THE ICENI

When the Romans invaded Britain, the Iceni, the main tribe in East Anglia, joined forces with them to defeat the Catuvellauni, a rival tribe. But the Romans then turned on the Iceni, torturing Queen Boadicea (or Boudicca). In AD 61, she led a revolt against Roman rule: her followers burned down London, Colchester and St Albans. The rebellion was put down and the queen took poison rather than submit. At Cockley Cley, near Swaffham, an Iceni camp has been excavated.

Illustration of Queen Boadicea leading her Iceni followers

A windmill on Wicken Fen

The Fens ❺

Cambridgeshire/Norfolk. ⟨⟩ *Ely.*
ℹ️ *29 St Mary's St, Ely (01353 662062).* ⚫ *Mon.*
www.eastcambs.gov.uk/tourism

This is the open, flat, fertile expanse that lies between Lincoln, Cambridge, Bedford and King's Lynn. Up until the 17th century it was a swamp, and settlement was possible only on "islands", such as Ely *(see p194).*

Through the 17th century, speculators, recognizing the value of the peaty soil for farmland, brought in Dutch experts to drain the fens. However, as the peat dried, it contracted, and the fens have slowly been getting lower. Powerful electric pumps now keep it drained.

Nine miles (14 km) from Ely is Wicken Fen, 243 ha (600 acres) of undrained fen providing a habitat for water life, wildfowl and wild flowers.

King's Lynn ❻

Norfolk. 🏠 *42,000.* ⟨⟩ ⟨⟩
ℹ️ *Custom House, Purfleet Quay (01553 763044).* 🖺 *Tue, Fri, Sat.*
www.west-norfolk.gov.uk

Formerly Bishop's Lynn, its name was changed at the Reformation *(see p50)* to reflect the changing political reality. In the Middle Ages it was one of England's most prosperous ports, shipping grain and wool from the surrounding countryside to Europe. There are still a few warehouses and merchants' houses by the River Ouse surviving from this period. At the north end of the town is **True's**

Trinity Guildhall, King's Lynn

North Norfolk Coastal Tour ❽

This tour takes you through some of the most beautiful areas of East Anglia; nearly all of the north Norfolk coast has been designated an Area of Outstanding Natural Beauty. The sea has dictated the character of the area. With continuing deposits of silt, once busy ports are now far inland and the shingle and sand banks that have been built up are home to a huge variety of wildlife. Do bear in mind when planning your journey that this popular route can get congested during summer.

TIPS FOR DRIVERS

Tour length: *28 miles (45 km).*
Stopping-off points: *Holkham Hall makes a pleasant stop for a picnic lunch. There are some good pubs in Wells-next-the -Sea*

THE WASH

Holme-next-the-Sea ②
A149
Brancaster
A149
Burnham Market
B1153
B1155
NORWICH

Hunstanton Cliffs ②
These magnificent cliffs tower 18 m (60 ft) above the beach. Their three bands of colour are made from carstone and red and white chalk.

Hunstanton
A149
B1454
Heacham
KING'S LYNN

LORD NELSON
GREENE KING

Caley Mill ①
The largest producer of English Lavender, this whole area is at its best in July and August when the fields are a blaze of purple.

Lord Nelson pub ③
Nelson *(p54),* born near Bur ham Market, dined here befo he went to sea for the last tim

Yard, a relic of the old fishermen's quarter.

The **Trinity Guildhall**, located in the Saturday Market Place, dates back to the 15th century and was formerly a prison. The handsome **Custom House**, overlooking the river, was built in the 17th century as a merchant exchange. It is now a museum dedicated to the town's colourful maritime history. The Tourist Information Centre is also located here. **St Margaret's Church**, on the Market Place, dates back to 1101, and the interior includes a fine Elizabethan screen. In 1741 the tall spire on the southwest tower collapsed in a storm.

> ### 🏛 Custom House
> Purfleet Quay. *Tel* 01553 763044.
> ⬭ *daily.* ♿ *ground floor.*

Sandringham House, where the Royal Family spend every Christmas

Sandringham ❼

Norfolk. *Tel* 01553 612908. 🚌 *from King's Lynn.* ⬭ *Easter–Oct: daily.* ⬤ *one wk Jul.* ♿ 🍴 *all year.* 📷 *all year.* **www**.sandringhamestate.co.uk

This sizeable Norfolk estate has been in royal hands since 1862 when it was bought by the Prince of Wales, who later became Edward VII. The 18th-century house was elaborately embellished and refurbished by the prince and now retains an appropriately Edwardian atmosphere.

The large stables are now a museum and contain several trophies that relate to hunting, shooting and horse racing – all favourite royal activities. A popular feature is a display of royal motor cars spanning nearly a century. In the park there are scenic nature trails.

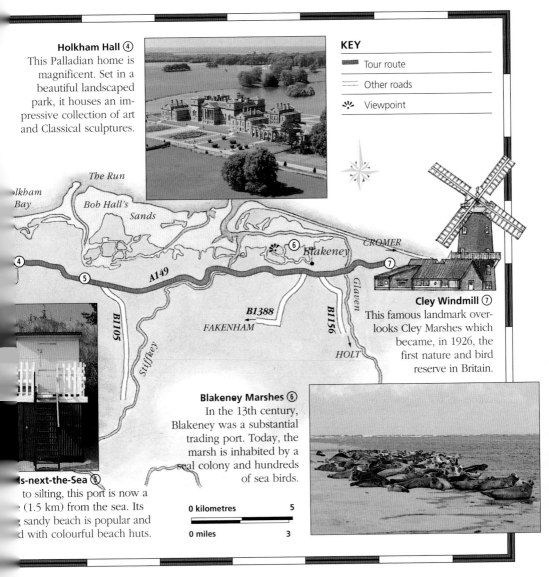

Holkham Hall ④
This Palladian home is magnificent. Set in a beautiful landscaped park, it houses an impressive collection of art and Classical sculptures.

KEY

▭ Tour route

═ Other roads

☀ Viewpoint

The Run

Ikham Bay

Bob Hall's Sands

④

⑤

A149

B1105

Stiffkey

Blakeney ⑥

CROMER

Glaven

⑦

Cley Windmill ⑦
This famous landmark overlooks Cley Marshes which became, in 1926, the first nature and bird reserve in Britain.

B1388

FAKENHAM

B1156

HOLT

Blakeney Marshes ⑥
In the 13th century, Blakeney was a substantial trading port. Today, the marsh is inhabited by a seal colony and hundreds of sea birds.

Is-next-the-Sea ⑤
to silting, this port is now a
(1.5 km) from the sea. Its
sandy beach is popular and
d with colourful beach huts.

0 kilometres   5

0 miles   3

The symmetrical red-brick façade of the 17th-century Blickling Hall

Blickling Hall **9**

(NT) Aylsham, Norfolk. **Tel** 01263 738 030. ⇄ Norwich, then bus. **House** ◯ mid-Mar–Oct: Wed–Thu (Aug: daily). **Garden** ◯ dawn–dusk daily. **Park** ◯ daily. 🎦 ♿ 🍴 🛈 **www**.nationaltrust.org.uk

Approached from the east, its symmetrical Jacobean front framed by trees and flanked by two yew hedges, Blickling Hall offers one of the most impressive vistas of any country house in the area.

Anne Boleyn, Henry VIII's tragic second queen, spent her childhood here, but very little of the original house remains. Most of the present structure dates from 1628, when it was home to James I's Chief Justice Sir Henry Hobart. Later in 1767 the 2nd Earl of Buckinghamshire, John Hobart, celebrated the Boleyn connection with reliefs in the Great Hall depicting Anne and her daughter, Elizabeth I. The Long Gallery is the most spectacular room to survive from the 1620s. Its ceiling depicts symbolic representations of learning.

The Peter the Great Room marks the 2nd earl's service as ambassador to Russia and was built to display a huge spectacular tapestry (1764) of the tsar on horseback, a gift from, Catherine the Great. It also has portraits (1760) of the ambassador and his wife by Gainsborough (see p163).

Norwich **10**

See pp200–201.

The Broads **11**

Norfolk. ⇄ Hoveton, Wroxham. 🚌 Norwich, then bus. 🛈 Station Rd, Hoveton (01603 782281) Apr–Oct, or 18 Colegate, Norwich (01603 610 734). **www**.broads-authority.gov.uk

These shallow lakes and waterways south and northeast of Norwich, joined by six rivers – the Bure, Thurne, Ant, Yare, Waveney and Chet – were once thought to have been naturally formed, but in actual fact they are medieval peat diggings which flooded when the water level rose in the 13th century.

In summer the 125 miles (200 km) of open waterways, uninterrupted by locks, teem with thousands of boating enthusiasts. You can either hire a boat yourself or take one of the many trips on offer to view the plants and wildlife of the area. Look out for Britain's largest butterfly, the swallowtail. Wroxham, the unofficial capital of the Broads, is the starting point for many of these excursions.

The waterways support substantial beds of strong and durable reeds, much in demand for thatching (see p33). They are cut in winter and carried to shore in the distinctive Broads punts.

For a more detailed look at the origins of the Broads and their varied wildlife, visit the **Norfolk Wildlife Trust** – a large thatched floating information centre on Ranworth Broad, with displays on all aspects of the area, and a bird-watching gallery.

In the centre of Ranworth is **St Helen's Church** which has a painted medieval screen, a well-preserved 14th-century illuminated manuscript and spectacular views over the entire area from its tower.

🦋 **Norfolk Wildlife Trust** Ranworth. **Tel** 01603 625540. ◯ Apr–Oct: daily. ♿ 🛈

Sailing boat, Wroxham Broad, Norfolk

Great Yarmouth ⑫

Norfolk. 🏘 *90,000.* ⮀ 🚌
ℹ️ *Marine Parade (01493 846345).*
🏛 *Wed, Fri (summer), Sat.*
www.great-yarmouth.co.uk

Herring fishing was once the major industry of this port, with 1,000 boats engaged in it just before World War I. Over-fishing led to a depletion of stocks and, for the port to survive, it started to earn its living from servicing container ships and North Sea oil rigs.

It is also the most popular seaside resort on the Norfolk coast and has been since the 19th century, when Dickens *(see p189)* gave it useful publicity by setting part of his novel *David Copperfield* here.

The **Elizabethan House Museum** has a large, eclectic display which illustrates the social history of the area.

In the old part of the town, around South Quay, are a number of charming houses including the 17th-century **Old Merchant's House**. It retains its original patterned plaster ceilings as well as examples of old ironwork and architectural fittings from

Fishing trawlers at Lowestoft's quays

nearby houses, which were destroyed during World War II. The guided tour of the house includes a visit to the adjoining cloister of a 13th-century friary.

🏛 **Elizabethan House Museum**
(NT) 4 South Quay. **Tel** 01493 855746. ⭕ *Apr–Oct: daily (pm only weekends).* 📷 🚻

🏠 **Old Merchant's House**
(EH) South Quay. **Tel** 01493 857900. ⭕ *Apr–Sep: pm daily.* 📷 🅿️ 🚻

WINDMILLS ON THE FENS AND BROADS

The flat, open countryside and the stiff breezes from the North Sea made windmills an obvious power source for East Anglia well into the 20th century, and today they are an evocative and recurring feature of the landscape. On the Broads and Fens, some were used for drainage, while others, such as that at Saxtead Green, ground corn. On the boggy fens they were not built on hard foundations, so few survived, but elsewhere, especially on the Broads, many have been restored to working order. The seven-storey Berney Arms Windmill is the tallest on the Broads. Thurne Dyke Drainage Mill is the site of an exhibition about the occasionally idiosyncratic mills and their more unusual mechanisms.

Corn mill at Saxtead Green, near Framlingham

Herringfleet Smock Mill, near Lowestoft

Lowestoft ⑬

Suffolk. 🏘 *55,000.* ⮀ 🚌
ℹ️ *East Point Pavilion, Royal Plain (01502 533600).* 🏛 *Tue–Sat.*
www.visit-lowestoft.co.uk

The most easterly town in Britain was long a rival to Great Yarmouth, both as a holiday resort and a fishing port. Its fishing industry has only just survived. The coming of the railway in the 1840s gave the town an advantage over other resorts, and the solid Victorian and Edwardian boarding houses are evidence of its popularity.

Lowestoft Museum, in a 17th-century house, has a good display of the fine porcelain made here in the 18th century, as well as exhibits on local archaeology and domestic life.

Environs: Somerleyton Hall is built in Jacobean style on the foundations of a smaller mansion. Its gardens are a real delight, and there is a genuinely baffling yew hedge maze.

🏛 **Lowestoft Museum**
Oulton Broad. **Tel** 01502 511457. ⭕ *May–Oct: 10:30am–5pm daily (from 2pm Sun).* 🚻 ♿ ltd. 📷 *by appt.* **www**.lowestoftmuseum.org

🏠 **Somerleyton Hall**
On B1074. **Tel** 01502 734901. ⭕ *Easter Sun–Oct: Thu, Sun & pub hols (Jul–Aug: also Tue, Wed).* 🚻 📷 ♿ 📷 *by appt.* 🖥
www.somerleyton.co.uk

Norwich ➓

In the heart of the fertile East Anglian countryside, Norwich, one of the best-preserved cities in Britain, is steeped in a relaxed provincial atmosphere. The city was first fortified by the Saxons in the 9th century and still has the irregular street plan of that time. With the arrival of Flemish settlers in the early 12th century and the establishment of a textile industry, the town soon became a prosperous market and was the second city of England until the Industrial Revolution in the 19th century *(see pp56–7).*

One of over a thousand carved bosses in the cathedral cloisters

a 13th-century flint arch, and the **Erpingham Gate** at the west end, built by Sir Thomas Erpingham, who led the triumphant English archers at the Battle of Agincourt in 1415 *(see p49).*

Beneath the east outer wall is the grave of Edith Cavell, the Norwich-born nurse who was arrested and executed in 1915 by the Germans for helping Allied soldiers escape from occupied Belgium.

The cobbled street, Elm Hill

Exploring Norwich

The oldest parts of the city are Elm Hill, one of the finest medieval streets in England, and Tombland, the old Saxon market place by the cathedral. Both have well-preserved medieval buildings, which are now incorporated into pleasant areas of small shops.

With a trading history spanning hundreds of years, the colourful market in the city centre is well worth a visit. A good walk meanders around the surviving sections of the 14th-century flint city wall.

⛪ Norwich Cathedral

The Close. *Tel 01603 218300.*
◯ daily. **Donations.** ♿ ▢ 🍴 ▢
www.cathedral.org.uk

This magnificent building was founded in 1096 by Bishop Losinga and built with stone from Caen in France and Barnack.

The precinct originally included a monastery, and the surviving cloister is the most extensive in England. The thin cathedral spire was added in the 15th century, making it, at 96 m (315 ft), the second tallest in England after Salisbury *(see pp264–5).* In the majestic

nave, soaring Norman pillars and arches support a 15th-century vaulted roof whose stone bosses, many of which illustrate well-known Bible stories, have recently been beautifully restored.

Easier to appreciate at close hand is the elaborate wood carving in the choir – the canopies over the stalls and the misericords beneath the seats, one showing a small boy being smacked. Not to be missed is the 14th-century Despenser Reredos in St Luke's Chapel. It was hidden for years under a carpenter's table to prevent its destruction by Puritans.

Two gates to the cathedral close survive: **St Ethelbert's,**

🏛 Castle Museum

Castle Meadow. *Tel 01603 493625.*
◯ daily (Sun pm only). ⬤ 1 Jan, 25 & 26 Dec. ♿ ▢ ▢
www.museums.norfolk.gov.uk

The brooding keep of this 12th-century castle has been a museum since 1894, when it ended 650 years of service as a prison. The most important Norman feature is a carved door that used to be the main entrance.

Exhibits include significant collections of archaeology,

A view of Norwich Cathedral's spire and tower from the southeast

COLMAN'S MUSTARD

It was said of the Colmans that they made their fortune from what diners left on their plate. In 1814 Jeremiah Colman started milling mustard at Norwich because it was at the centre of a fertile plain where mustard was grown. Today at 15 Royal Arcade a shop sells mustard and related items, while a small museum illustrates the history of the company.

A 1950s advertisement for Colman's Mustard

🏛 Strangers' Hall
Charing Cross. *Tel 01603 667229.*
◯ *Wed–Sat; call ahead for times
(tickets from Castle Museum).*
⬤ *24–31 Dec.*

This 14th-century merchant's house gives a glimpse into English domestic life through the ages. The house was lived in by immigrant weavers – the "strangers". It has a fine 15th-century Great Hall and a costume display featuring a collection of underwear.

🏛 The Sainsbury Centre for Visual Arts
University of E Anglia (on B1108).
Tel 01603 593199. ◯ *Tue–Sun.*
⬤ *23 Dec–20 Jan.* 🚼 ♿ 📷 *by arrangement.* 💻 📷 **www**.scva.ac.uk

This important art gallery was built in 1978 to house the collection of Robert and Lisa Sainsbury given to the University of East Anglia in 1973.

The collection's strength is in its modern European paintings, including works by Modigliani, Picasso and Bacon, and in its sculptures by Giacometti and Moore. There are also displays of ethnographic art from Africa, the Pacific and the Americas.

The centre, designed by Lord Norman Foster, one of Britain's most innovative architects, was among the first to display its steel structure openly.

natural history, fine art as well as the world's largest collection of ceramic teapots.

The art gallery is dominated by works from the Norwich School of painters. This group of early 19th century landscape artists painted directly from nature, getting away from the stylized studio landscapes that had been fashionable up to then. Chief among the group were John Crome (1768–1821), whom many compare with Constable (*see p204*), and John Sell Cotman (1782–1842), known for his watercolours. There are also regular exhibitions held here.

🔒 Church of St Peter Mancroft
Market Place. *Tel 01603 610443.*
◯ *10am–4pm Mon–Sat; 10am–4pm Sat (summer), 10am–1pm (winter);
Sun (services only).* **Donations**. ♿

This imposing Perpendicular church, built around 1455, so dominates the city centre that many visitors assume it is the cathedral. John Wesley (*see p279*) wrote of it, "I scarcely ever remember to have seen a more beautiful parish church".

The large windows make the church very light, and the dramatic east window still has most of its 15th-century glass. The roof is unusual in having wooden fan tracery – it is normally in stone – covering the hammerbeam construction. The famous peal of 13 bells rang out in 1588 to celebrate the defeat of the Spanish Armada (*see p51*) and is still heard every Sunday.

Its name derives from the Latin *magna crofta* (great meadow) which described the area in pre-Norman times.

🏛 Bridewell Museum
Bridewell Alley. *Tel 01603 629127.*
⬤ *until 2011.* 🚼 📷

One of the oldest houses in Norwich, this 14th-century flint-faced building was used for years as a jail for women and beggars. It now houses an exhibition of local industries, with displays of old machines and reconstructed shops. A section about the people of Norwich is being developed.

🏛 Guildhall
Gaol Hill. *Tel 01264 781611.* 💻

Above the city's ancient market place is the imposing 15th-century flint and stone Guildhall with its gable of check-ered flushwork (now a café).

Back of the New Mills (1814) by John Crome of the Norwich School

Purple heather in flower on Dunwich Heath

Southwold ⑭

Suffolk. 👥 3,900. 🚃 ℹ️ *High Street (01502 724729).* 🚌 *Mon, Thu. Shops closed Wed pm.* **www**.visit-southwold.co.uk

This picture-postcard seaside resort, with its charming white-washed villas clustered around small greens, has, largely by historical accident, remained unspoiled. The railway line which connected it with London was closed in 1929, which effectively isolated this Georgian town from an influx of day-trippers.

This was also once a large port, as testified by the size of the 15th-century **St Edmund King and Martyr Church**, worth a visit for the 16th-century painted screens.

On its tower is a small figure dressed in the uniform of a 15th-century soldier and known as Jack o'the Clock. **Southwold Museum** tells the story of the Battle of Sole Bay, which was fought offshore between the English and Dutch navies in 1672.

Jack o'the Clock, Southwold

Environs: The pretty village of **Walberswick** lies across the creek. By road it is a long detour and the only alternatives are a rowing-boat ferry across the harbour (summer only) or a footbridge across the river half a mile inland. Further inland at Blythburgh, the 15th-century **Holy Trinity Church** dominates the surrounding land. In 1944 a US bomber blew up over the church, killing Joseph Kennedy Jr, brother of the future American president.

🏛 **Southwold Museum**
9–11 Victoria St. **Tel** *01502 726097.* ◯ *Easter–Oct: 2–4pm daily (also am in Aug).* ♿

Dunwich ⑮

Suffolk. 👥 1,400.

This tiny village is all that remains of a "lost city" consigned to the sea by erosion. In the 7th century Dunwich was the seat of the powerful East Anglian kings. In the 13th century it was still the biggest port in Suffolk and some 12 churches were built. But the land was being eroded at about a metre (3 ft) a year, and the last original church collapsed into the sea in 1919.

Dunwich Heath, to the south, runs down to a sandy beach and is an important nature reserve. **Minsmere Reserve** has observation hides for watching a huge variety of birds.

🦅 **Dunwich Heath**
(NT) Nr Westleton. **Tel** *01728 648501.* ◯ *dawn–dusk.* ▯ ▮

🦅 **Minsmere Reserve**
Minsmere, Westleton. **Tel** *01728 648281.* ◯ *daily.* ● *25, 26 Dec.* ♿ ▯ ▮ **www**.rspb.org.uk

Aldeburgh ⑯

Suffolk. 👥 3,840. 🚃
ℹ️ *High St (01728 453637).*
www.suffolkcoastal.gov.uk/tourism

Best known today for the music festivals at Snape Maltings just up the River Alde, Aldeburgh has been a

Intricate carving on the exterior of the Tudor Moot Hall, Aldeburgh

port since Roman times (the Roman area is under water).

Erosion has resulted in the fine Tudor **Aldeburgh Museum**, once far inland, now being close to the beach. Its ground floor, originally the market, is now a museum. The large timbered court room above can only be reached by the original outside staircase.

The **church**, also Tudor, contains a large stained-glass window placed in 1979 as a memorial to Benjamin Britten.

🏛 **Aldeburgh Museum**
Moot Hall, Market Cross Pl. **Tel** 01728 454666. ◻ May–Oct: daily (pm); Easter–Apr: Sat, Sun (pm). 🖼 🛈

Framlingham Castle ⓱

(EH) Framlingham, Suffolk. **Tel** 01728 724189. 🚆 Wickham Market then taxi. ◻ daily (Nov–Mar: Thu–Mon). 🌑 1 Jan, 24–26 Dec. 🔌 🛈 🖼

Perched on a hill, the small village of Framlingham has long been an important strategic site, even before the present castle was built in 1190 by the Earl of Norfolk.

Little of the castle from that period survives except the powerful curtain wall and its towers; walk round the top of it for fine views of the town.

Mary Tudor, daughter of Henry VIII, was staying here in 1553 when she heard she was to become queen.

Environs: To the southeast, on the coast, is the 27 m (90 ft) keep of **Orford Castle**, built for Henry II as a coastal defence at around the same time as Framlingham. It is an early example of an English castle with a 16-sided keep; earlier they were square and later round. A short climb to the top of the castle gives fantastic views.

🏰 **Orford Castle**
(EH) Orford. **Tel** 01394 450472. ◻ daily (Oct–Mar: Thu–Mon). 🌑 1 Jan, 24–26 Dec. 🖼 🛈

Ipswich ⓲

Suffolk. 🏘 120,000. 🚆 🚌 🛈 St Stephen's Lane (01473 258070). 🛒 Tue, Thu–Sat. 🎭 IPART (music & arts): last wk Jun–1st wk Jul. **www**.visit-ipswich.com

Suffolk's county town has a largely modern centre but several buildings remain from earlier times. It rose to prominence after the 13th century as a port for the rich Suffolk wool trade *(see p207)*. Later, with the Industrial Revolution, it began to export coal.

The **Ancient House** in Buttermarket has a superb example of pargeting – the ancient craft of ornamental façade plastering. The town's museum and art gallery, **Christchurch Mansion**, is a Tudor house from 1548, where Elizabeth I stayed in 1561. It also boasts the best collection of Constable's paintings out of London *(see p204)*, including four marvellous Suffolk landscapes, as well as paintings by Gainsborough *(see p163)*.

Ipswich Museum contains replicas of the Mildenhall and Sutton Hoo treasures, the originals being in the British Museum *(see pp106–7)*.

In the centre of the town is **St Margaret's**, a 15th-century church built in flint and stone with a double hammerbeam roof and 17th-century painted ceiling panels. **Wolsey's Gate**, a Tudor gateway of 1527, provides a link with Ipswich's most famous son, Cardinal Wolsey *(see p173)*. He started to build an ecclesiastical college in the town, but fell from royal favour before it was finished.

🏛 **Christchurch Mansion**
Christchurch Pk. **Tel** 01473 433554. ◻ 10am–5pm daily. 🌑 1 Jan, Good Fri, 24–27 Dec. 🔌 limited. 🖼 by appt. 🛈 🛈

🏛 **Ipswich Museum**
High St. **Tel** 01473 433550. ◻ Tue–Sat. 🛈 🔌

Pargeting on the Ancient House in Ipswich

Constable Walk ⑲

This walk in Constable country follows one of the most picturesque sections of the River Stour. The route taken would have been familiar to the landscape painter John Constable (1776–1837). Constable's father, a wealthy merchant, owned Flatford Mill, which was depicted in many of the artist's important paintings. Constable claimed to know and love "every stile and stump, and every lane" around East Bergholt.

The River Stour, used as a backdrop for Constable's *Boatbuilding* (1814)

TIPS FOR WALKERS

Starting point: Park off Flatford Lane, East Bergholt (charge to park). ℹ 01206 299460; **(NT)** Bridge Cottage (01206 298260). **Getting there:** A12 to East Bergholt, then follow signs to Flatford. 🚆 Manningtree is within walking distance of Flatford. 🚌 from Ipswich or Colchester. **Stopping-off point:** Dedham. **Length:** 3 miles (5 km). **Difficulty:** Flat trail along riverside footpath with kissing gates.

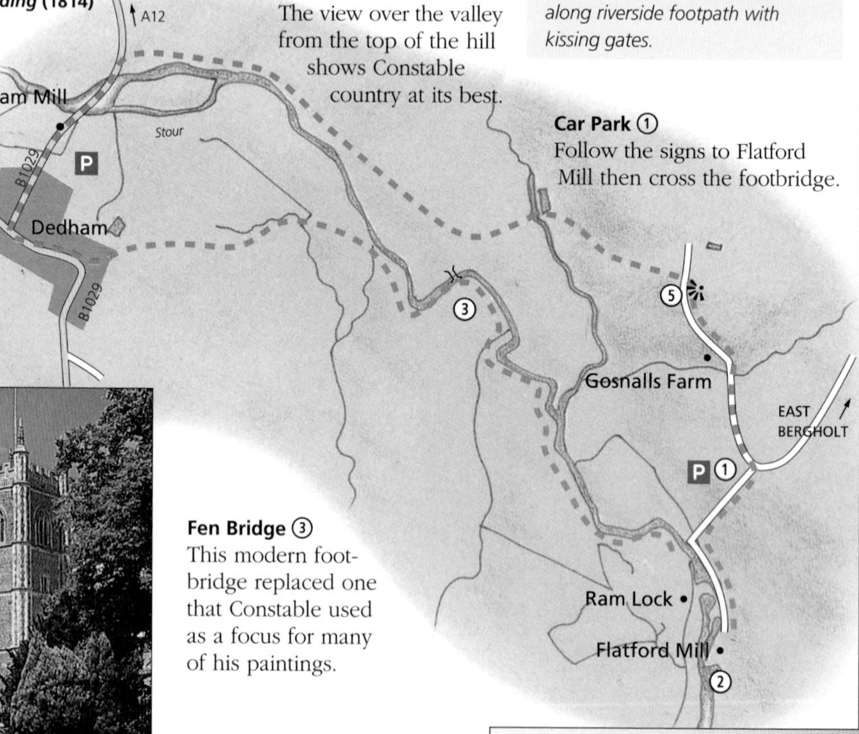

Viewpoint ⑤
The view over the valley from the top of the hill shows Constable country at its best.

Car Park ①
Follow the signs to Flatford Mill then cross the footbridge.

Dedham Mill

Stour

Dedham

EAST BERGHOLT

Gosnalls Farm

Fen Bridge ③
This modern footbridge replaced one that Constable used as a focus for many of his paintings.

Ram Lock •

Flatford Mill •

Dedham Church ④
The tall church tower appears in many of Constable's pictures including the *View on the Stour near Dedham* (1822).

KEY

- - - Route
▬▬ B road
═══ Minor road
☀ Viewpoint
P Parking

0 metres   500
0 yards   500

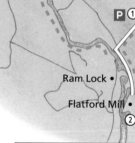

Willy Lott's Cottage ②
This cottage remains much the same as it did when featured in Constable's painting *The Hay-Wain* (see p83).

Colchester ⑳

Essex. 🏠 160,000. ⛴ 🚌 ℹ️ *Queen St (01206 282920).* 🛒 *Fri, Sat.* **www**.visitcolchester.com

The oldest recorded town in Britain, Colchester was the effective capital of south-east England when the Romans invaded in AD 43, and it was here that the first permanent Roman colony was established.

After Boadicea *(see p195)* burnt the town in AD 60, a 2 mile (3 km) wall was built, 3 m (10 ft) thick and 9 m (30 ft) high, to deter future attackers. You can still see these walls and the surviving Roman town gate, the largest in Britain.

During the Middle Ages Colchester developed into an important weaving centre. In the 16th century, a number of immigrant Flemish weavers settled in an area west of the castle, known as the **Dutch Quarter**, which still retains the original tall houses and steep, narrow streets.

Colchester was besieged for 11 weeks during the Civil War *(see p52)* before being captured by Cromwell's troops.

🏛 Tymperleys
Trinity St. *Tel 01206 282943.* ◻ *Apr–Oct: Tue–Sat.* ♿ *limited.* 📷
www.colchestermuseums.org.uk
Clock-making was an important craft in Colchester, and it is celebrated in this restored half-timbered, 15th-century mansion, also worth visiting for its formal Tudor garden.

🏛 Hollytrees Museum
High St. *Tel 01206 282940.* ◻ *daily.* 🔴 *1 Jan, 24–27 Dec.* ♿ 📷
www.colchestermuseums.org.uk
This elegant Georgian townhouse was built in 1719. Now a charming museum of social history, you can experience the day-to-day lives of Colchester people and changing technology over 300 years.

🏛 Castle Museum
High St. *Tel 01206 282939.* ◻ *9am–5pm daily (from 11am Sun).* 🔴 *1 Jan, 24–27 Dec.* 📷 ♿
www.colchestermuseums.org.uk
This is the oldest and largest Norman keep still standing in England. Twice the size of the White Tower at the Tower of

The Norman keep of the Castle Museum, Colchester

London *(see pp118–19)*, it was built in 1076 on the platform of a Roman temple dedicated to Claudius *(see p44)*, using stones and tiles from other Roman buildings. The museum's displays relate the story of the town from prehistoric times to the Civil War. There is also a medieval prison.

🏯 Layer Marney Tower
Off B1022. *Tel 01206 330784.* ◻ *Apr–Sep: Wed & Sun (Jul & Aug: Sun–Thu).* ♿ *limited.* 📷 *by appt.* 📷 **www**.layermarneytower.co.uk
This remarkable Tudor gatehouse is the tallest in Britain: its pair of six-sided, eight-storey turrets reach to 24 m (80 ft). It was intended to be part of a larger complex, but the designer, Sir Henry Marney, died before it was completed. The brickwork and terracotta ornamentation around the roof and windows are models of Tudor craftsmanship.

♣ Beth Chatto Garden
Elmstead Market. *Tel 01206 822007.* ◻ *Mar–Oct: 9am–5pm daily (pm only Sun); Nov–Feb: 9am–4pm Mon–Sat.* 🔴 *22 Dec–5 Jan.* ♿ 📷
www.bethchatto.co.uk
One of Britain's most eminent gardening writers, Beth Chatto began this experiment in the 1960s to test her belief that it is possible to create a garden in the most adverse conditions. The dry and windy slopes, boggy patches, gravel beds and wooded areas support an array of plants best suited to that particular environment.

Coggeshall ㉑

Essex. 🏠 4,000. 🛒 *Thu.* **www**.coggeshall-pc.gov.uk

This town has two of the most important medieval and Tudor buildings in the country. Dating from 1140, **Coggeshall Grange Barn** is the oldest surviving timber-framed barn in Europe. Inside is a display of historic farm wagons. The half-timbered merchant's house, **Paycocke's**, was built around 1500 and has a beautifully panelled interior. There is a display of Coggeshall lace.

🏯 Coggeshall Grange Barn
(NT) Grange Hill. 📞 *01376 562226.* ◻ *Apr–Oct: Tue, Thu, Sun & public hols (pm).* 🔴 *Good Fri.* ♿

🏯 Paycocke's
(NT) West St. *Tel 01376 561305.* ◻ *Apr–Oct: Tue, Thu, Sun & public hols (pm).* 🔴 *Good Fri.* ♿

Beth Chatto Garden, Colchester, in full summer bloom

Lavenham ㉒

Suffolk. 🚶 *1,800.*
ℹ *Lady St (01787 248207).*

Often considered the most perfect of all English small towns, Lavenham is a treasure trove of beautiful timber-framed houses ranged along streets whose pattern is virtually unchanged from medieval times. For 150 years, between the 14th and 16th centuries, Lavenham was the prosperous centre of the Suffolk wool trade. It still has many outstanding and well-preserved buildings; indeed no less than 300 of the town's buildings are listed, including the magnificent **Little Hall**.

Environs: Gainsborough's House, Sudbury, is a museum on this painter *(see p163).*

🏛 **Little Hall** Market Place. *Tel* 01787 247019. ◯ *Apr–Oct: Wed, Thu, Sat, Sun; public hols.* 🈶

🏛 **Gainsborough's House** Sudbury. *Tel 01787 372958.* ◯ *Mon–Sat.* ● *24 Dec–2 Jan, Good Fri.* ♿ 🚻 📷 🈶 www.gainsborough.org

LITTLE HALL

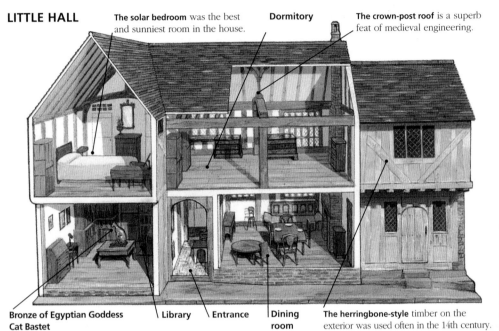

The solar bedroom was the best and sunniest room in the house.

Dormitory

The crown-post roof is a superb feat of medieval engineering.

Bronze of Egyptian Goddess Cat Bastet

Library

Entrance

Dining room

The herringbone-style timber on the exterior was used often in the 14th century.

Bury St Edmunds ㉓

Suffolk. 🚶 *34,000.* 🚆 🚌 **ℹ** *Angel Hill (01284 764667).* 🛒 *Wed, Sat.* www.stedmundsbury.gov.uk

St Edmund was the last Saxon king of East Anglia, decapitated by Danish raiders in 870. Legend has it that a wolf picked up the severed head – an image that appears in a number of medieval carvings. Edmund was canonized in 900 and buried in Bury, where in 1014 King Canute *(see p171)* built an **abbey** in his honour, the wealthiest in England until its destruction in the Dissolution of the Monasteries *(see p351).* The abbey ruins now lie in the town centre.

Nearby are two large 15th-century churches, built when the wool trade made the town wealthy. **St James's** was designated a cathedral in 1914. The best features of **St Mary's** are the north porch and the hammerbeam roof over the nave. A stone slab in the north-east corner marks the tomb of Mary Tudor *(see pp50–51).*

Just below the **market cross** in Cornhill – remodelled by Robert Adam *(see p28)* in 1714 – stands the large 12th-century **Moyse's Hall**, a merchant's house that serves as the local history museum, displaying archaeology from the area.

Environs: Three miles (5 km) southwest of Bury is the late 18th-century **Ickworth House**. This eccentric Neo-Classical mansion features an unusual rotunda with a

Illustration of St Edmund

The 18th-century rotunda of Ickworth House, Bury St Edmunds

domed roof flanked by two huge wings. The art collection includes works by Reynolds and Titian. There are also fine displays of silver, porcelain and sculpture, for example, John Flaxman's (1755–1826) moving *The Fury of Athamas*. The house is set in a large park.

The stallion unit at the National Stud, Newmarket

🏛 Moyse's Hall

Cornhill. *Tel* 01284 706183.
⬤ daily (last adm: 4pm). ⬤
public hols, 24 Dec. 🖼 🔌 📷

🏚 Ickworth House (NT)

Horringer. *Tel* 01284 735270. ⬤
Mar–Oct: Fri–Tue. 🖼 🔌 🍴 📷

Newmarket ㉔

Suffolk. 🏠 *17,000.* 🚆 🚌 ℹ️ *Palace House, Palace St (01638 667200).* 🛍
Tue, Sat. www.forest-heath.gov.uk

A walk down the short main street tells you all you need to know about this busy and wealthy little town. The shops sell horse feed and all manner of riding accessories; the clothes on sale are tweeds, jodhpurs and the soft brown hats rarely worn by anyone except racehorse trainers.

Newmarket has been the headquarters of British horse racing since James I decided that its open heaths were ideal for testing the mettle of his fastest steeds against those of his friends. The first ever recorded horse race was held here in 1622. Charles II shared his grandfather's enthusiasm and after the Restoration (*see p53*) would move the whole court to Newmarket, every spring and summer, for the sport – he is the only British king to have ridden a winner.

A horse being exercised on Newmarket Heath

The modern racing industry began to take shape here in the late 18th century. There are now over 2,500 horses in training in and around the town, and two racecourses staging regular race meetings from around April to October (*see pp66–7*). Training stables are occasionally open to the public but you can view the horses being exercised on the heath in the early morning. Tattersall's, the auction house for thoroughbreds, is in the centre of Newmarket.

The **National Stud** can also be visited. You will see the five or six stallions on stud, mares in foal and if you are lucky a newborn foal – most likely in April or May.

The **National Horseracing Museum** tells the history of the sport and contains many offbeat exhibits such as the skeleton of Eclipse, one of the greatest horses ever, unbeaten in 18 races and the ancestor of most of today's fastest performers. It also has a large display of sporting art.

🎯 National Stud

Newmarket. *Tel* 01638 663464. ⬤
Feb–Sep: daily; Oct: half term. 🖼 🔌
🖼 📷 📷 www.nationalstud.co.uk

🏛 National Horseracing Museum

99 High St, Newmarket. *Tel* 01638
667333. ⬤ Apr–Oct: daily. 🖼 🔌
🖼 📷 📷 www.nhrm.co.uk

THE RISE AND FALL OF THE WOOL TRADE

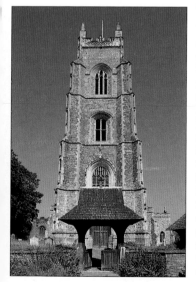

St Mary's Church, Stoke-by-Nayland, southeast of Bury St Edmunds

Wool was a major English product from the 13th century and by 1310 some ten million fleeces were exported every year. The Black Death (*see p48),* which swept Britain in 1348, perversely provided a boost for the industry: with labour in short supply, land could not be cultivated and was grassed over for sheep. Around 1350 Edward III decided it was time to establish a home-based cloth industry and encouraged Flemish weavers to come to Britain. Many settled in East Anglia, particularly Suffolk, and their skills helped establish a flourishing trade. This time of prosperity saw the construction of the sumptuous churches, such as the one at Stoke-by-Nayland, that we see today – East Anglia has more than 2,000 churches. The cloth trade here began to decline in the late 16th century with the development of water-powered looms. These were not suited to the area, which never regained its former wealth. Today's visitors are the beneficiaries of this decline, because the wool towns such as Lavenham and Bury St Edmunds never became rich enough to destroy their magnificent Tudor halls and houses and construct new buildings.

The façade of Anglesey Abbey

Anglesey Abbey 25

(NT) Lode, Cambridgeshire.
Tel 01223 810080. � Cambridge
then bus. **House** ◯ Mar–Oct: Wed–
Sun; **Garden** ◯ Wed–Sun. ▨ ⛓
limited. 🍴 🖺

The original Abbey was built
in 1135 for an Augustinian
order. But only the crypt – also
known as the monks' parlour
– with its vaulted ceiling on
marble and stone pillars, survived the Dissolution *(see p50)*.
   This was later incorporated
into a manor house whose
treasures include furniture
from many periods and a rare
seascape by Gainsborough
(see p206). The superb garden
was created in the 1930s by
Lord Fairhaven as an ambitious, Classical landscape of
trees, sculptures and borders.

Huntingdon 26

Cambridgeshire. 🏘 18,000. � 🖥
ℹ Princes St (01480 388588).
🛆 Wed, Sat.

More than 300 years after
his death, Oliver Cromwell
(see p52) still dominates this
small town. Born here in 1599,
a record of his baptism can be
seen in the County Records
Office in Huntingdon. You can
see his name and traces of
ancient graffiti scrawled all
over it which says "England's
plague for five years".
Cromwell Museum, his
former school, traces his life
with pictures and mementoes,
including his death mask.
   Cromwell remains one of the
most disputed figures in British
history. An MP before he was
30, he became embroiled in
the disputes between Charles
I and Parliament over taxes
and religion. In the Civil War
(see p52) he proved an
inspired general and, after
refusing the title of king, was
made Lord Protector in 1653,
four years after the King was
beheaded. Just two years after
his death the monarchy was
restored by popular demand,
and his body was taken out
of Westminster Abbey *(see
pp92–3)* to hang on gallows.
   There is a 14th-century
bridge across the River Ouse
which links Huntingdon with
Godmanchester, the site of a
Roman settlement.

🏛 **Cromwell Museum**
Grammar School Walk.
Tel 01480 375830. ◯ Tue–Sun
(Nov–Mar: pm only except Sat).
⬤ 1 Jan, 24–27 Dec, some public
hols. ⛓ 🖺

Cambridge 27

See pp210–15.

Audley End 28

(EH) Saffron Walden, Essex.
Tel 01799 522399. � Audley End
then taxi. **House** ◯ mid-Mar–Oct:
Wed–Sun. **Garden** ◯ Wed–Sun.
⬤ 24 Dec–31 Jan. ▨ ⛓ limited.
🗂 🍴 🖵 🖺
www.english-heritage.org.uk

This was the largest house in
England when built in 1603–14
for Thomas Howard, Lord
Treasurer and 1st Earl of Suffolk.
James I joked that Audley End
was too big for a king but not
for a Lord Treasurer. Charles
II, his grandson, disagreed
and bought it in 1667. He
seldom went there, however,
and in 1701 it was given back
to the Howards, who demolished two thirds of it.
   What remains is a Jacobean
mansion, retaining its original
hall and many fine plaster
ceilings. Robert Adam *(see
p28)* remodelled some of the
interior in the 1760s, and these
rooms have been restored
to his original designs. At the
same time, Capability Brown
(see p26) landscaped the magnificent 18th-century park.

The Chapel *was completed
in 1772 to a Gothic design.
The furniture was made to
complement the wooden
pillars and vaulting which
are painted to imitate stone.*

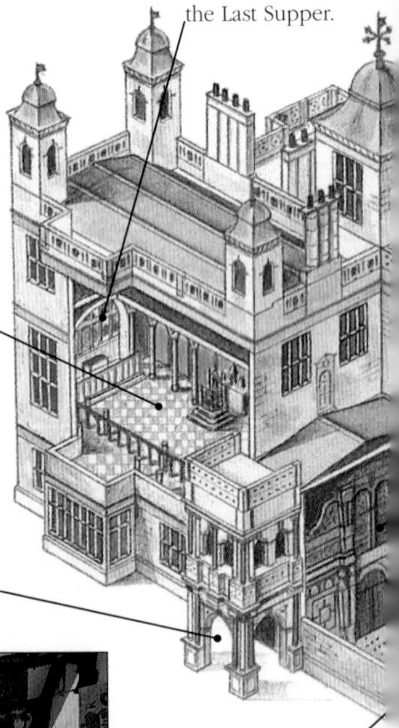

Stained glass window,
installed in 1771, represents
the Last Supper.

Main entrance

The Great Hall,
*hung with family
portraits, is the highligh
of the house, with the
massive oak screen and
elaborate hammerbea
roof surviving in their
Jacobean form.*

Epping Forest ㉙

Essex. 🚉 *Chingford.* 🚇 *Loughton, Theydon Bois.* ℹ️ *High Beach, Loughton (020–8508 0028) & Highbridge St, Waltam Abbey (01992 652295).*

As one of the large open spaces near London, the 2,400 ha (6,000 acre) forest is popular with walkers, just as, centuries ago, it was a favourite hunting ground for kings and courtiers – the word forest

Epping Forest contains oaks and beeches up to 400 years old

A depiction of the Battle of Maldon (991) on the *Maldon Embroidery*

denoted an area for hunting. Henry VIII had a lodge built in 1543 on the edge of the forest. His daughter Elizabeth I often used the lodge and it soon became known as **Queen Elizabeth's Hunting Lodge**.

This three-storey timbered building has been fully renovated and now houses an exhibition explaining the lodge's history and other aspects of the forest's life.

The tracts of open land and woods interspersed with a number of lakes, make an ideal habitat for a variety of plant, bird and animal life: deer roam the northern part, many of a special dark strain introduced by James I. The

Corporation of London bought the forest in the mid-19th century to ensure it remained open to the public.

🏛 Queen Elizabeth's Hunting Lodge

Rangers Rd, Chingford. **Tel** 020–8529 6681. ◯ Oct–Mar: Fri–Sun; Apr–Sep: Wed–Sun, pm only. ⬤ 1 Jan, 24–26 Dec. ♿ limited. 🎟 by appt. 🛈 🖾

Maldon ㉚

Essex. 🏘 *21,000.* 🚉 *Chelmsford then bus.* ℹ️ *Coach Lane (01621 856503).* 🛒 *Thu, Sat.* www.visitmaldon.co.uk

This delightful old town on the River Blackwater, its High Street lined with shops and inns from the 14th century on, was once an important harbour. One of its best-known industries is the production of Maldon sea salt, panned in the traditional way.

A fierce battle here in 991, when Viking invaders defeated the Saxon defenders, is told in *The Battle of Maldon,* one of the earliest known Saxon poems. The battle is also celebrated in the *Maldon Embroidery* on display in the **Maeldune Centre**. This 13-m- (42-ft-) long embroidery, made by locals, depicts the history of Maldon from 991 to 1991.

Environs: East of Maldon at Bradwell-on-Sea is the sturdy Saxon church of **St Peter's-on-the-Wall**, a simple stone building that stands isolated on the shore. It was built in 654, from the stones of a former Roman fort, by St Cedd, who used it as his cathedral. It was restored in the 1920s.

🏛 Maeldune Centre

High St. **Tel** 01621 851628. ◯ Apr–Oct: Mon–Sat; Nov–Mar: Thu & Fri; pm only. ⬤ 1 Jan, 24–26 Dec. 🎟

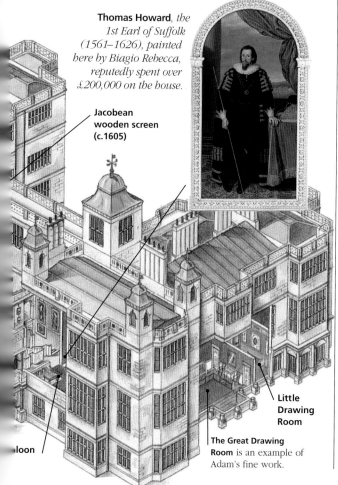

Thomas Howard, the 1st Earl of Suffolk (1561–1626), painted here by Biagio Rebecca, reputedly spent over £200,000 on the house.

Jacobean wooden screen (c.1605)

Little Drawing Room

The Great Drawing Room is an example of Adam's fine work.

...loon

Street-by-Street: Cambridge ㉗

Cambridge has been an important town since Roman times as it was sited at the first navigable point on the River Cam. In the 11th century religious orders began to be established in the town and, in 1209, a group of religious scholars broke away from Oxford University (*see pp222–27*) after academic and religious disputes and came here. Student life dominates the city but it is also a thriving market centre serving a rich agricultural region.

Carving, King's College Chapel

Cyclists in Cambridge

Newmarket

BRIDGE STREET

ST JOHN'S STREET

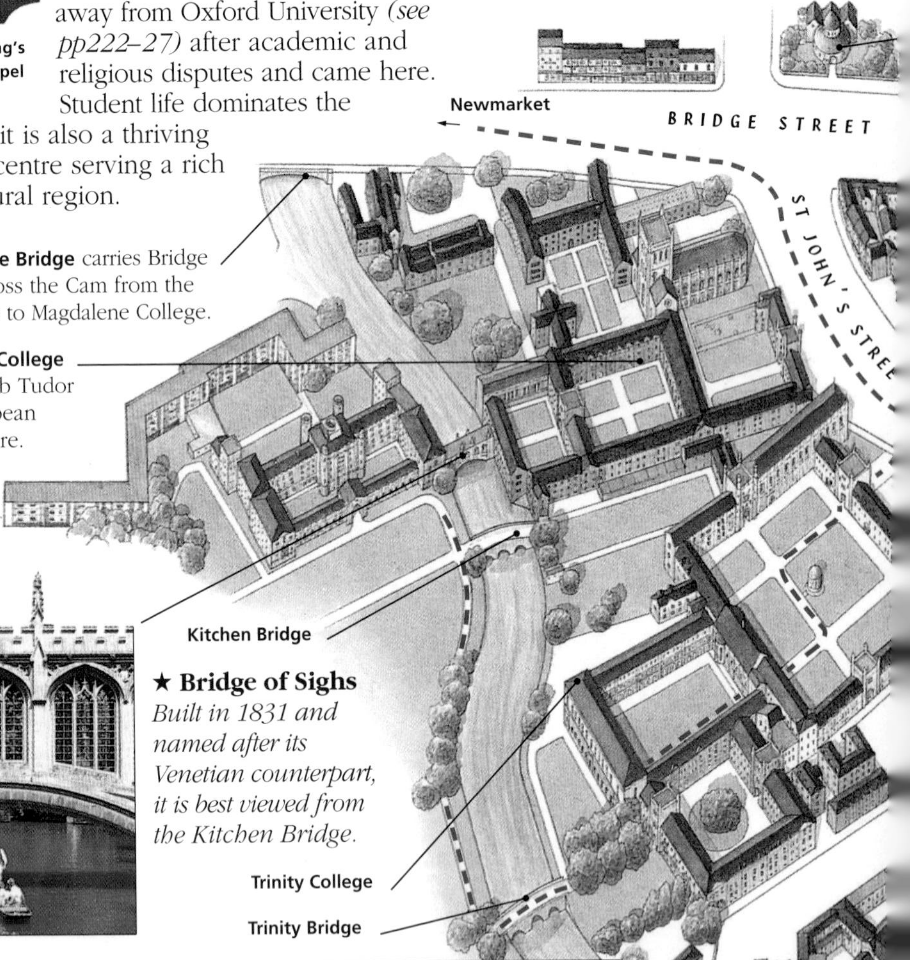

Magdalene Bridge carries Bridge Street across the Cam from the city centre to Magdalene College.

St John's College has superb Tudor and Jacobean architecture.

Kitchen Bridge

★ Bridge of Sighs
Built in 1831 and named after its Venetian counterpart, it is best viewed from the Kitchen Bridge.

Trinity College

Trinity Bridge

The Backs
This is the name given to the grassy strip lying between the backs of the big colleges and the banks of the Cam – a good spot to enjoy this classic view of King's College Chapel.

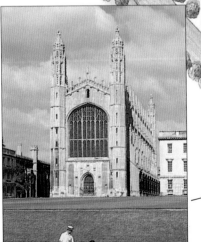

Clare College

Clare Bridge

Grantchester

KEY

– – – Suggested route

STAR SIGHTS

★ Bridge of Sighs

★ King's College Chapel

0 metres

0 yards   7

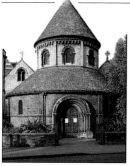

Round Church
The 12th-century Church of the Holy Sepulchre has one of the few round naves in the country. Its design is based on the Holy Sepulchre in Jerusalem.

Great St Mary's Church
This clock is over the west door of the university's official church. Its tower offers fine views.

1679

VISITORS' CHECKLIST

Cambridgeshire. 120,000. Stansted. Cambridge. Station Rd. Drummer St. Wheeler St (0871 2268006). 01223 457574. daily. Folk Festival: July; Strawberry Fair: June. **www**.visitcambridge.org

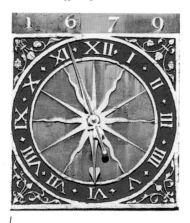

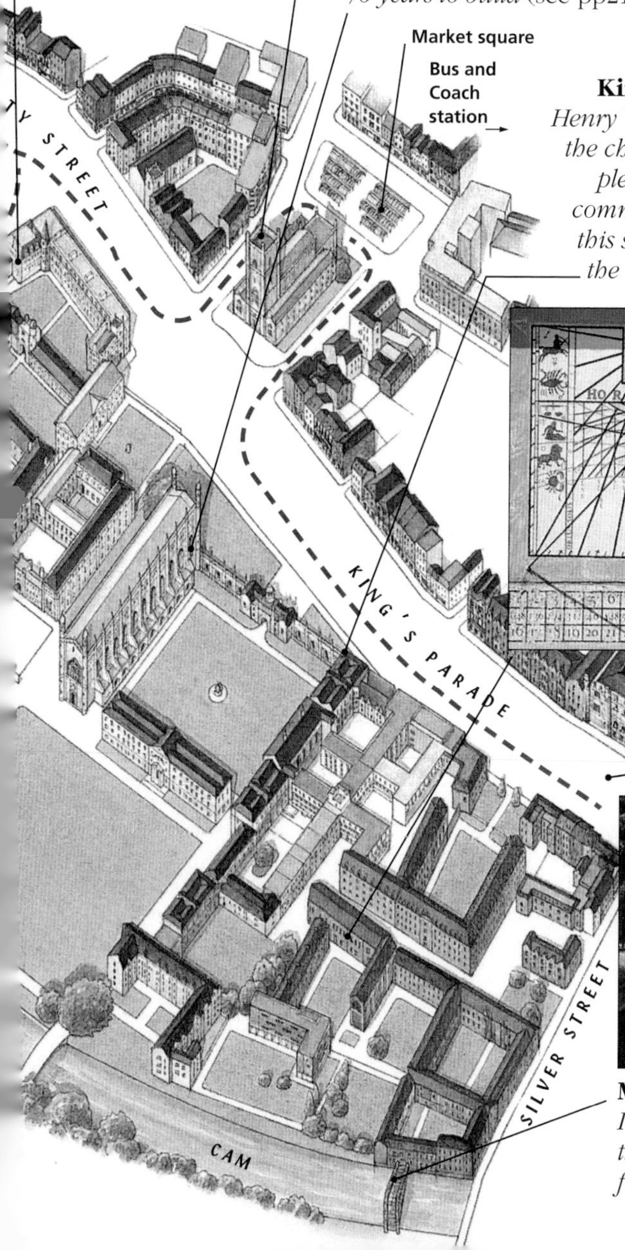

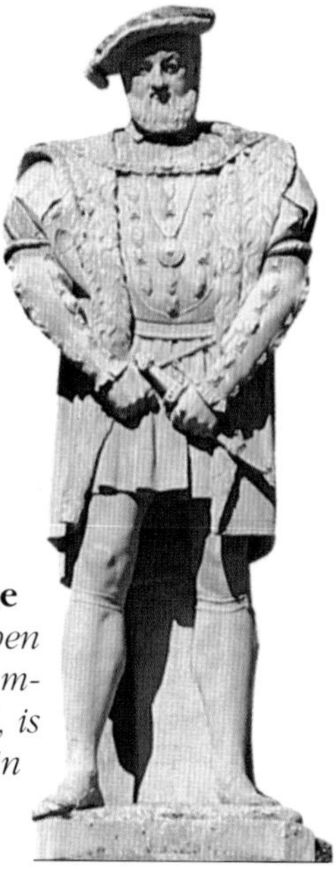

King's College
Henry VIII, king when the chapel was completed in 1515, is commemorated in this statue near the main gate.

Gonville and Caius (pronounced "keys"), founded in 1348, is one of the oldest colleges.

★ King's College Chapel
This late medieval masterpiece took 70 years to build (see pp212–13).

Market square
Bus and Coach station
Corpus Christi College
To London and railway station
STREET
KING'S PARADE
SILVER STREET
CAM

HORIZON

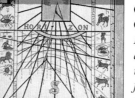

Queens' College
Its Tudor courts are among the university's finest. This 18th-century sundial is over the old chapel – now a reading room.

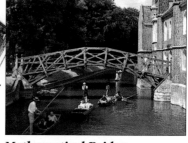

Mathematical Bridge
It is a myth that this bridge over the Cam at Queens' College was first built without nuts or bolts.

🏛 Fitzwilliam Museum

Trumpington St. **Tel** *01223 332900.*
◯ *Tue–Sun; public hols.* ⬤ *24–27
Dec, 1 Jan, Good Fri.* **Donation**. ♿
📷 *by arrangement.* ▭ 🛈
www.fitzmuseum.cam.ac.uk

One of Britain's oldest public museums, this massive Classical building has works of exceptional quality and rarity, especially antiquities, ceramics, paintings and manuscripts.

The core of the collection was bequeathed in 1816 by the 7th Viscount Fitzwilliam. Other gifts have since greatly added to the exhibits.

Works by Titian (1488–1576) and the 17th-century Dutch masters, including Hals, Cuyp and Hobbema's *Wooded Landscape* (1686), stand out among the paintings. French Impressionist gems include Monet's *Le Printemps* (1866) and Renoir's *La Place Clichy* (1880), while Picasso's *Still Life* (1923) is notable among the modern works. Most of the important British artists are represented, from Hogarth in the 18th century through Constable in the 19th to Ben Nicholson in the 20th.

The miniatures include the earliest surviving depiction of Henry VIII. In the same gallery are some dazzling illuminated manuscripts, notably the 15th-century *Metz Pontifical,* a French liturgical work.

The impressive Glaisher collection of European earthenware and stoneware includes a unique display of English delftware from the 16th and 17th centuries.

Handel's bookcase contains folios of his work, and nearby is Keats's original manuscript for *Ode to a Nightingale* (1819).

**Portrait of Richard James
(c.1740s) by William Hogarth**

Cambridge: King's College

**King's College
Coat of Arms**

Henry VI founded this college in 1441. Work on the chapel – one of the most important examples of late medieval English architecture – began five years later, and took 70 years to complete. Henry himself decided that it should dominate the city and gave specific instructions about its dimensions: 88 m (289 ft) long, 12 m (40 ft) wide and 29 m (94 ft) high. The detailed design is thought to have been by master stonemason Reginald Ely, although it was altered in later years.

★ Fan Vaulted Ceiling
This awe-inspiring ceiling, supported by 22 buttresses, was built by master stonemason John Wastell in 1515.

The Fellows' Building was designed in 1724 by James Gibbs, as part of an uncompleted design for a Great Court.

Henry VI's statue
This bronze statue of the college's founder was erected in 1879.

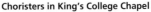

KING'S COLLEGE CHOIR

When he founded the chapel, Henry VI stipulated that a choir of six lay clerks and 16 boy choristers – educated at the College school – should sing daily at services. This still happens in term time but today the choir also gives concerts all over the world. Its broadcast service of carols has become a much-loved Christmas tradition.

Choristers in King's College Chapel

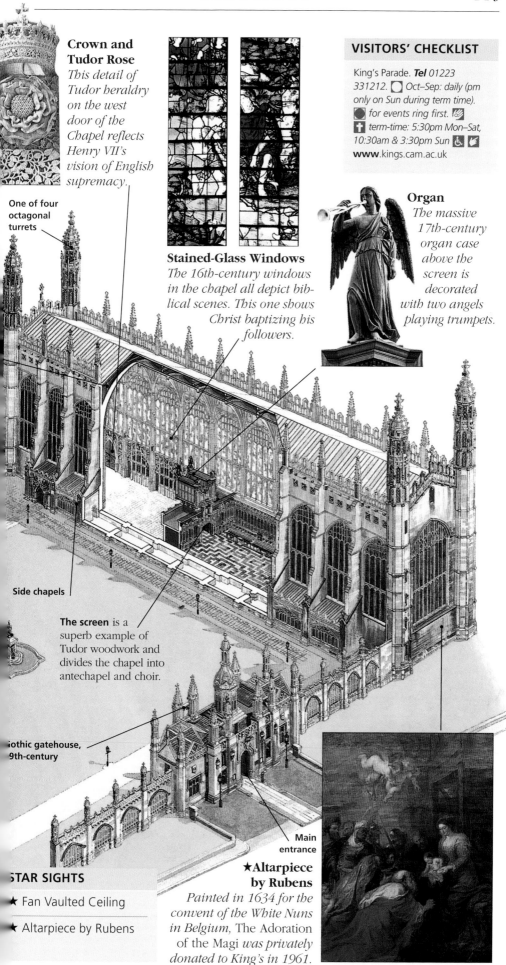

Crown and Tudor Rose
This detail of Tudor heraldry on the west door of the Chapel reflects Henry VII's vision of English supremacy.

One of four octagonal turrets

Stained-Glass Windows
The 16th-century windows in the chapel all depict biblical scenes. This one shows Christ baptizing his followers.

Organ
The massive 17th-century organ case above the screen is decorated with two angels playing trumpets.

Side chapels

The screen is a superb example of Tudor woodwork and divides the chapel into antechapel and choir.

Gothic gatehouse, 19th-century

Main entrance

STAR SIGHTS

★ Fan Vaulted Ceiling

★ Altarpiece by Rubens

★Altarpiece by Rubens
Painted in 1634 for the convent of the White Nuns in Belgium, The Adoration of the Magi *was privately donated to King's in 1961.*

Exploring Cambridge University

Cambridge University has 31 colleges *(see also pp210–11)*, the oldest being Peterhouse (1284) and the newest being Robinson (1979). Clustered around the city centre, many of the older colleges have peaceful gardens backing onto the River Cam, which are known as the "Backs". The layout of the older colleges, as at Oxford *(see pp226–7)*, derives from their early connections with religious institutions, although few escaped heavy-handed modification in the Victorian era. The college buildings are generally grouped around squares called courts and offer an unrivalled mix of over 600 years of architecture from the late medieval period through Wren's masterpieces and up to the present day.

The nave of the Wren Chapel at Pembroke College

The imposing façade of Emmanuel College

Emmanuel College
Built in 1677 on St Andrew's Street, Sir Christopher Wren's *(see p114)* chapel is the highlight of the college. Some of the intricate interior details, particularly the plaster ceiling and Amigoni's altar rails (1734), are superb. Founded in 1584, the college has a Puritan tradition. One notable graduate was the clergyman John Harvard, who emigrated to America in 1636 and left all his money to the Massachusetts college that now bears his name.

Senate House
King's Parade is the site of this Palladian building, which is used primarily for university ceremonies. It was designed by James Gibbs in 1722 as part of a grand square of university buildings – which was never completed.

Corpus Christi College
Just down from Senate House, this was founded in 1352 by the local trade guilds, anxious to ensure that education was not the sole prerogative of church and nobility. Its Old Court is remarkably well preserved and looks today much as it would have done when built in the 14th century.

The college is connected by a 15th-century gallery of red brick to St Bene't's Church (short for St Benedict's), whose large Saxon tower is the oldest structure in Cambridge.

King's College
See pp212–13.

Pembroke College
The college chapel was the first building completed by Wren *(see pp114–15)*. A formal classical design, it replaced a 14th-century chapel that was turned into a library. The college, just off Trumpington Street, also has fine gardens.

Jesus College
Although founded in 1497, some of its buildings on Jesus Lane are older, as the college took over St Radegond's nunnery, built in the 12th century. There are traces of Norman columns, windows and a well preserved hammerbeam roof in the college dining hall.

The chapel keeps the core of the original church but the stained glass windows are modern and contain work by William Morris *(see pp220–21)*.

Queens' College
Built in 1446 on Queens' Lane, the college was endowed in 1448 by Margaret of Anjou, queen of Henry VI, and again in 1465 by Elizabeth Woodville, queen of Edward IV, which explains the position of the apostrophe. Queens' has a

---

PUNTING ON THE CAM

Punting captures the essence of carefree college days: a student leaning on a long pole, lazily guiding the flat-bottomed river craft along, while others stretch out and relax. Punting is still popular both with students and visitors, who can hire punts from boat-yards along the river – with a chauffeur if required. Punts do sometimes capsize, and novices should prepare for a dip.

Punting by the King's College "Backs"

marvellous collection of Tudor buildings, notably the half-timbered President's Gallery, built in the mid-16th century on top of the brick arches in the charming Cloister Court. The Principal Court is 15th century, as is Erasmus's Tower, named after the Dutch scholar.

Pepys Library in Magdalene College

The college has buildings on both sides of the Cam, linked by the bizarre Mathematical Bridge, built in 1749 to hold together without the use of nuts and bolts – although they have had to be used in subsequent repairs.

Magdalene College
Pronounced "maudlin" – as is the Oxford college (see p226) – the college, on Bridge Street, was established in 1482. The diarist Samuel Pepys (1633–1703) was a student here and left his large library to the college on his death. The 12 red-oak bookcases have over 3,000 books. Magdalene was the last all-male Cambridge college and it admitted women students only in 1987.

St John's College
Sited on St John's Street, the imposing turreted brick and stone gatehouse of 1514, with its colourful heraldic symbols, provides a fitting entrance to the second largest Cambridge college and its rich store of 16th- and 17th-century buildings. Its hall, most of it Elizabethan, has portraits of the college's famous alumni, such as the poet William Wordsworth (see p366) and the statesman Lord Palmerston. St John's spans the Cam and boasts two bridges, one built in 1712 and the other, the Bridge of Sighs, in 1831, based on its Venetian namesake.

Peterhouse
The first Cambridge college, on Trumpington Street, is also one of the smallest. The hall still has original features from 1286 but its best details are later – a Tudor fireplace which is backed with 19th-century tiles by William Morris (see pp220–21). A gallery connects the college to the 12th-century church of St Mary the Less, which used to be called St Peter's Church – hence the college's name.

William Morris tiles, Peterhouse

VISITORS' CHECKLIST

Cambridge Colleges can usually be visited from 2–5pm daily, but there are no set opening hours. See noticeboards at each college for daily opening times. Some colleges charge admission.

Trinity College
The largest college, situated on Trinity Street, was founded by Henry VIII in 1547 and has a massive court and hall. The entrance gate, with statues of Henry and James I (added later), was built in 1529 for King's Hall, an earlier college incorporated into Trinity. The Great Court features a late Elizabethan fountain – at one time the main water supply. The chapel, built in 1567, has life-size statues of college members, notably Roubiliac's statue of the scientist Isaac Newton (1755).

University Botanic Garden
A delightful place for a leisurely stroll, just off Trumpington Street, as well as an important academic resource, the garden has been on this site since 1846. It has a superb collection of trees and a sensational water garden. The winter garden is one of the finest in the country.

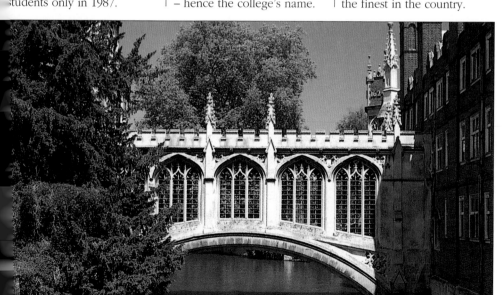

The Bridge of Sighs over the River Cam, linking the buildings of St John's College

THAMES VALLEY

BUCKINGHAMSHIRE · OXFORDSHIRE · BERKSHIRE
BEDFORDSHIRE · HERTFORDSHIRE

The mighty tidal river on which Britain's capital city was founded has modest origins, meandering from its source in the hills of Gloucestershire through the lush countryside towards London. Almost entirely agricultural land in the 19th century, the Thames Valley maintains its pastoral beauty despite the incursion of modern industry.

There are ancient royal connections with the area. Windsor Castle has been a residence of kings and queens for more than 900 years, and played a critical role in history in 1215, when King John set out from here to sign the *Magna Carta* at Runnymede on the River Thames. Further north, Queen Anne had Blenheim Palace built for her military commander, the 1st Duke of Marlborough. Elizabeth I spent part of her childhood at Hatfield House, and part of the Tudor palace still stands.

Several towns in this region, most notably Burford in Oxfordshire, developed as coach staging posts on the important trunk routes between London and the West Country. With the introduction of commuter transportation in the early 20th century, much of the area became an extension of suburbia and saw some imaginative experiments in Utopian town planning such as the garden city of Welwyn and the Quaker settlement at Jordons.

Oxford, the Thames Valley's principal city, owes its importance to the foundation of Britain's first university there in 1167; many of its colleges are gems of medieval architecture. In the 17th century, a number of battles during the Civil War *(see p52)* were fought around Oxford, which for a time was the headquarters of King Charles I, who was supported by the students. When the royalists were forced to flee Oxford, Cromwell made himself chancellor of the university.

Punting on the River Cherwell, Oxford

◁ **Medieval staircase in Christchurch College, Oxford**

Exploring the Thames Valley

The pleasant countryside of the Chiltern Hills and of the Thames Valley itself appealed to aristocrats who built stately homes close to London. Many of these are among the grandest in the country, including Hatfield House and Blenheim. Around these great houses grew picturesque villages, with half-timbered buildings and, as you move towards the Cotswolds, houses built in attractive buff-coloured stone. That the area has been inhabited for thousands of years is shown by the number of prehistoric remains, including the most remarkable chalk hillside figure, the White Horse of Uffington.

SIGHTS AT A GLANCE

Blenheim Palace pp228–9 ⑥
Burford ②
Gardens of the Rose ⑮
Great Tew ①
Hatfield House ⑬
Hughendon Manor ⑯
Kelmscott ③
Knebworth House ⑫
Oxford pp222–7 ⑤
Roald Dahl Museum ⑩
St Albans ⑭
Stowe ⑦
Vale of the White
    Horse ④
Waddesdon Manor ⑨
Windsor pp235–7 ⑱
Woburn Abbey ⑧
ZSL Whipsnade Zoo ⑪

Walks and Tours

Touring the Thames ⑰

A thatched cottage, Upper Swarford, Banbury

GETTING AROUND

As an important commuter belt, the Thames Valley is well served by public transport, as well as a good network of motorways and major roads into London. Mainline trains travel to all the major towns and there are many coach services that run from London to the major sights and attractions.

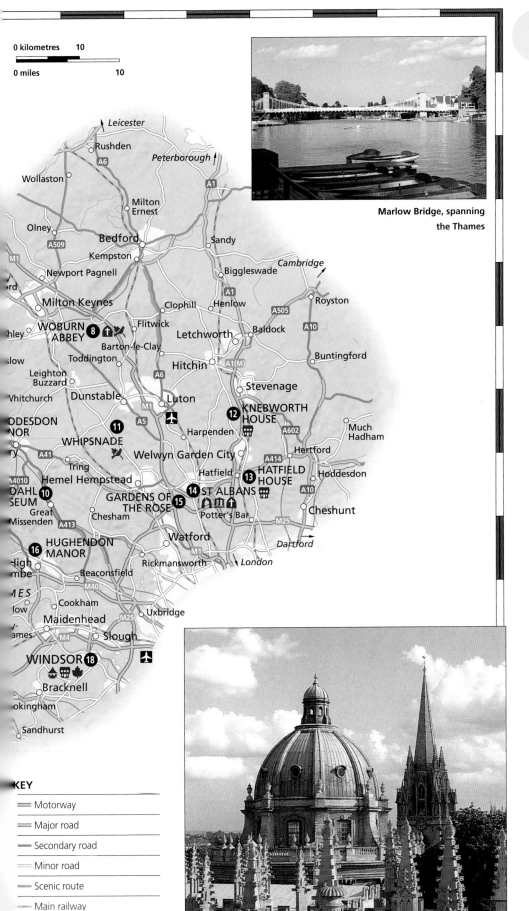

0 kilometres 10

0 miles 10

Leicester
Rushden
A6
Peterborough
Wollaston
Milton Ernest
Olney
Bedford
A509
Kempston
Sandy
M1
Newport Pagnell
Biggleswade
Cambridge
rd
Milton Keynes
Clophill
Henlow
A1
Royston
A505
hley
WOBURN ABBEY 8
Flitwick
Letchworth
Baldock
A10
Buntingford
slow
Barton-le-Clay
Toddington
Hitchin
A1(M)
Leighton Buzzard
A6
Stevenage
Whitchurch
Dunstable
Luton
KNEBWORTH HOUSE 12
Much Hadham
ODDESDON NOR
11
WHIPSNADE
A5
M1
Harpenden
A602
ry
A41
Tring
Welwyn Garden City
Hertford
A414
Hoddesdon
M4010
Hemel Hempstead
Hatfield
HATFIELD HOUSE 13
A10
DAHL SEUM 10
GARDENS OF THE ROSE
Chesham
ST ALBANS 15
14
Cheshunt
Great Missenden
A413
Potter's Bar
M25
HUGHENDON MANOR 16
Watford
Dartford
High mbe
M1
Rickmansworth
London
Beaconsfield
M40
MES
Cookham
low
Maidenhead
M25
Uxbridge
ames
M4
Slough
WINDSOR 18
Bracknell
okingham
Sandhurst

Marlow Bridge, spanning the Thames

KEY

Motorway

Major road

Secondary road

Minor road

Scenic route

Main railway

Minor railway

Radcliffe Camera, surrounded by Oxford's spires

Great Tew ❶

Oxfordshire. 🚶 *250.* 🚆 *Oxford or Banbury then taxi.* ℹ️ *Castle Quay Shopping Centre, Banbury (01295 259855).* **www.**visitnorth oxfordshire.com

This secluded village of ironstone was founded in the 1630s by Lord Falkland for estate workers. It was heavily restored between 1809 and 1811 in the Gothic style. Thatched cottages stand in gardens with clipped box hedges, and in the village centre is the 16th-century pub, the **Falkland Arms**, with its original period atmosphere.

Environs: Five miles (8 km) west are the **Rollright Stones**, three Bronze Age monuments. They comprise a stone circle of 77 stones, about 30 m (100 ft) in diameter, known as the King's Men; the remains of a burial chamber called the Whispering Knights; and the solitary King Stone.

Further north is **Banbury**, well known for its spicy flat cakes and its market cross, immortalized in the nursery rhyme, *Ride a Cock-horse to Banbury Cross.* The original medieval cross was destroyed but it was replaced in 1859.

🍺 **Falkland Arms Pub**
Great Tew. *Tel 01608 683653.* ⭘ *daily.* ⬤ *25 Dec.* 🍴 🎵

The 19th-century Banbury Cross

Burford ❷

Oxfordshire. 🚶 *1,000.* ℹ️ *Sheep St (01993 823558).*

A charming small town, Burford has hardly changed from Georgian times, when it was an important coach stop between Oxford and the West Country. Cotswold stone houses, inns and shops, many built in the 16th century, line its main street. **Tolsey Hall** is a Tudor house with an open ground floor where stalls are still set up. The house is located on the corner of Sheep Street, itself a reminder of the importance of the medieval wool trade *(see p207).*

Environs: Just east of Burford is **Swinbrook**, whose church contains the Fettiplace Monuments, six carved figures from the Tudor and Stuart periods.

Two miles (3 km) beyond are the ruins of **Minster Lovell Hall**, a 15th-century manor house whose unusual dovecote survives intact.

A few miles south of Burford is **Cotswold Wildlife Park**, home to a diverse collection of mammals, reptiles and birds. **Witney**, to the west, has a town hall dating from 1730.

🏛️ **Minster Lovell Hall**
(EH) Minster Lovell. ⭘ *daily.*

🐾 **Cotswold Wildlife Park**
Burford. *Tel 01993 823006.* ⭘ *daily.* ⬤ *25 Dec.* 📷 ♿ 🍴 🚻
www.cotswoldwildlifepark.co.uk

Kelmscott ❸

Oxfordshire. 🚶 *100.* ℹ️ *5 Market Place, Faringdon (01367 242191).* **www.**faringdon.org

The imaginative designer and writer William Morris lived in this pretty Thameside village from 1871 until his death in 1896. He shared his house, the classic Elizabethan **Kelmscott Manor**, with fellow painter Dante Gabriel Rossetti (1828–82), who left after an affair with Morris's wife Jane – the model for many pre-Raphaelite paintings.

Morris and his followers in the Arts and Crafts movement were attracted by the

Cotswold stone houses, Burford, Oxfordshire

The formal entrance of the Elizabethan Kelmscott Manor

medieval feel of the village and several cottages were later built in Morris's memory.

Today Kelmscott Manor has works of art by members of the movement – including some William de Morgan tiles. Morris is buried in the village churchyard, with a tomb designed by Philip Webb.

Two miles (3 km) to the east is **Radcot Bridge**, thought to be the oldest bridge still standing over the Thames. Built in the 13th century from the local Taynton stone, it was a strategic river crossing, and in 1387 was damaged in a battle between Richard II and his barons.

🕎 Kelmscott Manor
Kelmscott. *Tel* 01367 252486. ◯ *Apr–Sep: Wed & some Sat; Gardens & shop: Thu.* 🖼 ♿ limited. 🅿 🍴
www.kelmscottmanor.co.uk

Vale of the White Horse ❹

Oxfordshire. 🚉 *Didcot.* ℹ *25 Bridge St, Abingdon (01235 522711); 19 Church St, Wantage (01235 760176).* **www**.abingdon.gov.uk

This lovely valley gets its name from the huge chalk horse, 100 m (350 ft) from nose to tail, carved into the hillside above Uffington. It is believed to be Britain's oldest hillside carving and has sparked many legends: some say it was cut by the Saxon leader Hengist (whose name means stallion in German), while others believe it is to do with Alfred the Great, thought to have been born nearby.

It is, however, a great deal older than either of these stories suggest, having been dated at around 1000 BC.

Nearby is the Celtic earth ramparts of the Iron Age hill fort, **Uffington Castle**. A mile (1.5 km) west along the Ridgeway, an ancient trade route, *(see p37)*, is an even older monument, a large Stone Age burial mound which is known as **Wayland's Smithy**. This is immersed in legends that Sir Walter Scott *(see p512)* used in his novel *Kenilworth*.

The best view of the horse is to be had from Uffington village, which is also worth visiting for the **Tom Brown's School Museum**. This 17th-century school house contains exhibits devoted to the author Thomas Hughes (1822–96). Hughes set the early chapters of his Victorian novel, *Tom Brown's Schooldays,* here. The museum also contains material about excavations on White Horse Hill.

🏛 Tom Brown's School
Broad St, Uffington. ℹ *01367 820259.* ◯ *Easter–Oct: Sat, Sun & public hols (pm).* 🖼 ♿ limited. 🅿
www.museum.uffington.net

HILLSIDE CHALK FIGURES

It was the Celts who first saw the potential for creating large-scale artworks on the chalk hills of southern England. Horses – held in high regard by both the Celts and later the Saxons, and the objects of cult worship – were often a favourite subject, but people were also depicted, notably Cerne Abbas, Dorset *(see p269)* and the Long Man of Wilmington *(see p180)*. The figures may have served as religious symbols or as landmarks by which tribes identified their territory. Many chalk figures have been obliterated, because without any attention they are quickly overrun by grass. Uffington is "scoured", to prevent encroachment by grass, a tradition once accompanied by a fair and other festivities. There was a second flush of hillside carving in the 18th century, especially in Wiltshire. In some cases – for instance at Bratton Castle near Westbury – an 18th-century carving has been superimposed on an ancient one.

Britain's oldest hillside carving, the White Horse of Uffington

Street-by-Street: Oxford ❺

Oxford has long been a strategic point on the western routes into London – its name describes its position as a convenient spot for crossing the river (a ford for oxen). The city's first scholars, who founded the university, came from France in 1167. The development of England's first university created the spectacular skyline of tall towers and "dreaming spires".

Old Ashmolean
Now the Museum of the History of Science, this resplendent building was designed in 1683 to show Elias Ashmole's collection of curiosities. The displays were moved in 1845.

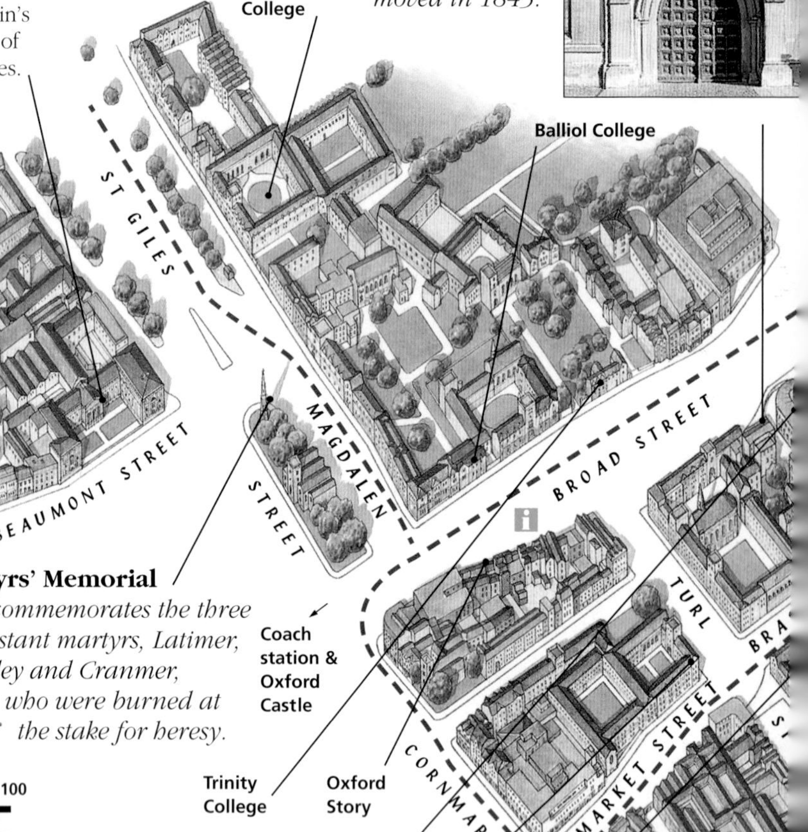

The Ashmolean Museum
displays one of Britain's foremost collections of fine art and antiquities.

St John's College

Balliol College

ST GILES

BEAUMONT STREET

MAGDALEN STREET

BROAD STREET

TURL

BRA

Martyrs' Memorial
This commemorates the three Protestant martyrs, Latimer, Ridley and Cranmer, who were burned at the stake for heresy.

Coach station & Oxford Castle

CORNMARKET STREET

MARKET STREET

0 meters 100
0 yards 100

KEY

▬ ▬ ▬ Suggested route

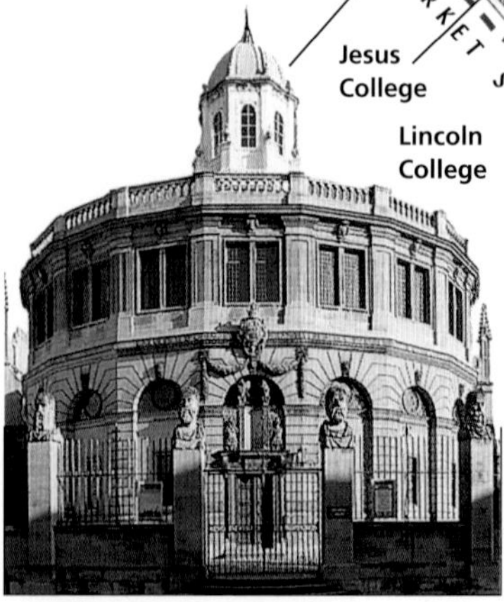

Trinity College

Oxford Story

Jesus College

Lincoln College

Covered market

Railway station

Lincoln College Library

Museum of Oxfor

ST A

PERCY BYSSHE SHELLEY

Shelley (1792–1822), one of the Romantic poets *(see p366)*, attended University College, Oxford, but was expelled after writing the revolutionary pamphlet *The Necessity of Atheism*. Despite that disgrace, the college has put up a memorial to him from his daughter-in-law.

Sheldonian Theatre
The first building designed by Wren (see p114) is the scene of Oxford University's traditional graduation ceremonies.

STAR SIGHTS

★ Radcliffe Camera

★ Christ Church

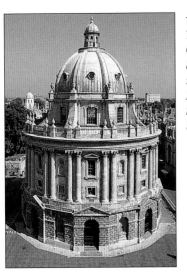

★ Radcliffe Camera
This Classical rotunda is Oxford's most distinctive building and is now a reading room of the Bodleian. It was one of the library's original buildings (see p227).

VISITORS' CHECKLIST

Oxfordshire. 🏛 134,248. 🚇 Botley Rd. 🚌 Gloucester Green. 🛈 15–16 Broad St (01865 25 2200). 🛒 Wed, 1st & 3rd Thu of mth (farmers' market), Thu (flea market). **www**.visitoxford.org

Bridge of Sighs
Resembling the steeply arched bridge in Venice of the same name, this picturesque landmark was built in 1914 and joins the old and new buildings of Hertford College.

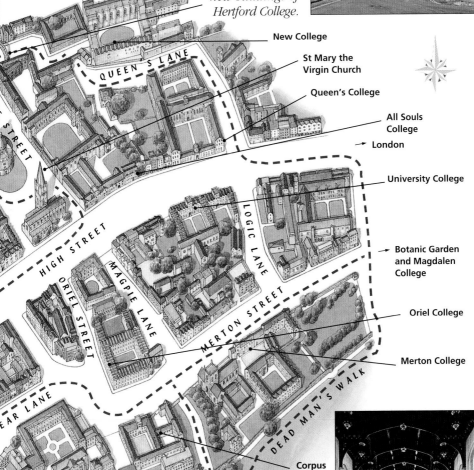

New College

St Mary the Virgin Church

QUEEN'S LANE

Queen's College

All Souls College

→ **London**

CATTE STREET

University College

HIGH STREET

LOGIC LANE

→ **Botanic Garden and Magdalen College**

ORIEL STREET

MAGPIE LANE

MERTON STREET

Oriel College

Merton College

DEAD MAN'S WALK

BEAR LANE

Corpus Christi College

★ Christ Church
Students still eat at long tables in all the college halls. Senior academics sit at the high table and grace is almost always said in Latin.

A bust on the Sheldonian Theatre

Exploring Oxford

Oxford is more than just a university city; it has one of Britain's most important car factories in the suburb of Cowley. Despite this, Oxford is dominated by institutions related to its huge academic community: like Blackwell's bookshop which has over 20,000 titles in stock. The two rivers, the Cherwell and the Isis (the name given to the Thames as it flows through the city), provide lovely riverside walks, or you can hire a punt and spend an afternoon on the Cherwell.

🏛 Ashmolean Museum

Beaumont St. **Tel** 01865 278000.
◯ Tue–Sun (Sun pm only) & public hols. ● 1 Jan, Good Fri, 25–28 Dec.
& ✏ Tue, Fri, Sat. 🖥 🛈
www.ashmolean.org

One of the best museums in Britain outside London, the Ashmolean – the first purpose-built museum in England – opened in 1683, based on a display known as "The Ark" collected by the two John Tradescants, father and son.

On their many voyages to the Orient and the Americas they collected stuffed animals and tribal artifacts. On their death, the collection was acquired by the antiquarian Elias Ashmole, who donated it to the university and had a building made for the exhibits on Broad Street – the Old Ashmolean, now the Museum of the History of Science. In the 1800s, part of the Tradescant collection was moved to the

University Galleries, a Neo-Classical building of 1845. This greatly expanded museum is now known as the Ashmolean.

What is left of the original curio collection is overshadowed by the other exhibits in the museum, in particular the paintings. These include Bellini's *St Jerome Reading in a Landscape* (late 15th century); Raphael's *Heads of Two Apostles* (1519); Turner's *Venice: The Grand Canal* (1840); Rembrandt's *Saskia Asleep* (1635); Michelangelo's *Crucifixion* (1557), Picasso's *Blue Roofs* (1901) and a large group of Pre-Raphaelites, including Rossetti and Millais. There are also fine Greek and Roman carvings and a collection of stringed musical instruments. Items of more local interest include a Rowlandson watercolour of Radcliffe Square in about 1790 and the Oxford Crown. This silver coin was minted here during the Civil War in 1644 *(see p52)* and forms part of the second-largest coin collection in Britain. Perhaps the single most important item is the gold enamelled ring known as the Alfred Jewel *(see p47),* which is over 1,000 years old.

A new building designed by Rick Mather, which opened in late 2009 provides the museum with twice as much space as it previously had.

The entrance to the Ashmolean Museum

🌿 Botanic Garden

Rose Lane. **Tel** 01865 286690.
◯ daily. ● Good Fri, 25 Dec.
▨ Mar–Oct. **Donation** Nov–Feb.
& www.botanic-garden.ox.ac.uk

Britain's oldest botanic garden was founded in 1621 – one ancient yew tree survives from that period. The entrance gates were designed by Nicholas Stone in 1633 and paid for, like the garden itself, by the Earl of Danby. His statue adorns the gate, along with those of Charles I and II. This small garden is a delightful spot for a stroll, with an original walled garden, a more recent herbaceous border and rock garden, and a new insectivorous house.

The 17th-century Botanic Gardens

🔒 Carfax Tower

Carfax Sq. **Tel** 01865 790522. ◯ daily. ● 1 Jan, 25 & 26 Dec. ▨ 🛈

The tower is all that remains of the 14th-century Church of St Martin, demolished in 1896 so that the adjoining road could be widened. Be there to watch the clock strike the quarter hours, and climb to the top for a panoramic view of the city. Carfax was the crossing point of the original north-to-south and east-to-west routes through Oxford and the word comes from the French *quatre voies,* or "four ways".

🎵 Holywell Music Room

Holywell St. ◯ concerts only. ▨ &

This was the first building in Europe designed, in 1752, specifically for public musical performances. Previously, concerts had been held in private houses for invited guests only. Its two splendid chandeliers originally adorned Westminster Hall at the coronation of George IV in 1820, and were given by the king to Wadham College, of which the music room technically forms a part. The room is regularly used for contemporary and classical concerts.

🏛 Museum of Oxford

St Aldates. *Tel 01865 252761.* ◔ *Tue–Sun.* ● *1 Jan, 24–26 Dec, 31 Dec.* ◻ www.moo.org.uk
A well-organized display in the Victorian town hall illustrates the long history of Oxford and its university. Exhibits include a Roman pottery kiln. The main features are a series of well-reconstructed rooms, including one from an Elizabethan inn and an 18th-century student's room.

⛪ Martyrs' Memorial

Magdalen St.
This commemorates the three Protestants burned at the stake on Broad Street – Bishops Latimer and Ridley in 1555, and Archbishop Cranmer in 1556. On the accession of Queen Mary in 1553 *(see p51)*, they were committed to the Tower of London, then sent to Oxford to defend their views before the doctors of divinity who, after the hearing, condemned them as heretics.

The memorial was designed in 1843 by George Gilbert Scott and based on the Eleanor crosses erected in 12 English towns by Edward I (1239–1307) to honour his queen.

⛪ Oxford Castle

44–46 Oxford Castle. *Tel 01865 260666.* ◔ *daily.* ♿ ▢ ◻
Following a £40-million development, this 1,000-year-old castle opened in 2005. It forms part of an urban space that includes shops, restaurants and a hotel.

🏛 Oxford Castle Unlocked

44–46 Oxford Castle. *Tel 01865 260666.* ◔ *daily.* ● *25 Dec.* ▢ ▭ ▨ ♿
The secrets of the castle are revealed in this exhibition that looks at the site's turbulent past. Climb St George's Tower for panoramic views over the city.

⛩ Sheldonian Theatre

Broad St. *Tel 01865 277299.* ◔ *call for details.* ● *Christmas period, Easter & public hols.* ▨ ♿ *limited.* www.sheldon.ox.ac.uk
Completed in 1669, this was designed by Christopher Wren *(see p114)*, and paid for by Gilbert Sheldon, the Archbishop of Canterbury, as a location for university degree ceremonies. The Classical design of the D-shaped building is based on the Theatre of Marcellus in Rome. The octagonal cupola was built in 1838 and boasts a famous view from its huge Lantern. The theatre's painted ceiling depicts the triumph of religion, art and science over envy, hatred and malice.

⛪ St Mary the Virgin Church

High St. *Tel 01865 279111.* ◔ *daily.* ● *Good Fri, 25, 26 Dec.* ▭ ◻ www.university-church.ox.ac.uk
This, the official university church, is said to be the most visited parish church in England. The oldest parts date from the early 13th century and include the tower, from which there are fine views. Its Convocation House served as the university's first

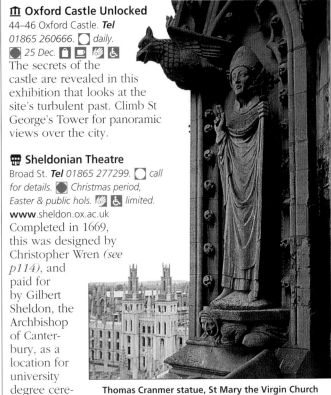

Thomas Cranmer statue, St Mary the Virgin Church

library until the Bodleian was founded in 1488 *(see p227)*. The church is where the three Oxford Martyrs were pronounced heretics in 1555. An architectural highlight is the Baroque south porch.

🏛 University Museum

Parks Rd. *Tel 01865 272950.* ◔ *daily.* ● *Easter, 24–26 Dec.* ♿ ◻ www.oum.ox.ac.uk

🏛 Pitt Rivers Museum

Parks Rd. *Tel 01865 270927.* ◔ *daily.* ● *Easter, 24–26 Dec.* ♿ ◻ www.prm.ox.ac.uk
Two of Oxford's most interesting museums adjoin each other. The first is a museum of natural history containing relics of dinosaurs as well as a stuffed dodo. This flightless bird has been extinct since the 17th century, but was immortalized by Lewis Carroll (an Oxford mathematics lecturer) in his book *Alice in Wonderland*. The Pitt Rivers Museum has an extensive ethnographic collection – masks and totems from Africa and the Far East – and archaeological displays, including exhibits collected by the explorer Captain Cook.

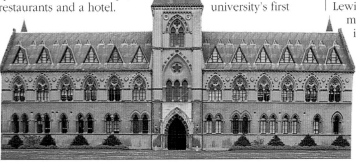

The impressive frontage of the University Museum and Pitt Rivers Museum

Exploring Oxford University

Many of the 36 colleges which go to make up the university were founded between the 13th and 16th centuries and cluster around the city centre. As scholarship was then the exclusive preserve of the church, the colleges were designed along the lines of monastic buildings but were often surrounded by beautiful gardens. Although most colleges have been altered over the years, many still incorporate a lot of their original features.

The spectacular view of All Souls College from St Mary's Church

All Souls College
Founded in 1438 on the High Street by Henry VI, the chapel on the college's north side has a classic hammerbeam roof, unusual misericords *(see p341)* on the choir stalls and 15th-century stained glass.

Christ Church College
The best way to view this, the largest of the Oxford colleges, is to approach through the meadows from St Aldate's. Christ Church dates from 1525 when Cardinal Wolsey founded it as an ecclesiastical college to train cardinals. The upper part of the tower in Tom Quad – a rectangular courtyard – was built by Wren *(see p114)* in 1682 and is the largest in the

city. When its bell, Great Tom, was hung in 1648, the college had 101 students, which is why the bell is rung 101 times at 9:05pm, to mark the curfew for students (which has not been enforced since 1963). The odd timing is because night falls here five minutes later than at Greenwich *(see p125)*. Christ Church has produced 13 British prime ministers in the last 200 years. Beside the main quad is the 12th-century Christ Church Cathedral, one of the smallest in England.

Lincoln College
One of the best-preserved of the medieval colleges, it was founded in 1427 on Turl Street, and the front quad and façade

are 15th century. The hall still has its original roof, including the gap where smoke used to escape. The Jacobean chapel is notable for its stained glass. John Wesley *(see p279)* was at college here and his rooms, now a chapel, can be visited.

Magdalen College
At the end of the High Street is perhaps the most typical and beautiful Oxford college. Its 15th-century quads in contrasting styles are set in a park by the Cherwell, crossed by Magdalen Bridge. Every May Day at 6am, the college choir sings from the top of Magdalen's bell tower (1508) – a 16th-century custom to mark the start of summer.

New College
One of the grandest colleges, it was founded by William of Wykeham in 1379 to educate clergy to replace those killed by the Black Death of 1348 *(see p49)*.

Magdalen Bridge spanning the River Cherwell

Its magnificent chapel on New College Lane, restored in the 19th century, has vigorous 14th-century misericords and El Greco's (1541–1614) famous painting of *St James*.

Queen's College
Most of the college buildings date from the 18th century and represent some of the finest work from that period in Oxford. Its superb library was built in 1695 by Henry Aldrich (1647–1710) The front screen with its bell-topped gatehouse is a feature of the High Street.

STUDENT LIFE

Students belong to individual colleges and usually live in them for the duration of their course. The university gives lectures, sets exams and awards degrees but much of the students' tuition and social life is based around their college. Many university traditions date back hundreds of years, like the graduation ceremonies at the Sheldonian, which are still held in Latin.

Graduation at the Sheldonian *(see p224)*

Merton College seen from Christ Church Meadows

VISITORS' CHECKLIST

Oxford Colleges can usually be visited from 2–5pm daily all year, but there are no set opening hours. See noticeboards outside each college entrance to check opening times.
Bodleian Library (Duke Humphrey's Library & Divinity School), Broad St. *Tel* 01865 277224. 🔲 9am–5pm Mon–Fri, 9am–4:45pm Sat. 🔘 23 Dec–3 Jan, Easter. 🎫 📷 ♿ **www**.bodley.ox.ac.uk

St John's College
The impressive frontage on St Giles dates from 1437, when it was founded for Cistercian scholars. The old library has lovely 17th-century bookcases and stained glass, while the Baylie Chapel has a display of 15th-century vestments.

Trinity College
The oldest part of the college on Broad Street, Durham Quad, is named after the earlier college of 1296, which was incorporated into Trinity in 1555. The late 17th-century chapel has a magnificent reredos and wooden screen.

Corpus Christi College
The whole of the charming front quad on Merton Street dates from 1517, when the college was founded. The quad's sundial, topped by a pelican – the college symbol – bears an early 17th-century calendar. The chapel has a rare 16th-century eagle lectern.

Merton College
Off Merton Street, this is the oldest college (1264) in Oxford. Much of its hall dates from then, including a sturdy decorated door. The chapel choir contains allegorical reliefs representing music, arithmetic, rhetoric and grammar. Merton's Mob Quad served as a model for the later colleges.

BODLEIAN LIBRARY
Founded in 1320, the library was expanded in 1426 by Humphrey, Duke of Gloucester (1391–1447) and brother of Henry V, when his collection of manuscripts would not fit into the old library. It was refounded in 1602 by Thomas Bodley, a wealthy scholar, who insisted on strict rules: the keeper was forbidden to marry. The library is one of the six copyright deposit libraries in the country – it is entitled to receive a copy of every book published in Britain.

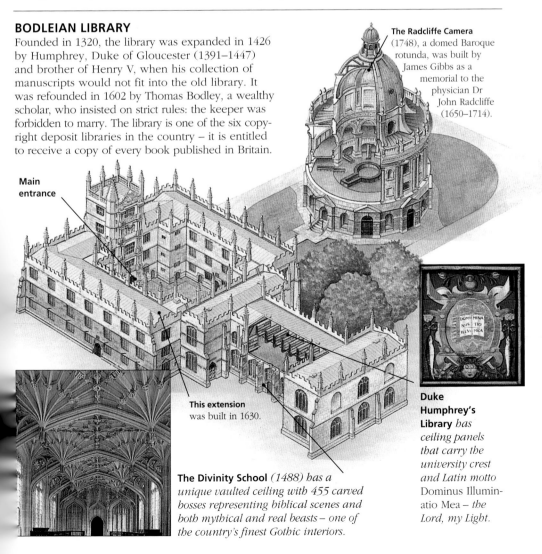

The Radcliffe Camera (1748), a domed Baroque rotunda, was built by James Gibbs as a memorial to the physician Dr John Radcliffe (1650–1714).

Main entrance

This extension was built in 1630.

The Divinity School *(1488) has a unique vaulted ceiling with 455 carved bosses representing biblical scenes and both mythical and real beasts – one of the country's finest Gothic interiors.*

Duke Humphrey's Library *has ceiling panels that carry the university crest and Latin motto* Dominus Illuminatio Mea *– the Lord, my Light.*

Blenheim Palace ❻

After John Churchill, the 1st Duke of Marlborough, defeated the French at the Battle of Blenheim in 1704, Queen Anne gave him the Manor of Woodstock and had this palatial house built for him in gratitude. Designed by both Nicholas Hawksmoor and Sir John Vanbrugh (see p398), it is a Baroque masterpiece. It was also the birthplace of Britain's World War II leader, Winston Churchill, in 1874.

★ **Long Library**
This 55 m (183 ft room was designe by Vanbrugh as a picture gallery. T portraits include of Queen Anne b Sir Godfrey Knell (1646–1723). Th stucco on the ceiling is by Isaac Mansfield (1725.

Winston Churchill and his wife, Clementine

The Grand Bridge was begun in 1708. It has a 31 m (101 ft) main span and contains rooms within its structure.

Chapel
The marble monument to the 1st Duke of Marlborough and his family was sculpted by Michael Rysbrack in 1733.

STAR SIGHTS

★ Long Library

★ Saloon

★ Park and Gardens

Water Terraces
These magnificent gardens were laid out in the 1920s by French architect Achille Duchêne in 17th-century style, with detailed patterned beds and fountains.

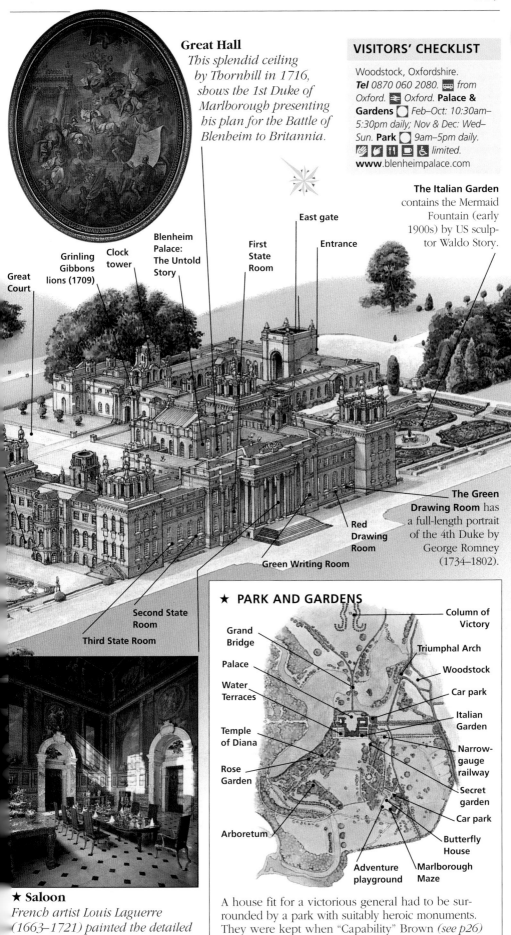

Great Hall
This splendid ceiling by Thornhill in 1716, shows the 1st Duke of Marlborough presenting his plan for the Battle of Blenheim to Britannia.

VISITORS' CHECKLIST

Woodstock, Oxfordshire.
Tel *0870 060 2080.* from
Oxford. Oxford. **Palace &
Gardens** Feb–Oct: 10:30am–
5:30pm daily; Nov & Dec: Wed–
Sun. **Park** 9am–5pm daily.
limited.
www.blenheimpalace.com

The Italian Garden
contains the Mermaid Fountain (early 1900s) by US sculptor Waldo Story.

East gate

Entrance

Blenheim Palace: The Untold Story

First State Room

Clock tower

Grinling Gibbons lions (1709)

Great Court

The Green Drawing Room has a full-length portrait of the 4th Duke by George Romney (1734–1802).

Red Drawing Room

Green Writing Room

Second State Room

Third State Room

★ PARK AND GARDENS

Grand Bridge

Palace

Water Terraces

Temple of Diana

Rose Garden

Arboretum

Column of Victory

Triumphal Arch

Woodstock

Car park

Italian Garden

Narrow-gauge railway

Secret garden

Car park

Butterfly House

Adventure playground

Marlborough Maze

★ Saloon
French artist Louis Laguerre (1663–1721) painted the detailed scenes on the walls and ceiling.

A house fit for a victorious general had to be surrounded by a park with suitably heroic monuments. They were kept when "Capability" Brown *(see p26)* re-landscaped the park (1764–74) and created the lake.

Canaletto's Entrance to the Arsenal **(1730) hangs at Woburn Abbey**

Stowe Gardens ❼

(NT) Buckingham, Buckinghamshire.
Tel 01494 755568. 🚋 Milton
Keynes then bus. 🔵 Mar–Nov: Wed–
Sun; Dec–Feb: Sat & Sun, public hols.
Stowe House 🔵 Access may be
restricted due to a 20-year restoration
project. 🎦 🔥 limited. ▣ 🔲 www.
nationaltrust.org.uk/stowegardens

This is the most ambitious
and important landscaped
garden in Britain, as well as
being one of the finest examples of the 18th-century
passion for improving on
nature to make it conform to
fashionable notions of taste.
  In the space of nearly 100
years the original garden, first
laid out around 1680, was
enlarged and transformed by
the addition of monuments,
Greek and Gothic temples,
grottoes, statues, ornamental
bridges, artificial lakes and
"natural" tree plantings.
  Most of the leading designers
and architects of the period
contributed to the design,
including Sir John Vanbrugh,
James Gibbs and Capability
Brown *(see p26)*.
  From 1593 to 1921 the property was owned by the Temple
and Grenville families – later
the Dukes of Buckingham –
until the large Palladian house
at its centre was converted
into an elite boys' school.
  The family were soldiers
and politicians in the liberal
tradition, and many of the
buildings and sculptures in
the garden symbolize Utopian
ideals of democracy and free-
dom. Some features deteriorated in the 19th century but a
major restoration programme
has returned much of the
statuary to its former glory.

Woburn Abbey ❽

Woburn, Bedfordshire. *Tel* 01525
290333. 🚋 Flitwick then taxi.
🔵 Mar–Sep: daily. ● Oct–Feb.
Grounds 🔵 daily. 🔲 🎦 🔥 ring
first. 🎦 by arrangement. 🍴
www.woburnabbey.co.uk

The Dukes of Bedford have
lived here for over 350 years
and were among the first
owners of an English stately
home to open their house to
the public some 40 years ago.
  The abbey was built in the
mid-18th century on the
foundations of a large 12th-
century Cistercian monastery.
Its mix of styles range from
Henry Flitcroft and Henry
Holland *(see p28)*. The abbey's
grounds are also popular for
their 142-ha (350-acre) safari
park and attractive deer park,
home to nine species including
the Manchurian Sika deer
from China.
  The home's magnificent
state apartments house an
important private art collection
which includes works by
Reynolds (1723–92) and
Canaletto (1697–1768).

Waddesdon Manor ❾

Nr Aylesbury, Buckinghamshire.
Tel 01296 653226. 🚋 Aylesbury
then taxi. **House** 🔵 Mar–Dec:
Wed–Sun; Jan–Feb: Sat & Sun.
Grounds 🔵 Mar–23 Dec: 10am–
5pm Wed–Sun & bank hol Mon. 🎦
🍴 ▣ 🔲 www.waddesdon.org.uk

Waddesdon Manor was built
between 1874–89 by Baron
Ferdinand de Rothschild and
designed by French architect
Gabriel-Hippolyte Destailleur.
  Built in the style of a French
16th-century chateau, the
manor houses one of the
world's finest collections of
French 18th-century decorative
art as well as Savonnierie
carpets and Sèvres porcelain.
  The garden, originally laid out
by French landscape gardener
Elie Lainé, is renowned for its
seasonal displays.

Roald Dahl Museum ❿

81–83 High St, Great Missenden,
Buckinghamshire. *Tel* 01494 892192.
🚋 Great Missenden. 🔵 10am–5pm
Tue–Sun & bank hols. 🔲 🎦 🔥
www.roalddahlmuseum.org

The magical world of Roald
Dahl's stories comes to life in
this award-winning museum.
A series of biographical
galleries explore the life and
work of the children's writer,
while the Story Centre's
interactive exhibits allow
children to make their own
animation film, record dreams
in a "dream bottle" or try their
hand at creative writing.

The 17th-century Palladian bridge over the Octagon Lake in Stowe Park

Hatfield House, one of the largest Jacobean mansions in the country

ZSL Whipsnade Zoo ⑪

Nr Dunstable, Bedfordshire. **Tel** 01582 872171. ⚡ Hemel Hempsted or Luton then bus. ◯ daily. ⬤ 25 Dec. 🗺 ♿ 🖥 www.zsl.org

The rural branch of London Zoo, this was one of the first zoos to minimize the use of cages, confining animals safely but without constriction.

At 240 ha (600 acres), it is Europe's largest conservation park, with more than 2,500 species. You can drive through some areas or go by steam train. Also popular are the adventure playground, the Cheetah Rock exhibit and the sea lions' underwater display.

Knebworth House ⑫

Knebworth, Hertfordshire. **Tel** 01438 812661. ⚡ Stevenage then taxi. ◯ Sat, Sun; two weeks at Easter: daily; Jul–Aug: daily. 🏠 🗺 ♿ limited. 🍴 🖥 www.knebworthhouse.com

A notable Tudor mansion, with a beautiful Jacobean banqueting hall, Knebworth was overlain with a 19th-century Victorian Gothic exterior by Lord Lytton, the head of the family. His eldest son, the 1st Earl of Lytton, was Viceroy of India, and exhibits illustrate the Delhi Durbar of 1877, when Queen Victoria became Empress of India.

A visit includes the house, gardens, park, and a dinosaur trail for children.

Hatfield House ⑬

Hatfield, Hertfordshire. **Tel** 01707 287010. ⚡ Hatfield. ◯ Easter Sat–Sep: Wed–Sun & public hols. 🏠 🗺 ♿ 🍴 www.hatfield-house.co.uk

One of England's finest Jacobean houses, Hatfield House was built between 1607 and 1611 for the powerful statesman Robert Cecil.

Its chief historical interest, though, lies in the surviving wing of the original Tudor Hatfield Palace, where Queen Elizabeth I (see pp50–51) spent much of her childhood. She held her first Council of State here when she was crowned in 1558. The palace was partly demolished in 1607 to make way for the new house, which contains mementoes of her life, including the *Rainbow* portrait painted around 1600 by Isaac Oliver. Visitors can attend medieval banquets in the old palace's Great Hall.

Originally laid out by Robert Cecil with help from John Tradescant, the gardens have been restored to reflect these Jacobean origins.

FAMOUS PURITANS

Three major figures connected with the 17th-century Puritan movement are celebrated in the Thames area. John Bunyan (1628–88), who wrote the allegorical tale *The Pilgrim's Progress*, was born at Elstow, near Bedford. A passionate Puritan orator, he was jailed for his beliefs for 17 years. The Bunyan Museum in Bedford is a former site of Puritan worship. William Penn (1644–1718), founder of Pennsylvania in the USA, lived, worshipped and is buried at Jordans, near Beaconsfield. A bit further north at Chalfont St Giles is the cottage where the poet John Milton (1608–74) stayed to escape London's plague. There he completed his greatest work, *Paradise Lost*. The house is now a museum based on his life and works.

18th-century engraving of John Bunyan

William Penn, founder of Pennsylvania

John Milton painted by Pieter van der Plas

St Albans ⑭

Today a thriving market town and a base for London commuters, St Albans was for centuries at the heart of some of the most stirring events in English history. A regional capital of ancient Britain, it became a major Roman settlement and then a key ecclesiastical centre – so important that during the Wars of the Roses *(see p49)*, two battles were fought for it. In 1455 the Yorkists drove King Henry VI from the town and six years later the Lancastrians retook it.

The martyr St Alban

Exploring St Albans

Part of the appeal of this ancient and fascinating town, little more than an hour's drive from London, is that its 2,000-year history can be traced vividly by visiting a few sites within easy walking distance of one another. There is a large car park within the walls of the Roman city of Verulamium, between the museum and St Michael's Church and across the road from the excavated theatre. From there it is a pleasant lakeside walk across the park, passing more Roman sites, Ye Olde Fighting Cocks inn, the massive cathedral and the historic High Street. Marking the centre of the town, the High Street is lined with several Tudor buildings and a clock tower dating from 1412, from which the curfew bell used to ring at 4am in the morning and 8:30pm at night.

♏ Verulamium

Just outside the city centre are the walls of Verulamium, one of the first British cities the Romans established after their invasion of Britain in AD 43. Boadicea *(see p195)* razed it

to the ground during her unsuccessful rebellion against the Romans in AD 62, but its position on Watling Street, an important trading route, meant that it was quickly rebuilt on an even larger scale and the city flourished until 410.

♏ Verulamium Museum

St Michael's St. **Tel** *01727 751810.*
⬡ *daily (pm only Sun).* ⬤ *25 Dec–2 Jan.* 🖼 🚻 🏠 **www**.stalbans museum.org.uk

This excellent museum tells the story of the city, but its main attraction is its splendid collection of well-preserved Roman artefacts, notably some breathtaking mosaic floors, including one depicting the head of a sea god, and another of a scallop shell. Other finds included burial urns and lead coffins.

On the basis of excavated plaster fragments, a Roman room has been painstakingly recreated, its walls painted in startlingly bright colours and geometric patterns.

Between here and St Albans Cathedral are a bath house with a mosaic, remnants of the ancient city wall and one of the original gates.

A scallop shell, one of the mosaic floors at the Verulamium Museum

⬛ Ye Olde Fighting Cocks

Abbey Mill Lane. **Tel** *01727 869152.*
⬡ *daily.* 🚻

Believed to be England's oldest surviving pub, Ye Olde Fighting Cocks is certainly, with its

One of the oldest surviving pubs in England

octagonal shape, one of the most unusual. It originated as the medieval dovecote of the old abbey and moved here after the Dissolution *(see p50)*.

♏ Roman Theatre

Bluehouse Hill. **Tel** *01727 835035.*
⬡ *daily.* ⬤ *1 Jan, 25, 26 Dec.* 🖼 🏠 **www**.romantheatre.co.uk

Just across the road from the museum are the foundations of the open-air theatre, first built around AD 140 but enlarged several times. It is one of only six known to have been built in Roman Britain. Alongside it are traces of a row of Roman shops and a house, from which many of the museum's treasures – such as a bronze statuette of Venus – were excavated in the 1930s.

⬆ St Michael's Church

St Michael's. **Tel** *01727 835037.*
⬡ *Apr–Sep: phone for details.* 🚻

This church was first founded during the Saxon reign and is built partly with bricks taken from Verulamium, which by then was in decline. Numerous additions have been made since then, including a truly splendid Jacobean pulpit.

The church contains an early 17th-century monument to the statesman and writer Sir Francis Bacon; his father owned nearby Gorhambury, a large Tudor house, now in ruins.

VISITORS' CHECKLIST

Hertfordshire. 🧍 *129,000.*
🚶 ➿ **i** *Market Pl (01727
864511).* 🏛 *Wed, Sat.*
www.stalbans.gov.uk

🔒 St Albans Cathedral

Sumpter Yard. **Tel** *01727 860780.*
⬜ *daily.* ♿ 📷 *11:30am & 2:30pm.*
www.stalbanscathedral.org.uk

This outstanding example of medieval architecture has some classic features such as the 13th- and 14th-century wall paintings on the Norman piers.

It was begun in 793, when King Offa of Mercia founded the abbey in honour of St Alban, Britain's first Christian martyr, put to death by the Romans in the third century for sheltering a priest. The

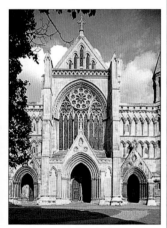

**The imposing west side of
St Albans Cathedral**

oldest parts, which still stand, were first built in 1077 and are easily recognizable as Norman by the round-headed arches and windows. They form part of the 84 m (276 ft) nave – the longest in England.

The pointed arches further east are Early English (13th century), while the decorated work of the 14th century was added when some of the Norman arches collapsed.

East of the crossing is what remains of St Alban's shrine – a marble pedestal made up of more than 2,000 tiny fragments. Next to it is the tomb of Humphrey, Duke of Gloucester *(see p227).*

It was here at the cathedral that the English barons drafted the *Magna Carta* document *(see p48),* which King John was then forced to sign.

The splendour of the Gardens of the Rose in June

Gardens of the Rose ⑮

Chiswell Green, Hertfordshire. **Tel** *01727 850461.* ➿ *St Albans then bus.* ⬜ *Jun–Sep: daily, but always call ahead.* ⬤ *sometimes Mon, Tue.*
🚻 ♿ ♿ 🛍 📷 **www**.rnrs.org

As well as being England's national symbol, the rose is the most popular flower with British gardeners.

The 5 ha (12 acre) garden of the Royal National Rose Society, with over 30,000 plants and 1,700 varieties, is at its peak in late June. The gardens trace the history of the flower as far back as the white rose of York, the red rose of Lancaster *(see p49)* and the Rosa Mundi – named by Henry II for his mistress Fair Rosamond after she was poisoned by Queen Eleanor in 1177. In 2005–7

the gardens were extensively redeveloped by leading garden designer Michael Balston.

Hughenden Manor ⑯

(NT) High Wycombe, Buckinghamshire. **Tel** *01494 755565.* ➿ *High Wycombe then bus.* ⬜ *Mar–Oct: Wed–Sun, 2 weeks in Dec.*
⬤ *Good Fri.* 🚻 ♿ ♿ *limited.* 🍴

The Victorian statesman and novelist Benjamin Disraeli, Prime Minister from 1874 to 1880, lived here for 33 years until his death. Originally a Georgian villa, Disraeli adapted it in 1862 to the Gothic style. Furnished as it was in his day, the house gives an idea of the life of a wealthy Victorian gentleman and shows some portraits of his contemporaries.

GEORGE BERNARD SHAW

Although a controversial playwright and known as a mischievous character, the Irish-born George Bernard Shaw (1856–1950) was a man of settled habits. He lived near St Albans in a house at Ayot St Lawrence, now called Shaw's Corner, for the last 44 years of his life, working until his last weeks in a summer-house at the bottom of his large garden. His plays, combining wit with a powerful political and social message, still seem fresh today. One of the most enduring is *Pygmalion* (1913), on which the musical *My Fair Lady* is based. The house and garden are now a museum of his life and works.

Touring the Thames 🔟

The Thames between Pangbourne and Eton is leafy and romantic and best seen by boat. But if time is short, the road keeps close to its bank for much of the way. Swans glide gracefully below ancient bridges, voles dive into the water for cover, and elegant herons stand impassive at the river's edge. Huge beech trees overhang the banks which are lined with fine houses, their gardens sloping to the water. The tranquil scene has inspired painters and writers through the ages as well as operating, until recently, as an important transport link.

Hambledon Mill ⑥
The white weather-boarded mill, which was operational until 1955, is one of the largest on the Thames as well as one of the oldest in origin. There are traces of the original 16th-century mill.

Beale Park ①
The philanthropist Gilbert Beale (1868–1967) created a 10 ha (25 acre) park to preserve this beautiful stretch of river intact and breed endangered birds like owls, ornamental water fowl, pheasants and peacocks.

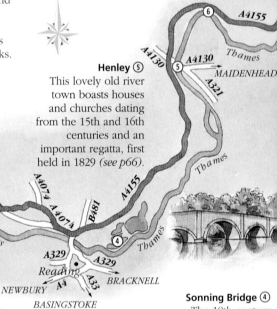

Henley ⑤
This lovely old river town boasts houses and churches dating from the 15th and 16th centuries and an important regatta, first held in 1829 (see p66).

Pangbourne ②
Kenneth Grahame (1859–1932), author of *The Wind in the Willows*, lived here. Pangbourne was used as the setting by artists Ernest Shepard in 1908 and Arthur Rackham in 1951 to illustrate the book.

Sonning Bridge ④
The 18th-century bridge is made up of 11 brick arches of varying width.

TIPS FOR DRIVERS

Tour length: 50 miles (75 km).
Stopping-off points: The picturesque town of Henley has a large number of riverside pubs which will make good stops for lunch. If you are boating you can often moor your boat alongside the river bank.

Whitchurch Mill ③
This charming village, linked to Pangbourne by a Victorian toll bridge, has a picturesque church and one of the many disused watermills that once harnessed the power of this stretch of river.

Cookham ⑦
This is famous as the home of Stanley Spencer (1891–1959), one of Britain's leading 20th-century artists. The former Methodist chapel, where Spencer worshipped as a child, has been converted into a gallery that contains some of his paintings and equipment. This work, entitled *Swan Upping* (1914–19), recalls a Thames custom.

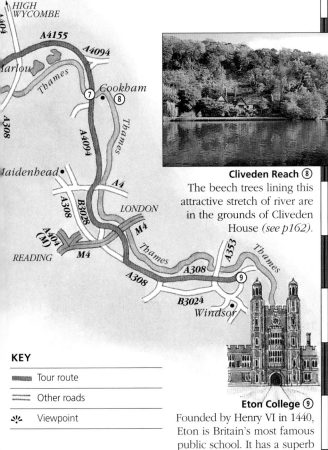

Cliveden Reach ⑧
The beech trees lining this attractive stretch of river are in the grounds of Cliveden House *(see p162)*.

Eton College ⑨
Founded by Henry VI in 1440, Eton is Britain's most famous public school. It has a superb Perpendicular chapel (1441) with a series of English wall paintings (1479–88).

KEY

- Tour route
- Other roads
- Viewpoint

0 kilometres 10

0 miles 5

Salter Bros hire boats, moored at Henley

BOATING TOURS

In summer, scheduled river services run between Henley, Windsor, Runnymede and Marlow. Several companies operate from towns along the route. You can hire boats by the hour or the day or, for a longer tour, you can rent cabin cruisers and sleep on board. Ring Salter Bros on 01753 865 832 for more information.

Windsor ⑱

Berkshire. 30,000
Windsor Royal Station (01753 743900). **www**.windsor.gov.uk

The town of Windsor is dwarfed by the enormous **castle** *(see pp236–7)* on the hill above – in fact its original purpose was to serve the castle's needs. The town is full of quaint Georgian shops, houses and inns. The most prominent building on the High Street is the **Guildhall** completed by Wren *(see p114)* in 1689, where Prince Charles and Camilla Parker-Bowles were married in 2005. **Eton College**, the most prestigious school in Britain, lies just a short walk away.

The huge 1,940-ha (4,800-acre) **Windsor Great Park** stretches from the castle three miles (5 km) to Snow Hill, where there is a statue of George III.

Environs: Four miles (7 km) to the southeast is the level grassy meadow, **Runnymede**. This is one of England's most historic sites, where in 1215 King John was forced by his rebellious barons to sign the *Magna Carta (see p48)*, thereby limiting his royal powers. The dainty memorial pavilion at the top of the meadow was erected in 1957.

Eton College
Tel *01753 671177. mid-Mar–Oct: 10:30am–4:30pm. Always call ahead.* **www**.etoncollege.com

King John signing the *Magna Carta*, Runnymede

Windsor Castle

Henry II rebuilt the castle

The oldest continuously inhabited royal residence in Britain, the castle, originally made of wood, was built by William the Conqueror in around 1080 to guard the western approaches to London. He chose the site as it was on high ground and just a day's journey from his base in the Tower of London. Successive monarchs have made alterations that render it a remarkable monument to royalty's changing tastes. King George V's affection for it was shown when he chose Windsor for his family surname in 1917. The castle is an official residence of the Queen and her family who stay here many weekends.

Albert Memorial Chapel
First built in 1240, it was rebuilt in 1485 and finally converted into a memorial for Prince Albert in 1863.

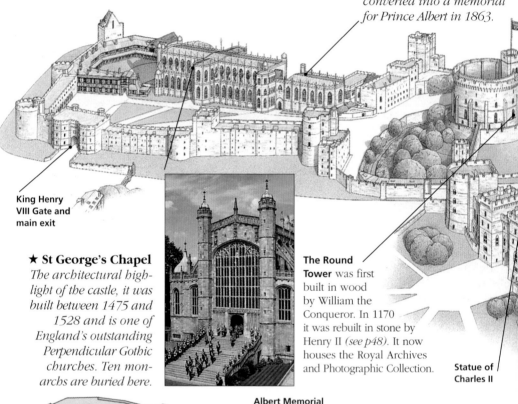

King Henry VIII Gate and main exit

★ **St George's Chapel**
The architectural highlight of the castle, it was built between 1475 and 1528 and is one of England's outstanding Perpendicular Gothic churches. Ten monarchs are buried here.

The Round Tower was first built in wood by William the Conqueror. In 1170 it was rebuilt in stone by Henry II *(see p48)*. It now houses the Royal Archives and Photographic Collection.

Statue of Charles II

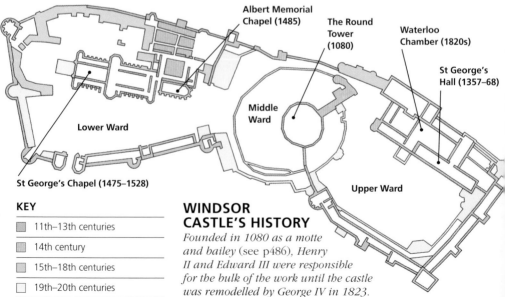

Albert Memorial Chapel (1485)

The Round Tower (1080)

Waterloo Chamber (1820s)

St George's Hall (1357–68)

Middle Ward

Lower Ward

St George's Chapel (1475–1528)

Upper Ward

KEY

- 11th–13th centuries
- 14th century
- 15th–18th centuries
- 19th–20th centuries

WINDSOR CASTLE'S HISTORY
Founded in 1080 as a motte and bailey (see p486), Henry II and Edward III were responsible for the bulk of the work until the castle was remodelled by George IV in 1823.

Drawings Gallery
This chalk etching of Christ by Michelangelo is part of the Royal Collection. Various pieces in the collection are on display here, including works by Holbein and Leonardo da Vinci among others.

VISITORS' CHECKLIST

Castle Hill. ***Tel*** *020 7766 7304.* *9:45am–5:15pm (Nov–Feb: to 4:15pm). (Last adm: 1 hr 15 mins before close.)* *Good Fri, 25 & 26 Dec.* *St Georges Chapel (closed for services).* **www**.royalcollection.org.uk

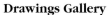

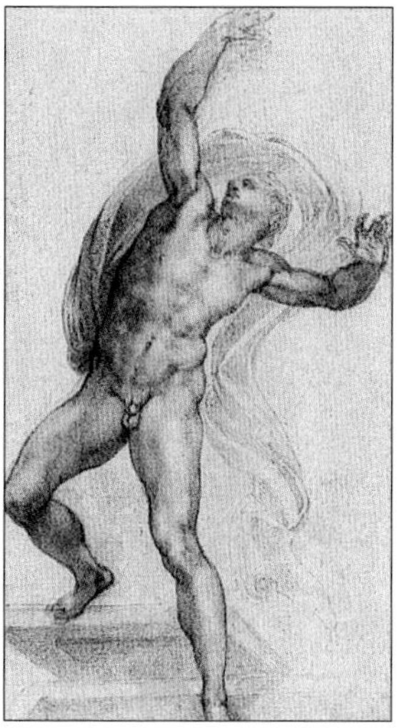

The Audience Chamber is where the Queen greets her guests.

The Queen's Ballroom

Queen Mary's Dolls' House, designed by Sir Edwin Lutyens, was given to Queen Mary in 1924. The wine cellar contains genuine vintage wine.

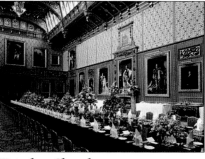

Waterloo Chamber
This banqueting hall was created as part of Charles Long's brief for the remodelling of the castle in 1823.

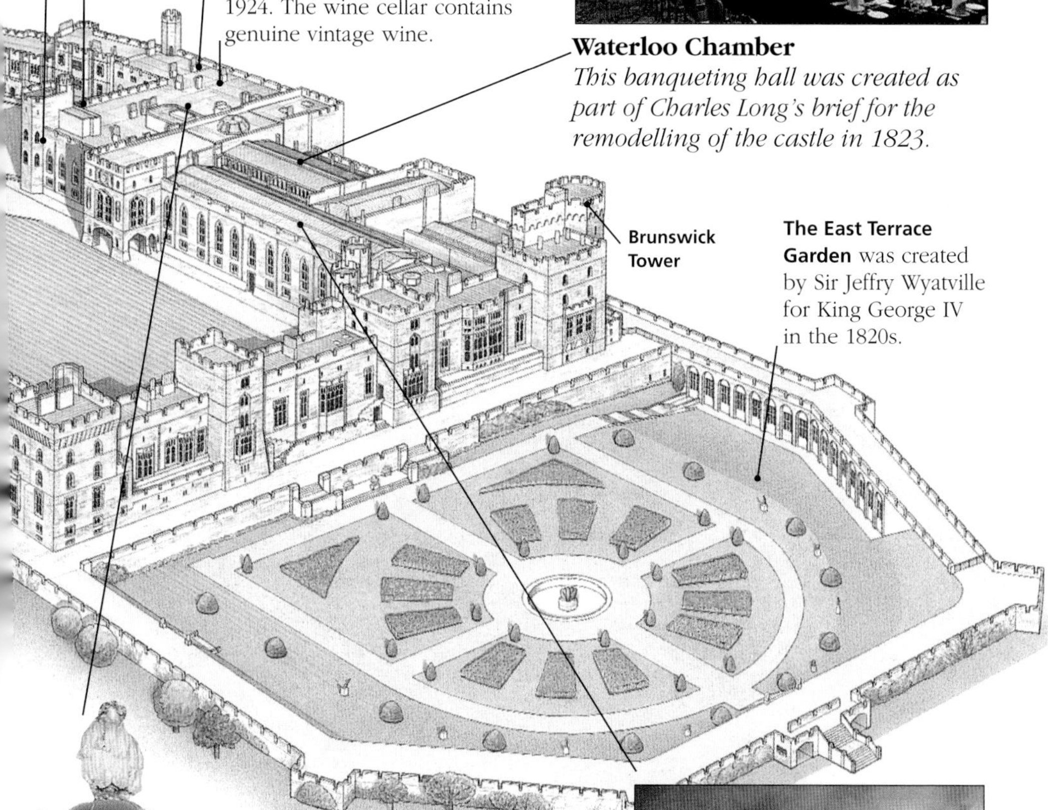

Brunswick Tower

The East Terrace Garden was created by Sir Jeffry Wyatville for King George IV in the 1820s.

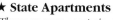

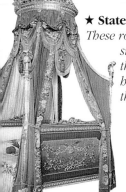

★ State Apartments
These rooms contain many treasures, such as this 18th-century bed in the King's State Bedchamber, hung in its present splendour for the visit in 1855 of Napoleon III.

STAR SIGHTS

★ St George's Chapel

★ State Apartments

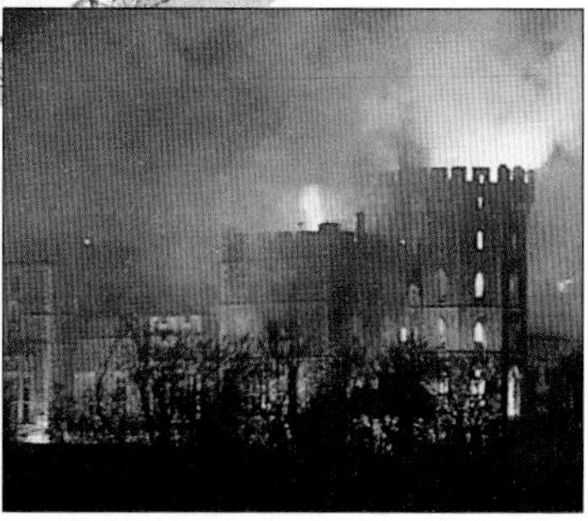

The Fire of 1992
A devastating blaze began during maintenance work on the State Apartments. St George's Hall was destroyed but has been rebuilt.

THE WEST COUNTRY

The West Country at a Glance

The West Country forms a long peninsula bounded by the Atlantic to the north
and the English Channel to the south,
tapering down to Land's End, mainland
Britain's westernmost point. Whether
exploring the great cities and cathedrals,
experiencing the awesome solitude of
the moors and their prehistoric
monuments, or simply enjoying
the miles of coastline and mild
climate, this region has an enduring appeal for holiday-makers.

Wells (see pp252–3) *is a
charming town nestling at the
foot of the Mendip Hills. It is
famous for its exquisite three-
towered cathedral with an
ornate west façade, featuring an
array of statues. Alongside stand
the moated Bishop's Palace and
the 15th-century Vicar's Close.*

Exmoor's (see
pp250–51)
*heather-clad moors
and wooded
valleys, grazed by
wild ponies and
red deer, lead
down to some
of Devon and
Somerset's
most dramatic
cliffs and coves.*

St Ives (see p277) *has a
branch of the Tate Gallery
that shows modern
works by artists
associated with the
area. Patrick Heron's
bold coloured glass
(1993) is on
permanent
display.*

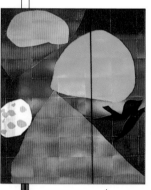

Devon

DEVON AND CORNWALL
(see pp272–95)

Cornwall

Dartmoor (see pp294–5) *is a wilderness of great natural beauty
covering an area of 365 sq miles
(945 sq km). Stone clapper bridges,
picturesque villages and weathered
granite tors punctuate the landscape.*

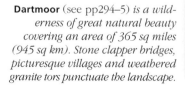

◁ **Stunning views of the Lizard Peninsula**

Bath (see pp258–9) *is named after the Roman baths that stand at the heart of the old city next to the splendid medieval abbey. It is one of Britain's liveliest and most rewarding cities, full of elegant Georgian terraces, built in local honey-coloured limestone by the two John Woods (Elder and Younger).*

Stonehenge (see pp262–3), *the world-famous prehistoric monument, was built in several stages from 3000 BC. Moving and erecting its massive stones was an extraordinary feat for its time. It is likely that this magical stone circle was a place of worship to the sun.*

WESSEX *(see pp246–71)*

Wiltshire

Somerset

Dorset

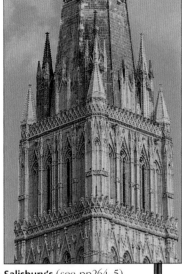

Salisbury's (see pp264–5) *cathedral with its soaring spire was the inspiration for one of John Constable's best-loved paintings. The picturesque Cathedral Close has a number of fine medieval buildings.*

0 kilometres 25

0 miles 25

Stourhead *garden (see pp266–7) was inspired by the paintings of Claude and Poussin. Created in the 18th century, the garden is itself a work of art. Contrived vistas, light and shade and a mixture of landscape and gracious buildings, such as the Neo-Classical Pantheon at its centre, are vital to the overall effect.*

Coastal Wildlife

The long and varied West Country coastline, ranging from the stark, granite cliffs of Land's End to the pebble-strewn stretch of Chesil Bank, is matched with an equally diverse range of wildlife. Beaches are scattered with colourful shells, while rock pools form miniature marine habitats teeming with life. Caves are used by larger creatures, such as grey seals, and cliffs provide nest sites for birds. In the spring and early summer, an astonishing range of plants grow on the foreshore and cliffs which can be seen at their best from the Southwest Coastal Path *(see p36)*. The plants in turn attract numerous moths and butterflies.

Cliff-tops of Land's End with safe ledges for nesting birds

Chesil Bank *is an unusual ridge of pebbles* (see p256) *stretching 18 miles (29 km) along the Dorset coast. The bank was created by storms and the pebbles increase in size from northwest to southeast due to varying strengths of coastal currents. The bank encloses a lagoon called the Fleet, habitat of the Abbotsbury swans, as well as a large number of wildfowl.*

The Painted Lady, *often seer on cliff-top coastal plants, migrates to Brita in the spring.*

High tides wash u driftwood and she

Cliff-top turf contains many species of wild flowers.

Thrift, *in hummocks of honey-scented flowers, is a familiar sight on cliff ledges in spring.*

Yellowhammers *are to be seen perched on cliff-top bushes.*

Marram grass roots help hold back sand against wind erosion.

A BEACHCOMBER'S GUIDE

The best time to observe the natural life of the shore is when the tide begins to roll back, befc the scavenging seagulls pick up the stranded cr fish and sandhoppers, and the seaweed dries u Much plant and marine life can be found in the secure habitat provided by rock pools.

Grey seals *come on land to give birth to their young. They can be spotted on remote beaches.*

COLLECTING SHELLS

Most of the edible molluscs, such as scallops and cockles, are known as bivalves; others, such as whelks and limpets, are known as gastropods.

Great scallop

Common cockle

Common whelk

Common limpet

Durdle Door *was formed by waves continually eroding the weaker chalk layers of this cliff (see p270) in Dorset, leaving the stronger oolite to create a striking arch, known in geology as an eyelet.*

Seaweed, *such as bladder wrack, can resemble coral or lichen when in water.*

Oystercatchers *have a distinctive orange beak. They hunt along the shore, feeding on all kinds of shellfish.*

Rocks are colonized by clusters of barnacles, mussels and limpets.

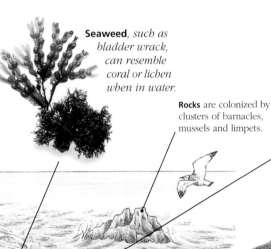

Starfish *can be aggressive predators on shellfish. The light-sensitive tips of their tentacles help them to "see" the way.*

Mussels *are widespread and can be harvested for food.*

Rock pools teem with crabs, mussels, shrimps and plant life.

The Velvet Crab, *often found hiding in seaweed, is covered with fine downy hair all over its shell.*

Grey mullet, *when newly hatched, can often be seen in rock pools.*

West Country Gardens

Gardeners have long been attracted to the West Country. Its mild climate is perfect for growing tender and exotic plants, many of which were brought from Asia in the 19th century. As a result, the region has some of England's finest and most varied gardens, covering the whole sweep of garden styles and history *(see pp26–7)*, from the clipped formality of Elizabethan Montacute, to the colourful and crowded cottage-garden style of East Lambrook Manor.

Lanhydrock's (p284) *clipped yews and low box hedges frame a blaze of colourful annuals.*

Trewithen (p281) *is renowned for its rare camellias, rhododendrons and magnolias, grown from seed collected in Asia. The huge garden is at its most impressive in March and June.*

Cotehele *(p293)* has a lovely lush valley garden.

DEVON AND CORNWALL *(see pp272–5)*

Trelissick *(p281)* has memorable views over the Fal Estuary through shrub-filled woodland.

Glendurgan *(p281)* is a plant-lover's paradise set in a steep, sheltered valley.

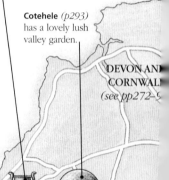

Mount Edgcumbe *(p292)* preserves its 18th-century French, Italian and English gardens.

Trengwainton (p276) *has a fine stream garden, whose banks are crowded with moisture-loving plants, beneath a lush canopy of New Zealand tree ferns.*

Overbecks *(near Salcombe) enjoys a spectacular site overlooking the Salcombe Estuary. There are secret gardens, terraces and rocky dells.*

CREATIVE GARDENING

Gardens are not simply collections of plants; they rely for much of their appeal on man-made features. Whimsical topiary, ornate architecture, fanciful statuary and mazes help to create an atmosphere of adventure or pure escapism. The many gardens dotted around the West Country offer engaging examples of the vivid imagination of designers.

Mazes *were created in medieval monasteries to teach patience and persistence. This laurel maze at Glendurgan was planted in 1833.*

Fountains *and flamboyant statuary have adorned gardens since Roman times. Such eye-catching embellishments add poetic and Classical touches to the design of formal gardens, such as Mount Edgcumbe.*

Knightshayes Court (p289) *is designed as a series of formal garden "rooms", planted for scent, colour or seasonal effect.*

WESSEX (*see pp246–71*)

East Lambrook Manor (*near South Petherton*) *is a riot of colours, as old-fashioned cottage plants grow without restraint.*

Stourhead (*see pp266–7*) is a magnificent example of 18th-century landscape gardening.

Athelhampton's (*p269*) gardens make use of fountains, statues, pavilions and columnar yews.

Montacute House (*p268*) has pavilions and a centuries-old yew hedge, and is renowned for its collection of old roses.

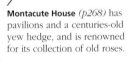

0 kilometres 25

0 miles 25

Parnham (*near Beaminster*), *like many West Country gardens, has several parts devoted to different themes. Here conical yews complement the formality of the stone balustrade; elsewhere there are woodland, kitchen, shade and Mediterranean gardens.*

Many garden buildings *are linked by an element of fantasy; while country houses had to conform to everyday practicalities, the design of many smaller buildings gave more scope for imagination. This fanciful Elizabethan pavilion on the forecourt at Montacute House was first and foremost decorative, but sometimes served as a lodging house.*

Topiary *can be traced back to the Greeks. Since that time the sculpting of trees into unusual, often eccentric shapes has been developed over the centuries. The yew topiary of 1920s Knightshayes features a fox being chased by a pack of hounds. The figures form a delightful conceit and come into their own in winter when little else is in leaf.*

WESSEX

WILTSHIRE · SOMERSET · DORSET

Т*he natural and diverse beauty of this predominantly rural region is characterized by rolling hills and charming villages. The area is enriched by a wealth of historical and architectural attractions, ranging from the prehistoric stone circle of Stonehenge to the Roman baths and magnificent Georgian townscape of Bath.*

Vast swathes of bare windswept downland give way to lush river valleys, and the contrast between the two may explain the origin in medieval times of the saying, "as different as chalk and cheese". The chalk and limestone hills provided pasture for sheep whose wool was exported to Europe or turned to cloth in mill towns such as Bradford-on-Avon. Meanwhile the rich cow-grazed pastures of the valleys produced the Cheddar cheese for which the region has become famous.

The area's potential for wealth was first exploited by prehistoric chieftains whose large, mysterious monuments, such as Stonehenge and Maiden Castle, are striking features of the landscape. From this same soil sprang King Arthur *(see p285)* and King Alfred the Great, about whom there are numerous fascinating legends. It was King Arthur who is thought to have led British resistance to the Saxon invasion in the 6th century. The Saxons finally emerged the victors and one of them, King Alfred, first united the West Country into one political unit, called the Kingdom of Wessex *(see p47)*.

Wilton House and Lacock Abbey, both former monasteries, were turned into splendid stately homes during the 16th century, due to the Dissolution of the Monasteries *(see pp50–51)*. Today, their previous wealth can be gauged by the size and grandeur of their storage barns.

Matching the many man-made splendours of the region, Wessex is rich in rare wildlife and plants.

Two visitors enjoying the Elizabethan gardens of Montacute House, Somerset

◁ **Eighteenth-century cottages lining Gold Hill, Shaftesbury**

Exploring Wessex

From the rolling chalk plains around Stonehenge
to the rocky cliffs of Cheddar Gorge and the
heather-covered uplands of Exmoor, Wessex
is a scenically varied microcosm of England.
Reflecting the underlying geology, each part
of Wessex contributes its own distinctive
architecture, with the Neo-Classically inspired
buildings of Bath giving way to the mellow brick
and timber of Salisbury and the thatched flint-
and-chalk cottages of the Dorset landscape.

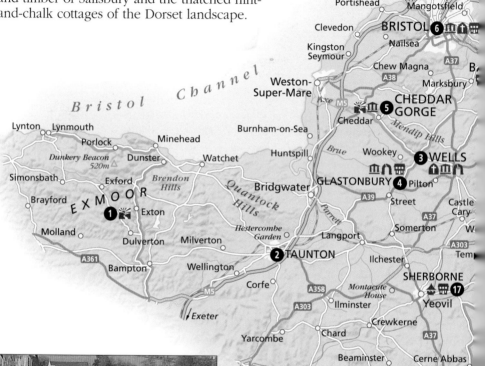

Bath's abbey and Georgian townscape

KEY

▬▬	Motorway
▭▭	Major road
━━	Secondary road
═══	Minor road
━━	Scenic route
┉┉	Main railway
┄┄	Minor railway
△	Summit

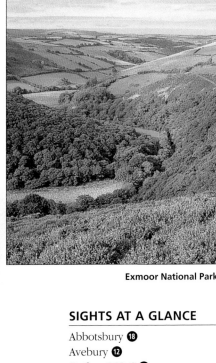

Exmoor National Park

SIGHTS AT A GLANCE

0 kilometres   20

0 miles   10

**Huge sarsen stones of Stonehenge,
dating from around 3000 BC**

GETTING AROUND

Bath and Bristol are served by fast mainline trains, other major towns and seaside resorts by regional railways and long-distance bus services. Popular sights such as Stonehenge feature on many tour operators' bus excursions. The rural heart of Wessex, however, has little in the way of public transport and unless you have the time to walk the region's footpaths, you will need a car.

Exmoor National Park ❶

The majestic cliffs plunging into the Bristol Channel along Exmoor's northern coast are interrupted by lush, wooded valleys carrying rivers from the high moorland down to sheltered fishing coves. Inland, wild rolling hills are grazed by sturdy Exmoor ponies, horned sheep and the local wild red deer. Buzzards are also a common sight wheeling over the bracken-clad terrain looking for prey. For walkers, Exmoor offers 1,000 km (620 miles) of wonderful public paths and varied, dramatic scenery, while the tamer perimeters of the National Park offer less energetic attractions – everything from traditional seaside entertainments to picturesque villages and ancient churches.

Curlew

View east along the South West Coast Path

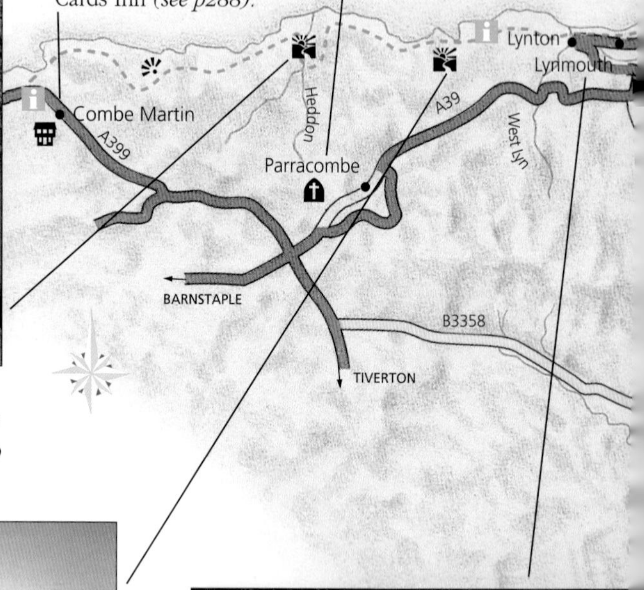

Combe Martin is a pretty setting for the Pack of Cards Inn *(see p288).*

Parracombe Old Church has a Georgian interior with a complete set of wooden furnishings.

Combe Martin

Heddon

Parracombe

A39

Lynton

Lynmouth

West Lyn

A399

BARNSTAPLE

TIVERTON

B3358

Heddon's Mouth
The River Heddon passes through woodland and meadows down to this attractive point on the coast.

The Valley of Rocks
Sandstone outcrops, eroded into fantastical shapes, characterize this natural gorge.

KEY

ℹ️	Tourist information
▬	A road
▭	B road
═	Minor road
– –	Coast path
☼	Viewpoint

Lynmouth
Above the charming fishing village of Lynmouth stands hill-top Lynton. The two villages are connected by a cliff railway (see p288).

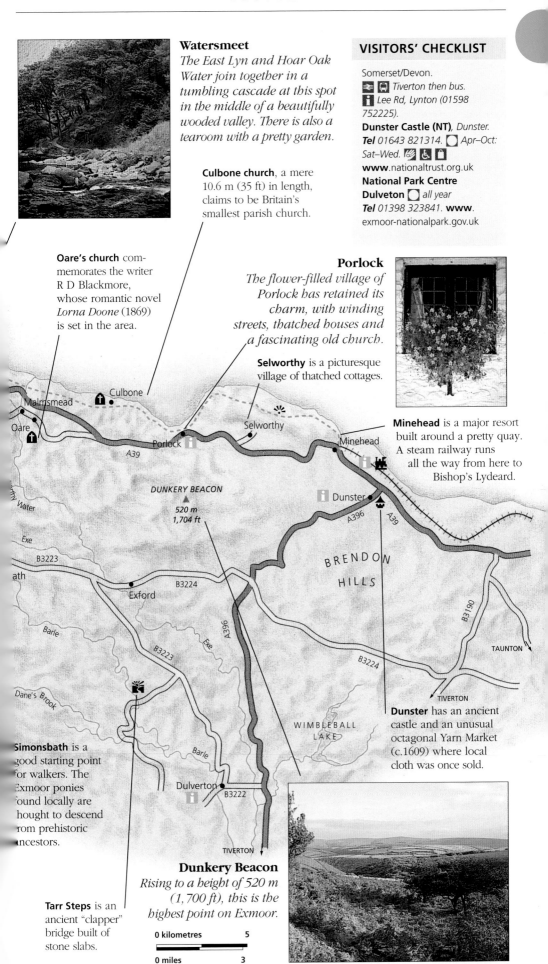

Watersmeet

The East Lyn and Hoar Oak Water join together in a tumbling cascade at this spot in the middle of a beautifully wooded valley. There is also a tearoom with a pretty garden.

Culbone church, a mere 10.6 m (35 ft) in length, claims to be Britain's smallest parish church.

Oare's church commemorates the writer R D Blackmore, whose romantic novel *Lorna Doone* (1869) is set in the area.

Porlock

The flower-filled village of Porlock has retained its charm, with winding streets, thatched houses and a fascinating old church.

Selworthy is a picturesque village of thatched cottages.

Minehead is a major resort built around a pretty quay. A steam railway runs all the way from here to Bishop's Lydeard.

Dunster has an ancient castle and an unusual octagonal Yarn Market (c.1609) where local cloth was once sold.

Simonsbath is a good starting point for walkers. The Exmoor ponies found locally are thought to descend from prehistoric ancestors.

Tarr Steps is an ancient "clapper" bridge built of stone slabs.

Dunkery Beacon

Rising to a height of 520 m (1,700 ft), this is the highest point on Exmoor.

VISITORS' CHECKLIST

Somerset/Devon.
🚉 🚌 *Tiverton then bus.*
ℹ️ *Lee Rd, Lynton (01598 752225).*
Dunster Castle (NT), *Dunster.*
Tel *01643 821314.* ☐ *Apr–Oct: Sat–Wed.* ♿ 🅿️
www.nationaltrust.org.uk
National Park Centre Dulveton ☐ *all year*
Tel *01398 323841.* **www**.exmoor-nationalpark.gov.uk

Map labels: Malmsmead, Culbone, Oare, Selworthy, Porlock, A39, Minehead, Worthy Water, DUNKERY BEACON 520 m 1,704 ft, Dunster, A396, A39, Exe, B3223, ath, Exford, B3224, BRENDON HILLS, Barle, Exe, A396, B3223, Dane's Brook, B3190, TAUNTON, WIMBLEBALL LAKE, B3224, TIVERTON, Barle, Dulverton, B3222, TIVERTON

0 kilometres 5
0 miles 3

Taunton ❷

Somerset. 🏃 77,000. ⚊ 🚻 ℹ️
Paul St (01823 336 344). 🛒 *Thu
(farmers'), Tue & Sat (livestock).*
www.heartofsomerset.com

Taunton lies at the heart of a
fertile region famous for its
apples and cider, but it was
the prosperous wool industry
that financed the massive
church of **St Mary Magdalene**
(1488–1514) with its glorious
tower. Taunton's **castle** was
the setting for the notorious
Bloody Assizes of 1685 when
"Hanging" Judge Jeffreys dispensed harsh retribution on
the Duke of Monmouth and
his followers for an uprising
against King James II. The

12th-century building now
houses the **Museum of Somerset**.
A star exhibit is the Roman
mosaic from a villa at Low
Ham, Somerset, showing the
story of Dido and Aeneas.

**Environs: Hestercombe
Garden** is one of Sir Edwin
Lutyens and Gertrude
Jekyll's great masterpieces.

🏛 **Museum of Somerset**
Castle Green. **Tel** *01823
320201.* ⏺ *call for details.* ⚫
*for refurbishment until summer
2010.* ♿ *ground floor.* 📷
🍁 **Hestercombe Garden**
Cheddon Fitzpaine. **Tel** *01823
413923.* ⏺ *daily.* 🖼📷📁
♿ **www**.hestercombe
gardens.com

SOMERSET CIDER

Somerset is one of the few
English counties where
real farmhouse cider,
known as "scrumpy",
is still made using
the traditional
methods. Cider
once formed
part of the farm
labourer's wages
and local folk-
lore has it that
various unsav-
oury additives,
such as iron
nails, were added to give
strength. Cider-making can
be seen at **Sheppy's** farm,
on the A38 near Taunton.

**Scrumpy
cider**

Wells ❸

Somerset. 🏃 10,000. 🚌 ℹ️ *Market
Place (01749 672552).* 🛒 *Wed
(farmers'), Sat.* **www**.wellstourism.com

Wells is named after St
Andrew's Well, the sacred
spring that bubbles up from
the ground near the 13th-
century **Bishop's
Palace**, residence
of the Bishop of
Bath and Wells. A
tranquil city, Wells
is famous for its
magnificent cathe-
dral which was
begun in the late
1100s. Penniless
Porch, where
beggars once
received alms,
leads from the
bustling market
place to the calm
of the cathedral
close. **Wells & Mendip Museum**
has prehistoric finds from nearby
Wookey Hole and other caves.

**Cathedral
clock
(1386–92)**

Environs: To the northeast of
Wells lies the impressive cave
complex of **Wookey Hole**,
which has an extensive range
of popular amusements.

🏛 **Wells & Mendip Museum**
8 Cathedral Green. **Tel** *01749 673477.*
⏺ *daily* 🖼 ♿ *limited.* 📷
www.wellsmuseum.org.uk
🪧 **Wookey Hole**
Off A371. **Tel** *01749 672243.* ⏺ *daily.*
🖼📷🍴📁 **www**.wookey.co.uk

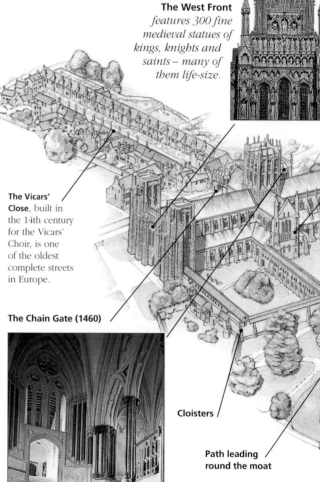

The West Front
*features 300 fine
medieval statues of
kings, knights and
saints – many of
them life-size.*

**The Vicars'
Close**, built in
the 14th century
for the Vicars'
Choir, is one
of the oldest
complete streets
in Europe.

The Chain Gate (1460)

Cloisters

**Path leading
round the moat**

This graceful flight of steps
*curves up to the octagonal
Chapter House which has delicate vaulting dating from 1306.
The 32 ribs springing from the
central column create a
beautiful palm-tree effect.*

Glastonbury Abbey, left in ruins in 1539 after the Dissolution

Bishops' tombs *circle the chancel. This sumptuous marble tomb, in the south aisle, is that of Bishop Lord Arthur Hervey, who was Bishop of Bath and Wells (1869–94).*

The palace moat *is home to swans which ring a bell by the gatehouse when they want to be fed. Feeding times are at 11am and 4pm.*

The Bishop's Palace (1230–40)

WELLS CATHEDRAL AND THE BISHOP'S PALACE

The Close. **Tel** 01749 674483.
○ daily. ♿ limited.
Bishop's Palace Tel 01749 678691.
○ Apr–Oct: Tue–Fri, Sun & public hols (Aug: daily). ♿

Wells has maintained much of its medieval character with its cathedral, Bishop's Palace and other buildings around the close forming a harmonious group. The most striking features of the cathedral are the west front and the "scissor arches" installed in 1338 to support the tower.

3th-century ruins of
he Great Hall

Glastonbury ❹

Somerset. 👥 9,000. 🚌 ℹ Tribunal, High St (01458 832954). 🚃 Tue.
www.glastonburytic.co.uk

Shrouded in Arthurian myth and rich in mystical association, the town of Glastonbury was once one of the most important destinations for pilgrims in England. Now thousands flock here for the annual rock festival *(see p63)* and for the summer solstice on Midsummer's Day (21 June).

Over the years history and legend have become intertwined, and the monks who founded **Glastonbury Abbey**, around 700, found it profitable to encourage the association between Glastonbury and the mythical "Blessed Isle" known as Avalon – alleged to be the last resting place of King Arthur and the Holy Grail *(see p285)*.

The great abbey was left in ruins after the Dissolution of the Monasteries *(see p50)*. Even so, some magnificent relics survive, including parts of the vast Norman abbey church, the unusual Abbot's Kitchen, with its octagonal roof, and the Victorian farmhouse, now the **Somerset Rural Life Museum**.

Growing in the abbey grounds is a cutting from the famous Glastonbury thorn which is said to have miraculously grown from the staff of St Joseph of Arimathea. According to myth, he was sent around AD 60 to convert England to Christianity. The English hawthorn flowers at Christmas as well as in May.

The **Lake Village Museum** has some interesting finds from the Iron Age settlements that once fringed the marshlands around **Glastonbury Tor**. Seen for miles around, the Tor is a hill crowned by the remains of a 14th-century church.

🏛 Somerset Rural Life Museum
Chilkwell St. **Tel** 01458 831197.
○ Tue–Sun (Nov–Apr: Tue–Sat & pub hols). ● 1 Jan, Good Fri, 24–26 Dec. ♿ limited. 🖥 closed winter.

🏛 Lake Village Museum
Tribunal, High St. **Tel** 01458 832954.
○ daily. ● 25, 26 Dec.

Cheddar Gorge ❺

Described as a "deep frightful chasm" by novelist
Daniel Defoe in 1724, Cheddar Gorge is a spectacular
ravine cut through the Mendip plateau by fast-flowing
streams during the interglacial phases of the last Ice
Age. Cheddar has given its name to a rich cheese
that originates from here and is now
produced worldwide. The caves in the
gorge provide the perfect environment
of constant temperature and high
humidity for storing and maturing
the cheese.

VISITORS' CHECKLIST

On B3135, Somerset. 🛈 01934
744071. 🚌 from Wells and
Weston-super-Mare. 🅿 🍴 ♿
Cheddar Caves & Gorge
Tel 01934 742343. ◯ daily. ●
24, 25 Dec. 📷 ♿ limited. 📷
🌐 www.cheddarcaves.co.uk
Cheddar Gorge Cheese Co.
Tel 01934 742810. ◯ daily.
♿ 📷 📷 www.cheddargorge
cheeseco.co.uk

**The Cheddar Gorge Cheese
Company** *is the only working
Cheddar dairy in Cheddar.
Visitors can see Cheddar being
made, and taste and buy cheese
in the new store.*

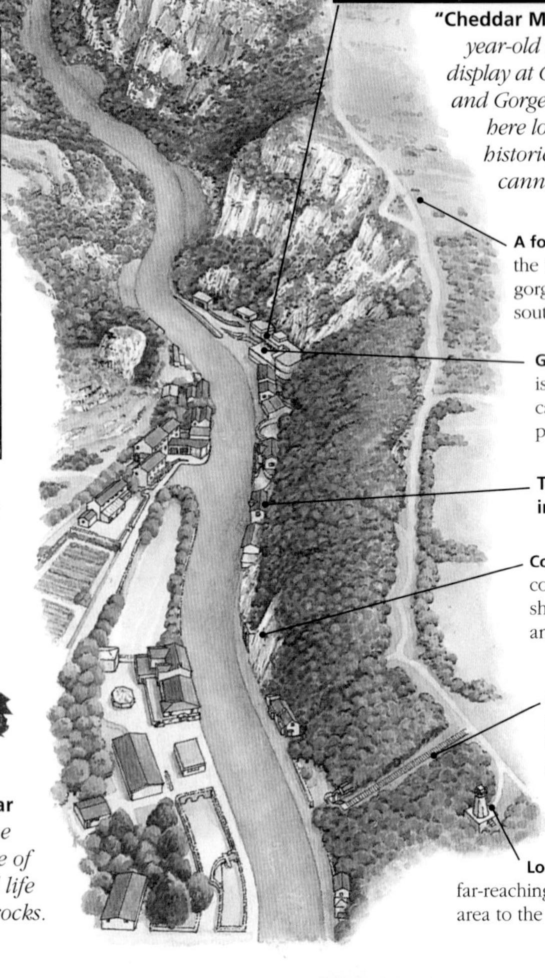

The B3135
road winds
round the base
of the 3 mile
(5 km) gorge.

"Cheddar Man", *a 9,000-
year-old skeleton, is on
display at Cheddar Caves
and Gorge. The museum
here looks at the pre-
historic world of our
cannibal ancestors.*

The gorge *is a narrow, winding
ravine with limestone rocks rising
almost vertically on either side
to a height of 140 m (460 ft).*

A footpath follows
the top of the
gorge on its
southern edge.

Gough's Cave
is noted for its
cathedral-like
proportions.

**Tourist
information**

Cox's Cave
contains unusuall
shaped stalactites
and stalagmites.

A flight of 274
steps leads
to the top
of the gorge.

**The rare Cheddar
Pink** *is among the
astonishing range of
plant and animal life
harboured in the rocks.*

Lookout Tower ha
far-reaching views over th
area to the south and wes

Bristol **6**

See pp256–7.

Bath **7**

See pp258–61.

Bradford-on-Avon **8**

Wiltshire. 🚶 *9,500.* 🚆 ℹ️ *St Margaret St (01225 865797).* ♠ *Thu.* **www**.bradfordonavon.co.uk

This lovely Cotswold-stone town with its steep flagged lanes is full of flamboyant houses built by wealthy wool and cloth merchants in the 17th and 18th centuries. One fine Georgian example is **Abbey House**, on Church Street. A little further along, **St Laurence Church** is a remarkably complete Saxon building founded in 705 *(see p47).* The

Typical Cotswold-stone architecture in Bradford-on-Avon

church was converted to a school and cottage in the 12th century and was rediscovered in the 19th century when a vicar recognized the characteristic cross-shaped roof.

At one end of the medieval **Town Bridge** is a small stone cell, built as a chapel in the 13th century but later used as a lock-up for 17th-century vagrants. A short walk away, near converted mill buildings and a stretch of the Kennet and Avon Canal, is the massive 14th-century **Tithe Barn** *(see p32).*

🏛 **Tithe Barn**
(EH) Pound Lane. ◯ *daily.* ● *25, 26 Dec.* ♿

Corsham **9**

Wiltshire. 🚶 *12,000.*
ℹ️ *31 High St (01249 714660).*
www.visitwiltshire.co.uk

The streets of Corsham are lined with stately Georgian houses in Cotswold stone. **St Bartholomew's Church** has an elegant spire and a lovely carved alabaster tomb (1960) to the late Lady Methuen, whose family founded Methuen publishers. The family acquired **Corsham Court** in 1745 with its picture gallery and a remarkable collection of Flemish, Italian and English paintings, including works by Van Dyck, Lippi and Reynolds. Peacocks wander through the grounds, adding their colour and elegance to the façade of the Elizabethan mansion.

Peacock in grounds, Corsham Court

🏛 **Corsham Court**
off A4. **Tel** 01249 712214. ◯ *mid-Mar–Sep: Tue–Thu, Sat, Sun; Oct–mid-Mar: Sat, Sun (pm).* ● *Dec.* ♿♿

Lacock **10**

Wiltshire. 🚶 *1,000.*

Maintained in its pristine state by the National Trust, with very few modern intrusions, Lacock is a picturesque and delightful village to explore. The meandering River Avon forms the boundary to the north side of the churchyard, while humorous stone figures look down from **St Cyriac Church**. Inside the 15th-century church is the splendid Renaissance-style tomb of Sir William Sharington (1495–1553). He acquired **Lacock Abbey** after the Dissolution of the Monasteries *(see p50),* but it was a later owner, John Ivory Talbot, who had the buildings remodelled in the Gothic

revival style, in vogue in the early 18th century. The abbey is famous for the window (in the south gallery) from which his descendant William Henry Fox Talbot, an early pioneer of photography, took his first picture in 1835, and for the sheets of snowdrops which cover the abbey grounds in early spring. A 16th-century barn at the abbey gates has been converted to the **Fox Talbot Museum**, which has displays on his experiments.

Environs: Designed by Robert Adam *(see pp32–3)* in 1769, **Bowood House** includes the laboratory where Joseph Priestley discovered oxygen in 1774, and a rich collection of sculpture, costumes and paintings. Italianate gardens surround the house while the lake-filled grounds, landscaped by Capability Brown *(see p30),* contain a Doric temple, grotto, cascade and an adventure playground.

🔑 **Lacock Abbey**
(NT) Lacock. **Tel** 01249 730459. ◯ *Mar–Oct: Wed–Mon (pm).* ● *Good Fri.* 🎟 ♿ *limited in house.* **www**.nationaltrust.org.uk

🏛 **Fox Talbot Museum**
(NT) Lacock. **Tel** 01249 730459. ◯ *daily (Nov–Feb: Sat & Sun only).* ● *Good Fri.* 🎟 ♿

🏛 **Bowood House**
Derry Hill, nr Calne. **Tel** 01249 812102. ◯ *Apr–Oct: daily.* 🎟 ♿ ⛱ 🖥 🏛

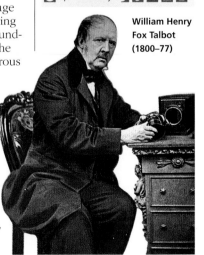

William Henry Fox Talbot (1800–77)

Bristol ❻

King Brennus, St John's Gate

It was in 1497 that John Cabot sailed from Bristol on his historic voyage to North America. The city, at the mouth of the Avon, became the main British port for transatlantic trade, pioneering the era of the ocean-going steam liner with the construction of Brunel's ss *Great Britain*. The city flourished as a major trading centre, growing rich on the distribution of wine, tobacco and, in the 17th century, slaves. Because of its docks and aero-engine factories, Bristol was heavily bombed during World War II and the city centre bears witness to the ideas of post-war planners. The docks have been shifted to deeper waters at Avonmouth and the old dock area has been transformed, taking on new life characterized by waterside cafés, shops and art galleries.

Exploring Bristol

The oldest part of the city lies around Broad, King and Corn streets, known as the Old Quarter. The lively St Nicholas covered market, part of which occupies the **Corn Exchange**, was built by John Wood the Elder (*see p258*) in 1743. Outside are the famous Bristol Nails, four bronze 16th–17th-century pedestals which Bristol merchants used as tables when paying for goods – hence the expression "to pay on the nail". **St John's Gate**, at the head of Broad Street, has medieval statues of Bristol's two mythical founders, King Brennus and King Benilus. Between Lewins Mead and Colston Street, **Christmas Steps** is a steep lane lined with specialist shops and cafés. The **Chapel of the Three Kings** at the top was founded in 1504.

A group of buildings around the cobbled King Street include the 17th-century timber-framed **Llandoger Trow** inn. It is here that Daniel Defoe is said to have met Alexander

Bow of Brunel's ss *Great Britain*

The Two Sisters (c.1889) by Renoir, City Museum and Art Gallery

Selkirk, whose true-life island exile served as the inspiration for Defoe's novel *Robinson Crusoe* (1719). Just up from here is the **Theatre Royal**, built in 1766, and home to the famous Bristol Old Vic.

Not far away, the renowned gallery the **Arnolfini**, on Narrow Quay, is a showcase for contemporary art, drama, dance and cinema.

On the Harbourside, **Explore-At-Bristol** (www.at-bristol.org.uk) combines an exciting, interactive science centre with an aquarium.

Not far from the Harbourside, elegant **Clifton** revels in ornate Regency crescents. The impressive **Clifton Suspension Bridge** by Brunel, completed in 1864, perfectly complements the drama of the steep Avon gorge. **Bristol Zoo Gardens** houses over 400 exotic and endangered species set in stunning gardens.

Memorial to William Canynge the Younger (1400–74)

🔒 St Mary Redcliffe

Redcliffe Way. **Tel** 0117 9291487. ◯ daily. ♿ 📷 by arrangement. 🖥 www.stmaryredcliffe.co.uk

This magnificent 14th-century church was claimed by Queen Elizabeth I to be "the fairest in England". The church owes much to the generosity of William Canynge the Elder and Younger, both famous mayors of Bristol. Inscriptions on the tombs of merchants and sailors tell of lives devoted to trade in Asia and the West Indies. Look out for the Bristol maze in the north aisle.

🏛 Brunel's ss *Great Britain*

Gas Ferry Rd. 📞 0117 9260680. ◯ daily. ● 24, 25 Dec. 🎟 ticket valid for one year. ♿ 📷 by appt. 🖥 📷 www.ssgreatbritain.com

Designed by Isambard Kingdom Brunel, this is the world's first large iron passenger ship. Launched in 1843, she travelled 32 times round the world before being abandoned in the Falkland Islands in 1886. The ship has recently been fully restored.

🏛 Georgian House

7 Great George St. **Tel** 0117 9211362. ◯ Sat–Wed. www.bristol-city.gov.uk/museums

Life in a wealthy Bristol merchant's house of the 1790s is illustrated by furnishings in the elegant drawing room and the servants' area.

🏛 Museum of Bristol

Princes Wharf, Harbourside. ◯ consult the website for more information. www.bristol-city.gov.uk/museums

After a massive rebuild, the old Industrial Museum will reopen in 2011 as the Museum of Bristol. The focus will be on the individual lives, stories and memories of the city's residents while retaining the best of the original building's industrial heritage. This project is part of the regeneration of Bristol's Harbourside.

Warehouses overlooking the Floating Harbour

🏛 Bristol Blue Glass Factory and Shop

Brislington. **Tel** *0117 972 0818.*
○ *daily.* **www**.bristol-glass.co.uk
The Bristol Blue Glass name is over 350 years old and represents the best tools, techniques and traditions from the past. Every piece of glass is free blown and hand-made, making each one unique and collectable. Glass blowing demonstrations take place at the visitor centre, where there is also a gallery shop.

🏛 City Museum and Art Gallery

Queen's Rd. **Tel** *0117 922 3571.* ○
daily. ● *24, 25 Dec.* & *limited.* 🖻
▣ **www**.bristol-city.gov.uk/museums
Varied collections include Egyptology, dinosaur fossils, Roman tableware, the largest collection of Chinese glass outside China and a fine collection of European paintings including works by Renoir and Bellini. Bristol artists include Sir Thomas Lawrence and Francis Danby.

♰ Bristol Cathedral

College Green. **Tel** *0117 9264879.*
○ *daily.* **Donation.** & *limited.*
www.bristol-cathedral.co.uk
Bristol's cathedral, begun in 1140, took an unusually long time to build. Rapid progress was made between 1298 and 1330, when the inventive choir was rebuilt; the transepts and tower were finished in 1515, and another 350 years passed before the Victorian architect, G E Street, built the nave. Humorous medieval carving abounds – a snail crawling across the stone foliage in the Berkeley Chapel, musical monkeys in the Elder Lady Chapel, and a fine set of wooden misericords in the choir.

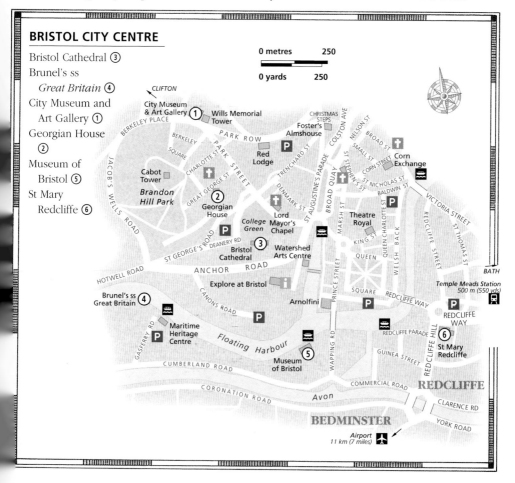

BRISTOL CITY CENTRE

Bristol Cathedral ③
Brunel's ss *Great Britain* ④
City Museum and Art Gallery ①
Georgian House ②
Museum of Bristol ⑤
St Mary Redcliffe ⑥

Street-by-Street: Bath **7**

Bath owes its magnificent Georgian town-scape to the bubbling pool of water at the heart of the Roman Baths. The Romans transformed Bath into England's first spa resort and it regained fame as a spa town in the 18th century. At this time the two John Woods (Elder and Younger), both architects, designed the city's Palladian-style buildings. Many houses bear plaques recording the numerous famous people who have resided here.

The Circus
This is a daring departure from the typical Georgian square, by John Wo the Elder (1705–5

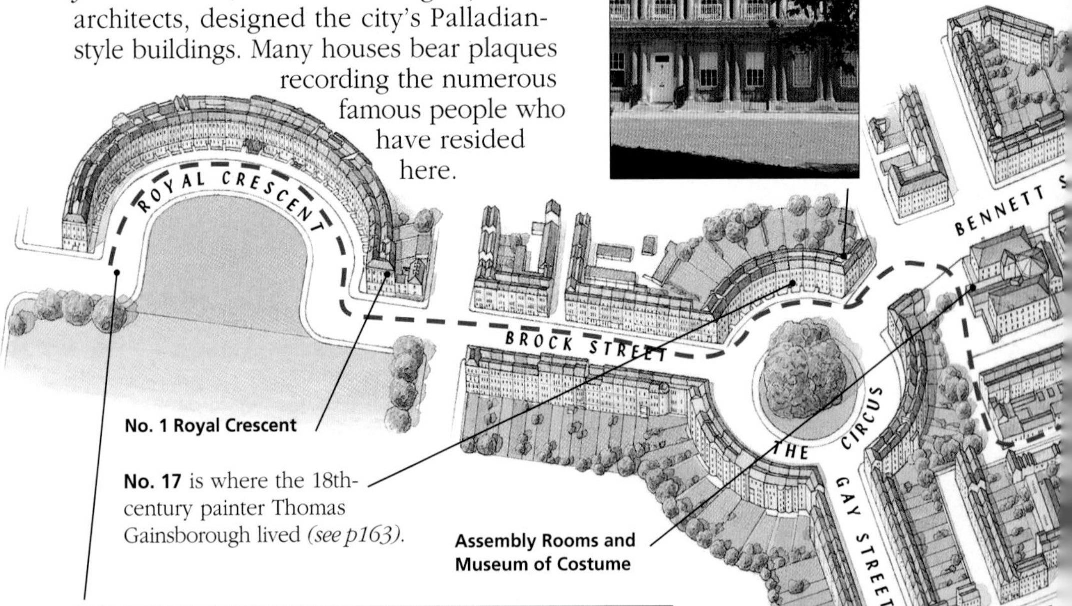

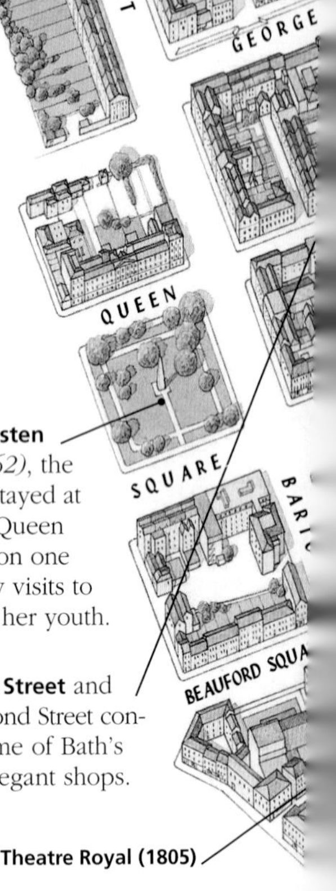

No. 1 Royal Crescent

No. 17 is where the 18th-century painter Thomas Gainsborough lived *(see p163)*.

Assembly Rooms and Museum of Costume

★ Royal Crescent
Hailed the most majestic street in Britain, this graceful arc of 30 houses (1767–74) is the masterpiece of John Wood the Younger. West of the Royal Crescent, Royal Victoria Park (1830) is the city's largest open space.

Jane Austen *(see p162)*, the writer, stayed at No. 13 Queen Square on one of many visits to Bath in her youth.

Milsom Street and New Bond Street contain some of Bath's most elegant shops.

Theatre Royal (1805)

KEY

- - - Suggested route

0 metres   100

0 yards   100

STAR SIGHTS

- ★ Royal Crescent
- ★ Roman Baths
- ★ Bath Abbey

Pump Rooms
These tearooms once formed the social hub of the 18th-century spa community. They contain this decorative drinking fountain.

Pulteney Bridge

This charming bridge (1769–74), designed by Robert Adam, is lined with shops and links the centre with the magnificent Great Pulteney Street. Look out for a rare Victorian pillar box on the east bank.

The Building of Bath Museum

★ Bath Abbey

The splendid abbey stands at the heart of the old city in the Abbey Church Yard, a paved courtyard enlivened by buskers. Its unique façade features stone angels climbing Jacob's Ladder to heaven.

★ Roman Baths

Built in the 1st century, this bathing complex is one of Britain's greatest memorials to the Roman era.

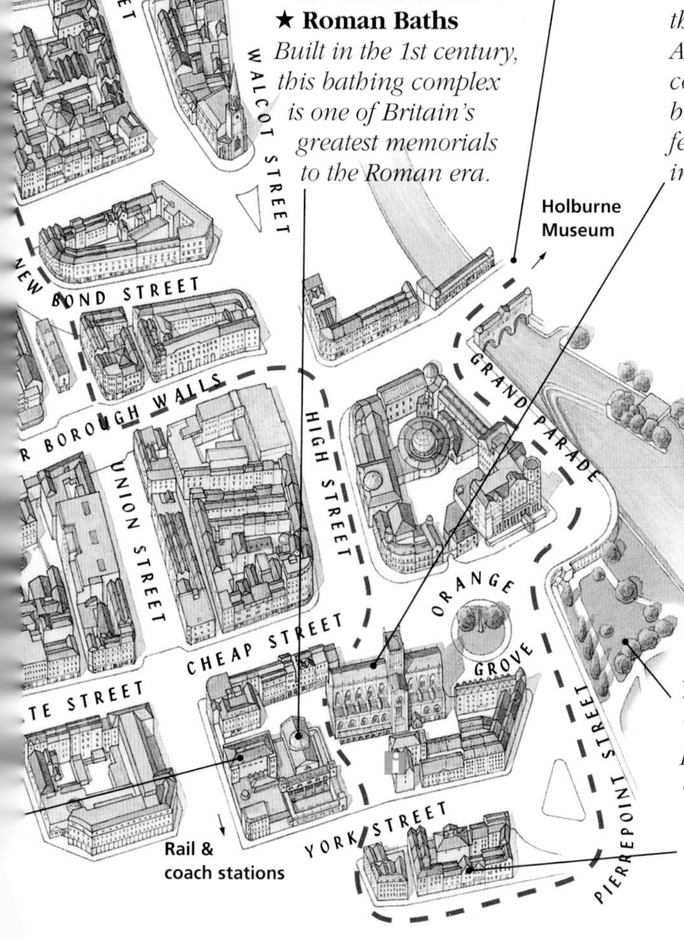

Holburne Museum

Parade Gardens

Courting couples came to this pretty riverside park for secret liaisons in the 18th century.

Rail & coach stations

Sally Lunn's House (1482) is one of Bath's oldest houses.

Exploring Bath

The beautiful and compact city of Bath is set among the rolling green hills of the Avon valley, and wherever you walk you will enjoy spendid views of the surrounding countryside. The traffic-free heart of this lively city is full of street musicians, museums, cafés and enticing shops, while the elegant honey-coloured Georgian houses, so characteristic of Bath, form an elegant backdrop to city life.

Piazza cellist

Bath Abbey, at the heart of the old city, begun in 1499

🔒 Bath Abbey

13 Kingston Bldgs, Abbey Churchyard. *Tel* 01225 422462. ◯ daily. ● during services. **Donation.** 🔗 🛈
www.bathabbey.org

This splendid abbey was supposedly designed by divine agency. According to legend, God dictated the form of the church to Bishop Oliver King in a dream; this story has been immortalized in the wonderfully eccentric carvings on the west front. The bishop began work in 1499, rebuilding a church that had been founded in the 8th century. Memorials cover the walls and the varied Georgian inscriptions make fascinating reading. The spacious interior is remarkable for the fan vaulting of the nave, an addition made by Sir George Gilbert Scott in 1874.

🏛 National Trust Assembly Rooms and Museum of Costume

Bennett St. *Tel* 01225 477789. ◯ daily. ● 25, 26 Dec. 🖾 for Museum of Costume. 🔗 🖵 🛈
www.museumofcostume.co.uk

The Assembly Rooms were built by Wood the Younger in 1769, as a meeting place for the fashionable elite and as an elegant backdrop for many glittering balls. Jane Austen's novel *Northanger Abbey* (1818) describes the atmosphere of gossip and flirtation here. In the basements is a collection of costumes in period settings. The display illustrates fashions from the 16th century to the present day.

🏛 No. 1 Royal Crescent

Royal Crescent. *Tel* 01225 428 126. ◯ Tue–Sun & public hols. ● Dec, Jan, Good Fri. 🛈 🖾
www.bath-preservation-trust.org.uk

This museum lets you inside the first house of this beautiful Georgian crescent, giving a glimpse of what life was like for 18th-century aristocrats, such as the Duke of York, who probably lived here. It is furnished down to such details as the dog-powered spit used to roast meat in front of the fire.

🏛 Holburne Museum of Art

Great Pulteney St. *Tel* 01225 466669. ◯ call for details. ● for refurbishment. 🖾 🔗 limited. 🖵 🛈 www.bath.ac.uk/holburne

This historic building is named after William Holburne of Menstrie (1793–1874), whose collections form the nucleus of the display of fine and decorative arts. Paintings can be seen by British artists such as Gainsborough and Stubbs.

ROMAN BATHS MUSEUM

Entrance in Abbey Churchyard. 🎟 01225 477785. ◯ daily. ● 25, 26 Dec. 🖾 🔗 limited. www.romanbaths.co.uk

According to legend, Bath owes its origin to the Celtic King Bladud who discovered the curative properties of its natural hot springs in 860 BC. Cast out from his kingdom as a leper, Bladud cured himself by imitating his swine and rolling in the hot mud at Bath.

In the first century, the Romans built baths around the spring, and a temple dedicated to the goddess Sulis Minerva, who combined the attributes of the Celt water goddess Sulis and the Roman goddess Minerva. Among the Roman relics is a bronze head of the goddess.

Medieval monks of Bath Abbey also exploited the springs properties, but it was when Queen Anne visited in 1702–3 that Bath reached its zenith as a fashionable watering place.

Gilded bronze head of Sulis Minerva

🏛 Building of Bath Museum

The Vineyards. **Tel** 01225 333895. ☐ Tue–Sun & public hols. ⬤ end-Nov–mid-Feb. 🖼 ♿ limited. 🅿 www.bath-preservation-trust.org.uk

This museum, housed in an old Methodist chapel, is an excellent starting point for exploring the city. It shows how, in the 18th century, Bath was transformed from a medieval wool town into one of Europe's most elegant spas. John Wood and his son designed the Classically inspired stone fronts of the Royal Crescent and the Circus, leaving individual property speculators to develop the houses behind. While the façades speak of harmony and order, the houses behind show the result of rampant individualism, with no two houses alike. The museum looks at every aspect of the buildings, from their construction to a new gallery of Georgian interiors.

🏛 American Museum

Claverton Manor, Claverton Down. **Tel** 01225 460503. ☐ Aug, mid-Nov–mid-Dec: daily (pm); Mar–Oct: Tue–Sun (pm) & pub hols. 🖼 ♿ limited. 🖥 🅿 www.american museum.org

Founded in 1961, this was the first American museum to be established in this country. Rooms in the 1820 manor house are decorated in many styles, from the rudimentary dwellings of the first settlers to opulent 19th-century homes. There are special sections on Shaker furniture, quilts and Native American art, and a replica of George Washington's Mount Vernon garden of 1785.

A 19th-century American Indian weathervane

RICHARD "BEAU" NASH (1674–1762)

Elected in 1704 as Master of Ceremonies, "Beau" Nash played a crucial role in transforming Bath into the fashionable centre of Georgian society. During his long career, he devised a never-ending round of games, balls and entertainment (including gambling) that kept the idle rich amused and ensured a constant flow of visitors.

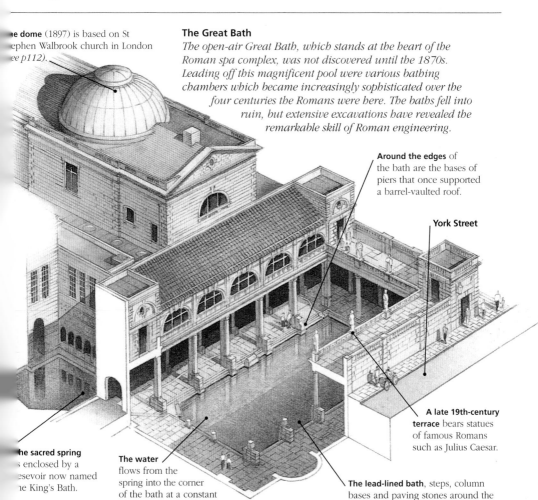

The dome (1897) is based on St Stephen Walbrook church in London (see p112).

The Great Bath

The open-air Great Bath, which stands at the heart of the Roman spa complex, was not discovered until the 1870s. Leading off this magnificent pool were various bathing chambers which became increasingly sophisticated over the four centuries the Romans were here. The baths fell into ruin, but extensive excavations have revealed the remarkable skill of Roman engineering.

Around the edges of the bath are the bases of piers that once supported a barrel-vaulted roof.

York Street

A late 19th-century terrace bears statues of famous Romans such as Julius Caesar.

The sacred spring is enclosed by a reservoir now named the King's Bath.

The water flows from the spring into the corner of the bath at a constant temperature of 46° C (115° F).

The lead-lined bath, steps, column bases and paving stones around the edge all date from Roman times.

Stonehenge ⑪

Built in several stages from about 3000 BC, Stonehenge is Europe's most famous prehistoric monument. We can only guess at the rituals that took place here, but the alignment of the stones leaves little doubt that the circle is connected with the sun and the passing of the seasons, and that its builders possessed a sophisticated understanding of both arithmetic and astronomy. Despite popular belief, the circle was not built by the Druids, an Iron Age priestly cult that flourished in Britain from around 250 BC – more than 1,000 years after Stonehenge was abandoned.

Stonehenge as it is today

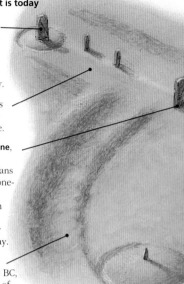

Finds from a burial mound near Stonehenge (Devizes Museum)

The Heel Stone casts a long shadow straight to the heart of the circle on Midsummer's day.

The Avenue forms a ceremonial approach to the site.

The Slaughter Stone, named by 17th-century antiquarians who believed Stonehenge to be a place of human sacrifice, was in fact one of a pair forming a doorway.

The Outer Bank, dug around 3000 BC, is the oldest part of Stonehenge.

BUILDING OF STONEHENGE

Stonehenge's monumental scale is more impressive given that the only tools available were made of stone, wood and bone. The labour involved in quarrying, transporting and erecting the huge stones was such that its builders must have been able to command immense resources and vast numbers of people. One method is explained below.

RECONSTRUCTION OF STONEHENGE

This illustration shows what Stonehenge probably looked like about 4,000 years ago.

A sarsen stone *was moved on rollers and levered into a pit.*

With levers *supported by timber packing, it was gradually raised.*

The stone *was then pulled upright by about 200 men hauling on ropes.*

The pit *round the was packed tightly stones and chalk.*

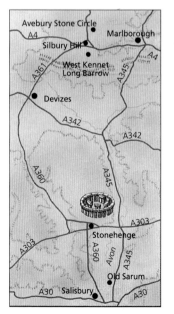

WILTSHIRE'S OTHER PREHISTORIC SITES

The open countryside of the Salisbury Plain made this area an important centre of prehistoric settlement, and today it is covered in many ancient remains. Ringing the horizon around Stonehenge are scores of circular barrows, or burial mounds, where members of the ruling class were honoured with burial close to the temple site. Ceremonial bronze weapons and other finds excavated around Stonehenge and the other local prehistoric sites can be seen in the museum at Salisbury *(see pp264–5)* and the main museum at Devizes.

Silbury Hill (NT) is Europe's largest prehistoric earthwork,

Silbury Hill

but despite extensive excavations its purpose remains a mystery. Built out of chalk blocks around 2750 BC, the hi covers 2 ha (5 acres) and rises to a height of 40 m (131 ft). Nearby **West Kennet Long Barrow** (NT) is the biggest

The **Sarsen Circle** was erected around 2500 BC and is capped by lintel stones held in place by mortice and tenon joints.

The **Bluestone Circle** was built around 2500 BC out of some 80 slabs quarried in south Wales. It was never completed.

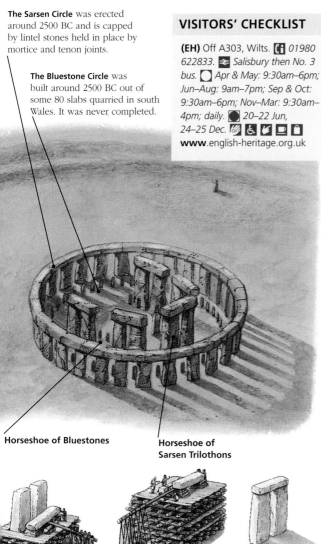

Sarsen stone forming part of the Avebury Stone Circle

Horseshoe of Bluestones

Horseshoe of Sarsen Trilothons

ternate ends *the lintel were ered up.*

The weight *of the lintel was supported by a timber platform.*

The lintel *was then levered sideways on to the uprights.*

chambered tomb in England, with numerous stone-lined "rooms" and a monumental entrance. Built as a communal cemetery around 3250 BC, it was in use for several centuries – old bodies were taken away to make room for newcomers.

Old Sarum is set within the massive ramparts of a 1st-century Romano-British hill fort. The Norman founders of Old Sarum built their own motte and bailey castle inside this ready-made fortification, and the remains of this survive along with the foundations of the huge cathedral of 1075. Above ground nothing remains of the town that once sat within the ramparts. The town's occupants moved to the fertile

river valley site that became Salisbury during the early 12th century (*see pp264–5*).

Old Sarum

(EH) Castle Rd. **Tel** 01722 335398. daily. 1 Jan, 24–26 Dec.

The chambered tomb of West Kennet Long Barrow (c.3250 BC)

Avebury ⑫

(EH/NT) Wiltshire. 600. Swindon then bus. Green St (01672 539250). daily. www.nationaltrust.org.uk

Built around 2500 BC, the **Avebury Stone Circle** surrounds the village of Avebury and was probably once some form of religious centre. Although the stones used are smaller than those at Stonehenge, the circle itself is wider. Superstitious villagers smashed many of the stones in the 18th century, believing the circle to have been a place of pagan sacrifice.

The original form of the circle is best appreciated by a visit to the excellent **Alexander Keiller Museum** to the west of the site, which illustrates in detail the construction of the circle. There is also a fascinating exhibition called "6,000 Years of Mystery", which explains the changing landscape of Avebury.

St James's Church has a Norman font carved with sea monsters, and a rare 15th-century choir screen.

Environs: A few minutes' drive east, **Marlborough** is an attractive town with a long and broad High Street lined with colonnaded Georgian shops.

Alexander Keiller Museum

(NT) Off High St. **Tel** 01672 538015. daily. 24–26 Dec. www.nationaltrust.org.uk

Salisbury ⑬

The "new" city of Salisbury was founded in 1220, when the old hill-top settlement of Old Sarum *(see p263)* was abandoned, being too arid and windswept, in favour of a new site among the lush water meadows where the rivers Avon, Nadder and Bourne meet. Locally sourced Purbeck marble and Chilmark stone were used for the construction of a new cathedral which was built mostly in the early 13th-century, over the remarkably short space of 38 years. Its magnificent landmark spire – the tallest in England – was an inspired afterthought added in 1280–1310.

The early 14th-century house of John A'Port, Queen's Street

Bishop's Walk and a sculpture by Elisabeth Frink (1930–93), Cathedral Close

Exploring Salisbury

The spacious and tranquil **Close**, with its schools, alms-houses and clergy housing, makes a fine setting for Salisbury's cathedral. Among the numerous elegant buildings here are the **Matrons' College**, built in 1682 as a home for widows and unmarried daughters of the clergy, and 13th-century **Malmesbury House** with its splendid early Georgian façade (1719), fronted by lovely wrought-iron gates. Other buildings of interest include the 13th-century **Medieval Hall**, the 13th-century **Wardrobe**, now a regimental museum, and the **Cathedral School**, housed in the 13th-century Bishop's Palace and famous for the quality of its choristers.

Beyond the walls of the Cathedral Close, Salisbury developed its chessboard layout, with areas devoted to different trades, perpetuated in street names such as Fish Row and Butcher Row. Leaving the Close through **High Street Gate**, you reach the busy High Street leading to the 13th-century **Church of St Thomas**, which has a lovely carved timber roof (1450), and a late 15th-century Doom painting, showing Christ seated in judgement and demons seizing the damned. Nearby in Silver Street, **Poultry Cross** was built in the 14th century as a covered poultry market. An intricate network of alleys fans out from this point with a number of fine timber-framed houses. In the large bustling **Market Place** the **Guildhall** is an unusual cream stone building from 1787–95, used for civic functions. More attractive are the brick and tile-hung houses on the north side of the square, many with Georgian façades concealing medieval houses.

The Cloisters are the largest in England. They were added between 1263 and 1284 in the Decorated style.

The Chapter House has an original of the *Magna Carta*. Its walls have stone friezes of the Old Testament.

The Trinity Chapel contains the grave of St Osmund who was bishop of Old Sarum from 1078–1099.

Choir stalls

Bishop Audley's Chantry, a magnificent 16th-century monument to the bishop, is one of several small chapels clustered round the altar.

Street signs reflecting trades of 13th-century Salisbury

⊞ Mompesson House
(NT) The Close. **Tel** 01722 420980.
◯ Apr–Oct: Sat–Wed. 🅿️ ♿ limited.
💻 www.nationaltrust.org.uk
Built by a wealthy Wiltshire
family in 1701, the handsomely
furnished rooms of this house
give an indication of
life for the Close's
inhabitants in the 18th
century. The delight-
ful garden, bounded
by the north wall of
the Close, has fine
herbaceous borders.

🏛 Salisbury and South Wiltshire Museum
The Close. **Tel** 01722 332151. ◯
Mon–Sat (Jul–Aug: Sun pm). 🅿️ 💻
📷 www.salisburymuseum.org.uk
In the medieval King's House,
this museum has displays on
early man, Stonehenge and
nearby Old Sarum (see p263).

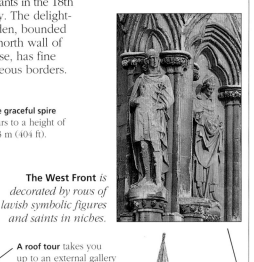

Environs: The town of Wilton
is renowned for its carpet
industry, founded by the 8th
Earl of Pembroke using French
Huguenot refugee weavers.
The town's ornate **church**
(1844) is a brilliant example
of Neo-Romanesque architecture, incorporating genuine
Roman columns, Flemish
Renaissance woodwork,
German and Dutch stained
glass and Italian mosaics.

Wilton House has been
home to the Earls of Pembroke
since it was converted from a
nunnery after the Dissolution
(see p50). The house, largely
rebuilt by Inigo Jones in the
17th century, includes one
of the original Tudor
towers, a fine collec-
tion of art and a
landscaped park
with a Palladian
bridge (1737). The
Single and Double
Cube State Rooms
have magnificently
frescoed ceilings and
gilded stucco work,
and were designed
to hang a series of
family portraits by
Van Dyck.

The graceful spire
soars to a height of
123 m (404 ft).

The West Front is
decorated by rows of
lavish symbolic figures
and saints in niches.

A roof tour takes you
up to an external gallery
at the base of the spire
with views of the town
and Old Sarum.

⊞ Wilton House
Wilton. **Tel** 01722 746729. ◯
Easter weekend, May–Aug: Sun–
Thu, bank hol Sat. 🅿️ ♿ 🍴 📷

The clock dating from
1386 is the oldest work-
ing clock in Europe.

The nave is divided into
ten bays by columns of
polished Purbeck marble.

**North
transept**

**Numerous
windows** add
to the airy
and spacious
atmosphere
of the interior.

SALISBURY CATHEDRAL
The Close. **Tel** 01722 555120. ◯ daily. **Donation.** ♿ 💻
📷 www.salisburycathedral.org.uk
The cathedral was mostly built between 1220
and 1258. It is a fine example of Early English
Gothic architecture, typified by tall, sharply
pointed lancet windows.

**Double Cube room, designed by
Inigo Jones in 1653**

*The Longleat Tree tapestry (1980)
depicting a 400-year history*

Longleat House ⑭

Warminster, Wiltshire. **Tel** 01985
844400. 🚇 Warminster then taxi.
House ⬤ daily. ⬤ 25 Dec.
Safari Park ⬤ Feb–Nov: daily. ⬤
♿ 🍴 🛍 🎁 **www**.longleat.co.uk

The architectural historian
John Summerson coined the
term "prodigy house" to
describe the exuberance and
grandeur of Elizabethan
architecture that is so well
represented at Longleat. The
house was started in 1540,
when John Thynne bought
the ruins of a priory on the
site for £53. Over the centuries subsequent owners have
added their own touches.
These include the Breakfast
Room and Lower Dining
Room (dating from the
1870s), modelled on the
Venetian Ducal Palace, and
erotic murals painted by
the present owner, the 7th
Marquess of Bath. Today,
the Great Hall is the only
remaining room which
belongs to Thynne's time.
   In 1949, the 6th Marquess
was the first landowner in
Britain to open his stately
home to the public, in order
to fund the maintenance and
preservation of the house
and its estate. Parts of the
grounds, landscaped by
Capability Brown *(see p26)*,
were turned into an expansive safari park in 1966,
where lions, tigers and other
wild animals roam freely.
This, along with other additions such as England's
longest hedge maze, the
Adventure Castle and Blue
Peter Maze, and special
events, now draw even more
visitors than the house.

Stourhead ⑮

Stourhead is among the finest examples of 18th-century
landscape gardening in Britain *(see pp26–7)*. The garden
was begun in the 1740s by Henry Hoare (1705–85),
who inherited the estate and transformed it into a breathtaking work of art. Hoare created the lake, surrounding
it with rare trees and plants, and Neo-
Classical Italianate temples, grottoes and
bridges. The Palladian-style house, built by
Colen Campbell *(see p28)*, dates from 1724.

Pantheon
*Hercules is among the
statues of Roman gods
housed in the elegant
Pantheon (1753).*

**Gothic Cottage
(1806)**

**Iron
Bridge**

A walk of 2 miles
(3 km) round the
lake provides
artistically
contrived
vistas.

The lake was created from
a group of medieval fishponds.
Hoare dammed the valley to
form a single expanse of water.

**Turf
Bridge**

**Temple of
Flora (1744)**

**★ Temple
of Apollo**
*The Classical
temples that dot the
garden were all
designed by
influential archi-
tect Henry Flitcroft
(1679–1769).*

Grotto
Tunnels lead to an artificial cave with a pool and a life-size statue of the guardian of the River Stour, sculpted by John Cheere in 1748.

VISITORS' CHECKLIST

(NT) Stourton, Wiltshire. ***Tel*** *01747 841152.* *Gillingham (Dorset) then taxi.* **House** *Mar–Oct: 11am–5pm Fri–Tue.* **Gardens** *9am–7pm (or dusk if earlier) daily.* *limited.* **www**.national-trust.org.uk/stourhead

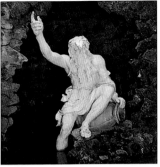

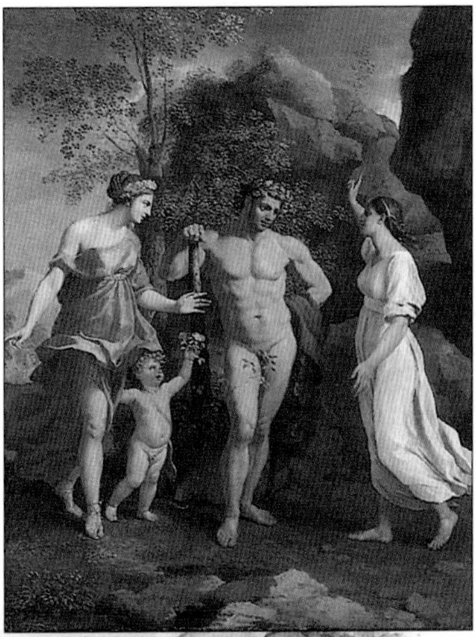

★ Stourhead House
Reconstructed after a fire in 1902, the house contains fine Chippendale furniture. The art collection reflects Henry Hoare's Classical tastes and includes The Choice of Hercules *(1637) by Nicolas Poussin.*

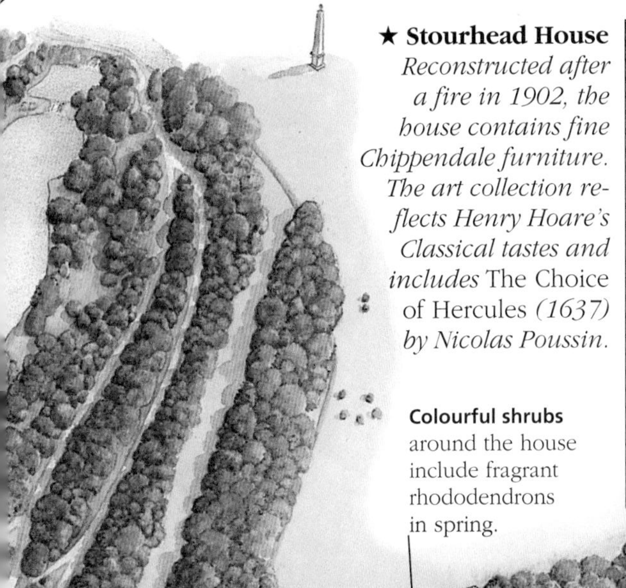

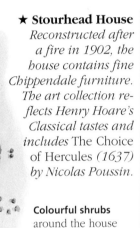

Colourful shrubs around the house include fragrant rhododendrons in spring.

Stourton village was incorporated into Hoare's overall design.

Pelargonium House is a historical collection of over 100 species and cultivars.

The reception offers information to help you enjoy your visit.

Entrance and car park

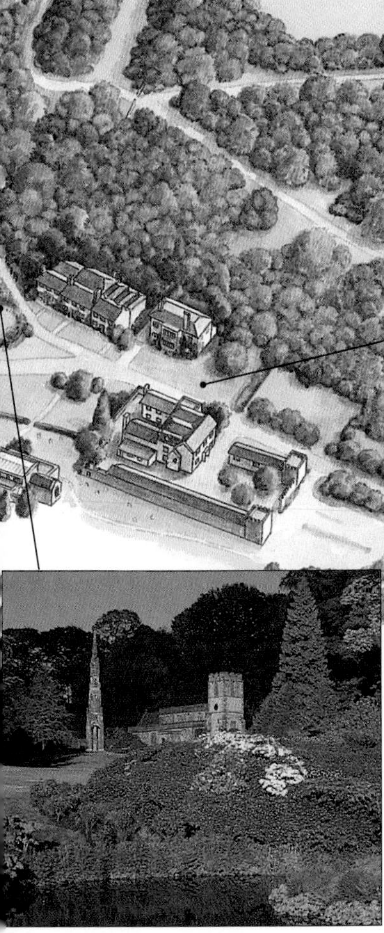

St Peter's Church
The parish church contains monuments to the Hoare family. The medieval Bristol Cross, nearby, was brought from Bristol in 1765.

STAR SIGHTS

★ Temple of Apollo

★ Stourhead House

Shaftesbury ⓰

Dorset. 👥 *8,000.* 🚌 ℹ️ *8 Bell St (01747 853514).* 🛍️ *Thu.*
www.ruraldorset.com

Hilltop Shaftesbury, with its cobbled streets and 18th-century cottages is often used as a setting for films to give a flavour of Old England. Picturesque **Gold Hill** is lined on one side by a wall of the demolished **abbey**, founded by King Alfred in 888. Only the excavated remains of the abbey church survive, and many masonry fragments are found in the local museum.

The Almshouse (1437) adjoining the Abbey Church, Sherborne

Sherborne ⓱

Dorset. 👥 *9,500.* 🚂 🚌 ℹ️ *Digby Rd (01935 815341).* 🛍️ *Thu, Sat.*
www.westdorset.com

Few other towns in Britain have such a wealth of unspoilt medieval buildings. Edward VI *(see p41)* founded the famous Sherborne School in 1550, saving intact the splendid **Abbey Church** and other monastic buildings that might otherwise have been demolished in the Dissolution *(see p50)*. Remains of the Saxon church can be seen in the abbey's façade, but the most striking feature is the 15th-century fan-vaulted ceiling.

Sherborne Castle, built by Sir Walter Raleigh *(see p51)* in 1594, is a wonderfully varied building that anticipates the flamboyant Jacobean style. Raleigh also lived briefly in the early 12th-century **Old Castle**, which now stands in ruins, demolished during the Civil War *(see p52)*.

Environs: West of Sherborne, past Yeovil, is the magnificent Elizabethan **Montacute House** *(see p245)*, set in 120 ha (300 acres) of grounds. It is noted for tapestries, and for the Tudor and Jacobean portraits in the vast Long Gallery.

♣ **Sherborne Castle**
Off A30. **Tel** *01935 813182.*
Castle ◯ *Apr–Oct: Tue–Thu, Sat, Sun & bank hols (pm).* **Grounds** ◯ *Apr–Oct: Thu–Tue.* 🖼️ 🖥️ 🚻
www.sherbornecastle.com

♣ **Old Castle**
(EH) Off A30. **Tel** *01935 812730.*
◯ *Easter–Oct: daily.* 🖼️ 🖥️ 🚻

🏛️ **Montacute House**
(NT) Montacute. **Tel** *01935 823289.*
House ◯ *Mar–Oct: Wed–Mon.*
Grounds ◯ *Apr–Nov: Wed–Mon.*
🖼️ 🍴 🚻

Abbotsbury ⓲

Dorset. 👥 *400.* ℹ️ *Bakehouse Market St (01305 871130).*
www.abbotsbury-tourism.co.uk

The name Abbotsbury recalls the town's 11th-century Benedictine abbey of which little but the huge tithe barn, built around 1400, remains.
  Nobody knows when the **Swannery** here was founded, but the earliest record dates to 1393. Mute swans come to nest in the breeding season, attracted by the reed beds along the Fleet, a brackish lagoon protected from

The Swannery at Abbotsbury

the sea by a high ridge of pebbles called **Chesil Bank** *(see p242)*. Its wild atmosphere makes an appealing contrast to the south coast resorts, although strong currents make swimming too dangerous. **Abbotsbury Sub-Tropical Gardens** are the frost-free home to many new plants, discovered by botanists travelling in South America and Asia.

🦢 **Swannery**
New Barn Rd. **Tel** *01305 871858.* ◯
mid-Mar–Oct: daily. 🖼️ 🚻 🖥️ 🚻

🌿 **Abbotsbury Sub-Tropical Gardens**
Off B3157. **Tel** *01305 871387.* ◯
daily. ⦿ *24 Dec–1 Jan.* 🖼️ 🚻 🖥️ 🚻

Weymouth ⓳

Dorset. 👥 *62,000.* 🚂 🚌 ⛴️
ℹ️ *King's Statue, The Esplanade (01305 785747).* 🛍️ *Thu.*

Weymouth's popularity as a seaside resort began in 1789, when George III paid the first of many summer visits here. The king's bathing machine can be seen in the old brewery complex, **Brewers' Quay**; his

Weymouth Quay, Dorset's south coast

statue is a prominent feature on the seafront. Here gracious Georgian terraces and hotels look across to the beautiful expanse of Weymouth Bay. Different in character is the old town around Custom House Quay with its fishing boats and old seamen's inns. Weymouth will host the sailing events at the 2012 London Olympics.

🏛 Brewers' Quay
Hope Sq. *Tel* 01305 777622. ◯ daily. ● 25 & 26 Dec, 2 wks in Jan. 🖫

Dorchester ⑳

Dorset. 🏘 16,000. 🚅 🛈 Antelope Walk (01305 267992). 🖴 Wed. **www**.visit-dorchester.co.uk

Dorchester, the county town of Dorset, is still recognizably the town in which Thomas Hardy based his novel *The Mayor of Casterbridge* (1886). Here, among the many 17th- and 18th-century houses lining the High Street, is the **Dorset County Museum**, where the original manuscript of the novel is displayed. Dorchester has the only example of a **Roman town house** in Britain. The remains reveal architectural details including a fine mosaic. There are also finds from Iron Age and Roman sites on the outskirts of the

A 55 m (180 ft) giant carved on the chalk hillside, Cerne Abbas (NT)

town. **Maumbury Rings** (Weymouth Avenue), is a Roman amphitheatre, originally a Neolithic henge. To the west, many Roman graves have been found below the Iron Age hill fort, **Poundbury Camp**.

Environs: Just southwest of Dorchester, **Maiden Castle** *(see p43)* is a massive monument dating from around 100 BC. In AD 43 it was the scene of a battle when the Romans fought the Iron Age people of southern England.

To the north lies the charming village of **Cerne Abbas** with its magnificent medieval tithe barn and monastic buildings. The huge chalk figure of a giant on the hillside here is a fertility figure thought to represent either

the Roman god Hercules or an Iron Age warrior.

East of Dorchester are the churches, thatched villages and rolling hills immortalized in Hardy's novels. Picturesque **Bere Regis** is the Kingsbere of *Tess of the D'Urbervilles*, where the tombs of the family whose name inspired the novel may be seen in the Saxon **church**. **Hardy's Cottage** is where the writer was born and **Max Gate** is the house he designed and lived in from 1885 until his death. His heart is buried with his family at

Hardy's statue, Dorchester

Stinsford church – his body was given a public funeral at Westminster Abbey *(pp92–3)*.

There are beautiful gardens *(see p245)* and a magnificent medieval hall at 15th-century **Athelhampton House**.

🏛 Dorset County Museum
High West St. *Tel* 01305 262735. ◯ Mon–Sat (Jul–Sep: daily). ● 25, 26 Dec. 🖫 valid for one year. 🖫 ltd. 🖫 **www**.dorsetcountymuseum.org

🏛 Hardy's Cottage
(NT) Higher Bockhampton. *Tel* 01305 262366. ◯ Apr–Oct: Sun–Thu. 🖫 🖫 garden only.

🏛 Max Gate
(NT) Alington Ave, Dorchester. *Tel* 01305 262538. ◯ Apr–Sep: Sun, Mon & Wed (pm). 🖫 🖫 🖫

🏛 Athelhampton House
Athelhampton. *Tel* 01305 848363. ◯ Sun–Thu (Nov–Feb: Sun). 🖫 🖫 gardens only. 🖫 🖫 🖫 **www**.athelhamptonhouse.co.uk

THOMAS HARDY (1840–1928)

The vibrant, descriptive novels and poems of Thomas Hardy, one of England's best-loved writers, are set against the background of his native Dorset. The Wessex countryside provides a constant and familiar stage against which his characters enact their fate. Vivid accounts of rural life record a key moment in history, when mechanization was about to destroy ancient farming methods, just as the Industrial Revolution had done in the towns a century before *(see pp54–5)*. Hardy's powerfully visual style has made novels such as *Tess of the D'Urbervilles* (1891) popular with modern film-makers, and drawn literary pilgrims to the villages and landscapes that inspired his fiction.

Nastassja Kinski in Roman Polanski's film *Tess* (1979)

Corfe Castle 21

(NT) Dorset. ***Tel*** *01929 481294.* *Wareham then bus.* *daily.* *25 & 26 Dec.* *limited.* *Mar–Oct; Nov–Feb by arrangement.* **www**.nationaltrust.org.uk

The spectacular ruins of Corfe Castle romantically crown a jagged pinnacle of rock above the charming unspoilt village that shares its name. The castle has dominated the landscape since the 11th century, first as a royal fortification, then as the dramatic ruins seen today. In 1635 the castle was purchased by Sir John Bankes, whose wife and her retainers – mostly women – courageously held out against 600 Parliamentary troops, in a six-week siege during the Civil War *(see pp52–3)*. The castle was eventually taken through treachery and in 1646 Parliament voted to have it "slighted" – deliberately blown up to prevent it being used again. From the ruins there are far-reaching views over the Isle of Purbeck and its coastline.

The ruins of Corfe Castle, dating mainly from Norman times

Isle of Purbeck 22

Dorset. *Wareham.* *Shell Bay, Studland.* *Swanage (01929 422885).* **www**.swanage.gov.uk

The Isle of Purbeck, which is in fact a peninsula, is the source of the grey shelly limestone, known as Purbeck marble, from which the castle and surrounding houses were built. The geology changes to the southwest at **Kimmeridge**, where the muddy shale is rich in fossils and recently discovered oil reserves. The Isle, a World Heritage site, is fringed with unspoilt beaches. **Studland Bay** (NT) – with its white sand and its sand-dune nature reserve, rich in birdlife – has been rated one of Britain's best beaches. Sheltered **Lulworth Cove** is almost encircled by white cliffs, and there is a fine cliff-top walk to Durdle Door *(see p243)*, a natural chalk arch.

The main resort in the area is **Swanage**, the port where Purbeck stone was transported by ship to London, to be used for everything from street paving to church building. Unwanted masonry from demolished buildings was shipped back and this is how Swanage got its wonderfully ornate **Town Hall** façade, designed by Wren around 1668.

Beach adjoining Lulworth Cove, Isle of Purbeck

Poole 23

Dorset. *142,000.* *The High St (01202 253253).* **www**.pooletourism.com

Situated on one of the largest natural harbours in the world, Poole is an ancient, still thriving, seaport. The quay is lined with old warehouses, modern apartments and a marina, overlooking a safe sheltered bay. The **Waterfront Museum**, partly housed in 15th-century cellars on the quay, has undergone a major refurbishment, and re-opened during 2007.

Nearby **Brownsea Island** (reached by boat from the quay) is given over to a woodland nature reserve with

a waterfowl and heron sanctuary. The fine views of the Dorset coast add to the appeal of the island.

🏛 Waterfront Museum
High St. **Tel** *01202 262600.*
⭕ *daily.* ⬤ *1 Jan, 25, 26 Dec.* ♿
www.poole.gov.uk

⚸ Brownsea Island
(NT) *Poole.* **Tel** *01202 707744.*
⭕ *Apr–Nov: daily (boat trips leave the quayside every 30 mins during the season).* 🎫 ♿ 📷 📹 🏠

Boats in Poole harbour

Wimborne Minster ㉔

Dorset. 🏠 *6,500.* 🚂 🛈 *29 High St (01202 886116).* ⛴ *Fri–Sun.*
www.ruraldorset.com

The fine collegiate church of Wimborne's **Minster** was founded in 705 by Cuthburga, sister of King Ina of Wessex. It fell prey to marauding Danish raiders in the 10th century, and the imposing grey church we see today dates from the refounding by Edward the Confessor *(see p47)* in 1043. Stonemasons made use of the local Purbeck marble, carving beasts, biblical scenes, and a mass of zig-zag decoration.

The 16th-century **Priest's House Museum** has rooms furnished in the style of different periods and an enchanting hidden garden.

Environs: Designed for the Bankes family after the destruction of Corfe Castle, **Kingston Lacy** was acquired by the National Trust in 1981. The estate has always been farmed by traditional methods

and is astonishingly rich in wildlife, rare flowers and butterflies. This quiet, forgotten corner of Dorset is grazed by rare Red Devon cattle and can be explored using paths and "green lanes" that date back to Roman and Saxon times. The fine 17th-century house on the estate contains an outstanding collection of paintings, including works by Rubens, Velázquez and Titian.

🏛 Priest's House Museum
High St. **Tel** *01202 882533.* ⭕ *Apr–Oct: Mon–Sat.* 🎫 ♿ *limited.* 📹 🏠

⛩ Kingston Lacy
(NT) *on B3082.* **Tel** *0845 0511700.*
House ⭕ *Apr–Oct: Wed–Sun; 2 wks at Christmas.* **Gardens**
⭕ *Apr–Oct: daily; Nov–Mar: Sat & Sun.* 🎫 ♿ *gardens only.* 🍴 🏠

Bournemouth ㉕

Dorset. 🏠 *165,000.* ✈ 🚄 🚌.
🛈 *westover road (01202 451700).*
www.bournemouth.co.uk

Bournemouth's popularity as a seaside resort is due to an almost unbroken sweep of sandy beach, extending from the mouth of Poole Harbour to Hengistbury Head. Most of the seafront is built up, with large seaside villas and exclusive hotels. To the west there are numerous clifftop parks and gardens, interrupted by beautiful wooded river ravines, known as "chines". The varied and colourful garden of **Compton Acres** was conceived as a museum of many different garden styles.

In central Bournemouth the amusement arcades, casinos, nightclubs and shops cater for the city's many visitors. In the summer, pop groups, TV comedians and the highly

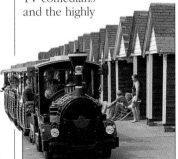

A toy train on the popular seafront at Bournemouth

Marchesa Maria Grimaldi **by Sir Peter Paul Rubens (1577–1640), Kingston Lacy**

regarded Bournemouth Symphony Orchestra perform at various venues in the city. The **Russell-Cotes Art Gallery and Museum**, housed in a late Victorian villa, has an extensive collection, with many fine Oriental and Victorian artefacts.

Environs: The magnificent **Christchurch Priory**, east of Bournemouth, is 95 m (310 ft) in length – the longest church in England. It was rebuilt between the 13th and 16th centuries and presents a sequence of different styles. The original nave, built around 1093, is an impressive example of Norman architecture, but the highlight is the intricate stone reredos, which features a Tree of Jesse, tracing the lineage of Christ. Next to the Priory are the ruins of a Norman **castle**.

Between Bournemouth and Christchurch, **Hengistbury Head** is well worth climbing for grassland flowers, butterflies and sea views, while **Stanpit Marsh**, to the west of Bournemouth, is an excellent spot for viewing herons and other wading birds.

❀ Compton Acres
Canford Cliffs Rd. **Tel** *01202 700778.* ⭕ *daily.* 🏠 🎫 ♿ 🍴
www.comptonacres.co.uk

🏛 Russell-Cotes Art Gallery and Museum
Eastcliff. **Tel** *01202 451800.*
⭕ *Tue–Sun.* ♿ 🍴 🏠 www.
russell-cotes.bournemouth.gov.uk

DEVON AND CORNWALL

DEVON · CORNWALL

M*iles of magnificently varied coastline dominate this magical corner of Britain. Popular seaside resorts alternate with secluded coves and unspoilt fishing villages rich in maritime history. In contrast there are lush, exotic gardens and the wild terrain of the moorland interior, dotted with tors and historic remains.*

Geographical neighbours, the counties of Devon and Cornwall are very different in character. Celtic Cornwall, with its numerous villages named after early Christian missionaries, is mostly stark and treeless at its centre. In many places it is still scarred by the remains of tin and copper mining that has played an important part in the economy for some 4,000 years. Yet this does not detract from the beauty and variety of the coastline dotted with lighthouses and tiny coves, and penetrated by deep tidal rivers.

Devon, by contrast, is a land of lush pasture divided into a patchwork of tiny fields and threaded with narrow lanes, whose banks support a mass of flowers from the first spring primroses to summer's colourful mixture of campion, foxglove, oxeye daisies and blue cornflowers. The leisurely pace of rural life here, and in Cornwall, contrasts with life in the bustling cities. Exeter with its magnificent cathedral, historic Plymouth, elegant Truro and Elizabethan Totnes are urban centres brimming with life and character.

The spectacular coastline and the mild climate of the region attract families, boating enthusiasts and surfers. For those in search of solitude, the Southwest Coastal Path provides access to the more tranquil areas. There are fishing villages and harbours whose heyday was in the buccaneering age of Drake and Raleigh *(see p51),* and inland the wild moorland of Bodmin and Dartmoor, which provided inspiration for many romantic tales. Many of these are associated with King Arthur *(see p285)* who, according to legend, was born at Tintagel on Cornwall's dramatically contorted north coast.

Beach huts on the seafront at Paignton, near Torquay

◁ **Fishing boats in Port Isaac, on Cornwall's north coast**

Exploring Devon and Cornwall

Romantic Moorland dominates the inland parts of Devon and Cornwall, ideal walking country with few roads and magnificent views stretching for miles. By contrast the extensive coastline is indented by hundreds of sheltered river valleys, each one seemingly isolated from the rest of the world – one reason why Devon and Cornwall can absorb so many visitors and yet still seem uncrowded. Wise tourists get to know one small part of Devon or Cornwall intimately, soaking up the atmosphere of the region, rather than rushing to see everything in the space of a week.

KEY

▬▬	Motorway
▭▭	Major road
▬	Secondary road
▭ ▭	Minor road
▬	Scenic route
▬ ▬	Main railway
──	Minor railway
△	Summit

SIGHTS AT A GLANCE

Appledore **16**
Barnstaple **17**
Bideford **15**
Bodmin **11**
Buckfastleigh **23**
Buckland Abbey **26**
Bude **13**
Burgh Island **24**
Clovelly **14**
Cotehele **27**
Dartmoor pp294–5 **29**
Dartmouth **21**
Eden Project pp282–3 **9**
Exeter **19**
Falmouth **6**
Fowey **10**
Helston and the
   Lizard Peninsula **5**
Lynton and Lynmouth **18**
Morwellham Quay **28**
Penzance **3**
Plymouth **25**
St Austell **8**
St Ives **2**
St Michael's Mount
   pp278–9 **4**
Tintagel **12**
Torbay **20**
Totnes **22**
Truro **7**

Walks and Tours

Penwith Tour **1**

The dramatic cliffs of Land's End, England's most westerly point

Lundy

Barnst
Bidefo
Hartland Point   CLOVEL
Hartland ○
Morewenstow ○
Holsw
Be
BUDE 13
Bude Bay   Marham
Week St Mary ○   Ash
Boscastle ○   A39   Boyto
Camelford ○   **⋒12 TINTAGEL**
Brown Willy   Launces
420m   △
Altarn
Polzeath ○   *Bodmin Moor*
Padstow ○   Bolventor ○
Colliford   Ca
Wadebridge ○   A30   Reservoir
St Neot ○
St Mawgan ○   A39   **BODMIN 11 ⋒⊞   A38**   Lisl
Newquay ○   St Columb   ○ Lanhydrock
Major   Lostwithiel ○   St G
Bugle ○   East Looe ○
Newlyn East ○   **EDEN PROJECT 9**   ○ Polperr
ST AUSTELL 8   **10**
St. Agnes ○   A39   *Trewithen* ⋒   **FOWEY**
A390   *Heligan* ○ Mevagissey
Portreath ○   **7 TRURO** ○ ⋒
Camborne ○   A30   Redruth ○   *Trelissick*   ○ Gorran Haven
Dodman Point
ST IVES 2   ⋒   Hayle ○   Penryn ○   Gerrans ○
Chysauster ○   Poldark   A394   **6 FALMOUTH**
St Just ○   **PENZANCE**   Mine ○   ⋒
PENWITH   ⋒⋒ 3   4 ⚓   **5 HELSTON** ○   Mawnan Smith
TOUR 1   **ST MICHAEL'S**
Sennen ○   Mousehole   **MOUNT**   Goonhilly
Mount's   ○ Earth Station
Bay   Mullion ○   ⋒   ○ Coverack
5 LIZARD PENINSULA
Lizard ○   *Lizard Point*

Sub-tropical gardens at Torquay, the popular seaside resort

GETTING AROUND

Large numbers of drivers, many towing caravans (trailers), travel along the M5 motorway and A30 trunk road from mid-July to early September and travel can be slow, especially on Saturdays. Once in Devon and Cornwall, allow ample time if you are travelling by car along the region's narrow and high-banked lanes.

The regular train services, running from Paddington to Penzance, along Brunel's historic Great Western Railway, stop at most major towns. Aside from this, you are dependent on taxis or infrequent local buses.

Typical thatched, stone cottages, Buckland-in-the-Moor, Dartmoor

0 kilometres 15

0 miles 10

Penwith Tour ●

This tour passes through a spectacular, remote Cornish landscape, dotted with relics of the tin mining industry, picturesque fishing villages and many prehistoric remains. The magnificent coastline varies between the gentle rolling moorland in the north and the rugged, windswept cliffs that characterize the dramatic south coast. The beauty of the area, combined with the clarity of light, has attracted artists since the late 19th century. Their work can be seen in Newlyn, St Ives and Penzance.

TIPS FOR DRIVERS

Tour length: 31 miles (50 km)
Stopping-off points: There are pubs and cafés in most villages. Sennen Cove makes a pleasant mid-way stop.

Zennor ①
The carved mermaid in the church recalls the legend of the mermaid who lured the local squire's son to her ocean lair.

Lanyon Quoit ②
One of many prehistoric monuments, this chambered tomb is visible on the left from the road to Madron.

Botallack Mine ⑧
Derelict enginehouses clinging to the cliffside are a vivid reminder of the region's former industry of tin-mining.

Trengwainton ③
These gardens are noted for their luxuriance (p244).

Land's End ⑦
England's most westerly point is noted for its dramatic and wild landscape. A local exhibition reveals its history, geology and wildlife.

Newlyn ④
Cornwall's largest fishing port gave its name to a school of artists founded in the 1880s (p278). Examples of their work can be seen in the art gallery here.

Merry Maidens ⑤
This Bronze Age stone circle is said to be 19 girls turned to stone for dancing on Sunday.

Minack Theatre ⑥
This Ancient Greek-style theatre (1923) overlooks a magical bay of Porthcurno. It forms a magnificent backdrop for productions in summer.

| 0 kilometres | | 3 |
| 0 miles | | 2 |

KEY

▩▩▩	Tour route
═══	Other roads
☀	Viewpoint

St Ives ❷

Cornwall. 👥 *11,000.* 🚃 🚌
ℹ️ *Street-an-Pol (01736 796297).*
www.visit-westcornwall.com

St Ives's **Barbara Hepworth Museum and Sculpture Garden** and **Tate St Ives** celebrate the work of a group of artists who set up a seaside art colony here from the 1920s. The former presents the sculptor's work in the house and garden where she lived and worked for many years. Tate St Ives, designed to frame a panoramic view of Porthmeor Beach, reminds visitors of the natural surroundings that inspired the art on display within. A new museum at the Leach Pottery (Tel: 01736 799703) celebrates the life and work of potter Bernard Leach, another luminary of the St Ives Society of Artists.

The Lower Terrace, Tate St Ives

The town of St Ives remains a typical English seaside resort, surrounded by a crescent of golden sands. Popular taste rules in the many other art galleries tucked down winding alleys with names such as Teetotal Street, a legacy of the town's Methodist heritage. Many galleries are converted cellars and lofts where fish were once salted and packed. In between are whitewashed cottages with tiny gardens brimming with flowers, their vibrant colours made intense by the unusually clear light that first attracted artists to St Ives.

🏛 **Barbara Hepworth Museum and Sculpture Garden**
Barnoon Hill. **Tel** *01736 796226.*
⭕ *daily (Nov–Feb: Tue–Sun).* ⬤
24–26 Dec. 📷 ♿ *by appt.* 📷

🏛 **Tate St Ives**
Porthmeor Beach. **Tel** *01736 796226.* ⭕ *daily (Nov–Feb: Tue–Sun).* ⬤ *24–26 Dec; occasionally for rehanging – phone to check.* 📷 ♿ 🍴 📷 **www**.tate.org.uk/stives

---

TWENTIETH-CENTURY ARTISTS OF ST IVES

Ben Nicholson and Barbara Hepworth formed the nucleus of a group of artists that made a major contribution to the development of abstract art in Europe. In the 1920s, St Ives together with Newlyn *(see p276)* became a place for aspiring artists. Among the prolific artists associated with the town are the potter Bernard Leach (1887–1979) and the painter Patrick Heron (1920–99), whose *Coloured Glass Window (see p240)* dominates the Tate St Ives entrance. Much of the art on display at Tate St Ives is abstract and illustrates new responses to the rugged Cornish landscape, the human figure and the ever-changing patterns of sunlight on sea.

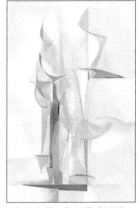

Barbara Hepworth *(1903–75) was one of the foremost abstract sculptors of her time.* Madonna and Child *(1953) can be seen in the church of St Ia.*

John Wells' *(1907–2000) key interests are in light, curved forms and birds in flight, as revealed in* Aspiring Forms *(1950).*

Ben Nicholson's *(1894–1982) work shows a change in style from simple scenes, such as the view from his window, to a preoccupation with shapes – as seen in this painting* St Ives, Cornwall *(1943–5). Later, his interest moved towards pure geometric blocks of colour.*

Penzance ③

Cornwall. 🏛 *15,000.* 🚶 🚌 🚢 🛈
Station Approach (01736 362207).
www.visit-westcornwall.com

Penzance is a bustling resort with a climate so mild that palm trees and sub-tropical plants grow happily in the lush **Morrab Gardens**. The town commands fine views of St Michael's Mount and a great sweep of clean sandy beach.

The main road through the town is Market Jew Street, at the top of which stands the magnificent domed Market House (1837), fronted by a statue of Sir Humphrey Davy (1778–1829). Davy, who came from Penzance, invented the miner's safety lamp which detected lethal gases.

Chapel Street is lined with curious buildings, none more striking than the flamboyant **Egyptian House** (1835), with its richly painted façade and lotus bud decoration. Just as curious is **Admiral Benbow Inn** (1696) on the same street, which has a pirate perched on the roof looking out to sea. The town's **Museum and Art Gallery** has pictures by the Newlyn School of artists.

Environs: A short distance south of Penzance, **Newlyn** *(see p276)* is Cornwall's largest fishing port, which has given its name to the local school of artists founded by Stanhope Forbes (1857–1947). They painted outdoors, aiming to capture the fleeting impressions of wind, sun and sea. Continuing south, the coastal road ends at **Mousehole** (pronounced Mowzall), a pretty, popular village with a

The Egyptian House (1835)

tiny harbour, tiers of cottages and a maze of narrow alleys.

North of Penzance, overlooking the magical Cornish coast, **Chysauster** is a fine example of a Romano-British village. The site has remained almost undisturbed since it

St Michael's Mount ④

(NT) Marazion, Cornwall. **Tel** *01736 710507; tide and ferry information 01736 710265.* 🚢 *from Marazion (Mar–Oct) or on foot at low tide.* ⭕ *Mar–Oct: Sun–Fri; Nov–Mar guided tours only (book ahead).* 📷 🍴 📷
🔒 **www.**stmichaelsmount.co.uk

St Michael's Mount emerges dramatically from the waters of Mounts Bay. According to ancient Roman historians, the mount was the island of Ictis, an important centre for the Cornish tin trade during the Iron Age. It is dedicated to the archangel St Michael who, according to legend, appeared here in 495.

When the Normans conquered England in 1066 *(see pp46–7)*, they were struck by the island's resemblance to their own Mont-St-Michel, whose Benedictine monks were invited to build a small abbey here. The abbey was absorbed into a fortress at the Dissolution *(see p351)*, when Henry VIII set up a chain of coastal defences to counter an expected attack from France. In 1659 St Michael's Mount was purchased by Colonel John St Aubyn, whose descendants subsequently turned the fortress into a magnificent house.

View of St Michael's Mount from Marazion

Harbourside village

Access to the island is by boat from Marazion or on foot by a cobbled causeway at low tide.

The rocky slopes were planted with sub-tropical trees and shrubs by the St Aubyn family.

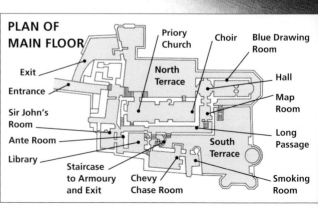

PLAN OF MAIN FLOOR

Exit

Entrance

Sir John's Room

Ante Room

Library

Staircase to Armoury and Exit

Chevy Chase Room

North Terrace

Priory Church

Choir

Blue Drawing Room

Hall

Map Room

South Terrace

Long Passage

Smoking Room

was abandoned during the 3rd century.

From Penzance, regular boat and helicopter services depart for the **Isles of Scilly**, a beautiful archipelago forming part of the same granite mass as Land's End, Bodmin Moor and Dartmoor. Along with tourism, flower-growing forms the main source of income here.

⌂ Penlee House Gallery and Museum
Morrab Rd.
Tel 01736 363625. ◯ May–Sep: 10am–5pm Mon–Sat; Oct–Apr: 10:30am–4:30pm Mon–Sat. ◼ 25–26 Dec, 1 Jan. ◻ ◻ but free admission on Sat. ♿ ◻
www.penleehouse.org.uk

⋒ Chysauster
(EH) Off B3311.
Tel 07831 757934.
◯ Apr–Oct: daily. ◻ ◻

THE GROWTH OF METHODISM

The hard-working and independent mining and fishing communities of the West Country had little time for the established church, but they were won over by the new Methodist religion, with its emphasis on hymn singing, open-air preaching and regular or "methodical" Bible reading. When John Wesley, the founder of Methodism, made the first of many visits to the area in 1743, sceptical Cornishmen pelted him with stones. His persistence, however, led to many conversions and by 1762 he was preaching to congregations of up to 30,000 people. Simple places of worship were built throughout the county; one favoured spot was the amphitheatre **Gwennap Pit**, at Busveal, south of Redruth. Methodist memorabilia can be seen in the Royal Cornwall Museum in Truro (*see p281*).

John Wesley (1703–91)

Castle Entrance

The South Terrace forms the roof of the large Victorian wing. Beneath it there are five floors of private quarters.

The Blue Drawing Room *was formed from the Lady Chapel in the mid-18th century and is decorated in charming Rococo Gothic style. It contains fine plaster work, furniture and paintings by Gainsborough and Thomas Hudson.*

The Armoury displays sporting weapons and military trophies brought back by the St Aubyn family from various wars.

The Priory Church, *rebuilt in the late 14th century, forms the summit of the island. Beautiful rose windows are found at both ends.*

The Chevy Chase Room *takes its name from a plaster frieze (1641) representing hunting scenes.*

Pinnacles of serpentine rock at Kynance Cove (NT), Lizard Peninsula

Helston and the Lizard Peninsula ❺

Cornwall. 🚌 *from Penzance.*
ℹ️ *Station Approach, Penzance
(01736 362207).*
www.visit-westcornwall.com

The attractive town of Helston makes a good base for exploring the windswept coastline of the Lizard Peninsula. The town is famous for its Furry Dance, which welcomes spring with dancing through the streets *(see p62);* the **Folk Museum** explains the history of this ancient custom. The Georgian houses and inns of Coinagehall Street are a reminder that Helston was once a thriving stannary town where tin ingots were brought for weighing and stamping before being sold. Locally mined tin was brought down river to a harbour at the bottom of this street until access to the sea was blocked in the 13th century by a shingle bar that formed across the estuary. The bar created the freshwater lake, Loe Pool, and an attractive walk skirts its wooded shores. In 1880, Helston's trade was taken over by a new harbour created to the east on the River Helford, at Gweek. Today, Gweek is the home of the **National Seal Sanctuary**, where sick seals are nursed before being returned to the sea.

Cornwall's tin mining industry, from Roman to recent times, is covered at the **Poldark Mine** where underground tours show the working conditions of 18th-century miners. Another major attraction is **Flambards Experience**, with its recreation of a Victorian village and of Britain during the Blitz.

Further south, huge satellite dishes rise from the heathland. The **Goonhilly Earth Station** visitors' centre here explores the world of satellite communications.

Local shops sell souvenirs carved from serpentine, a soft greenish stone which forms the unusual-shaped rocks that rise from the sandy beach at picturesque **Kynance Cove**.

🏛 **Folk Museum**
Market Place, Helston. **Tel** 01326
564027. ⬜ *Mon–Sat (am only).*
⬛ *Christmas week.* 🔲 ♿ *limited.*
🖥 www.kerrierleisure.org.uk

🦭 **National Seal Sanctuary**
Gweek. **Tel** 01326 221361.
⬜ *daily.* ⬛ *25 Dec.* 🔲 ♿ 🅿️
🖥 www.sealsanctuary.co.uk

🏛 **Poldark Mine**
Wendron. **Tel** 01326 573173.
⬜ *2 wks at Easter, Jul & Aug: daily;
Apr–Jun, Sep & Oct: Sun–Fri; Nov–
Mar: tours only, by appt.* 🔲 🖥 🅿️
www.poldark-mine.co.uk

🏛 **Flambards Experience**
Culdrose Manor, Helston. **Tel** 0845
6018684. ⬜ *Easter–Aug: daily;
Oct–Mar: Tue–Thu.* 🔲 ♿ 🍴 🅿️
www.flambards.co.uk

🏛 **Goonhilly Earth Station**
Nr Helston, off B3293. **Tel** 0800
679 593. ⬜ *daily.* 🔲 ♿ 🖥 🖵
🖥 www.goonhilly.bt.com

Falmouth ❻

Cornwall. 🏠 *22,000.* ✈ 🚌 🚢
ℹ️ *11 Market Strand (01326
312300).* **www.**acornishriver.co.uk

Falmouth stands at the point where seven rivers flow into a long stretch of water called the **Carrick Roads**. The drowned river valley is so deep that huge ocean-going ships can sail up almost as far as Truro. Numerous creeks are ideal for boating excursions to view the varied scenery and birdlife.

Falmouth has the third largest naturally deep harbour after Sydney and Rio de Janeiro, and it forms the most interesting part of this seaside resort. On the

---

CORNISH SMUGGLERS

In the days before income tax was invented, the main form of government income came from tax on imported luxury goods, such as brandy and perfume. Huge profits were to be made by evading these taxes, which were at their height during the Napoleonic Wars (1780–1815). Remote Cornwall, with its coves and rivers penetrating deep into the mainland, was prime smuggling territory; estimates put the number of people involved, including women and children, at 100,000. Some notorious families resorted to deliberate wrecking, setting up deceptive lights to lure vessels onto the sharp rocks, in the hope of plundering the wreckage.

harbour waterfront stands the recently constructed **National Maritime Museum Cornwall**, part of a projected large new waterside complex, to include cafés, shops and restaurants. With an exterior that is oak-clad to reflect the history of wooden boat sheds in the area, the museum is dedicated to the great maritime tradition of Cornwall, and contains Britain's finest public collection of historic and contemporary small craft. The building is designed to bring to life the stories of boats, maritime themes and Cornwall's heritage, as well as the story of the people whose lives depended on the sea. It aims to be accessible to the whole family.

The many old houses on the harbour include the striking **Customs House** and the chimney alongside, known as the "King's Pipe" because it was used for burning contraband tobacco seized from smugglers in the 19th century. **Pendennis Castle** and St Mawes Castle opposite, were built by King Henry VIII.

Environs: To the south, **Glendurgan** (see p244) and **Trebah** gardens are both set in sheltered valleys leading down to delightful sandy coves on the Helford River.

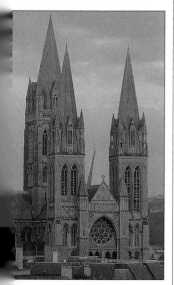

Truro Cathedral, designed by J L Pearson and completed in 1910

🏛 **National Maritime Museum Cornwall**
Discovery Quay, Falmouth. **Tel** 01326 313388. ◯ daily. ● 25, 26 Dec. ▦ ♿ ◻ 🛍 ◻ www.nmmc.co.uk

⚓ **Pendennis Castle**
(EH) The Headland. **Tel** 01326 316594. ◯ daily. ● 1 Jan, 24–26 Dec. ▦ ♿ limited. ☷ ◻ 🛍

🍁 **Glendurgan**
(NT) Mawnan Smith. **Tel** 01326 250906.
◯ mid-Feb–mid-Nov: Tue–Sat & pub hols (Aug: Mon–Sat). ● Good Fri. ▦ 🛍 ◻

🍁 **Trebah**
Mawnan Smith. **Tel** 01326 252200. ◯ daily. 🛍 ▦ ♿ ◻ www.trebah-garden.co.uk

Ship's figurehead, Falmouth

Truro ❼

Cornwall. 🏘 19,000. ⇌ 🚌 ℹ Boscawen St (01872 274555). 🍎 Wed (cattle), Wed & Sat (farmers' market). www.acornishriver.co.uk

Once a market town and port, Truro is now the administrative capital of Cornwall. Truro's many gracious Georgian buildings reflect its prosperity during the tin mining boom of the 1800s. In 1876 the 16th-century parish church was rebuilt to create the first new **cathedral** to be built in England since Wren built St Paul's (see pp114–15) in the 17th century. With its central tower, lancet windows and spires, the cathedral is an exuberant building that looks more French than English.

Truro's cobbled streets and alleys lined with craft shops are also a delight to explore. The **Royal Cornwall Museum** provides an excellent introduction to the history of the county with displays on tin mining, Methodism (see p279) and smuggling.

Environs: On the outskirts of the city lie **Trewithen** and **Trelissick** gardens (see p244). The former has a rich collection of Asiatic plants.

🏛 **Royal Cornwall Museum**
River St. **Tel** 01872 272205. ◯ Mon–Sat. ● public hols. ♿ ◻ 🛍 www.royalcornwallmuseum.org.uk

🍁 **Trewithen**
Grampound Rd. **Tel** 01726 883647. ◯ Mar–May: daily; Jun–Sep: Mon–Sat. ▦ ♿ 🛍 by arrangement. ◻ 🛍 www.trewithengardens.co.uk

🍁 **Trelissick**
(NT) Feock. **Tel** 01872 862090. ◯ Mar–May: daily; Jun–Sep: Mon–Sat. ▦ ♿ 🍴 ◻ 🛍

The "Cornish Alps": china-clay spoil tips north of St Austell

St Austell ❽

Cornwall. 🏘 20,000. ⇌ 🚌 ℹ Jet Service Station, Southbourne Rd (0845 094 0428). 🍎 Fri–Sun. www.cornish-riviera.co.uk

The busy industrial town of St Austell is the capital of the local china-clay industry which rose to importance in the 18th century. Clay is still a vital factor here; until recently, China was the only other place where such quality and quantity of clay could be found. Spoil tips are a prominent feature; on a sunny day they look like snow-covered peaks, meriting the local name the "Cornish Alps".

Environs: The famous **Lost Gardens of Heligan** are an amazing restoration project to recreate the extraordinary gardens created by the Tremayne family from the 16th century to World War I. At the **Wheal Martyn China Clay Museum**, nature trails weave through clay works that operated from 1878 until the 1920s.

🍁 **Lost Gardens of Heligan**
Pentewan. **Tel** 01726 845100. ◯ daily. ● 24 & 25 Dec. ▦ ♿ 🍴 ◻ 🛍 www.heligan.com

🏛 **Wheal Martyn China Clay Museum**
Carthew. **Tel** 01726 850362. ◯ Feb–Sep: daily. ▦ ♿ limited. ◻ 🛍 www.wheal-martyn.com

Eden Project ❾

Built in a china clay pit that had reached the end of its useful life, the Eden Project is a global garden for the 21st century, and a dramatic setting in which to tell the fascinating story of mankind's dependence on plants. Two futuristic conservatories called Biomes have been designed to mimic the environments of warmer climes: one hot and humid, the other warm and dry. The outer Biome is planted with species that thrive in the Cornish climate. The Eden Project seeks to educate by telling the story of plants, people and places. The relationship between humans and nature is interpreted by artists throughout the site. An impressive education centre, the Core, was opened in 2006 and is used for exhibitions, films and workshops.

④ Tropical South America
Some plants in this area reach enormous proportions. The leaves of the giant waterlily can be up to 2 m (6 ft) across.

③ West Africa
Iboga is central to the African religion Bwiti. Highly hallucinogenic, it is an integral part of initiation ceremonies.

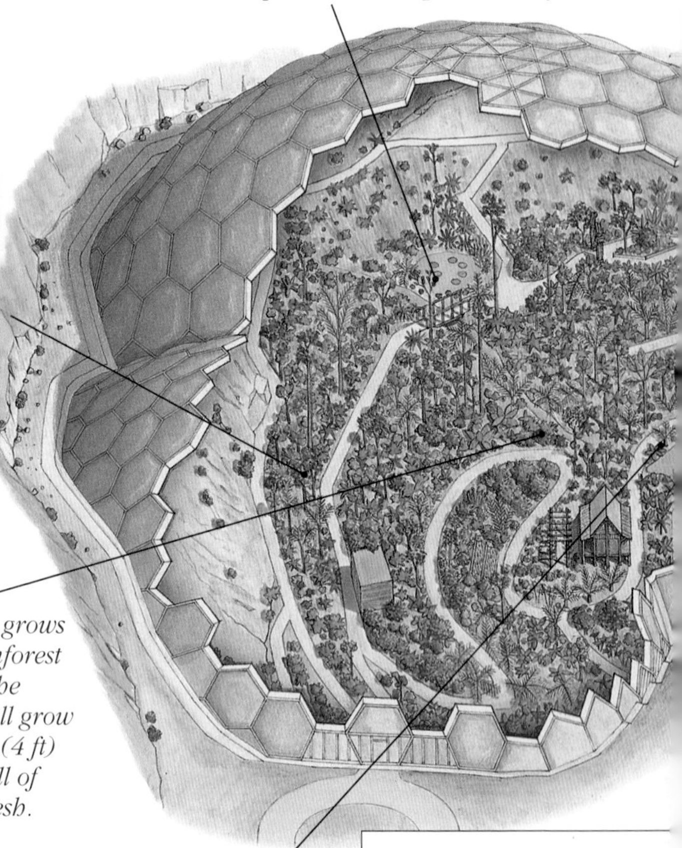

② Malaysia
The Titan arum grows within this rainforest display. The flower will grow to 1.5 m (4 ft) and smell of rotting flesh.

① Tropical Islands
Set apart from the rest of the world, these islands have many fascinating plants. The rare Madagascar Periwinkle (Catharanthus roseus) is thought to help cure leukemia.

THE SITE

Access to the outdoor and the covered Biomes is via the Visitor Centre.

Rainforest Biome
① Tropical Islands
② Malaysia
③ West Africa
④ Tropical South America
⑤ Crops & cultivation

Mediterranean Biome
⑥ The Mediterranean
⑦ South Africa
⑧ California
⑨ Crops & cultivation

VISITORS' CHECKLIST

Bodelva, St Austell, Cornwall.
Tel 01726 811911. St Austell.
dedicated bus service from St
Austell. Apr–Oct: 10am–
6pm daily (last adm 5pm); Nov–
Mar: 10am–4:30pm daily (last
adm 3pm). 24, 25 Dec.
For events details
see **www**.edenproject.com

Building Eden

*Cornwall's declining china clay industry has left behind
many disused pits. The Eden Project makes ingenious use
of this industrial landscape. After partly infilling a pit,
the massive Biomes were nestled into its base and walls.*

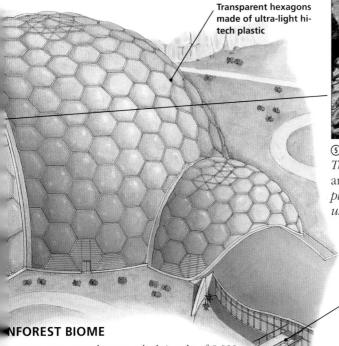

**Transparent hexagons
made of ultra-light hi-
tech plastic**

⑤ Crops and cultivation
*The coffee plant (Coffea
arabica) is one of the many
plants on display that are
used in our everyday lives.*

The entrance to both
the Rainforest and
Mediterranean Biomes is
via the Link, where two
restaurants are located.

...NFOREST BIOME

...vast conservatory houses a lush jungle of 8,000
...and plants. The dome is high enough to allow
...e rainforest trees to grow to their full height.

...loor Biome	㉕ Play
...llination	㉖ Flowers in the making
...ornish crops	㉗ Health
...ants for taste	㉘ Flowerless garden
...obal gardeners	
...er & brewing	
...pe & fibre	
...mp	
...eppe & Prairie	
...o-engineering	
...a	
...vender	
...echanical theatre	
...el	
...th & folkore	
...diversity & Cornwall	

KEY

▨ Land Train

The Stage
The Core
Eden Arena
Visitor Centre

0 metres   150
0 yards   150

View of Polruan across the estuary from Fowey

Fowey ⑩

Cornwall. 👥 *2,000.* ⛴
ℹ *5 South St (01726 833616).*
www.fowey.co.uk

Fowey (pronounced Foy), has been immortalized under the name of Troy Town in the humorous novels of Sir Arthur Quiller-Couch (1863–1944), who lived here in a house called **The Haven**. A resort favoured by many wealthy Londoners with a taste

DAPHNE DU MAURIER

The period romances of Daphne du Maurier (1907–89) are inextricably linked with the wild Cornish landscape where she grew up. *Jamaica Inn* established her reputation in 1936, and with the publication of *Rebecca* two years later she found herself one of the most popular authors of her day. *Rebecca* was made into a film directed by Alfred Hitchcock, starring Joan Fontaine and Lord Laurence Olivier.

for yachting and expensive seafood restaurants, Fowey is the most gentrified of the Cornish seaside towns. The picturesque charm of the flower-filled village is undeniable, with its tangle of tiny steep streets and its views across the estuary to Polruan. The church of **St Fimbarrus** marks the end of the ancient Saint's Way footpath from Padstow – a reminder of the Celtic missionaries who arrived on the shores of Cornwall to convert people to Christianity. Its flower-lined path leads to a majestic porch and carved tower. Inside there are some fine 17th-century memorials to the Rashleigh family whose seat, Menabilly, became Daphne du Maurier's home and featured as Manderley in *Rebecca* (1938).

Environs: For a closer look at the town of **Polruan** and the ceaseless activity of the harbour there is a number of river trips up the little creeks. At the estuary mouth are the twin towers from which chains were once hung to demast invading ships – an effective form of defence.

A fine stretch of coast leads further east to the picturesque fishing villages of **Polperro**, nestling in a narrow green ravine, and neighbouring **Looe**.

Upriver from Fowey is the tranquil town of **Lostwithiel**. Perched on a hill just to the north are the remains of the Norman **Restormel Castle**.

⚓ **Restormel Castle**
(EH) Lostwithiel. **Tel** 01208 872687.
◯ *Apr–Oct: daily.* 📷 🅿

Bodmin ⑪

Cornwall. 🚋 *Bodmin Parkway.* 🚌 *Bodmin.* ℹ *Mount Folly Sq, Bodmin (01208 76616).* **www.**bodminlive.com

Bodmin, Cornwall's ancient county town, lies on the sheltered western edge of the great expanse of moorland that shares its name. The history and archaeology of the town and moor is covered by **Bodmin Town Museum**, while **Bodmin Jail**, where public executions took place until 1909, is a gruesome tourist attraction. The churchyard is watered by the ever-gushing waters of a holy spring, and it was here that St Guron established a Christian cell in the 6th century. The **church** is dedicated to St Petroc, a Welsh missionary who founded a monastery here. The monastery has disappeared, but the bones of St Petroc remain, housed in a splendid 12th-century ivory casket in the church.

For a pleasant day out, ride the **Bodmin & Wenford Railway**, a steam train which departs from Bodmin Station, or take part in a Victorian murder

Jamaica Inn, Bodmin Moor

trial at **The Courtroom Experience**, run by the tourist office.

South of Bodmin is the **Lanhydrock** estate. Amid its extensive wooded acres and formal gardens *(see p244)* lies the massive Victorian manor house, rebuilt after a fire in 1881, but retaining some Jacobean features. The fine 17th-century plaster ceiling in the Long Gallery depicts scenes from the Bible.

The desolate wilderness of Bodmin Moor is noted for its network of prehistoric field boundaries. The main attraction, however, is the 18th-century **Jamaica Inn**, made famous by Daphne du Maurier's tale of smuggling and romance. Today there is a restaurant and bar based on du Maurier's novel, and a small museum. A 30-minute walk from the Inn is **Dozmary Pool**, reputed to be bottomless until it dried up in 1976.

The ruins of Tintagel Castle on the north coast of Cornwall

According to legend, the dying King Arthur's sword Excalibur was thrown into the pool.

To the east is **Altarnun**. Its spacious 15th-century church of **St Nonna** is known as the "Cathedral of the Moor".

🏛 **Bodmin Town Museum**
Mt Folly Sq, Bodmin. *Tel* 01208 77067. ○ Easter–Oct: Mon–Sat, Good Fri. ● pub hols. & ltd. 📷

🏚 **Bodmin Jail**
Berrycombe Rd, Bodmin. *Tel* 01208 76292. ○ daily. ● 25 Dec. 📷 🍽
🍴 💻 www.bodminjail.org

🏚 **Lanhydrock**
(NT) Bodmin. *Tel* 01208 265950.
House ○ Apr–Oct: Tue–Sun & public hols. **Gardens** ○ daily.
📷 🍽 & 🍴

Tintagel ⑫

Cornwall. 🏘 1,700. 🅸 Bossiney Rd (01840 779084). 🚌 Thu (summer). **www**.visitboscastleandtintagel.com

The romantic and mysterious ruins of **Tintagel Castle**, built around 1240 by Earl Richard of Cornwall, sit high on a hill-top surrounded by slate cliffs. Access to the castle is via two steep staircases clinging to the cliffside where pink thrift and purple sea lavender abound.

The earl was persuaded to build in this isolated, windswept spot by the popular belief, derived from Geoffrey of Monmouth's fictitious *History of the Kings of Britain*, that this was the birthplace of the legendary King Arthur.

Large quantities of fine eastern Mediterranean pottery dating from around the 5th century have been discovered, indicating that the site was an important trading centre, long before the medieval castle was built. Whoever lived here, perhaps the ancient Kings of Cornwall, could evidently afford a luxurious lifestyle.

A clifftop path leads from the castle to Tintagel's **church**, which has Norman and Saxon masonry. In Tintagel village the **Old Post Office** is a rare example of a 14th-century restored and furnished Cornish manor house.

Environs: A short distance to the east, **Boscastle** is a pretty National Trust village. The River Valency runs down the middle of the main street to the fishing harbour, which is sheltered from the sea by high slate cliffs. Access from the harbour to the sea is via a channel cut through the rocks.

🏰 **Tintagel Castle**
(EH) Off High St. *Tel* 01840 770328. ○ daily. ● 1 Jan, 24–26 Dec. 🍽
www.english-heritage.org.uk/tintagel

🏚 **Old Post Office**
(NT) Fore St. *Tel* 01840 770024. ○ Mar–Oct: daily. 📷 🍽

KING ARTHUR

Historians think the legendary figure of King Arthur has some basis in historical fact. He was probably a Romano-British chieftain or warrior who led British resistance to the Saxon invasion of the 6th century *(see pp46–7)*. Geoffrey of Monmouth's *History of the Kings of Britain* (1139) introduced Arthur to literature with an account of the many legends connected with him – how he became king by removing the sword Excalibur from a stone, his final battle with the treacherous Mordred, and the story of the Knights of the Round Table *(see p170)*. Other writers, such as Alfred, Lord Tennyson, took up these stories and elaborated on them.

King Arthur, from a 14th-century chronicle by Peter of Langtoft

Bude ⑬

Cornwall. 🏘 9,000. 🅸 Crescent car park (01288 354240). 🚌 Fri (summer). **www**.visitbude.info

Wonderful beaches around this area make Bude a popular resort for families. The expanse of clean golden sand that attracts visitors today once made Bude a bustling port. Shelly, lime-rich sand was transported along a canal to inland farms where it was used to neutralize the acidic soil. The canal was abandoned in 1880 but a short stretch survives, providing a haven for birds such as kingfishers and herons.

Kingfisher

Clovelly ⑭

Devon. 🏛 *350*. **Tel** *01237 431781*.
Town & Visitors' Centre ◯ *daily*.
● *25 & 26 Dec.* 🈵 ♿ *Visitors' Centre*. **www**.clovelly.co.uk

Clovelly has been a noted beauty spot since the novelist Charles Kingsley (1819–75) wrote about it in his stirring story of the Spanish Armada, *Westward Ho!* (1855). The whole village is privately owned and has been turned into a tourist attraction, with little sign of the flourishing fishing industry to which it owed its birth. It is a charming, picturesque village with steep, traffic-free cobbled streets rising up the cliff from the harbourside, white-washed houses and gardens brimming with brightly coloured flowers. There are superb views from the lookout points and fine coastal paths to explore from the tiny quay.

Hobby Drive is a scenic 3-mile (5-km) approach on foot to the village which runs through woodland along the coast. The road was constructed in 1811–29 to give

Bideford's medieval bridge, 203 m (666 ft) long with 24 arches

employment to local men who had been made redundant at the end of the Napoleonic Wars *(see pp54–5)*.

Bideford ⑮

Devon. 🏛 *14,000*. 🚌 ℹ️ *Kingsley Rd (01237 477676)*. 🚢 *Tue, Sat.*

Strung out along the estuary of the River Torridge, Bideford grew and thrived on importing tobacco from the New World. Some 17th-century merchants' houses survive in Bridgeland Street, including the splendid bay-windowed house at No. 28 (1693). Beyond is Mill Street, leading to the parish church

and the fine medieval bridge. The quay stretches from here to a pleasant park and a statue that commemorates Charles Kingsley, whose novels helped bring visitors to the area in the 19th century.

Environs: To the west of Bideford, the village **Westward Ho!** was built in the late 19th century and named after Kingsley's popular novel. The development failed, and the Victorian villas and hotels are now part of a holiday resort. Rudyard Kipling *(see p163)* was at school here and the hill to the south, known as **Kipling Tors**, was the background for *Stalky & Co* (1899).

Also to the west is **Hartland Abbey**, built as a monastery c.1157, now a family home. The BBC filmed parts of *Sense and Sensibility* here. Visitors can enjoy a museum, art and antiques, as well as gardens.

Henry Williamson's *Tarka the Otter* (1927) describes the otters of the **Torridge Valley** and naturalists are hoping to reintroduce otters here. Part of a Tarka Trail has been laid out along the Torridge and bicycles can be hired from the old railway station. The trail passes close to the magnificent **Rosemoor Garden**.

Day trips run from either Bideford or Ilfracombe (depending on the tide) to **Lundy** island, which is abundant in birds and wildlife.

🌷 **RHS Rosemoor Garden**
Great Torrington. **Tel** *01805 624067*. ◯ *daily*. ● *25 Dec.* 🈵 ♿ 🍴 🅿 **www**.rhs.org.uk

🏛 **Hartland Abbey**
nr. Bideford. **Tel** *01237 441264*.
◯ *Apr–May: Wed, Thu, Sun; Jun–Sep: Sun–Thu.* 🈵 🅿 🅿 ♿ *limited*. **www**.hartlandabbey.com

Fishing boats in Clovelly's harbour

videos on local trades such as fishing and shipbuilding.

🏛 **North Devon Maritime Museum**
Odun Rd. **Tel** 01237 474852. ◯
May–Sep: daily; Apr, Oct: pm. 🎥 ♿
ltd. 🖥 www.devonmuseums.net

Barnstaple ⓱

Devon. 🚶 33,000. ⛵ 🚌 ℹ The Square (01271 375000). 🅰 Mon–Sat. www.staynorthdevon.co.uk

Although Barnstaple is an important distribution centre for the whole region, its town centre remains calm due to the exclusion of traffic. The massive glass-roofed **Pannier Market** (1855) has stalls of organic fruit and vegetables, honey and eggs, much of it produced by farmers' wives to supplement their income. Nearby is **St Peter's Church** with its twisted broach spire, said to have been caused by a lightning strike which warped the timbers in 1810.

On the Strand is a wonderful arcade topped with a statue of Queen Anne, now the **Heritage Centre**. This was built as an exchange where merchants traded the contents of their cargo boats moored on the River Taw alongside. Nearby is the 15th-century bridge and the **Museum of Barnstaple and North Devon**, where displays cover local history and the 700-year-old pottery industry, as well as local wildlife, such as the otters. The 180-mile (290 km) Tarka Trail circuits around Barnstaple; 35 miles (56 km) of it can be cycled.

Barnstaple's Pannier Market

Environs: Just west of Barnstaple, **Braunton "Great Field"** covers over 120 ha (300 acres) and is a well-preserved relic of medieval open-field

Fishermen's cottages, Appledore

Appledore ⓰

Devon. 🚶 3,000. ℹ Bideford (01237 477676).

Appledore's remote position at the tip of the Torridge Estuary has helped to preserve its charms intact. Busy boatyards line the long riverside quay, which is also the departure point for fishing trips and ferries to the sandy beaches of Braunton Burrows on the opposite shore. Timeworn Regency houses line the main street which runs parallel to the quay, and behind is a network of narrow cobbled lanes with 18th-century fishermen's cottages. Several shops retain their original bow-windows and sell an assortment of crafts, antiques and souvenirs.

Uphill from the quay is the **North Devon Maritime Museum**, with an exhibition on the experiences of Devon emigrants in Australia and displays explaining the work of local shipyards. The tiny **Victorian Schoolroom** which is affiliated to the museum, shows various documentary

Statue of Queen Anne (1708)

cultivation. Beyond lies **Braunton Burrows**, one of the most extensive wild-dune reserves in Britain. It is a must for plant enthusiasts who would like to spot sea kale, sea holly, sea lavender and horned poppies growing in their natural habitat. The sandy beaches and pounding waves at nearby Croyde and Woolacombe, are favourites among surfing enthusiasts, but there are also calmer areas of warm shallow water and rock pools.

Arlington Court, north of Barnstaple, has a collection of model ships, magnificent perennial borders and a lake. The stables house a collection of horse-drawn vehicles. Carriage rides are available.

🏛 **Museum of Barnstaple and North Devon**
The Square. **Tel** 01271 346747. ◯ Mon–Sat. ⬤ 24 Dec–1 Jan. ♿ ltd. 🖥 www.devonmuseums.net

🚻 **Arlington Court**
(NT) Arlington. **Tel** 01271 850296. ◯ Easter–Oct: Sun–Fri. 🎥 ♿ limited. 🖥 🏠

DEVONSHIRE CREAM TEAS

Devon people claim all other versions of a cream tea are inferior to their own. The essential ingredient is Devonshire clotted cream which comes from Jersey cattle fed on rich Devon pasture – anything else is second best, or so it is claimed. Spread thickly on freshly baked scones, with lashings of homemade strawberry jam, this makes a seductive, delicious, but fattening, tea-time treat.

A typical cream tea with scones, jam and clotted cream

The village of Lynmouth

Lynton and Lynmouth ⑱

Devon. 🏘 2,000. 🚌 ℹ️ *Town Hall, Lee Rd, Lynton (0845 660 3232).* **www**.lynton-lynmouth-tourism.co.uk

Situated at the point where the East and West Lyn rivers meet the sea, Lynmouth is a picturesque, though rather commercialized, fishing village. The pedestrianized main street, lined with shops selling clotted cream and seaside souvenirs, runs parallel to the Lyn, now made into a canal with high embankments as a precaution against flash floods. One flood devastated the town at the height of the holiday season in 1952. The scars caused by the flood, which was fuelled by heavy rain on Exmoor, are now overgrown by trees in the pretty **Glen Lyn Gorge**, which leads north out of the village. Lynmouth's sister town, Lynton, is a mainly Victorian village perched on the clifftop 130 m (427 ft) above, giving lovely views across the Bristol Channel to the Welsh coast. It can be reached from the harbour front by a cliff railway, by road or by a steep path.

Environs: Lynmouth makes an excellent starting point for walks on Exmoor. There is a 2 mile (3 km) trail that leads southeast to tranquil **Watersmeet** *(see p251)*. On the western edge of Exmoor, **Combe Martin** *(see p250)* lies in a sheltered valley. On the main street, lined with Victorian villas, is the 18th-century Pack of Cards Inn, built by a gambler with 52 windows, for each card in the pack.

Exeter ⑲

Exeter is Devon's capital, a bustling and lively city with a great deal of character, despite the World War II bombing that destroyed much of its city centre. Built high on a plateau above the River Exe, the city is encircled by substantial sections of Roman and medieval wall, and the street plan has not changed much since the Romans first laid out what is now the High Street. Elsewhere the Cathedral Close forms a pleasant green, and there are cobbled streets and narrow alleys which invite leisurely exploration. For shoppers there is a wide selection of big stores and smaller speciality shops.

Exploring Exeter
The intimate green and the close surrounding Exeter's distinctive cathedral were the setting for Anthony Trollope's novel *He Knew He Was Right* (1869). Full of festive crowds listening to buskers in the summer, the close presents an array of architectural styles. One of the finest buildings here is the Elizabethan **Mol's Coffee House**. Among the other historic buildings that survived World War II are the magnificent **Guildhall** (1330) on the High Street (one of Britain's oldest civic buildings), the opulent **Custom House** (1681) by the quay, and the elegant 18th-century **Rougemont House** which stands near the remains of a Norman **castle** built by William the Conqueror *(see pp46–7)*.

The port area has been transformed into a tourist attraction with its early 19th-century warehouses converted into craft shops, antique galleries and cafés. Boats can be hired for cruising down the short stretch of canal. The **Quay House Interpretation Centre**

The timber-framed Mol's Coffee House (1596), Cathedral Close

West front and south tower, Cathedral Church of St Peter

(open daily April–October; weekends November–March) has audio-visual and other displays on the history of Exeter.

🏛 Cathedral Church of St Peter
Cathedral Close. **Tel** *01392 255573.* ⭕ *daily.* 🅿️ ♿ 🍴
Exeter's cathedral is one of the most gloriously ornamented in Britain. Except for the two Norman towers, the cathedral is mainly 14th century and built in the style aptly known as Decorated because of the swirling geometric patterns of the stone work. The West Front, the largest single collection (66) of medieval figure sculptures in England, includes kings, apostles and prophets. Started in the 14th century, it was completed by 1450. Inside, the splendid Gothic vaulting sweeps from one end of the church to the other, impressive in its uniformity and punctuated by gaily painted ceiling bosses.

Among the tombs around the choir is that of Edward II's treasurer, Walter de Stapledon (1261–1326), who was murdered by a mob in London. Stapledon raised much of the money needed to fund the building of this cathedral.

Collection of shells and other objects in the library of A La Ronde

VISITORS' CHECKLIST

Devon. 🏃 *111,000.* ✈ *5 miles (8 km) east.* ⇄ *Exeter St David's, Bonhay Rd; Exeter Central, Queen St.* 🚏 *Paris St.* ⓘ *Paris St (01392 265700).* ⛴ *daily.* **www**.exeter.gov.uk

North of Sidmouth lies the magnificent church at **Ottery St Mary**. Built in 1338–42 by Bishop Grandisson, the church is clearly a scaled-down version of Exeter Cathedral, which he also helped build. In the churchyard wall is a memorial to the poet Coleridge who was born in the town in 1772.

Nearby **Honiton** is famous for its extraordinarily intricate and delicate lace, made here since Elizabethan times.

To the north of Exeter, **Killerton** is home to the National Trust's costume collection. Here, displays of bustles and corsets and vivid tableaux illustrate aristocratic fashions from the 18th century to the present day.

Further north near Tiverton, is **Knightshayes Court**, a Victorian Gothic mansion with fine gardens *(see p245)*.

🏛 A La Ronde
(NT) Summer Lane, Exmouth. *Tel 01395 265514.* ◯ *Mar–Oct: Sat–Wed.* 📷 🅿 🏪

🏛 Killerton
(NT) Broadclyst. *Tel 01392 881345.* **House** ◯ *Mar–Sep: Wed–Mon; Aug & Christmas: daily; Oct: Wed–Sun.* **Garden** ◯ *daily.* 📷 ♿ 🅿 🏪

🌿 Knightshayes Court
(NT) Bolham. *Tel 01884 254665.* ◯ *mid-Feb–Oct: Sat–Thu, Good Fri.* **Gardens** ◯ *Apr–Nov: daily.* 📷 ♿ *limited.* 🍴 🏪

🏠 Underground Passages
Paris St. *Tel 01392 665 887.* ◯ *Jun–Sep: daily; Oct–May: Tue–Sun.* 🏪 📷
Under the city centre lie the remains of Exeter's medieval water-supply system. An excellent video and guided tour explain how the stone-lined tunnels were built in the 14th and 15th centuries on a slight gradient in order to bring in fresh water for townspeople from springs outside the town. The site was refurbished in 2007 and includes the new Heritage Centre.

🏠 St Nicholas Priory
The Mint. *Tel 01392 665858.* ◯ *for conservation work – phone for details*
Built in the 12th century, this building has retained many of its original features and rooms. These help visitors to trace its fascinating history from austere monastic beginnings, through its secular use as a Tudor residence for wealthy merchants, to its 20th-century incarnation as five separate business premises occupied by various tradesmen including a bootmaker and an upholsterer.

🏛 Royal Albert Memorial Museum and Art Gallery
Queen St. *Tel 01392 665858.* ◯ *call for details.* ● *for refurbishment until 2011.* 🏪 ♿ 📷
This museum has a wonderfully varied collection, including Roman remains, a zoo of stuffed animals, West Country art and a particularly good ethnographic display. Highlights include displays on silverware, watches and clocks.

Environs: South of Exeter on the A376, the eccentric **A La Ronde** is a 16-sided house built in 1796 by two spinster cousins, who decorated the interior with shells, feathers and souvenirs gathered while on tour in Europe.

Further east, the unspoilt Regency town of **Sidmouth** lies in a sheltered bay. There is an eclectic array of architecture, the earliest buildings dating from the 1820s when Sidmouth became a popular summer resort. Thatched cottages stand opposite huge Edwardian villas, and elegant terraces line the seafront. In summer the town hosts the famous International Festival of Folk Arts *(see p63)*.

19th-century head of an Oba, Royal Albert Museum

Mexican dancer at Sidmouth's International Festival of Folk Arts

Torbay ⓴

Torbay. ⚏ 🚉 *Torquay, Paignton.* ℹ️
*Vaughan Parade, Torquay (01803
211211).* **www**.englishriviera.co.uk

The seaside towns of Torquay,
Paignton and Brixham form
an almost continuous resort
around the great sweep of
sandy beach and blue waters
of Torbay. Because of its mild
climate, semi-tropical gardens
and exuberant Victorian hotel
architecture, this popular
coastline has been dubbed
the English Riviera. In the
Victorian era Torbay was
patronized by the wealthy.
Today, the theme is mass
entertainment, and there are
plenty of attractions, mostly
in and around Torquay.

Torre Abbey includes the
remains of a monastery founded in 1196. It is currently
undergoing a massive restoration programme, the first
phase of which focused on
the abbey's oldest part. Future
phases will redevelop the
abbey's galleries and restore
the historic gardens. **Torquay**

Museum nearby covers natural history and archaeology,
including finds from **Kents
Cavern**, on the outskirts of
the town. This is one of England's most important prehistoric sites, and the spectacular
caves include displays on
people and animals who lived
here up to 350,000 years ago.

The charming miniature
town of **Babbacombe Model
Village** is north of Torquay,
while a mile (1.5 km) inland
is the lovely village of
Cockington. Visitors travel by
horse-drawn carriage to the
preserved Tudor manor house,
church and thatched cottages.

In Paignton, the celebrated
Paignton Zoo teaches children about the planet's wildlife,
and from here you can take
the steam railway – an ideal
way to visit Dartmouth.

Continuing south from
Paignton, the pretty town of
Brixham was once England's
most prosperous fishing port.

🏛 **Torre Abbey**
King's Drive, Torquay. **Tel** *01803
293593.* ◯ *daily.* 🖼 📷 ♿ 🖥 🏠

Bayards Cove, Dartmouth

🏛 **Torquay Museum**
Babbacombe Rd, Torquay. **Tel** *01803
293975.* ◯ *daily (Nov–Easter: Mon–
Sat).* ● *Christmas wk.* 🖼 ♿ 🖥
🏠 **www**.torquaymuseum.org

🗼 **Kents Cavern**
Ilsham Rd, Torquay. 📅 *01803 215
136.* ◯ *daily.* ● *25 & 26 Dec.* 🖼
📷 🍴 🖥 **www**.kents-cavern.co.uk

🏛 **Babbacombe Model
Village**
Hampton Ave, Torquay. **Tel** *01803
315315.* ◯ *daily.* 🖼 ♿ 🖥

🦓 **Paignton Zoo**
Totnes Rd, Paignton. 📅 *01803 697
500.* ◯ *daily.* ● *25 Dec.* 🖼 ♿
🍴 🏠 **www**.paigntonzoo.org.uk

Dartmouth ㉑

Devon. 👥 *5,500.* 🚉 ℹ️ *Mayors Ave
(01803 834224).* ⚓ *Tue–Fri am.*
www.discoverdartmouth.com

Sitting high on the hill
above the River Dart is the
Royal Naval College, where
British naval officers have
trained since 1905. Dartmouth
has always been an important
port and it was from here that
English fleets set sail to join
the Second and Third Cru-
sades. Some 18th-century
houses adorn the cobbled
quay of Bayards Cove, while
carved timber buildings line
the 17th-century Butterwalk,
home to **Dartmouth Museum**.
To the south is **Dartmouth
Castle** (1388).

🏛 **Dartmouth Museum**
Butterwalk. **Tel** *01803 832923.* ◯
Mon–Sat. ● *1 Jan, 25 & 26 Dec.*
🖼 🏠 **www**.devonmuseums.net

⚓ **Dartmouth Castle**
(EH) Castle Rd. **Tel** *01803 833588.*
◯ *daily (Nov–Easter: Sat & Sun).*
● *1 Jan, 24–26 Dec.* 🖼 🏠

Torquay, on the "English Riviera"

Stained-glass window in Blessed Sacrament Chapel, Buckfast Abbey

Totnes ❷

Devon. 🏘 7,500. 🚉 🚌 🛳
ℹ️ *Town Mill (01803 863168).*
🛒 *Tue am (May–Sep), Fri, Sat.*
www.totnesinformation.co.uk

Totnes sits at the highest
navigable point on the River
Dart with a Norman **castle**
perched high on the hill
above. Linking the two is the
steep High Street, lined with
bow-windowed Elizabethan
houses. Bridging the street is
the **Eastgate**, part of the medieval town wall. Life in the
town's heyday is explored
in the **Totnes Elizabethan
Museum**, which also has a
room devoted to the mathe-
matician Charles Babbage
(1791–1871), who is regarded
as the pioneer of
modern computers.
There is a **Guildhall**,
and a **church** with
a delicately carved
and gilded rood
screen. On
Tuesdays in the
summer, market
stallholders dress in
Elizabethan costume.

Environs: A few miles
north of Totnes, **Dar-
tington Hall** has 10
ha (25 acres) of lovely
gardens and a famous
music school where concerts
are held in the timbered 14th-
century Great Hall.

**Stallholders in
Totnes market**

⛵ **Totnes Castle**
(EH) Castle St. *Tel 01803 864406.*
◻ *Apr–Oct: daily.* 🌙

🏛 **Totnes Elizabethan
Museum**
Fore St. *Tel 01803 863821.* ◻
Easter–Oct: Mon–Fri. 🌙 ♿ *limited.*

🏛 **Guildhall**
Rampart Walk. *Tel 01803 862147.*
◻ *Apr–Oct: Mon–Fri.* 🌙

🌿 **Dartington Hall Gardens**
Tel 01803 862367. ◻ *daily.*
www.dartingtonhalltrust.com

Buckfastleigh ❸

Devon. 🏘 3,300. 🚉 ℹ️ *Fore St
(01364 644522).*

This market town, situated
on the edge of Dartmoor *(see
pp294–5)*, is dominated by
Buckfast Abbey. The original
abbey, founded in
Norman times, fell
into ruin after the
Dissolution of the
Monasteries and
it was not until
1882 that
a small group
of French
Benedictine
monks set up
a new abbey
here. Work on the
present building
was financed by
donations and carried
out by the monks. The abbey
was completed in 1938 and
lies at the heart of a thriving
community. The fine mosaics
and modern stained-glass
window are also the work
of the monks.

Nearby is the **Buckfast
Butterfly Farm and Otter
Sanctuary**, and the **South
Devon Steam Railway** ter-
minus where steam trains
leave for Totnes.

🏛 **Buckfast Abbey**
Buckfastleigh. *Tel 01364 645500.*
◻ *daily.* ⬤ *Good Fri, 25–27 Dec.*
♿ 🍴 📷 **www**.buckfast.org.uk

🦋 **Buckfast Butterfly Farm
and Otter Sanctuary**
Buckfastleigh. *Tel 01364 642916.*
◻ *Easter–Nov: daily.* 🌙 ♿
www.ottersandbutterflies.co.uk

Burgh Island ❹

Devon. 🚉 *Plymouth, then taxi.* ℹ️
*The Quay, Kingsbridge (01548 853
195).* **www**.kingsbridgeinfo.co.uk

The short walk across the
sands at low tide from
Bigbury-on-Sea to Burgh Island
takes you back to the era of
the 1920s and 1930s. It was
here that the millionaire
Archibald Nettlefold built the
luxury **Burgh Island Hotel** in
1929. Created in Art Deco
style with a natural rock
sea-bathing pool, this was the
exclusive retreat of figures
such as the Duke of Windsor
and Noel Coward. The restored
hotel is worth a visit for the
photographs of its heyday and
the Art Deco fittings. You can
also explore the island and
Pilchard Inn (1336), reputed to
be haunted by the ghost of a
smuggler.

**The Art Deco style bar in Burgh
Island Hotel**

Plymouth ㉕

Plymouth. 🏛 250,000. ✈ ⇄ 🚍 🛳 ℹ *The Mayflower, The Barbican* (01752 306330). 🚢 daily. www.plymouth.gov.uk

The tiny port from which Drake, Raleigh, the Pilgrim Fathers, Cook and Darwin all set sail on pioneering voyages has now grown to a substantial city, much of it boldly rebuilt after wartime bombing. Old Plymouth clusters around the **Hoe**, the famous patch of turf on which Sir Francis Drake is said to have calmly finished his game of bowls as the Spanish Armada approached the port in 1588 *(see pp50–51).* Today the Hoe is a pleasant park and parade ground surrounded by memorials to naval men, including Drake himself. Alongside is Charles II's **Royal Citadel**, built to guard the harbour in

the 1660s. On the harbour is the **National Marine Aquarium**. Nearby is the **Mayflower Stone and Steps**, the spot where the Pilgrim Fathers set sail for the New World in England's third and successful attempt at colonization in 1620. The popular **Plymouth Mayflower Exhibition** explores the story of the Mayflower and the creation of the harbour. Interactive graphics are used to tell the tales of merchant families and emigration to the New World.

Environs: A boat tour of the harbour is the best way to see the dockyards where warships have been built since the Napoleonic Wars. There are also splendid views of various fine gardens, such as **Mount Edgcumbe Park** *(see p244),* scattered around the coastline. East of the city, the 18th-century **Saltram House** has two rooms

Drake's coat of arms

Mid-18th-century carved wood chimneypiece, Saltram House

by Adam *(see pp28–9)* and portraits by Reynolds, who was born in nearby Plympton.

🏰 **Royal Citadel**
(EH) The Hoe. **Tel** 0117 9750700. ◯ May–Sep: Tue & Thu. 🎫 only. ♿

🐟 **National Marine Aquarium**
Rope Walk, Coxside. **Tel** 01752 600 301. ◯ daily. ● 25 Dec. 🎫♿🅿 www.national-aquarium.co.uk

🏛 **Plymouth Mayflower Exhibition**
3–5 The Barbican. **Tel** 01752 306 330. ◯ daily (Nov–Apr: Mon–Sat).

🌿 **Mount Edgcumbe Park**
Cremyll, Torpoint. 🚢 from Torpoint car park. **Tel** 01752 822236. **House** ◯ Apr–Sep: Sun–Thu. **Grounds** ◯ all year. 🎫♿🅿📷🍴 www.mountedgcumbe.gov.uk

🏰 **Saltram House**
(NT) Plympton. **Tel** 01752 333500. **Gallery** ◯ Mar–Nov: Sat–Thu; Jan & Feb: Sat. **Gardens** ◯ all year. 🎫 ♿🍴🅿 open all year. 🚻

Buckland Abbey ㉖

(NT) Yelverton, Devon. **Tel** 01822 853607. 🚌 from Yelverton. ◯ Fri–Wed (Nov–Mar: Sat & Sun pm). ● Christmas–mid-Feb. 🎫♿🍴 🚻 www.nationaltrust.org.uk

Founded by the Cistercian monks in 1278, Buckland Abbey was converted to a house after the Dissolution of the Monasteries and became the home of Drake from 1581–96. Many of the monastic buildings survive in a garden setting, notably the 14th-century tithe barn *(see p28).* Drake's life is explained through paintings and memorabilia in the house.

View of Plymouth Harbour from the Hoe

Cotehele ㉗

(NT) St Dominick, Cornwall.
Tel 01579 351346. 🚉 *Calstock.*
House ◯ *Apr–Oct: Sat–Thu &
Good Fri.* **Grounds** ◯ *daily.* 🔲 ▨
♿ *limited.* 🍴 ▢

Magnificent woodland and
lush river scenery make Cotehele (pronounced Coteal) one
of the most delightful spots
on the River Tamar and a
rewarding day can be spent
exploring the estate. Far from
civilization, tucked into its
wooded fold in the Cornish
countryside, Cotehele has
slumbered for 500 years. The
main attraction is the house
and valley garden at its centre.
Built mainly between 1489
and 1520, it is a rare example
of a medieval house, set
around three courtyards with a
magnificent open hall, kitchen,
chapel and a warren of private
parlours and chambers. The
romance of the house is enhanced by colourful terraced
gardens to the east, leading via
a tunnel into a richly planted
valley garden. The path
through this garden passes a
large domed medieval dovecote and descends to a quay,
to which lime and coal were
once shipped. There are fine
views up and down the winding reed-fringed Tamar from
Prospect Tower, and a gallery
on the quayside specializes in
local arts and crafts. The estate
includes a village, a quay with
a small maritime museum,
working mill buildings, ancient
lime kilns and workshops
with 19th-century equipment.

Medieval dovecote in the gardens
of Cotehele estate

Spanish Armada and British fleets in the English Channel, 1588

SIR FRANCIS DRAKE

Sir Francis Drake (c.1540–1596) was the first Englishman to
circumnavigate the globe and he was knighted by Elizabeth I
in 1580. Four years later he introduced tobacco and potatoes
to England, after bringing home 190 colonists who had tried
to establish a settlement in Virginia. To many, however,
Drake was no more than an opportunistic rogue, renowned
for his exploits as a "privateer", the polite name for a pirate.
Catholic Spain was the bitter enemy and Drake further
endeared himself to queen and people by his part in the
victory over Philip II's Armada *(see pp50–51)*, defeated by
bad weather and the buccaneering spirit of the English.

Morwellham Quay ㉘

Near Tavistock, Devon.
Tel 01822 832766. 🚉 *Gunnislake.*
◯ *daily.* ● *1 Jan, 24–26 Dec.*
🔲 ▨ ♿ *limited.* ▨ ▢
www.morwellham-quay.co.uk

Morwellham Quay was a
neglected and overgrown
industrial site until 1970, when
members of a local trust began
restoring the abandoned cottages, schoolhouse, farmyards,
quay and copper mines to
their original condition.

Today, Morwellham Quay
is a thriving and rewarding
industrial museum, where
you can easily spend a whole
day partaking in the typical
activities of a Victorian
village, from preparing the
shire horses for a day's work,
to riding a tramway deep into
a copper mine in the hillside
behind the village. The
museum is brought to life by
characters in costumes, some
of whom give demonstrations
throughout the day. You can
watch, or lend a hand to the

Industrial relics at Morwellham
Quay in the Tamar Valley

cooper while he builds a
barrel, attend a lesson in the
schoolroom, take part in
Victorian playground games
or dress up in 19th-century
hooped skirts, bonnets, top
hats or jackets. The staff, who
convincingly play the part of
villagers, lead you through
their lives and impart a huge
amount of information about
the history of this small
copper-mining community.

Dartmoor National Park ❷⓿

The high, open moorland of central Dartmoor provides the eerie background for Conan Doyle's thriller, *The Hound of the Baskervilles* (1902). Here at Princetown, surrounded by weathered outcrops of granite tors is one of Britain's most famous prisons. Also dotting the landscape are scores of prehistoric remains which have survived because of the durability of granite. Elsewhere the mood is very different. Streams tumble through wooded and boulder-strewn ravines forming cascades and waterfalls, and thatched cottages nestle in the sheltered valleys around the margins of the moor. Many establishments offer cream teas and warming fires to weary walkers.

Buzzard

Characteristic moorland, eastern Dartmoor

Okehampton has the Museum of Dartmoor Life and a ruined 14th-century castle.

Lydford Gorge (NT) (open Apr–Oct) is a dramatic ravine, leading to a waterfall.

Brentor
This volcanic hill crowned by a tiny church (first built in 1130) is visible for miles.

The Ministry of Defence uses much of this area for training but access is available on non-firing days (0800 458 4868 to check).

High Moorland Visitor Centre

KEY

ℹ️	Information centre
▰▰▰	A road
▭▭▭	B road
▭ ▭ ▭	Minor road
☀	Viewpoint

0 kilometres   5

0 miles   5

Okehampton

MELDON RESERVOIR

LAUNCESTON   A386   West Okement   High Willhays   621 m   2,038 ft

Lydford

MINISTRY OF DEFENCE FIRING RANGES

Postbridge

Walkham   Two Bridges

A386   Merrivale   Blackbrook

Tavistock   Princetown

LISKEARD   Meavy

Yelverton   BURRATOR RESERVOIR

PLYMOUTH   Plym

PLYMOU

Ivy

Postbridge
Dartmoor's northern moor can be explored from the village of Postbridge. The gently rolling moorland is crossed by many dry-stone walls.

Dartmoor Ponies
These small, tough ponies have lived on the moor since at least the 10th century.

Grimspound is the impressive remains of a Bronze Age settlement.

Castle Drogo (NT) is a magnificent mock-castle built by the architect Sir Edwin Lutyens *(see p29)* in 1910–30.

VISITORS' CHECKLIST

Devon. ⚏ ⊟ *Exeter, Plymouth, Totnes then bus.* ⓘ *Dartmoor National Park Authority's Centre (01822890414),* **www**.dartmoor-npa.gov.uk. **Okehampton Castle**, Castle Lane, Okehampton. **Tel** 01837 52844. ◯ *Apr–Sept: daily.* 🎦 **Museum of Dartmoor Life**, West St, Okehampton. **Tel** 01837 52295. ◯ *10:15am–4:15pm Tue & Fri (closed for lunch).* ⚫ *24 Dec–1 Jan.* 🎦 ♿ *limited.* **Castle Drogo (NT)**, Drewsteignton. **Tel** 01647 433 306. ◯ *Apr–Nov: Wed–Mon.* **Gardens** ◯ *daily.* 🎦 ♿ *gardens only.* 🍴 🛒 🎁

Becky Falls is a 22-m (72-ft) waterfall set in delightful woodlands.

Drewsteignton   EXETER
Teign
EXETER
Moretonhampstead
WORTHY VOIR
Bovey
Manaton
A382
EXETER
Bovey Tracey
Buckland-in-the-Moor
A38
ENFORD RESERVOIR
Ashburton
Buckfastleigh
Dart
ON DAM RESERVOIR
A38

Hound Tor
Nearby lie the remains of a Medieval settlement abandoned in the 14th century.

Bovey Tracey has an extensive woodland reserve.

Haytor Rocks is one of the most popular of the many tors.

South Devon Steam Railway

Buckfast Abbey was founded by King Canute *(see p159)* in 1018.

Dartmoor Butterfly and Otter Sanctuary

Dartmeet marks the lovely confluence point of the East and West Dart rivers.

Buckland-in-the-Moor
One of the many picturesque villages on Dartmoor.

THE
MIDLANDS

The Midlands at a Glance

The Midlands is an area that embraces wonderful landscapes and massive industrial cities. Visitors come to discover the wild beauty of the rugged Peaks, cruise slowly along the Midlands canals on gaily painted narrowboats and explore varied and enchanting gardens. The area encompasses the full range of English architecture from mighty cathedrals and humble churches to charming spa towns, stately homes and country cottages. There are fascinating industrial museums, many in picturesque settings.

Cheshire

Staffordshir

Shropshire

Tissington Trail (see p337) *combines a walk through scenic Peak District countryside with an entertaining insight into the ancient custom of well-dressing.*

THE HEART OF ENGLAND
(see pp304–329)

Worcestershire

Herefordshire

Ironbridge Gorge (see pp314–15) *was the birthplace of the Industrial Revolution (see pp348–9). Now a World Heritage Centre, the site is a reminder of the lovely countryside in which the original factories were located.*

Gloucestershire

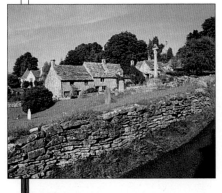

The Cotswolds (see pp304–5) *are full of delightful houses built from local limestone, on the profits of the medieval wool trade. Snowshill Manor (left) is situated near the unspoilt village of Broadway.*

| 0 kilometres | 25 |
| 0 miles | 2 |

◁ **The front of the half-timbered Lord Leycester Hospital, Warwick**

Chatsworth House (see pp334–5), *a magnificent Baroque edifice, is famous for its gorgeous gardens. The "Conservative" Wall, a greenhouse for exotic plants, is pictured above.*

Nottinghamshire

Lincolnshire

Lincoln Cathedral (see p341), *a vast, imposing building, dominates the ancient town. Inside are splendid misericords and the superb 13th-century Angel Choir, which has 30 carved angels.*

Derbyshire

EAST MIDLANDS
(see pp330–343)

Leicestershire

Burghley House (see pp342–3) *is a dazzling landmark for miles around in the flat East Midlands landscape, with architectural motifs from the European Renaissance.*

Warwick Castle (see pp322–3) *is an intriguing mixture of medieval power base and country house, complete with massive towers, battlements, a dungeon and state apartments, such as the Queen Anne Bedroom.*

rwickshire

Northamptonshire

Stratford-upon-Avon (see pp324–7) *has many picturesque houses connected with William Shakespeare's life, some of which are open to visitors. These black and white timber-framed buildings, which abound in the Midlands, are a typical example of Tudor architecture (see pp302–3).*

Canals of the Midlands

One of England's first canals was built by the 3rd Duke of Bridgewater in 1761 to link the coal mine on his Worsley estate with Manchester's textile factories. This heralded the start of a canal-building boom and by 1805, a 3,000 mile (4,800 km) network of waterways had been dug across the country, linking into the natural river system. Canals provided the cheapest, fastest way of transporting goods, until competition began to arrive from the railways in the 1840s. Cargo transport ended in 1963 but today nearly 2,000 miles (3,200 km) of canals are still navigable, for travellers who wish to take a leisurely cruise on a narrowboat.

The Grand Union Canal *(pictured in 1931) is 300 miles (485 km) long and was dug in the 1790s to link London with the Midlands.*

Lockside inns cater for narrowboats.

Lock-keepers were provided with canalside houses.

The Farmer's Bridge *is a flight of 13 locks in Birmingham. Locks are used to raise or lower boats from one level of the canal to another. The steeper the gradient, the more locks are needed.*

Heavy V-shaped timber gates close off the lock.

Water pressing against the gate keeps it shut.

The towpath is where horses pulled the canal boats before engines were invented. They were changed periodically for fresh animals.

Narrowboats *have straight sides and flat bottoms and are pointed at both ends. Cargo space took up most of the boat, with a small cabin for the crew. Exteriors were brightly painted.*

N[o] **7**   BILL O TOMS   NEW MARTON LOCK

MIDLANDS CANAL NETWORK

The industrial Midlands was the birthplace of the English canal system and still has the biggest concentration of navigable waterways.

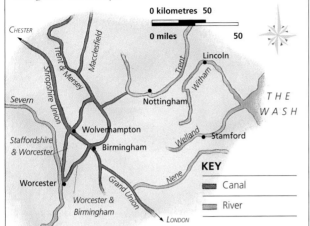

VISITORS' CHECKLIST

Companies specializing in canal boat holidays: Blake's Holidays *Tel* 01603 739400; Hoseasons *Tel* 01502 501010; Canal Cruising Co *Tel* 01785 813982; Black Prince Holidays *Tel* 01527 575115; Alvechurch Boat Centres Ltd *Tel* 0121 445 2909;
Canal museums: Phone to check opening times: National Waterways Museum *(see p329)*; Canal Museum, Stoke Bruerne, Towcester *Tel* 01604 862229; Boat Museum, Ellesmere Port. *Tel* 0151 3555017.
www.thewaterwaystrust.co.uk

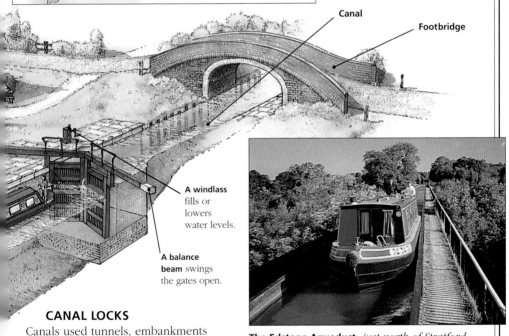

Canal

Footbridge

A windlass fills or lowers water levels.

A balance beam swings the gates open.

CANAL LOCKS

Canals used tunnels, embankments and locks for the speedy transportation of goods across country. Locks were used to convey boats up or down hills.

The Edstone Aqueduct, *just north of Stratford-upon-Avon, carries the canal in a cast iron trough. This is supported on brick piers for 180 m (495 ft), over roads and a busy railway line.*

CANAL ART

Canal boat cabins are very small and every inch of space is utilized to make a comfortable home for the occupants. Interiors were enlivened with colourful paintings and attractive decorations.

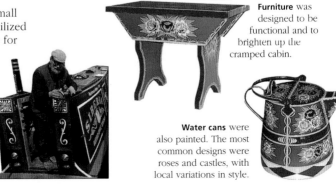

Furniture was designed to be functional and to brighten up the cramped cabin.

Narrowboats are often decorated with ornamental brass.

Water cans were also painted. The most common designs were roses and castles, with local variations in style.

Tudor Manor Houses

Many striking manor houses were built in central England during the Tudor Age *(see pp50–51)*, a time of relative peace and prosperity. The abolition of the monasteries meant that vast estates were broken up and sold to secular landowners, who built houses to reflect their new status *(see p28)*. In the Midlands,

The Lucy family arms

wood was the main building material, and the gentry flaunted their wealth by using timber panelling for flamboyant decorative effect.

The decorative moulding *on the south wing dates from the late 16th century. Ancient motifs, such as vines and trefoils, are combined with the latest imported Italian Renaissance styles.*

The rectangular moat *was for decoration rather than defence. It surrounds a recreated knot garden (see p26) that was laid out in 1972 using plants known to have been available in Tudor times.*

The Long Gallery *was the last part of the Hall to be built (c.1560–1562). It has original plasterwork portraying* Destiny *(left) and* Fortune.

Brickwork chimney

Jetties (overhanging upper stories)

TUDOR MANSIONS AND TUDOR REVIVAL

There are many sumptuously decorated Tudor mansions in the Midlands. In the 19th century Tudor Revival architecture became a very popular "Old English" style, intended to invoke family pride and values rooted in the past.

Hardwick Hall *in Derbyshire, whose huge kitchen is pictured, is one of the finest Tudor mansions in the country. These buildings are known as "prodigy" houses (see p342) due to their gigantic size.*

Charlecote Park, *Warwickshire, is a brick mansion built by Sir Thomas Lucy in 1551–59. It was heavily restored in Tudor style in the 19th century, but has a fine original gatehouse. According to legend, the young William Shakespeare (see pp324–7) was caught poaching deer in the park.*

The Parlour *was an informal reception room. Biblical scenes such as* Susannah and the Elders *(right) expressed religious faith and learning.*

Entrance

Wood panelling

Courtyard

The Great Hall *(c.1504–1508) is the oldest part of the house, and in Tudor times was the most important. The open-plan hall was the main communal area for dining and entertainment.*

The patterned glazing *in the great bay window is typically 16th century: small pieces of locally made glass were cut into diamond shapes and held in place by lead glazing bars.*

LITTLE MORETON HALL

The Moreton family home *(see p311)* was built between 1504 and 1610, from a number of box-shapes, fitted together. Wood panelling and jetties displayed the family's wealth.

Packwood House *in Warwickshire is a timber-framed mid-Tudor house with extensive 17th–century additions. The unusual garden of clipped yew trees dates from the 17th century and is supposed to represent the Sermon on the Mount.*

Moseley Old Hall, *Staffordshire, has a red brick exterior concealing its early 17th-century timber frame. The King's Room is where Charles II hid after the Battle of Worcester (see pp52–3).*

Wightwick Manor, *West Midlands, was built in 1887–93. It is a fine example of Tudor Revival architecture and has superb late 19th-century furniture and decorations.*

Building with Cotswold Stone

The Cotswolds are a range of limestone hills running over 50 miles (80 km) in a north-easterly direction from Bath *(see pp258–61)*. The thin soils are difficult to plough but ideal for grazing sheep, and the wealth engendered by the medieval wool trade was poured into building majestic churches and opulent town houses. Stone quarried from these hills was used to build London's St Paul's Cathedral *(see pp114–15)*, as well as the villages, barns and manor houses that make the landscape so picturesque.

Dragon, Deerhurst Church

Arlington Row Cottages *in Bibury, a typical Cotswold village, were built in the 17th century for weavers whose looms were set up in the attics.*

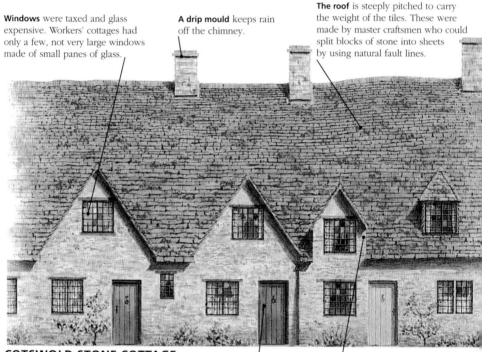

Windows were taxed and glass expensive. Workers' cottages had only a few, not very large windows made of small panes of glass.

A drip mould keeps rain off the chimney.

The roof is steeply pitched to carry the weight of the tiles. These were made by master craftsmen who could split blocks of stone into sheets by using natural fault lines.

Timber lintels and doors

Timber framing was cheaper than stone, and was used for the upper rooms in the roof.

COTSWOLD STONE COTTAGE

The two-storey Arlington Row Cottages are asymmetrical and built of odd-shaped stones. Small windows and doorways make them quite dark inside.

VARIATIONS IN STONE

Cotswold stone is warmer-toned in the north, pearly in central areas and light grey in the south. The stone seems to glow with absorbed sun-light. It is a soft stone that is easily carved and can be used for many purposes, from buildings to bridges, headstones and gargoyles.

"Tiddles" *is a cat's gravestone in Fairford churchyard.*

Lower Slaughter *gets its name from the Anglo-Saxon word* slough, *or muddy place. It has a low stone bridge, over the River Eye.*

COTSWOLD STONE TOWNS AND VILLAGES

The villages and towns on this map are prime examples of places built almost entirely from stone. By the 12th century almost all of the villages in the area were established. Huge deposits of limestone resulted in a wealth of stone buildings. Masons worked from distinctive local designs that were handed down from generation to generation.

① Winchcombe
② Broadway
③ Stow-on-the-Wold
④ Upper and Lower Slaughter
⑤ Bourton-on-the-Water
⑥ Sherborne
⑦ Northleach
⑧ Painswick
⑨ Bibury
⑩ Fairford

Wool merchants' houses were built of fine ashlar (dressed stone) with ornamental cornerstones, doorframes and windows.

The eaves here have a dentil frieze, so-called because it resembles a row of teeth.

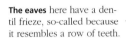

COTSWOLD STONE HOUSE

This early Georgian merchant's house in Painswick shows the fully developed Cotswold style, which borrows decorative elements from Classical architecture.

The door frame has a rounded pediment on simple pilasters.

STONE GARGOYLES

In Winchcombe's church, 15th-century gargoyles reflect a combination of pagan and Christian beliefs.

Pagan gods warded off pre-Christian evil spirits.

Fertility figures, always important in rural areas, were incorporated into Christian festivals.

Human faces often caricatured local church dignitaries.

Animal gods represented qualities such as strength in pagan times.

Dry-stone walling *is an ancient technique used in the Cotswolds. The stones are held in place without mortar.*

A stone cross *(16th century) in Stanton village, near Broadway, is one of many found in the Cotswolds.*

Table-top and "tea caddy", *fine 18th-century tombs, can be found in Painswick churchyard.*

The Cotswold Arm

Real
Bar Snacks
Restaurant
Beer Garden
Morning Coffee

THE HEART OF ENGLAND

CHESHIRE · GLOUCESTERSHIRE · HEREFORDSHIRE
SHROPSHIRE · STAFFORDSHIRE · WARWICKSHIRE · WORCESTERSHIRE

*B*ritain's great attraction is its variety, and nowhere is this more true than at the heart of the country, where the Cotswold hills, enfolding stone cottages and churches, give way to the flat, fertile plains of Warwickshire. Shakespeare country borders on the industrial heart of England, once known as the workshop of the world.

Coventry, Birmingham, the Potteries and their hinterlands have been manufacturing iron, textiles and ceramics since the 18th century. In the 20th century these industries have declined, and a new type of museum has developed to commemorate the towns' industrial heyday and explain the manufacturing processes which were once taken for granted. Ironbridge Gorge and Quarry Bank Mill, Styal, where the factories are now living museums, are fascinating industrial sites and enjoy beautiful surroundings.

These landscapes may be appreciated from the deck of a narrowboat, making gentle progress along the Midlands canals, to the region on the border with Wales known as the Marches. Here the massive walls of Chester and the castles at Shrewsbury and Ludlow recall the Welsh locked in fierce battle with Norman barons and the Marcher Lords. The Marches are now full of rural communities served by the peaceful market towns of Leominster, Malvern, Ross-on-Wye and Hereford. The cities of Worcester and Gloucester both have modern shopping centres, yet their majestic cathedrals retain the tranquillity of an earlier age.

Cheltenham has Regency terraces, Cirencester a rich legacy of Roman art and Tewkesbury a solid Norman abbey. Finally, there is Stratford-upon-Avon, where William Shakespeare, the Elizabethan dramatist, lived and died.

Leisurely village pastimes, reminiscent of a more tranquil age

◁ Cotswold stone: an extremely popular building material in the Heart of England

Exploring the Heart of England

The heart of England, more than any other region, takes its character from the landscape. Picturesque houses, pubs and churches, made from timber and Cotswold stone, create a harmonic appearance that delights visitors and adds greatly to the pleasures of exploration. The area around Birmingham and Stoke-on-Trent, however – once the industrial hub of England – contrasts sharply. The bleak concrete skyline may not appeal, but the area has a fascinating history that is reflected in the self-confident Victorian art and architecture, and a series of award-winning industrial heritage museums.

Arlington Row: stone cottages in the Cotswold village of Bibury

SIGHTS AT A GLANCE

0 kilometres 10

0 miles 10

GETTING AROUND

The Heart of England is easily reached by train, with mainline rail services to Cheltenham, Worcester, Birmingham, and Coventry. The M5 and M6 motorways are the major road routes but are frequently congested. Long-distance buses provide regular shuttle services to Cheltenham and Birmingham. Travelling within the region is best done by car. Rural roads are delightfully empty, although major attractions, such as Stratford-upon-Avon, may be very crowded during the summer.

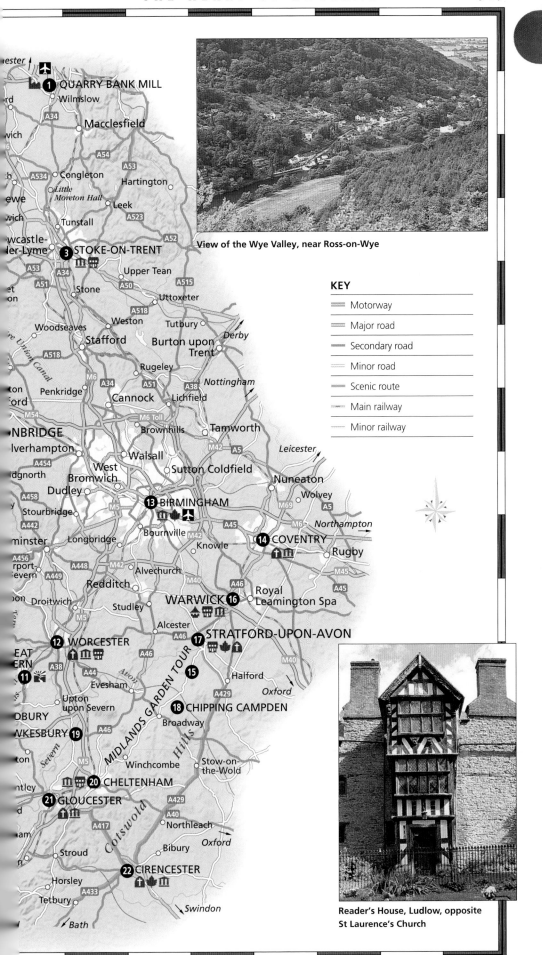

View of the Wye Valley, near Ross-on-Wye

KEY

Motorway
Major road
Secondary road
Minor road
Scenic route
Main railway
Minor railway

Reader's House, Ludlow, opposite
St Laurence's Church

Quarry Bank Mill, a working reminder of the Industrial Revolution

Quarry Bank Mill, Styal ❶

(NT) Cheshire. *Tel 01625 445896.*
🚆 *Manchester Airport, then bus.*
⭕ *Mar–Oct: daily; Nov–Jan: Wed–Sun (& Mon in school hols).* ⚫ *24 & 25 Dec.* 🐾♿ *limited.* 🍴📷
www.nationaltrust.org.uk

The history of the Industrial Revolution *(see pp54–5)* is brought vividly to life at Quarry Bank Mill, an early factory now transformed into a museum and private garden. Here, mill master Samuel Greg first used the waters of the Bollin Valley in 1784 to power the water frame, a machine for spinning raw cotton fibres into thread. By the 1840s, the Greg cotton empire was one of the biggest in Britain, and the mill produced bolts of material to be exported all over the world.

Today the massive old mill buildings have been restored to house a living museum of the cotton industry. This dominated the Manchester area for nearly 200 years, but was finally destroyed by foreign competition. The entire process, from the spinning and weaving to the bleaching, printing and dyeing, is shown through a series of reconstructions, demonstrations and hands-on displays. The weaving shed is full of clattering looms producing textiles. There are fascinating contraptions that demonstrate how water can be used to drive machinery, including an enormous wheel, 50 tons in weight and 7 m (24 ft) high, that is still used to power the looms.

The Greg family realized the importance of having a healthy, loyal and stable workforce. A social history exhibition explains how the mill workers were housed in the purpose-built village of Styal, in spacious cottages which had vegetable gardens and toilets. Details of their wages, working conditions and medical facilities are displayed on information boards.

There are guided tours of the nearby **Apprentice House**. Local orphans lived here, and were sent to work up to 12 hours a day at the mill when they were just six or seven years old. Visitors can try the beds in the house and even sample the medicine they were given. Quarry Bank Mill is surrounded by over 115 ha (284 acres) of woodland.

Chester ❷

Cheshire. 👥 *125,000.* 🚆 🚌
ℹ️ *Town Hall, Northgate St
(01244 402111).* 🏛️ *Mon–Sat.*
www.chestertourist.com

First settled by the Romans *(see pp44–5)*, who established a camp in AD 79 to defend fertile land near the River Dee, the main streets of Chester are now lined with timber buildings. These are the **Chester Rows**, which, with their two tiers of shops and continuous upper gallery, anticipate today's multi-storey shops by several centuries.

Although their oriel windows and decorative timber-work are mostly 19th century, the Rows were first built in the 13th and 14th centuries, and the original structures can be seen in many places. The façade of the 16th-century **Bishop Lloyd's House** in Watergate Street is the most richly carved in Chester. The Rows are at their most varied and attractive where Eastgate Street meets Bridge Street. Here, views of the cathedral and the town walls give the impression of a perfectly preserved medieval city. This illusion is helped by the Town Crier, who calls the hour and announces news in summer from the Cross, a reconstruction of the 15th-century stone crucifix that was destroyed in the Civil War *(see pp52–3)*.

Chester's 1897 clocktower

The **Grosvenor Museum,** south of the Cross, explains the town's history. To the north is the **cathedral**. The choir stalls have splendid misericords *(see p341)*, with

Examples of the intricate carving on Bishop Lloyd's House, a Tudor building in Watergate Street, Chester

The Chester Rows, where shops line the first-floor galleries

scenes including a quarrelling couple. In sharp contrast are the delicate spire-lets on the stall canopies. The cathedral is surrounded on two sides by the **city walls**, originally Roman but rebuilt at intervals. The best stretch is from the cathedral to Eastgate, where a wrought-iron **clock** was erected in 1897. The route to Newgate leads to a **Roman amphitheatre** built in AD 100.

🏛 **Grosvenor Museum**
Grosvenor St. *Tel 01244 402008.*
⬤ *Mon–Sat, Sun pm.* ⬤ *1 Jan, Good Fri, 25 & 26 Dec.* 🏠 ♿ limited. **www**.chester.gov.uk

🏛 **Roman Amphitheatre**
Little St John St. *Tel 01244 402009.*
⬤ *daily.*

Stoke-on-Trent ❸

Stoke-on-Trent. 🏙 *252,000.*
🚃 🚌 ℹ️ *Victoria Hall Cultural Quarter (01782 236000).* 🏠 *Mon–Sat.* **www**.visitstoke.co.uk

From the mid-18th century, Staffordshire became a leading centre for mass-produced ceramics. Its fame arose from the fine bone china and porcelain products of Wedgwood,

Minton, Doulton and Spode, but the Staffordshire potteries also make a wide range of utilitarian products such as baths, toilets and wall tiles.

In 1910 a group of six towns – Longton, Fenton, Hanley, Burslem, Tunstall and Stoke – merged to form the conurbation of Stoke-on-Trent, also known as the Potteries. Fans of the writer Arnold Bennett (1867–1931) may recognise this area as the "Five Towns", a term he used in a series of novels about the region (Fenton was excluded).

The **Gladstone Pottery Museum** is a Victorian complex of workshops, kilns, galleries and an engine house. There are demonstrations of traditional pottery techniques. The **Potteries Museum and Art Gallery** in Hanley has historic and modern ceramics.

Josiah Wedgwood began his earthenware firm in 1769 and built a workers' village, Etruria. The last surviving steam-powered pottery mill is on display at the **Etruria Industrial Museum**.

Environs: About 10 miles (16 km) north of Stoke-on-Trent is **Little Moreton Hall** (*see p303*), a Tudor manor house.

🏛 **Gladstone Pottery Museum**
Uttoxeter Rd, Longton.
Tel 01782 319 232. ⬤ *daily.*
⬤ *24 Dec–2 Jan.* 🏠 ♿ 🖥 🏠
www.stoke.gov.uk/gladstone

🏛 **Potteries Museum and Art Gallery**
Bethesda St, Hanley. *Tel 01782 232323.* ⬤ *daily.* ⬤ *25 Dec–1 Jan.* ♿ 🖥 🏠 **www**.stoke.gov.uk/museums

🏛 **Etruria Industrial Museum**
Lower Bedford St, Etruria. *Tel 01782 233144.* ⬤ *Jan–Mar: Mon–Wed; Apr–Dec: Sat–Wed.* ⬤ *25 Dec–1 Jan.* 🏠 🎫 *by arrangement.* 🖥 🏠

🏰 **Little Moreton Hall**
(NT) Congleton, off A34. *Tel 01260 272018.* ⬤ *Mar–Oct: Wed–Sun & public hols; Nov–Feb: Sat & Sun.* 🏠

STAFFORDSHIRE POTTERY

An abundance of water, marl, clay and easily mined coal to fire the kilns enabled Staffordshire to develop as a ceramics centre; and local supplies of iron, copper and lead were used for glazing. In the 18th century, pottery became widely accessible and affordable. English bone china, which used powdered animals' bones for strength and translucence, was shipped all over the world, and Josiah Wedgwood (1730–95) introduced simple, durable crockery – though his best known design is the blue jasperware decorated with white Classical themes. Coal-powered bottle kilns fired the clay until the 1950s Clean Air Acts put them out of business. They have been replaced by electric or gas-fired kilns.

Wedgwood candlesticks, 1785

Timber-framed, gabled mansions in Fish Street, Shrewsbury

Shrewsbury ❹

Shropshire. 🏛 96,000. ⇄ 🚌
ℹ️ The Square (01743 281200).
🗓 Tue, Wed, Fri, Sat. 🎪 Shrewsbury
Flower Show (mid Aug).

Shrewsbury is almost an island, enclosed by a great loop of the River Severn. A gaunt **castle** of red sandstone, first built in 1083, guards the entrance to the town, standing on the only section of land not surrounded by the river. Such defences were necessary on the frontier between England and the wilder Marches of Wales, whose inhabitants fiercely defied Saxon and Norman invaders (see pp46–7). The castle, rebuilt over the centuries, now houses the Shropshire Regimental Museum.

In AD 60 the Romans (see pp44–5) built the garrison town of Viroconium, modern Wroxeter, 5 miles (8 km) east of Shrewsbury. Finds from the excavations are displayed at **Shrewsbury Museum and Art Gallery**, including a decorated silver mirror from the 2nd century and other luxury goods imported by the Roman army.

The town's medieval wealth as a centre of the wool trade is evident in the many timber-framed buildings found along the High Street, Butcher Row,

Roman silver mirror in Rowley's House Museum

and Wyle Cop. Two of the grandest High Street houses, **Ireland's Mansions** and **Owen's Mansions**, are named after Robert Ireland and Richard Owen, the wealthy wool merchants who built them in 1575 and 1570 respectively. Similarly attractive buildings in Fish Street frame a view of the **Prince Rupert Hotel**, which was briefly the headquarters of Charles I's nephew, Rupert, in the English Civil War (see pp52–3).

Outside the loop of the river, the **Abbey Church** survives from the medieval monastery. It has a number of interesting memorials, including one to Lieutenant WES Owen MC, better known as the war poet Wilfred Owen (1893–1918), who taught at the local Wyle Cop school and was killed in the last days of World War I.

Environs: To the south of Shrewsbury, the road to Ludlow passes through the landscapes celebrated in the 1896 poem by AE Housman (1859–1936), *A Shropshire Lad*. Highlights include the bleak moors of **Long Mynd**, with 15 prehistoric barrows, and **Wenlock Edge**, wonderful walking country with glorious, far-reaching views.

⚓ **Shrewsbury Castle**
Castle St. **Tel** 01743 361196.
⬤ Tue–Sat. ⬤ late Dec–mid-Feb.
♿ 🏛 **Shrewsbury Museum and Art Gallery**
Barker St. **Tel** 01743 361196.
⬤ for refurbishment until 2011.
♿ limited. 🏛 **www**.shrewsbury
museums.com

Ironbridge Gorge ❺

See pp314–15.

Ludlow ❻

Shropshire. 🏛 10,000. ⇄ ℹ️ Castle
St (01584 875053). 🗓 Mon, Wed,
Fri, Sat. 🎪 music & drama (end Jun).
www.ludlow.org.uk

Ludlow attracts large numbers of visitors to its splendid castle, but there is much else to see in this town, with its small shops and its lovely Georgian and half-timbered Tudor buildings. Ludlow is an important area of geological research and the **museum**, just off the town centre, has fossils of the oldest known animals and plants.

The ruined **castle** is sited on cliffs high above the River Teme. Built in 1086, it was damaged in the Civil War (see pp52–3) and abandoned in 1689. *Comus*, a court masque using music and drama, by John Milton (1608–74) was first performed here in 1634 in the Great Hall.

The 13th-century south tower and hall of Stokesay Castle, near Ludlow

Prince Arthur (1486–1502), elder brother of Henry VIII *(see pp50–51)*, died at Ludlow Castle. His heart is buried in **St Laurence Church** at the other end of Castle Square, as are the ashes of the poet A E Housman. The east end of the church backs onto the **Bull Ring**, with its ornate timber buildings. Two inns vie for attention across the street: **The Bull**, with its Tudor back yard, and **The Feathers**, with its flamboyant façade, whose name recalls the feathers used in arrow-making, once a local industry.

Environs: About 5 miles (8 km) north of Ludlow, in a lovely setting, is **Stokesay Castle**, a fortified manor house with a colourful moated garden.

⚜ **Ludlow Castle**
The Square. *Tel 01584 873355.*
◯ *daily (Dec & Jan: Sat & Sun only).*
🎨 ♿ 🖥 🍴 🛍

🏛 **Ludlow Museum**
Castle St. *Tel 01584 873857.* ◯ *Apr–Oct: Mon–Sat (Jun–Aug: daily).* ♿

⚜ **Stokesay Castle**
(EH) Craven Arms, A49. *Tel 01588 672544.* ◯ *Mar–Oct: Wed–Sun; (Apr–Sep: daily); Nov–Feb: Thu–Sun.*
🎨 🖥 🛍

Leominster ⓻

Herefordshire. 🚶 11,000. 🚊
ℹ *Corn Sq (01568 616460).*
🛒 *Fri.* www.herefordshire.gov.uk

Farmers come to Leominster (pronounced "Lemster") from all over this rural region to buy supplies. There are two buildings of note in the town, which has been a wool-manufacturing centre for 700 years. In the town centre stands the magnificent **Grange Court**, carved with bold and bizarre figures in 1633. Nearby is the **priory**, whose imposing Norman portal is carved with an equally strange mixture of mythical birds and beasts. The lions, at least, can be explained: medieval monks believed the name of Leominster was derived from *monasterium leonis*, "the monastery of the lions". In fact, *leonis* probably comes from medieval, rather than Classical Latin, and it means

A view of Leominster, set on the River Lugg in rolling border country

"of the marshes". The aptness of this description can readily be seen in the green lanes around the town, following the lush river valleys.

Environs: South of the town, the magnificent gardens and parkland at **Hampton Court** have recently been restored and include island pavilions and a maze. To the west of the town, along the River Arrow, are the villages of **Eardisland** and **Pembridge**, with their well-kept gardens and timber-framed houses. **Berrington Hall**, 3 miles (5 km) north of Leominster,

Gatehouse of Stokesay Castle, near Ludlow

is a Neo-Classical house set in grounds by Capability Brown. Inside are beautifully preserved ceiling decorations and period furniture.

To the northeast of Leominster is **Tenbury Wells**, which enjoyed brief popularity as a spa in the 19th century. The River Teme flows through it, full of minnows, trout and other fish and beloved of the composer Sir Edward Elgar *(see p317)*, who came to seek inspiration on its banks. The river also feeds **Burford House Gardens**, on the western outskirts of Tenbury Wells, where the water is used to create streams, fountains and pools that are rich in unusual moisture-loving plants.

♣ **Hampton Court Gardens**
nr Hope Under Dinmore. *Tel 01568 797 777.* ◯ *Apr–21 Dec: 11am–5pm (to 4pm Nov–Dec) Tue–Sun.* 🎨 ♿
🍴 🛍 www.hamptoncourt.org.uk

🎪 **Berrington Hall**
(NT) Berrington. *Tel 01568 615721.*
◯ *mid-Mar–Oct: Sat–Wed; Nov–mid-Mar: Sat & Sun.* 🎨 🍴 🛍

♣ **Burford House Gardens**
Tenbury Wells. *Tel 01584 810777.*
◯ *daily.* ● *1 Jan, 25 & 26 Dec.* 🎨
♿ 🍴 🛍 www.burford.co.uk

Ironbridge Gorge ❺

Ironbridge Gorge was one of the most important centres of the Industrial Revolution *(see pp54–5)*. It was here, in 1709, Abraham Darby I (1678–1717) pioneered the use of inexpensive coke, rather than charcoal, to smelt iron ore. The use of iron in bridges, ships and buildings transformed Ironbridge Gorge into one of the world's great iron-making centres. Industrial decline in the 20th century led to the Gorge's decay, although today it has been restored as an exciting complex of industrial archaeology, with several museums strung along the wooded banks of the River Severn.

VISITORS' CHECKLIST

Shropshire. 🏠 2,900.
🚆 Telford then bus (Telford Travelink 01952 200005).
🛈 Ironbridge town (01952 884391). ◯ daily. ● 1 Jan, 24, 25 Dec. Some sites closed Nov–Apr, call for details.
♿ most sites. 📷 🎫 by arrangement. 🖵 🍴 🚻 🏧
www.ironbridge.org.uk

The Museum of Iron, topped by a cast- and wrought-iron clock

COALBROOKDALE MUSEUM OF IRON

The history of iron and the men who made it is traced in this remarkable museum. Abraham Darby I's discovery of how to smelt iron ore with coke allowed the mass production of iron, paving the way for the rise of large-scale industry. His original blast furnace forms the museum's centrepiece.

One of the museum's themes is the history of the Darby dynasty, a Quaker family who had a great impact on the Coalbrookdale community.

Ironbridge led the world in industrial innovation, producing the first iron wheels and cylinders for the first steam engine. Cast-iron statues, many of them commissioned for the 1851 Great Exhibition *(see pp56–7),* are among the many Coalbrookdale Company products on display. They include a bronze figure of Andromeda and many sculptures of stags and hounds.

One of the Darby family's homes in the nearby village of Coalbrookdale, **Rosehill House** (open during the summer), has been furnished in mid-Victorian style.

MUSEUM OF THE GORGE

This partly castellated, Victorian building was a warehouse for storing products from the ironworks before they were shipped down the River Severn. The warehouse is now home to the Museum of the Gorge, and has displays illustrating the history of the Severn and the development of the water industry.

Until the arrival of the railways in the mid-19th century, the Severn was the main form of transport and communication to and from the Gorge. Sometimes too shallow, at other times in flood, the river was not a particularly reliable means of transportation; by the 1890s river trading had stopped completely.

The highlight of the museum is a wonderful 12 m (40 ft) model of the Gorge as it would have appeared in 1796, complete with foundries, cargo boats and growing villages.

Europe (1860), statue in the Museum of Iron

JACKFIELD TILE MUSEUM

There have been potteries in this area since the 17th century, but it was not until the Victorian passion for decorative tiles that Jackfield became famous. There were two tile-making factories here – Maw and Craven Dunnill – that produced a tremendous variety of tiles from clay mined nearby.

Peacock Panel (1928), one of the tile museum's star attractions

Talented designers created an astonishing range of images. The Jackfield Tile Museum, in the old Craven Dunnill works, has a collection of the decorative floor and wall tiles that were produced here from the 1850s to the 1960s. On certain days, visitors can watch small-scale demonstrations of traditional methods of tile-making in the old factory buildings, including the kilns and the decoration workshops.

IRONBRIDGE GORGE SIGHTS

Blists Hill Victorian Town ⑥
Coalbrookdale
    Museum of Iron ①
Coalport China
    Museum ⑤
Iron Bridge ③
Jackfield Tile
    Museum ④
Museum of the Gorge ②

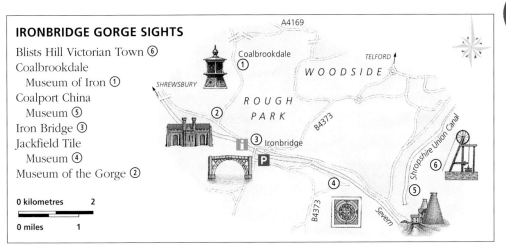

0 kilometres   2

0 miles   1

COALPORT CHINA MUSEUM

In the mid-19th century the Coalport Works was one of the largest porcelain manufacturers in Britain, and its name was synonymous with fine china. The Coalport Company still makes porcelain but has long since moved its operations to Stoke-on-Trent (see p311). Today the china workshops have been converted into a museum, where visitors can watch demonstrations of the various stages of making porcelain, including the skills of pot-throwing, painting and gilding. There is a superb collection of 19th-century china housed in one of the museum's distinctive bottle-shaped kilns.

Coalport China Museum with its bottle-shaped kiln

Nearby is the **Tar Tunnel**, an important source of natural bitumen discovered 110 m (360 ft) underground in the 1700s. It once yielded 20,500 litres (4,500 gal) of tar every week. Visitors can still explore part of the tunnel (Apr–Oct).

THE IRON BRIDGE

Abraham Darby III (grandson of the first man to smelt iron with coke) cast the world's first iron bridge in 1779, revolutionizing building methods in the process. Spanning the Severn, the bridge is a monument to the ironmasters' skills. The toll-house on the south bank charts its construction.

BLISTS HILL VICTORIAN TOWN

This enormous open-air museum recreates Victorian life in an Ironbridge Gorge town. A group of 19th-century buildings has been reconstructed on the 20 ha (50 acre) site of Blists Hill, an old coal mine that used to supply the ironworks in the Gorge. Here, people in period costume enact roles and perform tasks such as iron forging.

The site has period housing, a church and even a Victorian school. Visitors can change money into old coinage to buy items from the baker or even pay for a drink in the local pub.

The centrepiece of Blists Hill is a complete foundry that still produces wrought iron. One of the most spectacular sights is the Hay Inclined Plane, which was used to transport canal boats up and down a steep slope. Other attractions include steam engines, a saddlers, a doctors, a chemist, a candlemakers and a sweetshop.

Hereford 8

Herefordshire. 50,000. King St (01432 268430). Wed (cattle, general), Sat (general). www.visitherefordshire.co.uk

Once the capital of the Saxon kingdom of West Mercia, Hereford is today an attractive town which serves the needs of a primarily rural community. A cattle market is held here every Wednesday, and local produce is sold at the covered market in the town centre. Almost opposite, the Jacobean timber-framed **Old House** of 1621 is now a museum of local history.

In the **cathedral**, only a short stroll away, interesting features include the Lady Chapel, in richly ornamented Early English style, the *Mappa Mundi* (see below) and the Chained Library, whose 1,500 books are tethered by iron chains to bookcases as a precaution against theft. The story of these national treasures is told through models, original artifacts and interactive computer technology. The best place for an overall view of the cathedral is at the Bishop's Meadow, south of the centre, leading down to the banks of the Wye.

Hereford's many rewarding museums include the **City Museum and Art Gallery**, noted for its Roman mosaic and for watercolours by local artists, and the **Cider Museum and King Offa Distillery**. In the museum, visitors can discover the history of traditional cider making. The King Offa Distillery, which is open for visits and tastings, is the first distillery licensed to produce cider brandy for 200 years.

Hereford's 17th-century Old House, furnished in period style

Detail of figures on Kilpeck Church

Environs: During the 12th century, Oliver de Merlemond made a pilgrimage from Hereford to Spain. Impressed by several churches he saw on the way, he brought French masons over to England and introduced their techniques to this area. One result was **Kilpeck Church**, 6 miles (10 km) southwest, covered in lustful figures showing their genitals, and tail-biting dragons. At **Abbey Dore**, 4 miles (6 km) west, the Cistercian abbey church is complemented by the serene riverside gardens of **Abbey Dore Court**.

Old House
High Town. ***Tel*** *01432 260694.* *Apr–Sep: Tue–Sun; Oct–Mar: Tue–Sat; public hols.* *25 & 26 Dec, 1 Jan, Good Fri.* *limited.*
www.herefordshire.gov.uk/museums

City Museum and Art Gallery
Broad St. ***Tel*** *01432 260692.* *Apr–Sep: Tue–Sun; Oct–Mar: Tue–Sat, public hols.* *25 & 26 Dec, 1 Jan, Good Fri.*
www.herefordshire.gov.uk

Cider Museum and King Offa Distillery
Ryelands St. ***Tel*** *01432 354207.* *Tue–Sat & public hols.* *25 & 26 Dec, 1 Jan.* *limited.* *by arrangement.*
www.cidermuseum.co.uk

MEDIEVAL VIEW

Hereford Cathedral's most celebrated treasure is the *Mappa Mundi*, the Map of the World, drawn in 1290 by a clergyman, Richard of Haldingham. The world is depicted here on Biblical principles: Jerusalem is at the centre, the Garden of Eden figures prominently and monsters inhabit the margins of the world.

Central detail, *Mappa Mundi*

Ross-on-Wye 9

Herefordshire. 10,000. Edde Cross St (01989 562768). Thu, Sat; farmers' market 1st Fri of month. www.visitherefordshire.co.uk

The fine town of Ross sits on a cliff of red sandstone above the water meadows of the River Wye. There are wonderful views over the river from the cliff-top gardens,

The wooded Wye Valley near Ross

given to the town by a local benefactor, John Kyrle (1637–1724). Kyrle was lauded by the poet Alexander Pope (1688–1744) in his *Moral Essays on the Uses of Riches* (1732) for using his wealth in a practical way, and he came to be known as "The Man of Ross". There is a memorial to Kyrle in **St Mary's Church**.

Environs: From Hereford to Ross, the **Wye Valley Walk** follows 16 miles (26 km) of gentle countryside. From Ross it continues south for 33 miles (54 km), over rocky ground in deep, wooded ravines.

Goodrich Castle, 5 miles (8 km) south of Ross, is a 12th-century red sandstone fort on a rock above the river.

⚜ **Goodrich Castle**
(EH) Goodrich. *Tel 01600 890538.*
🔲 *daily (Nov–Feb: Wed–Sun).* 🖼 🔲
(Apr–Sep). **www**.english-heritage.org.uk

Ledbury ❿

Herefordshire. 🏃 *8,000.* 🚲 🚌
ℹ️ *The Masters House (01531 636147).* **www**.visitledbury.co.uk

Ledbury's main street is lined with timbered houses, including the **Market Hall** which dates from 1655. Church Lane, a cobbled lane running up from the High Street, has lovely 16th-century buildings: the **Heritage Centre** and **Butcher Row House** are both now museums. **St Michael and All Angels Church** has a massive detached bell tower, ornate Early English decoration and interesting monuments.

Medieval tile from the Priory at Great Malvern

🏛 **Heritage Centre**
Church Lane. 🔲 *Easter–Oct: daily.* ♿

🏛 **Butcher Row House**
Church Lane. 🔲 *Easter–Oct: daily.*

Great Malvern and the Malverns ⓫

Worcestershire. 🏃 *35,000.* 🚲 🚌
ℹ️ *21 Church St (01684 892289).*
🏪 *Fri; farmers' market 3rd Sat of month.* **www**.malvernhills.gov.uk

The ancient granite rock of the Malvern Hills rises from the plain of the River Severn, its 9 miles (15 km) of glorious scenery visible from afar. Composer Sir Edward Elgar (1857–1934) wrote many of his greatest works here, including the oratorio *The Dream of Gerontius* (1900), inspired by what the diarist John Evelyn (1620–1706) described as "one of the goodliest views in England". Elgar's home was in **Little Malvern**, whose truncated Church of St Giles, set on a steep, wooded hill, lost its nave when the stone was stolen during the Dissolution *(see p339).* **Great Malvern**, capital of the hills, is graced with 19th-century buildings which look like Swiss sanitoria: patients would stay at institutions such as Doctor Gulley's Water Cure Establishment. The water gushing from the hillside at St Ann's Well, above the town, is bottled and sold throughout Britain. The town is home to the famous Morgan cars (contact 01684 573104 to arrange a factory visit).

Malvern's highlight is the **Priory**, with its 15th-century stained-glass windows and medieval misericords. The old monastic fishponds below the church form the lake of the **Priory Park**. Here the theatre hosts performances of Elgar's music and plays by George Bernard Shaw.

A view of the Malverns range, formed of hard Pre-Cambrian rock

Worcester ⑫

Worcestershire. 🏛 *95,000.*
✈ 🚆 🛈 *High St (01905 726311).*
🏧 *Mon–Sat.*
www.visitworcester.com

Worcester is one of many
English cities whose character
has been transformed by
modern development. The
architectural highlight remains
the **cathedral**, off College
Yard, which suffered a collapsed tower in 1175 and a
disastrous fire in 1203, before
the present structure was
started in the 13th century.

The nave and central tower
were completed in the 1370s,
after building was severely
interrupted by the Black Death,
which decimated the labour
force *(see p48)*. The most
recent and ornate addition
was made in 1874, when Sir
George Gilbert Scott *(see p465)*
designed the High Gothic
choir, incorporating 14th-
century carved misericords.

There are many interesting
tombs, including King John's,

**Charles I holding a symbol of the
Church on Worcester's Guildhall**

a masterpiece of medieval
carving, in front of the altar.
Prince Arthur, Henry VIII's
brother *(see p313)*, who died
at the age of 15, is buried in
the chantry chapel south of
the altar. Underneath, the
huge Norman crypt survives
from the first cathedral (1084).

From the cathedral cloister,
a gate leads to College Green
and out into Edgar Street and

its Georgian houses. Here the
Worcester Porcelain Museum
displays Royal Worcester porcelain dating back to 1751.
On the High Street, north of
the cathedral, the **Guildhall**
of 1723 is adorned with
statues of Stuart monarchs,
reflecting the city's Royalist
allegiances. In Cornmarket
is **Ye Olde King Charles
House**, in which Prince
Charles, later Charles II, hid
after the Battle of Worcester
in 1651 *(see pp52–3)*.

Some of Worcester's finest
timber buildings are found
in Friar Street: **The Greyfriars**,
built around 1480, has been
restored in period style. The
Commandery was originally
an 11th-century hospital. It
was rebuilt in the 15th century
and used by Prince Charles
as a base during the Civil
War. Now a museum, it has
a fine hammerbeam roof.

Elgar's Birthplace was the
home of composer Sir Edward
Elgar *(see p318)* and contains
memorabilia of his life.

🏛 **Worcester Porcelain
Museum**
Severn St. **Tel** *01905 746000.* ⬜
daily. ⬤ *25 Dec.* 📷 ♿ 🖊 🍴 🛍

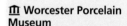 **The Greyfriars**
(NT) Friar St. **Tel** *01905 23571.*
⬜ *Mar–Dec: Wed–Sat; Jul & Aug:
Wed–Sun & public hols.* 📷

🏛 **Commandery**
Sidbury. **Tel** *01905 361821.*
⬜ *daily (Nov–Mar: Mon–Thu &
Sat).* ⬤ *1 Jan, 25–26 Dec.* 🗄 📷

🏛 **Elgar's Birthplace**
Lower Broadheath. **Tel** *01905
333224.* ⬜ *daily.* ⬤ *24 Dec–
mid-Jan.* 📷 ♿ *limited.* 🗄
www.elgarfoundation.org

Birmingham ⑬

Birmingham. 🏛 *1,000,000.*
🚶 ✈ 🚆 🛈 *The Rotunda
(0844 888 3883).* 🏧 *Mon–Sat.*
www.visitbirmingham.com

Brum, as it is affectionately
known to its inhabitants, grew
up as a major centre of the
Industrial Revolution in the
19th century. A vast range
of manufacturing trades was
based in Birmingham and
was responsible for the rapid
development of grim factories
and cramped housing. Since

Worcester Cathedral, overlooking the River Severn

The Last of England, Ford Madox Brown, Birmingham Art Gallery

the clearance of several of these areas after World War II, Birmingham has raised its cultural profile. The city succeeded in enticing Sir Simon Rattle to conduct the City of Birmingham Symphony Orchestra, and persuaded the former Royal Sadler's Wells Ballet (now the Birmingham Royal Ballet) to leave London for the more up-to-date facilities of Birmingham. The **National Exhibition Centre**, 8 miles (13 km) east of the centre, draws thousands of people to its conference, lecture and exhibition halls.

Set away from the massive Bullring shopping centre, Birmingham's 19th-century civic buildings are excellent examples of Neo-Classical architecture. Among them are the **City Museum and Art Gallery**, where the collection includes outstanding works by pre-Raphaelite artists such as Sir Edward Burne-Jones (1833–98), who was born in Birmingham, and Ford Madox Brown (1821–93). The museum also organizes some interesting

temporary exhibitions of art, such as works by J M W Turner (1775–1851).

Birmingham's extensive canal system is now used mainly for leisure boating (*see pp300–1*), and several former warehouses have been converted into museums and galleries. **Thinktank – The Birmingham Museum of Science and Discovery** celebrates the city's contributions to the world of railway engines, aircraft, and the motor trade. The old jewellery quarter has practised its traditional crafts here since the 16th century.

Suburban Birmingham has many attractions, including the **Botanical Gardens** at Edgbaston, and **Cadbury World** at Bournville, where there is a visitor centre dedicated to chocolate (booking ahead is advisable). Bournville village was built in 1890 by the Cadbury brothers for their workers and is a pioneering example of a garden suburb.

🏛 City Museum and Art Gallery
Chamberlain Sq. *Tel 0121 303 2834.* ◯ call for details. ● 25 & 26 Dec. ♿ ▢ 🗋

🏛 Thinktank
Millennium Point. *Tel 0121 202 2222.* ◯ daily. ● 24–26 Dec.

🌼 Botanical Gardens
Westbourne Rd, Edgbaston. *Tel 0121 454 1860.* ◯ daily. ● 25 Dec. 🗋 🖼 ♿ 🗋 by appt. 🍴

🏛 Cadbury World
Linden Rd, Bournville. *Tel 0845 450 3599.* ◯ daily (Nov–Jan: call for details). ● first two weeks Jan. 🖼 ♿

Coventry ⑭

Coventry. 🏃 *300,000.* ⤢ 🚉 ℹ *Cathedral Tower (024 7622 7264).* ◒ *Mon–Sat.* **www**.visitcoventry.co.uk

As an armaments centre, Coventry was a prime target for German bombing raids in World War II, and in 1940 the **cathedral** in the city centre was hit. After the war the first totally modern cathedral by Sir Basil Spence (1907–76) was built alongside the ruins. It includes sculptures by

Epstein's *St Michael Subduing the Devil*, on Coventry Cathedral

Sir Jacob Epstein and a tapestry by Graham Sutherland.

The **Herbert Gallery and Museum** has displays on the 11th-century legend of Lady Godiva, who rode naked through the streets. The recently renovated **Coventry Transport Museum** has the largest collection of Britain's road transport in the world, including cars, cycles and models, and features the fastest car in the world as well as interactive displays.

🏛 Herbert Gallery and Museum
Jordan Well. *Tel 024 7683 2386.* ◯ daily (Sun: pm) 1 Jan. ▢ 🗋

🏛 Coventry Transport Museum
Hales St. *Tel 024 7623 4270.* ◯ daily. ● 24–26 Dec. ♿ ▢ 🗋 **www**.transport-museum.com

Stately civic office buildings in Victoria Square, Birmingham

Midlands Garden Tour ⑮

The charming Cotswold stone buildings perfectly complement the lush gardens for which the region is famous. This picturesque route from Warwick to Cheltenham is designed to show every type of garden, from tiny cottage plots, brimming with bell-shaped flowers and hollyhocks, to the deer-filled, landscaped parks of stately homes. The route follows the escarpment of the Cotswold Hills, taking in spectacular scenery and some of the prettiest Midlands villages on the way.

Plum tree in blossom

Cheltenham Imperial Gardens ⑨
These colourful public gardens on the Promenade were laid out in 1817–18 to encourage people to walk from the town to the spa *(see p328)*.

Sudeley Castle ⑧
The restored castle is complemented by box hedges, topiary and an Elizabethan knot garden *(see p26)*. Catherine Parr, Henry VIII's widow, died here in 1548.

Broadway ⑤
Wisteria and cordoned fruit trees cover 17th-century cottages, fronted by immaculate gardens.

Stanway House ⑦
This Jacobean manor has many lovely trees in its grounds and a pyramid above a cascade of water.

Snowshill Manor ⑥
This Cotswold stone manor contains an extraordinary collection, from bicycles to Japanese armour. There are walled gardens and terraces full of *objets d'art* such as the clock (left). The colour blue is a recurrent theme.

Warwick Castle ①
The castle's gardens (see pp322–3) include the Mound, planted in medieval style, with grass, oaks, yew trees and box hedges.

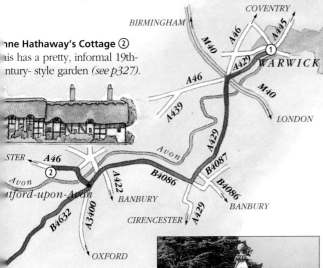

Anne Hathaway's Cottage ②
This has a pretty, informal 19th-century-style garden (see p327).

Hidcote Manor Gardens ③
Started in the early years of the last century, these beautiful gardens pioneered the idea of a garden as a series of outdoor "rooms", enclosed by high yew hedges and planted according to themes.

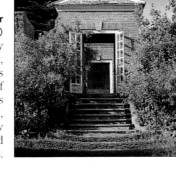

Kiftsgate Court Garden ④
This charmingly naturalistic garden lies opposite Hidcote Manor. It has many rare and unusual plants on a series of hillside terraces, including the enormous "Kiftsgate" Rose, nearly 30 m (100 ft) high.

KEY

≈≈≈	Motorway
▬▬▬	Tour route
═══	Other roads
☀	Viewpoint

0 kilometres   5

0 miles   5

Warwick ⑯

Warwickshire. 👥 28,000.
≈ 🚌 ℹ The Courthouse,
Jury St (01926 492212). 🛍 Sat.
www.warwickshire.gov.uk

Warwick suffered a major fire in 1694, but some medieval buildings survived. **St John's House Museum** in St John's is a charming Jacobean mansion housing reconstructions of a Victorian parlour, kitchen and classroom. At the west end of the High Street, a row of medieval guild buildings were transformed in 1571 by the Earl of Leicester, who founded the **Lord Leycester Hospital** as a refuge for his old soldiers.

The arcaded **Market Hall** (1670) is part of the Warwickshire Museum, renowned for its unusual tapestry map of the county, woven in 1558.

In Church Street, to the south of St Mary's Church, is the **Beauchamp Chapel** (1443–64). It is a superb example of Perpendicular architecture and has tombs of the Earls of Warwick. There is a view of **Warwick Castle** (see pp322–3) from St Mary's tower.

🏛 **St John's House Museum**
St John's. *Tel* 01926 412132.
◯ May–Sep: Tue–Sun; Oct–Apr: Tue–Sat; bank hol Mon. ♿ limited.

🏚 **Lord Leycester Hospital**
High St. *Tel* 01926 491422. ◯ Tue–Sun & public hols. ● Good Fri, 25 Dec. **Gardens** ◯ same as house but Easter–Sep only. 📷 🚻 ♿ ltd. 🅿

🏛 **Market Hall**
Market Place. *Tel* 01926 412500.
◯ Tue–Sat (May–Sep: Tue–Sun).
♿ limited. 🅿

The Lord Leycester Hospital, now a home for ex-servicemen

Warwick Castle

Neville family at prayer (c.1460)

Warwick's magnificent castle is the finest medieval fortress in the country. The original Norman castle was rebuilt in the 13th and 14th centuries, when huge outer walls and towers were added, mainly to display the power of the great feudal magnates, the Beauchamps and, in the 1400s, the Nevilles, the Earls of Warwick. The castle passed in 1604 to the Greville family who, in the 17th and 18th centuries, transformed it into a great country house. In 1978 the owners of Madame Tussaud's (*see p104*) bought the castle and set up tableaux of wax portraits to illustrate its history.

The Ghost Tower is where the ghost of Sir Fulke Greville, murdered in London by a servant in 1628, is said to walk.

The Mound has remains of the motte and bailey castle (*see p486*) and the 13 century keep.

Royal Weekend Party
The portrait of the valet is part of the award-winning exhibition of the Prince of Wales's visit in 1898.

The Mill and Engine House

★ Great Hall and State Rooms
Medieval apartments were transformed into the Great Hall and State Rooms. A mark of conspicuous wealth, they display a collection of family treasures from around the world.

Kingmaker Attraction
Dramatic displays recreate medieval life as "Warwick the Kingmaker", Richard Neville, prepared for battle in the Wars of the Roses.

View of Warwick Castle, south front, by Antonio Canaletto (1697–1768)

VISITORS' CHECKLIST

Castle Lane, Warwick. **Tel** 0870 4422000. ☐ Apr–Sep: 10am– 6pm daily; Oct–Mar: 10am–5pm daily (last adm: 30 mins before closing). ● 25 Dec. 🖼 ⬚ &
limited. ⬚ 🍴 ⬚ ⬚

Ramparts and towers, of local grey sandstone, were added in the 14th and 15th centuries.

★ **Guy's Tower**
Completed around 1393, the tower had lodgings for guests and members of the Earl of Warwick's retinue.

Dream of Battle Show creates the drama, noise and adrenaline-charged terror of medieval battle through the dreams of 14-year-old Squire William.

Entrance

STAR SIGHTS

★ Great Hall and State Rooms

★ Guy's Tower

The Gatehouse is defended by portcullises and "murder holes" through which boiling pitch was dropped onto attackers beneath.

The underground dungeon

Caesar's Tower

TIMELINE

1068 Norman motte and bailey castle built	**1264** Simon de Montfort, champion of Parliament against Henry III, attacks Warwick Castle	*Shield (1745)*	**1478** Castle reverts to Crown after murder of Richard Neville's son-in-law	**1890s–1910** Visits from future Edward VII

1000	1200	1400	1600	1800

Richard Neville

1268–1445 Much of the present castle built by the Beauchamp family, Earls of Warwick

1449–1471 Richard Neville, Earl of Warwick, plays leading role in Wars of the Roses

1604 James I gives castle to Sir Fulke Greville

1600–1800 Interiors remodelled and gardens landscaped

1642 Siege of the Castle of Royalist Troops

1871 Fire damages the Great Hall

Street-by-Street: Stratford-upon-Avon ⓱

Situated on the west bank of the River Avon, in the heart of the Midlands, is one of the most famous towns in England. Stratford-upon-Avon dates back to at least Roman times but its appearance today is that of a small Tudor market town, with mellow, half-timbered architecture and tranquil walks beside the tree-fringed Avon. This image belies its popularity as the most visited tourist attraction outside London, with eager hordes flocking to see buildings connected to William Shakespeare or his descendants.

A 1930s jester

Bancroft Gardens
There is an attractive boat-filled canal basin here and a 15th-century causeway.

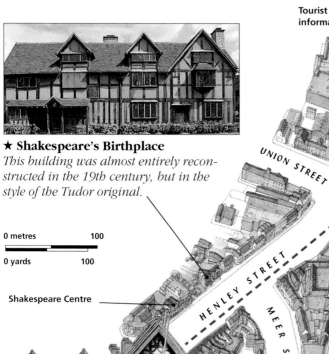

Tourist information

To train station

★ Shakespeare's Birthplace
This building was almost entirely recon-structed in the 19th century, but in the style of the Tudor original.

0 metres   100

0 yards   100

Shakespeare Centre

UNION STREET

BRIDGE STREET

WATER

HIGH STREET

HENLEY STREET

MEER STREET

WOOD STREET

ELY STREET

Harvard House
The novelist Marie Corelli (1855–1924) had this house restored. Next door is the 16th-century Garrick Inn.

STAR SIGHTS

- ★ Shakespeare's Birthplace
- ★ Hall's Croft
- ★ Holy Trinity Church

Town Hall
Built in 1767, there are traces of 18th-century graffiti on the front of the building saying God Save the King.

Royal Shakespeare Theatre and Swan Theatre
Closed for redevelopment from April 2007 to 2010, the RSC will instead perform at the Courtyard Theatre.

VISITORS' CHECKLIST

Warwickshire. 22,000.
20 miles (32 km) NW of
Stratford-upon-Avon.
Alcester Rd. Bridge St.
Bridge Foot **Tel** 0870 160
7930. Fri. Shakespeare's
Birthday: Apr; Stratford Festival:
Jul. **www**.shakespeare.org.uk

Nash's House
The foundations of New Place, where Shakespeare died, form the garden beside this house.

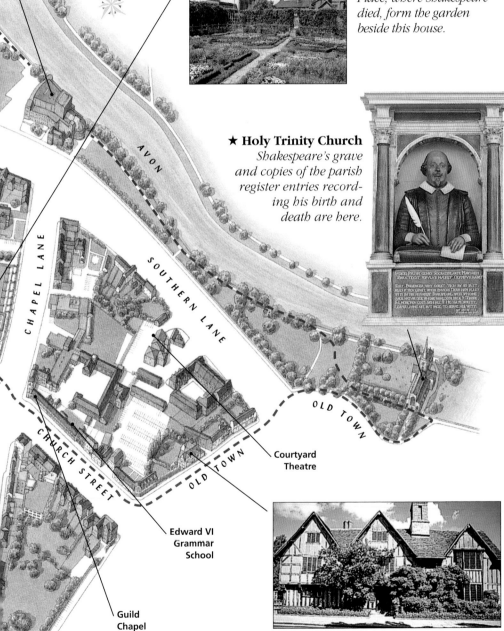

★ Holy Trinity Church
Shakespeare's grave and copies of the parish register entries recording his birth and death are here.

Courtyard
Theatre

Edward VI
Grammar
School

Guild
Chapel

KEY

- - - Suggested route

★ Hall's Croft
John Hall, Shakespeare's son-in-law, was a doctor. This delightful house includes an exhibition of medicine in Shakespeare's time.

Exploring Stratford-upon-Avon

Mosaic of Shakespeare on the beautiful Old Bank (1810)

William Shakespeare was born in Stratford-upon-Avon on St George's Day, 23 April 1564. Admirers of his work have been coming to the town since his death in 1616. In 1847 a public appeal successfully raised the money to buy the house in which he was born. As a result Stratford has become a literary shrine to Britain's greatest dramatist. It also has a thriving cultural reputation as the provincial home of the prestigious Royal Shakespeare Company, whose dramas are usually performed in Stratford before playing a second season in London (*see pp152–3*).

Anne Hathaway's Cottage, home of Shakespeare's wife

Around Stratford

The centre of Stratford-upon-Avon has many buildings that are connected with William Shakespeare and his descendants. On the High Street corner is the **Cage**, a 15th-century prison. It was converted into a house where Shakespeare's daughter Judith lived, and is now a shop. At the end of the High Street, the **Town Hall** has a statue of Shakespeare on the façade given by David Garrick (1717–79), the actor who in 1769 organized the first Shakespeare festival.

The High Street leads into Chapel Street where the half-timbered **Nash's House** is a museum of local history. It is also the site of **New Place**, where Shakespeare died in 1616, and which is now a herb and knot garden (*see p26*). In Church Street opposite, the **Guild Chapel** (1496) has a *Last Judgement* painting (c.1500) on the chancel wall. Shakespeare is thought to have attended the **Edward VI Grammar School** (above the former Guildhall) next door.

A left turn into Old Town leads to **Hall's Croft**, home of Shakespeare's daughter Susanna, which displays 16th- and 17th-century medical artefacts. An avenue of lime trees leads to **Holy Trinity Church**, where Shakespeare is buried. A walk along the river follows the Avon to **Bancroft Gardens**, which lies at the junction of the River Avon and the Stratford Canal.

🏛 Shakespeare's Birthplace

Henley St. **Tel** *01789 204016.* ◯ *daily.* ● *23–26 Dec.* 🗖 🕭 *limited.* 🖰 www.shakespeare.org.uk

Bought for the nation in 1847, when it was a public house, Shakespeare's Birthplace was converted back to Elizabethan style. Objects associated with Shakespeare's father, John, a glovemaker and wool merchant, are on display. There is a birth room, in which Shakespeare was supposedly born, and another room has a window etched with visitors' autographs, including that of Sir Walter Scott (*see p512*).

Holy Trinity Church, seen across the River Avon

⛪ Harvard House

High St. **Tel** *01789 204507.* ☐ *May, Jun & Sep: Fri–Sun; Jul & Aug: Wed–Sun.* 🖼 **www**.shakespeare.org.uk

Built in 1596, this ornate house was the home of Katherine Rogers, whose son, John Harvard, emigrated to America and in 1638 left his estate to a new college, later renamed Harvard University. The house contains a Museum of British Pewter and displays relating to John Harvard.

Environs: No tour of Stratford would be complete without a visit to **Anne Hathaway's Cottage**. Before her marriage to William Shakespeare she lived at Shottery, 1 mile (1.5 km) west of Stratford. Despite fire damage in 1969, the cottage is still impressive, with some original 16th-century furniture. The Hathaway descendants lived here until the early 20th century *(see p321).*

⛪ Anne Hathaway's Cottage

Cottage Lane. **Tel** *01789 292100.* ☐ *daily.* ● *23–26 Dec.* 🖼 ☐ **www**.shakespeare.org.uk

Kenneth Branagh in *Hamlet*

THE ROYAL SHAKESPEARE COMPANY

The Royal Shakespeare Company is renowned for its new interpretations of Shakespeare's work. The company performs at the 1932 Royal Shakespeare Theatre, a windowless brick building adjacent to the Swan Theatre, built in 1986 to a design based on an Elizabethan playhouse. Next to it is a building displaying sets, props and costumes. The RSC also performs at the 150-seat theatre, known as the Other Place, and in London *(see pp152–3).*

Grevel House, the oldest house in Chipping Campden

Chipping Campden ⑱

Gloucestershire. 🚶 *2,500.* ℹ *High St (01386 841206).* **www**.visitchippingcampden.com

This perfect Cotswold town is kept in pristine condition by the Campden Trust. Set up in 1929, the Trust has kept alive the traditional skills of stonecarving and repair that make Chipping Campden such a unified picture of golden-coloured and lichen-patched stone. Visitors travelling from the northwest along the B4035 first see a group of ruins: the remains of **Campden Manor**, begun around 1613 by Sir Baptist Hicks, 1st Viscount Campden. The manor was burned by Royalist troops to stop it being sequestered by Parliament at the end of the Civil War *(see pp52–3),* but the almshouses opposite the gateway were spared. They were designed in the form of the letter "I" (which is Latin for "J"), a symbol of the owner's loyalty to King James I.

The town's **Church of St James**, one of the finest in the Cotswolds, was built in the 15th century, financed by merchants who bought wool from Cotswold farmers and exported it at a high profit. Inside the church there are many elaborate tombs, and

a magnificent brass dedicated to William Grevel, describing him as "the flower of the wool merchants of England". He built **Grevel House** (c.1380) in the High Street, the oldest in a fine row of buildings, which is distinguished by a double-storey bay window.

Viscount Campden donated the **Market Hall** in 1627. His contemporary, Robert Dover, founded in 1612 the "Cotswold Olimpicks", long before the modern Olympic Games had been established. The 1612 version included such painful events as the shin-kicking contest. It still takes place on the first Friday after each Spring Bank Holiday, followed by a torchlit procession into town ready for the Scuttlebrook Wake Fair on the next day. The setting for the games is a spectacular natural hollow on **Dover's Hill** above the town, worth climbing on a clear day for the marvellous views over the Vale of Evesham.

The 17th-century Market Hall in Chipping Campden

Tewkesbury's abbey church overlooks the town, crowded onto the bank of the River Severn

Tewkesbury ⑲

Gloucestershire. 🏘 11,000.
ℹ Church St (01684 855040).
🕋 Wed, Sat. **www**.visitcotswolds
andsevernvale.gov.uk

This lovely town sits on the confluence of the rivers Severn and Avon. It has one of England's finest Norman abbey churches, **St Mary the Virgin**, which locals saved during the Dissolution of the Monasteries (*see p50*) by paying Henry VIII £453. Around the church, with its bulky tower and Norman façade, timbered buildings are crammed within the bend of the river. Warehouses are a reminder of past wealth, and Borough Mill on Quay Street, the only mill left harnessed to the river's energy, still grinds corn.

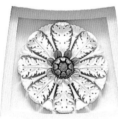

Pump Room detail,
Cheltenham

Environs: Boat trips run from the river to **Twyning**'s riverside pub, 6 miles (10 km) north.

Cheltenham ⑳

Gloucestershire. 🏘 107,000. 🚆 🚍
ℹ 77 Promenade (01242 522878).
🕋 Sun; farmers' market 2nd & last Fri of month. **www**.visitcheltenham.com

Cheltenham's reputation for elegance was first gained in the late 18th century, when high society flocked to the spa

town to "take the waters", following the example set by George III (*see pp54–5*). Many gracious terraced houses were built, in a Neo-Classical style, along broad avenues. These survive around the Queen's Hotel, near **Montpellier**, a lovely Regency arcade lined with craft and antique shops, and in the **Promenade**, with its smart department stores and couturiers. A more modern atmosphere prevails in the newly built Regency Arcade, where the star attraction is the 1987 **clock** by Kit Williams: visit on the hour to see fish blowing bubbles over the onlookers' heads. The **Museum and Art Gallery** is worth a visit to see its unusual collection of furniture and other crafts made by members of the influential Arts and Crafts Movement (*see p29*), whose strict principles of utilitarian design were laid down by William Morris (*see p220*).

The **Pittville Pump Room** (1825–30), modelled on the Greek Temple of Ilissos in Athens, is frequently used for performances during the town's renowned annual festivals of music (July) and literature (October).

The event that really attracts the crowds is the Cheltenham Gold Cup – the premier event of the National Hunt season – held in March (*see p66*).

🏛 **Museum and Art Gallery**
Clarence St. **Tel** 01242 237431.
◯ Mon–Sat. ● 1 Jan, 25 Dec & public hols. ♿ ☕ by arrangement.
▢ 📷 **www**.cheltenham museum.org.uk

🚰 **Pittville Pump Room**
Pittville Park. **Tel** 01242 523852.
◯ Wed–Mon. ● 1 Jan, 25 & 26 Dec, public hols & frequently for functions: call to check. ♿
www.pittvillepumproom.org.uk

Fantasy clock, by Kit Williams, in Cheltenham's Regency Arcade

Gloucester Cathedral's nave

Gloucester ㉑

Gloucestershire. 🏘 *110,000.*
⇄ 🚉 🛈 *28 Southgate St
(01452 396572).* 🚆 *Wed, Sat.*
www.visitgloucester.info

Gloucester has played a
prominent role in the history
of England. It was here that
William the Conqueror
ordered a vast survey of all the
land in his kingdom, that was
to be recorded in the *Domesday Book* of 1086 *(see p48).*

The city was popular with
the Norman monarchs and in
1216 Henry III was crowned
in its magnificent **cathedral**.
The solid, dignified nave was
begun in 1089. Edward II *(see
p439),* who was murdered in
1327 at Berkeley Castle, 14
miles (22 km) to the southwest, is buried in a tomb near
the high altar. Many pilgrims
came to honour Edward's
tomb, leaving behind gener-
ous donations, and Abbot
Thoky was able to begin
rebuilding in 1331. The result
was the wonderful east
window and the cloisters,
where the fan vault was
developed and then copied
in other churches all over
the country.

The impressive buildings
around the cathedral include
College Court, with its **House
of the Tailor of Gloucester**
museum, in the house that
the children's author Beatrix
Potter used as the setting *(see
p367)* for her illustrations of
that story. A museum complex
has been created in the
Gloucester Docks, part of
which is still a port, linked
to the Bristol Channel by the

Gloucester and Sharpness
Canal (opened in 1827). In
the old port, and housed in
a Victorian warehouse, the
National Waterways Museum
relates the history of canals.
A new gallery, Move It, looks
at how canals were built.

🏛 **House of the Tailor of
Gloucester**
College Court. **Tel** *01452 422856.*
⭕ *Mon–Sat (Sun: pm only).*
⬤ *public hols.* 🔲 🈸

🏛 **National Waterways
Museum**
Llanthony Warehouse, Gloucester
Docks. **Tel** *01452 318200.*
⭕ *daily.* ⬤ *25 Dec.*
🔲 🈸 🔲 🈸
www.nwm.org.uk

Cirencester ㉒

Gloucestershire. 🏘 *20,000.* 🚍
🛈 *Market Place (01285 654180).*
🚆 *Mon, Tue (cattle) & Fri.*
www.cotswold.gov.uk

Known as the capital of the
Cotswolds, Cirencester has as
its focus a market place, where
there is a market every Monday and Friday. Overlooking
the market is the **Church of St
John Baptist**, whose "wine-
glass" pulpit (1515) is one
of the few pre-Reformation
pulpits to survive in England.
To the west, **Cirencester Park**
was laid out by the 1st Earl
of Bathurst from 1714, with
help from the poet Alexander
Pope *(see p317).* The mansion
is surrounded by a massive
yew hedge. Clustering round

the park entrance are the
17th- and 18th-century wool
merchants' houses of Cecily
Hill, built in grand Italianate
style. Much humbler Cots-
wold houses are to be found
in Coxwell Street, and
underlying this is a Roman
town, evidence of which
emerges whenever the
ground is dug.

The **Corinium Museum**,
since its renovation in 2004,
is a must-see site. It features
excavated objects in a series
of tableaux illustrating life in
a Roman household.

🌿 **Cirencester Park**
Cirencester Park. **Tel** *01285
653135.* ⭕ *daily.* 🈸
www.cirencesterpark.co.uk

🏛 **Corinium Museum**
Park St. **Tel** *01285 655611.*
⭕ *daily (Sun pm only).* ⬤ *1 Jan,
25 & 26 Dec.* 🈸 🈸 🔲 🔲
www.cotswold.gov.uk

Cirencester's fine parish church,
one of the largest in England

ART AND NATURE IN THE ROMAN WORLD

Cirencester was an important centre of mosaic production
in Roman days. Fine examples of the local style are shown
in the Corinium Museum and mosaics range from Classical
subjects, such as Orpheus taming lions and tigers with the
music of his lyre, to the naturalistic depiction of a hare. At

Chedworth Roman Villa, 8
miles (13 km) north, mosaics
are inspired by real life. In
the *Four Seasons* mosaic,
Winter shows a peasant,
dressed in a woollen hood
and a wind-blown cloak,
clutching a recently caught
hare in one hand and a
branch for fuel in the other.

Hare mosaic, Corinium Museum

EAST MIDLANDS

DERBYSHIRE · LEICESTERSHIRE · LINCOLNSHIRE
NORTHAMPTONSHIRE · NOTTINGHAMSHIRE

Three very different kinds of landscape greet visitors to the East Midlands. In the west, wild moors rise to the craggy heights of the Peak District. These give way to the low-lying plain and the massive industrial towns at the region's heart. In the east, hills and limestone villages stretch to a long, flat seaboard.

The East Midlands owes much of its character to a conjunction of the pastoral with the urban. The spa resorts, historical villages and stately homes coexist within a landscape shaped by industrialization. Throughout the region there are swathes of scenic countryside – and grimy industrial cities.

The area has been settled since prehistoric times. The Romans mined lead and salt, and they built a large network of roads and fortresses. Anglo-Saxon and Viking influence is found in many of the place names. During the Middle Ages profits from the wool industry enabled the development of towns such as Lincoln, which still has many fine old buildings. The East Midlands was the scene of ferocious battles during the Wars of the Roses and the Civil War, and insurgents in the Jacobite Rebellion reached as far as Derby.

In the west of the region is the Peak District, Britain's first national park. Created in 1951, it draws crowds in search of the wild beauty of the heather-covered moors, or the wooded dales of the River Dove. The peaks are very popular with rock climbers and hikers.

The eastern edge of the Peaks descends through stone-walled meadows to sheltered valleys. The Roman spa of Buxton adds a final note of elegance before the flatlands of Derbyshire, Leicestershire and Nottinghamshire are reached. An area of coal mines and factories since the late 18th century, the landscape is being transformed, as part of a ten-year-long project, into The National Forest.

Well-dressing dance, an ancient custom at Stoney Middleton in the Peak District

◁ **West front of Chatsworth House, a superb Baroque stately home in the Peak District**

Exploring the East Midlands

The East Midlands is a popular tourist destination, easily accessible by road, but best explored on foot. Numerous well-marked trails pass through the Peak District National Park. There are superb country houses at Chatsworth and Burghley and the impressive historic towns of Lincoln and Stamford to discover.

SIGHTS AT A GLANCE

Burghley pp342–3 **8**
Buxton **1**
Chatsworth pp334–5 **2**
Lincoln pp340–41 **7**
Matlock Bath **3**
Northampton **10**
Nottingham **6**
Stamford **9**

Walks and Tours
Peak District Tour **5**
Tissington Trail **4**

GETTING AROUND

The M6, M1 and A1 are the principal road routes to the East Midlands, but they are subject to frequent delays because of the volume of traffic they carry. It can be faster and more interesting to find cross-country routes to the region, for example through the attractive countryside and villages around Stamford and Northampton. Roads in the Peak District become very congested during the summer and an early start to the day is advisable. Lincoln and Stamford are well served by fast mainline trains from London. Rail services in the Peak District are far more limited, but local lines run as far as Matlock and Buxton.

KEY

▬▬ Motorway

▭▭▭ Major road

▬ Secondary road

═══ Minor road

▬ Scenic route

▬▬ Main railway

──── Minor railway

△ Summit

View of Burghley House from the north courtyard

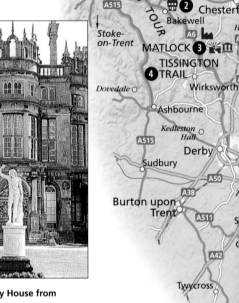

Barnsley
Manchester — A628
Peak District National Park
Kinder Scout 636m
Edale
Sheffield
PEAK DISTRICT TOUR
Hathersage
Eyam
BUXTON **1**
CHATSWORTH **2** Chesterfield
A515
Bakewell
A6
Stoke-on-Trent
MATLOCK **3**
TISSINGTON TRAIL **4**
Dovedale
Wirksworth
Ashbourne
Kedleston Hall
A515
Derby
Sudbury
A50
A38
Burton upon Trent
A511
A42
Twycross
Birmingham

Peak District countryside seen from the Tissington Trail

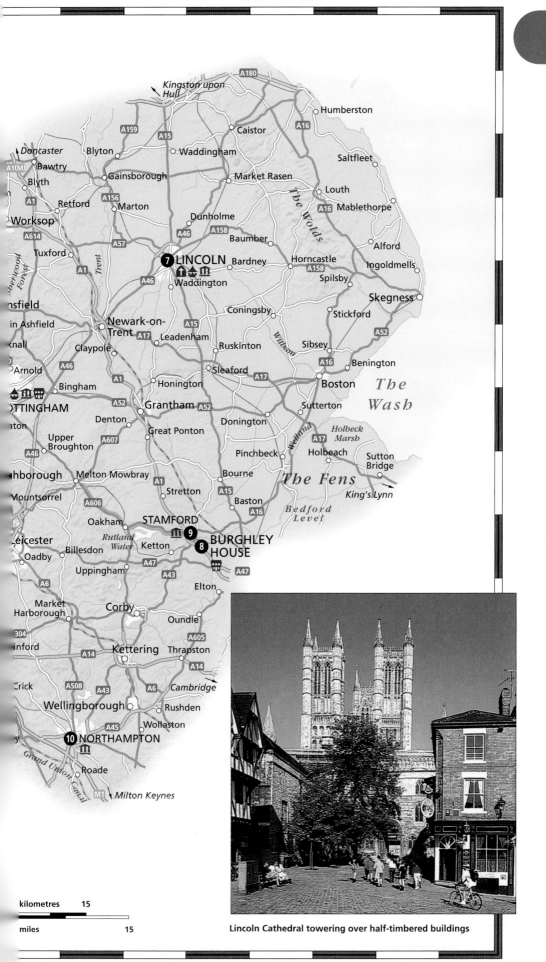

Kingston upon Hull
A180
Humberston
A159
A16
A15
Caistor
Doncaster
Blyton
Waddingham
Saltfleet
Bawtry
A1(M)
Gainsborough
Market Rasen
Louth
Blyth
A156
A16
Mablethorpe
Retford
Marton
A1
Dunholme
Alford
Worksop
A46
A158
Baumber
A614
A57
Ingoldmells
Tuxford
A158
7 LINCOLN
Bardney
Horncastle
Spilsby
Waddington
Skegness
Mansfield
Newark-on-Trent
Coningsby
Stickford
A52
in Ashfield
A17
Leadenham
Ruskinton
knall
A15
Sibsey
Arnold
A46
Sleaford
A16
Benington
A1
Honington
A17
Boston
NOTTINGHAM
A52
Grantham
A52
Sutterton
The Wash
aton
Denton
Donington
Upper Broughton
A607
Great Ponton
Holbeck Marsh
A46
Pinchbeck
A17
Holbeach
Sutton Bridge
hborough
Melton Mowbray
Bourne
The Fens
Mountsorrel
A1
Stretton
A15
King's Lynn
A606
Baston
Bedford Level
Oakham
STAMFORD
A16
Leicester
Rutland Water
9
Oadby
Billesdon
Ketton
8 BURGHLEY HOUSE
Uppingham
A47
A43
A47
A6
Elton
Market Harborough
Corby
Oundle
304
A605
inford
A14
Kettering
Thrapston
Crick
A14
A508
A43
A6
Cambridge
Wellingborough
Rushden
A45
Wollaston
10 NORTHAMPTON
Grand Union Canal
Roade
M1
Milton Keynes

kilometres 15

miles 15

Lincoln Cathedral towering over half-timbered buildings

Buxton Opera House, a late 19th-century building restored in 1979

Buxton ❶

Derbyshire. 👥 20,000. 🚆 🚌
ℹ️ Pavilion Gardens (01298 25106).
📮 Tue, Sat. www.highpeak.gov.uk

Buxton was developed as a spa town by the 5th Duke of Devonshire during the late 18th century. It has many fine Neo-Classical buildings, including the **Devonshire Royal Hospital** (1790), originally stables, at the entrance to the town. The **Crescent** was built (1780–90) to rival Bath's Royal Crescent (see p258).

At its southwest end, the tourist information office is housed in the former town baths. Here, a spring where water surges from the ground at a rate of 7,000 litres (1,540 gallons) an hour can be seen. Buxton water is bottled and sold but there is a public fountain at **St Ann's Well**, opposite.

Steep gardens known as the Slopes lead from the Crescent to the small, award-winning **Museum and Art Gallery**, with geological and archaeological displays. Behind the Crescent, overlooking the Pavilion Gardens, is the striking 19th-century iron and glass **Pavilion**, and the splendidly restored **Opera House**, where a Music and Arts Festival is held in summer.

🏛️ **Buxton Museum and Art Gallery**
Terrace Rd. *Tel* 01298 24658. ◯
Easter–Sep: Tue–Sun; Oct–Easter: Tue–Sat. ◯ 25 Dec–2 Jan. ♿ 📷
www.derbyshire.gov.uk

🏛️ **Pavilion Gardens**
St John's Rd. *Tel* 01298 23114.
◯ daily. ◯ 25 Dec. ♿ 🍴 📷 📷

Chatsworth House and Gardens ❷

Chatsworth is one of Britain's most impressive stately homes. Between 1687 and 1707, the 4th Earl of Devonshire replaced the old Tudor mansion with this Baroque palace. The house has beautiful gardens, landscaped in the 1760s by Capability Brown (see p26) and developed by the head gardener, Joseph Paxton (see pp56–7), in the mid-19th century.

First house built in 1552 by Bess of Hardwick

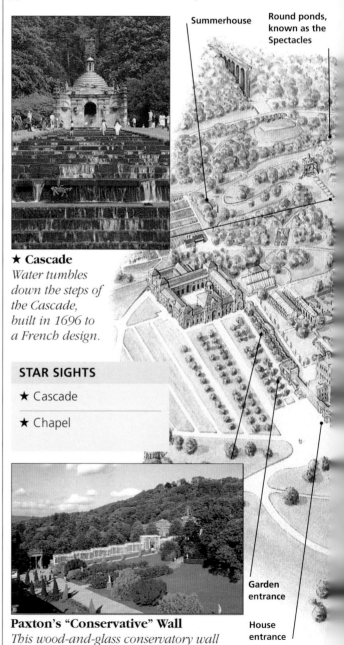
Summerhouse
Round ponds, known as the Spectacles

★ **Cascade**
Water tumbles down the steps of the Cascade, built in 1696 to a French design.

STAR SIGHTS
★ Cascade
★ Chapel

Garden entrance
House entrance

Paxton's "Conservative" Wall
This wood-and-glass conservatory wall was designed in 1848 by Joseph Paxton, the creator of Chatsworth's Great Conservatory (now demolished).

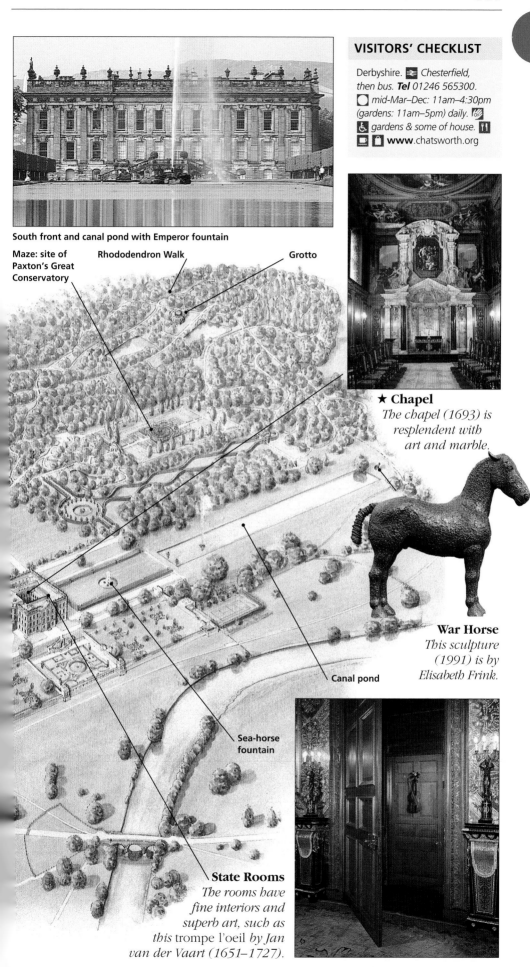

South front and canal pond with Emperor fountain

Maze: site of
Paxton's Great
Conservatory

Rhododendron Walk

Grotto

★ **Chapel**
The chapel (1693) is
resplendent with
art and marble.

War Horse
This sculpture
(1991) is by
Elisabeth Frink.

Canal pond

Sea-horse
fountain

State Rooms
The rooms have
fine interiors and
superb art, such as
this trompe l'oeil by Jan
van der Vaart (1651–1727).

Matlock ❸

Derbyshire. 👥 *23,000.* ⛴
ℹ️ *Crown Square (01629 583388).*
www.visitderbyshire.co.uk

Matlock was developed as a spa from the 1780s. Interesting buildings include the massive structure (1853) on the hill above the town, built as a hydrotherapy centre but now council offices. On the hill opposite is the mock-Gothic **Riber Castle**.

From Matlock, the A6 winds through the outstandingly beautiful **Derwent Gorge** to **Matlock Bath**. Here, cable cars ascend to the **Heights of Abraham** pleasure park, with caves, nature trail and extensive views. Lead-mining is the subject of the **Peak District Mining Museum**, and visitors can inspect the old **Temple Mine** nearby. **Sir Richard Arkwright's Cromford Mill** (1771), a world heritage site and the first ever water-powered cotton spinning mill, lies at the southern end of the gorge *(see p339).*

🎟 Heights of Abraham
On A6. *Tel 01629 582365.* ☐ Feb–Nov: daily. 🚫 ♿ limited. 🏠 🅿️
www.heightsofabraham.com

🏛 Peak District Mining Museum
The Pavilion, off A6. *Tel 01629 583834.* ☐ daily. 🚫 ♿ 🅿️ 🏠

⛏ Temple Mine
Temple Rd, off A6. *Tel 01629 583834.* ☐ call for details. 🚫

⛏ Cromford Mill
Mill Lane, Cromford. *Tel 01629 824297.* ☐ daily. ● 25 Dec. 🚫 ♿ 🍴 🏠 **www**.cromfordmill.co.uk

Cable cars taking visitors to the Heights of Abraham

Tissington Trail ❹

See p337.

Peak District Tour ❺

See pp338–9.

Nottingham ❻

Nottinghamshire. 👥 *269,000.* ⛴
🚌 ℹ️ *Smithy Row (0844 477 5678).*
🅿️ *daily.* **www**.nottinghamcity.gov.uk

The name of Nottingham often conjures up the image of the evil Sheriff, adversary of Robin Hood. **Nottingham Castle** stands on a rock riddled with underground passages. The castle houses a museum, with displays on the city's history, and what was Britain's first municipal art gallery, featuring works by Sir Stanley Spencer (1891–1959) and Dante Gabriel Rossetti (1828–82). At the foot of the castle, Britain's oldest tavern, the **Trip to Jerusalem** (1189), is still in business. Its name may refer to the 12th- and 13th-century crusades, but much of it is 17th-century.

There are several museums near the castle, including **Tales of Robin Hood**, which tells the story of the outlaw, and the **Museum of Nottingham Life**, which looks at life in Nottingham over the last 300 years.

Nottingham's redeveloped city centre includes an award-winning Old Market Square.

Environs: Stately homes within a few miles of Nottingham include the Neo-Classical **Kedleston Hall** *(see pp28–9).* "Bess of Hardwick", Countess of Shrewbury *(see p334),* built the spectacular **Hardwick Hall** *(see p302).*

🏰 Nottingham Castle and Museum
Friar Lane. *Tel 0115 9153700.* ☐ daily. ● 1 Jan, 24–27 Dec. 🚫 ♿ 🅿️ of the caves. 🖥 🏠

🏛 Tales of Robin Hood
30–38 Maid Marion Way. *Tel 0115 9483284.* ☐ daily. ● 25 & 26 Dec. 🚫 ♿ 🅿️ 🏠

🏛 Museum of Nottingham Life
Castle Boulevard. *Tel 0115 915 3600.* ☐ daily. ● 1 Jan, 24–26 Dec. ♿ 🏠 **www**.nottinghamcity. gov.uk

🏯 Kedleston Hall
(NT) off A38. *Tel 01332 842191.* ☐ Mar–Oct: Sat–Wed (pm). 🚫 ♿ 🍴 🏠

🏯 Hardwick Hall
(NT) off A617. *Tel 01246 850430.* ☐ Apr–Oct: Wed, Thu, Sat, Sun & public hols. 🚫 ♿ limited. 🍴 🏠

ROBIN HOOD OF SHERWOOD FOREST

England's most colourful folk hero was a legendary swordsman, whose adventures are depicted in numerous films and stories. He lived in Sherwood Forest, near Nottingham, with a band of "merry men", robbing the rich to give to the poor. As part of an ancient oral tradition, Robin Hood figured mainly in ballads; the first written records of his exploits date from the 15th century. Today historians think that he was not one person, but a composite of many outlaws who refused to conform to medieval feudal constraints.

Victorian depiction of Friar Tuck and Robin Hood

Tissington Trail ④

The full-length Tissington Trail runs for 13 miles (22 km), from the village of Ashbourne to Parsley Hay, where it meets the High Peak Trail. This is a short version, taking an easy route along a dismantled railway line around Tissington village and providing good views of the beautiful White Peak countryside. The Derbyshire custom of well-dressing is thought to have originated in pre-Christian times. It was revived in the early 17th century, when the Tissington village wells were decorated in thanksgiving for deliverance from the plague, in the belief that the fresh water had had a medicinal effect. Well-dressing is still an important event in the Peakland calendar, and can be seen in other villages where the water supplies were prone to dry up.

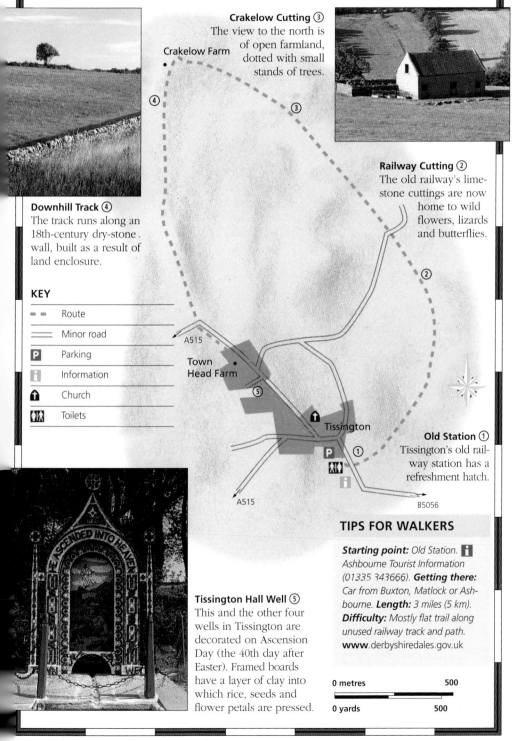

Crakelow Cutting ③
The view to the north is of open farmland, dotted with small stands of trees.

Crakelow Farm

Railway Cutting ②
The old railway's limestone cuttings are now home to wild flowers, lizards and butterflies.

Downhill Track ④
The track runs along an 18th-century dry-stone wall, built as a result of land enclosure.

KEY

– –	Route
═══	Minor road
P	Parking
i	Information
⛪	Church
🚻	Toilets

A515

Town Head Farm

⑤

Tissington

Old Station ①
Tissington's old railway station has a refreshment hatch.

A515

B5056

Tissington Hall Well ⑤
This and the other four wells in Tissington are decorated on Ascension Day (the 40th day after Easter). Framed boards have a layer of clay into which rice, seeds and flower petals are pressed.

TIPS FOR WALKERS

Starting point: Old Station. **i**
Ashbourne Tourist Information (01335 343666). **Getting there:** Car from Buxton, Matlock or Ashbourne. **Length:** 3 miles (5 km). **Difficulty:** Mostly flat trail along unused railway track and path.
www.derbyshiredales.gov.uk

0 metres	500
0 yards	500

Peak District Tour 5

Detail, Buxton Opera House

The Peak District's natural beauty and sheep-grazed crags contrast with the factories of nearby valley towns. Designated Britain's first National Park in 1951, the area has two distinct types of landscape. In the south are the gently rolling hills of the limestone White Peak. To the north, west and east are the wild, heather-clad moorlands of the Dark Peak peat bogs, superimposed on millstone grit.

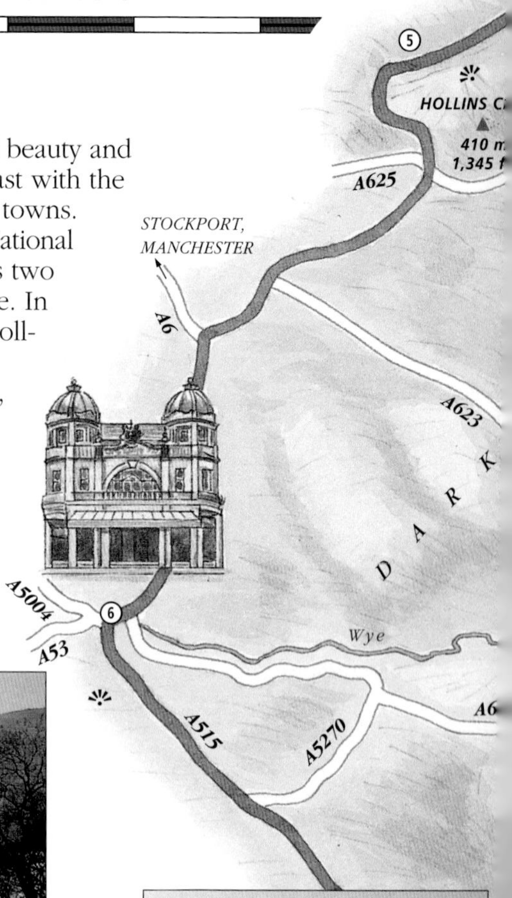

Edale 5
The high plateau of scenic Edale mark the starting point of the 256 mile (412 km) Pennine Way footpath *(see p36)*.

Buxton 6
This lovely spa town's opera house *(see p334)* is known as the "theatre in the hills" because of its magnificent setting.

TIPS FOR DRIVERS

Tour length: 40 miles (60 km).
Stopping-off points: There are refreshments at Crich Tramway Village and Arkwright's Mill in Cromford. Eyam has good old-fashioned tea shops. The Nag's Head in Edale is a charming Tudor inn. Buxton has many pubs and cafés.

Arbor Low 7
This stone circle, known as the "Stonehenge of the North", dates from around 2000 BC and consists of 46 recumbent stones enclosed by a ditch.

KEY

▨▨	Tour route
═══	Other roads
☀	Viewpoint

Dovedale 8
Popular Dovedale is one of the prettiest of the Peak District's river valleys, with its stepping stones, thickly wooded slopes and wind-sculpted rocks. Izaac Walton (1593–1683), author of *The Compleat Angler,* used to fish here.

5

HOLLINS C.
▲
410 m
1,345 f

A625

STOCKPORT, MANCHESTER

A6

A623

D A R K

A5004

6

A53

Wye

A515

A5270

A6

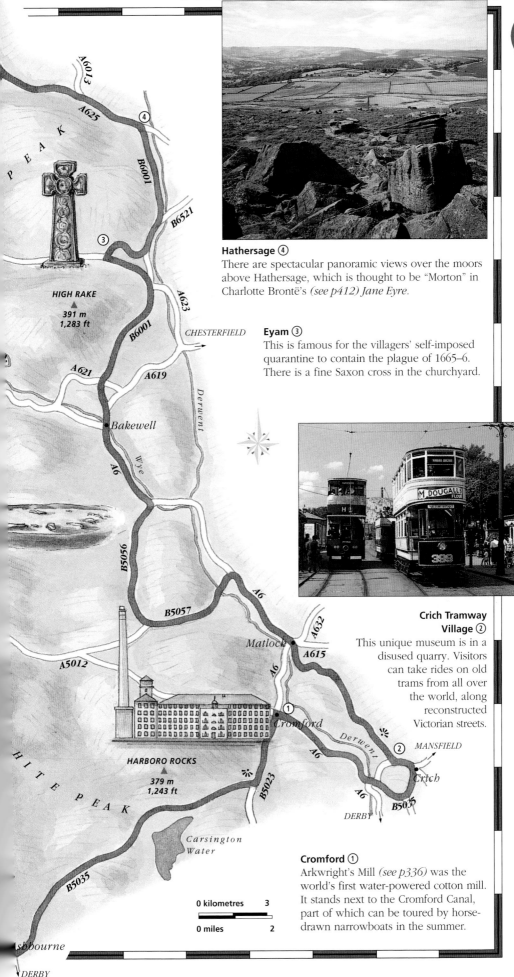

Hathersage ④
There are spectacular panoramic views over the moors above Hathersage, which is thought to be "Morton" in Charlotte Brontë's *(see p412) Jane Eyre.*

Eyam ③
This is famous for the villagers' self-imposed quarantine to contain the plague of 1665–6. There is a fine Saxon cross in the churchyard.

HIGH RAKE
391 m
1,283 ft

CHESTERFIELD

Bakewell

HARBORO ROCKS
379 m
1,243 ft

Matlock

Cromford ①

Crich

MANSFIELD

DERBY

Carsington Water

Crich Tramway Village ②
This unique museum is in a disused quarry. Visitors can take rides on old trams from all over the world, along reconstructed Victorian streets.

Cromford ①
Arkwright's Mill *(see p336)* was the world's first water-powered cotton mill. It stands next to the Cromford Canal, part of which can be toured by horse-drawn narrowboats in the summer.

0 kilometres 3
0 miles 2

shbourne

DERBY

Street-by-Street: Lincoln **❼**

Carving
in Angel
Choir

Surrounded by the flat landscape of the Fens, Lincoln rises dramatically on a cliff above the River Witham, the three towers of its massive cathedral visible from afar. The Romans *(see pp44–5)* founded the first fortress here in AD 50. By the time of the Norman Conquest *(see p47)*, Lincoln was one of the most important cities in England (after London, Winchester and York). The city's wealth was due to its strategic importance for the export of wool from the Lincolnshire Wolds to Europe. Lincoln has managed to retain much of its historic character. Many remarkable medieval buildings have survived, most of which are along the aptly named Steep Hill, leading to the cathedral.

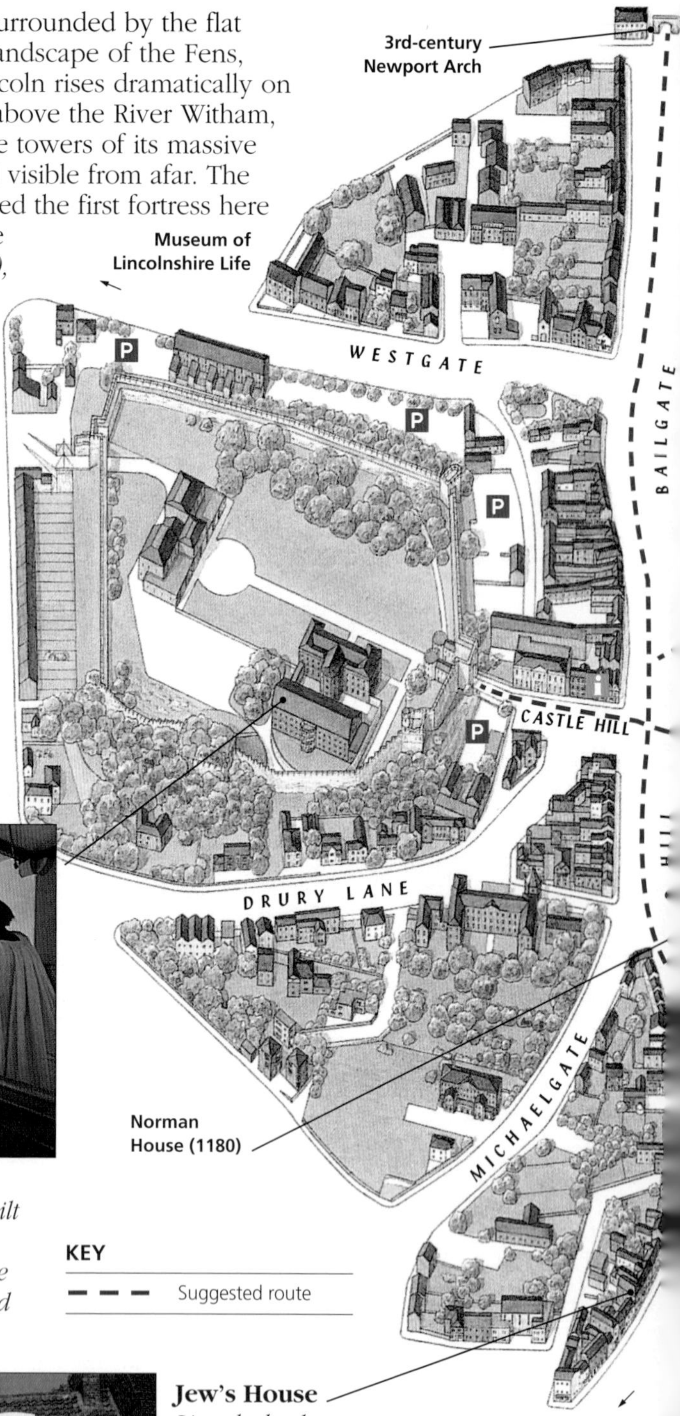

3rd-century
Newport Arch

Museum of
Lincolnshire Life

WESTGATE

BAILGATE

CASTLE HILL

DRURY LANE

MICHAELGATE

Norman
House (1180)

★ Lincoln Castle
The early Norman castle, rebuilt at intervals, acted as the city prison from 1787 to 1878. The chapel's coffin-like pews served to remind felons of their fate.

KEY

– – – –   Suggested route

Jew's House
Lincoln had a large medieval Jewish community. This mid-12th-century stone house, one of the oldest of its kind, was owned by a Jewish merchant.

15th-century Stone-
bow Gate and bus
and railway stations

0 meters	100
0 yards	100

STAR SIGHTS

★ Lincoln Castle

★ Lincoln Cathedral

VISITORS' CHECKLIST

Lincoln. 🚶 90,000. ✈ Humberside, 30 miles (48 km); E Midlands, 51 miles (82 km). 🚉 St Mary St. 🚌 Melville St. ℹ Castle Hill (01522 873800). **www**.lincoln.gov.uk

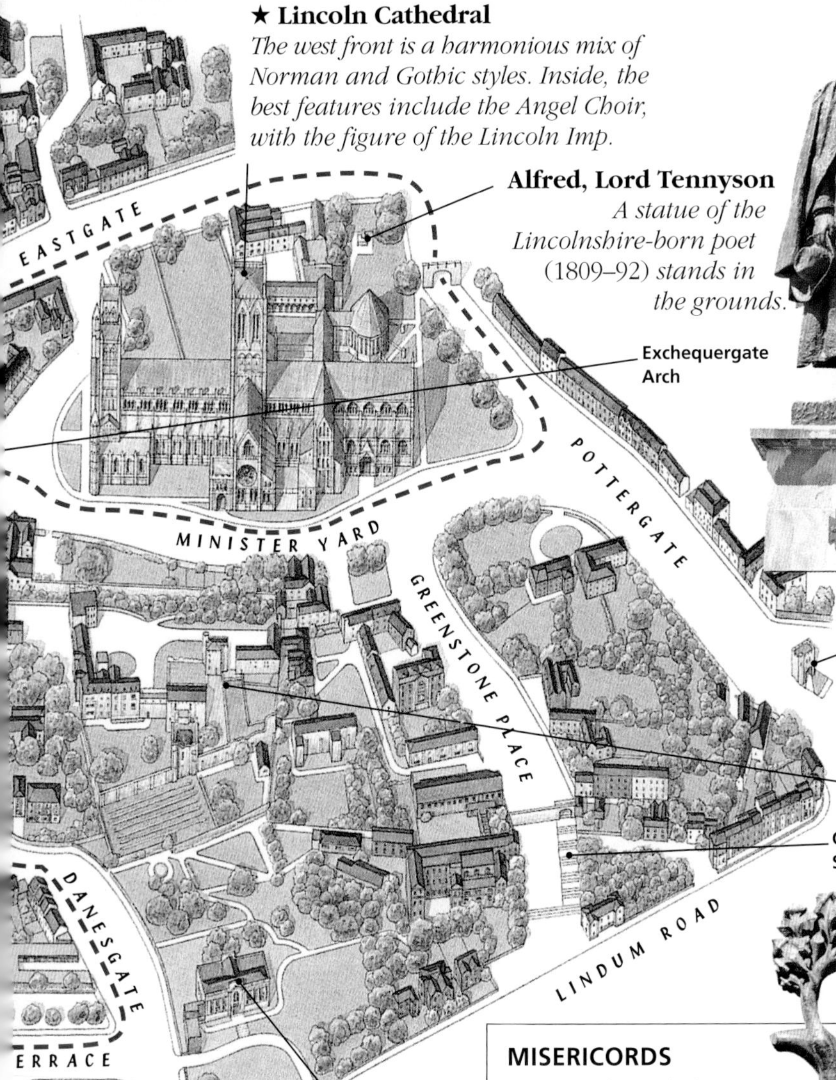

★ Lincoln Cathedral

The west front is a harmonious mix of Norman and Gothic styles. Inside, the best features include the Angel Choir, with the figure of the Lincoln Imp.

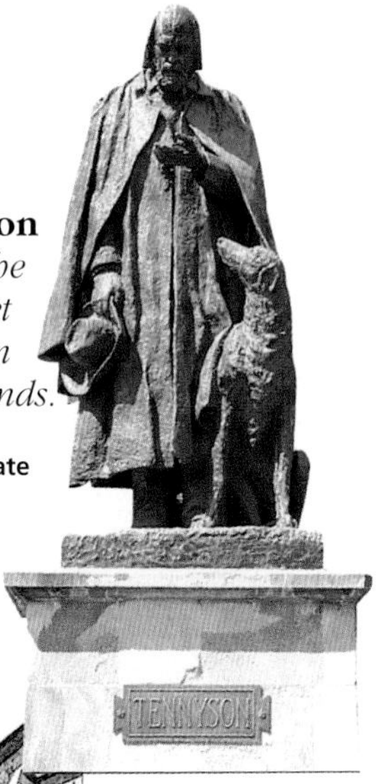

Alfred, Lord Tennyson

A statue of the Lincolnshire-born poet (1809–92) stands in the grounds.

TENNYSON

Exchequergate Arch

The 14th-century Pottergate Arch

Victorian Arboretum

Ruins of Medieval Bishop's Palace

Greenstone Stairs

St Francis of Assisi

MISERICORDS

Misericords are ledges that project from the underside of the hinged seat of a choir stall, which provide support while standing. Lincoln Cathedral's misericords in the early Perpendicular-style canopied choir stalls are some of the best in England. The wide variety of subjects includes parables, fables, myths, biblical scenes and irreverent images from daily life.

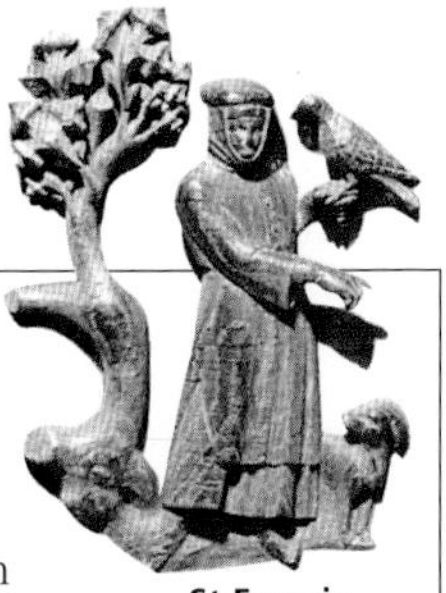

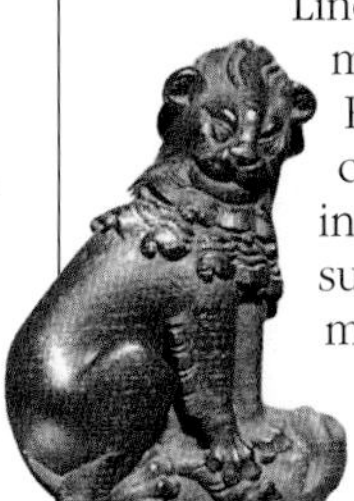

One of a pair of lions

Usher Art Gallery

This is packed with clocks, ceramics, and silver. There are paintings by Peter de Wint (1784–1849) and J M W Turner (see p91).

Burghley House 8

Portrait of Sir Isaac Newton, Billiard Room

William Cecil, 1st Lord Burghley (1520–98) was Queen Elizabeth I's adviser and confidant for 40 years and built the wonderfully dramatic Burghley House in 1555–87. The roof line bristles with stone pyramids, chimneys disguised as Classical columns and towers shaped like pepper pots. The busy skyline resolves itself into a symmetrical pattern when viewed from the west, where a lime tree stands, one of many planted by Capability Brown (see p26) when the surrounding deer park was landscaped in 1760. The interior walls are lavishly decorated with Italian paintings of Greek gods enacting their dramas. An Elizabethan "Garden of Surprises" and an education and visitor centre opened in 2007.

★ Old Kitchen
Gleaming copper pans hang from the walls of the fan-vaulted kitchen, little altered since the Tudor period.

North Gate
Intricate examples of 19th-century wrought-iron work adorn the principal entrances.

The Billiard Room
has many fine portraits inset in oak panelling.

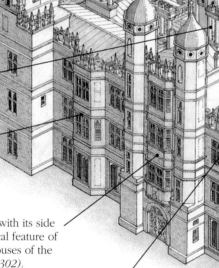

Cupolas were very fashionable details, inspired by European Renaissance architecture.

A chimney has been disguised as a Classical column.

Mullioned windows were added in 1683 when glass became less expensive.

The Gatehouse, with its side turrets, is a typical feature of the "prodigy" houses of the Tudor era (see p302).

West Front
Featuring the Burghley crest, the West Front was finished in 1577 and formed the original main entrance.

STAR SIGHTS

★ Old Kitchen

★ Heaven Room

★ Hell Staircase

VISITORS' CHECKLIST

Off A1 SE of Stamford, Lincs. **Tel**
01780 752451. ⇄ *Stamford.*
○ *Apr–Oct: 11am–5pm daily.*
● *4 days Sep (horse trials).*
& ⓘ ⓘ www.burghley.co.uk

★ **Heaven Room**
*Gods tumble from the sky,
and satyrs and nymphs play
on the walls and ceiling in
this masterpiece by Antonio
Verrio (1639–1707).*

**Obelisk and
clock (1585)**

The Great Hall has
a double hammer-
beam roof and was
a banqueting hall in
Elizabethan days.

The wine cooler
(1710) is thought
to be the largest
in existence.

**The Fourth George
Room,** one of a suite,
is panelled in oak
stained with ale.

★ **Hell Staircase**
*Verrio painted the
ceiling to show Hell
as the mouth of a
cat crammed with
tormented sinners.
The staircase, of
local stone, was
installed in 1786.*

Stamford ❾

Lincolnshire. 👥 *18,000.* ⇄ 🚌 ⓘ
27 St Mary's St (01780 755611). 🛒
Fri. **www**.southkesteven.gov.uk

Stamford is a showpiece town,
famous for its churches and
Georgian townhouses. The
town retains a medieval street
plan, with a warren of winding
streets and cobbled alleys.

The spires of the medieval
churches (five survive of the
original eleven) give Stamford
the air of a miniature Oxford.

Barn Hill, leading up from
All Saints Church, is the best
place for a view of Stamford's
Georgian architecture in all
its variety. Below it is Broad
Street, where the **Stamford
Museum** covers the history of
the town. Exhibits include a
model of Britain's fattest man,
Daniel Lambert, who was 336
kg (53 stone) and died while
attending Stamford Races in
1809, and the 6-m- (20-ft-)
long Stamford Tapestry.

🏛 Stamford Museum
Broad St. **Tel** 01780 766317. ○
*Apr–Sep: daily (Sun: pm); Oct–Mar:
Mon–Sat.* & ⓘ www.lincoln
shire.gov.uk/stamfordmuseum

Northampton ❿

Northamptonshire. 👥 *187,000.* ⇄
🚌 ⓘ *Sessions House, George Row
(01604 838800).* 🛒 *Mon–Sat (Thu:
antiques).* **www**.northampton.gov.uk

This market town was once a
centre for shoe-making, and
the **Central Museum and Art
Gallery** holds the world's
largest collection of footwear.
One of many fine old buildings is the Victorian Gothic
Guildhall. Six miles west of
the town is **Althorp House**,
family home of Diana Princess
of Wales. Visitors can tour
the house, grounds, see
an exhibition on Diana and
her island resting place.

**🏛 Central Museum and Art
Gallery**
Guildhall Rd. **Tel** 01604 838111. ○
daily (Sun: pm). ● *25, 26 Dec.* & ⓘ
🏛 Althorp House
Great Brington (off A428). **Tel** 01604
770107. ○ *Jul & Aug.* ● *31 Aug.*
📷 ▢ & ⓘ www.althorp.com

THE NORTH COUNTRY

The North Country at a Glance

Rugged coastlines, spectacular walks and climbs, magnificent stately homes and breathtaking cathedrals all have their place in the north of England, with its dramatic history of Roman rule, Saxon invasion, Viking attacks and border skirmishes. Reminders of the industrial revolution are found in towns such as Halifax, Liverpool and Manchester, and peace and inspiration in the dramatic scenery of the Lake District, with its awe-inspiring mountains and waters.

Hadrian's Wall (see pp422–3), *built around 120 to protect Roman Britain from the Picts to the north, cuts through rugged Northumberland National Park scenery.*

NORTHUMBRI
(see pp414–42

Northumberla

Durha

The Lake District (see pp354–69) *is a combination of superb peaks, tumbling rivers and falls and shimmering lakes such as Wast Water.*

Cumbria

Yorkshire Dales National Park (see pp384–86) *creates a delightful environment for walking and touring the farming landscape, scattered with attractive villages such as Thwaite, in Swaledale.*

Lancashire

LANCASHIRE
AND THE LAKES
(see pp354–379)

Manchester

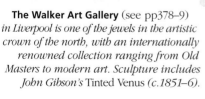

The Walker Art Gallery (see pp378–9) *in Liverpool is one of the jewels in the artistic crown of the north, with an internationally renowned collection ranging from Old Masters to modern art. Sculpture includes John Gibson's* Tinted Venus *(c.1851–6).*

Liverpool

◁ **The 11th-century Alnwick Castle, Alnwick, Northumberland, from across the River Aln**

Durham Cathedral (see pp428–9), *a striking Norman structure with an innovative southern choir aisle and fine stained glass, has towered over the city of Durham since 995.*

Fountains Abbey (see pp390–91), *one of the finest religious buildings in the north, was founded in the 12th century by monks who desired simplicity and austerity. Later the abbey became extremely wealthy.*

Castle Howard (see pp398–9), *a triumph of Baroque architecture, offers many magnificent settings, including this Museum Room (1805–10), designed by CH Tatham.*

Cleveland

North Yorkshire

ORKSHIRE
AND THE
HUMBER
REGION
pp380–413)

East Riding of Yorkshire

Leeds

York (see pp404–409) *is a city of historical treasures, ranging from the medieval to Georgian. Its magnificent minster has a large collection of stained glass and the medieval city walls are well preserved. Other sights include churches, narrow alleyways and notable museums.*

0 kilometres   25

0 miles   25

The Industrial Revolution in the North

The face of Northern England in the 19th century was dramatically altered by the development of the coal mining, textile and shipbuilding industries. Lancashire, Northumberland and the West Riding (*see p381*) of Yorkshire all experienced population growth and migration to cities. The hardships of urban life were partly relieved by the actions of several wealthy industrial philanthropists, but many people lived in extremely deprived conditions. Although most traditional industries have now declined sharply or disappeared as demand has moved elsewhere, a growing tourist industry has developed in many of the former industrial centres.

Back-to-backs *or colliers' rows, such as these houses at Easington, were provided by colliery owners from the 1800s onwards. They comprised two small rooms for cooking and sleeping, and an outside toilet.*

Coal mining *was a family industry in the North of England with women and children working alongside the men.*

1815 Sir Humphrey Davy invented a safety oil lamp for miners. Light shone through a cylindrical gauze sheet which prevented the heat of the flame igniting methane gas in the mine. Thousands of miners benefited from this device.

1750	1800
PRE-STEAM	STEAM AGE
1750	1800

1781 Leeds-Liverpool Canal opened. The building of canals facilitated the movement of raw materials and finished products, and aided the process of mechanization immeasurably.

1830 Liverp
and Manchester railw opened, connecting two the biggest cities outs London. Within a month railway carried 1, passeng

Halifax's Piece Hall (see p413), *restored in 1976, is the most impressive surviving example of industrial architecture in northern England. It is the only complete 18th-century cloth market building in Yorkshire. Merchants sold measures of cloth known as "pieces" from rooms lining the cloisters inside.*

Hebden Bridge (see p412), *a typical West Riding textile mill town jammed into the narrow Calder Valley, typifies a pattern of workers' houses surrounding a central mill. The town benefited from its position when the Rochdale Canal (1804) and then the railway (1841) took advantage of this relatively low-level route over the Pennines.*

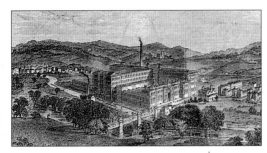

Saltaire (see p411) *was a model village built by the wealthy cloth merchant and mill-owner Sir Titus Salt (1803–76), for the benefit of his workers. Seen here in the 1870s, it included houses and facilities such as shops, gardens and sportsfields, with almshouses, a hospital, school and chapel. A disciplinarian, Salt banned alcohol and pubs from Saltaire.*

George Hudson *(1800–71) built the first railway station in York (see p408) in 1840–42. In the 1840s he owned more than a quarter of the railways in Britain and was known as the "railway king".*

1842 Coal Mines Act prevented women and children from working in harsh conditions in the mines.

Port Sunlight (see p379) *was founded by William Hesketh Lever (1851–1925) to provide housing for workers at his Sunlight soap factory. Between 1889 and 1914 he built 800 cottages. Amenities included a pool.*

Strikes to improve working conditions were common. Violence flared in July 1893 when colliery owners locked miners out of their pits and stopped their pay after the Miners' Federation resisted a 25 per cent wage cut. Over 300,000 men struggled without pay until November, when work resumed at the old rate.

SUNLIGHT SOAP

FOR REST & LEISURE

1850		1900
FULL MECHANIZATION		
1850		1900

Power loom weaving *transformed the textile industry while creating unemployment among skilled hand loom weavers. By the 1850s, the West Riding had 30,000 power looms, used in cotton and woollen mills. Of 79,000 workers, over half were to be found in Bradford alone.*

Furness dry dock *was built in the 1890s when the shipbuilding industry moved north, in search of cheap labour and materials. Barrow-in-Furness, Glasgow (see pp516–19) and Tyne and Wear (see p424) were the new centres.*

Joseph Rowntree *(1836–1925) founded his chocolate factory in York in 1892, having formerly worked with George Cadbury. As Quakers, the Rowntrees believed in the social welfare of their workers (establishing a model village in 1904), and, with Terry's confectionary (1767), they made a vast contribution to York's prosperity. Today, Nestlé Rowntree is the world's largest chocolate factory and York is Britain's chocolate capital.*

North Country Abbeys

Northern England has some of the finest and best preserved religious houses in Europe. Centres of prayer, learning and power in the Middle Ages, the larger of these were designated abbeys and were governed by an abbot. Most were located in rural areas, considered appropriate for a spiritual and contemplative life. Viking raiders had destroyed many Anglo-Saxon religious houses in the 8th and 9th centuries *(see pp46–7)* and it was not until William the Conqueror founded the Benedictine Selby Abbey in 1069 that monastic life revived in the north. New orders, Augustinians in particular, arrived from the Continent and by 1500 Yorkshire had 83 monasteries.

Cistercian monk

Ruins of St Mary's Abbey today

The Liberty of St Mary was the name given to the land around the abbey, almost a city within a city. Here, the abbot had his own market, fair, prison and gallows – all exempt from the city authorities.

ST MARY'S ABBEY

Founded in York in 1086, this Benedictine abbey was one of the wealthiest in Britain. Its involvement in the wool trade in York and the granting of royal and papal privileges and land led to a relaxing of standards by the early 12th century. The abbot was even allowed to dress in the same style as a bishop, and was raised by the pope to the status of a "mitred abbot". As a result, 13 monks left in 1132, to found Fountains Abbey *(see pp390–91)*.

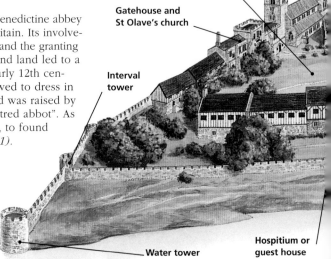
Gatehouse and St Olave's church
Interval tower
Water tower
Hospitium or guest house

MONASTERIES AND LOCAL LIFE

As one of the wealthiest landowning sections of society, the monasteries played a vital role in the local economy. They provided employment, particularly in agriculture, and dominated the wool trade, England's largest export during the Middle Ages. By 1387 two thirds of all wool exported from England passed through St Mary's Abbey, the largest wool trader in York.

Cistercian monks tilling their land

WHERE TO SEE ABBEYS TODAY

Fountains Abbey *(see pp390–91)*, founded by Benedictine monks and later taken over by Cistercians, is the most famous of the numerous abbeys in the region. Rievaulx *(see p393)*, Byland *(see p392)* and Furness *(see p368)* were all founded by the Cistercians, and Furness became the second wealthiest Cistercian house in England after Fountains. Whitby Abbey *(see p396)*, sacked by the Vikings, was later rebuilt by the Benedictine order. Northumberland is famous for its early Anglo-Saxon monasteries, such as Ripon, Lastingham and Lindisfarne *(see pp418–19)*.

Mount Grace Priory (see p394) *founded in 1398, is the best-preserved Carthusian house in England. The former individual gardens and cells of each monk are still clearly visible.*

THE DISSOLUTION OF THE MONASTERIES (1536–40)

By the early 16th century, the monasteries owned one-sixth of all English land and their annual income was four times that of the Crown. Henry VIII ordered the closure of all religious houses in 1536, acquiring their wealth in the process. His attempt at dissolution provoked a large uprising of Catholic northerners led by Robert Aske later that year. The rebellion failed and Aske and others were executed for conspiracy. The dissolution continued under Thomas Cromwell, who became known as "the hammer of the monks".

Thomas Cromwell (c.1485–1549)

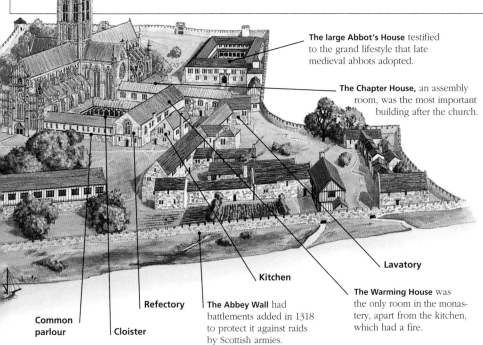

The large Abbot's House testified to the grand lifestyle that late medieval abbots adopted.

The Chapter House, an assembly room, was the most important building after the church.

Lavatory

Kitchen

The Warming House was the only room in the monastery, apart from the kitchen, which had a fire.

Refectory

The Abbey Wall had battlements added in 1318 to protect it against raids by Scottish armies.

Common parlour

Cloister

Kirkham Priory, *an Augustinian foundation of the 1120s, enjoys a tranquil setting on the banks of the River Derwent, near Malton. The finest feature of the ruined site is the 13th-century gatehouse which leads into the priory complex.*

Kirkstall Abbey *was founded in 1152 by monks from Fountains Abbey. The well-preserved ruins of this Cistercian house near Leeds include the church, the late Norman chapter house and the abbot's lodging. This evening view was painted by Thomas Girtin (1775–1802).*

…sby Abbey *lies beside the River …wale, outside the pretty market town of Richmond. Among the …ains of this Premonstratensian …ouse, founded in 1155, are the …-century refectory and sleeping …ers and 14th-century gatehouse.*

The Geology of the Lake District

Piece of Lake District slate

The Lake District contains some of England's most spectacular scenery. Concentrated in just 900 sq miles (231 sq km) are the highest peaks, deepest valleys and longest lakes in the country. Today's landscape has changed little since the end of the Ice Age 10,000 years ago, the last major event in Britain's geological history. But the glaciated hills which were revealed by the retreating ice were once part of a vast mountain-chain whose remains can also be found in North America. The mountains were first raised by the gradual fusion of two ancient landmasses which, for millions of years, formed a single continent. Eventually the continent broke into two, forming Europe and America, separated by the widening Atlantic Ocean.

Honister Pass, *with its distinctive U-shape, is an example of a glaciated valley, once completely filled with ice.*

GEOLOGICAL HISTORY

The oldest rock formed as sediment under an ocean called Iapetus. Some 450 million years ago, Earth's internal movements made two continents collide, and the ocean disappear.

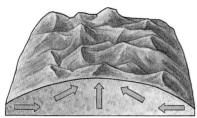

1 **The collision** *buckled the former sea bed into a mountain range. Magma rose from Earth's mantle, altered the sediments and cooled into volcanic rock.*

2 **In the Ice Age,** *glaciers slowly excavated huge rock basins in the mountainsides, dragging debris to the valley floor. Frost sculpted the summits.*

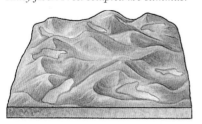

3 **The glaciers retreated** *10,000 years ago, their meltwaters forming lakes in valleys dammed by debris. As the climate improved, plants colonized the fells.*

RADIATING LAKES

The diversity of lakeland scenery owes much to its geology: hard volcanic rocks in the central lakes give rise to rugged hills, while soft slates to the north produce a more rounded topography. The lakes form a radial pattern, spreading out from a central volcanic rock zone.

Scafell Pike is the highest peak in England. One of the three Scafell Pikes, its two neighbours are Broad Crag and Ill Crag.

Great Gable

▲ *Old Man of Coniston*

Coniston Water

Wast Water *is the deepest of the lakes. Its southeastern cliffs are streaked with granite scree – the debris formed each year as rock shattered by the winter frost tumbles down during the spring thaw.*

MAN ON THE MOUNTAIN

The sheltered valley floors with their benign climate and fertile soils are ideal for settlement. Farmhouses, dry-stone walls, pasture and sheep pens are an integral part of the landscape. Higher up, the absence of trees and bracken are the result of wind and a cooler climate. Old mine workings and tracks are the relics of once-flourishing industries.

Plantations *of coniferous trees are a recent feature of the landscape. Some see them as harming traditional views and disturbing the ecology.*

Summer grazing

Copper and graphite mines

Tracks

Dry-stone walls *(see p305)*

Slate *and other local stone has long been incorporated into buildings: slate roofs, stone walls, lintels and bridges.*

Hedges

400–500m (130–170ft)

300–400m (100–130 ft)

Sheep pens for winter grazing

waite

▲ *Blencathra*

nt Water

▲ *Helvellyn*

Ullswater

▲ *Place Fell*

High Street

Windermere

Skiddaw *is composed of slate, formed when the muddy sediment of the ancient ocean floor was altered by extreme pressure.*

Striding Edge *is a long, twisting ridge which leads to the summit of Helvellyn. It was sharpened by the widening of the valleys on either side caused by the build up of glaciers.*

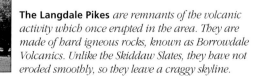

The Langdale Pikes *are remnants of the volcanic activity which once erupted in the area. They are made of hard igneous rocks, known as Borrowdale Volcanics. Unlike the Skiddaw Slates, they have not eroded smoothly, so they leave a craggy skyline.*

LANCASHIRE AND THE LAKES

CUMBRIA · LANCASHIRE

*T*he landscape painter John Constable (1776–1837) declared that the Lake District, now visited by 18 million people annually, had "the finest scenery that ever was". The Normans built many religious houses here, and William II created estates for English barons. Today, the National Trust is its most important landowner.

Within the 30 mile (45 km) radius of the Lake District lies an astonishing number of fells and lakes. Today, all looks peaceful, but from the Roman occupation to the Middle Ages, the northwest was a turbulent area, as successive kings and rulers fought over the territory. Historians can revel in the various Celtic monuments, Roman remains, stately homes and monastic ruins. Although the scenery is paramount, there are many outdoor activities as well as spectator sports, such as Cumbrian wrestling, and wildlife to observe.

Lancashire's portfolio of tourist attractions includes the fine county town of Lancaster, bright Blackpool with its autumn illuminations and fairground attractions, and the peaceful seaside beaches to the south. Inland, the most appealing regions are the Forest of Bowland, a sparse expanse of heathery grouse moor, and the picturesque Ribble Valley. Further south still are the industrial conurbations of Manchester and Merseyside, where the attractions are more urban.

There are many fine Victorian buildings in Manchester, where the industrial quarter of Castlefield has been revitalized. Liverpool, with its restored Albert Dock, is best known as the seaport city of the Beatles. It has a lively club scene and is increasingly used as a film location. Both cities have good art galleries and museums.

Jetty at Grasmere, one of the most popular regions of the Lake District

◁ Restored Albert Dock, lining the River Mersey in Liverpool

Exploring Lancashire and the Lakes

The Lake District's natural scenery outweighs any of its man-made attractions. Its natural features are the result of geological upheavals over millennia *(see pp352–3),* and four of its peaks are more than 1,000 m (3,300 ft). Human influences have left their mark too: the main activities are quarrying, mining, farming and tourism.

The Lakes are most crowded in summer when activities include lake trips and hill-walking. The best bases are Keswick and Ambleside, while there are also good hotels on the shores of Windermere and Ullswater and in the Cartmel area.

Lancashire's Bowland Forest is an attractive place to explore on foot, with picturesque villages. Further south, Manchester and Liverpool have excellent museums and galleries.

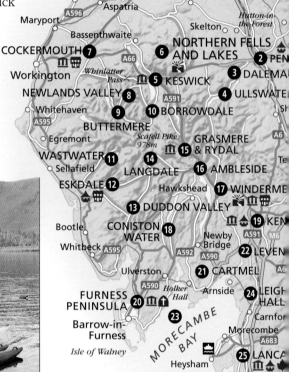

Watersports on Derwentwater in the Northern Fells and Lakes area

GETTING AROUND

For many, the first glimpse of the Lake District is from the M6 near Shap Fell, but the A6 is a more dramatic route. You can reach Windermere by train, but you need to change at Oxenholme, on the mainline route from Euston to Carlisle. Penrith also has rail services and bus links into the Lakes. L'al Ratty, the miniature railway up Eskdale, and the Lakeside & Haverthwaite railway, which connects with the steamers on Windermere,

make for enjoyable outings. Regular buses link all the main centres where excursions are organized. One of the most enterprising is the Mountain Goat minibus, in Windermere and Keswick.

Lancaster, Liverpool and Manchester are on the main rail and bus routes and also have airports. For Blackpool, you need to change trains in Preston. Wherever you go in the area, one of the best means of getting around is on foot.

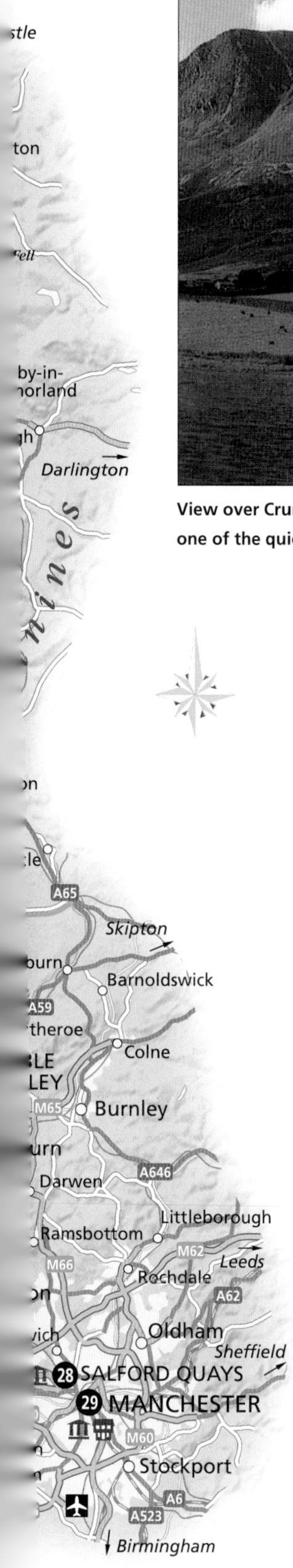

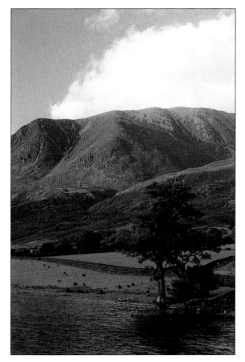

View over Crummock Water, north of Buttermere, one of the quieter Western Lakes

KEY

- Motorway
- Major road
- Secondary road
- Minor road
- Scenic route
- Main railway
- Minor railway
- △ Summit

0 kilometres 20

0 miles 10

SIGHTS AT A GLANCE

Ambleside 16
Blackpool 27
Borrowdale 10
Buttermere 9
Carlisle 1
Cartmel 21
Cockermouth 7
Coniston Water 18
Dalemain 3
Duddon Valley 13
Eskdale 12
Furness Peninsula 20
Grasmere and Rydal 15
Kendal 19
Keswick 5
Lancaster 25
Langdale 14
Leighton Hall 24
Levens Hall 22
Liverpool pp376–9 30
Manchester pp372–5 29
Morecambe Bay 23
Newlands Valley 8
Northern Fells and Lakes pp360–61 6
Penrith 2
Ribble Valley 26
Salford Quays 28
Ullswater 4
Wastwater 11
Windermere 17

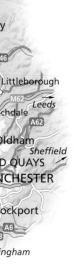

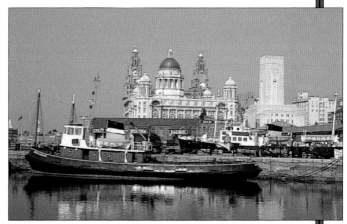

Preserved docks and Liver Building, Liverpool

Carlisle ❶

Cumbria. 👥 *102,000.* ✈ *mainly private.* 🚆 🚌 ℹ *The Old Town Hall, Green Market (01228 625600).* www.historic-carlisle.org.uk

Due to its proximity to the Scottish border, this city has long been a defensive site. Known as Luguvalium by the Romans, it was an outpost of Hadrian's Wall *(see pp422–3)*. Carlisle was sacked and pillaged repeatedly by the Danes, the Normans and border raiders, and suffered damage as a Royalist stronghold under Cromwell *(see p52)*.

Today, Carlisle is the capital of Cumbria. In its centre are the timber-framed Guildhall and market cross, and forti-fications still exist around its West Walls, drum-towered gates and its Norman **castle**. The castle tower has a small museum devoted to the King's Own Border Regi-ment. The cathedral dates from 1122 and features a decorative east window. Carlisle's **Tullie House Museum** recreates the city's past with sections on Roman history and Cumbrian wildlife. Nearby lie the evocative ruins of

Saxon iron sword in the Tullie House Museum

Façade of Hutton-in-the-Forest with medieval tower on the right

Lanercost Priory (c.1166) and the remains of the unique **Birdoswald Roman Fort**.

⛪ **Carlisle Castle**
(EH) Castle Way. *Tel 01228 591922.* ⬜ *daily.* ⬤ *24–26 Dec, 1 Jan.* 📷 ♿ *limited.* 📷 📷

🏛 **Tullie House Museum**
Castle St. *Tel 01228 618718.* ⬜ *daily (Sun: pm).* 📷 ♿ 📷 🍴

⛪ **Lanercost Priory**
(EH) Nr Brampton. *Tel 016977 3030.* ⬜ *Mar–Sep: daily, Oct: Thu–Mon; Nov & Dec: Sat & Sun.* 📷 📷 ♿ *limited.*

⛪ **Birdoswald Roman Fort**
(EH) Gilsland, Brampton. *Tel 016977 47602.* ⬜ *Mar–Oct: daily.* 📷 ♿ *limited.* 📷 📷

Penrith ❷

Cumbria. 👥 *15,000.* ℹ *Robinson's School, Middlegate (017688 67466).* 🚌 *Tue, Sat, Sun.* www.visiteden.co.uk

Timewarp shopfronts on the market square and a 14th-century **castle** of sandstone are Penrith's main attractions.

There are some strange hog-back stones in St Andrew's churchyard, allegedly a giant's grave, and the 285 m (937 ft) Beacon provides stunning views of distant fells.

Environs: Just northeast of Penrith at Little Salkeld is a famous Bronze Age circle (with 66 tall stones) known as **Long Meg and her Daughters**. Six miles (9 km) northwest of Penrith lies **Hutton-in-the-Forest**. The oldest part of this house is the 13th-century tower. Inside is a magnificent Italianate staircase, a sumptuously panelled 17th-century Long Gallery, a delicately stuccoed Cupid Room dating from the 1740s, and several Victorian rooms. Outside, you can walk around the walled garden and topiary terraces, or explore the woods.

⛪ **Penrith Castle**
(EH) Ullswater Rd. ⬜ *daily.* ♿ *in grounds.*

🏰 **Hutton-in-the-Forest**
Off B5305. *Tel 017684 84449.* **House** ⬜ *Easter–Sep: Wed, Thu, Sun & pub hols (pm).* **Grounds** ⬜ *Apr–Oct: Sun–Fri.* 📷 ♿ *ltd.* 📷 📷

Dalemain ❸

Penrith, Cumbria. *Tel 017684 86450.* 🚆 🚌 *Penrith then taxi.* ⬜ *Apr–Oct: Sun–Thu.* 📷 ♿ *limited.* 📷 📷 📷 www.dalemain.com

A seemly Georgian façade gives this fine house near Ullswater the impression of architectural unity, but hides a much-altered medieval and Elizabethan structure with a maze of rambling passages. Public rooms include a superb Chinese drawing room with

---

TRADITIONAL CUMBRIAN SPORTS

Cumberland wrestling is one of the most interesting sports to watch in the summer months. The combatants, often clad in longjohns and embroidered velvet pants, clasp one another in an armlock and attempt to topple each other over. Technique and good balance outweigh physical force. Other traditional Lakeland sports include fell-racing, a gruelling test of speed and stamina up and down local peaks at ankle-breaking speed. Hound-trailing is also a popular sport in which specially bred hounds follow an aniseed trail over the hills. Sheep-dog trials, steam fairs, flower shows and gym-khanas take place in summer. The Egremont Crab Fair in September holds events such as greasy-pole climbing.

Cumberland wrestlers

Sheep resting at Glenridding, on the southwest shore of Ullswater

hand-painted wallpaper, and a panelled 18th-century drawing room. Several small museums occupy various outbuildings, and the gardens contain a fine collection of fragrant shrub roses and a huge silver fir.

Sumptuous Chinese drawing room at Dalemain

Ullswater ❹

Cumbria. 🚆 *Penrith*. 🛈 *Main car park, Glenridding, Penrith (017684 82414)*. **www**.lake-district.gov.uk

Often considered the most beautiful of all Cumbria's lakes, Ullswater stretches from gentle farmland near Penrith to dramatic hills and crags at its southern end. The main western shore road can be very busy. In summer, two restored Victorian steamers ply

regularly from Pooley Bridge to Glenridding. One of the best walks crosses the eastern shore from Glenridding to Hallin Fell and the moorland of Martindale. The western side passes Gowbarrow, where Wordsworth's immortalized "host of golden daffodils" bloom in spring (*see p366*).

Keswick ❺

Cumbria. 🏠 *5,000.* 🛈 *Moot Hall, Market Sq (017687 72645)*. **www**.keswick.org

Popular as a tourist venue since the advent of the railway in Victorian times, Keswick now has guest houses, a summer repertory theatre, outdoor equipment shops and a serious parking problem in high season. Its most striking central building is the **Moot Hall**, dating from 1813, now used as the tourist office. The town prospered on wool and leather until, in Tudor times, deposits of graphite were discovered. Mining then took over as the main industry and Keswick became an important centre for pencil manufacture. In World War II, hollow pencils were made to hide espionage maps on thin paper. The factory includes the **Pencil Museum** with interesting

audiovisual shows. Among the many fine exhibits at the **Keswick Museum and Art Gallery** are the original manuscripts of Lakeland writers, musical stones and many other curiosities.

To the east of the town lies the ancient stone circle of Castlerigg, thought to be older than Stonehenge.

🏛 **Pencil Museum**
Carding Mill Lane. **Tel** *017687 73626.* ◯ *daily.* ● *1 Jan, 25, 26 Dec.* 📷 ♿ 🛈 www.pencilmuseum.co.uk

🏛 **Keswick Museum and Art Gallery**
Fitz Park, Station Rd. **Tel** *017687 73263.* ◯ *Easter–Oct: Tue–Sat & public hols.* ♿ 🛈

Outdoor equipment shop in Keswick

Northern Fells and Lakes ❻

The rare red squirrel, native to the area

Many visitors praise this northern area of the Lake District National Park for its scenery and geological interest (*see pp352–3*). It is ideal walking country, and nearby Derwentwater, Thirlmere and Bassenthwaite provide endless scenic views, rambles and opportunities for watersports. Large areas surrounding the regional centre of Keswick (*see p359*) are accessible only on foot, particularly the huge mass of hills known as Back of Skiddaw – located between Skiddaw and Caldbeck – or the Helvellyn range, east of Thirlmere.

The Whinlatter Pass is an easy route from Keswick to the farmland of Lorton Vale. It gives a good view of Bassenthwaite Lake and a glimpse of Grisedale Pike.

Bassenthwaite is best viewed from the east shore; however accessibility is limited. Parking is easier from the west side.

Lorton Vale

The lush, green farmland south of Cockermouth creates a marked contrast with the more rugged mountain landscapes of the central Lake District. In the village of Low Lorton is the private manor house of Lorton Hall, dating from the 15th century.

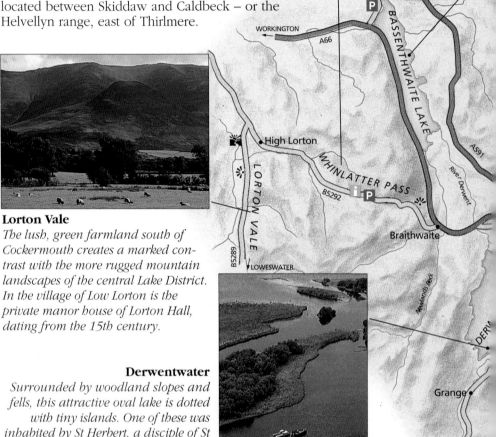

Derwentwater

Surrounded by woodland slopes and fells, this attractive oval lake is dotted with tiny islands. One of these was inhabited by St Herbert, a disciple of St Cuthbert (see p419), who lived there as a hermit until 687. A boat from Keswick provides a lake excursion.

THE MAJOR PEAKS

The Lake District hills are the highest in England. Although they seem small by Alpine or world standards, the scale of the surrounding terrain makes them look extremely grand. Some of the most important peaks are shown on the following pages. Each peak is regarded as having its own personality. This section shows the Skiddaw fells, which are north of Keswick.

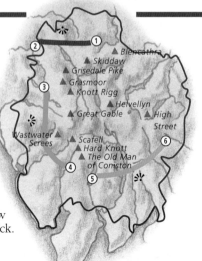

KEY

— From ① Blencathra to ② Cockermouth (*see opposite*)

— From ③ Grisedale Pike to ④ the Old Man of Coniston (*see pp362–3*)

— From ⑤ the Old Man of Coniston to ⑥ Windermere and Tarn Crag (*see pp364–5*)

— National Park boundary

VISITORS' CHECKLIST

Keswick, Cumbria. 🚌 *Keswick.* ℹ️
Mkt Sq, Keswick (017687 72645).
(NT) Castlerigg Stone Circle
⭕ *daily.* **www**.keswick.org

Skiddaw

At 931 m (3,054 ft) Skiddaw is England's fourth highest peak. Its rounded shape makes it a four- to five-hour walk for anyone reasonably fit and suitably equipped.

Blencathra, also known as Saddleback because of its twin peaks (868 m; 2,847 ft), is a challenging climb, especially in winter.

St John's in the Vale

This valley contains Castle Rock for climbers, and its old legends were used by Sir Walter Scott (see p512) in The Bridal of Triermain. *Lakeland poet John Richardson is buried in the churchyard.*

KEY

ℹ️	Information
▬	Major road
▭	Minor road
☀️	Viewpoint

Thirlmere was created as a reservoir to serve Manchester in 1879.

Castlerigg Stone Circle

Described by Keats (see p123) as "a dismal cirque of Druid stones upon a forlorn moor", these ancient stones overlook Skiddaw, Helvellyn and Crag Hill.

0 kilometres	5
0 miles	3

Crummock Water, one of the quieter "western lakes"

Cockermouth ➐

Cumbria. 🚶 8,000. 🚉
Workington. 🚌 ℹ Town Hall,
Market St (01900 822634).
www.western-lakedistrict.co.uk

Colourwashed terraces and restored workers' cottages beside the river are especially attractive in the busy market town of Cockermouth, which dates from the 12th century. The place not to miss is the handsome **Wordsworth House**, in the Main Street, where the poet was born (see p366). This fine Georgian building still contains a few of the family's possessions, and is furnished in the style of the late 18th century. Wordsworth mentions the attractive terraced garden, which overlooks the River Derwent, in his *Prelude*. The local parish church contains a Wordsworth memorial window.

Cockermouth **castle** is partly ruined but still inhabited and closed to the public. The town has small museums of printing, toys and a mineral collection, and an art gallery. The **Jennings Brewery** invites visitors for tours and tastings.

🏛 **Wordsworth House**
(NT) Main St. **Tel** 01900 820884. ⬜
Mar–Oct: Mon–Sat. 📷 non-members.
📷 www.wordsworthhouse.org.uk
🍺 **Jennings Brewery**
Castle Brewery. **Tel** 0845 1297185.
⬜ Mon–Sat (Jul, Aug: daily). 📷
📷 www.jenningsbrewery.co.uk

Newlands Valley ➑

Cumbria. 🚉 Workington then bus. 🚌
Cockermouth. ℹ Town Hall, Market
St, Cockermouth (01900 822634);
Market Sq, Keswick (017687 72645).
www.lake-district.gov.uk

From the gently wooded shores of Derwentwater, the Newlands Valley runs through a scattering of farms towards rugged heights of 335 m (1,100 ft) at the top of the pass, where steps lead to the waterfall, Moss Force. Grisedale Pike, Grasmoor and Knott Rigg all provide excellent fell walks. Local mineral deposits of copper, graphite, lead and even small amounts of gold and silver were extensively mined here from Elizabethan times onwards. **Little Town** was used as a setting by Beatrix Potter (see p367) in *The Tale of Mrs Tiggywinkle*.

Kitchen, with an old range and tiled floor, at Wordsworth House

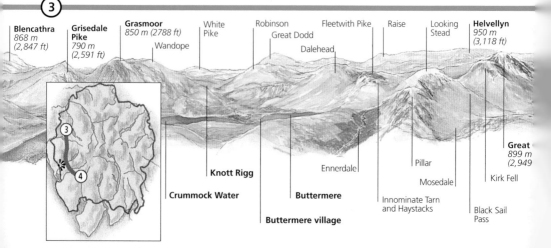

Blencathra
868 m
(2,847 ft)

Grisedale Pike
790 m
(2,591 ft)

Grasmoor
850 m (2788 ft)
Wandope

White Pike

Robinson
Great Dodd
Dalehead

Fleetwith Pike

Raise

Looking Stead

Helvellyn
950 m
(3,118 ft)

Knott Rigg

Crummock Water

Buttermere
Buttermere village

Ennerdale

Innominate Tarn and Haystacks

Pillar
Mosedale

Great
899 m
(2,949

Kirk Fell

Black Sail Pass

③
④

Buttermere **9**

Cumbria. 🚉 *Penrith.* 🚌 *Cocker-mouth.* 🚌 *Penrith to Keswick; Keswick to Buttermere.* ℹ️ *Town Hall, Market St, Cockermouth (01900 822634).*

Interlinking with Crummock Water and Loweswater, Buttermere and its surroundings contain some of the most appealing countryside in the region. Often known as the "western lakes", the three are remote enough not to become too crowded. Buttermere is a jewel amid grand fells: High Stile, Red Pike and Haystacks. Here the ashes of the celebrated hill-walker and author of fell-walking books, A W Wainwright, are scattered.

The village of Buttermere, with its handful of houses and inns, is a popular starting point for walks round all three lakes. Loweswater is hardest to reach and therefore the quietest, surrounded by woods and hills. Nearby Scale Force is the highest waterfall in the Lake District, plunging 36 m (120 ft).

Verdant valley of Borrowdale, a favourite with artists

Borrowdale **10**

Cumbria. 🚉 *Workington.* 🚌 *Cockermouth.* ℹ️ *Town Hall, Market St, Cockermouth (01900 822634).*

This romantic valley, subject of a myriad sketches and watercolours before photography stole the scene, lies beside the densely wooded shores of Derwentwater under towering crags. It is a popular trip from Keswick and a great variety of walks are possible along the valley.

The tiny hamlet of **Grange** is one of the prettiest spots, where the valley narrows dramatically to form the "Jaws of Borrowdale". Nearby Castle Crag has superb views.

From Grange you can complete the circuit of Derwentwater along the western shore, or move southwards to the more open farmland around Seatoller. As you head south by road, look out for a National Trust sign *(see p29)* to the **Bowder Stone**, a delicately poised block weighing nearly 2,000 tonnes, which may have fallen from the crags above or been deposited by a glacier millions of years ago.

Two attractive hamlets in Borrowdale are **Rosthwaite** and **Stonethwaite**. Also worth a detour, preferably on foot, is Watendlath village, off a side road near the famous beauty spot of **Ashness Bridge**.

WALKING IN THE LAKE DISTRICT

Typical Lake District stile over dry-stone wall

Two long-distance footpaths pass through the Lake District's most spectacular scenery. The 70 mile (110 km) Cumbrian Way runs from Carlisle to Ulverston via Keswick and Coniston. The western section of the Coast-to-Coast Walk *(see pp36–7)* passes through this area. There are hundreds of shorter walks along lake shores, nature trails or following more challenging uphill routes. Walkers should stick to paths to avoid erosion, and check weather conditions at National Park information centres.

④

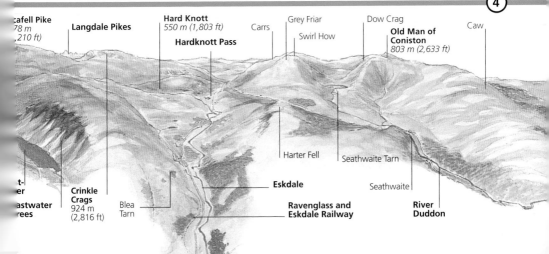

Scafell Pike 978 m (3,210 ft)
Langdale Pikes
Hard Knott 550 m (1,803 ft)
Hardknott Pass
Carrs
Grey Friar
Swirl How
Dow Crag
Old Man of Coniston 803 m (2,633 ft)
Caw

Wast-water Trees
Crinkle Crags 924 m (2,816 ft)
Blea Tarn
Eskdale
Harter Fell
Seathwaite Tarn
Seathwaite
Ravenglass and Eskdale Railway
River Duddon

Convivial Wasdale Head Inn at Wasdale Head

Wastwater ⑪

Cumbria. ⎚ Whitehaven. ℹ 12 Main St, Egremont (01946 820693).

A silent reflection of truly awesome surroundings, black, brooding **Wastwater** is a mysterious, evocative lake. The road from Nether Wasdale continues along its northwest side. Along its eastern flank loom walls of sheer scree over 600 m (2,000 ft) high. Beneath them the water looks inky black, whatever the weather, plunging an icy 80 m (260 ft) from the waterline to the bottom to form England's deepest lake. You can walk along the screes, but it is an uncomfortable and dangerous scramble. Boating on the lake is banned for conservation reasons, but fishing permits are available from the nearby National Trust camp site.

At **Wasdale Head** lies one of Britain's grandest views: the austere pyramid of **Great Gable**, centrepiece of a fine mountain composition, with the huge forms of Scafell and **Scafell Pike**. The scenery is utterly unspoilt, and the only buildings lie at the far end of the lake: an inn and a tiny church commemorating fallen climbers. Here the road ends, and you must turn back or take to your feet, following signs for Black Sail Pass and Ennerdale, or walk up the grand fells ahead. Wasdale's irresistible backdrop was the inspiration of the first serious British mountaineers, who flocked here during the 19th century, insouciantly clad in tweed jackets, carrying little more than a length of rope slung over their shoulders.

Eskdale ⑫

Cumbria. ⎚ Ravenglass then narrow-gauge railway to Eskdale (Easter–Oct: daily; Dec–Feb: phone to check). ℹ 12 Main St, Egremont (01946 820693). www.eskdale.info

The pastoral delights of Eskdale are best encountered over the gruelling **Hardknott Pass**, which is the most taxing drive in the Lake District, with steep gradients. You can pause at the 393-m (1,291-ft) summit to explore the Roman **Hardknott Fort** or enjoy the lovely view. As you descend into Eskdale, rhododendrons and pines flourish in a landscape of small hamlets, narrow lanes and gentle farmland. The main settlements below are the attractive village of Boot and coastal Ravenglass, both with old corn mills.

Just south of Ravenglass is the impressive **Muncaster Castle**, the richly furnished home of the Pennington family. Another way to enjoy the scenery is to take the miniature railway (La'l Ratty) from Ravenglass to Dalegarth.

⛫ **Muncaster Castle**
Ravenglass. **Tel** 01229 717614.
Castle ◯ mid-Feb–mid-Nov:
Sun–Fri (pm) & public hols.
Garden ◯ Feb–Dec: daily. 🏠 🖼
🚻 ground floor and garden. ⬛
www.muncaster.co.uk

Remains of the Roman Hardknott Fort, Eskdale

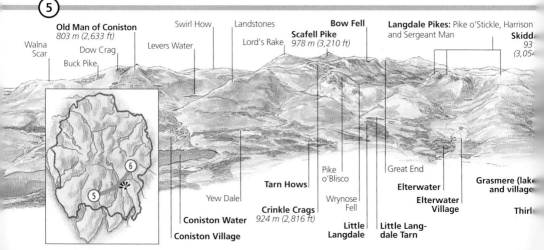

⑤

Walna Scar

Old Man of Coniston
803 m (2,633 ft)

Dow Crag

Buck Pike

Swirl How

Levers Water

Landstones

Lord's Rake

Scafell Pike
978 m (3,210 ft)

Bow Fell

Langdale Pikes: Pike o'Stickle, Harrison and Sergeant Man

Great End

Skidd⋯
93⋯
(3,05⋯

⑥

⑤

Yew Dale

Tarn Hows

Pike o'Blisco

Wrynose Fell

Elterwater

Elterwater Village

Grasmere (lake⋯ and village

Thirl⋯

Coniston Water

Coniston Village

Crinkle Crags
924 m (2,816 ft)

Little Langdale

Little Lang-dale Tarn

Autumnal view of Seathwaite, in the Duddon Valley, a popular centre for walkers and climbers

Duddon Valley ⑬

Cumbria. ⤭ *Foxfield, Ulverston.*
ℹ *The Square, Broughton-in-Furness
(01229 716115; Easter–Oct only).*
www.southlakeland.gov.uk

Also known as Dunnerdale,
this picturesque tract of
countryside inspired 35 of
Wordsworth's sonnets *(see
p366)*. The prettiest stretch lies
between Ulpha and Cockley
Beck. In autumn the colours
of heather moors and a light
sprinkling of birch trees are
particularly beautiful. Stepping
stones and bridges span the
river at intervals, the most
charming being Birk's Bridge,
near Seathwaite. At the southern end of the valley, where

the River Duddon meets the
sea at Duddon Sands, is the
pretty village of Broughton-
in-Furness. Note the stone
slabs used for fish on market
day in the square.

Langdale ⑭

Cumbria. ⤭ *Windermere.* ℹ *Market
Cross, Ambleside (015394 32582).*
www.southlakeland.gov.uk

Stretching from Skelwith
Bridge, where the Brathay
surges powerfully over waterfalls, to the summits of Great
Langdale is the two-pronged
Langdale Valley. Walkers and
climbers throng here to take
on **Pavey Ark, Pike o'Stickle,**

Crinkle Crags and **Bow Fell**.
The local mountain rescue
teams are the busiest in Britain.
   Great Langdale is the more
spectacular valley and it is
often crowded, but quieter
Little Langdale has many
attractions too. It is worth
completing the circuit back to
Ambleside via the southern
route, stopping at Blea Tarn.
Reedy **Elterwater** is a picturesque spot, once a site of the
gunpowder industry. Wrynose
Pass, west of Little Langdale,
climbs to 390 m (1,281 ft), a
warm-up for Hardknott Pass
further on. At its top is Three
Shires Stone, marking the
former boundary of the old
counties of Cumberland,
Westmorland and Lancashire.

⑥

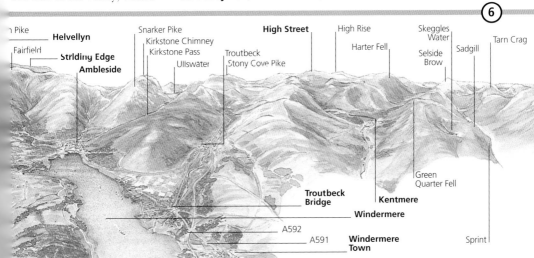

Rydal Water, one of the major attractions of the Lake District

Ambleside ⓰

Cumbria. 🏘 *3,400.* 🚌
ℹ️ *Central Buildings, Market Cross
(015394 32582).* 🚌 *Wed.*
www.lake-district.gov.uk

Ambleside has good road
connections to all parts of the
Lakes and is an attractive
base, especially for walkers
and climbers. Mainly Victorian
in character, it has a good
range of outdoor clothing,
crafts and specialist food
shops. An enterprising little
cinema and a summer
classical music festival add
life in the evenings. Sights in
town are small-scale: the
remnants of the Roman fort
of Galava, AD 79, Stock Ghyll
Force waterfall and **Bridge
House**, now a National Trust
information centre.

Environs: Within easy reach
are the wooded Rothay valley
and **Touchstone Interiors** at
Skelwith Bridge, with their
contemporary design products.
At nearby Troutbeck is the
restored farmhouse of
Townend, dating from 1626,

The tiny Bridge House over Stock
Beck in Ambleside

Grasmere and Rydal ⓯

Cumbria. **Grasmere** 🏘 *700.*
Rydal 🏘 *100.* 🚌 *Grasmere.*
ℹ️ *Central Buildings, Market Cross,
Ambleside (015394 32582).*
www.lake-district.gov.uk

The poet William Wordsworth
lived in both these villages on
the shores of two lakes. Fairfield, Nab Scar and Loughrigg
Fell rise steeply above their
reedy shores and offer good
opportunities for walking.
Grasmere is now a sizable settlement, and the famous Grasmere sports *(see p358)* attract
large crowds every August.
   The Wordsworth family is
buried in St Oswald's Church,
and crowds flock to the annual
ceremony of strewing the
church's earth floor with fresh
rushes. Most visitors head for
Dove Cottage, where the poet
spent his most creative years.
The museum in the barn behind includes such artefacts
as the great man's socks. The
Wordsworths moved to a
larger house, **Rydal Mount**, in

Rydal in 1813 and lived here
until 1850. The grounds have
waterfalls and a summerhouse.
Dora's Field nearby is a blaze
of daffodils in spring and Fairfield Horseshoe offers an
energetic, challenging walk.

🏛 **Dove Cottage and the
Wordsworth Museum**
Off A591 nr Grasmere. *Tel 015394
35544.* ⬜ *daily.* ⬤ *24–26 Dec,
mid-Jan–mid-Feb.* 🚫🔲🔲🔲
www.wordsworth.org.uk

🏛 **Rydal Mount**
Rydal. *Tel 015394 33002.* ⬜ *Mar–
Oct: daily; Nov–Feb: Wed–Mon.*
⬤ *Dec & Jan.* 🔲🔲 *limited.* 🔲

WILLIAM WORDSWORTH (1770–1850)

Best known of the Romantic poets, Wordsworth was born in
the Lake District and spent most of his life there. After school
in Hawkshead and a period at Cambridge, a
legacy enabled him to pursue his literary
career. He settled at Dove Cottage with
his sister Dorothy and in 1802 married
an old school friend, Mary Hutchinson.
They lived simply, walking, bringing up
their children and receiving visits from
poets such as Coleridge and de Quincey.
Wordsworth's prose works include one of
the earliest guidebooks to the Lake District.

BEATRIX POTTER AND THE LAKE DISTRICT

Although best known for her children's stories with characters such as Peter Rabbit and Jemima Puddle-duck, which she also illustrated, Beatrix Potter (1866–1943) became a champion of conservation in the Lake District after moving there in 1906. She married William Heelis, devoted herself to farming, and was an expert on Herdwick sheep. To conserve her beloved countryside, she donated land to the National Trust.

Cover illustration of _Jemima Puddleduck_ (1908)

whose interior gives an insight into Lakeland domestic life.

 **Touchstone Interiors**
Skelwith Bridge. **Tel** 015394 34002.
◯ daily. ● 24–26 Dec.

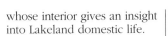 **Townend**
(NT) Troutbeck, Windermere. **Tel** 015394 32628. ◯ Apr–Oct: Wed–Sun; Sun & bank hol Mon: pm.

Windermere ❶

Cumbria. ⌖ Windermere. 🅿 Victoria St. ⓘ Victoria St (015394 46499) or Glebe Rd, Bowness-on-Windermere (015394 42895).
www.southlakeland.gov.uk

At over 10 miles (16 km) long, this dramatic watery expanse is England's largest mere. Industrial magnates built mansions around its shores long before the railway arrived. Stately **Brockhole**, now a national park visitor centre, was one such grand estate. When the railway reached Windermere in 1847, it enabled crowds of workers to visit the area on day trips.

Today, a year-round car ferry service connects the lake's east and west shores (it runs between Ferry Nab and Ferry House), and summer steamers link Lakeside, Bowness and Ambleside on the north-south axis. Belle Isle, a wooded island on which a unique round house stands, is one of the lake's most attractive features, but landing is not permitted. **Fell Foot Park** is at the south end of the lake, and there are good walks on the northwest shore. A quite stunning viewpoint is Orrest Head 238 m (784 ft) northeast of Windermere town.

Environs: Bowness-on-Windermere, on the east shore, is a hugely popular centre. Many of its buildings display Victorian details, and St Martin's Church dates back to the 15th century. The **Windermere Steamboat Museum** has a collection of superbly restored craft, and one of these, _Swallow_, makes regular lake trips. The **World of Beatrix Potter** recreates her characters in an exhibition, and a film tells her life story.

Beatrix Potter wrote many of her books at **Hill Top**, the 17th-century farmhouse at Near Sawrey, northwest of Windermere. Hill Top is furnished with many of Potter's possessions, and left as it was in her lifetime. The **Beatrix Potter Gallery** in Hawkshead holds annual exhibitions of her manuscripts and illustrations.

ⓘ **Brockhole Visitor Centre**
On A591. **Tel** 015394 46601.
◯ Feb–Nov: daily.

🍁 **Fell Foot Park**
(NT) Newby Bridge. **Tel** 015395 31273. ◯ daily.

 **Windermere Steamboat Museum**
Rayrigg Rd, Windermere. **Tel** 015394 45565. ◯ late Mar–Nov: daily.

 **World of Beatrix Potter**
The Old Laundry, Crag Brow. **Tel** 015394 88444. ◯ daily. ● 25 Dec, last three wks in Jan. limited. **www**.hop-skip-jump.com

🎠 **Hill Top**
(NT) Near Sawrey, Ambleside. **Tel** 015394 36269. ◯ Apr–Oct: Sat–Thu.

 **Beatrix Potter Gallery**
(NT) The Square, Hawkshead. **Tel** 015394 36355. ◯ Apr–Oct: Sat–Wed.

Boats moored along the shore at Ambleside, the north end of Windermere

Peaceful Coniston Water, the setting of Arthur Ransome's novel, *Swallows and Amazons* (1930)

Coniston Water ⓲

Cumbria. 🚆 *Windermere then bus.*
🚌 *Ambleside then bus.* 🛈
*Coniston car park, Ruskin Ave (015394
41533).* **www**.conistontic.org

For the finest view of this
stretch of water just outside
the Lake District, you need to
climb. The 19th-century art
critic, writer and philosopher
John Ruskin, had a fine view
from his house, **Brantwood**,
where his paintings and
memorabilia can be seen
today. Contemporary art
exhibitions and events take
place throughout the year.

An enjoyable excursion is
the summer lake trip from
Coniston Pier on the National
Trust steam yacht, *Gondola*,
calling at Brantwood.
Coniston was also the scene
of Donald Campbell's fatal
attempt on the world water
speed record in 1967. The
green slate village of Coniston,
once a centre for copper-
mining, now caters for
local walkers.

Also interesting is the traffic-
free village of **Hawkshead** to
the northwest, with its quaint
alleyways and timber-framed
houses. To the south is the
vast Grizedale Forest, dotted
with woodland sculptures.

Just north of Coniston Water
is the man-made **Tarn Hows**,
a landscaped tarn surrounded
by woods. There is a pleasant
climb up the 803 m (2,635 ft)
Old Man of Coniston.

🏛 **Brantwood**
Off B5285, nr Coniston. *Tel 015394
41396.* ◯ *mid-Mar–mid-Nov: daily;
mid-Nov–mid-Mar: Wed–Sun.* 🖼 🍴
🖥 🎟 **www**.brantwood.org.uk

Kendal ⓳

Cumbria. 🏘 *26,000.* 🚆 🛈 *Town
Hall, Highgate (01539 725758).* 🏪
Wed, Sat. **www**.southlakeland.gov.uk

A busy market town, Kendal
is the administrative centre of
the region and the southern
gateway to the Lake District.
Built in grey limestone, it has
an arts centre, the **Brewery**,
and a central area which is best
enjoyed on foot. **Abbot Hall**,

Kendal mint cake, the famous lakeland energy-booster for walkers

built in 1759, has paintings by
Turner and Romney as well as
Gillows furniture. In addition,
the hall's stable block contains
the **Museum of Lakeland
Life**, with occasional lively
workshops demonstrating local
crafts and trades. There are
dioramas of geology and wildlife in the **Museum of Natural
History and Archaeology**.
About 3 miles (5 km) south
of the town is 14th-century

Sizergh Castle, with a fortified
tower, carved fireplaces and a
lovely garden.

🏛 **Abbot Hall Art Gallery &
Museum of Lakeland Life**
Kendal. *Tel 01539 722464.* ◯ *mid-
Jan–20 Dec: Mon–Sat.* 🖼 ♿ *gallery.*
🎫 *by arrangement.* 🖥 🎟
www.abbothall.org.uk

🏛 **Kendal Museum of
Natural History and
Archaeology**
Station Rd. *Tel 01539 721374.*
◯ *Thu–Sat.* 🖼 🎟 **www**.
kendalmuseum.org.uk

♣ **Sizergh Castle**
(NT) off A591 & A590. *Tel 015395
60951.* ◯ *Apr–Oct: Sun–Thu.* 🖼
♿ *ground floor & grounds.* 🖥 🎟

Furness Peninsula ⓴

Cumbria. 🚆 🚌 *Barrow-in-Furness.*
🛈 *Forum 28, Duke St, Barrow-in-
Furness (01229 876505).*
www.barrowtourism.co.uk

Barrow-in-Furness (*see
p349*) is the peninsula's
main town. Its **Dock
Museum**, built over a
Victorian dock where ships
were repaired, traces the
history of Barrow using
interactive computer displays.

Ruins of the red sandstone
walls of **Furness Abbey**
remain in the wooded Vale
of Deadly Nightshade, with a
small exhibition of monastic
life. The historic town of
Ulverston received its charter
in 1280. Stan Laurel, of Laurel

and Hardy fame, was born here in 1890. His memorabilia **museum** has a cinema. In the nearby village of Gleaston is the **Gleaston Water Mill**, a 400-year-old, working corn mill.

🏛 Dock Museum
North Rd, Barrow-in-Furness. **Tel** 01229 876400. ◯ Easter–Oct: Tue–Sun; Nov–Easter: Wed–Sun (Sat, Sun: pm); public hols. ♿ ▯ 🏠 www.dockmuseum.org.uk

🏠 Furness Abbey
Vale of Deadly Nightshade. **Tel** 01229 823420. ◯ Easter–Sep: daily; Oct–Easter: Thu–Mon. ● 1 Jan, 24–26 Dec. 🏠 ▧ ♿ limited.

🏚 Gleaston Water Mill
Gleaston. **Tel** 01229 869244. ◯ Tue–Sun.

🏛 Laurel and Hardy Museum
Upper Brook St, Ulverston. **Tel** 01229 582292. ◯ daily. ● Jan, 25 Dec. ▧ ♿

Staircase at Holker Hall

Cartmel ㉑

Cumbria. 🏘 700. 🛈 Main St, Grange-over-Sands (015395 34026). www.grangeoversands.net

The highlight of this pretty village is its 12th-century **priory**, one of the finest Cumbrian churches. Little remains of the original priory except the gatehouse in the village centre. The restored church has an attractive east window, a stone-carved 14th-century tomb, and beautiful misericords.

Cartmel also boasts a small racecourse. The village has given its name to its surroundings, a hilly district of green farmland with mixed woodland and limestone scars.

A major local attraction is **Holker Hall**, former residence of the Dukes of Devonshire. Inside are lavishly furnished rooms, with fine marble fireplaces, and a superb oak staircase. Outside are stunning gardens and a deer park.

🏚 Holker Hall
Cark-in-Cartmel. **Tel** 015395 58328. ◯ Mar–Oct: Sun–Fri. ▧ ♿ limited. 🎦 by arrangement. ▯ 🏠 www.holker-hall.co.uk

Levens Hall ㉒

Nr Kendal, Cumbria. **Tel** 015395 60321. 🚌 from Kendal or Lancaster. ◯ Apr–mid-Oct: Sun–Thu. 🏠 ▧ ♿ gardens only. ▯ www.levenshall.co.uk

The outstanding attraction of this Elizabethan mansion is its topiary, but the house itself has much to offer. Built around a 13th-century tower, it contains a fine collection of Jacobean furniture and watercolours by Peter de Wint (1784–1849). Also of note are the ornate ceilings, Charles II dining chairs, the earliest example of English patchwork and the gilded hearts on the drainpipes.

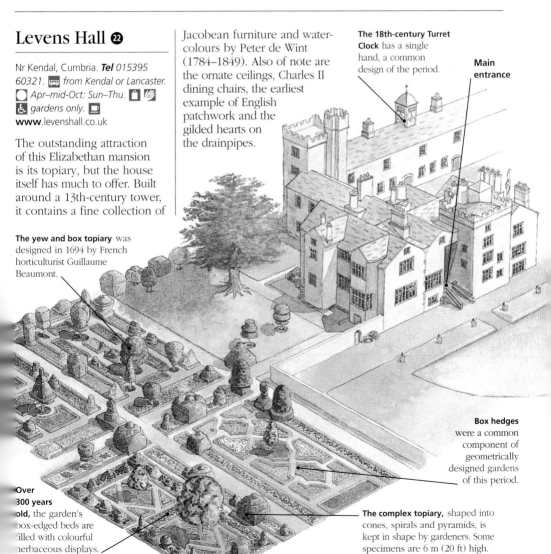

The yew and box topiary was designed in 1694 by French horticulturist Guillaume Beaumont.

The 18th-century Turret Clock has a single hand, a common design of the period.

Main entrance

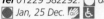
Over 300 years old, the garden's box-edged beds are filled with colourful herbaceous displays.

Box hedges were a common component of geometrically designed gardens of this period.

The complex topiary, shaped into cones, spirals and pyramids, is kept in shape by gardeners. Some specimens are 6 m (20 ft) high.

Morecambe Bay, looking northwest towards Barrow-in-Furness

Morecambe Bay ㉓

Lancs. ⊠ *Morecambe*. ⊠ *Heysham (to Isle of Man).* 🛈 *Marine Rd. (01524 582808).* **www**.lancaster.gov.uk

The best way to explore Morecambe Bay is by train from Ulverston to Arnside. The track follows a series of low viaducts across a huge expanse of glistening tidal flats where thousands of wading birds feed and breed. The bay is one of the most important bird reservations in the country. On the Cumbrian side of the bay, retirement homes have expanded the sedate Victorian resort of Grange-over-Sands, which grew up after the arrival of the railway in 1857. Nearby, **Hampsfield Fell** and **Humphrey Head Point** give fine views along the bay.

Leighton Hall ㉔

Carnforth, Lancashire. **Tel** *01524 734 474.* 🚌 *to Yealand Conyers (from Lancaster).* ◯ *May–Sep: 2–5pm Tue–Fri & bank hols (also Sun in Aug).* 🚫 🚌 *ground floor only.* 🎦 📷 🎁 **www**.leightonhall.co.uk

Leighton Hall's estate dates back to the 13th century, but most of the building is 19th-century, including its Neo-Gothic façade. It is owned by the Gillow family, of the Lancastrian furniture business, whose products are now prized antiques. Excellent pieces can be seen here, including a ladies' work-box inlaid with biblical scenes. In the afternoon, weather permitting, the hall's large collection of birds of prey display their aerial prowess.

Lancaster ㉕

Lancashire. 👥 *50,000.* ⊠ 🚌 🛈 *Castle Hill (01524 32878).* 🏪 *Mon–Sat.* **www**.lancaster.gov.uk

This county town of Lancashire is tiny compared to Liverpool or Manchester (now counties in their own right), but it has a long history. The Romans named it after their camp over the River Lune. Originally a defensive site, it developed into a prosperous port largely on the proceeds of the slave trade. Today, its university and cultural life still thrive. The Norman **Lancaster Castle** was expanded in the 14th and 16th centuries. It has been a crown court and a prison since the 13th century. The Shire Hall is decorated with 600 heraldic shields. Some fragments from Hadrian's Tower (which has a collection of torture instruments) are 2,000 years old.

The nearby priory church of **St Mary** is on Castle Hill. Its main features include a Saxon doorway and carved 14th-century choir stalls. There is an outstanding museum of furniture in the 17th-century **Judge's Lodgings**, while the **Maritime Museum**, in the Georgian custom house on St George's Quay, contains displays on the port's history. The **City Museum**, based in the old town hall, concentrates on the history of Lancaster.

The splendid **Lune Aqueduct** carries the canal over the River Lune on five wide arches. Other attractions are found in **Williamson Park**, site of the 1907 Ashton Memorial. This folly was built by the local linoleum magnate and politician, Lord Ashton.

Tawny eagle at Leighton Hall

CROSSING THE SANDS

Morecambe Bay sands are very dangerous. Travellers used to cut across the bay at low tide to shorten the long trail around the Kent estuary. Many perished as they were caught by rising tides or quicksand, and sea fogs hid the paths. Locals who knew the bay became guides, and today you can travel with a guide from Kents Bank to Hest Bank near Arnside.

The High Sheriff of Lancaster Crossing Morecambe Sands (anon)

There are fine views from the top of this 67 m (220 ft) domed structure. Opposite is the tropical butterfly house and the pavilion café.

⚓ Lancaster Castle
Castle Parade. **Tel** 01524 64998. ◯ daily. ● mid-Dec–early Jan. 🎫 🎟 only (limited when court is in session). 🖥 www.lancastercastle.com

🏛 Judge's Lodgings
Church St. **Tel** 01524 32808. ◯ Apr–Jun, Oct: daily (Sat & Sun: pm only); Jul–Sep: daily. ● Nov–Good Fri. 🎫 🎟 ♿ limited.

🏛 Maritime Museum
Custom House, St George's Quay. **Tel** 01524 382264. ◯ daily (Nov–Easter: pm). ● 24–26, 31 Dec, 1 Jan. 🎫 ♿ 🖥 🖥 www.lancashire.gov.uk

🏛 City Museum
Market Sq. **Tel** 01524 64637. ◯ Mon–Sat. ● 24 Dec–2 Jan. ♿ 🖥

🌷 Williamson Park
Wyresdale Rd. **Tel** 01524 33318. ◯ daily. 🎫 ♿ limited. 🖥 🖥 www.williamsonpark.com

Ribble Valley ㉖

Lancashire. 🚃 Clitheroe. 🅸 Market Place, Clitheroe (01200 425566). 🅰 Tue, Thu, Sat. www.ribblevalley.gov.uk

Clitheroe, a small market town with a hilltop castle, is a good centre for exploring the Ribble Valley's rivers and old villages, such as Slaidburn. Ribchester has a **Roman Museum**, and there is a ruined **Cistercian abbey** at Whalley. To the east is 560 m (1,830 ft) Pendle Hill, with a Bronze Age burial mound at its peak.

🏛 Roman Museum
Ribchester. **Tel** 01254 878261. ◯ daily. 🎫 ♿ 🎟 by arrangement. 🖥

🏰 Whalley Abbey
Whalley. **Tel** 01254 828400. ◯ daily. ● 24 Dec–2 Jan. 🎫 ♿ 🖥 🖥 www.whalleyabbey.co.uk

Blackpool ㉗

Lancashire. 🏛 150,000. ✈ 🚃 🚌 🅸 Clifton St (01253 478222). www.visitblackpool.com

British holiday patterns have changed in the past few decades, and Blackpool is no longer the apogee of seaside entertainment, but it remains a unique experience. A wall of

Coming from the Mill (1930) by L S Lowry (See p375)

amusement arcades, piers, bingo halls and fast-food stalls stretch behind the sands. At night, entertainers strut their stuff under the bright lights. The town attracts thousands of visitors in September and October when the Illuminations trace the skeleton of the 158 m (518 ft) Blackpool Tower. Blackpool's resort life dates back to the 18th century, but it burst into prominence when the railway first arrived in 1840, bringing Lancastrian workers to their holiday resort.

Blackpool Tower, painted gold for its centenary in 1994

Salford Quays ㉘

Salford. 🚃 Harbour City (from Manchester). 🅸 The Lowry, Pier 8 (0161 848 8601). www.visitsalford.info

The Quays, to the west of Manchester city centre (15 minutes by tram), were once the terminal docks for the **Manchester Ship Canal**. After the docks closed in 1982, the area became sadly run down but since the 1990s a massive redevelopment plan has changed the area dramatically. A world-class business, cultural and residential area of great architectural and regional significance has been created and more people are now employed at the Quays than in its heyday as a major seaport.

There is a wealth of entertainment, leisure and cultural facilities on offer, including **The Lowry** (*see p375*), the **Manchester United Museum** (*see p375*), the **Imperial War Museum North** (*see p375*), the **Salford Museum and Art Gallery** and The Lowry Outlet Mall, as well as numerous bars, restaurants and shops. There are various water-based activities and ship-canal cruises. The Quays was also a venue for the Commonwealth Games in 2002, and now hosts the Triathlon World Cup.

🏛 Salford Museum and Art Gallery
Peel Park, The Crescent. **Tel** 0161 778 0800. ◯ Mon–Fri, Sat–Sun pm. ● 25, 26 Dec.

Manchester ㉙

Sign for the John Rylands Library

Manchester dates back to Roman times, when in AD 79, Agricola set up a base called Mancunium. It rose to prominence in the late 18th century, when Richard Arkwright introduced cotton processing. By 1830, the first railway linked Manchester and Liverpool, and in 1894 the Manchester Ship Canal (*see p371*) opened, allowing cargovessels inland. Civic buildings sprang up from the proceeds of cotton wealth, but these were in stark contrast to the slums of the millworkers. Social discontent led writers, politicians and reformers to espouse liberal or radical causes.

The achievements of football team Manchester United and the international success of bands such as The Smiths and The Stone Roses, gave Manchester a cachet of cool during the 1980s and 1990s. Devastation caused by an IRA car-bombing of the city centre in 1996 was seized as an opportunity to redevelop the main shopping areas. This regeneration has since spread to other areas of the city, notably the old dockside area of Salford Quays.

Urbis, an interactive attraction on life in cities

Exploring Manchester

Manchester is a fine, compact city with much to see in its central areas. The Victorian era of cotton wealth has gifted the city an imposing heritage of industrial architecture, much of which is providing sites for development. The former central railway station, for example, is now **Manchester Central**, a huge exhibition and conference complex. Among other fine 19th-century buildings are the dramatic **John Rylands Library** on Deansgate, founded over 100 years ago by the widow of a local cotton millionaire, and the 1856 Renaissance-style **Free Trade Hall**, now the Radisson Edwardian hotel, which stands on the site of the Peterloo Massacre.

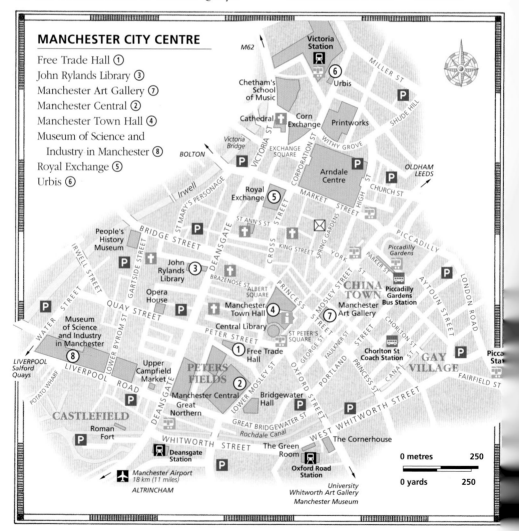

MANCHESTER CITY CENTRE

Free Trade Hall ①
John Rylands Library ③
Manchester Art Gallery ⑦
Manchester Central ②
Manchester Town Hall ④
Museum of Science and
    Industry in Manchester ⑧
Royal Exchange ⑤
Urbis ⑥

M62
Victoria Station
MILLER ST
Chetham's School of Music
Urbis ⑥
Cathedral
SHUDE HILL
Corn Exchange
Printworks
Victoria Bridge
BOLTON
VICTORIA ST
EXCHANGE ST
EXCHANGE SQUARE
WITHY GROVE
CORPORATION ST
Arndale Centre
OLDHAM LEEDS
Irwell
ST MARY'S PARSONAGE
Royal Exchange ⑤
MARKET STREET
HIGH ST
CHURCH ST
People's History Museum
BRIDGE STREET
GARTSIDE STREET
ST ANN'S ST
DEANSGATE
CROSS STREET
KING STREET
SPRING GARDENS
YORK ST
PARKER ST
PICCADILLY
Piccadilly Gardens
IRWELL STREET
QUAY STREET
John Rylands Library ③
BRAZENOSE ST
ALBERT SQUARE
PRINCESS ST
MOSLEY STREET
CHINA TOWN
Piccadilly Gardens Bus Station
AYTOUN STREET
LONDON ROAD
WATER ST
Opera House
Manchester Town Hall ④
Manchester Art Gallery ⑦
CHORLTON ST
Museum of Science and Industry in Manchester ⑧
LOWER BYROM ST
LIVERPOOL ROAD
QUAY STREET
Central Library
PETER STREET
ST PETER'S SQUARE
GEORGE'S ST
FAULKNER ST
PORTLAND STREET
PRINCESS ST
CANAL ST
Chorlton St Coach Station
GAY VILLAGE
FAIRFIELD ST
Picca Sta
LIVERPOOL
Salford Quays
POTATO WHARF
Upper Campfield Market
① Free Trade Hall
PETERS FIELDS
② Manchester Central
LOWER MOSLEY ST
OXFORD STREET
WEST WHITWORTH STREET
CASTLEFIELD
Roman Fort
DEANSGATE
Great Northern
Bridgewater Hall
GREAT BRIDGEWATER ST
Rochdale Canal
WHITWORTH STREET
The Green Room
The Cornerhouse
Deansgate Station
Oxford Road Station
Manchester Airport
18 km (11 miles)
ALTRINCHAM
University
Whitworth Art Gallery
Manchester Museum

| 0 metres | 250 |
| 0 yards | 250 |

The Neo-Gothic Town Hall by Alfred Waterhouse

🏛 Manchester Town Hall

Albert Square. **Tel** 0161 234 5000.
⭕ Mon–Fri. ♿

Manchester's majestic town hall was designed by Liverpool-born Alfred Waterhouse (1830–1905), an architect who would later find fame with his Natural History Museum in London. Waterhouse won the commission for the building in an architectural competition, his design finding favour for making best use of the awkward triangular site.

The building was completed in 1877 in an English Gothic style with its roots in the 13th century. Tours take place at 2pm every other Saturday but visitors can also explore the building on their own. Sign in inside the main entrance, where a statue of General Agricola, the Roman who founded Manchester in AD 79, looks down on passersby. The highlight is the Great Hall adorned by 12 murals painted by Ford Maddox Brown, the celebrated Pre-Raphaelite painter.

Throughout the building the decoration includes numerous examples of cotton flowers and bees, the latter a symbol of Manchester's industriousness. In the square in front of the town hall is Manchester's **Albert Memorial**,
dedicated to the consort of Queen Victoria, which is similar in style but predates the one in London's Hyde Park.

🏛 Royal Exchange

St Ann's Square.
Tel 0161 833 9833.
⭕ Mon–Sat. ♿
🖥 🏠 www.royal
exchange.co.uk

Built in 1729, the Manchester Royal Exchange, as it was then known, was once claimed to be the "biggest room in the world". It was built as the main trading hall of the cotton industry and at the end of the 19th century it was reckoned that over 80 percent of world trade in cloth was controlled from these premises. During the Second World War the building was severely damaged by bombs. This coincided with the decline of the cotton trade in the United Kingdom and when the Exchange was rebuilt it was reduced to half its original size. The doors were finally closed to trading in 1968. A daring scheme saw the main hall converted into a theatre in the mid-1970s with the auditorium enclosed in a high-tech structure supported by the old building's pillars; it nestles like a lunar module beneath the great dome. The rest of the Exchange building contains an arcade, shops and cafés.

🏛 Urbis

Cathedral Gdns. **Tel** 0161 605 8200.
⭕ 10am–6pm daily. 🎟 for temporary exhibitions only.
♿ 🍴 🖥 🏠 www.urbis.org.uk

The Urbis, opened in 2002, explores life around the world in different cities. It's housed in a striking ski slope-shaped glass building. The visit begins with a glass-elevator ride up the incline, then proceeds via an introductory film show down through three staggered floors of interactive exhibits.

The lower level houses temporary exhibitions on an urban theme, for which there is usually an admission fee. The interactive galleries, on levels two to four, explore the people, place and pulse of the modern city.

Across the plaza from Urbis is **Manchester Cathedral**, which largely dates from the 19th century but stands on a site that has been occupied by a church for over a millennium.

VISITORS' CHECKLIST

Manchester. 🚶 2.5 million.
✈ Off M56 11 miles (18 km)
S Manchester. 🚆 Piccadilly,
Victoria, Oxford Rd. 🚌 Chorlton
St. ℹ 0871 222 8223. 🖥 daily.
www.visitmanchester.com

THE PETERLOO MASSACRE

In 1819, the working conditions of Manchester's factory workers were so bad that social tensions reached breaking point. On 16 August, 50,000 people assembled in St Peter's Field to protest at the oppressive Corn Laws. Initially peaceful, the mood darkened and the poorly trained mounted troops panicked, charging the crowd with their sabres. Eleven were killed and many wounded. The incident was called Peterloo (the Battle of Waterloo had taken place in 1815). Reforms such as the Factory Act came in that year.

G Cruikshank's Peterloo Massacre cartoon

Museum of Science and Industry, set in old passenger railway buildings

🏛 Manchester Art Gallery

Mosley St & Princess St. *Tel 0161 235 8888.* ○ *Tue–Sun.* ● *Mon (except Bank Holidays), 24–26, 31 Dec, 1 Jan, Good Fri.* ✔ ♿ 🍴 🖵 📷
www.manchestergalleries.org

The gallery reopened in summer 2002, doubling its display space after a £35 million makeover and a brand new extension by architect Sir Michael Hopkins. The original building was designed by Sir Charles Barry (1795–1860) in 1824, and contains an excellent collection of British art, notably Pre-Raphaelites such as Holman Hunt and Dante Gabriel Rossetti. Early Italian, Flemish and French Schools are also represented.

The gallery has a fine collection of decorative arts, from the Greeks to Picasso to contemporary craftworkers, in the Gallery of Craft & Design. There is also a changing programme of special exhibitions in two fantastic new galleries on the top floor. Most exhibitions are free and there is a programme of accompanying events for adults and families.

A new and lively space called the Clore Interactive Gallery offers a combination of real artworks and hands-on activities for children.

🏛 Museum of Science and Industry

Liverpool Rd. *Tel 0161 832 2244.* ○ *daily.* ● *24–26 Dec.* ♿ 🖵 🍴 📷 www.msim.org.uk

One of the largest science museums in the world, the spirit of scientific enterprise and industrial might of Manchester's heyday is conveyed here. Among the best sections are the Power Hall, a collection of working steam engines, the Electricity Gallery, tracing the history of domestic power, and an exhibition on the Liverpool and Manchester Railway. A collection of planes that made flying history are displayed in the Air and Space Gallery.

🏛 Manchester Museum

Oxford Road. *Tel 0161 275 2634,* ○ *daily.* ♿ 🍴 🖵 📷 www.museum.man.ac.uk.

Part of Manchester University, this venerable museum (opened 1885) houses around six million items from all ages and all over the world, but it specializes in Egyptology and zoology. The collection of ancient Egyptian artefacts is one of the largest in the United Kingdom and numbers about 20,000 objects including monumental stone sculpture and a number of mummies, displayed together with their coffins and funerary

Lawrence Alma-Tadema, *Etruscan Vase Painters*, Manchester Art Gallery

goods. There are also various sections that deal with funerary masks, tomb models and mummified animals. The zoological collections number over 600,000 objects, ranging from stuffed animals to a cast of one of the most complete skeletons of a T Rex dinosaur, which was added to the museum in November 2004.

The original museum building was designed by Alfred Waterhouse, the same architect responsible for the city's magnificent Town Hall *(see p373)*.

🏛 Whitworth Art Gallery

University of Manchester, Oxford Rd. *Tel 0161 275 7450.* ○ *daily (Sun: pm).* ● *24 Dec–2 Jan, Good Fri.* ♿ 🖵 📷 www.whitworth.man.ac.uk

Jacob Epstein's *Genesis*, Whitworth Art Gallery

The Stockport-born machine tool manufacturer and engineer Sir Joseph Whitworth bequeathed money for this gallery, originally intended to be a museum of industrial art and design that would inspire the city's textile trade. Founded in 1889, it has been a part of the University of Manchester since 1958. The fine red-brick building is from the Edwardian period, while the modern interior dates from the 1960s.

The gallery houses a superb collection of drawings, sculpture, contemporary art, textiles and prints. Jacob Epstein's *Genesis* nude occupies the entrance, and there is an important collection of British watercolours by Turner *(see p91)*, Girtin and others. Look out for the Japanese woodcuts and the Collection of historic and modern wallpapers, built up from donations from wallpaper manufacturers, as well as through the gallery's active Collecting Policy.

There is a well-developed Education Department that organizes a full programme of activities for groups and individuals of all ages and abilities, for both formal and informal learning.

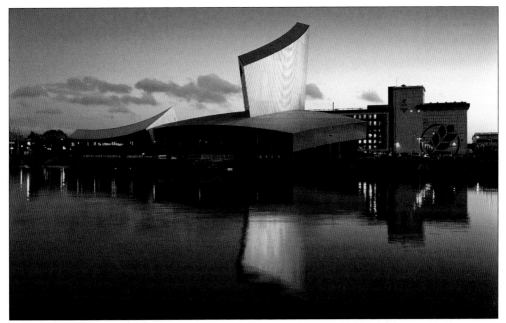

Exterior of the Imperial War Museum North, designed by Daniel Libeskind to represent a globe shattered by conflict

🏛 Lowry Centre

Pier 8, Salford Quays. *Tel 0870 787 5788.* ⭕ *daily. Admission free, but donations requested.* 🔧 🍴 🖥 🛗
www.thelowry.com.

On a prominent site beside the Manchester Ship Canal, the Lowry is a shimmering, silvery arts and entertainment complex that combines two theatres, a restaurant, terrace bars and cafes, art galleries and a shop.

The centre is named after celebrated reclusive artist Laurence Stephen Lowry (1887–1976), who was born locally and lived all his life in the Manchester area. A rent collector by day, in his leisure hours he painted cityscapes dominated by the smoking chimneys of industry beneath heavy soot filled skies.

However, he is most famous as a painter of "matchstick men", the term frequently applied to the crowds of slight and ghostly figures peopling his canvases. Some of Lowry's work is displayed in one of the galleries here; another hosts regularly changing temporary exhibitions. There is also a room where a 20-minute documentary "Meet Mr Lowry" is screened throughout the day.

The centre provides many facilities and activities for children, and is perfect for a family day out.

🏛 Imperial War Museum North

Trafford Wharf Road, Salford Quays. *Tel 0161 836 4000.* ⭕ *daily.*
⚫ *24–26 Dec.* 🎫 🔧 🍴 🖥 🛗
www.iwm.org.uk.

This most striking piece of modern architecture comes courtesy of Daniel Libeskind, the architect nominated to design a replacement for New York's World Trade Centre. His Manchester building is a waterfront collision of three great aluminium shards, representing a globe shattered by conflict. Inside, a vast, irregular space is used to display a small but well presented collection of military hardware and ephemera, with nine "silos" devoted to exhibits on people's experiences of war.

On the hour the lights are extinguished for an audio-visual display using the angled walls of the main hall.

As visitors leave they are invited to take the elevator up the 55-metre (180-ft) "Air Shard" for views over the city.

🏛 Manchester United Museum

Salford Quays. *Tel 0161 868 8000.* ⭕ *daily. Tours must be booked in advance.* 🎫 🖥 🛗
www.manutd.com

Premier League football (soccer) team Manchester United's ground Old Trafford also includes a purpose-built museum. In addition to the historic displays there is much interactive fun such as a chance to test your own penalty-taking skills.

The museum tour takes in the dressing rooms, the trophy room and the players' lounge and culminates in a walk down the tunnel tracing the route taken by players at every home game.

Manchester United Museum on the grounds of Old Trafford football stadium

Liverpool 30

Traces of settlement on Merseyside date back to the 1st century. In 1207 "Livpul", a fishing village, was granted a charter by King John. The population was only 1,000 in Stuart times, but during the 17th and 18th centuries Liverpool's westerly seaboard gave it a leading edge in the lucrative Caribbean slave trade. The first docks opened in 1715 and eventually stretched 7 miles (11 km) along the Mersey. Liverpool's first ocean steamer set out from here in 1840, and would-be emigrants to the New World poured into the city from Europe, including a flood of Irish refugees from the potato famine. Many settled permanently in Liverpool and a large, mixed community developed. Today, the port handles even greater volumes of cargoes than in the 1950s and 1960s, but container ships use Bootle docks. Despite economic and social problems, the irrepressible "Scouse" or Liverpudlian spirit re-emerged in the Swinging Sixties, when four local lads stormed the pop scene. Many people still visit Liverpool to pay homage to the Beatles, but the city is also known for its orchestra, the Liverpool Philharmonic, its sport (football and the Grand National steeplechase) and its universities.

Liver Bird on the Royal Liver Building

Victorian ironwork, restored and polished, at Albert Dock

Exploring Liverpool

Liverpool's waterfront by the Pier Head, guarded by the mythical Liver Birds (a pair of cormorants with seaweed in their beaks) on the **Royal Liver Building**, is one of the most easily recognized in Britain. Nearby are the famous ferry terminal across the River Mersey and the revitalized

LIVERPOOL CITY CENTRE

Beatles Story ⑥
Cavern Quarter ①
Merseyside Maritime
   Museum ⑧
Metropolitan Cathedral ⑤
Museum of Liverpool Life ⑨
Royal Liver Building ⑩

St George's Hall ④
Tate Liverpool ⑦
Town Hall ⑪
The Walker pp378–9 ③
World Museum Liverpool ②

docklands. Other attractions include top-class museums and fine galleries, such as the **Walker** (see pp378–9). Its wealth of interesting architecture includes some fine Neo-Classical buildings in the city centre, such as the gargantuan **St George's Hall**, and two cathedrals.

Albert Dock
🛈 0151 708 7334. ◯ daily. ● 1 Jan, 25 Dec. 🔲 some attractions. ♿ www.albertdock.com

There are five warehouses surrounding Albert Dock, all designed by Jesse Hartley in 1846. The docks were closed by 1972. After a decade of dereliction, these Grade I listed buildings were restored in a development that includes museums, galleries, shops, restaurants, bars and businesses.

Albert Dock quay beside the River Mersey

🏛 Merseyside Maritime Museum
Albert Dock. **Tel** 0151 478 4499. ◯ daily. ♿ limited. 🔲 📷 www.liverpoolmuseums.org.uk

Devoted to the history of the Port of Liverpool, this large complex has good sections on shipbuilding and the Cunard and White Star liners. The area on the Battle of the Atlantic in World War II includes models and charts. Another gallery deals with emigration to the New World. The **HM Customs and Excise National Museum** is also located here, and examines the history of the subject, including smuggling, as well as customs and excise today. Next door is the new **International Slavery Museum**. Across the quayside is the rebuilt Piermaster's House and the Cooperage.

Ship's bell in the Maritime Museum

🏛 Museum of Liverpool Life
Pier Head, Albert Dock. **Tel** 0151 478 4080. ● for refurbishment until 2010. ♿ 📷

Many aspects of Liverpool culture converge here. Exhibits cover the history of Liverpool, its people and their contribution to international life. The *City Soldier's* gallery explores life in the King's Regiment in times of war and peace. Other interactive exhibits and accounts of daily life tell stories of sporting and political events since the 1800s.

🏛 Beatles Story
Britannia Vaults. **Tel** 0151 709 1963. ◯ daily. ● 25, 26 Dec. 🔲 ♿ 📷 www.beatlesstory.com

In a walk-through exhibition, this museum records the history of The Beatles' meteoric rise to fame, from their first record, *Love Me Do,* through Beatlemania to their last live appearance together in 1969, and their eventual break-up. The hits that mesmerized a generation can be heard.

🏛 Tate Liverpool
Albert Dock. **Tel** 0151 702 7400. ◯ Tue–Sun (Jun–Aug: daily). ● 1 Jan, Good Fri, 24–26 Dec. 🔲 some exhibitions. ♿ 📷 by arrangement. 🔲 📷 www.tate.org.uk/liverpool

Tate Liverpool has one of the best contemporary art collections outside London. Marked by bright blue and orange panels and arranged over three floors, the gallery was converted from an old warehouse by architect James Stirling. It opened in 1988 as Tate Britain's (see p91) first outstation.

THE BEATLES

Liverpool has produced many good bands and a host of singers, comedians and entertainers before and since the 1960s. But the Beatles – John Lennon, Paul McCartney, George Harrison and Ringo Starr – were the most sensational, and locations associated with the band, however tenuous, are revered as shrines in Liverpool. Bus and walking tours trace the hallowed ground of the Salvation Army home at *Strawberry Fields* and *Penny Lane* (both outside the city centre), as well as the boys' old homes. The most visited site is Mathew Street, near Moorfields Station, where the Cavern Club first throbbed to the Mersey Beat. The original site is now a shopping arcade, but the bricks have been used to create a replica. Nearby are statues of the Beatles and *Eleanor Rigby*.

Liverpool: The Walker

**Italian dish
(c. 1500)**

Founded in 1877 by Sir Andrew Barclay Walker, a local brewer and Mayor of Liverpool, this gallery houses one of the finest art collections in Britain. Paintings range from early Italian and Flemish works to Rubens, Rembrandt, Poussin, and French Impressionists such as Degas's *Woman Ironing* (c.1892–5). Among the strong collection of British artists from the 18th century onward are works by Millais and Turner and Gainsborough's *Countess of Sefton* (1769). There is 20th-century art by Hockney and Sickert, and the sculpture collection includes works by Henry Moore.

Interior at Paddington
(1951) Lucian Freud's friend Harry Diamond posed for six months for this picture, intended by the artist to "make the human being uncomfortable".

Seashells *(1874)*
Albert Moore painted female figures based on antique statues. Influenced by Whistler (see p519), he adopted subtle shading.

15

4

5

14

8

13

9

12

10

Big Art for
Little Artists
Gallery

Ground floor

11

First flo

Façade was
designed by
H H Vale and
Cornelius
Sherlock.

Main entrance

GALLERY GUIDE

*All the picture galleries are on the first floor.
Rooms 1–2 house medieval and Renaissance paintings; Rooms 3 and 4 have 17th-century Dutch, French, Italian and Spanish art. British 18th- and 19th-century works are in Rooms 5–9. Rooms 11–15 have 20th-century and contemporary British art, and Room 10 has Impressionists and Post-Impressionists.*

The Sleeping Shepherd Boy
(c.1835) The great Neo-Classica sculptor of the mid-19th century John Gibson (1790–1866), use traditional colours to give his statuary a smooth appearance.

**The 7th-century Kingston Brooch
in World Museum Liverpool**

🏛 World Museum Liverpool

William Brown St. **Tel** *0151 478
4393.* ○ *10am–5pm daily.*
● *1 Jan, 24–26 Dec.* 🚻 🖥️ 🅿️
www.liverpoolmuseums.org.uk
Six floors of exhibits in this
excellent museum include
collections of Egyptian, Greek
and Roman pieces, natural
history, archaeology, space and
time. Highlights include the
hands-on Weston Discovery
Centre, a planetarium, the
Close Natural History Centre,
an aquarium, a world cultures
gallery and a Bug House.

⛪ Anglican Cathedral

St James' Mount. **Tel** *0151 709
6271.* ○ *daily.* 🚻 🖥️ 🅿️
www.liverpoolcathedral.org.uk
Although Gothic in style, this
building was only completed
in 1978. The largest Anglican
cathedral in the world is a fine
red sandstone edifice designed
by Sir Giles Gilbert Scott. The
foundation stone was laid
in 1904 by Edward VII but,
dogged by two world wars,
building work dragged on to
modified designs.

⛪ Metropolitan Cathedral of Christ the King

Mount Pleasant. **Tel** *0151 709 9222.*
○ *daily.* **Donation.** 🚻 🅿️ www.
liverpoolmetrocathedral.org.uk
Liverpool's Roman Catholic
cathedral rejected traditional
forms in favour of a striking
modern design. Early plans,
drawn up by Pugin and later
by Lutyens *(see p29)* in the
1930s, proved too expensive.
The final version, brainchild
of Sir Frederick Gibberd and
built from 1962–7, is a circular
building surmounted by a
stylized crown of thorns 88 m
(290 ft) high. It is irreverently
known as "Paddy's Wigwam"
by non-Catholics (a reference
to Liverpool's large Irish
population). Inside, the stained-
glass lantern, designed by John
Piper and Patrick Reyntiens,
floods the circular nave with
diffused blueish light. There
is a fine bronze of Christ by
Elisabeth Frink (1930–94).

Environs: A spectacular richly
timbered building dating from
1490, **Speke Hall** lies 6 miles
(10 km) east of Liverpool's
centre, surrounded by lovely
grounds. The oldest parts of
the hall enclose a cobbled
courtyard dominated by two
yew trees, Adam and Eve.
Birkenhead on the Wirral
peninsula has been linked to
Liverpool by ferry for over
800 years. Now, road and rail
tunnels supplement access.
The Norman Priory is still in
use on Sundays, and stately
Hamilton Square was designed
from 1825–44 by J Gillespie
Graham, one of the architects
of Edinburgh's New Town.
On the Wirral side is **Port
Sunlight Village** *(see p349)*, a
Victorian garden village built
by enlightened soap manufacturer William Hesketh Lever
for his factory workers. He also
founded the **Lady Lever Art
Gallery** here for his collection
of works of art, including Pre-
Raphaelite paintings.

🏛 Speke Hall

(NT) The Walk, Speke. **Tel** *0151 427
7231.* ○ *Apr–Oct: Wed–Sun (pm);
Nov–mid-Dec: Sat, Sun (pm); public
hols.* 🎟️ 🚻 *limited.* 🖥️ 🅿️
www.nationaltrust.org.uk

🏛 Port Sunlight Village & Heritage Centre

95 Greendale Rd, Port Sunlight, Wirral.
Tel *0151 644 6466.* ○ *Apr–Oct:
10am–4pm; Nov–Mar: 11am–4pm
daily.* ● *Christmas wk.* 🎟️ 🖊️ 🚻
🖥️ 🅿️ **www**.portsunlightvillage.com

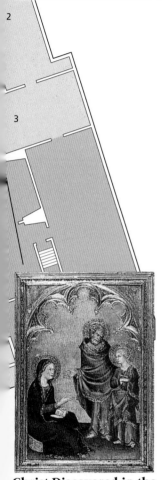

**Christ Discovered in the
Temple** *(1342)*
*Simone Martini's Holy
Family conveys emotional
tension through highly
expressive body language.*

KEY TO FLOOR PLAN

- ▢ 13th–17th-century European
- ▢ 18th–19th-century British, Pre-Raphaelites and Victorian
- ▢ Impressionist/Post-Impressionist
- ▢ 20th-century and contemporary British
- ▢ Sculpture gallery
- ▢ Craft and design gallery
- ▢ Special exhibitions
- ▢ Non-exhibition space

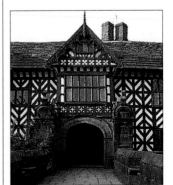

**Entrance to the half-timbered
manor house of Speke Hall**

YORKSHIRE AND THE HUMBER REGION

NORTH YORKSHIRE · EAST RIDING OF YORKSHIRE

With the historic city of York at its heart, this is an area of picturesque moorland and valleys. To the north lie the Yorkshire Dales and the North York Moors; eastwards, a coastline of beaches; and southwards, a landscape of lush meadows.

Yorkshire was originally made up of three separate counties, formerly known as "Ridings". Today it covers over 5,000 sq miles (12,950 sq km). The northeast section has dramatic limestone scenery that was carved by glaciers in the Ice Age. Farming was the original livelihood, and the dry-stone walls weaving up precipitous scars and fells were used to divide the land. Imposed on this were the industries of the 19th century; blackened mill chimneys and crumbling viaducts are as much a part of the scenery as the grand houses of those who profited from them.

Close to the Humber, the landscape is very different, dominated historically by the now flagging fishing industry, and geographically by lush, sprawling meadows. Its coastline is exceptional, and further north are the attractions of wide, sandy beaches and bustling harbour towns. Yet it is the contrasting landscapes that make the area so appealing, ranging from the bleak moorland of the Brontë novels to the ragged cliff coast around Whitby, and the flat expanse of Sunk Island.

The city of York, where Roman and Viking relics exist side by side, is second only to London in the number of visitors that tread its streets. Indeed the historical centre of York is the region's foremost attraction. Those in search of a real taste of Yorkshire, however, should head for the countryside. In addition to excellent touring routes, a network of rewarding walking paths range from mellow ambles along the Cleveland Way to rocky scrambles over the Pennine Way at Pen-y-Ghent.

Lobster pots on the quayside at the picturesque fishing port of Whitby

◁ The peaceful valley of Rosedale, North York Moors

Exploring Yorkshire and the Humber Region

Yorkshire covers a wide area, once made up of three counties or "Ridings". Until the arrival of railways, mining and the wool industry in the 19th century, the county was a farming area. Dry-stone walls dividing fields still pepper the northern part of the county, alongside 19th-century mill chimneys and country houses. Among the many abbeys are Rievaulx and the magnificent Fountains. The medieval city of York is a major attraction, as are Yorkshire's beaches. The Humber region is characterized by the softer, rolling countryside of the Wolds, and its nature reserves attract enormous quantities of birds.

Rosedale village in the North York Moors

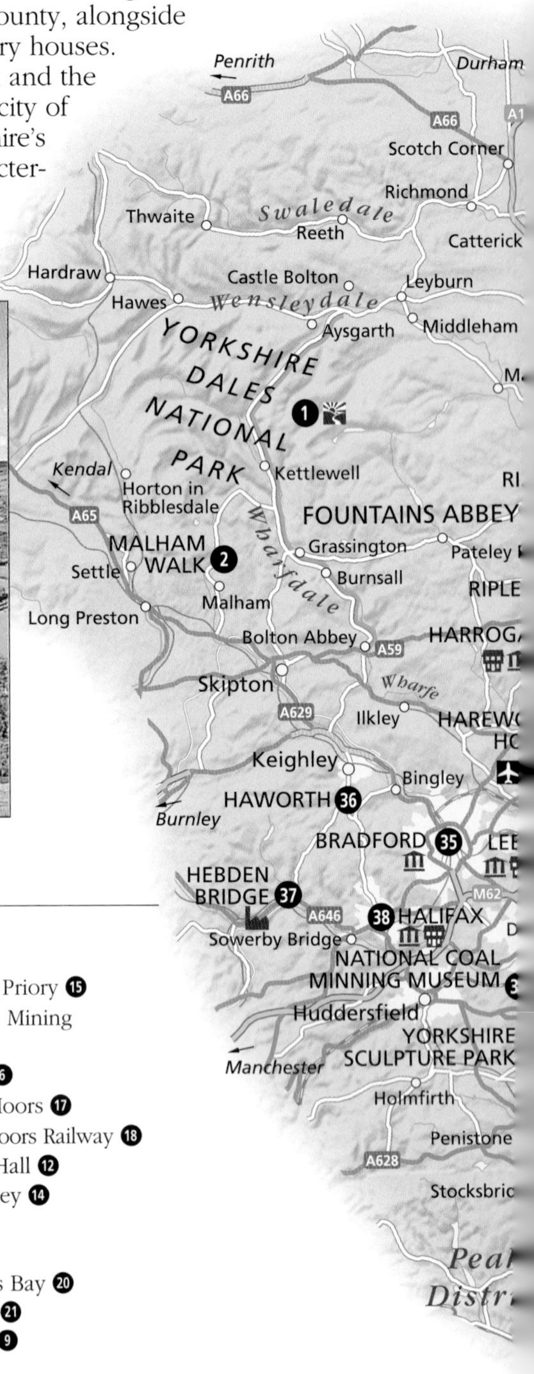

SIGHTS AT A GLANCE

Penrith
A66
Durham
A66
A1
Scotch Corner
Richmond
Thwaite
Swaledale
Reeth
Catterick
Hardraw
Castle Bolton
Leyburn
Hawes
Wensleydale
Aysgarth
Middleham
M
YORKSHIRE
DALES
NATIONAL
Kendal
PARK
Kettlewell
RI
Horton in
Ribblesdale
A65
Wharfedale
FOUNTAINS ABBEY
MALHAM
Settle
WALK
Grassington
Pateley
Burnsall
RIPLE
Malham
Long Preston
Bolton Abbey
A59
HARROG
Skipton
Wharfe
RIPLE
A629
Ilkley
HAREW(
HC
Keighley
Bingley
HAWORTH **36**
Burnley
BRADFORD **35**
LEE
HEBDEN
BRIDGE **37**
A646
38 HALIFAX
D
Sowerby Bridge
NATIONAL COAL
MINNING MUSEUM
Huddersfield
YORKSHIRE
Manchester
SCULPTURE PARK
Holmfirth
Penistone
A628
Stocksbrit
Pea
Distr

0 kilometres   15

0 miles   10

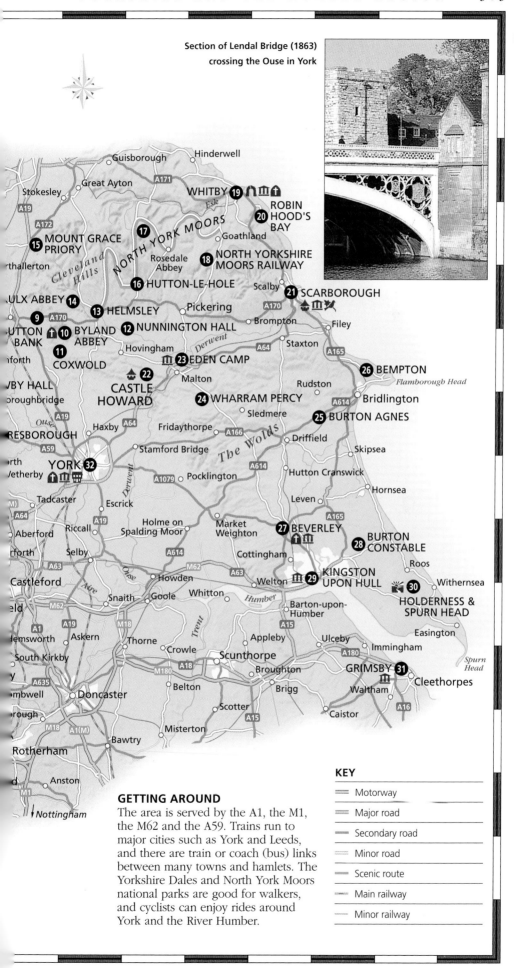

Section of Lendal Bridge (1863) crossing the Ouse in York

Guisborough
Hinderwell
Stokesley
Great Ayton
A171
WHITBY 19
A19
A172
MOUNT GRACE 15 PRIORY
17
NORTH YORK MOORS
ROBIN 20 HOOD'S BAY
Goathland
thallerton
Cleveland Hills
Rosedale Abbey
18 NORTH YORKSHIRE MOORS RAILWAY
ULX ABBEY 14
16 HUTTON-LE-HOLE
Scalby
21 SCARBOROUGH
9 A170
13 HELMSLEY
Pickering
A170
Brompton
Filey
UTTON 10 BANK
BYLAND ABBEY
12 NUNNINGTON HALL
Hovingham
Derwent
A64
Staxton
A165
forth
11 COXWOLD
23 EDEN CAMP
BY HALL
22
Malton
Rudston
26 BEMPTON
Flamborough Head
roughbridge
CASTLE HOWARD
24 WHARRAM PERCY
A614
Bridlington
RESBOROUGH
A19
Haxby
A64
Sledmere
25 BURTON AGNES
Fridaythorpe
A166
Driffield
Skipsea
A59
Stamford Bridge
The Wolds
rth
YORK 32
A1079
Pocklington
A614
Hutton Cranswick
Hornsea
Jetherby
Derwent
Leven
Tadcaster
Escrick
A165
M)
Riccall
Holme on Spalding Moor
Market Weighton
27 BEVERLEY
BURTON 28 CONSTABLE
A64
A19
Aberford
rforth
Selby
A614
Cottingham
Roos
Castleford
Aire
A63
M62
Howden
A63
Welton
KINGSTON 29 UPON HULL
30
Withernsea
eld
M62
Snaith
Goole
Whitton
Humber
HOLDERNESS & SPURN HEAD
A1
A19
M18
Barton-upon-Humber
Easington
emsworth
Askern
Thorne
Crowle
Appleby
A15
Ulceby
Immingham
Spurn Head
South Kirkby
M180
A18
Scunthorpe
Broughton
A180
y
A635
Belton
Brigg
GRIMSBY 31
Cleethorpes
mbwell
Doncaster
Scotter
Waltham
rough
M18
A1(M)
Bawtry
Misterton
A15
Caistor
A16
Rotherham
d
Anston
M1
Nottingham

GETTING AROUND

The area is served by the A1, the M1, the M62 and the A59. Trains run to major cities such as York and Leeds, and there are train or coach (bus) links between many towns and hamlets. The Yorkshire Dales and North York Moors national parks are good for walkers, and cyclists can enjoy rides around York and the River Humber.

KEY

Motorway
Major road
Secondary road
Minor road
Scenic route
Main railway
Minor railway

Yorkshire Dales ❶

The Yorkshire Dales is a farming landscape, formed
from three principle dales, Swaledale, Wharfedale and
Wensleydale, and a number of small ones, such as
Deepdale. Glaciation in the Ice Age helped carve out
these steep-sided valleys, and this scenery contrasts with
the high moorlands. However, 12 centuries of settlement
have altered the landscape in the form of cottages, castles
and villages which create a delightful environment for
walking. A national park since 1954, the area provides
recreation while serving local community needs.

Monk's Wynd – one of Richmond's
narrow, winding streets

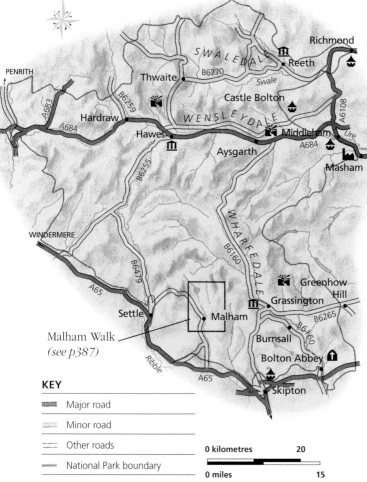

KEY

▥▥▥	Major road
▦▦▦	Minor road
═══	Other roads
▬▬▬	National Park boundary

0 kilometres   20

0 miles   15

Malham Walk
(see p387)

Exploring Swaledale

Swaledale's prosperity was
founded largely on wool, and
it is famous for its herd of
sheep that graze on the wild
higher slopes in the harshest
weather. The fast-moving river
Swale that gives the northernmost dale its name travels from
bleak moorland down magnificent waterfalls into the richly
wooded lower slopes, passing
through the village of Reeth
and the town of Richmond.

♠ Richmond Castle

(EH) Tower Street. **Tel** 01748 822493.
◐ Oct–Apr: Thu–Mon; May–Sep:
daily. 🅿 ♿ limited. 🚻
Swaledale's main point of entry
is the medieval market town
of Richmond, which has the
largest cobbled marketplace in
England. Alan Rufus, the
Norman 1st Earl of Richmond,
began building the castle in
1071, and some of the masonry
on the curtain walls probably
dates from that time. It has a
fine Norman keep, 30 m (100
ft) high with walls 3.3 m (11
ft) thick. An 11th-century arch
leads into a courtyard containing Scolland's Hall (1080), one
of England's oldest buildings.
  Richmond's marketplace was
once the castle's outer bailey.
Its quaint, narrow streets gave
rise to the song, *The Lass of
Richmond Hill* (1787), written
by Leonard McNally for his
wife, Frances I'Anson, who
was brought up in Hill House

The green, rolling landscape of Deepdale, near Dent

on Richmond Hill. Turner *(see p91)* depicted the town many times. The Georgian Theatre (1788) is the only one of its age still surviving.

🏛 Swaledale Folk Museum
Reeth Green. *Tel 01748 884118.*
⭕ *Easter–Oct: Wed–Fri, Sun & public hols; Nov–Easter: Sun.* 🈸 🖵 🏠
Reeth, a town that became known as the centre of the lead-mining industry, houses this museum in a former Methodist Sunday school (1830). Included in it are mining and wool-making artifacts (wool from the hardy Swaledale sheep was another mainstay of the economy) and brass band memorabilia.

🈳 Buttertubs
Near Thwaite, on the B6270 Hawes road, are a series of potholes that streams fall into. These became known as the Buttertubs when farmers going to market lowered their butter into the holes to keep it cool.

Buttertubs, near Thwaite

Exploring Wensleydale
The largest of the Yorkshire dales, Wensleydale is famous for its cheese and more recently for James Herriot's books and the television series, *All Creatures Great and Small.* It is easy walking country for anyone seeking an alternative to major moorland hikes.

🏛 Dales Countryside Museum
Station Yard, Hawes. *Tel 01969 666210.* ⭕ *daily.* 🈲 *24–26 Dec, 1 Jan.* 🈸 👍 🏠
In a former railway goods warehouse in Hawes, capital of Upper Wensleydale, is a

Barrels at the Theakston Brewery

fascinating museum, filled with items from life and industry in the 18th- and 19th-century Upper Dales. This includes cheese- and butter-making equipment. Wensleydale cheese was created by monks at nearby Jervaulx Abbey. There is also a rope-making works a short walk away.

Hawes itself is the highest market town in England, at 259 m (850 ft) above sea level. It is a thriving centre where thousands of sheep and cattle are auctioned each summer.

🈳 Hardraw Force
🈸 *at Green Dragon Inn, Hardraw.*
At the tiny village of Hardraw, nearby, is England's tallest single-drop waterfall, with no outcrops to interrupt its 29 m (96 ft) fall. It became famous in Victorian times when the daredevil Blondin walked across it on a tightrope. Today, you can walk right under this fine waterfall, against the rock face, and look through the stream without getting wet.

🈳 Aysgarth Waterfalls
ℹ️ *National Pk Centre (01969 662910).* ⭕ *Fri–Sun.*
An old packhorse bridge gives a clear view of the point at which the previously placid River Ure suddenly begins to plunge in foaming torrents over wide limestone shelves. Turner painted the impressive lower falls in 1817.

🏛 Theakston Brewery
Masham. *Tel 01765 680000.* ⭕ *daily.* 🈲 *23 Dec–early Jan.* 🈸 🚭 🏠 www.theakstons.co.uk
The pretty town of Masham is the home of Theakston brewery, creator of the potent ale Old Peculier. The history

VISITORS' CHECKLIST

N Yorkshire. 🚆 Skipton.
🚌 ℹ️ *01756 792809.*
www.yorkshiredales.org.uk

of this local family brewery from its origin in 1827 is on display in the visitors' centre. Masham village itself has an attractive square once used for sheep fairs, surrounded by 17th- and 18th-century houses. There is a medieval church.

⛫ Bolton Castle
Castle Bolton, nr Leyburn. *Tel 01969 623981.* ⭕ *daily.* 🈲 *23–25 Dec.* 🈸 🖵 🏠 www.boltoncastle.co.uk
Situated in the village of Castle Bolton, this castle was built in 1379 by the 1st Lord Scrope, Chancellor of England. It was used as a fortress from 1568 to 1569 when Mary, Queen of Scots *(see p511)* was held prisoner here by Elizabeth I *(see pp50–51).*

⛫ Middleham Castle
(EH) Middleham, nr Leyburn. *Tel 01969 623899.* ⭕ *Apr–Sep: 10am–6pm daily; Oct–Mar: 10am–4pm Mon–Wed, Sat & Sun.* 🈲 *1 Jan, 24–26 Dec.* 🏠 🈸 👍 *limited.*
Owned by Richard Neville, Earl of Warwick, it was built in 1170. The castle is better known as home to Richard III *(see p49)* when he was made Lord of the North. It was once one of the strongest fortresses in the north but became un-inhabited during the 15th century, when many of its stones were used for nearby buildings. The keep provides a fine view of the landscape.

Remains of Middleham Castle, once residence of Richard III

Extensive ruins of Bolton Priory, dating from 1154

Exploring Wharfedale

This dale is characterized by gritstone moorland, contrasting with quiet market towns along meandering sections of river. Many consider Grassington a central point for exploring Wharfedale, but the showpiece villages of Burnsall, overlooked by a 506 m (1,661 ft) fell, and Buckden, 701 m (2,302 ft), near Buckden Pike, also make excellent bases.

Nearby are the Three Peaks of Whernside, 736 m (2,416 ft), Ingleborough, 724 m (2,376 ft) and Pen-y-Ghent 694 m (2,278 ft). They are known for their potholes and tough terrain, but this does not deter keen walkers from attempting to climb them all in one day. If you sign in at the Pen-y-Ghent café at Horton-in-Ribblesdale, at the centre of the Three Peaks, and complete the 20 mile (32 km) course, reaching the summit of all three peaks in less than 12 hours, you can qualify for membership of the Three Peaks of Yorkshire Club.

Burnsall

St Wilfrid's, Burnsall. *Tel 01756 720331.* ◯ *Apr–Oct: daily to dusk.* ⓑ
Preserved in St Wilfrid's church graveyard are the original village stocks, gravestones from Viking times and a headstone carved in memory of the Dawson family by sculptor Eric Gill (1882–1940). The village has a five-arched bridge and hosts Britain's oldest fell race every August.

🏛 Grassington Museum

The Square, Grassington.
◯ *Mar–Oct: daily (pm).* 🎫
ⓑ *limited.*
This folk museum is set in two 18th-century lead miners' cottages. Its exhibits illustrate the domestic and working history of the area, including farming and lead mining.

🏴 Bolton Priory

Bolton Abbey, Skipton. *Tel 01756 718009.* ◯ *daily.* ⓑ
One of the most beautiful areas of Wharfedale is around the village of Bolton Abbey, set in an estate owned by the Dukes of Devonshire. While preserving its astounding beauty, its managers have incorporated over 30 miles (46 km) of footpaths, many suitable for the disabled and young families.

The ruins of Bolton Priory, established by Augustinian canons in 1154 on the site of a Saxon manor, are extensive. They include a church, chapter house, cloister and prior's lodging. These all demonstrate the wealth accumulated by the canons from the sale of wool from their flocks of sheep. The priory nave is still used as a parish church. Another attraction of the estate is the "Strid", a point where the River Wharfe surges spectacularly through a gorge, foaming yellow and gouging holes out of the rocks.

🏞 Stump Cross Caverns

Greenhow Hill, Pateley Bridge. *Tel 01756 752780.* ◯ *Mar–Nov: daily; Dec–Feb: Sat, Sun & pub hols.* 🎫 ▢
🗄 www.stumpcrosscaverns.co.uk
These caves were formed over a period of half a million years: trickles of underground water formed intertwining passages and carved them into fantastic shapes and sizes. Sealed off in the last Ice Age, the caves were only discovered in the 1850s, when lead miners sank a mine shaft into the caverns.

♟ Skipton Castle

High St. *Tel 01756 792442.* ◯ *daily (Sun: pm).* ⬤ *25 Dec.* 🎫 ▢ 📷
www.skiptoncastle.co.uk
The market town of Skipton is still one of the largest auctioning and stockraising centres in the north. Its 11th-century castle was almost entirely rebuilt by Robert de Clifford in the 14th century. Beautiful Conduit Court was added by Henry, Lord Clifford, in Henry VIII's reign. The central yew tree was planted by Lady Anne Clifford in 1659 to mark restoration work to the castle after Civil War damage.

Conduit Court (1495) and yew tree at Skipton Castle

Malham Walk ❷

The Malham area, shaped by glacial erosion 10,000 years ago, has one of Great Britain's most dramatic limestone landscapes. The walk from Malham village can take over four hours if you pause to enjoy the viewpoints and take a detour to Gordale Scar. Those who are short of time tend to go only as far as Malham Cove. This vast natural amphitheatre, formed by a huge geological tear, is like a giant boot-heel mark in the landscape. Above lie the deep crevices of Malham Lings, where rare flora such as hart's-tongue flourishes. Unusual plants grow in the lime-rich Malham Tarn, said to have provided inspiration for Charles Kingsley's *The Water Babies* (1863). Coot and mallard visit the tarn in summer and tufted duck in winter.

Sandpiper at Malham Tarn

Where the path meets the road ⑤
From here, you can catch a bus back to Malham village.

🚻 Malham Tarn House

Malham Tarn ④
Yorkshire's second-largest lake lies 305 m (1,000 ft) above sea level in a designated nature reserve.

Malham Lings ③
This fine limestone pavement was formed when Ice Age meltwater seeped into cracks in the rock, then froze and expanded.

Gordale Scar ⑥
Guarded by steep limestone cliffs, this deep gorge was created by meltwater from Ice Age glaciers.

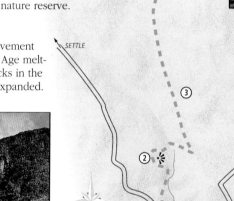

Malham Cove ②
The black streak in the centre of this 76 m (250 ft) cove is the site of a former waterfall.

Malham ①
An attractive riverside village, it has an information centre with details of drives and walks.

KEY

▬ ▬ Walk route

═══ Minor road

🌟 Viewpoint

🅿 Parking

ℹ️ Tourist information

🚻 Toilets

0 kilometres   1

0 miles   ¹/₂

TIPS FOR WALKERS

Starting point: *Malham.* ***Getting there:*** *Leave M65 at Junction 14 and take A56 to Skipton, then follow signs to Malham which is off A65.* ***Length:*** *7 miles (11 km).* ***Difficulty:*** *Malham Cove is steep but the Tarn area is flatter.*
ℹ️ *01729 830363.*

A 1920s poster advertising the spa town of Harrogate

Harrogate ❸

North Yorkshire. 🏠 69,000.
🚆 🚌 ℹ️ The Royal Baths,
Crescent Rd (0845 389 3223).
www.harrogate.gov.uk

Between 1880 and World
War I, Harrogate was the
north's leading spa town, with
nearly 90 medicinal springs.
It was ideal for aristocrats
who, after a tiring London
season, were able to stop
for a health cure before
journeying on to grouse-
shooting in Scotland.
   Today, Harrogate's main
attractions are its spa town
atmosphere, fine architecture,
public gardens and its conven-
ience as a centre for visiting
North Yorkshire and the Dales.
   The naturally welling spa
waters may not currently be
in use, but you can still go
for a Turkish bath in one of
the country's most attractive
steam rooms. The entrance at

the side of the Royal Bath
Assembly Rooms (1897) is
unassuming, but once inside,
the century-old **Harrogate
Turkish Baths** are a visual
feast of tiled Victoriana.
   The town's spa history is
recorded in the **Royal Pump
Room Museum**. At the turn
of the century, the waters
were thought to be rich in
iron early in the day. So,
between 7am and 9am the
1842 octagonal building
would have been filled with
rich and fashionable people
drinking glasses of water.
Poorer people could take
water from the pump outside.
Today you can sample the
waters and enjoy the
museum's exhibits, including
a Penny Farthing bicycle.
   Harrogate is also known for
the rainbow-coloured flower-
beds in **The Stray**, a common
space to the south of the town
centre, and for the ornamental
RHS Harlow Carr Gardens,

owned by the Royal Horticultural Society. Visitors can enjoy
the delicious cakes at **Betty's
Café Tea Rooms**.

🛁 **Harrogate Turkish Baths**
The Royal Baths, Crescent Rd.
Tel 01423 556746. ⭕ **Men:** Mon,
Wed & Fri: (pm); Sat. **Women:** Mon
(am); Tue & Thu: (pm); Fri (am); Sun.
Mixed (in bathing suits): Tue (am);
(couples only in bathing suits): Wed
& Fri (both eve); Sun (eve). 🖼️

🏛 **Royal Pump Room Museum**
Crown Pl. **Tel** 01423 556188.
⭕ daily (Sun: pm only).
⚫ 1 Jan, 24–26 Dec. 🖼️ ♿ 🎁

🛁 **Betty's Café Tea Rooms**
1 Parliament St. **Tel** 01423 814070.
⭕ daily. ⚫ 1 Jan, 25–26 Dec.
www.bettysandtaylors.co.uk

🌿 **RHS Harlow Carr Gardens**
Crag Lane. **Tel** 01423 702746. ⭕
daily. 🖼️ ♿ 🍴 🖥️ www.rhs.org.uk

Knaresborough ❹

North Yorkshire. 🏠 14,000. 🚆 🚌
from Harrogate. ℹ️ 9 Castle
Courtyard, Market Place (01423
866886). 🚌 Wed.

Perched precipitously above
the River Nidd is one
of England's oldest towns,
mentioned in the Domesday
Book of 1086 (see p48). Its
historic streets – which link the
church, John of Gaunt's ruined
castle, and the market place
with the river – are now lined
with fine 18th-century houses.
   Nearby is **Mother Shipton's
Cave**, reputedly England's
oldest tourist attraction. It first
went on show in 1630 as the
birthplace of Ursula Sontheil,

Mother Shipton's cave, with
objects encased in limestone

The south front of Newby Hall

a famous local prophetess. Today, people can view the effect the well near her cave has on objects hung below the dripping surface. Almost any item, from umbrellas to soft toys, will become encased in limestone within a few weeks.

※ Mother Shipton's Cave
Prophesy House, High Bridge. **Tel** 01423 864600. ◯ Easter–Oct: daily; Feb–Easter: Sat, Sun. ◉ Nov–Jan. 🖼 📷 📼 🏠

Ripley ❺

North Yorkshire. 🏠 150. 🚌 from Harrogate or Ripon. 🛈 Town Hall (01773 841488).
www.harrogate.gov.uk

Since the 1320s, when the first generation of the Ingilby family lived in an early incarnation of **Ripley Castle**, the village has been made up almost exclusively of castle employees. The influence of one 19th-century Ingilby had the most visual impact. In the 1820s, Sir William Amcotts Ingilby was so entranced by a village in Alsace Lorraine that he created a similar one in French Gothic style, complete with an *Hotel de Ville*. Present-day Ripley has a cobbled market square, and quaint cottages line the streets.

Ripley Castle, with its 15th-century gatehouse, was where Oliver Cromwell *(see p52)* stayed following the Battle of Marston Moor. The 28th generation of Ingilbys live here, and it is open for tours. The attractive grounds contain two lakes and a deer park, as well as more formal gardens.

♣ Ripley Castle
Ripley. **Tel** 01423 770152. ◯ Apr–Oct: daily; Nov–Mar: Tue, Thu, Sat–Sun; Dec–Feb: Sat–Sun. ◉ 25 Dec. 🖼 ♿ 📷 📼 🏠

Newby Hall ❻

Nr Ripon, North Yorkshire. **Tel** 01423 322583. ◯ Apr–Jun & Sep: Tue–Sun; Jul & Aug: daily. 🖼 ♿ 🍴 🏠
www.newbyhall.com

Newby Hall stands on land once occupied by the de Nubie family in the 13th century, and has been in the hands of the current family since 1748. The central part of the present house was built in the late 17th century in the style of Sir Christopher Wren.

Visitors will find 25 acres of gardens to explore. Laid out in a series of compartmented areas off a main axis, each garden is planted to come into flower during a different season. There is also a Woodland Discovery Walk, where contemporary scultpture is displayed.

For children, there is an adventure garden with activities and a miniature railway that runs through the gardens alongside the river Ure. River boat rides are also available. Each year a number of special events are staged, including Plant Fairs, a Historic Vehicle Rally and two Craft Fairs.

Fountains Abbey ❼

See pp390–91.

Ripon ❽

North Yorkshire. 🏠 14,000. 🚌 from Harrogate. 🛈 Minster Rd (0845 389 0178). ◉ Thu.
www.visitripon.org

Ripon, a charming small city, is best known for the cathedral and "the watch", which has been announced since the Middle Ages by the Wakeman. In return for protecting Ripon citizens, he would charge an annual toll of two pence per household. Today, a man still blows a horn in the Market Square each evening at 9pm, and every Thursday a handbell is rung to open the market.

The **Cathedral of St Peter and St Wilfrid** is built above a 7th-century Saxon crypt. At less than 3 m (10 ft) high and just over 2 m (7 ft) wide, it is held to be the oldest complete crypt in England. The cathedral is known for its collection of misericords *(see p341)*, which include both pagan and Old Testament examples. The architectural historian Sir Nikolaus Pevsner (1902–83) considered the cathedral's West Front the finest in England.

Ripon's **Prison and Police Museum**, housed in the 1686 "House of Correction", looks at police history and the conditions in Victorian prisons.

🏛 Prison and Police Museum
St Marygate. **Tel** 01765 690799. ◯ Apr–Oct: daily (pm only). ◉ Nov–Mar. 🖼 ♿ 🏠
www.riponmuseums.co.uk

Ripon's Wakeman, blowing his horn in the Market Square

Fountains Abbey ⑦

Nestling in the wooded valley of the River Skell are the extensive sandstone ruins of Fountains Abbey and the outstanding water garden of Studley Royal. Fountains Abbey was founded by Benedictine monks in 1132 and taken over by Cistercians three years later. By the mid-12th century it had become the wealthiest abbey in Britain, though it fell into ruin during the Dissolution *(see p50)*. In 1720, John Aislabie, the MP for Ripon and Chancellor of the Exchequer, developed the land and forest of the abbey ruins. He began work, continued by his son William, on the famous water garden, the statuary and Classical temples in the grounds. This makes a dramatic contrast to the simplicity of the abbey.

Fountains Hall
Built by Sir Stephen Proctor around 1611, with stones from the abbey ruins, its design is attributed to architect Robert Smythson. It included a great hall with a minstrels' gallery and an entrance flanked by Classical columns.

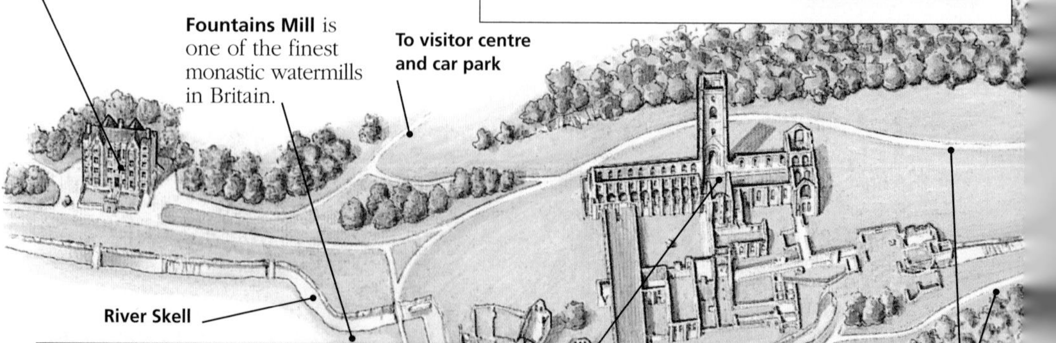

THE ABBEY

The abbey buildings were designed to reflect the Cistercians' desire for simplicity and austerity. The abbey frequently dispensed charity to the poor and the sick, as well as travellers.

The Chapel of Nine Altars *at the east end of the church was built from 1203 to 1247. It is ornate, compared to the rest of the abbey, with an 18-m (60-ft) high window complemented by another at the western end of the nave.*

Chapter house

Cloister

Abbot's house

Kitchen

Monks' infirmary hall

Refectory

Lay brothers' infirmary

Lay brothers' refectory

Cellarium and dormitory undercroft, *with vaulting 90 m (300 ft) long, was used for storing fleeces which the abbey monks sold to Venetian and Florentine merchants.*

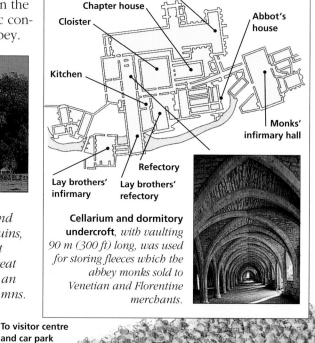

Fountains Mill is one of the finest monastic watermills in Britain.

To visitor centre and car park

River Skell

Paths leading to the estate park

★ **Abbey** *This was built by using stones taken from the Skell valley.*

STAR SIGHTS

★ Abbey

★ Temple of Piety

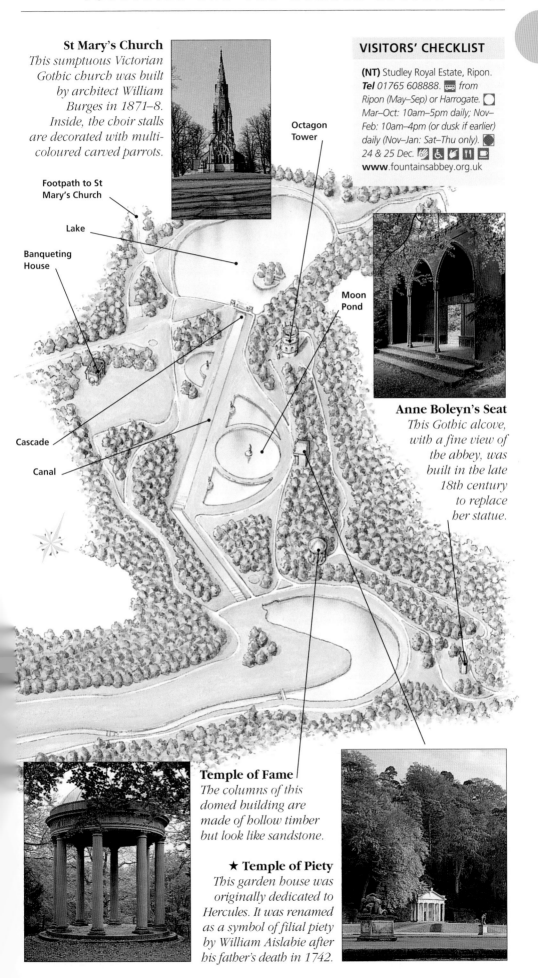

St Mary's Church
This sumptuous Victorian Gothic church was built by architect William Burges in 1871–8. Inside, the choir stalls are decorated with multi-coloured carved parrots.

Footpath to St Mary's Church

Lake

Banqueting House

Cascade

Canal

Octagon Tower

Moon Pond

VISITORS' CHECKLIST

(NT) Studley Royal Estate, Ripon. **Tel** 01765 608888. ▭ from Ripon (May–Sep) or Harrogate. ◯ Mar–Oct: 10am–5pm daily; Nov–Feb: 10am–4pm (or dusk if earlier) daily (Nov–Jan: Sat–Thu only). ● 24 & 25 Dec. ▨ & ◪ ▮ ▣ www.fountainsabbey.org.uk

Anne Boleyn's Seat
This Gothic alcove, with a fine view of the abbey, was built in the late 18th century to replace her statue.

Temple of Fame
The columns of this domed building are made of hollow timber but look like sandstone.

★ Temple of Piety
This garden house was originally dedicated to Hercules. It was renamed as a symbol of filial piety by William Aislabie after his father's death in 1742.

The 19th-century white horse, seen on one of the walks around Sutton Bank

Sutton Bank ⑨

North Yorkshire. 🚋 *Thirsk.* ℹ️
Sutton Bank (01845 597426).

Notorious among motorists for its 1 in 4 gradient, which climbs for about 107 m (350 ft), Sutton Bank itself is well known for its panoramic views. On a clear day you can see from the Vale of York to the Peak District *(see pp338–9)*. William and his sister Dorothy Wordsworth stopped here to admire the vista in 1802, on their way to visit his future wife, Mary Hutchinson, at Brompton. Apart from Sutton Bank, where you can walk round the white horse, the area is less wild than the coastal side, and suitable for children.

Byland Abbey ⑩

(EH) *Coxwold, York.* **Tel** *01347 868 614.* 🚌 *from York or Helmsley.* 🚋 *Thirsk.* ⭕ *Apr–Jul & Sep: Thu–Mon; Aug: daily.* 🎫 ♿ *limited.* **www**.
english-heritage.org.uk/yorkshire

This Cistercian monastery was founded in 1177 by monks from Furness Abbey in Cumbria. It featured what was then the largest Cistercian church in Britain, 100 m (328 ft) long and 41 m (135 ft) wide across the transepts. The layout of the monastery, including cloisters and the west front of the church, is still visible, as is the green and yellow glazed tile floor. Fine workmanship is shown in carved stone details and in the capitals, kept in the small museum.

In 1322 the Battle of Byland was fought nearby, and King Edward II *(see p40)* narrowly escaped capture when the invading Scottish army learned that he was dining with the Abbot. In his hurry to escape, the king had to leave many treasures behind, which were looted by the invading soldiers.

Coxwold ⑪

North Yorkshire. 🚶 *160.* ℹ️ *49 Market Place, Thirsk (01845 522755).* **www**.herriotcountry.com

Situated just inside the bounds of the North York Moors National Park *(see p395)*, this charming village nestles at the foot of the Howardian Hills. Its pretty houses are built from local stone, and the 15th-century church has some fine Georgian

Shandy Hall, home of author Laurence Sterne, now a museum

box pews and an impressive octagonal tower. But Coxwold is best known as the home of the author Laurence Sterne (1713–68), whose writings include *Tristram Shandy* and *A Sentimental Journey*.

Sterne moved here in 1760 as the church curate. He rented a rambling house that he named **Shandy Hall** after a Yorkshire expression meaning eccentric. Originally built as a timber-framed, open-halled house in the 15th century, it was modernized in the 17th century and Sterne later added a façade. His grave lies beside the porch at Coxwold's church.

The miniature Queen Anne drawing room at Nunnington Hall

Shandy Hall
Coxwold. *Tel 01347 868465.*
May–Sep: Wed & Sun (pm).
limited. **Gardens** Sun–Fri.
www.hambleton.gov.uk

Nunnington Hall ⓬

(NT) Nunnington, York. *Tel 01439 748283.* Malton, then bus or taxi.
Tue–Sun.
ground floor.

Set in alluring surroundings, this 17th-century manor house is a combination of architectural styles, including features from the Elizabethan and Stuart periods. Both inside and outside, a notable architectural feature is the use of the broken pediment (the upper arch is left unjoined).

Nunnington Hall was a family home until 1952, when Mrs Ronald Fife donated it to the National Trust. A striking feature is the panelling in the Oak Hall. Formerly painted, it extends over the three-arched screen to the Great Staircase. Nunnington's collection of 22 miniature furnished period rooms is popular with visitors.

A mid-16th-century tenant Dr Robert Huickes, physician to Henry VIII *(see pp50–51)*, is best known for advising Elizabeth I that she should not, at the age of 32, consider having any children.

Helmsley ⓭

North Yorkshire. 2,000. from Malton or Scarborough. Helmsley Castle (01439 770173). Fri.
www.ryedale.gov.uk/tourism

This pretty market town is noted for its **castle**, now an imposing ruin. Built from 1186 to 1227, its main function and strength as a fortress is illustrated by the remaining keep, tower and curtain walls. The original D-shaped keep had one part blasted away in the Civil War *(see p52)*, but remains the dominant feature. The castle was so impregnable that there were few attempts to force entry. However, in 1644, after holding out for a three-month seige against Sir Thomas Fairfax, the Parliamentary general, the castle was finally taken.

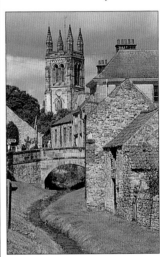
Helmsley church tower

Rievaulx Abbey ⓮

(EH) Nr Helmsley, North Yorkshire. *Tel 01439 798228.* Thirsk or Scarborough, then bus or taxi. Apr–Sep: daily; Oct–Mar: Thu–Mon.
24–26 Dec, 1 Jan. limited.

Rievaulx is perhaps the finest abbey in the area, due to both its dramatic setting in the steep wooded valley of the River Rye and its extensive remains. It is surrounded by steep banks that form natural barriers from the outside world. Monks of the French Cistercian order from Clairvaux founded this, their first major monastery in Britain, in 1132. The main buildings were finished before 1200. The layout of the chapel, kitchens and infirmary give an idea of monastic life.

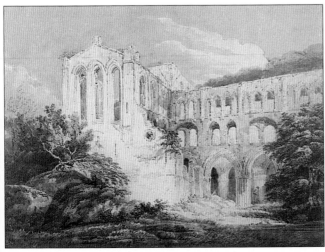
Rievaulx Abbey, painted by Thomas Girtin (1775–1802)

Mount Grace Priory ruins, with farm and mansion in foreground

Mount Grace Priory ⓯

(EH/NT) On A19, NE of Northallerton, North Yorks. **Tel** 01609 883494. ⚞ Northallerton then bus. ◯ Apr–Sep: Thu–Mon; Oct–Mar: Thu–Sun. 🖾 ♿ ground floor, shop & grounds. 🔒 **www**.english-heritage.org.uk/yorkshire

Founded by Thomas Holland, Duke of Surrey, and in use from 1398 until 1539, this is the best-preserved Carthusian or charterhouse monastery *(see pp350–51)* in England. The monks took a vow of silence and lived in solitary cells, each with his own garden and an angled hatch so that he would not even see the person serving his food. They only met at matins, vespers and feast-day services. Attempts at escape by those who could not endure the rigour of the rules were punished by imprisonment.

The ruins of the priory include the former prison, gatehouse and outer court, barns, guesthouses, cells and the church. The 14th-century church, the best-preserved section of the site, is particularly small, as it was only rarely used by the community. A cell has been reconstructed to give an impression of monastic life.

Hutton-le-Hole ⓰

North Yorkshire. 🚶 400. ⚞ Malton then bus. ℹ The Ropery, Pickering (01751 473791). **www**.ryedale.gov.uk/tourism

This picturesque village is characterized by a spacious green, grazed by roaming sheep, and surrounded by houses, an inn and shops. Lengths of white wood, replacing stone bridges, span the moorland stream. Its cottages, some with date panels over the doors, are made from limestone, with red pantiled roofs. In the village centre is the excellent

Wheelwright's workshop at Ryedale Folk Museum

Ryedale Folk Museum, which records the lifestyle of an agricultural community using Romano-British artifacts and reconstructed buildings.

🏛 **Ryedale Folk Museum** Hutton-le-Hole. **Tel** 01751 417367. ◯ late Jan–mid-Dec: daily. 🖾 ♿ 🔒

North York Moors ⓱

See p395.

North Yorkshire Moors Railway ⓲

Pickering & Grosmont, North Yorkshire. **Tel** 01751 472508. ◯ Apr–Oct: daily; Nov–Mar: some weekends (call for details). 🖾 ♿ 🖥 🔒 **www**.nymr.co.uk

Designed in 1831 by George Stephenson as a route along the North York Moors and links with the Esk Valley, Pickering and Whitby *(see p382)*, this railway was considered an engineering miracle. Due to budget constraints, Stephenson was not able to build a tunnel, so had to lay the route down the mile-long (1.5 km) incline between Beck Hole and Goathland. The area around Fen Bog had to be stabilized using timber, heather, brushwood and fleeces so that a causeway could be built over it. A horse was used to pull a coach along the track at 10 miles (16 km) per hour. After horsepower came steam, and for almost 130 years the railway linked Whitby to the rest of the country. In the early 1960s the line was closed but in 1967, a group of locals began a campaign to relaunch it, and in 1973 it was officially reopened. Today, the 18 mile (29 km) line runs from Pickering via Levisham, Newtondale Halt and Goathland before stopping at Grosmont, through the scenic heart of the North York Moors.

North York Moors ⓱

The area between Cleveland, the Vale of York and the Vale of Pickering is known as the North York Moors National Park. The landscape consists of bleak yet beautiful moors interspersed with lush green valleys. Agriculture is still the main source of income here as it has been for centuries, and until the advent of coal, the communities' local source of fuel was turf. In the 19th century, the geology of the area created extractive industries which included ironstone, lime, coal and building stone.

Mallyan Spout
A footpath leads to this waterfall from Goathland.

Farndale
During springtime, this area is famous for the beauty and profusion of its daffodils.

"Fat Betty" White Cross Crosses and standing stones are a feature of the Moors.

Goathland
A centre for forest and moorland walks, it has 19th-century houses and good accommodation.

THE MOORS CENTRE, DANBY

EGTON BRIDGE

WHITBY

West Beck

LEAEHOLM

Wheeldale Gill

THORGILL

Seven

Hartoft Beck

Rutmoor Beck

Blawarth Beck

Dove

Rosedale Abbey
Named after the priory that has long since gone, this beautiful village still has some remains of the kilns from its 19th-century ironstone mining industry.

Hutton-le-Hole
This lovely village has the excellent Ryedale Folk Museum.

Spaunton

Wade's Causeway
Often called the Roman Road, its origins and destination are unknown. Long considered Roman in date, this is now less certain, although it may date from towards the end of the Roman occupation.

VISITORS' CHECKLIST

North Yorkshire. 🚆 Pickering. 🚌 Pickering (Easter–Oct). **Moorsbus Tel** 01845 597000. ℹ Pickering (01751 473791); Moors Centre (01439 772737). **www**.visit northyorkshiremoors.co.uk

Lastingham
Lastingham's church, dating from 1078, has a Norman crypt with stone carving.

0 kilometres 2

0 miles 2

Whitby ⑲

Jet comb (c.1870)

Whitby's known history dates back to the 7th century, when a Saxon monastery was founded on the site of today's famous 13th-century abbey ruins. In the 18th and early 19th centuries it became an industrial port and shipbuilding town, as well as a whaling centre. In the Victorian era, the red-roofed cottages at the foot of the east cliff were filled with workshops crafting jet into jewellery and ornaments. Today, the tourist shops that have replaced them sell antique-crafted examples of the distinctive black gem.

VISITORS' CHECKLIST

North Yorkshire. 🏘 13,500. ✈ Teeside, 50 miles (80 km) ÑW Whitby. 🚆 Station Sq. 🛈 Langborne Rd (01723 383637). 🚌 Tue, Sat. 🎪 Whitby Festival: Jun; Angling Festival: Apr; Lifeboat Day: Jul or Aug; Folk Week: 17–23 Aug; Whitby Regatta: Aug. **www**. discoveryorkshirecoast.com

Exploring Whitby

Whitby is divided into two by the estuary of the River Esk. The Old Town, with its pretty cobbled streets and pastel-hued houses, huddles round the harbour. High above it is St Mary's Church with a wood interior reputedly fitted by ships' carpenters. The ruins of the 13th-century Whitby Abbey, nearby, are still used as a landmark by mariners. From them you get a fine view over the still-busy harbour, strewn with colourful nets. A pleasant place for a stroll, the harbour is overlooked by an imposing bronze clifftop statue of the explorer Captain James Cook (1728–79), who was apprenticed as a teenager to a Whitby shipping firm.

Lobster pots lining the quayside of Whitby's quaint harbour

Medieval arches above the nave of Whitby Abbey

🏛 Whitby Abbey

(EH) Abbey Lane. **Tel** 01947 603568. ☐ Mar–Oct: daily; Nov–Feb: Thu–Mon. 🗺🔖🛗🛈

The monastery founded in 657 was sacked by Vikings in 870. In the 11th century it was rebuilt as a Benedictine Abbey. The ruins date mainly from the 13th century. A visitor centre has recently been added.

🛈 St Mary's Parish Church

East Cliff. **Tel** 01947 603421. ☐ daily. Stuart and Georgian alterations to this Norman church have left a mixture of twisted wood columns and maze-like 18th-century box pews. The 1778 triple-decker pulpit has rather avant-garde decor – ear-trumpets used by a Victorian rector's deaf wife.

🏛 Captain Cook Memorial Museum

Grape Lane. **Tel** 01947 601900. ☐ Mar–Oct & Feb half-term: daily. 🗺🛈 **www**.cookmuseumwhitby.co.uk

The young James Cook slept in the attic of this 17th-century harbourside house when he was apprenticed nearby. The museum has displays of period furniture in the style described in the inventories of the house, and watercolours by artists who travelled on his voyages.

🏛 Whitby Museum and Pannett Art Gallery

Pannett Park. **Tel** 01947 602908 (museum), 01947 602051 (gallery). ☐ Tue–Sun & public hols. ☐ Sun: am; 24 Dec–2 Jan. 🗺 museum only. 🛗 limited. 🛈

The Pannett Park grounds, museum and gallery were a gift of Whitby solicitor, Robert Pannett (1834–1920), to house his art collection. Among the museum's treasures are objects illustrating local history, such as jet jewellery, and Captain Cook artifacts.

The three-storey extension at the museum, completed in 2005, houses a costume gallery and photography and map collections.

🛈 Caedmon's Cross

East Cliff.

On the path side of the abbey's clifftop graveyard is the cross of Caedmon, an illiterate labourer who worked at the abbey in the 7th century. He experienced a vision that inspired him to compose cantos of Anglo-Saxon religious verse, which are still sung today.

Cross of Caedmon (1898)

Robin Hood's Bay 20

North Yorkshire. 👥 *1,400.*
🚂 🚌 *Whitby.* ℹ️ *Langbourne Rd, Whitby (01723 383637).*
www.discoveryorkshirecoast.com

Legend has it that Robin Hood *(see p336)* kept his boats here in case he needed to make a quick getaway. The village has a history as a smugglers' haven, and many houses have ingenious hiding places for contraband. The cobbled main street is so steep that visitors need to leave their vehicles in the car park. In the village centre, attractive, narrow streets full of colour-washed stone cottages huddle around a quaint quay. There is a rocky beach with rock pools for children to play in. At low tide, the pleasant walk south to Boggle Hole takes 15 minutes, but you need to keep an eye on the tides.

Cobbled alley in the Bay Town area of Robin Hood's Bay

The fishing port and town of Scarborough nestling round the harbour

Scarborough 21

North Yorkshire. 👥 *54,000.* 🚂
🚌 ℹ️ *Valley Bridge Rd (01723 383636).* 🚢 *Mon–Sat.* **www**.
discoveryorkshirecoast.com

The history of Scarborough as a resort can be traced back to 1626, when it became known as a spa. In the Industrial Revolution *(see pp348–9)* it was nicknamed "the Queen of the Watering Places", but the post-World War II trend for holidays abroad has meant fewer visitors. The town has two beaches; the South Bay amusement arcades contrast with the quieter North Bay. Playwright Alan Ayckbourn premiers his work at the Stephen Joseph theatre, and Anne Brontë *(see p412)* is buried in St Mary's Church.

Bronze and Iron Age relics have been found on the site of **Scarborough Castle**. The **Rotunda** (1828–9), which underwent a major refurbishment during 2007, was one of Britain's first purpose-built museums. Works by the local artist Atkinson Grimshaw (1836–93) hang in **Scarborough Art Gallery**. The **Sea-Life and Marine Sanctuary**'s baby seals are its main attraction.

🏰 **Scarborough Castle**
(EH) Castle Rd. **Tel** *01723 372451.*
🕐 *Apr–Sep: daily; Oct–mid-Mar: Thu–Mon.* ⬤ *1 Jan, 24–26 Dec.*
📷 ♿ 🛍️

🏛️ **Rotunda Museum**
Vernon Rd. **Tel** *01723 374839.*
🕐 *Jun–Sep: Tue–Sun; Oct–May: Tue, Sat, Sun & public hols.*
⬤ *1 Jan, 25 & 26 Dec.* 🛍️ 📷

🏛️ **Scarborough Art Gallery**
The Crescent. **Tel** *01723 374753.*
🕐 *Tue–Sun.* ⬤ *1 Jan, 25 & 26 Dec.* 🛍️ 📷 🖥️ **www**.scarborough museums.org.uk

🐠 **Sea-Life and Marine Sanctuary**
Scalby Mills Rd. **Tel** *01723 376125.*
🕐 *daily.* ⬤ *25 Dec.* 📷 ♿ 🖥️ 🛍️
www.sealifeeurope.com

THE GROWING POPULARITY OF SWIMMING

During the 18th century, sea-bathing came to be regarded as a healthy pastime, and from 1735 onwards men and women, on separate stretches of the coast, could be taken out into the sea in bathing huts, or "machines". In the 18th century, bathing was segregated although nudity was permitted. The Victorians brought in fully clothed bathing, and 19th-century workers from Britain's industrial heartlands used the new steam trains to visit the coast for their holidays. At this time, British seaside resorts such as Blackpool *(see p371)* and Scarborough expanded to meet the new demand.

A Victorian bathing hut on wheels

Castle Howard ②

Pillar detail in the Great Hall, carved by Samuel Carpenter

Still owned and lived in by the Howard family, Castle Howard was created by Charles, 3rd Earl of Carlisle. In 1699, he commissioned Sir John Vanbrugh, a man of dramatic ideas but with no previous architectural experience, to design a palace for him. Vanbrugh's grand designs of 1699 were put into practice by architect Nicholas Hawksmoor *(see p28)*, and the main body of the house was completed by 1712. The West Wing was built in 1753–9, using a design by Thomas Robinson, son-in-law of the 3rd Earl. In the 1980s, Castle Howard was used as the location for the television version of Evelyn Waugh's novel *Brideshead Revisited* (1945) and again for the film version in 2008.

Temple of the Four Winds
Vanbrugh's last work, designed in 1724, has a dome and four Ionic porticoes. Situated in the grounds at the end of the terrace, it is typical of an 18th-century "landscape building".

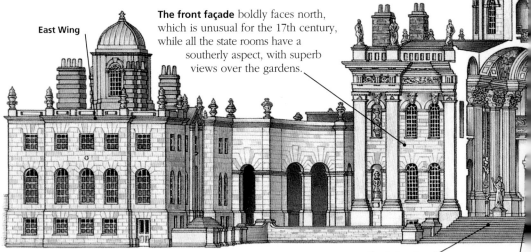

East Wing

The front façade boldly faces north, which is unusual for the 17th century, while all the state rooms have a southerly aspect, with superb views over the gardens.

North Front

★ Great Hall
Rising 20 m (66 ft), from its 515 sq m (5,500 sq ft) floor to the dome, the Great Hall has columns by Samuel Carpenter (1660–1713), wall paintings by Pellegrini and a circular gallery.

SIR JOHN VANBRUGH

Vanbrugh (1664–1726) trained as a soldier, but became better known as a playwright, architect and member of the Whig nobility. He collaborated with Hawksmoor over the design of Blenheim Palace, but his bold architectural vision, later greatly admired, was mocked by the establishment. He died while working on the garden buildings and grounds of Castle Howard.

Chapel Stained Glass

Admiral Edward Howard altered the chapel in 1870–75. The windows were designed by Edward Burne-Jones and made by William Morris & Co.

VISITORS' CHECKLIST

A64 from York. **Tel** 01653 648 444. York then bus, or Malton then taxi. **House** Mar–Oct: 11am–4pm daily. **Grounds** 10am–4:30pm daily. **www.**castlehoward.co.uk

Bust of the 7th Earl

J H Foley sculpted this portrait bust, which stands at the top of the Grand Staircase in the West Wing, in 1870.

★ Long Gallery

Displayed here are paintings and sculptures commissioned by the Howard family, including works by Reynolds and Pannini.

West Wing

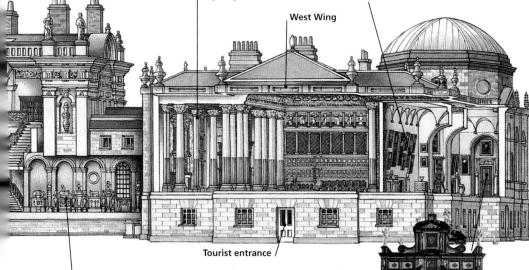

Tourist entrance

Antique Passage

Antiquities collected in the 18th and 19th centuries by the various Earls of Carlisle are on display here. The plethora of mythical figures and gods reflects contemporary interest in Classical civilizations.

STAR SIGHTS

- ★ Great Hall
- ★ Long Gallery

Museum Room

Furniture here includes Regency chairs, a bronze collection and this 17th-century cabinet.

Eden Camp ㉓

Malton, North Yorkshire. **Tel** 01653 697777. 🚆 Malton then taxi. ⬤ mid-Jan–late Dec: daily. 🄸 ▨ ♿ ▣
www.edencamp.co.uk

This is an unusual, award-winning theme museum which pays tribute to the British people during World War II. Italian and German prisoners of war were kept at Eden Camp between 1939 and 1948. Today, some original huts built by Italian prisoners in 1942 are used as a museum, with period tableaux and a soundtrack. Each hut adopts a theme to take the visitor through civilian life in war-time, from Chamberlain's radio announcement of the outbreak of hostilities to the coming of peace. Visitors, including schoolchildren and nostalgic veterans, can see the Doodle-bug V-1 bomb which crashed outside the Officers' Mess, take tea in the canteen or experience a night in the Blitz. A tour can last for several hours.

British and American flags by the sign for Eden Camp

Wharram Percy ㉔

(EH) North Yorkshire. **Tel** 01904 601 901. 🚆 Malton, then taxi. ⬤ daily.
www.english-heritage.org.uk

This is one of England's most important medieval village sites. Recent excavations have unearthed evidence of a 30-household community, with two manors, and the remains of a medieval church. There is also a millpond which has beautiful wild flowers in late spring. Wharram Percy is set in a pretty valley, sign-posted off the B1248 from Burdale, in the heart of the green, rolling Wolds. It is about 20 minutes' walk from the car park, and makes an ideal picnic stop.

Alabaster carving on the chimney-piece at Burton Agnes

Burton Agnes ㉕

On A614, nr Driffield, East Yorks. **Tel** 01262 490324. 🚆 Driffield, then bus. ⬤ Apr–Oct: daily. ▨ ♿ limited. ▣ 🄸 www.burton-agnes.com

Of all the grand houses in this area, Burton Agnes Hall is a firm favourite. This is partly because the attractive, red-brick Elizabethan mansion has such a homely atmosphere. One of the first portraits you see in the Small Hall is of Anne Griffith, whose father, Sir Henry, built the house. There is a monument to him in the local church.

Burton Agnes has remained in the hands of the original family and has changed little since it was built, between 1598 and 1610. You enter it by the turreted gatehouse, and the entrance hall has a fine Elizabethan alabaster chimney piece. The massive oak stair-case is an impressive example of Elizabethan woodcarving.

In the library is a collection of Impressionist and Post-Impressionist art, pleasantly out of character with the rest of the house, including works by André Derain, Renoir and Augustus John. The extensive grounds include a purpose-built play area for children.

Bempton and Flamborough Head ㉖

East Yorkshire. 🚶 4,300. 🚆 Bempton. 🚌 Bridlington. 🄸 25 Prince St, Bridlington (01262 673474).
www.eastriding.gov.uk

Bempton, which consists of 5 miles (8 km) of steep chalk cliffs between Speeton and Flamborough Head, is the largest seabird-breeding colony in England, and is famous for its puffins. The ledges and fissures provide ideal nest-sites for more

Nesting gannet on the chalk cliffs at Bempton

than 100,000 pairs of birds. Today, eight different species, including skinny black shags and kittiwakes, thrive on the Grade 1 listed Bempton cliffs. Bempton is the only mainland site for goose-sized gannets, well known for their dramatic fishing techniques. May, June and July are the best bird-watching months.

The spectacular cliffs are best seen from the north side of the Flamborough Head peninsula.

Beverley ㉗

East Riding of Yorkshire. 🚶 *30,000.*
ℹ️ *34 Butcher Row (01482 391672).*
🚪 *Sat.* **www.**eastriding.gov.uk

The history of Beverley dates back to the 8th century, when Old Beverley served as a retreat for John, later Bishop of York, who was canonized for his healing powers. Over the centuries Beverley grew as a medieval sanctuary town. Like York, it is an attractive combination of both medieval and Georgian buildings.

The best way to enter Beverley is through the last of five medieval town gates, the castellated North Bar (rebuilt

Minstrel Pillar in St Mary's Church

1409–10). The bars were constructed so that market goods had to pass through them and a toll (levy) paid.

The skyline is dominated by the twin towers of the magnificent **minster**. This was co-founded in 937 by Athelstan, King of Wessex, in place of the church that John of Beverley had chosen as his final resting place in 721. The decorated nave is the earliest surviving building work which dates back to the early 1300s. It is particularly famous for its 16th-century choir stalls and 68 misericords (*see p341*).

The minster contains many early detailed stone carvings, including a set of four from about 1308 that illustrate figures with ailments such as toothache and lumbago. On the north side of the altar is the richly carved 14th-century Gothic Percy tomb, thought to be that of Lady Idoine Percy. Also on the north side is the Fridstol, or Peace Chair, said to date from 924-39, the time of Athelstan. Anyone who sat on it would be granted 30 days' sanctuary. Within the North Bar, **St Mary's Church** has a 13th-century chancel and houses Britain's largest number of medieval

The inspiration for Lewis Carroll's White Rabbit, St Mary's Church

stone carvings of musical instruments. The brightly painted 16th-century Minstrel Pillar is particularly notable. Painted on the panelled chancel ceiling are portraits of monarchs after 1445. On the richly sculpted doorway of St Michael's Chapel is the grinning pilgrim rabbit said to have inspired Lewis Carroll's White Rabbit in *Alice in Wonderland*.

There is a great day out to be had at **Beverley Races**, with various theme days throughout the season and excellent food and drink.

🅿️ **Beverley Races**
York Rd. *Tel 01482 867488.*
⭕ *20 meetings Apr–Sep.*
♿ 🚻 @ info@
beverleyracecourse.co.uk

Beverley Minster, one of Europe's finest examples of Gothic architecture

Burton Constable 28

Nr Hull, East Yorkshire. *Tel 01964 562400.* Hull then taxi.
Easter–Oct: Sat–Thu.
www.burtonconstable.com

The Constable family have been leading landowners since the 13th century, and have lived at Burton Constable Hall since work began on it in 1570. It is an Elizabethan house, altered in the 18th century by Thomas Lightholer, Thomas Atkinson and James Wyatt. Today, its 30 rooms include Georgian and Victorian interiors. It has a fine collection of Chippendale furniture and family portraits dating from the 16th century. Most of the collections of prints, textiles and drawings belong to Leeds City Art Galleries. The family still lives in the south wing.

Painting of Burton Constable (c.1690) by an anonymous artist

The Princes' Dock in Kingston upon Hull's restored docks area

Kingston upon Hull 29

Kingston upon Hull. 270,000.
Paragon St. (01482 223559). Mon–Sat.
www.hullcc.gov.uk

There is a lot more to Hull than the heritage of a thriving fishing industry. The restored town centre docks are attractive, and Hull's Old Town, laid out in medieval times, is all cobbled, winding streets and quaintly askew red-brick houses. You can follow the "Seven Seas" Fish Trail, a path of inlaid metal fishes on the city's pavements that illustrates the many different varieties that have been landed in Hull, from anchovy to shark.

In Victoria Square is the **Maritime Museum**. Built in 1871 as the offices of the Hull Dock Company, it traces the city's maritime history. Among its exhibits are an ornate whale-bone and vertebrae bench and a display of complicated rope knots such as the Eye Splice and the Midshipman's Hitch.

An imposing Elizabethan building, **Hands on History**, explores Hull's story through a collection of some of its families' artifacts.

In the heart of the Old Town, the **William Wilberforce House** is one of the surviving examples of the High Street's brick merchants' dwellings. Its first-floor oak-panelled rooms date from the 17th century, but most of the house is dedicated to the Wilberforce family. The house has recently undergone a huge refurbishment costing around £1.6 million.

Nearby is the **Streetlife Transport Museum**, Hull's most popular and noisiest museum, loved by children. It features Britain's oldest tramcar. New to Hull, at the mouth of the River Hull, **The Deep** is the world's only submarium, in a stunning building and dramatic setting. With lots of exciting sea life and state-of-the-art technology, it is ideal for families.

Maritime Museum
Queen Victoria Sq *Tel 01482 613903.* daily (Sun: pm).
www.hullcc.gov.uk/museums

Hands on History
South Churchside. *Tel 01482 613902.* daily (Sun: pm).
23-27 Dec, 1 Jan, Good Fri.

WILLIAM WILBERFORCE (1758–1833)

William Wilberforce, born in Hull to a merchant family, was a natural orator. After studying Classics at Cambridge, he entered politics and in 1784 gave one of his first public addresses in York. The audience was captivated, and Wilberforce realized the potential of his powers of persuasion. From 1785 onwards, adopted by the Pitt government as spokesman for the abolition of slavery, he conducted a determined and conscientious campaign. But his speeches won him enemies, and in 1792, threats from a slave-importer meant that he needed a constant armed guard. In 1807 his bill to abolish the lucrative slave trade became law.

A 19th-century engraving of Wilberforce by J Jenkins

🏛 **William Wilberforce Hse**
High St, Hull. *Tel 01482 613921.*
○ *daily (Sun: pm).* 🅿 ᪥ *limited.*

🏛 **Streetlife Transport Museum**
High St, Hull. *Tel 01482 613956.*
○ *Mon–Sat, Sun pm.* ᪥ 🅿

🐬 **The Deep**
Hull (via Citadel Way). *Tel 01482 381 000.* ○ *daily.* ● *24, 25 Dec.* ᪥ 📷
📺 🅿 **P** www.thedeep.co.uk

Holderness and Spurn Head 30

East Riding of Yorkshire. 🚂 *Hull (Paragon St) then bus.* 🛈 *120 Newbegin, Hornsea (01964 536404).*

This curious flat area east of Hull, with straight roads and delicately waving fields of oats and barley, in many ways resembles Holland, except that its mills are derelict. Beaches stretch for 30 miles (46 km) along the coastline. The main resort towns are **Withernsea** and **Hornsea**.

The Holderness landscape only exists because of erosion higher up the coast. The sea continues to wash down tiny bits of rock which accumulate. Around 1560, this began to form a sandbank, and by 1669 it had became large enough to be colonized as Sonke Sand. The last bits of silting mud and debris joined the island to the mainland as recently as the 1830s. Today, you can drive through the eerie, lush wilderness of Sunk Island on the way east to Spurn Head. This is located at the tip of the Spurn Peninsula,

a 3.5 mile (6 km) spit of land that has also built up as the result of coastal erosion elsewhere. Flora, fauna and birdlife have been protected here by the Yorkshire Wildlife Trust since 1960. Walking here gives the eerie feeling that the land could be eroded from under your feet at any time. A surprise discovery at the end of Spurn Head is a tiny community of pilots and lifeboat crew, constantly on call to guide ships into Hull harbour, or help cope with disasters.

Fishing boat at Grimsby's National Fishing Heritage Centre

Grimsby 31

NE Lincs. 🏘 *92,000.* 🚂 🚌 🛈
Alexandra Dock, Cleethorpes (01472 323222). **www**.nelincs.gov.uk

Perched at the mouth of the River Humber, Grimsby was founded in the Middle Ages by a Danish fisherman

by the name of Grim, and rose to prominence in the 19th century as one of the world's largest fishing ports. Its first dock was opened in 1800 and, with the arrival of the railways, the town secured the means of transporting its catch all over the country. Even though the traditional fishing industry had declined by the 1970s, dock area redevelopment has ensured that Grimsby's unique heritage is retained.

This is best demonstrated by the award-winning **National Fishing Heritage Centre**, a museum that recreates the industry in its 1950s heyday, capturing the atmosphere of the period. Visitors sign on as crew members on a trawler and, by means of a variety of vivid interactive displays, travel from the back streets of Grimsby to the Arctic fishing grounds. On the way, they can experience the roll of the ship, the smell of the fish and the heat of the engine. The tour can be finished off with a guided viewing of the restored 1950s trawler, the *Ross Tiger.*

Other attractions in Grimsby include an International Jazz Festival every September, a restored Victorian shopping street called Abbeygate, a market, a wide selection of restaurants, and the nearby seaside resorts of Cleethorpes, Mablethorpe and Skegness.

🏛 **National Fishing Heritage Centre**
Heritage Sq, Alexandra Dock. *Tel 01472 323345.* ○ *Easter–Oct: daily.* ● *25 & 26 Dec.* 📷 ᪥ ✏ 📺 🅿

Isolated lighthouse at Spurn Head, at the tip of Spurn Peninsula

Street-by-Street: York 32

The city of York has retained so much of its medieval structure that walking into its centre is like entering a living museum. Many of the ancient timbered houses, perched on narrow, winding streets, such as the Shambles, are protected by a conservation order. Much of the centre is pedestrianised and there are always student bikes bouncing over cobbled streets. Its strategic position led to its development as a railway centre in the 19th century.

Monk Bar coat of arms

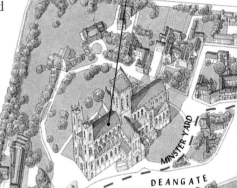

★ York Minster
England's largest medieval church was begun in 1220 (see pp406–

Stonegate
The medieval red devil is a feature of this street, built over a Roman road.

Thirsk ←

Helmsley

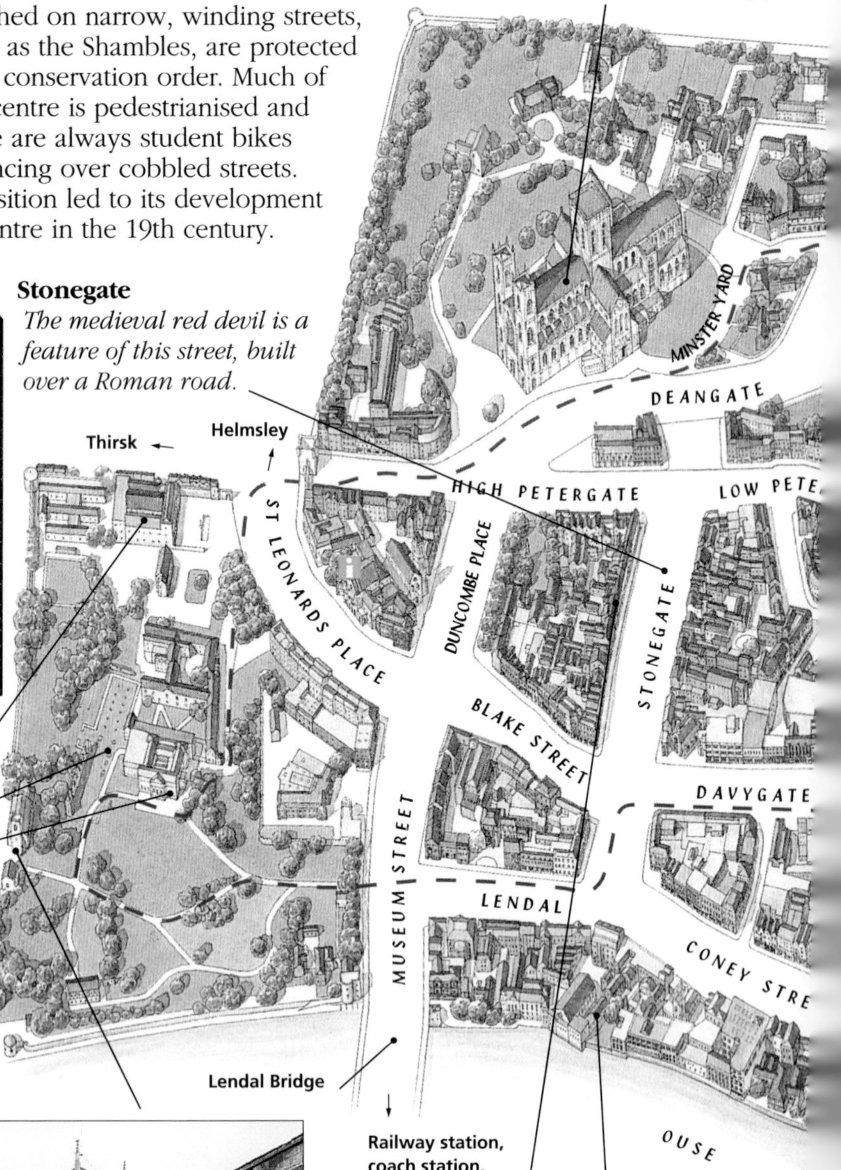

York Art Gallery

St Mary's Abbey

Yorkshire Museum is home to some of the most fascinating archeology in the country.

DEANGATE

HIGH PETERGATE

LOW PETE

ST LEONARDS PLACE

DUNCOMBE PLACE

STONEGATE

BLAKE STREET

DAVYGATE

MUSEUM STREET

LENDAL

CONEY STRE

MINSTER YARD

Lendal Bridge

OUSE

Railway station, coach station, National Railway Museum, and Leeds

Ye Old Starre Inne is one of the oldest pubs in York.

St Olave's Church
The 11th-century church, next to the gatehouse of St Mary's Abbey (see p350), was founded by the Earl of Northumbria in memory of St Olaf, King of Norway. To the left is the Chapel of St Mary on the Walls.

Guildhall
This two-headed medieval roof boss is on the 15th-century Guildhall, situated beside the River Ouse and restored after bomb damage during World War I.

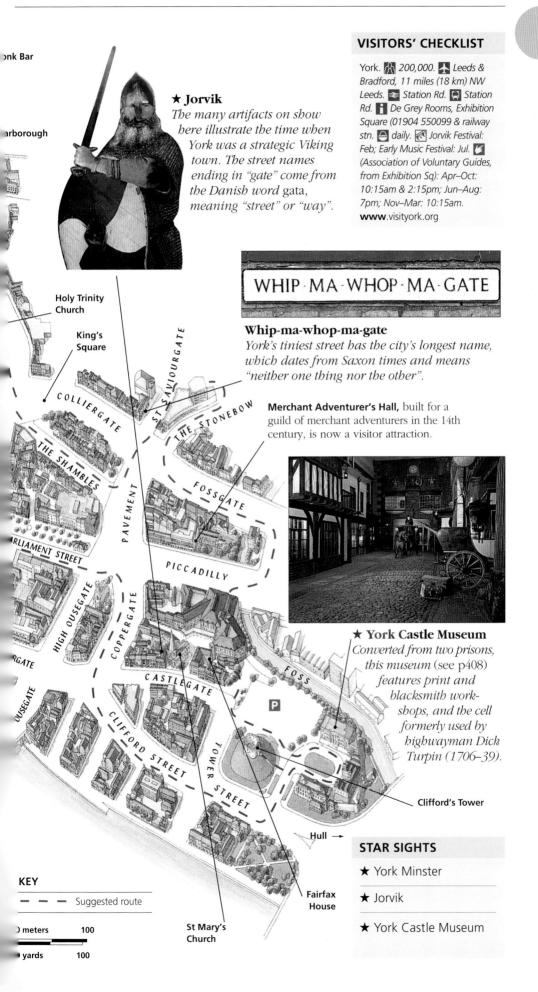

★ **Jorvik**

The many artifacts on show here illustrate the time when York was a strategic Viking town. The street names ending in "gate" come from the Danish word gata, *meaning "street" or "way".*

onk Bar

arborough

Holy Trinity Church

King's Square

COLLIERGATE

THE SHAMBLES

ST SAVIOURGATE

THE STONEBOW

FOSSGATE

PAVEMENT

RLIAMENT STREET

PICCADILLY

HIGH OUSEGATE

COPPERGATE

RGATE

CASTLEGATE

FOSS

OUSEGATE

CLIFFORD STREET

TOWER STREET

St Mary's Church

Fairfax House

Hull →

VISITORS' CHECKLIST

York. 👥 *200,000.* ✈ *Leeds & Bradford, 11 miles (18 km) NW Leeds.* 🚆 *Station Rd.* 🚌 *Station Rd.* ℹ️ *De Grey Rooms, Exhibition Square (01904 550099 & railway stn.* 🎭 *daily.* 🎊 *Jorvik Festival: Feb; Early Music Festival: Jul.* 🚶 *(Association of Voluntary Guides, from Exhibition Sq): Apr–Oct: 10:15am & 2:15pm; Jun–Aug: 7pm; Nov–Mar: 10:15am.* **www**.visityork.org

WHIP·MA·WHOP·MA·GATE

Whip-ma-whop-ma-gate

York's tiniest street has the city's longest name, which dates from Saxon times and means "neither one thing nor the other".

Merchant Adventurer's Hall, built for a guild of merchant adventurers in the 14th century, is now a visitor attraction.

★ **York Castle Museum**

Converted from two prisons, this museum (see p408) features print and blacksmith work-shops, and the cell formerly used by highwayman Dick Turpin (1706–39).

Clifford's Tower

STAR SIGHTS

★ York Minster

★ Jorvik

★ York Castle Museum

KEY

- - - Suggested route

meters   100

yards   100

York Minster

Central sunflower in rose window

The largest Gothic cathedral north of the Alps, York Minster is 158 m (519 ft) long and 76 m (249 ft) wide across the transepts, and houses the largest collection of medieval stained glass in Britain *(see p409)*. The word "minster" usually means a church served by monks, but priests always served at York. The first minster began as a wooden chapel used to baptize King Edwin of Northumbria in 627. There have been several cathedrals on or near the site, including an 11th-century Norman structure. The present minster was begun in 1220 and completed 250 years later. In July 1984, the south transept roof was destroyed by fire. Restoration cost £2.25 million.

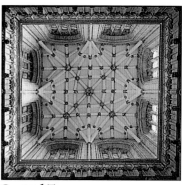

Central Tower
This lantern tower was reconstructed in 1420–65 (after partial collapse in 1407) from a design by the master stonemason William Colchester.

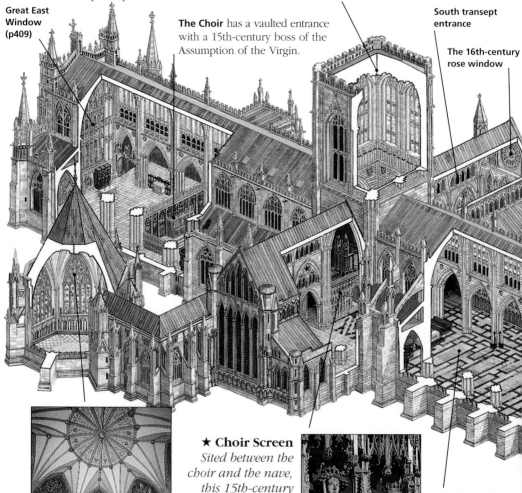

Great East Window (p409)

The Choir has a vaulted entrance with a 15th-century boss of the Assumption of the Virgin.

South transept entrance

The 16th-century rose window

★ **Choir Screen**
Sited between the choir and the nave, this 15th-century stone screen depicts kings of England from William I to Henry VI, and has a canopy of angels.

The Nave, begun 1291, was sever[e] damaged by fire 1840. Rebuildi[ng] costs were heav[y] but it was re-open[ed] with a new peal [of] bells in 18[—]

★ **Chapter House**
A Latin inscription near the entrance of the wooden-vaulted Chapter House (1260–85) reads: "As the rose is the flower of flowers, so this is the house of houses".

VISITORS' CHECKLIST

Deangate, York. **Tel** *01904 557216.* ☐ *Mon–Sat: 9am–5pm (from 9:30am Nov–Mar); Sun: noon–3:45pm. Opening times may change subject to major services.* ● *Good Fri, Easter Sun, 24 & 25 Dec.* to *Minster, Undercroft & the Tower.* ✝ *Mon–Sat: 7:30am, 7:45am, 12:30pm (also at noon Sat), 5:15pm (evensong); Sun: 8am, 10am, 11:30am, 4pm.* ♿ *main floors.*
www.yorkminster.org

Timbered interior of the Merchant Adventurers' Hall

The western towers, with their 15th-century decorative panelling and elaborate pinnacles, contrast with the simpler design of the north transept. The southwest tower is the minster belfry.

Great West Door

West Window

STAR SIGHTS

★ Chapter House

★ Choir Screen

🏰 Monk Bar

This is one of York's finest original medieval gates, situated at the end of Goodramgate. It is vaulted on three floors, and the portcullis still works. In the Middle Ages, the rooms above it were rented out, and it was a prison in the 16th century. Its decorative details include men holding stones ready to drop on intruders.

🏛 York Art Gallery

Exhibition Sq. **Tel** *01904 687687.* ☐ *daily.* ● *1 Jan, 24–26 Dec.*
www.yorkartgallery.org.uk
This Italianate building of 1879 holds a wide-ranging collection of paintings from western Europe dating from the early 14th century. There is also a collection of British and foreign studio pottery, including work by Bernard Leach, William Staite Murray and Shoji Hamada.

A 15th-century French portrait of St Anthony in York Art Gallery

🏰 Clifford's Tower

(EH) Clifford's St. **Tel** *01904 646940.* ☐ *daily.* ● *1 Jan, 24–26 Dec.*
www.english-heritage.org.uk
Sited on top of a mound that William the Conqueror built for his original wooden castle, destroyed by fire during anti-Jewish riots in 1190, Clifford's Tower dates from the 13th century. Built by Henry III, it was named after the de Clifford family, who were constables of the castle.

🏛 DIG – An Archaeological Adventure

St Saviourgate. **Tel** *01904 543403.* ☐ *daily (best to book in advance).* ● *24–25 Dec.*
Housed in a restored medieval church, this centre invites visitors to become archaeological detectives and discover how archaeologists have pieced together clues from the past to unravel the history of the Viking age in York.

🏰 Merchant Adventurers' Hall

(EH) Fossgate. **Tel** *01904 654818.* ☐ *Easter–Sep: daily; Oct–Easter: Mon–Sat.* ● *24 Dec–3 Jan.*
www.theyorkcompany.co.uk
Built by the York Merchants' Guild, which controlled the northern cloth trade in the 15th–17th centuries, this building has fine timberwork. The Great Hall is probably the best example of its kind in Europe. Among its paintings is an unattributed 17th-century copy of Van Dyck's portrait of Charles I's queen, Henrietta Maria. Below the Great Hall is the hospital, which was used by the guild until 1900, and a private chapel.

Exploring York

The appeal of York is its many layers of history. A medieval city constructed on top of a Roman one, it was first built in AD 71, when it became capital of the northern province and was known as Eboracum. It was here that Constantine the Great was made emperor in 306, and reorganized Britain into four provinces. A hundred years later, the Roman army had withdrawn. Eboracum was renamed Eoforwic, under the Saxons, and then became a Christian stronghold. The Danish street names are the reminder that it was a Viking centre from 867, and one of Europe's chief trading bases. Between 1100 and 1500 it was England's second city. The glory of York is the minster *(see pp406–7)*. The city also boasts 18 medieval churches, 3 mile long (4.8 km) medieval city walls, elegant Jacobean and Georgian architecture and fine museums.

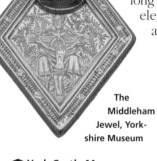

The Middleham Jewel, Yorkshire Museum

Grand staircase and fine plaster ceiling at Fairfax House

🏛 York Castle Museum

The Eye of York. *Tel 01904 687687.* ◯ daily. ● 1 Jan, 25 & 26 Dec. 🎦 🦽 ground floor only. 🖥 🎴 www.york.castle.museum.org.uk

Housed in two 18th-century prisons, the museum has a fine folk collection, started by Dr John Kirk of the market town of Pickering. Opened in 1938, its period displays include a Jacobean dining room, a moorland cottage, and a 1950s front room. It also contains an exhibition on the traditions of birth, marriages and death in Britain from 1700 to 2000.

The most famous exhibits include the reconstructed Victorian street of Kirkgate, complete with shopfronts, and the Anglo Saxon York Helmet, discovered in 1982.

🔒 York Minster

See pp406–7.

🏛 Jorvik

Coppergate. *Tel 01904 543400.* ◯ daily. ● 25 Dec. 🎦 🦽 ring first. 🎴 www.jorvik-viking-centre.co.uk

This centre is built on the site of the original Viking settlement which archaeologists uncovered at Coppergate. Using new technology, a dynamic vision of 10th-century York is recreated, with smells bringing the Viking world to life. At the centre's sister attraction, DIG, visitors can take part in an archaeological excavation.

🏛 Yorkshire Museum and St Mary's Abbey

Museum Gardens. *Tel 01904 687687.* ◯ daily. 🎦 🦽 🎴

Yorkshire Museum was in the news when it purchased the 15th-century Middleham Jewel for £2.5 million, one of the finest pieces of English Gothic jewellery found this century. Other exhibits include 2nd-century Roman mosaics and an Anglo-Saxon silver gilt bowl.

St Mary's Abbey *(see p350)* in the riverside grounds is where the medieval York Mystery Plays are set every few years.

🏛 Fairfax House

Castlegate. *Tel 01904 655543.* ◯ mid-Feb–Dec: daily (Sun: pm only). ● 24, 26 & 31 Dec, Jan, early Feb. 🎦 🎴 🦽 limited. 🎴 www.fairfaxhouse.co.uk

From 1755 to 1762 Viscount Fairfax built this fine Georgian town house for his daughter, Anne. The house was designed by John Carr *(see p28)*, and restored in the 1980s. Between 1920 and 1965 it was a cinema and dancehall. Today, visitors can see the bedroom of Anne Fairfax (1725–93), and a fine collection of 18th-century furniture, porcelain and clocks.

🏛 National Railway Museum

Leeman Rd. *Tel 01904 621261.* ◯ daily. ● 24–26 Dec. 🦽 🖥 🎴 www.nrm.org.uk

In what is the world's largest railway museum, nearly 200 years of history are explored using a variety of visual aids. Visitors can try wheel-tapping and shunting in the interactive gallery, or find out what made Stephenson's *Rocket* so successful. Exhibits include uniforms, rolling stock from 1797 onward and Queen Victoria's Royal Train carriage, as well as the very latest rail innovations.

Reproduction of Stephenson's Rocket (right) and 1830s first-class carriage in York's National Railway Museum

The Stained Glass of York Minster

York Minster houses the largest collection of medieval stained glass in Britain, some of it dating from the late 12th century. The glass was generally coloured during production, using metal oxides to produce the desired colour, then worked on by craftsmen on site. When a design had been produced, the glass was first cut, then trimmed to shape. Details

Window detail

were painted on, using iron oxide-based paint which was fused to the glass by firing in a kiln. Individual pieces were then leaded together to form the finished window.

Part of the fascination of the minster glass is its variety of subject matter. Some windows were paid for by lay donors who specified a particular subject, others reflect ecclesiastical patronage.

Miracle of St Nicholas *(late 12th century) was put in the nave over 100 years after it was made. It shows a Jew's conversion.*

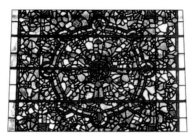

The Five Sisters *in the north transept are the largest examples of grisaille glass in Britain. This popular 13th-century technique involved creating fine patterning on clear glass and decorating it with black enamel.*

St John the Evangelist, *in part of the Great West Window (c.1338), is holding an eagle, itself an example of stickwork, where paint is scraped off to reveal clear glass.*

Noah's Ark *with its distinct boat-like shape is easily identified in the Great East Window.*

Edward III *is a fine example of the 14th-century "soft" style of painting, achieved by stippling the paint.*

The Great East Window *(1405–8), the size of a tennis court, is the largest area of medieval painted glass in the world. The Dean and Chapter paid master glazier John Thornton four shillings a week for this celebration of the Creation.*

Walter Skirlaw, *whose bishopric was revoked in favour of Richard Scrope, donated this window on its completion in 1408.*

Harewood House ❸

Leeds. **Tel** 0113 2181010. 🚋 Leeds then bus. ◯ mid-Mar–Nov: daily. 🖼 ♿ 🗺 by arrangement. 🖥 🗂
www.harewood.org

Designed by John Carr in 1759, Harewood House is the Yorkshire home of the Earl and Countess of Harewood.

The grand Palladian exterior is impressive, with interiors created by Robert Adam and an unrivalled collection of 18th-century furniture made specifically for Harewood by Yorkshire-born Thomas Chippendale (1711–79). There is a collection of paintings by Italian and English artists, including Reynolds and Gainsborough, and two watercolour rooms. The grounds by Capability Brown (see p26) include the **Harewood Bird Garden**, which has exotic species and a breeding programme of certain endangered varieties.

Bali starling, one of Harewood's rare birds

Leeds ❸④

Leeds. 🏛 750,000. ✈ 🚋 🚌 ℹ️ Leeds City Station (0113 2425242). 🏪 Mon–Sat.
www.leedsliveitloveit.com

The third-largest of Britain's provincial cities, Leeds was at its most prosperous during the Victorian period. The most impressive legacy from this era is a series of ornate, covered shopping arcades. Also of note is the **Town Hall**, designed by Cuthbert Brodrick and opened by Queen Victoria in 1858.

Today, although Leeds is primarily an industrial city, it also offers a thriving cultural scene. Productions at **The Grand** by Opera North, one of Britain's top operatic companies, are of a high quality.

The **City Art Gallery** has impressive collections of British 20th-century art and of Victorian paintings, including works by local artist Atkinson Grimshaw (1836–93). Among the late 19th-century French art are works by Signac, Courbet and Sisley. The Henry Moore Institute, added in 1993, is devoted to the research and display of sculpture of all periods. It comprises a study centre, library, galleries and an archive of material on Moore and other sculptural pioneers.

The **Armley Mills Museum**, in a 19th-century woollen mill, explores the industrial heritage of Leeds. Filled with original equipment, recorded sounds and models in 19th-century workers' clothes, it traces the history of the ready-to-wear industry. The **Leeds City Museum** charts the history of Leeds with ethnographical and archaeological exhibits.

A striking waterfront development by the River Aire has attracted two museums. The **Royal Armouries Museum**, from the Tower of London, tells the story of arms and armour around the world in battle, sport and fashion. The **Thackray Medical Museum** is an interactive display of medical advances, from a re-created Victorian slum to modern-day medical challenges.

For children, **Tropical World** features crystal pools, a rainforest house, butterflies and tropical fish. There is also a farm and a Rare Breeds

The County Arcade, one of Leeds' restored shopping arcades

centre in the grounds of the Tudor-Jacobean **Temple Newsam House**, which has major art and furniture collections including Chippendale pieces.

🏛 **City Art Gallery**
The Headrow. **Tel** 0113 2478248.
◯ daily (Sun: pm). 🖥 ♿ 🗺

🏛 **Armley Mills Museum**
Canal Rd, Armley. **Tel** 0113 2637 861. ◯ Tue–Sun (Sun: pm), pub hols.
● 1 Jan, 25, 26 Dec. 🖼 ♿ 🗂

🏛 **Leeds City Museum**
Millennium Sq. **Tel** 0113 2243732.
◯ daily. ● pub hols. ♿ 🖥 🗂

🏛 **Royal Armouries**
Armouries Drive. **Tel** 0113 2201999.
◯ daily. ● 24, 25 Dec. ♿ 🍴 🗂

🏛 **Thackray Medical Museum**
Beckett St. 🅵 0113 2457084. ◯ daily. ● 1 Jan, 24–26, 31 Dec. 🖼 ♿ 🗂 www.thackraymuseum.org

🌺 **Tropical World**
Canal Gdns, Princes Ave. **Tel** 0113 2661850. ◯ daily. ● 25, 26 Dec. 🖼 ♿ 🖥 🗂

🏯 **Temple Newsam House**
Off A63. **Tel** 0113 2645535. ◯ Tue–Sun. ● 25 & 26 Dec, Jan. 🖼 🖥 🗂

Working loom at the Armley Mills Museum in Leeds

The Other Side (1990–93) by David Hockney at Bradford's 1853 Gallery in Saltaire

Bradford ⑤

Bradford. 🏛 *492,000.* ✈ ≋ 🚌
🛈 *City Hall, Centenary Square
(01274 433678).* 🛍 *Mon–Sat.*
www.visitbradford.com

In the 16th century, Bradford was a thriving market town, and the opening of its canal in 1774 boosted trade. By 1850, it was the world's capital for worsted (fabric made from closely twisted wool). Many of the city's well-preserved civic and industrial buildings date from this period, such as the Wool Exchange on Market Street. In the 1800s a number of German textile manufacturers settled in what is now called Little Germany. Their houses are characterized by decorative stone carvings that illustrated the wealth and standing of the occupants.

The **National Media Museum**, founded in 1983, explores the technology and art of these media. There is a television section called TV Heaven, where visitors can ask to watch their favourite programme. They are also encouraged to see themselves read the news on TV. The giant IMAX screen uses the world's largest film format. Film subjects include journeys

Daguerreotype camera by Giroux (1839)

into space, the ocean and the natural world.

The **Colour Museum** traces dyeing and textile printing from ancient Egypt to the present day with an emphasis on hands-on elements. **Bradford Industrial Museum** is housed in an original spinning mill. As well as seeing and hearing all the mill machinery, you can ride on a horse-drawn tram. Saltaire, a Victorian industrial village *(see p349)*, is on the outskirts of the city. Built by Sir Titus Salt for his Salts Mill workers, it was completed in 1873. The **1853 Gallery** has the world's largest collection of works by David Hockney, born in Bradford.

🏛 **National Media Museum**
Pictureville. *Tel 01274 202030.*
◯ *daily (school hols); Tue–Sun (school terms); public holidays.* ◉ *24–26 Dec.*
🛍 ♿ 🍴 **www.**nmpft.org.uk

🏛 **Colour Museum**
1 Providence St. *Tel 01274 390955.*
◯ *Tue–Sat.* ◉ *24 Dec–2 Jan.*
🛍 🎨 ♿
www.colour-experience.org

🏛 **Bradford Industrial Museum**
Moorside Mills, Moorside Rd. *Tel 01274 435900.* ◯ *Tue–Sat, Sun (pm), public hols.* ◉ *25 & 26 Dec.* ♿ 🅿
www.bradfordmuseums.org

🏛 **1853 Gallery**
Salts Mill, Victoria Rd. *Tel 01274 531 163.* ◯ *daily.* ◉ *25 & 26 Dec.* ♿
🍴 📷 🅿 **www.**saltsmill.org.uk

BRADFORD'S INDIAN COMMUNITY

Immigrants from the Indian subcontinent originally came to Bradford in the 1950s to work in the mills, but with the decline of the textile industry many began small businesses. By the mid 1970s there were 1,400 such enterprises in the area. Almost one fifth were in the food sector, born out of simple cafés catering for mill-workers whose families were far away. As Indian food became more popular, these restaurants thrived, and today there are over 200 serving the highly spiced dishes of the Indian subcontinent.

Balti in a Bradford restaurant

Haworth Parsonage, home to the Brontë family, now a museum

Haworth ❸❻

Bradford. 🏘 5,000. 🚃 Keighley.
🛈 2–4 West Lane (01535 642329).
www.visithaworth.com

The setting of Haworth, in
bleak Pennine moorland
dotted with farmsteads, has
changed little since it was
home to the Brontë family. The
village boomed in the 1840s,
when there were more than
1,200 hand-looms in operation,
but it is more famous today
for the Brontë connection.
  You can visit the **Brontë
Parsonage Museum**, home
from 1820–61 to novelists
Charlotte, Emily and Anne,
their brother Branwell and
their father, the Revd Patrick
Brontë. Built in 1778–9, the
house remains decorated as it
was during the 1850s. Eleven
rooms, including the children's
study and Charlotte's room,
display letters, manuscripts,

furniture and personal objects.
  The nostalgic Victorian
**Keighley and Worth Valley
Railway** runs through
Haworth. It stops at Oakworth
station, where parts of *The
Railway Children* were filmed.
At the end of the line is the
Railway Museum at Oxenhope.

**🏛 Brontë Parsonage
Museum**
Church St. **Tel** 01535 642323.
⭕ daily. ⭘ 24–27 Dec; Jan. 🅿 ♿
♿ limited. **www**.bronte.org.uk

**Charlotte Brontë's childhood story
book, for her sister, Anne**

Hebden Bridge ❸❼

Calderdale. 🏘 12,500. 🚃 🛈
New Rd (01422 843831). 🚌 Thu.
www.hebdenbridge.co.uk

Hebden Bridge is a delightful
South Pennines former mill
town, surrounded by steep
hills and former 19th-century
mills. The houses seem to
defy gravity as they cling to
the valley sides. Due to the
gradient, one house is made
from two bottom floors, and
the top two floors form
another unit. To separate
ownership of these "flying
freeholds", an Act of
Parliament was devised.
  There is a superb view of
Hebden Bridge from nearby
Heptonstall, where the poet
Sylvia Plath (1932–63) is
buried. The village contains
a Wesleyan chapel (1764).

Halifax ❸❽

Calderdale. 🏘 88,000. 🚃 🚌
🛈 Piece Hall (01422 368725). 🚌
Thu–Sat. **www**.visitcalderdale.com

Halifax's history has been
influenced by textiles since
the Middle Ages, but today's
visual reminders date mainly
from the 19th century. The
town inspired William Blake's
vision of "dark Satanic mills"
in his poem *Jerusalem* (1820).
The wool trade helped to
make the Pennines into
Britain's industrial backbone.
  Until the mid-15th century
cloth production was modest,
but vital enough to contribute
towards the creation of the
13th-century Gibbet Law,
which stated that anyone
caught stealing cloth could be
executed. There is a replica of
the gibbet used for decapi-
tation at the bottom of Gibbet
Street. Many of Halifax's 18th-
and 19th-century buildings
owe their existence to wealthy
cloth traders. Sir Charles Barry
(1795–1860), architect of the
Houses of Parliament, was
commissioned by the Crossley
family to design the Town Hall
They also paid for the land-
scaping of the People's Park
by the creator of the Crystal
Palace, Sir Joseph Paxton
(1801–65). Thomas Bradley's

THE BRONTË SISTERS

Charlotte Brontë (1816–55)

During a harsh, motherless childhood, Charlotte, Emily and Anne
retreated into fictional worlds of
their own, writing poems and
stories. As adults, they had to work
as governesses, but still published
a poetry collection in 1846. Only
two copies were sold, but in the
following year Charlotte's *Jane Eyre*,
became a bestseller, arousing interest in Emily's *Wuthering Heights*
and Anne's *Agnes Grey*. After her
siblings' deaths in 1848–9, Charlotte published her last novel,
Villette, in 1852. She married the Revd Nicholls, her father's
curate, in 1854, but died shortly afterwards.

Large Two Forms (1966–9) by Henry Moore in Bretton Country Park

18th-century **Piece Hall** was where wool merchants once sold their cloth, trading in one of the 315 "Merchants' Rooms". It has a massive Italianate courtyard, now beautifully restored. Today, Halifax's market takes place here.

Eureka! is a hands-on children's museum, with exhibits such as the Giant Mouth Machine. **Shibden Hall Museum** is a fine period house, parts of which date to the 15th century.

Environs: The nearby village of **Sowerby Bridge** was an important textile centre from the Middle Ages to the 1960s. Today visitors come to enjoy the scenic canals.

🏛 **Eureka!**
Discovery Rd. 🆔 *01422 330069.*
◯ *daily.* ● *24–26 Dec.* 🈂🚻🚻📷
www.eureka.org.uk

🏛 **Shibden Hall Museum**
Listers Rd. *Tel 01422 352246.*
◯ *daily (Sun: pm).* ● *24 Dec–2 Jan.* 🏠🈂📷

National Coal Mining Museum ㉟

Wakefield. *Tel 01924 848806.* 🚉
Wakefield then bus. ◯ *daily (last tour 3:15pm – booking advised). Children under 5 not allowed underground.*
● *24–26 Dec, 1 Jan.* 🚻🈂📷🏠
www.ncm.org.uk

Housed in the old Caphouse Colliery, this museum offers the chance to go into a real mine shaft: warm clothing is advised. An underground tour takes you 137 m (450 ft) down,

equipped with a hat and a miner's lamp. Enter narrow seams and see exhibits such as life-size working models. Other displays depict mining from 1820 to the present day.

Yorkshire Sculpture Park ㊵

Wakefield. *Tel 01924 832631.*
🚉 *Wakefield then bus.* ◯ *daily.*
● *24, 25, 29–31 Dec.* 🚻📷🏠
www.ysp.co.uk

This is one of Europe's leading open-air galleries, situated in 200 ha (500 acres) of 18th-century parkland dotted with changing exhibitions of the work of Henry Moore, Anthony Caro, Eduardo Chillida, Barbara Hepworth, Antony Gormley and others. The indoor display spaces include the ambitious visitor centre, which leads on to the stunning new Underground Gallery exhibition space.

Magna ㊶

Rotherham. *Tel 01709 720002.*
🚉 *Rotherham Central or Sheffield then bus (No. 69).* ◯ *Mar–Sep: daily; Oct–Feb: Tue–Sun.*
● *24 & 25 Dec.* 🈂🚻🍴📷🏠
www.visitmagna.co.uk

A former steel works has been imaginatively converted into a huge science adventure centre, with an emphasis on interactive exhibits, noise and spectacle designed to appeal to 4–15-year-olds. In the Air, Fire, Water and Earth Pavilions visitors can get close to a tornado, operate real diggers or discover what it's like to detonate a rock face. There are also multimedia displays on the lives of steelworkers and on how a giant furnace operated, as well as a show that features robots with artificial intelligence that evolve and learn as they hunt each other down.

The Face of Steel display at Magna

NORTHUMBRIA

NORTHUMBERLAND · COUNTY DURHAM

Engsland's northeast extremity is a tapestry of moorland, ruins, castles, cathedrals and huddled villages. With Northumberland National Park and Kielder Water reservoir to the north, a rugged eastern coastline, and the cities of Newcastle and Durham to the south, the area combines a dramatic history with abundant natural beauty.

The empty peaceful hills, elusive wildlife and panoramic vistas of Northumberland National Park belie the area's turbulent past. Warring Scots and English, skirmishing tribes, cattle drovers and whisky smugglers have all left traces on ancient routes through the Cheviot Hills. Slicing through the southern edge of the park is the famous reminder of the Romans' 400-year occupation of Britain, Hadrian's Wall, the northern boundary of their empire.

Conflict between Scots and English continued for 1,000 years after the Romans departed, and even after the 1603 union between the two crowns. A chain of massive crenellated medieval castles punctuates the coastline, while other forts that once defended the northern flank of England along the River Tweed lie mostly in ruins. Seventh-century Northumbria was the cradle of Christianity under St Aidan, but this was sharply countered by Viking violence from 793 onward, as the Scandinavian invaders raided the monasteries. But a reverence for Northumbrian saints is in the local psyche, and St Cuthbert and the Venerable Bede are both buried in Durham Cathedral. The influence of the Industrial Revolution, concentrated around the mouths of the rivers Tyne, Wear and Tees, made Newcastle upon Tyne the north's main centre for coal mining and shipbuilding. Today, the city is famous for its "industrial heritage" attractions and urban regeneration schemes.

Section of Hadrian's Wall, built by the Romans in about 120, looking east from Cawfields

◁ The towers of Durham Cathedral, rising above the River Wear

Exploring Northumbria

Historic sites are plentiful along Northumbria's coast.
South of Berwick-upon-Tweed, a causeway leads to the
ruined priory and castle on Lindisfarne, and there are
major castles at Bamburgh, Alnwick and Warkworth. The
hinterland is a region of wide open spaces, with wilderness
in the Northumberland National Park, and fascinating Roman
remains of Hadrian's Wall at Housesteads and elsewhere.
The glorious city of Durham is dominated by its castle and
cathedral, and Newcastle upon Tyne has a lively nightlife.

SIGHTS AT A GLANCE

Alnwick Castle **5**
Bamburgh **4**
Barnard Castle **17**
Beamish Open Air Museum **13**
Berwick-upon-Tweed **1**
Cheviot Hills **8**
Corbridge **10**
Durham pp428–9 **14**
Farne Islands **3**
Hadrian's Wall pp422–3 **11**
Hexham **9**
Kielder Water **7**
Lindisfarne **2**
Middleton-in-Teesdale **16**
Newcastle upon Tyne **12**
Warkworth Castle **6**

Walks and Tours

North Pennines Tour **15**

The wilderness of Upper Coquetdale in the sparsely
populated Cheviot Hills

0 kilometres   10

0 miles   10

The rugged coastline of Northumberland, with Bamburgh Castle in the distance

GETTING AROUND

North of Newcastle, the A1068 meets the A1 linking the sights of the Northumbrian coast, and continuing on to Scotland. Two spectacular inland routes, the A696 and the A68, merge near Otterburn to skirt the Northumberland National Park. A mainline railway links Durham, Newcastle and Berwick, but a car is necessary to explore Northumbria comprehensively.

KEY

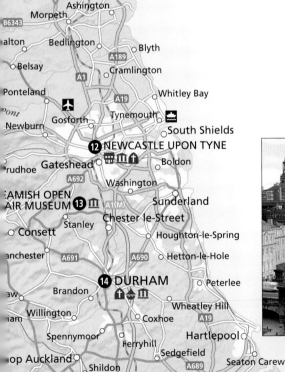

Guildhall, Newcastle upon Tyne

View over Berwick-upon-Tweed's three bridges

Berwick-upon-Tweed ❶

Northumberland. 🏘 *13,000.* 🚆
ℹ️ *106 Mary Gate (01289 330733).*
🏴 *Wed, Sat.*
www.berwick-upon-tweed.gov.uk

Between the 12th and 15th centuries Berwick-upon-Tweed changed hands 14 times in the wars between the Scots and English. Its position, at the mouth of the river which divides the two nations, made the town strategically vital.

The English finally gained permanent control in 1482 and maintained Berwick as a fortified garrison. Ramparts dating from 1555, 1.5 miles (2.5 km) long and 7 m (23 ft) thick, offer superb views over the Tweed. Within the 18th-century barracks are the **King's Own Scottish Borderers Regimental Museum**, an **art gallery**, and **By Beat of Drum**, charting the history of British infantrymen.

🏛 **King's Own Scottish Borderers Regimental Museum**
The Barracks. **Tel** *01289 307427.*
⭕ *Easter–Oct: Mon–Sat;*
Nov–Easter: Wed–Sun. ⚫ *22 Dec–3 Jan, public hols.* 🈂️🏠

Lindisfarne ❷

Northumberland. 🚆 *Berwick-upon-Tweed then bus.* ℹ️ *106 Mary Gate, Berwick-upon-Tweed (01289 330733).* **www**.lindisfarne.org.uk

Twice daily a long, narrow neck of land sinks under the North Sea tide for five hours, separating Lindisfarne, or Holy Island, from the coast. At low tide, visitors stream over the causeway to the island made famous by St Aidan, St Cuthbert and the Lindisfarne gospels. Nothing remains of the Celtic monks' monastery, finally abandoned in 875 after successive Viking attacks, but the magnificent arches of the 11th-century **Lindisfarne Priory** are still visible.

After 1540, stones from the priory were used to build **Lindisfarne Castle**, which was restored and made into a private home by Sir Edwin Lutyens *(see p29)* in 1903. It includes a walled garden by Gertrude Jekyll *(see p27).*

⛪ **Lindisfarne Castle**
(NT) Holy Island. **Tel** *01289 389244.* ⭕ *Mar–Oct & Feb half–term: Tue–Sun. Opening times depend on tide – phone to check.* 🈂️

Farne Islands ❸

(NT) Northumberland. ⛴ *from Seahouses (Apr–Oct).* ℹ️ *106 Mary Gate, Berwick-upon-Tweed (01289 330733).*

There are between 15 and 28 Farne Islands off the coast from Bamburgh, some of them periodically covered by sea. Nature wardens and lighthouse keepers share them with seals, puffins and other seabirds. Boat tours depart from **Seahouses** harbour and can land on Staple and Inner Farne, site of St Cuthbert's 14th-century chapel, or Longstone, where Grace Darling's lighthouse is located.

Lindisfarne Castle (1540), the main landmark on the island of Lindisfarne

Celtic Christianity

St Cuthbert on a sea voyage

The Irish monk St Aidan arrived in Northumbria in 635 from the island of Iona, off western Scotland, to evangelize the north of England. He founded the monastery on the island of Lindisfarne, and it became one of the most important centres for Christianity in England. This and other monastic communities thrived in Northumbria, becoming rich in scholarship, although the monks lived simply. It also emerged as a place of pilgrimage after miracles were reported at the shrine of St Cuthbert, Lindisfarne's most famous bishop. But the monks' pacifism made them defenceless against 9th-century Viking raids.

St Aidan's Monastery *was added to over the centuries to become Lindisfarne Priory. This 8th-century relic with interlaced animal decorations is from a cross at the site.*

The Venerable Bede *(673– 735), the most brilliant early medieval scholar, was a monk at the monastery of St Paul in Jarrow. He wrote* The Ecclesiastical History of the English People *in 731.*

St Aidan *(600–651), an Irish missionary, founded a mon- astery at Lindisfarne and became Bishop of Northumbria in 635. This 1960 sculpture of him, by Kathleen Parbury, is in Lindisfarne Priory grounds.*

St Cuthbert *(635–87) was the monk and miracle worker most revered of all. He lived as a hermit on Inner Farne (a chapel was built there in his memory) and later became Bishop of Lindisfarne.*

Lindisfarne Priory *was built by Benedictines in the 11th century, on the site of St Aidan's earlier monastery.*

THE LINDISFARNE GOSPELS

Held in the British Library, this book of richly illustrated portrayals of Gospel stories is one of the masterpieces of the "Northumbrian Renaissance" which left a permanent mark on Christian art and history-writing. The work was carried out by monks at Lindisfarne under the direction of Bishop Eadfrith, around 700. Monks managed to save the book and took it with them when they fled from Lindisfarne in 875 after suffering Viking raids. Other treasures were plundered.

Elaborately decorated initial to the *Gospel of St Matthew* **(c.725)**

Illustration of Grace Darling from the 1881 edition of *Sunday at Home*

Bamburgh ❹

Northumberland. 🏃 *1,100.* 🚉
Berwick. ℹ️ *Seahouses (01665
720884; Apr–Oct); 106 Mary Gate,
Berwick-upon-Tweed (01289 330733).*

Due to Northumbria's history
of hostility against the Scots,
there are more strongholds and
castles here than in any other
part of England. Most were
built from the 11th to the 15th
centuries by local warlords,
as was Bamburgh's red
sandstone **castle**. Its coastal
position had been fortified
since prehistoric times, but the
first major stronghold was
built in 550 by a Saxon chieftain, Ida the Flamebearer.

In its heyday between 1095
and 1464, Bamburgh
was the royal castle
that was used by the
Northumbrian kings for
coronations. By the end
of the Middle Ages it had
fallen into obscurity, then
in 1894 it was bought by
Newcastle arms tycoon
Lord Armstrong, who re-
stored it. Works of art are
exhibited in the cavernous
Great Hall, and there are
suits of armour and
medieval artifacts in
the basement.

Bamburgh's other
main attraction is the
tiny **Grace Darling
Museum** which cele-
brates the bravery of
the 23-year-old, who,
in 1838, rowed through tem-
pestuous seas with her father,
the keeper of the Longstone
lighthouse, to rescue nine
people from the wrecked
Forfarshire steamboat.

⛵ **Bamburgh Castle**
Bamburgh. **Tel** *01668 214515.*
⬜ *Mar–Oct: daily.* 🏞️ 🚻 💻 ℹ️
www.bamburghcastle.com
🏛️ **Grace Darling Museum**
Radcliffe Rd. ⬜ *Easter–Oct: daily.* 🚻

Alnwick Castle ❺

Alnwick, Northumberland. **Tel** *01665
510777.* 🚉 🚗 *Alnmouth.* ⬜
April–Oct: daily. 🏞️ 🚻 *limited.* 💻
ℹ️ **www**.alnwickcastle.com

Dominating the market town
on the River Aln is another
great fortress, Alnwick Castle.
Described by the Victorians
as the "Windsor of the north",
it is the main seat of the Duke
of Northumberland, whose
family, the Percys, have lived
here since 1309.

This border strong-
hold has survived
many battles, but now
peacefully dominates
the pretty market
town of Alnwick,
overlooking landscape
designed by Capability
Brown. The stern
medieval exterior
belies the treasure
house within,
furnished in palatial
Renaissance style with
a collection of Meissen
china and paintings by
Titian, Van Dyck and
Canaletto. The Postern
Tower contains early
British and Roman
relics. The **Regimental
Museum of Royal Northum-
berland Fusiliers** is in the
Abbot's Tower. Other attractions are the Percy State
coach, the dungeon and
superb countryside views.

Carrara marble
fireplace (1840) at
Alnwick Castle

Warkworth Castle ❻

(EH) Warkworth, nr Amble. **Tel**
01665 711423. ⬜ *Nov–Mar:
Sat–Mon; Apr–Oct: daily.* ⬤ *1 Jan,
24–26 Dec.* ℹ️ 🏞️ 🚻 *limited.*

Warkworth Castle sits on a
green hill overlooking the
River Coquet. It was one
of the Percy family homes.
Shakespeare's *Henry IV*
features the castle in the
scenes between the Earl of
Northumberland and his son,
Harry Hotspur. Much of the
present-day castle remains
date from the 14th century.
The unusual turreted, cross
shaped keep, also added in
the 14th century, is a central
feature of the castle tour.

**Warkworth Castle reflected in the
River Coquet**

Kielder Water ❼

Yarrow Moor, Falstone, Hexham.
Tel *0870 2403549.* ⬜ *daily.* 🚻
www.visitkielder.com

One of the top attractions
of Northumberland, Kielder
Water lies close to the
Scottish border, surrounded
by spectacular scenery. With
a perimeter of 27 miles (44
km), it is Europe's largest
man-made lake, and offers
facilities for sailing, windsurfing, canoeing, water-skiing
and fishing. In summer, the
cruiser *Osprey* departs from
Leaplish on trips around the
lake. The Kielder Water
Exhibition, next to the Tower
Knowe Visitor Centre, depicts
the history of the valley from
the Ice Age to the present day.

Cheviot Hills ❽

These bare, lonely moors, smoothed into rounded humps by Ice Age glaciers, form a natural border with Scotland. Walkers and outdoor enthusiasts find a near-wilderness unmatched anywhere else in England.

This remotest extremity of the Northumberland National Park nevertheless has a long and vivid history. Roman legions, warring Scots and English border raiders, cattle drovers and whisky smugglers have all left traces along the ancient routes and tracks they carved out here.

VISITORS' CHECKLIST

Northumberland. ⚞ Hexham. ℹ
Wooler (01668 282123), Eastburn,
South Park. **Tel** 01434 605555.

The Cheviots' isolated burns and streams are among the last habitats in England for the shy, elusive otter.

Chew Green Camp, which to the Romans was ad fines, or, "towards the last place", has fine views from the remaining fortified earthworks.

The Pennine Way starts in Derbyshire and ends at Kirk Yetholm in Scotland. The final stage (shown here) goes past Byrness, crosses the Cheviots and traces the Scottish border.

Uswayford Farm track

Uswayford Farm, is perhaps the most remote farm in England, and one of the hardest to reach. It is set in deserted moorland.

Map labels: B6351, BERWICK-UPON-TWEED, A697, Kirk Yetholm, Wooler, College Burn, Harthope Burn, A697, KIDLAND FOREST, Beamish, CHEVIOT HILLS, Usway Burn, Clennell Street track, Uswayford, Alwin, Alwinton, Harbottle, Byrness, Holystone, A68, Rede, B6341, Grassless Burn, Otterburn, Elsdon, A696, NEWCASTLE-UPON-TYNE

KEY

▬ A roads

▭ B roads

━ Minor roads

--- Pennine Way

☀ Viewpoint

Alwinton, *a tiny village built mainly from grey stone, is situated beside the River Coquet. It is an access point for many fine walks in the area, and the wild landscape is deserted except for sheep.*

kilometres 5

miles 5

Hexham ⑨

Northumberland. 👥 *14,000.* 🚆 🚌 ℹ️ *Wentworth Car Park (01434 652220).* 🛍️ *Tue.* www.hadrianswallcountry.org

The busy market town of Hexham was established in the 7th century, growing up around the church and monastery built by St Wilfrid, but the Vikings sacked and looted it in 876. In 1114, Augustinians began work on a priory and abbey on the original church ruins to create **Hexham Abbey**, which still towers over the market square. The Saxon crypt, built partly with stones from the former Roman fort at Corbridge, is all

Ancient stone carvings at Hexham Abbey

that remains of St Wilfrid's Church. The south transept has a 12th-century night stair: stone steps leading from the dormitory. In the chancel is the Frith Stool, a Saxon throne in the centre of a circle which protected fugitives.

Medieval streets, many with Georgian and Victorian shopfronts, spread out from the market square, The 15th-century Moot Hall was once a council chamber and the old gaol (jail) contains a **museum** of border history.

Hadrian's Wall ⑪

On the orders of Emperor Hadrian, work began in AD 120 on a 73 mile (117 km) wall to be erected across northern England, to mark and defend the northern limits of the British province and the northwest border of the Roman Empire. Troops were stationed at milecastles along the wall, and large turrets, later forts, were built at 5 mile (8 km) intervals. The wall, now the responsibility of English Heritage, was abandoned in 383 as the Empire crumbled, but much of it remains.

Location of Hadrian's Wall

Carvoran Fort is probably pre-Hadrianic. Little of the fort survives, but the Roman Army museum nearby covers the wall's history.

Great Chesters Fort was built facing east to guard Caw Gap, but there are few remains today. To the south and east of the fort are traces of a civil settlement and a bathhouse.

Vindolanda *is the site of several forts. The first timber fort dated from AD 90 and a stone fort was not built until the 2nd century. The museum has a collection of Roman writing tablets providing details of food, clothes and work.*

Housesteads Settlement *includes the remains of terrace shops or taverns.*

Emperor Hadrian *(76–138) came to Britain in 120 to order a stronger defence system. Coins were often cast to record emperors' visits, such as this bronze sestertius. Until 1971, the penny was abbreviated to* d, *short for* denarius, *a Roman coin.*

Cawfields, *2 miles (3 km) north of Haltwhistle, is the access point to one of the highest and most rugged sections of the wall. To the east, the remains of a milecastle sit on Whin Sill crag.*

🏠 Hexham Abbey
Market Place. **Tel** 01434 602031.
⬜ daily. ♿ 🖥 🅿

🏛 Border History Museum
Old Gaol, nr Hallgate. **Tel** 01434
652349. ⬜ Feb–Oct: daily; Nov:
Mon, Tue, Sat. 🎫 ♿ 🅿

Corbridge ⑩

Northumberland. 🏘 4,000. 🚆
ℹ Hill St (01434 632815).

This quiet town conceals
a few historic buildings
constructed with stones from
the Roman garrison town of

**The parson's 14th-century fortified
tower house at Corbridge**

nearby Corstopitum. Among
these are the thickset Saxon
tower of St Andrew's Church
and the 14th-century fortified
tower house built to protect
the local clergyman. Excavations of Corstopitum, now
known as **Corbridge Roman
Site and Museum**, have
exposed earlier forts, a well-
preserved granary, temples,
fountains and an aqueduct.

🏛 Corbridge Roman Site and Museum
(EH) Tel 01434 632349. ⬜ Apr–Oct:
daily; Nov–Mar: Sat & Sun. ⬛ 24–26
Dec, 1 Jan. 🎫 ♿ limited. 📷 🅿

THE WALL COAST-TO-COAST

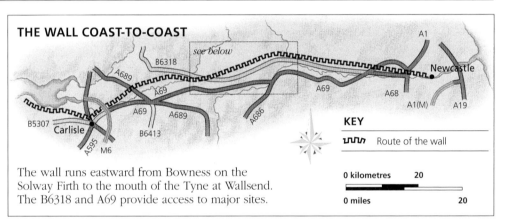

KEY

ᒐᒐᒐ Route of the wall

0 kilometres 20

0 miles 20

The wall runs eastward from Bowness on the
Solway Firth to the mouth of the Tyne at Wallsend.
The B6318 and A69 provide access to major sites.

Carrawburgh Fort, a 500-man
garrison, guarded the Newbrough
Burn and North Tyndale approaches.

Limestone Corner Milecastle is
sited at the northernmost part of
the wall and has magnificent views
of the Cheviot Hills (see p421).

Sewingshields Milecastle, *with
magnificent views west to Housesteads,
is one of the best places for walking.
This reconstruction shows the layout
of a Roman milecastle on the wall.*

Chesters Fort was a
bridgehead over the
North Tyne. In the
museum are altars, sculp-
tures and inscriptions.

Chesters Bridge crossed the
Tyne. The original Hadrianic
bridge was rebuilt in 207. The
remains of this second bridge
abutment can still be seen.

Housesteads Fort *is the best-
preserved site on the wall, with
fine views over the countryside.
The excavated remains include
the commanding officer's house
and a Roman hospital.*

0 metres 500

0 yards 500

Newcastle upon Tyne ⑫

🏛 273,000. ✈ ⇄ 🚉 ⛴ ℹ
Quayside (0191 2778000). 🅿 Sun.
www.visitnewcastlegateshead.com

Newcastle owes its name to its Norman **castle** which was founded in 1080 by Robert Curthose, the eldest son of William the Conqueror (*see p47*). The Romans had bridged the Tyne and built a fort on the site 1,000 years earlier. During the Middle Ages it was used as a base for English campaigns against the Scots. From the Middle Ages, the city flourished as a coal mining and exporting centre. It was known in the 19th century for engineering, steel production and later as the world's foremost shipyard. The city's industrial base has recently declined, but "Geordies", as inhabitants of the city are known, have refocused their civic pride on the ultra-modern Metro Centre shopping mall at Gateshead, southwest of the city, and Newcastle United soccer team.

Bridges crossing the Tyne at Newcastle

The city's lively night scene includes clubs, pubs and ethnic restaurants. The visible trappings of its past are reflected in the magnificent **Tyne Bridge** and in **Earl Grey's Monument**, as well as the grand façades in the city centre thoroughfares, such as Grey Street. On the quayside there are some dramatic new features, notably **Baltic**, the contemporary art centre, **The Sage Gateshead**, the international centre for music, and the tilting **Gateshead Millennium Bridge**.

⚓ **The Castle**
St Nicholas St. **Tel** 0191 232 7938. ◯ daily. ⬤ 1 Jan, Good Fri, 24–26 Dec. 📷 🔲
Curthose's original wooden "new castle" was rebuilt in stone in the 12th century. Only

Beamish, The North of England Open Air Museum ⑬

This giant open air museum, spread over 120 ha (300 acres) of County Durham, recreates an authentic picture of family, working and community life in the northeast in the 19th and early 20th centuries. It has a 1913 Town Street, colliery village with drift mine, working farm and railway station. A tramway serves the different parts of the museum, which carefully avoids romanticizing the past.

Tram symbol

The station, which dates back to 1913, has a platform, a signal box, a wrought-iron footbridge and a goods yard.

Home Farm recreates the atmosphere of an old-fashioned farm. Rare breeds of cattle and sheep, more common before the advent of mass breeding, can be seen.

🚻 🔲
School

Miners' houses were tiny, oil-lit dwellings, backing onto vegetable gardens and owned by the colliery.

Chapel

the thickset, crenellated keep remains intact with two suites of royal apartments. A series of staircases spiral up to the renovated battlements, from which there are fine views over the city and the Tyne.

🔒 St Nicholas Cathedral

St Nicholas Sq. *Tel 0191 2321939.*
◯ *daily.* ♿
This is one of Britain's tiniest cathedrals. There are remnants inside of the original 11th-century Norman church on which the present 14th- and 15th-century structure was founded. Its most striking feature is its ornate "lantern tower" – half tower, half spire – of which there are only three others in Britain.

🚏 Bessie Surtees' House

(EH) 41–44 Sandhill. *Tel 0191 2611585.* ◯ *Mon–Fri.* ● *25 Dec– 2 Jan, public hols.* ♿ *limited.* 📷
The story of beautiful, wealthy Bessie, who lived here before

Reredos of the Northumbrian saints in St Nicholas Cathedral

eloping with penniless John Scott, later Lord Chancellor of England, is the romantic tale behind these half-timbered 16th- and 17th-century houses. The window through which Bessie escaped now has a blue glass pane.

🚏 Tyne Bridge

Newcastle–Gateshead.
◯ *daily.* ♿
Opened in 1928, this steel arch was the longest of its type in Britain with a span of 162 m (531 ft). Designed by Mott, Hay and Anderson, it soon became the city's most potent symbol.

🚏 Earl Grey's Monument

Grey St.
Benjamin Green created this memorial to the 2nd Earl Grey, Liberal Prime Minister from 1830 to 1834.

🏛 Baltic

The Centre for Contemporary Art Gateshead. *Tel 0191 478 1810.* ◯ *daily.* 📷 🍴 💻 www.balticmill.com
This former grain warehouse has been converted by architect Dominic Williams into a major new international centre for contemporary art, one of the biggest in Europe, with amazing views of Tyneside from its rooftop restaurant.

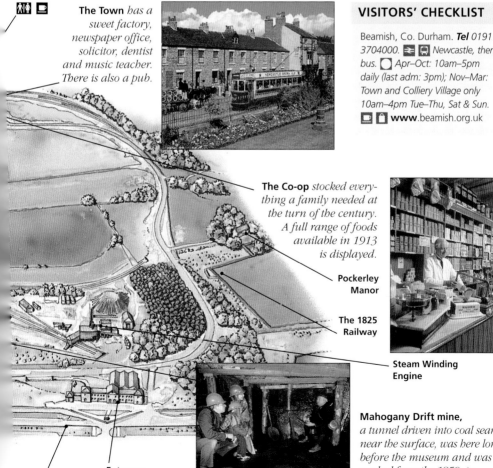

🚻 💻

The Town *has a sweet factory, newspaper office, solicitor, dentist and music teacher. There is also a pub.*

The Co-op *stocked everything a family needed at the turn of the century. A full range of foods available in 1913 is displayed.*

Pockerley Manor

The 1825 Railway

Steam Winding Engine

🅿 **Entrance** 🚻 📷 💻

Mahogany Drift mine, *a tunnel driven into coal seams near the surface, was here long before the museum and was worked from the 1850s to 1958. Visitors are given guided tours underground.*

Houses built by the London Lead Company in Middleton-in-Teesdale

Durham ⑭

See pp428–9.

North Pennines Tour ⑮

See p427.

Cotherstone cheese, a speciality of the Middleton-in-Teesdale area

Middleton-in-Teesdale ⑯

Co. Durham. 🏘 *1,100.* 🚆 *Darling-ton.* ℹ️ *10 Market Place (01833 690909).* **www**.visitteesdale.co.uk

Clinging to a hillside amid wild Pennine scenery on the River Tees is this old lead mining town. Many of its rows of grey stone cottages were built by the London Lead Company, a paternalistic, Quaker-run organization who influenced every corner of its employees' daily lives.

The company began mining in 1753, and soon it virtually owned the town. Workers were expected to observe strict temperance, send their children to Sunday school and conform to the many company maxims. Today, mining has all but ceased in Teesdale, with Middleton standing as a monument to the 18th-century idea of the "company town". The offices of the London Lead Company can still be seen, as well as Nonconformist chapels from the era and a memorial fountain made of iron.

The crumbly Cotherstone cow's milk cheese, a speciality of the surrounding dales, is available in the shops.

Barnard Castle ⑰

County Durham. 🏘 *5,000.* 🚆 *Darlington.* ℹ️ *Woodleigh, Flatts Rd (01833 690909).* 🛒 *Wed.* **www**.teesdalediscovery.com

Barnard Castle, known in the area as "Barney", is a little town full of character, with old shopfronts and a cobbled market overlooked by the ruins of the Norman castle from which it takes its name. The original Barnard Castle was built around 1125–40 by Bernard Balliol, ancestor of the founder of Balliol College, Oxford *(see p222).* Later, the market town grew up around the fortification.

Today, Barnard Castle is known for the extraordinary French-style château to the east of the town, surrounded by acres of formal gardens. Started in 1860 by the local aristocrat John Bowes and his French wife Josephine, an artist and actress, it was never a private residence, but always intended as a museum and public monument. The château finally opened in 1892, by which time the couple were both dead. Nevertheless, the **Bowes Museum** stands as a monument to his wealth and her extravagance.

The museum houses a strong collection of Spanish art which includes El Greco's *The Tears of St Peter,* dating from the 1580s, and Goya's *Don Juan Meléndez Váldez,* painted in 1797. Clocks, porcelain, furniture, musical instruments, toys and tapestries are among its treasures.

🏛 **Bowes Museum**
Barnard Castle. **Tel** *01833 690606.* 🔵 *daily.* ⚫ *1 Jan, 25 & 26 Dec.* 🎫 ♿ 📷 *(summer).* 🖥 📖
www.bowesmuseum.org.uk

The Bowes Museum, a French-style château near Barnard Castle

North Pennines Tour ⑮

Starting just to the south of Hadrian's Wall, this tour explores the South Tyne Valley, and Upper Weardale. It crosses one of England's wildest and most remote tracts of moorland, then heads north again. The high ground is mainly blanketed with heather, dotted with sheep or criss-crossed with dry-stone walls, a feature of this region. Harriers and other birds hover above, and streams tumble into valleys of tightly huddled villages.

Sheep grazing on the moors

Celts, Romans and other settlers have left imprints on the North Pennines. The wealth of the area was based on lead mining and stone quarrying which has long co-existed with farming.

Haltwhistle ①
In the Church of the Holy Cross is the tombstone of John Ridley, brother of Protestant martyr, Nicholas Ridley, burnt at the stake in 1555 *(see p222)*.

Haydon Bridge ③
There are some delightful walks near this spa town where the painter John Martin was born in 1789. Nearby Langley Castle is worth a visit.

Hexham ④
A pretty old town *(see p422)*, Hexham has a fine abbey.

Blanchland ⑤
Some houses in this lead-mining village are built on the site of a 12th-century abbey, using the original stone.

Bardon Mill ②
To the north is the Roman fort and civilian settlement of Vindolanda *(see p422)*.

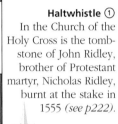

Allendale ⑦
With its capital at Allendale Town, this is an area of spectacular scenery, with many walking and trout fishing opportunities.

KEY

▬▬▬	Tour route
═══	Other roads
☀	Viewpoint

Stanhope ⑥
An 18th-century castle overlooks the market square. The giant stump of a fossilized tree, said to be 250 million years old, guards the graveyard.

TIPS FOR DRIVERS

Length: 50 miles (80 km)
Stopping-off points: Several pubs in Stanhope serve bar meals, and the Durham Dales Centre provides teas all year round. Horsley Hall Hotel at Eastgate serves meals all day.

0 kilometres   5

0 miles   5

Map labels: CARLISLE A69 · South Tyne · North Tyne · A69 · NEWCASTLE UPON TYNE · A69 · River Tyne · A686 · B6305 · B6531 · B6307 · West Dipton Burn · Ham Burn · B6305 · A686 · Allendale Town · Devil's Water · B6306 · Derwent reservoir · River East Allen · B6295 · Beldon Burn · B6278 · Edmund-byers · B6278 · Allenheads · Rookhope Burn · A689 · Cowshill · Wearhead · Killhope Burn · Eastgate · A689 · A689 · River Wear · DURHAM → · Burnhope Burn · Westgate

Durham ⑭

The city of Durham was built on Island Hill or "Dunholm" in 995. This rocky peninsula, which defies the course of the River Wear's route to the sea, was chosen as the last resting place for the remains of St Cuthbert. The relics of the Venerable Bede were brought to the site 27 years later, adding to its attraction for pilgrims. Durham Cathedral was treated by architects as an experiment for geometric patterning, while the Castle served as the Episcopal Palace until 1832, when Bishop William van Mildert gave it up and surrendered part of his income to found Britain's third university. The 23 ha (57 acre) peninsula has many foot-paths, views and fine buildings.

Cathedral Sanctuary knocker

★ Cathedral
Built from 1093 to 1274, it is a striking Norman structure.

Old Fulling Mill, a largely 18th-century building, houses a museum of archaeology.

Prebend's footbridge was built in 1777. A sculpture by Colin Wilbourn is situated at the "island" end.

College Green

Monastic kitchen

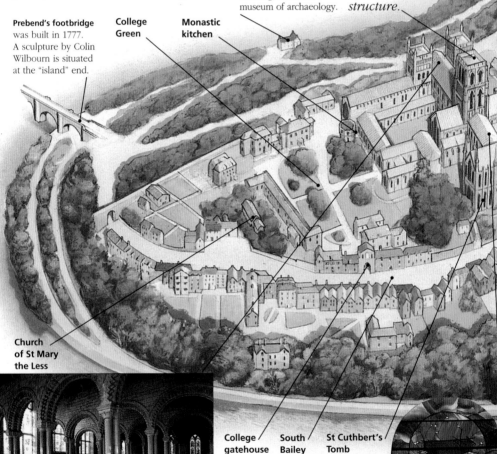

Church of St Mary the Less

College gatehouse

South Bailey

St Cuthbert's Tomb

"Our Daily Bread" Window
This modern stained-glass window in the north nave aisle was donated in 1984 by a local department store.

Galilee Chapel
Architects began work on the exotic Galilee Chapel in 1170, drawing inspiration from the Great Mosque of Cordoba in Andalusia. It was altered by Bishop Langley (d.1437) whose tomb is by the west door.

STAR SIGHTS

★ Cathedral

★ Castle

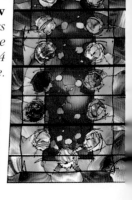

★ Castle

Begun in 1072, the castle is a fine Norman fortress. The keep, sited on a mound, is now part of the university.

Palace Green

Town Hall (1851)

St Nicholas' Church (1857)

VISITORS' CHECKLIST

Co.Durham. **≷** *Station Approach.* **ℹ** *Millennium Pl (0191 384 3720).* **Cathedral. *Tel* 0191 386 4266.** ⏱ *9:30am–6:15pm daily (to 5:30pm Sun, to 8pm July & Aug).* **♿ Castle. *Tel* 0191 334 3800.** ⏱ *univ hols: daily; term: Mon, Wed, Sat & Sun (pm)* ✔ *manda-tory.* **www**.durhamcastle.com

Tunstal's Chapel

Situated at the end of the Tunstal's Gallery, the castle chapel was built c.1542. Its fine woodwork includes this unicorn misericord (see p341).

University buildings *were built by Bishop John Cosin in the 17th century.*

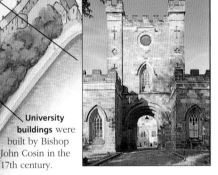

Castle Gatehouse

Traces of Norman stone-work can be seen in the outer arch, while the sturdy walls and upper floors are 18th century, rebuilt in a style dubbed "gothick" by detractors.

rch of St y le Bow

Kingsgate otbridge, *uilt from* *–3, leads to North Bailey.*

CATHEDRAL ARCHITECTURE

The vast dimensions of the 900-year-old columns, piers and vaults, and the inventive giant lozenge and chevron, trellis and dogtooth patterns carved into the stone columns, are the main innovative features of Durham Cathedral. It is believed that 11th- and 12th-century architects such as Bishop Ranulph Flambard tried to unify all parts of the structure. This can be seen in the south aisle of the nave below.

Ribbed vaults, *criss-crossing above the nave, are now common in church ceilings. One of the major achievements of Gothic architec ture, they were first built at Durham.*

The lozenge *shape is a pattern from prehistoric carving, but never before seen in a cathedral.*

Chevron patterns *on some of the piers in the nave are evidence of Moorish influence.*

WALES

Wales at a Glance

Wales is a country of outstanding natural beauty with varied landscapes. Visitors come to climb dramatic mountain peaks, go walking in the forests, fish in the broad rivers and enjoy the miles of unspoilt coastline. The country's many seaside resorts have long been popular with English holidaymakers. As well as outdoor pursuits there is the vibrancy of Welsh culture, with its strong Celtic roots, to be experienced. Finally there are many fine castles, ruined abbeys, mansions and cities full of magnificent architecture.

Anglesey

Caernarfonshire &
Merionethshire

Beaumaris Castle *was intended to be a key part of Edward I's "iron ring" to contain the rebellious Welsh (see p436). Begun in 1295 but never completed, the castle (see p438) has a sophisticated defence structure that is unparalleled in Wales.*

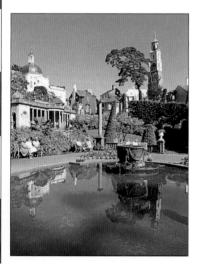

Portmeirion (see pp454–5) *is a private village whose astonishing buildings seem rather incongruous in the Welsh landscape. The village was created by the architect Sir Clough Williams-Ellis to fulfill a personal ambition. Some of the buildings are assembled from pieces of architecture taken from sites around the country.*

Card

Carmarthens

Pembrokeshire

St David *is the smallest city in Britain. The cathedral (see pp464–5) is the largest in Wales, and its nave is noted for its carved oak roof and beautiful rood screen. Next to the cathedral is the medieval Bishop's Palace, now a ruin.*

◁ **Caernarfon's colourful quayside marina**

Llanberis and Snowdon
(see p451) *is an area
famous for dangerous, high
peaks, long popular with
climbers. Mount Snowdon's
summit is most easily
reached from Llanberis. Its
Welsh name,* Yr Wyddfa
Fawr, *means "great tomb"
and it is the legendary
burial place of a giant slain
by King Arthur (see p285).*

Conwy Castle *guards one of the
best-preserved medieval fortified
towns in Britain (see pp446–7).
Built by Edward I, the castle
was besieged and came close
to surrender in 1294. It was
taken by Owain Glyndûr's
supporters in 1401.*

Flintshire
erconwy
Colwyn
Denbighshire

NORTH WALES
(see pp440–55)

Wrexham

Powys

SOUTH AND MID-WALES
(see pp456–75)

Monmouthshire

diff, Swansea & Environs

The Brecon Beacons *(see pp468–9) is a national park,
a lovely area of mountains, forest and moorland in South
Wales, which is a favourite with walkers and naturalists.
Pen-y-Fan is one of the principal summits.*

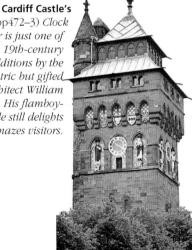

Cardiff Castle's
*(see pp472–3) Clock
Tower is just one of
many 19th-century
additions by the
eccentric but gifted
architect William
Burges. His flamboy-
ant style still delights
and amazes visitors.*

0 kilometres   25

0 miles   25

A PORTRAIT OF WALES

*L*ong popular with British holidaymakers, the many charms of Wales are now becoming better known internationally. They include spectacular scenery and a vibrant culture specializing in male-voice choirs, poetry and a passionate love of team sports. Governed from Westminster since 1536, Wales has its own distinct Celtic identity and in 1999 finally gained partial devolution.

Much of the Welsh landmass is covered by the Cambrian Mountain range, which effectively acts as a barrier from England. Wales is warmed by the Gulf Stream and has a mild climate, with more rain than most of Britain. The land is unsuitable for arable farming, but sheep and cattle thrive; the drove roads, along which sheep used to be driven across the hills to England, are now popular walking trails. It is partly because of the rugged terrain that the Welsh have managed to maintain their separate identity and their ancient language.

Welsh is an expansive, musical language, spoken by only one-fifth of the 2.7 million inhabitants, but in parts of North Wales it is still the main language of conversation. There is an official bilingual policy: road signs are in Welsh and English, even in areas where Welsh is little spoken. Welsh

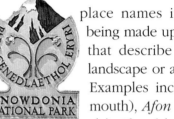

One of Wales's splendid National Parks

place names intrigue visitors, being made up of native words that describe features of the landscape or ancient buildings. Examples include *Aber* (river mouth), *Afon* (river), *Fach* (little), *Llan* (church) *Llyn* (lake) and *Nant* (valley).

Wales was conquered by the Romans, but not by the Saxons. The land and the people therefore retained Celtic patterns of settlement and husbandry for six centuries before the Norman Conquest in 1066. This allowed time for the development of a distinctive Welsh nation whose homogeneity continues to this day.

The early Norman kings subjugated the Welsh by appointing "Marcher Lords" to control areas bordering England. A string

Rugby: the popular Welsh sport

of massive castles provides evidence of the turbulent years when Welsh insurrection was a constant threat. It was not until 1535 that Wales formally became part of Britain, and it would take nearly 500 years before the people of Wales regained partial autonomy.

Religious non-conformism and radical politics are deeply rooted in Welsh consciousness. Saint David converted the country to Christianity in the 6th century. Methodism, chapel and teetotalism became firmly entrenched in

Mountain sheep: a familiar sight in rural Wales

A *gorsedd* (assembly) of bards at the eisteddfod

ancient bards: minstrels and poets, who may have been associated with the Druids. Bardic tales of quasi-historical figures and magic were part of the oral tradition of the Dark Ages. They were first written down in the 14th century as the *Mabinogion,* which has inspired Welsh poets up to the 20th century's Dylan Thomas. The male-voice choirs found in many towns, villages and factories, particularly in the industrial south, express the Welsh musical heritage. Choirs compete in eisteddfods: festivals that celebrate Welsh culture.

the Welsh psyche during the 19th century. Even today some pubs stay closed on Sundays. A long-standing oral tradition in Wales has produced many outstanding public speakers, politicians and actors. Welsh labour leaders have played important roles in the British trade union movement and the development of socialism.

Welsh heritage is steeped in song, music, poetry and legend rather than handicrafts, although one notable exception is the carved Welsh lovespoon – a craft recently revived. The well-known Welsh love of music derives from the

Welsh lovespoon

In the 19th century, the opening of the South Wales coalfield in Mid-Glamorgan – for a time the biggest in the world – led to an industrial boom, with mass migration from the countryside to the iron and steelworks. This prosperity was not to last: apart from a brief respite in World War II, the coal industry has been in terminal decline for decades, causing severe economic hardship. Today tourism is being promoted in the hope that the wealth generated, by outdoor activities in particular, will be able to take "King Coal's" place.

Conwy's picturesque, medieval walled town, fronted by a colourful harbour

The History of Wales

St David, patron saint of Wales

Wales has been settled since prehistoric times, its history shaped by many factors, from invasion to industrialization. The Romans set up bases in the mountainous terrain, but it was effectively a separate Celtic nation when Offa's Dyke was built as the border with England in 770. Centuries of cross-border raids and military campaigns followed before England and Wales were formally united by the Act of Union in 1535. The rugged north-west, the former stronghold of the Welsh princes, remains the heartland of Welsh language and culture.

Owain Glyndwr, heroic leader of Welsh opposition to English rule

THE CELTIC NATION

Ornamental Iron Age bronze plaque from Anglesey

Wales was settled by waves of migrants in prehistoric times. By the Iron Age (see pp42–3), Celtic farmers had established hillforts and their religion, Druidism. From the 1st century AD until the legions withdrew around 400, the Romans built fortresses and roads, and mined lead, silver and gold. During the next 200 years, Wales was converted to Christianity by missionaries from Europe. St David (see pp464–5), the Welsh patron saint, is said to have turned the leek into a national symbol. He per-suaded soldiers to wear leeks in their hats to distinguish themselves from Saxons dur-ing a 6th-century skirmish.

The Saxons (see pp46–7) failed to conquer Wales, and in 770 the Saxon King Offa built a defensive earthwork along the unconquered ter-ritory (see p461). Beyond Offa's Dyke the people called

themselves *Y Cymry* (fellow countrymen) and the land *Cymru*. The Saxons called the land "Wales" from the Old English *wealas*, meaning foreigners. It was divided into kingdoms of which the main ones were Gwynedd in the north, Powys in the centre and Dyfed in the south. There were strong trade, cultural and linguistic links between each.

MARCHER LORDS

The Norman invasion of 1066 (see p47) did not reach Wales, but the border territory ("the Marches") was given by William the Conqueror to three powerful barons based at Shrewsbury, Hereford and Chester. These Marcher Lords made many incursions into Wales and controlled most of the lowlands. But the Welsh

Edward I designating his son Prince of Wales in 1301

princes held the mountainous northwest and exploited English weaknesses. Under Llywelyn the Great (d.1240), North Wales was almost com-pletely independent; in 1267 his grandson, Llywelyn the Last, was acknowledged as Prince of Wales by Henry III.

In 1272 Edward I came to the English throne. He built fortresses and embarked on a military campaign to con-quer Wales. In 1283 Llywelyn was killed in a skirmish, a shattering blow for the Welsh. Edward introduced English law and proclaimed his son Prince of Wales (see p444).

OWAIN GLYNDWR'S REBELLION

Welsh resentment against the Marcher Lords led to rebellion. In 1400 Owain Glyndŵr (c.1350–1416), a descendant of the Welsh princes, laid waste to English-dominated towns and castles. Declaring himself Prince of Wales, he found Celtic allies in Scotland, Ireland, France and Northumbria. In 1404 Glyndŵr captured Harlech and Cardiff, and formed a parliament in Machynlleth (see p462). In 1408 the French made a truce with the English king, Henry IV. The rebellion then failed and Glyndŵr went into hiding until his death.

UNION WITH ENGLAND

Wales suffered greatly during the Wars of the Roses *(see p49)* as Yorkists and Lancastrians tried to gain control of the strategically important Welsh castles. The wars ended in 1485, and the Welshman Henry Tudor, born in Pembroke, became Henry VII. The Act of Union in 1535 and other laws abolished the Marcher Lordships, giving Wales parliamentary representation in London instead. English practices replaced inheritance customs and English became the language of the courts and administration. The Welsh language survived, partly helped by the church and by Dr William Morgan's translation of the Bible in 1588.

Miners from South Wales pictured in 1910

Vernacular Bible, which helped to keep the Welsh language alive

INDUSTRY AND RADICAL POLITICS

The industrialization of south and east Wales began with the development of open-cast coal mining near Wrexham and Merthyr Tydfil in the 1760s. Convenient ports and the arrival of the railways helped the process. By the second half of the 19th century open-cast mines had been superseded by deep pits in the Rhondda Valley.

Living and working conditions were poor for industrial and agricultural workers. A series of "Rebecca Riots" in South Wales between 1839 and 1843, involving tenant farmers (dressed as women) protesting about tithes and rents, was forcibly suppressed. The Chartists, trade unions and the Liberal Party had much Welsh support.

The rise of Methodism *(see p279)* roughly paralleled the growth of industry: 80 per cent of the population was Methodist by 1851. The Welsh language persisted, despite attempts by the British government to discourage its use, which included punishing children caught speaking it.

WALES TODAY

In the 20th century the Welsh became a power in British politics. David Lloyd George, although not born in Wales, grew up there and was the first British Prime Minister to come from a Welsh family. Aneurin Bevan, a miner's son who became a Labour Cabinet Minister, helped create the National Health Service *(see p59)*.

Welsh nationalism continued to grow: in 1926 Plaid Cymru, the Welsh Nationalist Party, was formed. In 1955 Cardiff was recognized as the capital of Wales *(see p470)* and four years later the red dragon became the emblem on Wales' new flag. Plaid Cymru won two parliamentary seats at Westminster in 1974, and in a 1998 referendum the Welsh espoused limited home rule. The National Assembly for Wales is housed in the stunning Y Senedd, on the waterfront in Cardiff Bay.

The 1967 Welsh Language Act made Welsh compulsory in schools, and the television channel S4C (Sianel 4 Cymru), formed in 1982, broadcasts many programmes in Welsh.

From the 1960s the steel and coal industries declined, creating mass unemployment. This has been partly alleviated by the emergence of high-tech industries, and by growth in tourism: Cardiff is home to many major tourist attractions including the Millennium Stadium and Cardiff Bay, Europe's largest waterfront development *(see pp470–71)*.

Girl in traditional Welsh costume

Castles of Wales

A French 15th-century painting of Conwy Castle

Wales is rich in romantic medieval castles. Soon after the Battle of Hastings, in 1066 *(see p47)*, the Normans turned their attentions to Wales. They built earth and timber fortifications, later replaced by stone castles, initiating a building programme that was pursued by the Welsh princes and invading forces. Construction reached its peak during the reign of Edward I *(see p436)*. As the need for security lessened in the later Middle Ages, some castles became stately homes.

The north gatehouse was planned to be 18 m (60 ft) high, providing lavish royal accommodation, but its top storey was never built.

The inner ward was lined with a hall, granary, kitchens and stables.

Rounded towers, with fewer blind spots than square ones, gave better protection.

Arrow slit

BEAUMARIS CASTLE

The last of Edward I's Welsh castles *(see p444)*, this perfectly symmetrical, concentric design was intended to combine impregnable defence with comfort. Invaders would face many obstacles before reaching the inner ward.

Moat

Curtain wall

WHERE TO SEE WELSH CASTLES

In addition to Beaumaris, in North Wales there are medieval forts at Caernarfon *(see p444)*, Conwy *(see p446)* and Harlech *(see p454)*. Edward I also built Denbigh, Flint (near Chester) and Rhuddlan (near Rhyll). In South and mid-Wales, Caerphilly (near Cardiff), Kidwelly (near Carmarthen) and Pembroke were built between the 11th and 13th centuries. Spectacular sites are occupied by Cilgerran (near Cardigan), Criccieth (near Porthmadog) and Carreg Cennen *(see p468)*. Chirk Castle, near Llangollen, is a good example of a fortress that has since become a stately home.

Caerphilly, *6 miles (10 km) north of Cardiff, is a huge castle with concentric stone and water defences that cover 12 ha (30 acres).*

Harlech Castle (see p454) *is noted for its massive gatehouse, twin towers and the fortified stairway to the sea. It was the headquarters of the Welsh resistance leader Owain Glyndŵr (see p436) from 1404–8.*

CASTELL-Y-BERE

This native Welsh castle at the foot of Cader Idris *(see p440)* was founded by Llywelyn the Great in 1221 *(see p422)*, to secure internal borders rather than to resist the English.

Entrance

The D-shaped, elongated tower is a typical feature of Welsh castles.

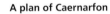

The castle's construction follows the shape of the rock. The curtain walls are too low and insubstantial to be of much practical use.

Drawbridge

The Chapel Tower has a beautiful medieval chapel.

The protected dock, on a channel that originally led to the sea, received supplies during sieges.

inner wall, with an ...er passage, was higher ...a the curtain wall to ...mit simultaneous firing.

Twin-towered gatehouse

EDWARD I AND MASTER JAMES OF ST GEORGE

In 1278 Edward I brought over from Savoy a master stonemason who became a great military architect, James of St George. Responsible for planning and building at least 12 of Edward's fine Welsh castles, James was paid well and liberally pensioned off, indicating the esteem in which he was held by the king.

Edward I *(see p436) was the warrior king whose castles played a key role in the subjugation of the Welsh people.*

A plan of Caernarfon Castle *illustrates how its position, on a promontory surrounded by water, has determined the building's shape and defence.*

Caernarfon Castle *(see p444), birthplace of the ill-fated Edward II (see p327), was intended to be the official royal residence in North Wales, and has palatial private apartments.*

Castell Coch *was restored in Neo-Gothic style by Lord Bute and William Burges (see p472). Mock-castles were built by many Victorian industrialists.*

Conwy Castle *(see p447), like many other castles, required forced labour on a massive scale for its construction.*

NORTH WALES

ABERCONWY & COLWYN · ANGLESEY · CAERNARFONSHIRE &
MERIONETHSHIRE · DENBIGHSHIRE · FLINTSHIRE · WREXHAM

The North Wales landscape has a dramatic quality reflected in its history. In prehistoric times, Anglesey was a stronghold of the religious elite known as the Druids. Roman and Norman invasions concentrated on the coast, leaving the mountains to the Welsh. These wild areas are the centre of Welsh language and culture.

Defence and conquest have been constant themes in Welsh history. North Wales was the scene of ferocious battles between the Welsh princes and Anglo-Norman monarchs determined to establish English rule. The string of formidable castles which still stand in North Wales are as much a testament to Welsh resistance as to the wealth and strength of the invaders. Several massive fortresses, including Beaumaris, Caernarfon and Harlech, almost surround the rugged high country of Snowdonia, an area that even today maintains an untamed quality.

Sheep and cattle farming are the basis of the rural economy here, though there are also large areas of forestry. Along the coast, tourism is a major activity. Llandudno, a purpose-built Victorian resort, popularized the sandy northern coastline in the 19th century. The area continues to attract large numbers of visitors, though major development is confined to the narrow coastal strip that lies between Prestatyn and Llandudno, leaving the island of Anglesey and the remote Llyn Peninsula largely untouched.

The Llyn Peninsula remains one of the strongholds of the Welsh language, along with rather isolated inland communities, such as Dolgellau and Bala.

No part of North Wales can truly be called industrial, though there are still remnants of the once-prosperous slate industry in Snowdonia, where the stark, grey quarries provide a striking contrast to the natural beauty of the surrounding mountains. At the foot of Snowdon (the highest mountain in Wales), the villages of Beddgelert, Betws-y-Coed and Llanberis are popular bases for walkers who come to enjoy the spectacular views and striking beauty of this remote region.

Caernarfon Castle, one of the forbidding fortresses built by Edward I

◁ **The River Dee at Llangollen, still an area of unspoilt natural beauty**

Exploring North Wales

The dominant feature of North Wales is Snowdon, the highest mountain in Wales. Snowdonia National Park extends dramatically from the Snowdon massif south beyond Dolgellau, with thickly wooded valleys, mountain lakes, moors and estuaries. To the east are the softer Clwydian Hills, and unspoilt coastlines can be enjoyed on Anglesey and the beautiful Llyn Peninsula.

A lighthouse perched on the sea cliffs of Anglesey

KEY

▰▰▰	Major road
▬▬	Minor road
═══	Secondary road
────	Scenic route
┄┄┄	Main railway
-------	Minor railway
△	Summit

Carmel Head
Cemaes A5025 Amlwch
Holyhead Bay
Llyn Alaw
A5111
Moelfre
Benllech
LLANDUDNO
Great Ormes Head
Holyhead
A n g l e s e y
Pentraeth
BEAUMARIS ②
CONWY
Holy Island
Gwalchmai
Penmaen
A5
Llangefni A5025
Llanfairfechan
Rhosneigr
Bangor
Bethesda
Dolgarrog
Aberffraw A4080 Port Dinorwic
Carnedd Llyw
1064m
Newborough
Llan
CAERNARFON ① A4086
Llanberis
Capel Curig
Caernarfon Bay
LLANBERIS AND SNOWDON ⑩
BETWS CO
Penygroes
Snowdon 1085m
Dolwydde
Llanllyfni
A498
A470
BEDDGELERT ⑪
BLAEN FFEST
⑨
A499
A487
Ffestini
Llanaelhaearn
A498
Tan-y-Bwlch
Maentwrog
Nefyn
Porthmadog
Tudweiliog A4417
LLYN PENINSULA
Criccieth
PORTMEIRION ⑬
Traws
⑫ A499
Pwllheli
Tremadog Bay
A470
Plas-yn-Rhiw B4413
Llanbedrog
HARLECH ⑭
Rhinog Fawr 720m
Abersoch
Aberdaron
Porth Neigwl
Llanbedr
Y Llethr 754m
Braich y Pwll
C a r d i g a n   B a y
A496
Snowdoni National
Bardsey Island
Llanaber
DOLGELLAU ⑮
Barmouth
Cader Idri 892m
Barmouth Bay
Fairbourne
A493
Llwyngwril
A4
Abergynolwyn
Tywyn
A493
Aberystwyth ↓
⑯ ABERDYFI

The peaks and moorland of Snowdonia

GETTING AROUND

The main route into North Wales from the northwest of England is the A55, a good dual carriageway which bypasses several places that used to be traffic bottlenecks, including Conwy. The other main route through the region is the A5 Shrewsbury to Holyhead road, which follows a trail through the mountains pioneered by the 19th-century engineer Thomas Telford *(see p447)*. Rail services run along the coast to Holyhead, connecting with ferries across the Irish Sea to Dublin and Dun Laoghaire. Scenic branch lines travel from Llandudno Junction to Blaenau Ffestiniog (via Betws-y-Coed) and along the southern Llyn Peninsula.

SIGHTS AT A GLANCE

Aberdyfi 16
Bala 7
Beaumaris 2
Beddgelert 11
Betws-y-Coed 8
Blaenau Ffestiniog 9
Caernarfon 1
Conwy pp446–7 3
Dolgellau 15
Harlech 14
Llanberis and Snowdon 10
LLandudno 4
LLangollen 6
Llyn Peninsula 12
Portmeirion pp454–5 13
Ruthin 5

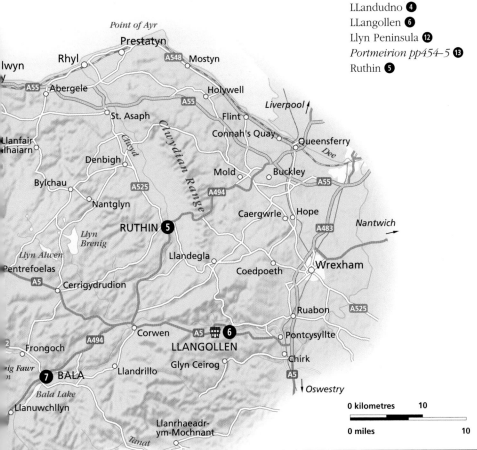

The imposing castle built at Conwy by Edward I in the 13th century

Caernarfon Castle, built by Edward I as a symbol of his power over the conquered Welsh

Caernarfon ❶

Caernarfonshire & Merionethshire
(Gwynedd). 🏃 10,000. 🚌
🛈 Castle St (01286 672232).
✉ Sat. www.gwynedd.gov.uk

One of the most famous
castles in Wales, Caernarfon
Castle, looms over this busy
town. Both town and castle
were created after Edward
I's defeat of the last native
Welsh prince, Llywelyn ap
Gruffydd (Llywelyn the Last)
in 1283 (see p436). The town
walls merge with modern
streets that spread beyond
the medieval centre to a
market square.

THE INVESTITURE

In 1301 the future Edward
II became the first English
Prince of Wales (see p436),
a title since held by the
British monarch's eldest
son. In 1969 the investi-
ture in Caernarfon Castle
of Prince Charles (above)
as Prince of Wales drew
500 million TV viewers.

Overlooking the town and its
harbour, **Caernarfon Castle**
(see p439), with its polygonal
towers, was built as a seat of
government for North Wales.
Caernarfon was a thriving
port in the 19th century, and
during this period the castle
ruins were restored by the
architect Anthony Salvin.
Displays in the castle include
the Royal Welch Fusiliers
Museum, and exhibitions
tracing the history of the
Princes of Wales and
exploring the theme
"Chieftains and Princes".

Situated on the hill above
the town are the ruins of
Segontium, a Roman fort
built in about AD 78. Local
legend claims that the first
Christian Emperor of Rome,
Constantine the Great, was
born here in 280.

♜ Caernarfon Castle
Y Maes. **Tel** 01286 677617.
🔾 daily. 🈳 🔲 call for details. 🔲
www.caernarfon.com

♫ Segontium
(NT) Beddgelert Rd. **Tel** 01286
675625. 🔾 Tue–Sun (Sun: pm).
● 1 Jan, 24, 26 Dec. 🔲 limited.
🔲 www.segontium.org.uk

Beaumaris ❷

Anglesey (Gwynedd). 🏃 2,000. 🚍
🛈 Llanfair PG, Station Site, Holyhead
Rd, Anglesey (01248 713177).
www.visitanglesey.co.uk

Handsome Georgian and
Victorian architecture gives
Beaumaris the air of a resort
on England's southern coast.
The buildings reflect this

sailing centre's past role as
Anglesey's chief port, before
the island was linked to the
mainland by the road and
railway bridges built across
the Menai Strait in the 19th
century. This was the site
of Edward I's last, and
possibly greatest, **castle**
(see p438), which was
built to command this
important ferrying point
to the mainland of Wales.

Ye Olde Bull's Head inn,
on Castle Street, was built in
1617. Its celebrated literary
patrons have included Dr
Samuel Johnson (1709–84)
and Victorian novelist Charles
Dickens (see p189).

The town's **Courthouse**,
was built in 1614 and the
recently restored 1829 **Gaol**
preserves its soundproofed
punishment room and a huge
treadmill for prisoners. Two
public hangings took place
here. Richard Rowlands,
the last victim, protested his
innocence and cursed the
church clock as he was
led to the gallows, declaring
that its four faces would
never show the same times
again. It failed to show
consistent times until it had
an overhaul in 1980.

♜ Beaumaris Castle
Castle St. **Tel** 01248 810361.
🔾 daily. 🈳 🚹
www.beaumaris.com

⛪ Courthouse
Castle St. **Tel** 01248 811691.
🔾 Apr–Sep: daily. 🈳 🚹 🔲

⛪ Gaol
Bunkers Hill. **Tel** 01248 810921.
🔾 Apr–Sep: daily. 🈳 🚹 limited.
🔲 www.angleseyheritage.org

ALICE IN WONDERLAND

The Gogarth Abbey Hotel, Llandudno, was the summer home of the Liddells. Their friend, Charles Dodgson (1832–98), would entertain young Alice Liddell with stories of characters such as the White Rabbit and the Mad Hatter. As Lewis Carroll, Dodgson wrote his magical tales in *Alice's Adventures in Wonderland* (1865) and *Through the Looking-Glass* (1871).

Arthur Rackham's illustration (1907) of *Alice in Wonderland*

Conwy ❸

See pp446–7.

Llandudno ❹

Gwynedd. 🏘 *19,000.* ⛢ ⊟ 🛈 *Library Building, Mostyn St (01492 577577).* **www**.visitllandudno.org.uk

Llandudno's crescent-shaped bay

Llandudno retains much of the holiday spirit of the 19th century, when the new railways brought crowds to the coast. Its **pier**, more than 700 m (2,295 ft) long, and its canopied walkways recall the heyday of seaside holidays. The town is also proud of its association with the author Lewis Carroll *(see above).* The exhibits at the **Llandudno Museum** explore Llandudno's history from Roman times onwards.

Llandudno's cheerful seaside atmosphere owes much to a strong sense of its Victorian roots – unlike many British seaside towns, which embraced the flashing lights and funfairs of the 20th century. To take full advantage of its sweeping beach, Llandudno was laid out between its two headlands, Great Orme's Head and Little Orme's Head.

Great Orme's Head, now a Country Park and Nature Reserve, rises to 207 m (670 ft) and has a long history. In the Bronze Age copper was mined here; the **copper mines** and their excavations are open to the public. The **church** on the headland was built from timber in the 6th century by St Tudno, rebuilt in stone in the 13th century, restored in 1855 and is still in use. Local history and wildlife can be traced in an information centre on the summit.

There are two effortless ways to reach the summit: on the **Great Orme Tramway**, one of only three cable-hauled street tramways in the world (the others are in San Francisco and Lisbon), or by the **Llandudno Cable Car**. Both operate only in summer.

🏛 **Llandudno Museum**
Gloddaeth St. **Tel** *01492 876517.* ◯ *Easter–Oct: 10:30am–1pm, 2–5pm Tue–Sun.* ♿ *limited.*

⛏ **Great Orme Copper Mines**
Off A55. **Tel** *01492 870447.* ◯ *mid-Mar–Oct: daily.* 📷 ♿ *limited.* 🖥 🎁 **www**.greatormemines.info

Ruthin ❺

Denbighshire (Clwyd). 🏘 *5,000.* ▦ 🛈 *Craft Centre, Park Rd (01824 703992).* 🛒 *1st Tue of every month; Thu (indoor).* **www**.borderlands.co.uk

Ruthin's long-standing prosperity as a market town is reflected in its fine half-timbered medieval buildings. These include the National Westminster and Barclays banks in St Peter's Square. The former was a 15th-century courthouse and prison, the latter the home of Thomas Exmewe, Lord Mayor of London in 1517–18. **Maen Huail** ("Huail's stone"), a boulder outside Barclays, is said to be where King Arthur *(see p285)* beheaded Huail, his rival in a love affair.

St Peter's Church, on the edge of St Peter's Square, was founded in 1310 and has a Tudor oak roof in the north aisle. Next to the Castle Hotel is the 17th-century pub **The Seven Eyes** (formerly the Myddleton Arms), whose seven unusual, Dutch-style, dormer windows are known locally as the "eyes of Ruthin".

The "eyes of Ruthin", an unusual feature in Welsh architecture

Street-by-Street: Conwy ❸

Conwy is one of Britain's most underrated historic towns. Until the early 1990s it was famous as a traffic bottleneck, but thanks to a town bypass, its concentration of architectural riches – unparalleled in Wales – can now be appreciated. The castle dominates: a brooding, intimidating monument built by Edward I *(see p438)*. But Conwy is set apart from other medieval towns by its amazingly well-preserved town walls. Fortified with 21 towers and three gateways, the walls form an almost unbroken shield around the old town.

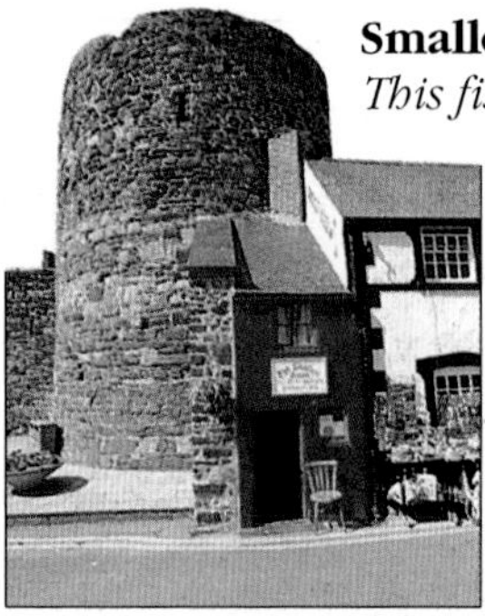

Smallest House
This fisherman's cottage on the quayside, just over 3 m (10 ft) high, is said to be the smallest house in Britain.

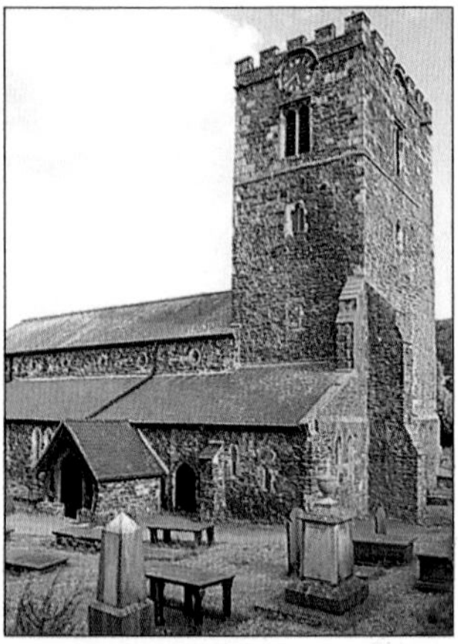

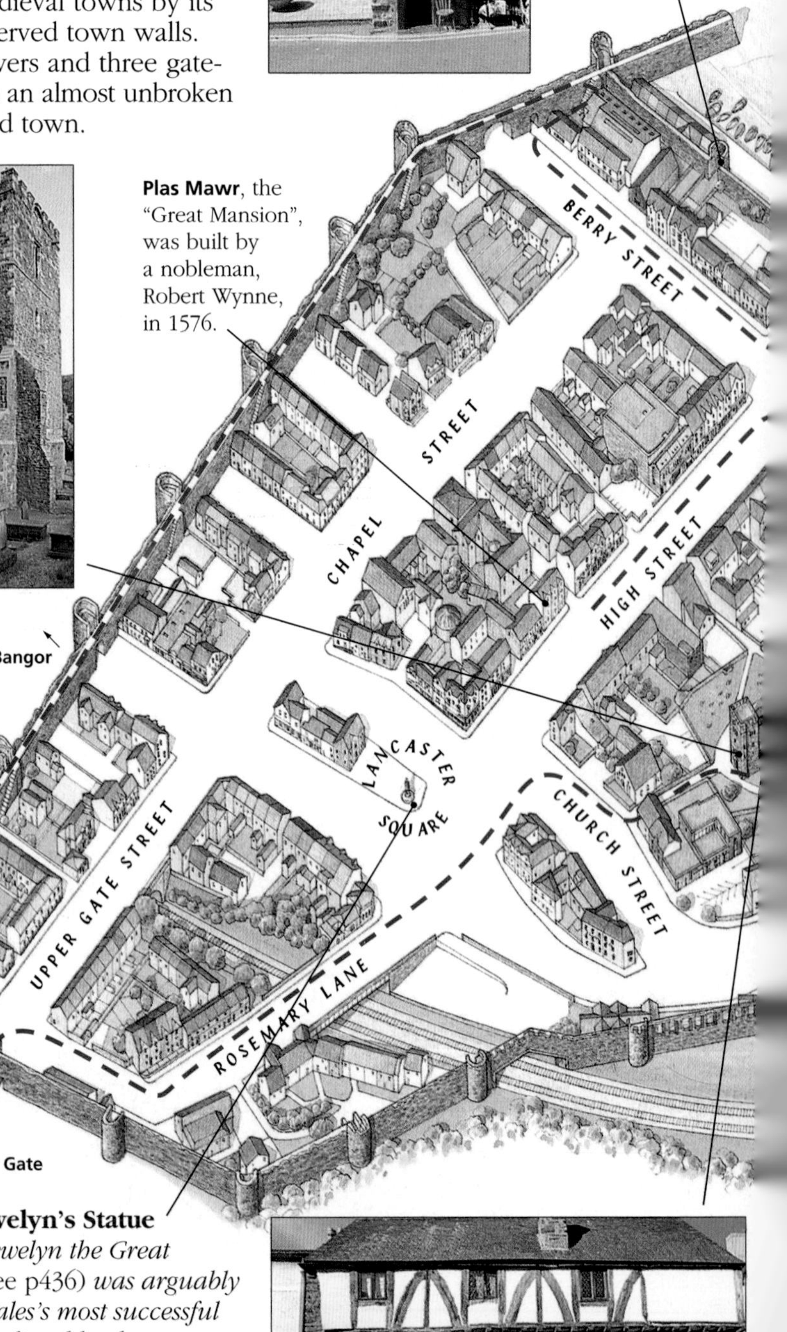

Plas Mawr, the "Great Mansion", was built by a nobleman, Robert Wynne, in 1576.

St Mary's Church
This medieval church, on the site of a 12th-century Cistercian abbey, is set in peaceful grounds.

Bangor

BERRY STREET

CHAPEL STREET

HIGH STREET

LANCASTER SQUARE

CHURCH STREET

UPPER GATE STREET

ROSEMARY LANE

Upper Gate

Llywelyn's Statue
Llywelyn the Great (see p436) was arguably Wales's most successful medieval leader.

Aberconwy House
This restored 14th-century house was once the home of a wealthy merchant.

THOMAS TELFORD

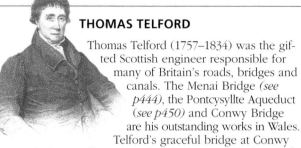

Thomas Telford (1757–1834) was the gifted Scottish engineer responsible for many of Britain's roads, bridges and canals. The Menai Bridge *(see p444)*, the Pontcysyllte Aqueduct *(see p450)* and Conwy Bridge are his outstanding works in Wales. Telford's graceful bridge at Conwy has aesthetic as well as practical qualities. Completed in 1826 across the mouth of the Conwy estuary, it was designed in a castellated style to blend with the castle. Before the bridge's construction the estuary could only be crossed by ferry.

VISITORS' CHECKLIST

Conwy. 8,000. Conwy. 01492 592248. **Aberconwy House (NT). Tel** 01492 592246. Wed–Mon. Nov–Mar. **Conwy Castle Tel** 01492 592358. daily. **Smallest House Tel** 01492 593484. Apr–Oct: daily. www.gonorthwales.co.uk

★ Town Walls
These remarkably well-preserved medieval walls are 1,280 m (4,200 ft) long and over 9 m (30 ft) high.

Chester

NEW BRIDGE

CASTLE STREET

HILL STREET

Telford's bridge

Railway bridge

0 metres 50
0 yards 50

Entrance to castle

KEY
– – – Suggested route

STAR SIGHTS
★ Town Walls
★ Conwy Castle

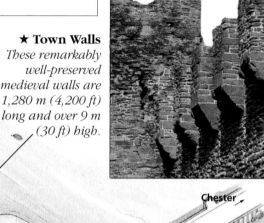

★ Conwy Castle
This atmospheric watercolour, Conwy Castle *(c.1770), is by the Nottingham artist Paul Sandby.*

Pontcysyllte Aqueduct, built in 1795–1805, carrying the Llangollen Canal

Llangollen ⑥

Denbighshire. 👥 *5,000.* 🚉 ℹ️
y Capel, Castle St (01978 860828).
🛒 *Tue.* www.llangollen.org.uk

Best known for its annual
Eisteddfod (festival), this pretty
town sits on the River Dee,
which is spanned by a 14th-
century bridge. The town
became notorious in the 1700s,
when two Irishwomen, Sarah
Ponsonby and Lady Eleanor
Butler, the "Ladies of Llangollen", set up house together in
the half-timbered **Plas Newydd**.
Their unconventional dress and
literary enthusiasms attracted
such celebrities as the Duke
of Wellington *(see p162)* and
William Wordsworth *(see
p366)*. The ruins of a 13th-
century castle, **Castell Dinas
Brân**, occupy the summit of
a hill overlooking the house.

Environs: Boats on the
Llangollen Canal sail from
Wharf Hill in summer and
cross the spectacular 300 m
(1,000 ft) long Pontcysyllte
Aqueduct, built by Thomas
Telford *(see p447)*.

🏛 **Plas Newydd**
(NT) Hill St. **Tel** *01248 715272.*
⭕ *Easter–Oct: Sat–Wed.* 🏷️ ♿
limited. 🖼️ 📷

Bala ⑦

Gwynedd. 👥 *2,000.* 🚌 *from Llangollen.* ℹ️ *Penllyn, Pensarn Rd (01678
521021).* www.visitsnowdonia.info

Bala Lake, Wales's largest
natural lake, lies between the
Aran and Arenig mountains
at the fringes of Snowdonia
National Park. It is popular
for water-sports and boasts a
unique fish called a *gwyniad*,
which is related to the salmon.

The little grey-stone town
of Bala is a Welsh-speaking
community, its houses strung
out along a single street at
the eastern end of the lake.
Thomas Charles (1755–1814),
a Methodist church leader,
once lived here. A plaque on
his former home recalls Mary
Jones who walked 28 miles
(42 km) barefoot from Abergynolwyn to buy a Bible. This
led to Charles establishing the
Bible Society, providing cheap
bibles to the working classes.

The narrow-gauge **Bala
Lake Railway** follows the
lake shore from Llanuwchllyn,
4 miles (6 km) southwest.

Betws-y-Coed ⑧

Conwy. 👥 *600.* 🚉 ℹ️ *Royal Oak
Stables (01690 710426).*
www.betws.org.uk

This village near the peaks of
Snowdonia has been a hill-
walking centre since the 19th
century. To the west are the

**WORLD CULTURES
IN LLANGOLLEN**

Llangollen's International
Eisteddfod *(see p63)* in
the first half of July draws
musicians, singers and
dancers from around the
world. First held in 1947
as a gesture of post-war
international unity, it now
attracts over 12,000
performers from nearly 50
countries to the six-day-
long competition-cum-fair.

Choristers at the Eisteddfod,
a popular Welsh festival

Swallow Falls, where the
River Llugwy flows through a
wooded glen. The bizarre **Ty
Hyll** ("Ugly House"), is a *tŷ
unnos* ("one-night house");
traditionally, houses erected
between dusk and dawn on
common land were entitled
to freehold rights, and the
owner could enclose land as
far as he could throw an axe
from the door. To the east is
Waterloo Bridge, built by
Thomas Telford to celebrate
the victory against Napoleon.

🏛 **Ty Hyll**
Capel Curig. **Tel** *01690 720287.*
House ⭕ *Easter–Sep: daily.*
Grounds ⭕ *Easter–Sep: daily;
Oct–Easter: Mon–Fri.* 🏷️ ♿ *limited.*

The ornate Waterloo Bridge, built in 1815 after the famous battle

A view of the Snowdonia countryside from Llanberis Pass, the most popular route to Snowdon's peak

Blaenau Ffestiniog ❾

Gwynedd. 🚶 5,500. 🚆 🛈 Betws-y-Coed (01690 710426); Jun–Sep: 01766 830360. 🏛 Tue (Jun–Sep).

Blaenau Ffestiniog, once the slate capital of North Wales, sits among mountains riddled with quarries. The **Llechwedd Slate Caverns**, overlooking Blaenau, opened to visitors in the early 1970s, marking a new role for the declining industrial town. The electric Miners' Tramway takes passengers on a tour into the original caverns.

On the Deep Mine tour, visitors descend on Britain's steepest passenger incline railway to the underground chambers, while sound effects recreate the atmosphere of a working quarry. The dangers included landfalls and floods, as well as the more gradual threat of slate dust breathed into the lungs.

There are slate-splitting demonstrations on the surface, a quarryman's cottage and a re-creation of a Victorian village to illustrate the cramped and basic living conditions endured by workers between the 1880s and 1945.

The popular narrow-gauge **Ffestiniog Railway** *(see pp452–3)* runs from Blaenau to Porthmadog.

🏛 **Llechwedd Slate Caverns**
Off A470. **Tel** 01766 830306.
⬜ daily. 💷 ♿ except the Deep Mine. 🅿 🛈 www.llechwedd-slate-caverns.co.uk

Llanberis and Snowdon ❿

Gwynedd. 🚶 2,100. 🛈 High St, Llanberis (01286 870765).
www.gwynedd.gov.uk

Snowdon, which at 1,085 m (3,560 ft) is the highest peak in Wales, is the main focus of the vast Snowdonia National Park, whose scenery ranges from this rugged mountain country to moors and sandy beaches.

The easiest route to Snowdon's summit begins in Llanberis: the 5 mile (8 km) **Llanberis Track**. From Llanberis Pass, the Miners' Track (once used by copper miners) and the Pyg Track are alternative paths. Walkers should beware of sudden weather changes and dress accordingly. The narrow-gauge **Snowdon Mountain Railway**, which opened in 1896, is an easier option.

Llanberis was a major 19th-century slate town, with grey terraces hewn into the hills. Other attractions are the 13th-century shell of **Dolbadarn Castle**, and, above Lake Peris, the **Electric Mountain**, which has tours of Europe's biggest hydro-electric pumped storage station.

🏰 **Dolbadarn Castle**
Off A4086 nr Llanberis.
Tel 01286 870765. ⬜ daily.

🛈 **Electric Mountain**
Llanberis. **Tel** 01286 870636.
⬜ daily. ⬤ Jan. 💷 ♿ 🅿 🛈
www.fhc.co.uk

BRITAIN'S CENTRE OF SLATE

Welsh slates provided roofing material for Britain's new towns in the 19th century. In 1898, the slate industry employed nearly 17,000 men, a quarter of whom worked at Blaenau Ffestiniog. Foreign competition and new materials later took their toll. Quarries such as Dinorwig in Llanberis and Llechwedd in Blaenau Ffestiniog now survive on the tourist trade.

The dying art of slate-splitting

The village of Beddgelert, set among the mountains of Snowdonia

Beddgelert ⓫

Gwynedd. 🏠 *500.*
ℹ️ *Canolfan-Hebog (01766 890615).*
www.eryri-npa.gov.uk

Beddgelert enjoys a spectacular location in Snowdonia. The village sits on the confluence of the Glaslyn and Colwyn rivers at the approach to two mountain passes: the beautiful Nant Gwynant Pass, which leads to Snowdonia's highest reaches, and the Aberglaslyn Pass, a narrow wooded gorge which acts as a gateway to the sea.

Business was given a boost by Dafydd Pritchard, the landlord of the Royal Goat Hotel, who in the early 19th century adapted an old Welsh legend to associate it with Beddgelert. Llywelyn the Great *(see p436)* is said to have left his faithful hound Gelert to guard his infant son while he went hunting. He returned to find the cradle overturned and Gelert covered in blood. Thinking the dog had savaged his son, Llywellyn slaughtered Gelert, but then discovered the boy, unharmed, under the cradle. Nearby was the corpse of a wolf, which Gelert had killed to protect the child. To support the tale, Pritchard created **Gelert's Grave** (*bedd Gelert* in Welsh) by the River Glaslyn, a mound of stones a short walk south of the village.

Environs: There are many fine walks in the area: one leads south to the Aberglaslyn Pass and along a disused part of the Welsh Highland Railway. The **Sygun Copper Mine**, 1 mile (1.5 km) northeast of Beddgelert, offers self-guided tours of caverns recreating the life of Victorian miners.

⛏ Sygun Copper Mine
On A498. **Tel** *01766 890595.*
◯ *Mar–Oct: daily; Feb half term.*
♿ &. limited. 🔲 🔲
www.syguncoppermine.co.uk

Ffestiniog Railway

Railway crest

The Ffestiniog narrow-gauge railway takes a scenic 14 mile (22 km) route from Porthmadog Harbour to the mountains and the slate town of Blaenau Ffestiniog *(see p451).* Designed to carry slate from the quarries to the quay, the railway replaced a horse-drawn tramway constructed in 1836, operating on a 60 cm (2 ft) gauge. After closure in 1946, it was reconstructed by volunteers and re-opened in sections from 1955–82.

Steam traction *trains were first used on the Ffestiniog Railway in 1863. There are some diesel engines but most trains on the route are still steam-hauled.*

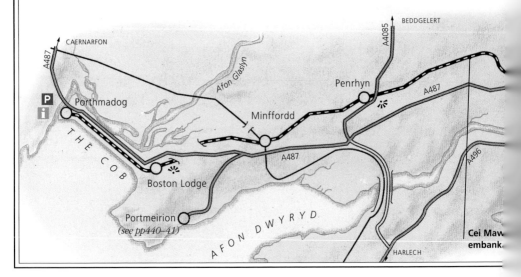

Llyn Peninsula ⑫

Gwynedd. ⛴ 🏠 *Pwllheli*. ⛴
Aberdaron to Bardsey Island. ℹ️
*Min-y-don, Station Sq, Pwllheli (01758
613000).* **www**.nwt.co.uk

This 24-mile (38-km) finger
of land points southwest from
Snowdonia into the Irish Sea.
Although it has popular
beaches, notably at Pwllheli,
Criccieth, Abersoch and Nefyn,
the coast's overriding feature is
its untamed beauty. Views are
at their most dramatic in the far
west and along the mountain-
backed northern shores.

The windy headland of
Braich-y-Pwll, to the west of
Aberdaron, looks out towards
Bardsey Island, the "Isle of
20,000 Saints". This became a
place of pilgrimage in the 6th
century, when a monastery
was founded here. Some of
the saints are said to be buried
in the churchyard of the ruined
13th-century **St Mary's Abbey**.
Close by is **Porth Oer**, a small
bay also known as "Whistling
Sands" (the sand is meant to
squeak, or whistle, underfoot).

East of Aberdaron is the
4 mile (6.5 km) bay of **Porth
Neigwl**, known in English as
Hell's Mouth, the scene of
many shipwrecks due to the
bay's treacherous currents.
Hidden in sheltered grounds
above Porth Neigwl bay,
1 mile (1.5 km) northeast of
Aberdaron, is **Plas-yn-Rhiw**,
a small, medieval manor house
with Tudor and Georgian
additions and lovely gardens.

The former quarrying village
and "ghost town" of **Llithfaen**,
tucked away below the sheer
cliffs of the mountainous
north coast, is now a centre
for Welsh language studies.

🎫 **Plas-yn-Rhiw**
(NT) off B4413. **Tel** *01758 780219.*
◯ *Apr–Oct: Thu–Sun; May, Jun &
Sep: Thu–Mon; Jul & Aug: Wed–Mon.*
📷 ♿ *limited.*

Llithfaen village, now a language centre, on the Llyn Peninsula

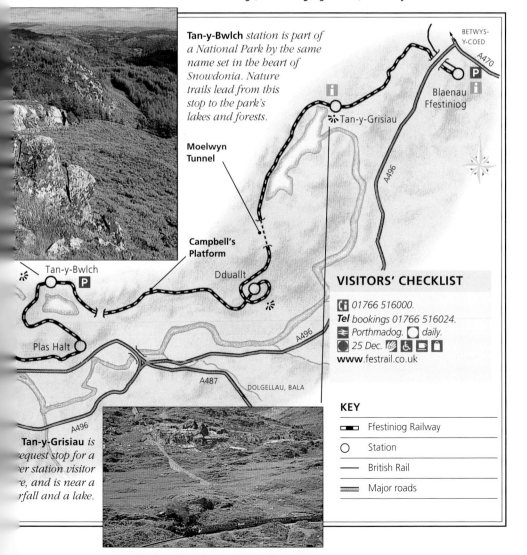

Tan-y-Bwlch *station is part of
a National Park by the same
name set in the heart of
Snowdonia. Nature
trails lead from this
stop to the park's
lakes and forests.*

**Moelwyn
Tunnel**

**Campbell's
Platform**

Tan-y-Bwlch

Plas Halt

Tan-y-Grisiau *is
request stop for a
er station visitor
e, and is near a
rfall and a lake.*

Dduallt

BETWYS-
Y-COED

Tan-y-Grisiau

Blaenau
Ffestiniog

A470

A496

A496

A487

A496

DOLGELLAU, BALA

VISITORS' CHECKLIST

📇 *01766 516000.*
Tel *bookings 01766 516024.*
🚆 *Porthmadog.* ◯ *daily.*
● *25 Dec.* 📷 ♿ 🎧 🏠 🚻
www.festrail.co.uk

KEY

▭▭	Ffestiniog Railway
◯	Station
—	British Rail
▬▬	Major roads

Portmeirion ⑬

Gwynedd. **Tel** 01766 770000.
≋ Minffordd. ◯ daily ● 25 Dec.
🖐 ♿ limited. 🎫 🍴 🖥 📷
www.portmeirion-village.com

This bizarre Italianate village on a private peninsula at the top of Cardigan Bay was created by Welsh architect Sir Clough Williams-Ellis (1883–1978). He fulfilled a childhood dream by building a village "to my own fancy on my own chosen site". About 50 buildings surround a central piazza, in styles from Oriental to Gothic. Visitors can stay at the luxurious hotel or in one of the charming village cottages. Portmeirion has been an atmospheric location for many films and television programmes, including the popular 1960s television series *The Prisoner*.

Sir Clough Williams-Ellis at Portmeirion

Hercules *is a life-size 19th-century copper statue near the Town Hall, where a 17th-century ceiling, rescued from a demolished mansion, depicts his legend.*

Fountain Cottage is where Noel Coward (1899–1973) wrote *Blithe Spirit.*

The *Amis Reunis* is a stone replica of a boat that sank in the bay.

Swimming pool

The Portmeirion Hotel *overlooks the bay. In 2005 its dining room was redesigned by Sir Terence Conran.*

Harlech ⑭

Gwynedd. 🏚 1,300. ≋ 🚶 *High St (01766 780658).* ⌂ Sun (summer).
www.gwynedd.gov.uk

This small town with fine beaches is dominated by **Harlech Castle**, a medieval fortress (*see p438*) built by Edward I between 1283 and 1289. The castle sits on a precipitous crag, with superb views of Tremadog Bay and the Llyn Peninsula to the west, and Snowdonia to the north. When the castle was built, the sea reached a fortified stairway cut into the cliff, so that supplies could arrive by ship, but now the sea has receded. A towering gatehouse protects the inner ward, enclosed by walls and four round towers.

Despite its defences, Harlech Castle fell to Owain Glyndŵr (*see p436*) in 1404, and served as his court until its recapture four years later. The song *Men of Harlech* is thought to have been inspired by the castle's heroic resistance during an eight-year siege in the Wars of the Roses (*see p49*).

⚓ **Harlech Castle**
Castle Sq. **Tel** 01766 780552.
◯ daily. ● 1 Jan, 24–26 Dec.
🖐 📷 www.harlech.com

Dolgellau ⑮

Gwynedd. 🏚 2,650. 🚶 *Eldon Sq (01341 422888).* ⌂ Fri (livestock).

The dark local stone gives a stern, solid look to this market town, where the Welsh language and customs are still very strong. It lies in the long shadow of the 892 m (2,927 ft) mountain of Cader Idris where, according to legend, anyone who spends a night on its summit will awake a poet or a madman – or not at all.

Dolgellau was gripped by gold fever in the 19th century, when high-quality gold was

Harlech Castle's strategic site overlooking mountains and sea

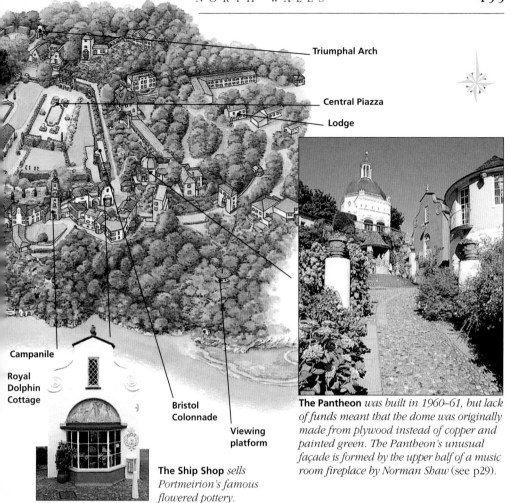

Triumphal Arch

Central Piazza

Lodge

Campanile

Royal Dolphin Cottage

Bristol Colonnade

Viewing platform

The Pantheon *was built in 1960–61, but lack of funds meant that the dome was originally made from plywood instead of copper and painted green. The Pantheon's unusual façade is formed by the upper half of a music room fireplace by Norman Shaw (see p29).*

The Ship Shop *sells Portmeirion's famous flowered pottery.*

Dolgellau's grey-stone buildings, dwarfed by the mountain scenery

discovered in the Mawddach Valley nearby. The deposits were not large enough to sustain an intensive mining industry for long. Nevertheless, up until 1999, small amounts were mined and crafted locally into fine jewellery.

Dolgellau is a good centre for walking, whether you wish to take gentle strolls through beautiful leafy countryside or strenuous hikes across extreme terrain with dramatic mountain views. The lovely **Cregennen Lakes** are set high in the hills above the thickly wooded **Mawddach Estuary** to the northwest; north are the harsh, bleak **Rhinog moors**, one of Wales's last true wildernesses.

Aberdyfi ⑯

Gwynedd. 🏠 *900.* 🚉 🅸 *Wharf Gardens (01654 767321).* **www**.gwynedd.gov.uk

Perched on the mouth of the Dyfi Estuary, this little harbour resort and sailing centre makes the most of its splendid but rather confined location, its houses occupying every yard of a narrow strip of land between mountain and sea. In the 19th century, local slate was exported from here, and between the 1830s and the 1860s about 100 ships were built in the port. *The Bells of Aberdovey*, a song by Charles Dibdin for his opera *Liberty Hall* (1785), tells the legend of Cantref-y-Gwaelod, thought to have been located here, which was protected from the sea by dykes. One stormy night, the sluice gates were left open by Prince Seithenyn, when he was drunk, and the land was lost beneath the waves. The submerged church bells are said to peal under the water to this day.

Neat Georgian houses by the sea, Aberdyfi

SOUTH AND MID-WALES

CARDIFF, SWANSEA & ENVIRONS · CARDIGANSHIRE
CARMARTHENSHIRE · MONMOUTHSHIRE · POWYS · PEMBROKESHIRE

South and mid-Wales are less homogeneous regions than North Wales. Most of the population lives in the southeast corner. To the west is Pembrokeshire, the loveliest stretch of Welsh coastline. To the north the industrial valleys give way to the wide hills of the Brecon Beacons and the rural heartlands of central Wales.

South Wales's coastal strip has been settled for many centuries. There are prehistoric sites in the Vale of Glamorgan and Pembrokeshire. The Romans established a major base at Caerleon, and the Normans built castles all the way from Chepstow to Pembroke. In the 18th and 19th centuries, coal mines and ironworks opened in the valleys of South Wales, attracting immigrants from all over Europe. Close communities developed here, focused on the coal trade, which turned Cardiff from a sleepy coastal town into the world's busiest coal-exporting port.

The declining coal industry has again changed the face of this area: slag heaps have become green hills, and the valley towns struggle to find alternative forms of employment. Coal mines such as Blaenafon's Big Pit are now tourist attractions; today, many of the tour guides taking visitors underground are ex-miners, who can offer a first-hand glimpse of the hard life found in mining communities before the pits closed.

The southern boundary of the Brecon Beacons National Park marks the beginning of rural Wales. With a population sparser than anywhere in England, this is an area of small country towns, hill-sheep farms, forestry plantations and spectacular man-made lakes.

The number of Welsh-speakers increases and the sense of Welsh culture becomes stronger as you travel further from the border with England, with the exception of an English enclave in south Pembrokeshire.

The changing face of the coal industry: former miners take visitors down the Big Pit in Blaenafon

◁ Magnificent coastal scenery near St David's, Pembrokeshire

Exploring South and Mid-Wales

Magnificent coastal scenery marks the Pembrokeshire
Coast National Park and cliff-backed Gower Peninsula,
while Cardigan Bay and Carmarthen Bay offer quieter
beaches. Walkers can enjoy grassy uplands in the Brecon
Beacons and gentler country in the leafy Wye Valley. Urban
life is concentrated in the southeast of Wales, where old
mining towns line the valleys north of Cardiff, the capital.

**Cliffs of the Pembrokeshire
Coast National Park**

GETTING AROUND

The M4 motorway is the major route
into Wales from the south of England,
and there are good road links west of
Swansea running to the coast. The
A483 and A488 give access to mid-
Wales from the Midlands. Frequent
rail services connect London with
Swansea, Cardiff and the ferry
port of Fishguard.

MACHYNLLETH

Aberdyfi

Borth   Ta

A487

ABERYSTWYTH **7**

*Cardigan
Bay*

Devil's B

Llanon   Pontrhydfend

Strata Florida

ABERAERON **8**   Tregaro

New Quay   Llanarth

Llanarth

Ystrad Aeron

Aberporth   A487   Lampete

Cardigan   Llanybydder   Pumsaint

Goodwick   Newport   Newcastle   *Teifi*   Llandysul

Fishguard   A487   Emlyn   Rhos   *C a m b*

Crymych   Llano

Pembrokeshire Coast National Park

Letterston   Cynwyl Elfed   Llandeilo

9 ST. DAVIDS   Treffgarne   Carmarthen   A40   Carreg Cenne

*St. Brides
Bay*   Haverfordwest   A40   Whitland   A48   *Tywi*

*Skomer
Island*   Narberth   St. Clears   Cross Hands

Milford   Kilgetty   Laugharne   Kidwelly   Pontarddulais

Dale   Haven   Neyland   Saundersfoot   Pembrey

Broad Sound   Pembroke   **10** TENBY   *Carmarthen
Bay*   Llanelli   Cly

Manorbier   *Caldey
Island*   Gorseinon   M4

St Govan's Head   Llanrhidian   SWANSEA

Gower

Rhossili   *peninsula*   Mumbles

Port-Eynon

SIGHTS AT A GLANCE

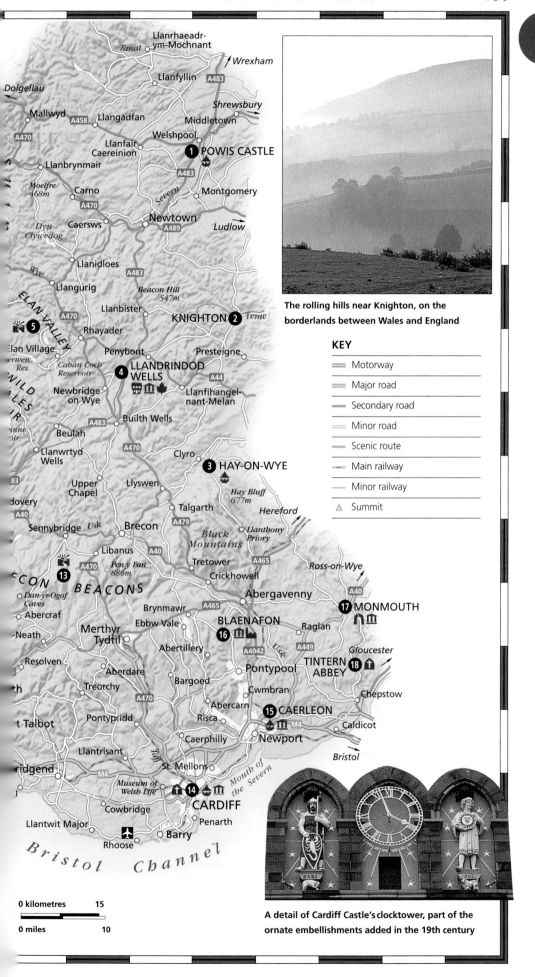

Dolgellau

Tanat

Llanrhaeadr-
ym-Mochnant

Llanfyllin

A483

Wrexham

Shrewsbury

Mallwyd

A458

Llangadfan

Middletown

A470

Llanfair
Caereinion

Welshpool

1 POWIS CASTLE

Llanbrynmair

A483

Moelfre
468m

Carno

Montgomery

A470

Llyn
Clywedog

Caersws

Newtown

A489

Ludlow

Llanidloes

A483

Llangurig

Wye

Beacon Hill
547m

ELAN VALLEY

A470

Llanbister

KNIGHTON 2

Teme

5

Rhayader

Penybont

Presteigne

Elan Village

erwen
Res.

WILD
WALES

Caban Coch
Reservoir

LLANDRINDOD
WELLS 4

A44

Llanfihangel-
nant-Melan

Newbridge
on Wye

Builth Wells

anne
oir

A483

A470

Beulah

Clyro

Llanwrtyd
Wells

Llyswen

3 HAY-ON-WYE

83

dovery

Upper
Chapel

Hay Bluff
677m

A40

Sennybridge

Usk

Brecon

Talgarth

A479

Hereford

Libanus

A40

Black
Mountains

Llanthony
Priory

13

Pen y Fan
886m

Tretower

A465

Ross-on-Wye

BECON

BEACONS

Crickhowell

Dan-yr-Ogof
Caves

Brynmawr

A465

Abergavenny

A40

Abercraf

Ebbw Vale

BLAENAFON

Raglan

17 MONMOUTH

Neath

Merthyr
Tydfil

Abertillery

16

A4042

A449

Gloucester

Resolven

Aberdare

Usk

TINTERN
ABBEY 18

Treorchy

Bargoed

Pontypool

Chepstow

A470

Abercarn

Cwmbran

t Talbot

Pontypridd

Risca

15 CAERLEON

Caerphilly

Newport

Caldicot

Llantrisant

Taff

M4

Bristol

ridgend

M4

St. Mellons

Mouth of
the Severn

Museum of
Welsh Life

14

Cowbridge

CARDIFF

Llantwit Major

Penarth

Rhoose

Barry

Bristol Channel

The rolling hills near Knighton, on the
borderlands between Wales and England

KEY

Motorway

Major road

Secondary road

Minor road

Scenic route

Main railway

Minor railway

△ Summit

0 kilometres 15

0 miles 10

A detail of Cardiff Castle's clocktower, part of the
ornate embellishments added in the 19th century

Italianate terraces and formal gardens at Powis Castle, adding a Mediterranean air to the Welsh borderlands

Powis Castle ❶

(NT) Welshpool, Powys. ☎ *01938 551944.* ☒ *Welshpool then bus.* ○ *Apr–Jun & Sep–Oct: Thu–Mon; Jul–Aug: Wed–Mon & public hols; Nov & Mar: Sat & Sun.* ▨ ♿ *limited.* ☐ ♁ www.castlewales.com/powis

Powis Castle – the spelling is an archaic version of "Powys" – has outgrown its military roots. Despite its sham battlements and dominant site, 1 mile (1.6 km) to the southwest of the town of Welshpool, this red-stone building has served as a country mansion for centuries. It began life in the 13th century as a fortress, built by the princes of Powys to control the border with England.

The castle is entered through one of few surviving medieval features: a gateway, built in 1283 by Owain de la Pole. The gate is flanked by two towers.

The castle's lavish interiors soon banish all thoughts of war. A **Dining Room**, decorated with fine 17th-century panelling and family portraits, was originally designed as the castle's Great

Hall. The **Great Staircase**, added in the late 17th century and elaborately decorated with carved fruit and flowers, leads to the main apartments: an early 19th-century library, the panelled **Oak Drawing Room** and the Elizabethan **Long Gallery**, where ornate plasterwork on the fireplace and ceiling date from the 1590s. In the **Blue Drawing Room** there are three 18th-century Brussels tapestries.

The Herbert family bought the property in 1587 and were proud of their Royalist connections; the panelling in

The richly carved 17th-century Great Staircase

the **State Bedroom** bears the royal monogram. Powis Castle was defended for Charles I in the Civil War *(see pp52–3),* but fell to Parliament in 1644. The 3rd Baron Powis, a supporter of James II, had to flee the country when William and Mary took the throne in 1688 *(see pp52–3).*

The castle's **Clive Museum** has an exhibition concerning "Clive of India" (1725–74), the general and statesman who helped strengthen British control in India in the mid-18th century. The family's link with Powis Castle was established by the 2nd Lord Clive, who married into the Herbert family and became the Earl of Powis in 1804.

The gardens at Powis are among the best-known in Britain, with their series of elegant Italianate terraces, adorned with statues, niches, balustrades and hanging gardens, all stepped into the steep hillside beneath the castle walls. Created between 1688 and 1722, these are the only formal gardens of this period in Britain that are still kept in their original form *(see pp26–7).*

Knighton ❷

Powys. 🏛 3,500. 🚃 ℹ️ Offa's Dyke Centre, West St (01547 528753). 🏪 Thu. **www**.offasdyke.demon.co.uk

Knighton's Welsh name, Tref y Clawdd ("The Town on the Dyke"), reflects its status as the only original settlement on **Offa's Dyke**. In the 8th century, King Offa of Mercia (central and southern England) constructed a ditch and bank to mark out his territory, and to enable the enforcement of a Saxon law: "Neither shall a Welshman cross into English land without the appointed man from the other side, who should meet him at the bank and bring him back again without any offence being committed." Some of the best-preserved sections of the 6-m- (20-ft-) high earthwork lie in the hills around Knighton. The Offa's Dyke Footpath runs for 177 miles (285 km) along the border between England and Wales.

Knighton is set on a steep hill, sloping upwards from **St Edward's Church** (1877) with its medieval tower, to the summit, where a castle once stood. The main street leads via the market square, marked by a 19th-century clock tower, along **The Narrows**, a Tudor street with little shops. **The Old House** on Broad Street is a medieval "cruck" house (curved timbers form a frame to support the roof), with a hole in the ceiling instead of a chimney.

Hay-on-Wye ❸

Powys. 🏛 1,300. ℹ️ Oxford Rd (01497 820144). 🏪 Thu. **www**.hay-on-wye.co.uk

Book-lovers from all over the world come to this quiet border town in the Black Mountains. Hay-on-Wye has

Knighton's clock

over 30 second-hand bookshops stocking millions of titles, and in early summer hosts a prestigious Festival of Literature. The town's love affair with books began when a bookshop was opened in the 1960s by Richard Booth, who claims the (fictitious) title of King of Independent Hay and lives in **Hay Castle**, a 17th-century mansion in the grounds of the original 13th-century castle. Hay's oldest inn, the 16th–century **Three Tuns** on Bridge Street, is still functioning and has an attractive half-timbered façade.

Environs: Hay sits on the approach to the Black Mountains and is surrounded by rolling hills. To the south are the heights of Hay Bluff and the Vale of Ewyas, where the 12th-century ruins of **Llanthony Priory** (see p469) retain fine pointed arches.

⛪ **Hay Castle**
Tel 01497 820503. ⭘ daily. ⬤ 25 Dec. 🖼 grounds only. ♿

Llandrindod Wells ❹

Powys. 🏛 5,000. 🚃 ℹ️ Memorial Gardens (01597 822600). 🏪 farmers' market last Thu of month; Fri.

Llandrindod is a perfect example of a Victorian town, with canopied streets, delicate wrought ironwork,

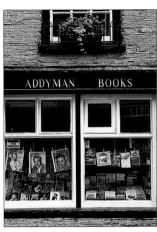

One of Hay-on-Wye's bookshops

gabled villas and ornamental parklands. This purpose-built spa town became Wales's premier inland resort of the 19th century. Its sulphur and magnesium spring waters were taken to treat skin complaints and a range of other ailments.

The town now makes every effort to preserve its Victorian character, with a lake and the well-tended **Rock Park Gardens**. The restored 19th-century **Pump Room** in Temple Gardens is where, during the last full week of August, residents don period costume and cars are banned from the town centre.

The **Radnorshire Museum** traces the town's past as one of a string of 19th-century Welsh spas which included Builth, Llangammarch and **Llanwrtyd** (now a pony trekking centre).

🏛 **Radnorshire Museum**
Temple Street. **Tel** 01597 824513. ⭘ Phone for opening times. ⬤ 1 Jan, 25 & 26 Dec. 🖼 ♿

Victorian architecture on Spa Road, Llandrindod Wells

Craig Goch, one of the original chain of Elan Valley reservoirs

Elan Valley 5

Powys. ⚡ *Llandrindod.*
i *Rhayader (01597 810898).*
www.elanvalley.org.uk

A string of spectacular reservoirs, the first of the country's man-made lakes, has made this one of Wales's most famous valleys. **Caban Coch, Garreg Ddu, Pen-y-Garreg** and **Craig Goch**, were created between 1892 and 1903 to supply water to Birmingham, 73 miles (117 km) away. They form a chain of lakes about 9 miles (14 km) long, holding 50 billion litres (13 billion gallons) of water. Victorian engineers selected these high moorlands on the Cambrian Mountains, for their high annual rainfall of 1,780 mm (70 inches). The choice created bitter controversy and resentment: more than 100 people had to move from the valley that was flooded in order to create Caban Coch.

Unlike their more utilitarian modern counterparts, these dams were built during an era when decoration was seen as an integral part of any design. Finished in dressed stone, they have an air of grandeur which is lacking in the huge **Claerwen** reservoir, a stark addition built during the early 1950s to double the lakes' capacity. Contained by a 355 m (1,165 ft) dam, it lies 4 miles (6 km) along the B4518 that runs through Elan Valley and offers magnificent views.

The remote moorlands and woodlands surrounding the lakes are an important habitat for wildlife; the red kite can often be seen here. The **Elan Valley Visitors' Centre**, beside the Caban Coch dam, describes the construction of the lakes, as well as the valley's own natural history. **Elan Village**, set beside the centre, is an unusual example of a model workers' village, built during the 1900s to house the water-works staff. Outside the centre is a statue of the poet Percy Bysshe Shelley *(see p222)*, who stayed in the valley at the mansion of Nantgwyllt in 1810 with his wife, Harriet. The house now lies underneath the waters of Caban Coch, along with the rest of the old village. Among the buildings submerged were the village school and a church.

The trail from Machynlleth to Devil's Bridge, near Aberystwyth

Machynlleth 6

Powys. 🏚 *2,200.* ⚡ **i** *Penrallt St (01654 702401).* 🜚 *Wed.*
www.exploremidwales.com

Half-timbered buildings and Georgian façades appear among the grey-stone houses in Machynlleth. It was here that Owain Glyndŵr, Wales's last native leader *(see p436),* held a parliament in 1404. The restored **Parliament House** has displays on his life and a brass-rubbing centre.

The ornate **Clock Tower**, in the middle of Maengwyn Street, was erected in 1874 by the Marquess of Londonderry to mark the coming of age of his heir, Lord Castlereagh. The Marquess lived in **Plas Machynlleth**, a 17th-century house in parkland off the main street, which is now a centre of Celtic heritage and culture.

Parliament House sign, Machynlleth

Environs: In an old slate quarry 2.5 miles (4 km) to the north, a "village of the future" is run by the **Centre for Alternative Technology**. A water-balanced cliff railway takes summer visitors to view low-energy houses and organic gardens, to see how to make the best of Earth's resources.

🏛 **Parliament House**
Maengwyn St. *Tel 01654 702827.*
🅾 *Easter–Sep: Mon–Sat.* 🔈 🅿

🏛 **Centre for Alternative Technology** On A487. *Tel 01654 705950.* 🅾 *daily.* ● *early Jan.* 🖼 🖼 🔈 ▥ 🅿 www.cat.org.uk

Aberystwyth 7

Ceredigion. 🏚 *11,000.* ⚡ 🚌
i *Terrace Rd (01970 612125).*
www.ceredigion.gov.uk

This seaside and university town claims to be the cultural capital of mid-Wales. By the standards of this rural area, "Aber" is a big place, its population increased for much of the year by students.

To Victorian travellers, Aberystwyth was the "Biarritz

of Wales". There have been no great changes along the promenade, with its gabled hotels, since the 19th century. **Constitution Hill**, a steep outcrop at the northern end, can be scaled in summer on the electric **Cliff Railway**, built in 1896. At the top, in a *camera obscura*, a lens

Buskers on Aberystwyth's seafront

projects views of the town. The ruined **Aberystwyth Castle** (1277) is located south of the promenade. In the town centre, the **Ceredigion Museum**, set in a former music hall, traces the history of the town.

To the northeast of the town centre, **The National Library of Wales**, next to Aberystwyth University, has a valuable collection of ancient Welsh manuscripts.

SAVIN'S HOTEL

When the Cambrian Railway opened in 1864, businessman Thomas Savin put £80,000 into building a new hotel in Aberystwyth for package tourists. The scheme made him bankrupt, but the seafront building, complete with mock-Gothic tower, was bought by campaigners attempting to establish a Welsh university. The "college by the sea" opened in 1872, and is now the Theological College.

Mosaics on the college tower

Environs: During the summer the narrow-gauge Vale of Rheidol Railway runs 12 miles (19 km) to **Devil's Bridge**, where a dramatic series of waterfalls plunges through a wooded ravine and a steep trail leads to the valley floor.

🏛 Ceredigion Museum
Terrace Rd. *Tel 01970 633088.* ◯ Mon–Sat. ⬤ Good Fri, 25 Dec–2 Jan. 📷 ♿ www.ceredigion.gov.uk

Aberaeron ❽

Ceredigion. 👥 *1,500.*
🚆 *Aberystwyth, then bus.*
ℹ *The Quay (01545 570602).*
www.tourism.ceredigion.gov.uk

Aberaeron's harbour, lined with Georgian houses, became a trading port and shipbuilding centre in the early 19th century. Its orderly streets were laid out in pre-railway days, when the ports along Cardigan Bay enjoyed considerable wealth. The last boat was built here in 1994 and its harbour is now full of holiday sailors. The harbour can be crossed via a wooden footbridge.

On the quayside, the popular Honey Bee Ice Cream Parlour serves world-renowned ice creams to a loyal clientele. There is also a centre of local crafts in the town, Clos Pengarreg.

Rows of brightly painted Georgian houses lining the purpose-built harbour at Aberaeron

St Davids ❾

St David, the patron saint of Wales, founded a monastic settlement in this remote corner of southwest Wales in about 550, which became one of the most important Christian shrines. The present cathedral, built in the 12th century, and the Bishop's Palace, added a century later, are set in a grassy hollow below St Davids town, officially Britain's smallest city. The date of St David's death, 1 March, is commemorated throughout Wales.

Icon of Elijah, south transept

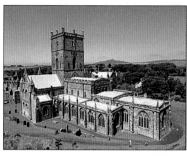

St Davids' Cathedral, the largest in Wales

★ Great Hall
The open arcade and decorated parapet were added by Bishop Gower (1328–47) to unify different sections of the palace.

The Private Chapel was a late 14th-century addition, built, like the rest of the palace, over a series of vaults.

Entrance

BISHOP'S PALACE
The bishop's residence, built between 1280 and 1350 and now in ruins, had lavish private apartments.

Palace latrines

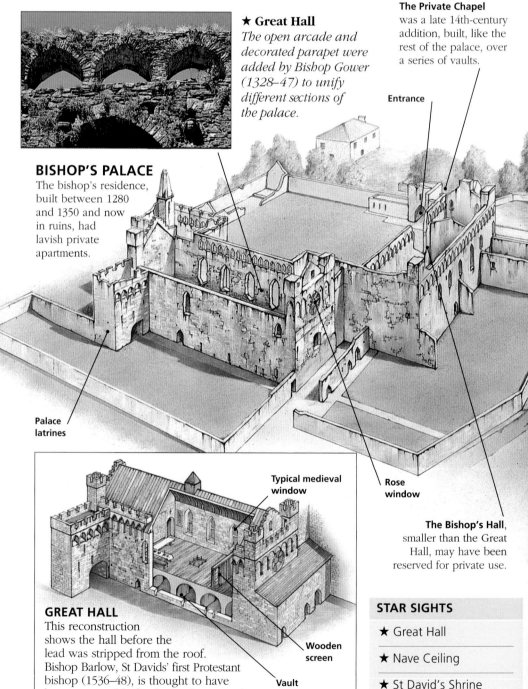

Typical medieval window

Rose window

The Bishop's Hall, smaller than the Great Hall, may have been reserved for private use.

GREAT HALL
This reconstruction shows the hall before the lead was stripped from the roof. Bishop Barlow, St Davids' first Protestant bishop (1536–48), is thought to have been responsible for the lead's removal.

Wooden screen

Vault

STAR SIGHTS

★ Great Hall

★ Nave Ceiling

★ St David's Shrine

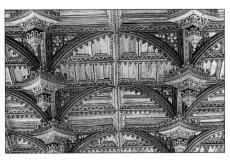

★ Nave Ceiling

The roof of the nave is lowered and hidden by an early 16th-century oak ceiling. A beautiful 14th-century rood screen divides the nave from the choir.

VISITORS' CHECKLIST

Cathedral Close, St Davids.
Tel 01437 720199.
🚆 *Haverfordwest then bus.*
🕙 *9am–5:30pm daily (Sun: pm).*
♿ 🅿 📷 🖼
www. stdavidscathedral.org.uk

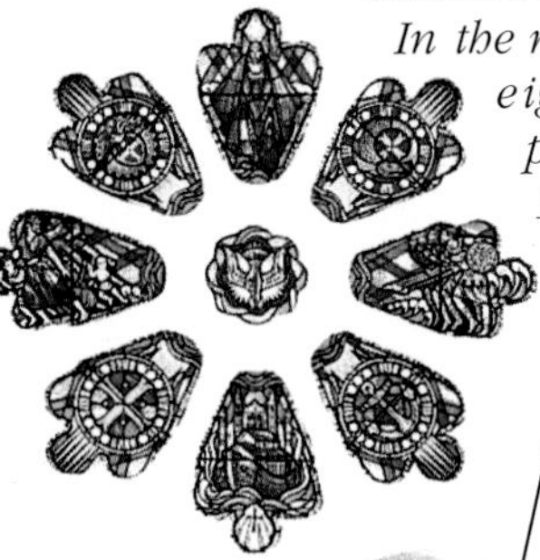

Stained-Glass Window

In the nave's west end, eight panels, produced in the 1950s, radiate from a central window showing the dove of peace.

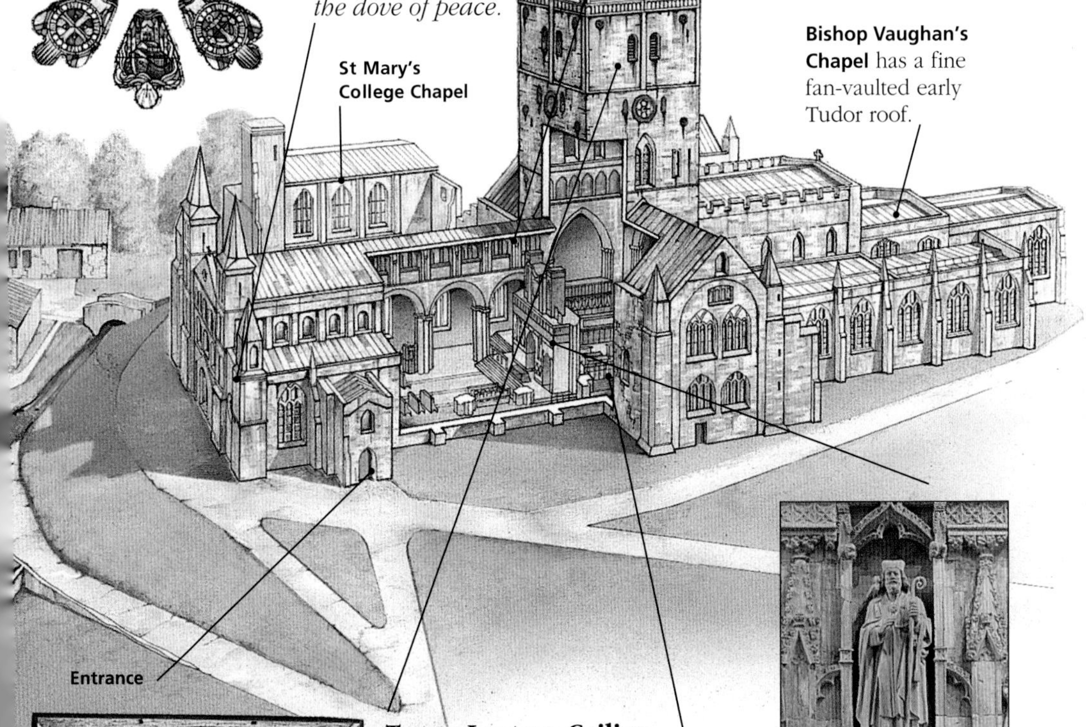

CATHEDRAL

St David was one of the founders of the 6th-century monastic movement, so this was an important site of pilgrimage. Three visits here equalled one to Jerusalem.

St Mary's College Chapel

Bishop Vaughan's Chapel has a fine fan-vaulted early Tudor roof.

Entrance

Tower Lantern Ceiling

The medieval roof was decorated with episcopal insignia when restored in the 1870s by Sir George Gilbert Scott.

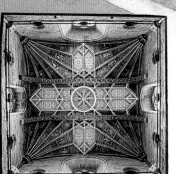

★ St David's Shrine

A statue of the saint is placed near the shrine. Thought to symbolize the Holy Spirit, a dove is said to have landed on David's shoulder as he spoke to a gathering of bishops.

Sixteenth-Century Choir Stalls

The royal coat of arms on one of the carved choir stalls shows that the sovereign is a member of St Davids' Chapter. There are some interesting misericords (see p341) in these stalls.

Tenby ⑩

Pembrokeshire. 5,000.
Upper Park Road (01834 842 402). **www**.pembrokeshire.gov.uk

Tenby has successfully trodden the fine line between over-commercialization and popularity, refusing to submit its historic character to the garish excesses of some seaside towns. Georgian houses overlook its handsome harbour, which is backed by a well-preserved medieval clifftop town of narrow streets and passages. The old town was defended by a headland fortress, now ruined, flanked by two wide beaches and a ring of 13th-century walls. These survive to their full height in places, along with a fortified gateway, the **Five Arches**.

The three-storeyed **Tudor Merchant's House** is a 15th-century relic of Tenby's highly prosperous seafaring days, with original fireplaces and chimneys. There are regular boat trips from the harbour to **Caldey Island**, 3 miles (5 km) offshore, home of a perfume-making monastic community.

Tudor Merchant's House
(NT) Quay Hill.
Tel *01834 842279.*
Mar–Oct: Sun–Fri.
for pre-booked parties.

A partly medieval restaurant next to the Tudor Merchant's House

Swansea and the Gower Peninsula ⑪

Swansea. *230,000.*
Plymouth St (01792 468321).
Mon–Sat. **www**.swansea.gov.uk

Swansea, Wales's second city, is set along a wide, curving bay. The city centre was rebuilt after heavy bombing in World War II but, despite the modern buildings, a traditional Welsh atmosphere prevails. This is particularly noticeable in the excellent food market, full of Welsh delicacies such as laverbread and locally caught cockles.

Swansea's most celebrated son, the poet Dylan Thomas

The award-winning **Maritime Quarter** redevelopment has transformed the old docklands, and is worth a visit.

A statue of copper magnate John Henry Vivian (1779–1855) overlooks the marina. The Vivians, a leading Swansea family, founded the **Glynn Vivian Art Gallery**, which has exquisite Swansea pottery and porcelain. Archaeology and Welsh history feature at the **Swansea Museum**, the oldest museum in Wales.

The life and work of local poet Dylan Thomas (1914–53) is celebrated in the recently opened **Dylan Thomas Centre**. A permanent exhibition, Man and Myth, includes the original drafts of his poems, letters and memorabilia. His statue overlooks the Maritime Quarter. Thomas spent his childhood in the city's suburbs. **Cwmdonkin Park** was the scene of an early poem, *The Hunchback in the Park,* and its water garden has a memorial stone quoting from his *Fern Hill.*

Swansea's austere **Guildhall** (1934) has a surprisingly rich interior. The huge panels, by Sir Frank Brangwyn (1867–1956), on the theme of the British Empire, were originally painted for the House of Lords.

Picturesque fishermen's cottages at the Mumbles seaside resort

Swansea Bay leads to the **Mumbles**, a popular water-sports centre at the gateway to the 19-mile-long (30 km) Gower Peninsula, which in 1956 was the first part of Britain to be declared an Area of Outstanding Natural Beauty. A string of sheltered, south-facing bays leads to Oxwich and Port-Eynon beaches.

Rhossili's enormous beach leads to north Gower and a coastline of low-lying burrows, salt marshlands and cockle beds. The peninsula is littered with ancient sites such as **Parc Le Breose**, a prehistoric burial chamber.

Near Camarthen is the **National Botanic Garden of Wales**, with formal gardens centred on The Great Glasshouse which contains a Mediterranean ecosystem.

Glynn Vivian Art Gallery
Alexandra Rd. ***Tel*** *01792 516900.*
Tue–Sun & public hols.
limited. *by arrangement.*
www.glynnviviangallery.org

Swansea Museum
Victoria Rd. ***Tel*** *01792 653763.*
Tue–Sun & public hols. *limited.*
www.swanseaheritage.net

Dylan Thomas Centre
Somerset Pl. ***Tel*** *01792 463980.*
daily. *by arrangement.*
www.swansea.gov.uk

Guildhall
St Helen's Rd. ***Tel*** *01792 635489.*
Mon–Fri. *public hols.*

National Botanic Garden of Wales
Middleton Hall, Llanarthne.
Tel *01558 668768.* *daily.*
25 Dec.
www.gardenofwales.org.uk

Wild Wales Tour ⑫

This tour weaves across the Cambrian Mountains' windswept moors, green hills and high, deserted plateaux. New roads have been laid to the massive Llyn Brianne Reservoir, north of Llandovery, and the old drover's road across to Tregaron has a tarmac surface. But the area is still essentially a "wild Wales" of hidden hamlets, isolated farmsteads, brooding highlands and traditional, quiet market towns.

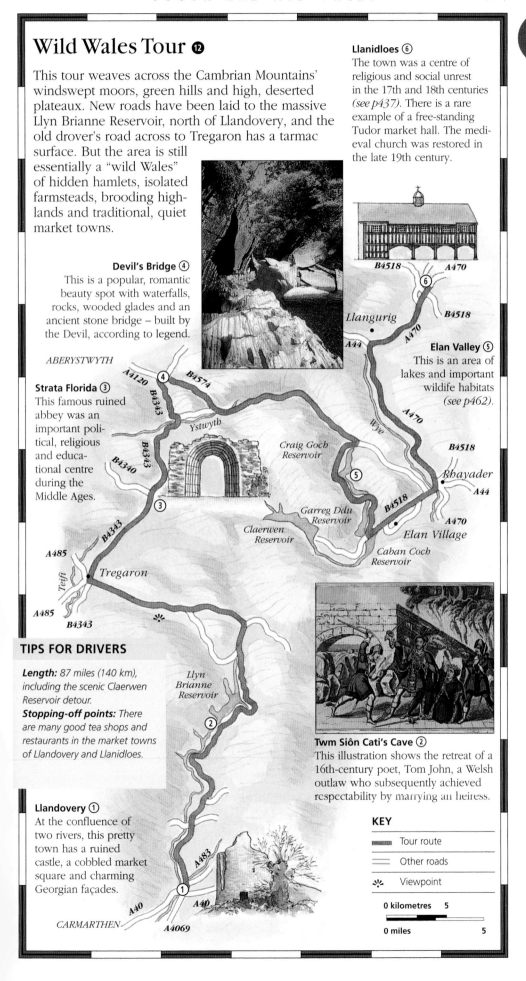

Llanidloes ⑥
The town was a centre of religious and social unrest in the 17th and 18th centuries (*see p437*). There is a rare example of a free-standing Tudor market hall. The medieval church was restored in the late 19th century.

Devil's Bridge ④
This is a popular, romantic beauty spot with waterfalls, rocks, wooded glades and an ancient stone bridge – built by the Devil, according to legend.

ABERYSTWYTH

Strata Florida ③
This famous ruined abbey was an important political, religious and educational centre during the Middle Ages.

Elan Valley ⑤
This is an area of lakes and important wildife habitats (*see p462*).

A4120 ④ *B4574*

B4343

Ystwyth

B4343

B4340 *B4343*

③

B4343 *Teifi*

A485

Tregaron

A485

B4343

Llangurig

A44 *A470*

Wye *A470*

Craig Goch Reservoir

⑤ *B4518*

Rhayader

A44

Garreg Ddu Reservoir

Claerwen Reservoir

B4518

A470

Elan Village

Caban Coch Reservoir

B4518 *A470*

⑥

B4518

TIPS FOR DRIVERS

Length: 87 miles (140 km), including the scenic Claerwen Reservoir detour.

Stopping-off points: There are many good tea shops and restaurants in the market towns of Llandovery and Llanidloes.

Llyn Brianne Reservoir

②

Twm Siôn Cati's Cave ②
This illustration shows the retreat of a 16th-century poet, Tom John, a Welsh outlaw who subsequently achieved respectability by marrying an heiress.

Llandovery ①
At the confluence of two rivers, this pretty town has a ruined castle, a cobbled market square and charming Georgian façades.

A483

①

A40 *A40*

CARMARTHEN *A4069*

KEY

▬▬▬	Tour route
═══	Other roads
☼	Viewpoint

0 kilometres 5

0 miles 5

Brecon Beacons ⓭

Trekking in the Beacons

The Brecon Beacons National Park covers 520 sq miles (1,345 sq km) from the Wales–England border almost all the way to Swansea. There are four mountain ranges within the park: the Black Mountain (to the west), Fforest Fawr, the Brecon Beacons and the Black Mountains (to the east). Much of the area consists of high, open country with smooth, grassy slopes on a bedrock of red sandstone. The park's southern rim has limestone crags, wooded gorges, waterfalls and caves. Visitors can enjoy many outdoor pursuits, from fishing in the numerous reservoirs to pony trekking, caving and walking.

Llyn y Fan Fach
This remote, myth-laden glacial lake is a 4 mile (6.5 km) walk from Llanddeusant.

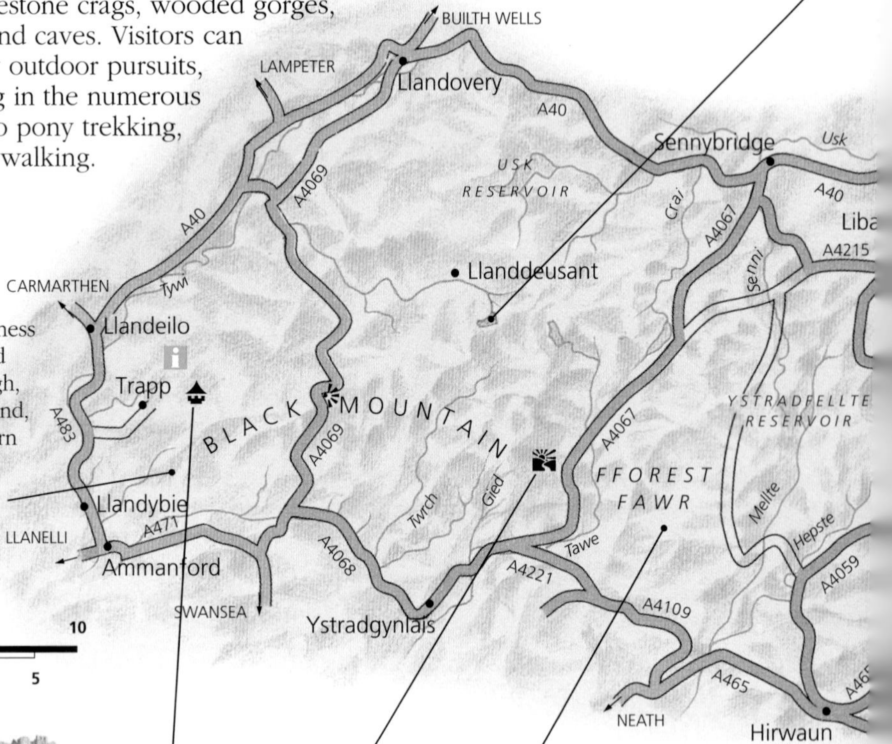

The Black Mountain, a largely unexplored wilderness of knife-edged ridges and high, empty moorland, fills the western corner of the National Park.

BUILTH WELLS
LAMPETER
Llandovery
A40
Sennybridge
Usk
USK RESERVOIR
Cray
A4067
A40
Liba
A4215
Llanddeusant
Senni
CARMARTHEN
Tywi
Llandeilo
Trapp
BLACK MOUNTAIN
A40
A4069
A4069
A4067
YSTRADFELLTE RESERVOIR
FFOREST FAWR
Melte
Hepste
A483
Llandybie
A471
Twrch
Gfed
A4059
LLANELLI
Ammanford
A4068
Tawe
A4221
A4109
SWANSEA
Ystradgynlais
A465
NEATH
A465
Hirwaun

0 kilometres   10
0 miles   5

Fforest Fawr ("Great Forest") is named after an area that was a medieval royal hunting ground.

Dan-yr-Ogof Caves
A labyrinth of caves runs through the Brecon Beacons. Guided tours of two large caves are offered here.

Carreg Cennen Castle
Spectacularly sited, the ruined medieval fortress of Carreg Cennen (see p438) stands on a sheer limestone cliff near the village of Trapp.

KEY

▬▬	A road
▭▭	B road
⁓⁓	Minor road
‒ ‒	Footpath
☆	Viewpoint

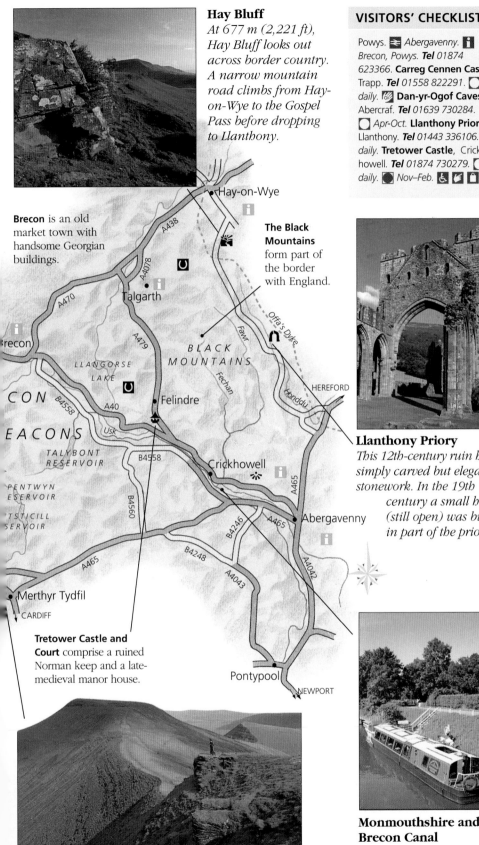

Hay Bluff

At 677 m (2,221 ft), Hay Bluff looks out across border country. A narrow mountain road climbs from Hay-on-Wye to the Gospel Pass before dropping to Llanthony.

VISITORS' CHECKLIST

Powys. ⇌ Abergavenny. ℹ Brecon, Powys. **Tel** 01874 623366. **Carreg Cennen Castle**, Trapp. **Tel** 01558 822291. ◯ daily. 🖼 **Dan-yr-Ogof Caves**, Abercraf. **Tel** 01639 730284. ◯ Apr–Oct. **Llanthony Priory**, Llanthony. **Tel** 01443 336106. ◯ daily. **Tretower Castle**, Crickhowell. **Tel** 01874 730279. ◯ daily. ◯ Nov–Feb. ♿ 🚻 🛈 ▯

Brecon is an old market town with handsome Georgian buildings.

The Black Mountains form part of the border with England.

Llanthony Priory

This 12th-century ruin has simply carved but elegant stonework. In the 19th century a small hotel (still open) was built in part of the priory.

Hay-on-Wye

A438

Talgarth

A470

A4078

A479

BLACK MOUNTAINS

Fawr

Offa's Dyke

Fechan

Honddu

HEREFORD

recon

LLANGORSE LAKE

CON

B4558

A40

Felindre

Usk

EACONS

TALYBONT RESERVOIR

PENTWYN ESERVOIR

TSTICILL SERVOIR

B4558

B4560

Crickhowell

A465

A4246

A465

Abergavenny

Merthyr Tydfil

CARDIFF

B4248

A4043

A4042

Tretower Castle and Court comprise a ruined Norman keep and a late-medieval manor house.

Pontypool

NEWPORT

Pen y Fan

At 886 m (2,907 ft), Pen y Fan is the highest point in South Wales. Its distinctive, flat-topped summit, once a Bronze Age burial ground (see pp42–3), can be reached by footpaths from Storey Arms on the A470.

Monmouthshire and Brecon Canal

This peaceful waterway, completed in 1812, was once used to transport raw materials between Brecon and Newport. It is now popular with leisure boats.

Cardiff 14

Cardiff was first occupied by the Romans, who built a fort here in AD 75 *(see pp44–5)*. Little is known of its subsequent history until Robert FitzHamon *(see p472)*, a knight in the service of William the Conqueror, was given land here in 1093. By the 13th century, the settlement was substantial enough to be granted a royal charter, but it remained a quiet country town until the 1830s when the Bute family, who inherited land in the area, began to develop it as a port. By 1913 this was the world's busiest coal-exporting port, profiting from rail links with the South Wales mines. Its wealth paid for grandiose architecture, while the docklands became a raucous boom-town. Cardiff was confirmed as the first Welsh capital in 1955, by which time demand for coal was falling and the docks were in decline. The city is now being transformed by urban renewal programmes.

Fireplace detail in the Banqueting Hall, Cardiff Castle

City Hall's dome, adorned with a dragon, the emblem of Wales

Exploring Cardiff

Cardiff is a city with two focal points. The centre, laid out with Victorian and Edwardian streets and gardens, is the first of these. There is a Neo-Gothic castle and Neo-Classical civic buildings, as well as indoor shopping malls and a 19th-century **covered market**. Canopied arcades, lined with shops, lead off the main streets, the oldest being the **Royal Arcade** of 1858. The **Millennium Stadium** (on the site of Cardiff Arms Park, the first home of Welsh rugby) opened in 1999 with the Rugby World Cup, and is open for tours most days.

To the south of the centre, the docklands are now being transformed into the second focal point by the creation of a freshwater lake and waterfront. **Y Senedd**, which opened in 2006, houses the National Assembly for Wales. Free guided tours are available but

booking is essential. Other attractions in the area are **Techniquest**, a hands-on science museum, and the impressive **Wales Millennium Centre**. A leading cultural venue, it stages a range of arts performances including musicals, ballet and stand-up comedy. It is also home to the Welsh National Opera.

The wooden **Norwegian Church** was first erected in 1868 for Norwegian sailors bringing wooden props for use in the coal pits of the South Wales valleys. Once surrounded by warehouses, it was taken apart and rebuilt during the dockland development.

Also in Cardiff Bay, the Red Dragon Centre houses the **Doctor Who Up Close Exhibition**, featuring many of the props and costumes seen in the TV series, which is shot in Cardiff (open daily; www. doctorwhoexhibitions.com). The **Cardiff Bay Visitor Centre** (www.cardiffharbour.com), on the waterfront, offers great views of the bay and displays about the history and development of the area.

♙ Cardiff Castle
See pp472–3.

⊞ City Hall and Civic Centre
Cathays Park. **Tel** *029 2087 1727.*
◻ *Mon–Fri.* ● *public hols.* ♿ ☞
www.cardiffcityhall.com
Cardiff's civic centre of Neo-Classical buildings in white Portland stone is set among parks and avenues around Alexandra Gardens. The City Hall (1905), one of its first buildings, is dominated by its 60 m (200 ft) dome and clock

The entrance to the Wales Millennium Centre

tower. Members of the public can visit the first-floor Marble Hall, which is furnished with Siena marble columns and statues of Welsh heroes, among them St David, Wales's patron saint (see pp464–5). Cardiff University is based in the Civic Centre.

🏛 National Museum Cardiff

Cathays Park. **Tel** 029 2039 7951. ◯ Tue–Sun, public hols. ◉ 1, 2 Jan & 24, 25 Dec. 🚻 📷 by appt. 💻 🛈 www.museum wales.ac.uk

Opened in 1927, the museum occupies an impressive civic building with a colonnaded portico, guarded by a statue of David Lloyd George (see p437). The art collection is among the finest in Europe, with works on display by Renoir, Monet and Van Gogh.

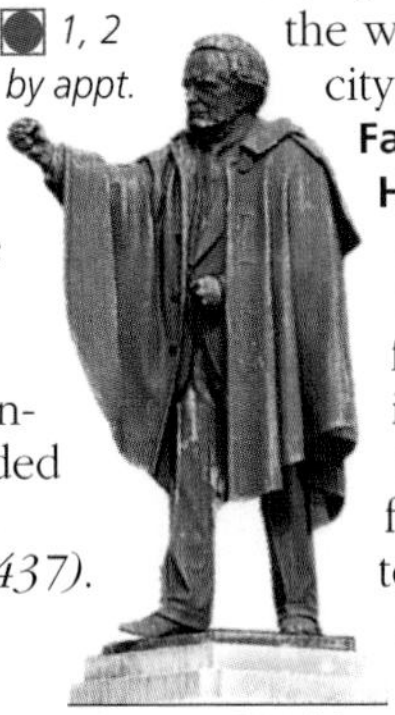

Statue of Welsh politician David Lloyd George

🏛 Craft in the Bay

The Flourish, Lloyd George Ave, Cardiff Bay. **Tel** 029 2048 4611. ◯ 10:30am–5:30pm daily. 🚻 💻

An extensive craft gallery, organized by the Makers' Guild in Wales, opened here in June 2002. The building now houses a wide variety of craft displays and demonstrations, including textile weaving and ceramic making.

Environs: Established during the 1940s at St Fagans, on the western edge of the city, the open-air **St Fagans' National History Museum** was one of the first of its kind. Buildings from all over Wales, including workers' terraced cottages, farmhouses, a tollhouse, row of shops, chapel and old schoolhouse have been carefully reconstructed within the 40-ha (100-acre) parklands, along with a recreated Celtic village. There is also a Tudor mansion which can be visited, boasting

its own beautiful gardens in the grounds.

Llandaff Cathedral lies in a deep, grassy hollow beside the River Taf at Llandaff, 2 miles (3 km) northwest of the city centre. The cathedral was first a medieval building, occupying the site of a 6th-century monastic community.

Restored after suffering severe bomb damage during World War II, it was eventually reopened in 1957 with the addition of Sir Jacob Epstein's huge, stark statue, *Christus,* which is mounted on a concrete arch.

🏛 St Fagans' National History Museum

St Fagans. **Tel** 029 2057 3500. ◯ daily. 🚻 🍴 www.museumwales.ac.uk

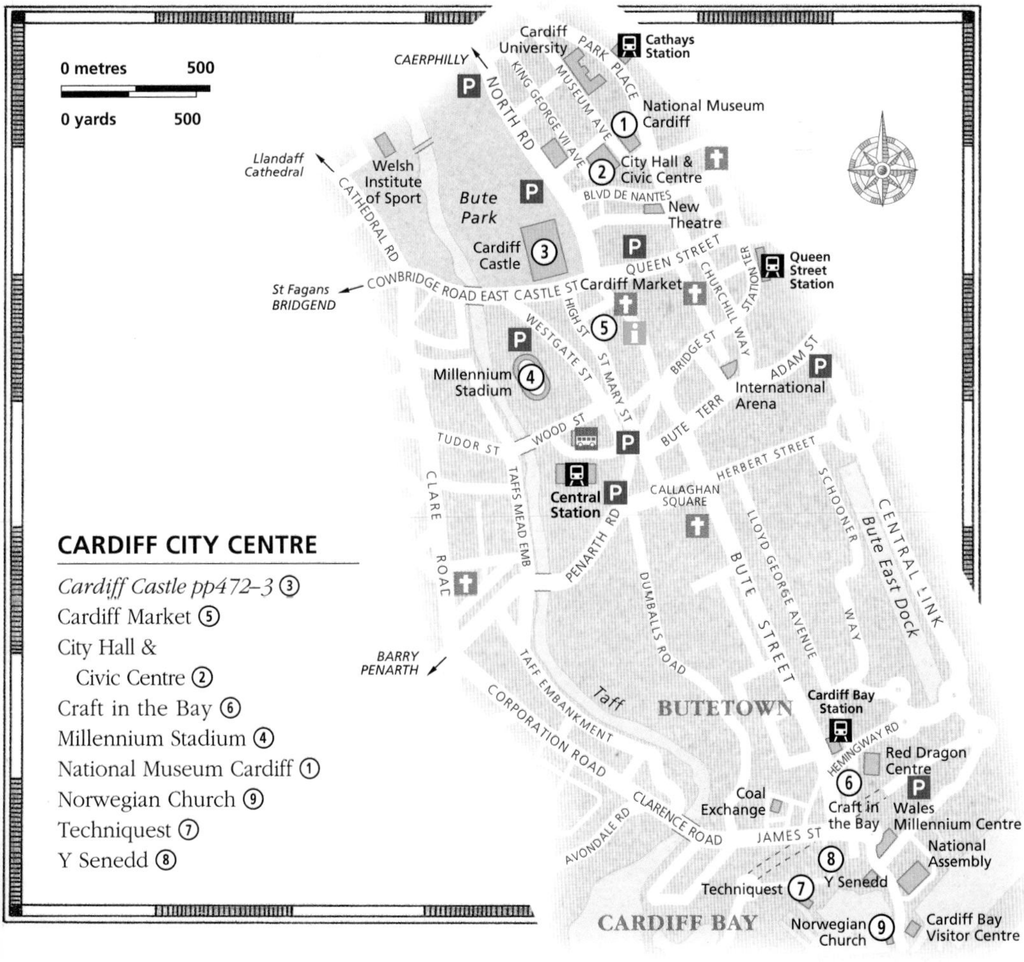

CARDIFF CITY CENTRE

Cardiff Castle

Cardiff Castle began life as a Roman fort, whose remains are separated from later work by a band of red stone. A keep was built within the Roman ruins in the 12th century. Over the following 700 years, the castle passed to several powerful families and eventually to John Stuart, son of the Earl of Bute, in 1776. His great-grandson, the 3rd Marquess of Bute, employed the "eccentric genius", architect William Burges, who created an ornate mansion between 1869 and 1881, rich in medieval images and romantic detail.

Arab Room
The gilded ceiling, with Islamic marble and lapis lazuli decorations, was built in 1881.

Animal Wall
A lion and other creatures guard the wall to the west of the castle. They were added between 1885 and 1930.

Herbert Tower

★ **Summer Smoking Room**
This was part of a complete bachelor suite in the Clock Tower, that also included a Winter Smoking Room.

Clock Tower

Main entrance to apartments

TIMELINE

AD 75 Roman fort constructed	**1107** Castle inherited by Mabel FitzHamon, whose husband is made Lord of Glamorgan	**1423–49** Beauchamp family adds the Octagon Tower and Great Hall ceiling	**1869** 3rd Marquess of Bute begins reconstruction
	1183 Castle damaged during Welsh uprising	**1445–1776** Castle passes in turn to Nevilles, Tudors and Herberts	

1000	**1200**	**1400**	**1600**	**1800**

1093 First Norman fort built by Robert FitzHamon of Gloucester	**1308–1414** Despenser family holds castle		**1776** Bute family acquires the castle
			1947 The castle is given in trust to the city of Cardiff

Chaucer Room wall detail

★ Banqueting Hall
*The design and decoration of
this room depicts the castle's
history, making impressively
ingenious use of the murals
and castellated fireplace.*

The Octagon Tower, also
called the Beauchamp
Tower, is the setting for
Burges's Chaucer Room,
decorated with themes
from the *Canterbury
Tales (see p186).*

★ Roof Garden
*Using tiles, shrubs and
a central fountain,
Burges aimed to create
a Mediterranean feel
in this indoor garden,
turning it into the
crowning glory of the
castle's apartments.*

**The Bute
Tower** had
a suite of
private rooms
added in 1873,
including a
dining room,
bedroom and
sitting room.

STAR SIGHTS

★ Banqueting Hall

★ Library

★ Summer Smoking
   Room

★ Roof Garden

★ Library
*Carved figures representing ancient characters
of Greek, Assyrian, Hebrew and Egyptian
alphabets decorate the library's chimneypiece.*

Remains of Caerleon's amphitheatre, built in the 2nd century

Caerleon ⓯

Newport (Gwent). ⚑ *11,000.*
🛈 *5 High St (01633 422656).*
www.caerleon-tourism.org

Together with York (*see
pp404–5*) and Chester (*see
pp310–11*), Caerleon was one
of only three fortress settlements in Britain built for the
Romans' elite legion-
ary troops. From AD
74 Caerleon (*Isca* to
the Romans, after the
River Usk, which
flows beside the town)
was home to the 2nd
Augustan Legion,
which had been sent
to Wales to crush the
native Silures tribe.
The remains of their
base now lie bet-
ween the modern
town and the river.

**An altar at Caerleon's
Legion Museum**

The excavations at Caerleon
are of great social and military significance. The Romans
built not just a fortress for
their crack 5,500-strong infantry division but a complete
town to service their needs,
including a stone amphi-
theatre. Judging by the results
of the excavation work
carried out since the archae-
ologist Sir Mortimer Wheeler
unearthed the amphitheatre in
1926, Caerleon is one of the
largest and most important
Roman military sites in Europe.
The defences enclosed an
area of 20 ha (50 acres), with
64 rows of barracks, arranged
in pairs, a hospital, and a
bath-house complex.

Outside the settlement, the
amphitheatre's large stone
foundations have survived in an
excellent state of preservation.

Six thousand spectators could
enjoy the blood sports and
gladiators' combat.

More impressive still is the
fortress baths complex, which
opened to the public in the
mid-1980s. The baths were
designed to bring all the home
comforts to an army posted to
barbaric Britain. The Roman
troops could take a dip in the
open-air swimming
pool, play sports in
the exercise yard
or covered hall, or
enjoy a series of
hot and cold baths.

Nearby are the
foundations of the
only Roman
legionary barracks
on view in Europe.
The many excavated
artifacts, including a
collection of en-
graved gemstones,
are displayed at the **National
Roman Legion Museum**.

🏛 **National Roman Legion
Museum**
High St. *Tel 01633 423134.* ⭘
Mon–Sat, Sun (pm). ● *1 Jan, 24–
26 Dec.* ♿ 📷 www.nmgw.ac.uk

**Big Pit Mining Museum, reminder
of a vanished industrial society**

Blaenafon ⓰

Torfaen. ⚑ *6,000.* 🛈 *Monmouth
Rd, Abergavenny (01873 853254).*
www.blaenafontic.com

Commercial coal-mining has
now all but ceased in the
South Wales valleys – an area
which only 100 years ago was
gripped by the search for its
"black gold". Though coal is
no longer produced at **Big
Pit** in Blaenafon, the **Mining
Museum** provides a vivid
reminder of this tough industry. The Big Pit closed as a
working mine in 1980, and
opened three years later as
a museum. Visitors follow a
marked-out route around the
mine's surface workings to
the miners' baths, the blacksmith's forge, the workshops
and the engine house. There
is also a replica of an underground gallery, where mining
methods are explained. But
the climax of any visit to Big
Pit is beneath the ground.
Kitted out with helmets, lamps
and safety batteries, visitors
descend by cage 90 m (300 ft)
down the mineshaft and then
are guided by ex-miners on a
tour of the underground workings and pit ponies' stables.

Blaenafon also has remains
of the iron-smelting industry.
Across the valley from Big Pit
stand the 18th-century smelting
furnaces and workers' cottages
that were once part of the
Blaenavon Ironworks, and
which are now a museum.

🏛 **Big Pit Mining Museum**
Blaenafon. *Tel 01495 790311.* ⭘
*mid-Feb–Nov: daily; Dec & Jan: phone
for details.* ♿ *phone first.* 📷📷📷
🏛 **Blaenavon Ironworks**
North St. *Tel 01495 792615.*
⭘ *mid-Mar–Oct: daily.* 📷📷📷

Monmouth ⓱

Monmouthshire (Gwent). ⚑ *12,000.*
🚌 🛈 *Priory St (01600 713899).* ♻
Fri, Sat. www.visitwyevalley.com

This market town, which sits
at the confluence of the Wye
and Monnow rivers, has
many historical associations.
The 11th-century castle, behind
Agincourt Square, is in ruins
but the **Regimental Museum,**

Monnow Bridge in Monmouth, once a watchtower and jail

Tintern Abbey ⑱

Monmouthshire (Gwent). *Tel 01291 689251.* 🚃 *Chepstow then bus.* 🔵 *daily* ⬤ *1 Jan, 24–26 Dec.* 🎁 ♻️ ♿ *www.*cadw.wales.gov.uk

Ever since the 18th century, travellers have been enchanted by Tintern's setting in the steep and wooded Wye Valley and by the majestic ruins of its abbey. Poets were often inspired by the scene. Wordsworth's sonnet, *Lines composed a few miles above Tintern Abbey*, embodied his romantic view of landscape:

> *once again*
> *Do I behold these steep and*
> *lofty cliffs,*
> *That on a wild, secluded*
> *scene impress*
> *Thoughts of more deep*
> *seclusion*

The abbey was founded in 1131 by Cistercian monks, who cultivated the surrounding lands (now forest), and developed it as an influential religious centre. By the 14th century this was the richest abbey in Wales, but along with other monasteries it was dissolved in 1536. Its skeletal ruins are now roofless and exposed, the soaring arches and windows giving them a poignant grace and beauty.

beside it, remains open to the public. The castle was the birthplace of Henry V *(see p49)* in 1387. Statues of Henry V (on the façade of Shire Hall) and Charles Stewart Rolls stand in the Square. Rolls, born at nearby Hendre, co-founded Rolls-Royce cars, and died in a flying accident in 1910.

Lord Horatio Nelson *(see p54)*, the famous admiral, visited Monmouth in 1802. An excellent collection of Nelson memorabilia, gathered by Lady Llangattock, mother of Charles Rolls, is displayed at the **Nelson Museum**.

Monmouth was the county town of the old Monmouthshire. The wealth of elegant Georgian buildings, including the elaborate **Shire Hall**, which dominates Agincourt Square, reflect its former status. The most famous architectural feature in Monmouth is **Monnow Bridge**, a narrow 13th-century gateway on its western approach, thought to be the only surviving fortified bridge gate in Britain.

For a lovely view over the town, climb the Kymin, a 256 m (840 ft) hill crowned by a **Naval Temple** built in 1801.

🏰 Monmouth Castle and Regimental Museum
The Castle. *Tel 01600 772175.* 🔵 *Apr–Oct: daily (pm); Nov–Mar: Sat & Sun (pm).* ⬤ *25 Dec.* ♿ *www.* monmouthcastlemuseum.org.uk

🏛 Nelson Museum
Priory St. *Tel 01600 710630.* 🔵 *daily (Sun: pm).* ♿ 🎁

Tintern Abbey in the Wye Valley, in the past a thriving centre of religion and learning, now a romantic ruin

SCOTLAND

Scotland at a Glance

Stretching from the rich farmlands of the Borders to a chain of isles only a few degrees south of the Arctic Circle, the Scottish landscape has a diversity without parallel in Britain. As you travel northwest from Edinburgh, the land becomes more mountainous and its archaeological treasures more numerous. In the far northwest, Scotland's earliest relics stand upon the oldest rock on Earth.

Western Isles

Skye (see pp534–5) *renowned for its dramatic scenery, has one of Scotland's most striking coast-lines. On the east coast, a stream plunges over Kilt Rock, a cliff of hexagonal basalt columns named after its likeness to an item of Scottish national dress.*

THE HIGHLAND AND ISLANDS *(see pp524–49)*

Argyll and Bute

Clyde Valley

Ayrsh

The Trossachs (see pp494–5) *are a beautiful range of hills straddling the border between the Highlands and the Lowlands. At their heart, the forested slopes of Ben Venue rise above the still waters of Loch Achray.*

Culzean Castle (see pp522–3) *stands on a cliff's edge on the Firth of Clyde, amid an extensive country park. One of the jewels of the Lowlands, Culzean is a magnificent showcase of work by the Scottish-born architect, Robert Adam (see p28).*

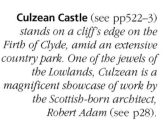

◁ **Loch Lomond, the Lowlands**

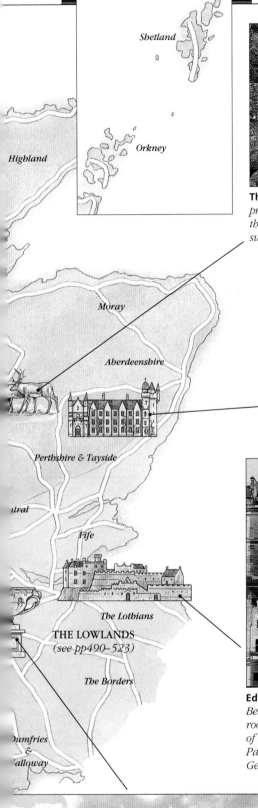

Shetland

Orkney

Highland

Moray

Aberdeenshire

Perthshire & Tayside

Fife

The Lothians

THE LOWLANDS
(see pp490–523)

The Borders

Dumfries
&
Galloway

The Cairngorms (see pp544–45) *cover an area prized for its beauty and diversity of wildlife, though there are also many historical relics to be found, such as this early 18th-century arch at Carrbridge.*

Royal Deeside (see pp540–41) *in the Grampians has been associated with British royalty since Queen Victoria bought Balmoral Castle in 1852.*

Edinburgh (see pp504–11) *is the capital of Scotland. Between its medieval castle and the Palace of Holyroodhouse stretches the Royal Mile – a concentration of historic sights, ranging from the old Scottish Parliament buildings to the house of John Knox. Georgian terraces predominate in the New Town.*

The Burrell Collection (see pp520–21), *on the southern outskirts of Glasgow, is a museum of some of the city's greatest art treasures. It is housed in a spacious, glass building opened in 1983.*

0 kilometres   50

0 miles   50

A PORTRAIT OF SCOTLAND

From the grassy hills of the Borders to the desolate Cuillin Ridge of Skye, the landscape of Scotland is breathtaking in its variety. Lonely glens, sparkling lochs and ever-changing skies give the land a challenging character, which is reflected in the qualities of the Scottish people. Tough and self-reliant, they have made some of Britain's finest soldiers, its boldest explorers and most astute industrialists.

The Scots are proud of their separate identity and their own systems of law and education and, in 1998, voted overwhelmingly for their own parliament. Many Scots welcomed this as a long-awaited reversal of the Act of Union that united the English and Scottish parliaments in 1707. But despite their national pride, they are not a homogeneous people, the main division is between traditionally Gaelic-speaking Highlanders, and the Lowlanders who spoke Scots, a form of Middle English which is now extinct. Today, though Gaelic survives (chiefly in the Western Isles), most people speak regional dialects or richly accented English. Many Scottish surnames derive from Gaelic: the prefix "mac" means "son of". A Norse heritage can be found in the far north, where Shetlanders welcome the annual return of the sun during the Viking fire festival, Up Helly Aa.

A hammer-thrower at the Braemar Games

In the 16th century, a suspicion of authority and dislike of excessive flamboyance attracted many Scots to the Presbyterian church with its absence of bishops and its stress on simple worship. The Presbyterian Church of Scotland was established in 1689, though a substantial Catholic minority remained which today predominates in the crofting (small-scale farming) communities of the Western Isles. Now sparsely populated, the Isles preserve a rural culture that once dominated the Highlands, a region that is the source of much that is distinctively Scottish. The clan system originated there, along with the tartans, the bagpipes and such unique sports as tossing the caber – a large tree trunk. Highland sports, along with traditional dances, are still performed at annual games *(see p64)*.

Edinburgh bagpiper

Resourcefulness has always been a prominent Scottish virtue, and Scotland has produced a disproportionately high number of Britain's geniuses. James Watt designed the first effective steam engine to power the Industrial Revolution, while Adam Smith became the 18th century's most influential economist. In the 19th century, James Simpson discovered the anaesthetic qualities of

The Viking festival, Up Helly Aa, in Lerwick, Shetland

A traditional stone croft on the Isle of Lewis

With some of the harshest weather conditions in Europe it is perhaps less surprising that Scotland has bred numerous explorers, including polar explorer William Speirs Bruce and African missionary David Livingstone. There is also a strong intellectual and literary tradition, from the 18th-century philosopher David Hume, through novelists Sir Walter Scott and Robert Louis Stevenson, to the poetry of Robert Burns. Today Scotland hosts a variety of arts festivals, such as Edinburgh's.

chloroform, James Young developed the world's first oil refinery and Alexander Bell revolutionized communications by inventing the telephone. The 20th century saw one of the greatest advances in medicine with the discovery of penicillin by Alexander Fleming.

The Scots are also known for being shrewd businessmen, and have always been prominent in finance: both the Bank of England and the Royal Bank of France were founded by Scots, while Andrew Carnegie created one of 19th century-America's biggest business empires.

Detail of Edinburgh's Festival Fringe office

With a population density only one-fifth of England and Wales, Scotland has vast tracts of untenanted land which offer numerous outdoor pleasures. It is richly stocked with game, and the opening of the grouse season on 12 August is a highlight on the social calendar. Fishing and hill-walking are popular and in winter thousands flock to the Cairngorms and Glencoe for skiing. Though the weather may be harsher than elsewhere, the Scots will claim that the air is purer – and that enjoying rugged conditions is what distinguishes them from their soft southern neighbours.

The blue waters of Loch Achray in the heart of the Trossachs, north of Glasgow

The History of Scotland

Bonnie Prince Charlie, by G Dupré

Since the Roman invasion of Britain, Scotland's history has been characterized by its resistance to foreign domination. The Romans never conquered the area, and when the Scots extended their kingdom to its present boundary in 1018, a long era of conflict began with England. After many wars, the Scots finally accepted union with the "auld enemy": first with the union of crowns, and then with the Union of Parliament in 1707. In 1999 the inauguration of the Scottish Parliament was a dramatic change.

An elaborately carved Pictish stone at Aberlemno, Angus

EARLY HISTORY

There is much evidence in Scotland of important prehistoric population centres, particularly in the Western Isles, which were peopled mostly by Picts who originally came from the Continent. By the time Roman Governor Julius Agricola invaded in AD 81, there were at least 17 independent tribes, including the Britons in the southwest, for him to contend with.

The Romans reached north to the Forth and Clyde valleys, but the Highlands deterred them from going further. By 120, they had retreated to the line where the Emperor Hadrian had built his wall to keep the Picts at bay (not far from today's border). By 163 the Romans had retreated south for the last time. The Celtic influence began when

"Scots" arrived from Ireland in the 6th century, bringing the Gaelic language with them.

The Picts and Scots united under Kenneth McAlpin in 843, but the Britons remained separate until 1018, when they became part of the Scottish kingdom.

THE ENGLISH CLAIM

The Norman Kings regarded Scotland as part of their territory but seldom pursued the claim. William the Lion of Scotland recognized English sovereignty by the Treaty of Falaise (1174), though English control never spread to the northwest. In 1296 William Wallace, supported by the French (the start of the Auld Alliance, which lasted two centuries), began the long war of independence. During this bitter conflict, Edward I seized the sacred Stone of Destiny from Scone *(see p498)*, and took it to Westminster Abbey. The war lasted for more than 100 years. Its great hero was Robert the Bruce, who defeated the English in 1314 at Bannockburn. The English held the upper hand after that, even though the Scots would not accept their rule.

John Knox statue in Edinburgh

THE ROAD TO UNION

The seeds of union between the crowns were sown in 1503 when James IV of Scotland married Margaret Tudor, daughter of Henry VII. When her brother, Henry VIII, came to the throne, James sought to assert independence but was defeated and killed at Flodden Field in 1513. His granddaughter, Mary, Queen of Scots *(see p511)*, married the French Dauphin in order to cement the Auld Alliance and gain assistance in her claim to

Bruce in Single Combat at Bannockburn (1906) by John Hassall

the throne of her English cousin, Elizabeth I. She had support from the Catholics wanting to see an end to Protestantism in England and Scotland. However, fiery preacher John Knox won support for the Protestants and established the Presbyterian Church in 1560. Mary's Catholicism led to the loss of her Scottish throne in 1568, and her subsequent flight to England, following defeat at Langside. Finally, after nearly 20 years of imprisonment she was executed for treason by Elizabeth in 1587.

The factories on Clydeside, once creators of the world's greatest ships

UNION AND REBELLION

On Elizabeth I's death in 1603, Mary's son, James VI of Scotland, succeeded to the English throne and became James I, king of both countries. Thus the crowns were united, though it was 100 years before the formal Union of Parliaments in 1707. During that time, religious differences within the country

Articles of Union between England and Scotland, 1707

reached boiling point. There were riots when the Catholic-influenced Charles I restored bishops to the Church of Scotland and authorized the printing of a new prayer book. This culminated in the signing, in Edinburgh in 1638, of the National Covenant, a document that condemned all Catholic doctrines. Though the Covenanters were suppressed, the Protestant William of Orange took over the English throne in 1688 and the crown passed out of Scottish hands.

In 1745, Bonnie Prince Charlie *(see p535)*, descended from the Stuart kings, tried to seize the throne from the Hanoverian George II. He

marched far into England, but was driven back and defeated at Culloden field *(see p537)* in 1746.

INDUSTRIALIZATION AND SOCIAL CHANGE

In the late 18th and 19th centuries, technological progress transformed Scotland from a nation of crofters to an industrial powerhouse. In the notorious Highland Clearances *(see p531)*, from the 1780s on, landowners ejected tenants from their smallholdings and gave the land over to sheep and other livestock. The first ironworks was established in 1760 and was soon followed by coal mining, steel production and shipbuilding on the Clyde. Canals were cut, railways and bridges built.

A strong socialist movement developed as workers sought to improve their conditions. Keir Hardie, an Ayrshire coal miner, in 1892 became the first socialist elected to parliament, and in 1893 founded the Independent Labour Party. The most enduring symbol of this time is the spectacular Forth rail bridge *(see p502)*.

SCOTLAND TODAY

Although the status of the country appeared to have been settled in 1707, a strong nationalist sentiment remained

and was heightened by the Depression of the 1920s and '30s which had severe effects on the heavily industrialized Clydeside. This was when the Scottish National Party formed, advocating self-rule. The Nationalists asserted themselves in 1950 by stealing the Stone of Scone from Westminister Abbey.

The discovery of North Sea oil in 1970 encouraged a nationalist revival and, in 1979, the Government promised to establish a separate assembly if 40 per cent of the Scottish electorate endorsed the plan in a referendum. This figure was finally surpassed in 1998, and the Scottish Parliament was duly inaugurated in 1999.

A North Sea oil rig, helping to provide prosperity in the 1970s

Clans and Tartans

The clan system, by which Highland society was divided into tribal groups led by autocratic chiefs, can be traced to the 12th century, when clans were already known to wear the chequered wool cloth later called tartan. All members of the clan bore the name of their chief, but not all were related by blood. Though they had noble codes of hospitality, the clansmen had to be warriors to protect their herds, as can be seen from their mottoes. After the Battle of Culloden (see p537), all the clan lands were forfeited to the Crown, and the wearing of tartan was banned for nearly 100 years.

The Mackays, *also known as the Clan Morgan, won lasting renown during the Thirty Years War.*

The MacLeods *are of Norse heritage. The clan chief still lives in Dunvegan Castle, Skye (see p534).*

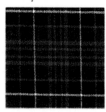

The MacDonalds *were the most power-ful of all the clans, holding the title of Lords of the Isles.*

The Mackenzies *received much of the lands of Kintail (see p530) from David II in 1362.*

CLAN CHIEF

The chief was the clan's patriarch, judge and leader in war, commanding absolute loyalty from his clansmen who gave military service in return for his protection. The chief summoned his clan to do battle by sending a runner across his land bearing a burning cross.

Bonnet with eagle feathers, clan crest and plant badge.

Dirk

Sporran, or pouch, made of badger's skin.

Feileadh-mor, or "great plaid" (the early kilt), wrapped around waist and shoulder.

Basket-hilted sword

The Campbells *were a widely feared clan who fought the Jacobites in 1746 (see p537).*

The Black Watch, *raised in 1729 to keep peace in the Highlands, was one of the Highland regiments in which the wearing of tartan sur-vived. After 1746, civilians were punished by exile for up to seven years for wearing tartan.*

The Sinclairs *came from France in the 11th century and became Earls of Caithness in 1455.*

The Frasers *came to Britain from France with William the Conqueror (see p47) in 1066.*

George IV, *dressed as a Highlander, visited Edinburgh in 1822, the year of the tartan revival. Many tartan "setts" (patterns) date from this time, as the original ones were lost.*

The Gordons *were famously good soldiers; the clan motto is "by courage, not by craft".*

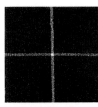

The Stuarts *were Scotland's royal dynasty. Their motto was "no one harms me with impunity".*

CLAN TERRITORIES

The territories of 10 prominent clans are marked here with their clan crests. Dress tartans tend to be colourful, while hunting tartans are darker.

The Douglas *clan were prominent in Scottish history, though their origin is unknown.*

PLANT BADGES

Each clan had a plant associated with its territory. It was worn on the bonnet, especially on the day of battle.

Scots pine was worn by the MacGregors of Argyll.

Rowan berries were worn by the Clan Malcolm.

Ivy was worn by the Clan Gordon of Aberdeenshire.

Spear thistle, now a national symbol, was a Stuart badge.

Cotton grass was worn by the Clan Henderson.

HIGHLAND CLANS TODAY

Once the daily dress of the clansmen, the kilt is now largely reserved for formal occasions. The one-piece *feileadh-mor* has been replaced by the *feileadh-beag*, or "small plaid", made from approximately 7 m (23 ft) of material with a double apron fastened at the front with a silver pin. Though they exist now only in name, the clans are still a strong source of pride for Scots, and many still live in areas traditionally belonging to their clans. Many visitors to Britain can trace their Scots ancestry (*see p31*) to the Highlands.

Modern Highland formal dress

Evolution of the Scottish Castle

There are few more romantic sights in the British Isles than a Scottish castle on an island or at a lochside. These formidable retreats, often in remote settings, were essential all over the Highlands, where incursions and strife between the clans were common. From the earliest Pictish *brochs (see p43)* and Norman-influenced motte and bailey castles, the distinctively Scottish stone tower-house evolved, first appearing in the 14th century. By the mid-17th century fashion had become more important than defence, and there followed a period in which numerous huge Scottish palaces were built.

Detail of the Baroque façade, Drumlanrig

MOTTE AND BAILEY

These castles first appeared in the 12th century. They stood atop two adjacent mounds enclosed by a wall, or palisade, and defensive ditches. The higher mound, or motte, was the most strongly defended as it held the keep and chief's house. The lower bailey was where the people lived. Of these castles little more than earthworks remain today.

Keep, with chief's house, lookout and main defence

All that remains today of Duffus Castle, Morayshire

Duffus Castle, *(c.1150), was atypically made of stone rather than wood. Its fine defensive position dominates the surrounding flatlands north of Elgin.*

Motte of earth or rock, sometimes partially man-made

Bailey enclosing dwellings and storehouses

EARLY TOWER-HOUSE

Designed to deter local attacks rather than a major assault, the first tower-houses appeared in the 13th century, though their design lived on for 400 years. They were built initially on a rectangular plan, with a single tower divided into three or four floors. The walls were unadorned, with few windows. Defensive structures were on top, and extra space was made by building adjoining towers. Extensions were made as vertically as possible, to minimize the area open to attack.

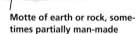

Crenellated parapet for sentries

Featureless, straight walls with arrow slits for windows

Claypotts Castle (c.1570) with uniquely projecting garrets above its towers

Braemar Castle (c.1630), a conglomeration of extended towers

Neidpath Castle, *standing upon a steep rocky crag above the River Tweed, is an L-shaped tower-house dating from the late 14th century. Once a stronghold for Charles II, its walls still bear damage from a siege conducted by Oliver Cromwell (see p52).*

Small, inconspicuous doorway

LATER TOWER-HOUSE

Though the requirements of defence were being replaced by those of comfort, the style of the early tower-house remained popular. By the 17th century, wings for accommodation were being added around the original tower (often creating a courtyard). The battlements and turrets were kept more for decorative than defensive reasons.

Drum Castle *(see p541)*, a 13th-century keep with a mansion house extension from 1619

Priest's room with secret access

The original 15th-century tower-house

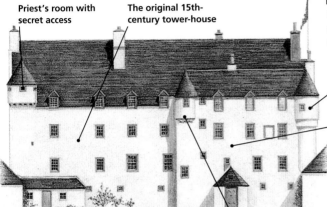

Round angle tower, containing stairway

A 16th-century horizontal extension

Traquair House (see p513), *by the Tweed, is reputedly the oldest continuously inhabited house in Scotland. The largely unadorned, roughcast exterior dates to the 16th century, when a series of extensions were built around the original 15th-century tower-house.*

Decorative, corbelled turret

Blair Castle *(see p543)*, incorporating a medieval tower

CLASSICAL PALACE

By the 18th century, the defensive imperative had passed and castles were built in the manner of country houses, rejecting the vertical tower-house in favour of a horizontal plan (though the building of imitation fortified buildings continued into the 19th century with the mock-Baronial trend). Outside influences came from all over Europe, including Renaissance and Gothic revivals, and echoes of French châteaux.

Dunrobin Castle (c.1840), Sutherland

Larger windows due to a lesser need for defence

Balustrades instead of battlements

Decorative cupola

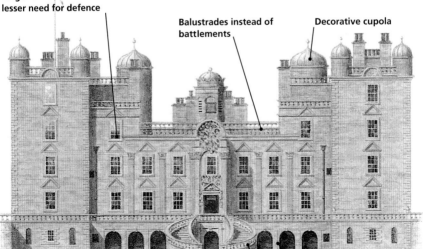

Drumlanrig Castle (see p514) *was built in the 17th century. There are many traditional Scots aspects as well as such Renaissance features as the decorated stairway and façade.*

Renaissance-style colonnade

Baroque horseshoe stairway

The Flavours of Scotland

At its best, Scottish food is full of the natural flavour of the countryside. Served with few sauces or spices, its meat is lean and tasty. Beef doesn't get better than Aberdeen Angus, the lamb is full flavoured, and the venison superb. Scottish salmon and trout are renowned, but there are also excellent mussels, lobster and crabs. Wheat does not grow here, so oatcakes and bannocks (flat, round loaves) replace bread. The Scots have a sweet tooth, not just for cakes and shortbread but also for toffee and butterscotch.

Smoked Salmon

Pedigree Aberdeen Angus cattle grazing the Scottish moors

THE LOWLANDS

The pasturelands of southern Scotland nourish dairy cattle and sheep, producing cheeses such as Bonnet, Bonchester and Galloway Cheddar. To accompany them are summer fruits such as loganberries, tayberries and strawberries that ripen in the Carse of Gowrie beside the River Tay. Oats, the principal cereal, appears in much Scottish cookery, from porridge to oatcakes. Pearl barley is also a staple, used in Scotch Broth (made with mutton and vegetables) or in a milk pudding. Oats are also used in the making of haggis, a round sausage of sheep or venison offal – the "chieftain o' the puddin' race", as the poet Robert Burns described it. It is often served with "neeps and tatties" (mashed swede and potato).

THE HIGHLANDS

From the Highlands comes wonderful game, including grouse, partridge, capercaillie (a large type of grouse) and deer. Fish are smoked around the coast, the west coast producing kippers, the east coast Finnan haddock, notably Arbroath Smokies. Smoked white fish is the main ingredient of Cullen Skink, a soup served on Burns' Night.

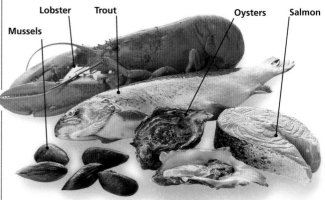
Mussels   Lobster   Trout   Oysters   Salmon
Selection of fresh Scottish fish and seafood

TRADITIONAL SCOTTISH FOOD

Kippers (oak-smoked herrings) are one way to start the day in Scotland, and porridge – traditionally served with salt rather than sugar – is another, although oatcakes or some other kind of griddled scone are usually present. A bowl of porridge would once last all week, just as one-pot Scotch broths bubbled in iron cauldrons over peat fires for days. Sometimes broths were made with kale or lentils, or they might contain an old boiling fowl and leeks, in which case they were known as cock-a-leekie. Any leftover meat went into making stovies, a potato and onion hash. The evening meal in Scotland is traditionally "high tea" taken in the early evening which might start with smoked fish, cold meats and pies, followed by shortbread, fruit cake or drop scones, all washed down with cups of tea.

Oats

Haggis with neeps and tatties
This is the definitive Scottish dish, traditionally served on Burns' Night (25 January).

HOW WHISKY IS MADE

Traditionally made from just barley, yeast and stream water, Scottish whisky (from the Gaelic *usquebaugh*, or the "water of life") takes a little over three weeks to produce, though it must be given at least three years to mature. Maturation usually takes place in oak casks, often in barrels previously used for sherry. The art of blending was pioneered in Edinburgh in the 1860s.

Barley grass

1 *Malting is the first stage. Barley grain is soaked in water and spread on the malting floor. With regular turning the grain germinates, producing a "green malt". Germination stimulates the production of enzymes which turn the starches into fermentable sugars.*

2 *Drying of the barley halts germination after 12 days of malting. This is done over a peat fire in a pagoda-shaped malt-kiln. The peat-smoke gives flavour to the malt and eventually to the mature whisky. The malt is gleaned of germinated roots and then milled.*

3 *Mashing of the ground malt, or "grist", occurs in a large vat, or "mash tun", which holds a vast quantity of hot water. The malt is soaked and begins to dissolve, producing a sugary solution called "wort", which is then extracted for fermentation.*

4 *Fermentation occurs when yeast is added to the cooled wort in wooden vats, or "washbacks". The mixture is stirred for hours as the yeast turns the sugar into alcohol, producing a clear liquid called "wash".*

5 *Distillation involves boiling the wash twice so that the alcohol vaporizes and condenses. In copper "pot stills", the wash is distilled – first in the "wash still", then in the "spirit still". Now purified, with an alcohol content of 57 per cent, the result is young whisky.*

6 *Maturation is the final process. The whisky mellows in oak casks for a legal minimum of three years. Premium brands give the whisky a 10- to 15-year maturation, though some are given up to 50 years.*

Traditional drinking vessels, or *quaichs,* **made of silver**

Blended whiskies *are made from a mixture of up to 50 different single malts.*

Single malts *vary according to regional differences in the peat and stream water used.*

THE LOWLANDS

CLYDE VALLEY · CENTRAL SCOTLAND · FIFE · THE LOTHIANS
AYRSHIRE · DUMFRIES AND GALLOWAY · THE BORDERS

*S*outheast of the Highland boundary fault line lies a part of
Scotland very different in character from its northern neighbour.
If the Highlands embody the romance of Scotland, the Lowlands
*have traditionally been her powerhouse. Lowlanders have always pros-
pered in agriculture and, more recently, in industry and commerce.*

Being the region of Scotland closest to the English border, the
Lowlands inevitably became
the crucible of Scottish history. For centuries after the
Romans built the Antonine
Wall *(see p44)* across the Forth–
Clyde isthmus, the area was
engulfed in conflict. The Borders
are scattered with the castles of
a territory in uneasy proximity
to rapacious neighbours, and
the ramparts of Stirling Castle
overlook no fewer than seven different battlefields fought over in the
cause of independence.

The ruins of medieval abbeys, such
as Melrose, also bear witness to the
dangers of living on the invasion route
from England, though the woollen
trade founded by their monks still
flourishes in Peebles and Hawick.

North of the Borders lies Edinburgh,
the cultural and administrative capital of Scotland. With its Georgian
squares dominated by a medieval castle, it is one of Europe's most elegant
cities. While the 18th and 19th centuries saw a great flowering of the
arts in Edinburgh, the city of
Glasgow became a merchant
city second only to London.
Fuelled by James Watt's development of the steam engine in
the 1840s, Glasgow became the cradle
of Scotland's Industrial Revolution,
which created a prosperous cotton
industry and launched the world's
greatest ships.

Both cities retain this dynamism
today: Edinburgh annually hosts the
world's largest arts festival, and
Glasgow is acclaimed as a model of
industrial renaissance.

A juggler performing at the annual arts extravaganza, the Edinburgh Festival

◁ Glamis Castle, 12 miles (19 km) north of Dundee, with its typically Scottish turreted exterior

Exploring the Lowlands

The Lowlands are traditionally all the land south of the fault line stretching northeast from Loch Lomond to Stonehaven. Confusingly, they include plenty of wild upland country. The region illustrates the diversity of Scotland's scenery. The wooded valleys and winding rivers of the borders give way to the stern hills of the Cheviots and Lammermuirs. Fishing villages cling to the rocky east coast, while the Clyde coast and its islands are dotted with holiday towns. Inland lies the Trossachs, a romantic area of mountain, loch and woodland east of Loch Lomond that is a magnet for walkers (*see pp36–7*) and well within reach of Glasgow.

Loch Katrine seen from the Trossachs

SIGHTS AT A GLANCE

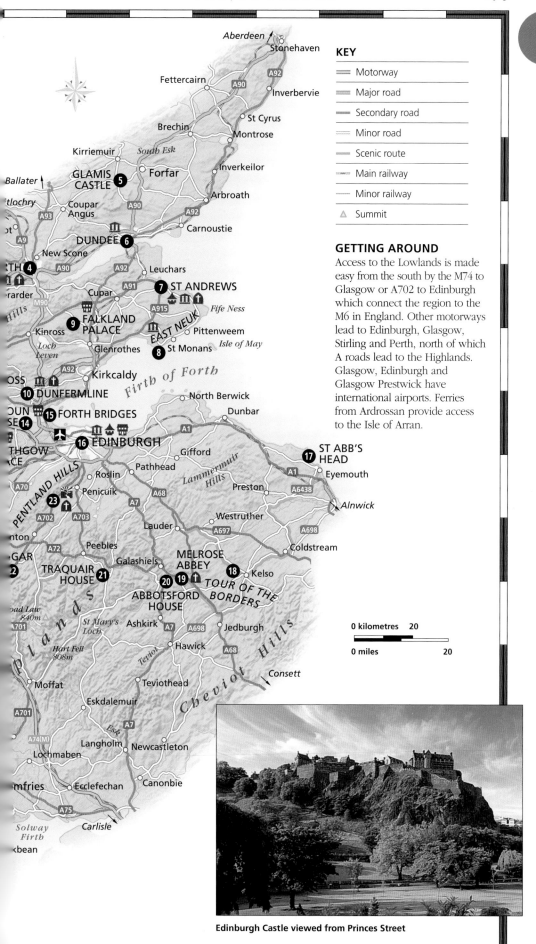

Fettercairn
A90
Inverbervie
A92
Brechin
St Cyrus
Montrose
Kirriemuir
South Esk
Inverkeilor
GLAMIS **5**
CASTLE
Forfar
Ballater
Arbroath
tlochry
Coupar
Angus
A90
A92
t
A93
Carnoustie
DUNDEE **6**
New Scone
TH **4**
A90
A92
Leuchars
A9
Cupar
7 ST ANDREWS
rarder
A91
M90
A915
Fife Ness
FALKLAND **9**
PALACE
Kinross
EAST NEUK
Pittenweem
Glenrothes
Loch
Leven
8 St Monans
Isle of May
A92
Kirkcaldy
Firth of Forth
OSS
t
10 DUNFERMLINE
North Berwick
OUN **15** FORTH BRIDGES
Dunbar
SE **14**
A1
THGOW
CE
16 EDINBURGH
Gifford
17 ST ABB'S
HEAD
A1
Eyemouth
A70
Roslin
Pathhead
Lammermuir
Hills
Preston
A6438
PENTLAND HILLS
Penicuik
A68
23
t
A7
Westruther
Alnwick
A702
A703
Lauder
A697
A698
nton
Peebles
Coldstream
A72
GAR
Galashiels
MELROSE
ABBEY
2
TRAQUAIR **21**
HOUSE
20 **19** **18** Kelso
ABBOTSFORD
HOUSE
TOUR OF THE
BORDERS
ad Law
840m
St Mary's
Loch
Ashkirk
A7
A698
Jedburgh
A701
Hart Fell
808m
Hawick
A68
Teviot
Moffat
Teviothead
Consett
Cheviot Hills
Eskdalemuir
A701
Esk
A7
Langholm
Newcastleton
Lochmaben
mfries
Ecclefechan
Canonbie
A75
Solway
Firth
Carlisle
kbean

KEY

	Motorway
	Major road
	Secondary road
	Minor road
	Scenic route
	Main railway
	Minor railway
△	Summit

GETTING AROUND

Access to the Lowlands is made easy from the south by the M74 to Glasgow or A702 to Edinburgh which connect the region to the M6 in England. Other motorways lead to Edinburgh, Glasgow, Stirling and Perth, north of which A roads lead to the Highlands. Glasgow, Edinburgh and Glasgow Prestwick have international airports. Ferries from Ardrossan provide access to the Isle of Arran.

0 kilometres 20

0 miles 20

Edinburgh Castle viewed from Princes Street

The Trossachs ❶

Combining the ruggedness of the Grampians with the pastoral tranquillity of the Borders, this beautiful region of craggy hills and sparkling lochs is the colourful meeting place of the Lowlands and Highlands. Home to a wide variety of wildlife, including the golden eagle, peregrine falcon, red deer and the wildcat, the Trossachs have inspired numerous writers, including Sir Walter Scott

Golden eagle

(see p512) who made the area the setting for several of his novels. It was the home of Scotland's folk hero, Rob Roy, who was so well known that, in his own lifetime, he was fictionalized in *The Highland Rogue* (1723), a novel attributed to Daniel Defoe.

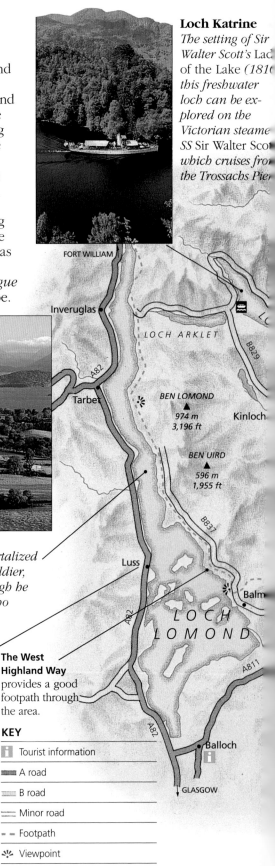

Loch Katrine
The setting of Sir Walter Scott's Lady of the Lake (1810 this freshwater loch can be explored on the Victorian steame SS Sir Walter Scott which cruises from the Trossachs Pier

FORT WILLIAM

Inveruglas

LOCH ARKLET

B829

A82

Tarbet

BEN LOMOND
▲
974 m
3,196 ft

Kinloch

BEN UIRD
▲
596 m
1,955 ft

B837

Loch Lomond
Britain's largest freshwater lake was immortalized in a ballad composed by a local Jacobite soldier, dying far from home. He laments that though he will return home before his companions who travel on the high road, he will be doing so on the low road (of death).

Luss

LOCH
LOMOND

A82

Balm

A811

The West Highland Way provides a good footpath through the area.

KEY

ℹ️	Tourist information
▬▬	A road
▬▬	B road
═══	Minor road
– –	Footpath
☀	Viewpoint

A82

● Balloch
ℹ️

GLASGOW

Luss
With its exceptionally picturesque cottages, Luss is one of the prettiest villages in the Lowlands. Surrounded by grassy hills, it occupies one of the most scenic parts of Loch Lomond's western shore.

0 kilometres   5

0 miles   5

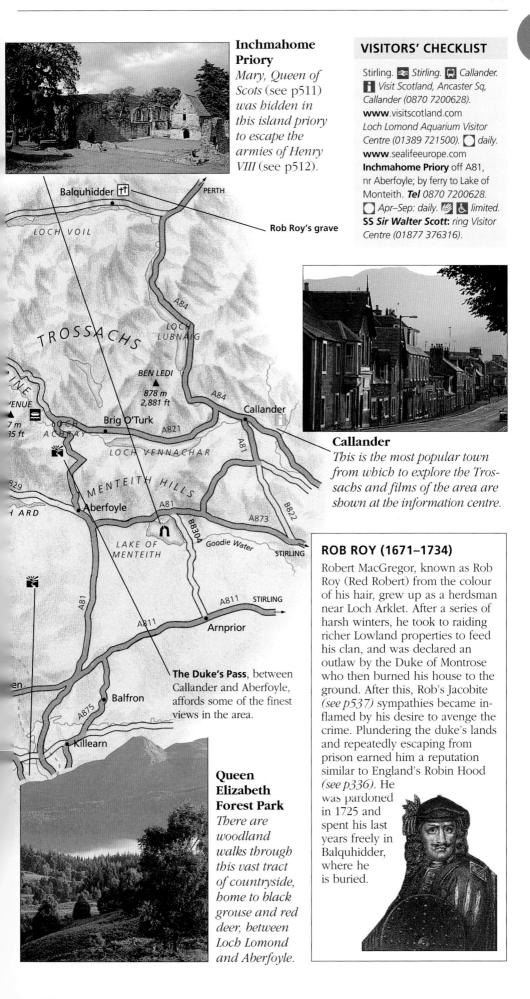

Inchmahome Priory

Mary, Queen of Scots (see p511) was hidden in this island priory to escape the armies of Henry VIII (see p512).

VISITORS' CHECKLIST

Stirling. Stirling. Callander.
Visit Scotland, Ancaster Sq, Callander (0870 7200628).
www.visitscotland.com
Loch Lomond Aquarium Visitor Centre (01389 721500). daily.
www.sealifeeurope.com
Inchmahome Priory off A81, nr Aberfoyle; by ferry to Lake of Monteith. **Tel** 0870 7200628. Apr–Sep: daily. limited.
SS Sir Walter Scott: ring Visitor Centre (01877 376316).

Balquhidder

PERTH

Rob Roy's grave

LOCH VOIL

A84

TROSSACHS

LOCH LUBNAIG

BEN LEDI
878 m
2,881 ft

A84

Callander

Brig O'Turk

A821

A81

LOCH ACHRAY

LOCH VENNACHAR

MENTEITH HILLS

Aberfoyle

A81

A873

B822

LAKE OF MENTEITH

Goodie Water

STIRLING

B8304

A81

A811

STIRLING

A811

Arnprior

The Duke's Pass, between Callander and Aberfoyle, affords some of the finest views in the area.

Balfron

A875

Killearn

Callander

This is the most popular town from which to explore the Trossachs and films of the area are shown at the information centre.

ROB ROY (1671–1734)

Robert MacGregor, known as Rob Roy (Red Robert) from the colour of his hair, grew up as a herdsman near Loch Arklet. After a series of harsh winters, he took to raiding richer Lowland properties to feed his clan, and was declared an outlaw by the Duke of Montrose who then burned his house to the ground. After this, Rob's Jacobite *(see p537)* sympathies became inflamed by his desire to avenge the crime. Plundering the duke's lands and repeatedly escaping from prison earned him a reputation similar to England's Robin Hood *(see p336).* He was pardoned in 1725 and spent his last years freely in Balquhidder, where he is buried.

Queen Elizabeth Forest Park

There are woodland walks through this vast tract of countryside, home to black grouse and red deer, between Loch Lomond and Aberfoyle.

The 17th-century town house of the Dukes of Argyll, Stirling

Stirling ❷

Stirling. 🏛 *41,000.* 🚉 🚌 ℹ️ *41 Dunbarton Rd (08707 200614).* **www.**visitscottishheartlands.com

Situated between the Ochil Hills and the Campsie Fells, Stirling grew up around its castle, historically one of Scotland's most important fortresses. Below the castle the Old Town is still protected by the original 16th-century walls, built to keep Mary Queen of Scots safe from Henry VIII. The medieval **Church of the Holy Rude**, on Castle Wynd, where the infant James VI was crowned in 1567, has one of Scotland's few surviving hammerbeam oak roofs. The ornate façade of **Mar's Wark** is all that remains of a grand palace which, though never completed, was commissioned in 1570 by the 1st Earl of Mar. It was destroyed by the Jacobites *(see p537)* in 1746. Opposite stands the beautiful 17th-century town house of the Dukes of Argyll.

Environs: Two miles (3 km) south, the **Bannockburn Heritage Centre** stands by the field where Robert the Bruce defeated the English *(see p482)*. After the battle, he dismantled the castle so it would not fall back into English hands. A bronze equestrian statue commemorates the man who is an icon of Scottish independence.

ℹ️ **Bannockburn Heritage Centre**
(NTS) Glasgow Rd. **Tel** 01786 812664. ⬤ Mar–Oct: 10am–5:30pm daily; other times by appointment. ⬤ 24 Dec–Feb.

Stirling Castle

Rising high on a rocky crag, this magnificent castle, which dominated Scottish history for centuries, now remains one of the finest examples of Renaissance architecture in Scotland. Legend says that King Arthur *(see p285)* wrested the original castle from the Saxons, but there is no evidence of a castle before 1124. The present building dates from the 15th and 16th centuries and was last defended, against the Jacobites *(see p537)*, in 1746. From 1881 to 1964 the castle was a depot for recruits into the Argyll and Sutherland Highlanders, though now it serves no military function.

Gargoyle on castle wall

Robert the Bruce
In the esplanade, this modern statue shows Robert the Bruce sheathing his sword after the Battle of Bannockburn in 1314.

Prince's Tower

Forework

Entrance

Stirling Castle in the Time of the Stuarts, painted by Johannes Vorsterman (1643–99)

★ Palace

The otherwise sparse interiors of the royal apartments contain the Stirling Heads. These Renaissance roundels depict 38 figures, thought to be contemporary members of the royal court.

VISITORS' CHECKLIST

Castle Wynd, Stirling. **Tel** *01786 450000.* ◯ *9:30am–6pm (Oct–Mar: to 5pm) daily. (Palace closed for restoration until 2011.)* ◑ *25–26 Dec.* 🎫 📷 *except museum.* ♿ *limited.* 🎟 🍴 🛍 📖 www. historic-scotland.gov.uk

The King's Old Building houses the Regimental Museum of the Argyll and Sutherland Highlanders.

★ Chapel Royal

Seventeenth-century frescoes by Valentine Jenkins adorn the chapel, reconstructed in 1594.

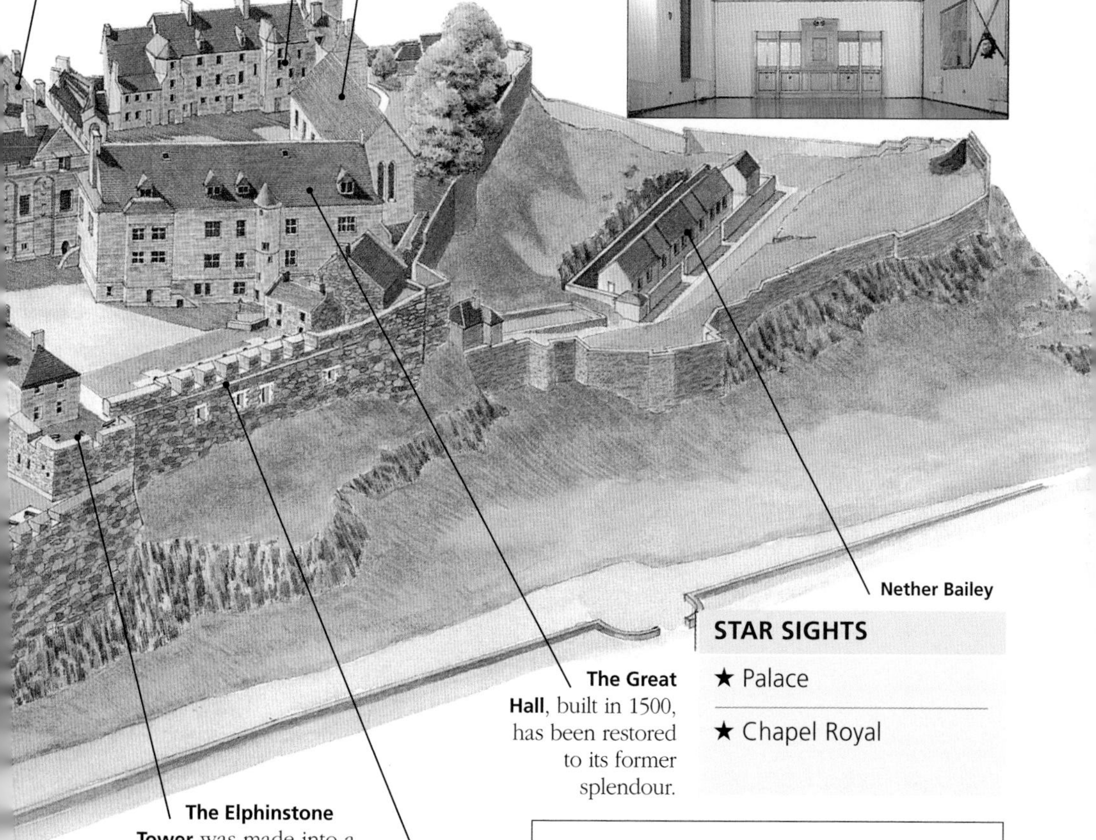

Nether Bailey

STAR SIGHTS

★ Palace

★ Chapel Royal

The Great Hall, built in 1500, has been restored to its former splendour.

The Elphinstone Tower was made into a gun platform in 1714.

Grand Battery

Seven guns stand on this parapet, built in 1708 during a strengthening of defences following the revolution of 1688 (see p53).

STIRLING BATTLES

At the highest navigable point of the Forth and holding the pass to the Highlands, Stirling occupied a key position in Scotland's struggles for independence. Seven battlefields can be seen from the castle; the 67-m (220-ft) Wallace Monument at Abbey Craig recalls William Wallace's defeat of the English at Stirling Bridge in 1297, foreshadowing Bruce's victory in 1314 *(see p482).*

The Victorian Wallace Monument

Perth seen from the east across the Tay

Doune Castle ❸

Doune, Stirling. **Tel** 01786 841742.
🚆 🚌 Stirling then bus. ◯ Apr–Sep:
9:30am–5:30pm daily; Oct–Mar:
9:30am–4:30pm Sat–Wed; last entry
30 mins before close. ● 21 Dec–
8 Jan. 🎫 ♿ limited.
www.historic-scotland.gov.uk

Built as the residence of
Robert, Duke of Albany, in the
14th century, **Doune Castle** was
a Stuart stronghold until it fell
into ruin in the 18th century.
Now fully restored, it is one of
the most complete castles of its
time and offers a unique insight
into the royal household.

The Gatehouse, once a
self-sufficient residence, leads
through to the central courtyard from which the Great
Hall can be entered. Complete
with its reconstructed open-
timber roof, minstrels' gallery
and central fireplace, the Hall
adjoins the Lord's Hall and
Private Room. A number of
private stairs and narrow

passages reveal the ingenious
ways the royal family tried to
hide during times of danger.
The castle was the setting for
the 1975 film, *Monty Python
and the Holy Grail.*

Perth ❹

Perthshire. 👥 45,000. 🚆 🚌
ℹ️ West Mill St (01738 450600).
www.perthshire.co.uk

Once the capital of medieval
Scotland, Perth's rich heritage
is reflected in many of its buildings. It was in the **Church of
Saint John**, founded in 1126,
that John Knox *(see p483)*
delivered many of his fiery
sermons. The Victorianized **Fair
Maid's House**, on North Port,
is one of the oldest houses in
town (c.1600) and was the
fictional home of the heroine
of Sir Walter Scott's *(see p512)
The Fair Maid of Perth* (1828).

In **Balhousie Castle**, the
Museum of the Black Watch
commemorates the first

Highland regiment, while the
Perth Museum & Art Gallery
has displays on local industry
and exhibitions of Scottish art.

Environs: Two miles (3 km)
north of Perth, the Gothic
mansion of **Scone Palace**
stands on the site of an abbey
destroyed in 1559. Between
the 9th and 13th centuries,
Scone guarded the sacred
Stone of Destiny *(see pp482–3),*
now kept in Edinburgh Castle
(see pp506–7). Some of Mary,
Queen of Scots' *(see p511)*
embroideries are on display.

⚓ **Balhousie Castle**
RHQ Black Watch, Hay St. **Tel** 0131
310 8530. ◯ 10am–4:30pm Mon–
Sat (Oct–Apr: to 3:30pm Mon–Fri).

🏛 **Perth Museum & Art
Gallery**
78 George St. **Tel** 01738 632488.
◯ 10am–5pm daily (from 1pm Sun;
Sep–Apr: Mon–Sat only). ♿

⚓ **Scone Palace**
A93 to Braemar. **Tel** 01738 552300.
◯ Apr–Oct: 9:30am–5pm daily (to
4pm Sun). Grounds close at 6pm.
🎫 ♿ **www**.scone-palace.co.uk

Glamis Castle ❺

Forfar, Angus. **Tel** 01307 840393.
🚆 🚌 Dundee then bus. ◯ Mar–
Oct: 10:30am–4:30pm daily; Nov &
Dec: 10am–6pm daily (last tour 4pm).
🎫 🎥 **www**.glamis-castle.co.uk

With the pinnacled fairytale
outline of a Loire chateau,
the imposing medieval tower-
house of **Glamis Castle** began

Glamis Castle with statues of James VI (left) and Charles I (right)

as a royal hunting lodge in the 11th century but underwent extensive reconstruction in the 17th century. It was the childhood home of Queen Elizabeth the Queen Mother, and her former bedroom can be seen with a youthful portrait by Henri de Laszlo (1878–956).

Many rooms are open to the public, including Duncan's Hall, the oldest in the castle and Shakespeare's setting for the king's murder in *Macbeth*. Together, the rooms present an array of china, paintings, tapestries and furniture spanning five centuries. In the grounds stand a pair of wrought-iron gates made for the Queen Mother on her 80th birthday in 1980.

Dundee ❻

Dundee City. 🚶 *144,000.* ✈ ⇄ 🚌
ℹ️ *Discovery Point, Discovery Quay (01382 527527).* 🛒 *Tue, Fri–Sun; farmers' market 3rd Sat of month.* **www**.angusanddundee.co.uk

Famous for its cake, marmalade and the DC Thomson publishing empire (creators of children's magazines *Beano* and *Dandy*), **Dundee** was also a major ship-building centre in the 18th and 19th centuries, a period which can be atmospherically recreated by a trip to the Victoria Docks.

HMS *Unicorn*, built in 1824, is the oldest British-built warship still afloat and is still fitted as it was on its last voyage. Berthed at Riverside is the royal research ship **Discovery**, built here in 1901 for Captain

View of St Andrews over the ruins of the cathedral

Scott's first voyage to the Antarctic. Housed in a Victorian Gothic building, the **McManus Galleries** provide a glimpse of Dundee's industrial heritage, as well as exhibitions on archaeology and Victorian art. The **Howff Burial Ground**, near City Square, has intriguing Victorian tombstones.

🏛 **HMS** *Unicorn*
Victoria Docks, City Quay. *Tel 01382 200900.* ◻ *Apr–Oct: daily; Nov–Mar: Wed–Sun.* 📷 ♿ *limited.*

🏛 **Discovery**
Discovery Point. *Tel 01382 309060.* ◻ *daily (Sun pm).* 📷 ♿ **www**.rrsdiscovery.com

🏛 **McManus Galleries**
Albert Sq. *Tel 01382 432350.* ◻ *call for opening times.* ♿ **www**.dundeecity.gov.uk

St Andrews ❼

Fife. 🚶 *16,000.* ⇄ *Leuchars.* 🚌 *Dundee.* ℹ️ *70 Market St (01334 472021).* **www**.visit-standrews.co.uk

Scotland's oldest university town and one-time ecclesiastical capital, **St Andrews** is now a shrine to golfers from all over the world *(see below)*. Its three main streets and numerous cobbled alleys, full of crooked housefronts, dignified university buildings and medieval churches, converge on the venerable ruins of the 12th-century **cathedral**. Once the largest in Scotland, the cathedral was later pillaged for stones to build the town. **St Andrew's Castle** was built for the bishops of the town in 1200. The dungeon can still be seen. The city's golf courses to the west are each open for a modest fee. The **British Golf Museum** tells how the city's Royal and Ancient Golf Club became the ruling arbiter of the game.

St Mary's College insignia, St Andrews University

♔ **St Andrew's Castle**
The Scores. *Tel 01334 477196.* ◻ *Apr–Sep: 9:30–6:30pm daily; Oct–Mar: 9:30–4:30pm daily.* ⬤ *1 & 2 Jan, 25 & 26 Dec.* 📷 ♿

🏛 **British Golf Museum**
Bruce Embankment. *Tel 01334 460 046.* ◻ *Mar–Oct: 9:30am–5:30pm Mon–Sat, 10am–5pm Sun; Nov–Mar: 10am–4pm daily.* 📷 ♿

THE ANCIENT GAME OF GOLF

Scotland's national game was pioneered on the sandy links around St Andrews. The earliest record dates from 1457, when golf was banned by James II on the grounds that it was interfering with his subjects' archery practice.

Mary, Queen of Scots *(see p511)* enjoyed the game and was berated in 1568 for playing straight after the murder of her husband Darnley.

Mary, Queen of Scots at St Andrews in 1563

The central courtyard of Falkland Palace, bordered by rose bushes

East Neuk ⑧

Fife. ⚡ *Leuchars.* 🚌 *Glenrothes & Leuchars.* ℹ️ *70 Market Street, St Andrews (01334 472021).*

A string of pretty fishing villages scatters the shoreline of the **East Neuk** (the eastern "corner") of Fife, stretching from Earlsferry to Fife Ness. Much of Scotland's medieval trade with Europe passed through these ports, a connection reflected in the Flemish-inspired crow-stepped gables of many of the cottages. Although the herring industry has declined and the area is now a peaceful holiday centre, the sea still dominates village life. Until the 1980s, fishing boats were built at St Monans, a charming town of narrow twisting streets, while Pittenweem is the base for the East Neuk fishing fleet.

The town is also known for **St Fillan's Cave**, the retreat of a 9th-century hermit whose relic was used to bless the army of Robert the Bruce *(see p482)* before the Battle of Bannockburn. A church stands among the cobbled lanes and colourful cottages of Crail; the stone by the church gate is said to have been hurled to the mainland from the Isle of May by the Devil.

Several 16th- to 19th-century buildings in the village of Anstruther contain the **Scottish Fisheries Museum** which tells the area's history with the aid of interiors, boats and displays on whaling. From the village you can embark for the nature reserve on the **Isle of May** which teems with seabirds and grey seals. The statue of Alexander Selkirk in Lower Largo recalls the local boy whose adventures inspired Daniel Defoe's *Robinson Crusoe* (1719). Disagreeing with his captain, he was dumped on a desert island for four years.

🏛️ **Scottish Fisheries Museum**
St Ayles, Harbourhead, Anstruther. *Tel 01333 310628.* ⬜ *Apr–Sep: 10am–5:30pm Mon–Sat (to 4:30pm Oct–Mar), 11am–5pm Sun (from noon Oct–Mar).* ⬤ *25 & 26 Dec, 1 & 2 Jan.* 📷 ♿ www.scotfishmuseum.org

THE PALACE KEEPER

Due to the size of the royal household and the necessity for the king to be itinerant, the office of Keeper was created by the medieval kings who required custodians to maintain and replenish the resources of their many palaces while they were away. Now redundant, it was a hereditary title and gave the custodian permanent and often luxurious lodgings.

James VI's bed in the Keeper's Bedroom, Falkland Palace

Falkland Palace ⑨

(NTS) *Falkland, Fife. Tel 01337 857397.* ⚡ 🚌 *Ladybank, Kirkcaldy, then bus.* ⬜ *Mar–Oct: 10am–5pm daily (Sun: pm).* 🎫 📷 ♿
www.nts.org.uk

This stunning Renaissance palace was designed as a hunting lodge of the Stuart kings. Although its construction was begun by James IV in 1500, most of the work was carried out by his son, James V *(see p510)*, in the 1530s. Under the influence of his two French wives he employed French workmen to redecorate the façade of the East Range with dormers, buttresses and medallions, and to build the beautifully proportioned South Range. The palace fell into ruin during the years of the Commonwealth *(see p52)* and was occupied briefly by Rob Roy *(see p495)* in 1715.

After buying the estates in 1887, the 3rd Marquess of Bute became the Palace Keeper and restored it. The richly panelled interiors are filled with superb furniture and portraits of the Stuart monarchs. The royal tennis court is the oldest in Britain.

Dunfermline ⑩

Fife. 🏘️ *55,000.* ⚡ 🚌 ℹ️ *1 High St (01383 720999).*
www.standrews.com/fife

Scotland's capital until 1603, Dunfermline is dominated by the ruins of the 12th-century abbey and palace which recall its royal past. In the 11th century, the town was the seat of King Malcolm III, who founded a priory on the present site of the **Abbey Church**. With its Norman nave and 19th-century choir, the church contains the tombs of 22 Scottish kings and queens, including Robert the Bruce *(see p482)*.

The ruins of King Malcolm's **palace** soar over the beautiful gardens of Pittencrieff Park. Dunfermline's most famous son, philanthropist Andrew Carnegie (1835–1919), had been forbidden entrance to the park as a boy. After making his fortune, he bought the entire Pittencrieff estate and gave it to the people of Dunfermline. He was born in the town, though moved to Pennsylvania in his teens. There he made a vast fortune in the iron and steel industry. The **Carnegie Birthplace Museum** is still furnished as it was when he lived there, and tells the story of his meteoric career.

🏛 **Carnegie Birthplace Museum**
Moodie St. **Tel** *01383 724302.* ⬤ *Apr–Oct: 11am–5pm Mon–Sat; 2–5pm Sun.* 🖼 ♿

The 12th-century Norman nave of Dunfermline Abbey Church

Culross ⑪

(NTS) Fife. 🚶 *450.* 🚃 *Dunfermline.* 🚌 *Dunfermline.* ⓘ *NTS, The Palace (01383 880359).* ⬤ *Easter–Sep: noon–5pm daily.* **Garden** ⬤ *10am–dusk all year.* 🖼 ♿ *limited.* 🖼 📷 🎭 *Music & Arts Festival: early Aug.*

An important religious centre in the 6th century, the town of Culross is said to have been the birthplace of St

Mungo in 514. Now a beautifully preserved 16th- and 17th-century village, Culross prospered in the 16th century with the growth of its coal and salt industries, most notably under Sir George Bruce. He took charge of the Culross colliery in 1575 and created a drainage system called the "Egyptian Wheel" which cleared a mile-long (1.5 km) mine beneath the River Forth.

During its subsequent decline Culross stood unchanged for over 150 years. The National Trust for Scotland began restoring the town in 1932 and now provides a guided tour, which starts at the **Visitors' Centre**.

Built in 1577, Bruce's **palace** has the crow-stepped gables, decorated windows and red pantiles typical of the period. The interior retains its original early 17th-century painted ceilings. Crossing the Square, past the **Oldest House**, dating from 1577, head for the **Town House** to the west. Behind it, a cobbled street known as the Back Causeway (with its raised section for nobility) leads to the turreted **Study**, built in 1610 as a house for the Bishop of Dunblane. The main room is open to visitors and should be seen for its original Norwegian ceiling. Continuing northwards to the ruined abbey, fine church and Abbey House, don't miss the Dutch-gabled **House with the Evil Eyes**.

The 16th-century palace of industrialist George Bruce, Culross

Linlithgow Palace ⑫

Linlithgow, West Lothian. **Tel** *01506 842896.* 🚃 🚌 ⬤ *Apr–Sep: 9:30am–5:30pm daily; Oct–Mar: 9:30am–4:30pm daily.* ⬤ *25, 26 Dec, 1, 2 Jan.* 🖼 ♿ *limited.* **www**.historic-scotland.gov.uk

On the edge of Linlithgow Loch stands the former royal palace of **Linlithgow**. Today's remains are mostly of the palace of James I in 1425. The scale of the building is demonstrated by the 28 m (94 ft) long Great Hall, with its huge fireplace and windows. Mary, Queen of Scots *(see p511)*, was born here in 1542.

Falkirk Wheel ⑬

Lime Rd, Falkirk. **Tel** *08700 500208 (booking line).* 🚃 *Falkirk.* ⬤ *Feb–Nov:* **Boat trips** *range from 5 trips daily in winter to 3 trips per hour in summer.* **Visitor Centre** *daily. Nov–Feb: phone for times.* 🖼 *boat trip.* 🖼 📷 **www**.thefalkirkwheel.co.uk

This impressive boat lift is the first ever to revolve, and the centrepiece of Scotland's canal regeneration scheme. Once important for commercial transport, the Union and the Forth and Clyde canals were blocked by several roads in the 1960s. Now the Falkirk Wheel gently swings boats between the two waterways creating an uninterrupted link between Glasgow and Edinburgh. Visitors can ride the wheel on boats that leave from the Visitor Centre.

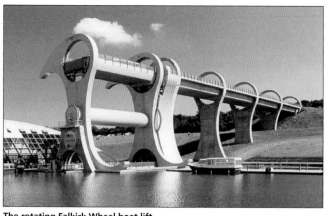
The rotating Falkirk Wheel boat lift

Hopetoun House ⑭

West Lothian. *Tel 0131 331 2451.*
🚆 *Dalmeny then taxi.* ◯ *mid-Mar–late Sep: 10:30am–5pm (last entry 4pm).* ⬛ 🚻 ⬛ *limited.*
📷 *for groups – book ahead.* ⬛
www.hopetounhouse.com

An extensive parkland by the Firth of Forth, designed in the style of Versailles, is the setting for one of Scotland's finest stately homes. The original house was built by 1707; it was later absorbed into William Adam's grand extension. The dignified, horse-shoe-shaped plan and lavish interior plasterwork represent Neo-Classical 18th-century architecture at its finest. The drawing rooms, with their Rococo plasterwork and highly ornate mantelpieces, are particularly impressive. The Marquess of Linlithgow, whose family still occupies part of the house, is a descendant of the 1st Earl of Hopetoun, for whom the house was built.

A wooden panel above the main stair, depicting Hopetoun House

Forth Bridges ⑮

Edinburgh. 🚆 🚌 *Dalmeny, Inverkeithing.* ℹ️ *1 High Street, Dunfermline (01383 720999).*

The small town of South Queensferry is dominated by the two great bridges that span the mile (1.6 km) across the River Forth to North Queensferry. The spectacular rail bridge, the first major steel-built bridge in the world, was opened in 1890 and

The shattered crags and cliffs of St Abb's Head

remains one of the greatest engineering achievements of the late Victorian era. Its massive cantilevered sections are held together by more than 6.5 million rivets, and the painted area adds up to some 55 ha (135 acres). The saying "like painting the Forth Bridge" has become a byword for non-stop, repetitive endeavour. The bridge also inspired *The Bridge* (1986) by writer Iain Banks.

The neighbouring road bridge was the largest suspension bridge outside the USA when it opened in 1964, a distinction now held by the Humber Bridge in England. A new bridge is due to open across the Forth in 2016.

South Queensferry got its name from the 11th-century Queen Margaret *(see p507)*, who used the ferry here on her journeys between Edinburgh and the royal palace at Dunfermline *(see p501)*.

Edinburgh ⑯

See pp504–11.

St Abb's Head ⑰

(NTS) Scottish Borders. 🚆 *Berwick-upon-Tweed.* 🚌 *from Edinburgh.*

The jagged cliffs of St Abb's Head, rising 91 m (300 ft) from the North Sea near the southeastern tip of Scotland, offer a spectacular view of thousands of seabirds wheeling and diving below. This 80 ha (200 acre) nature reserve is an important site for cliff-nesting sea birds and becomes, during the May to June breeding season, the home of more than 50,000 birds, including fulmars, guillemots, kittiwakes and puffins that throng the headland near the fishing village of St Abbs. The village has one of the few unspoiled working harbours on Britain's east coast. A clifftop trail begins at the **Visitors' Centre**, where displays include identification boards and a touch table where young visitors can get to grips with wings and feathers.

🏠 **Visitors' Centre**
St Abb's Head. *Tel 018907 71443.*
◯ *Apr–Oct: 10am–5pm daily.* 📷

The huge, cantilevered Forth Rail Bridge, seen from South Queensferry

A Tour of the Borders ⑱

Because of their proximity to England, the Scottish Borders are scattered with the ruins of many ancient buildings destroyed in the conflicts between the two nations. Most poignant of all are the Border abbeys, whose magnificent architecture bears witness to their former spiritual and political power. Founded during the 12th-century reign of David I, the abbeys were destroyed by Henry VIII *(see p512)*.

Kelso Abbey ②
The largest of the Border Abbeys, Kelso was once the most powerful ecclesiastical establishment in Scotland.

Melrose Abbey ⑥
Once one of the richest abbeys in Scotland, it is here that Robert the Bruce's heart is buried *(see p512)*.

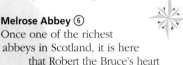

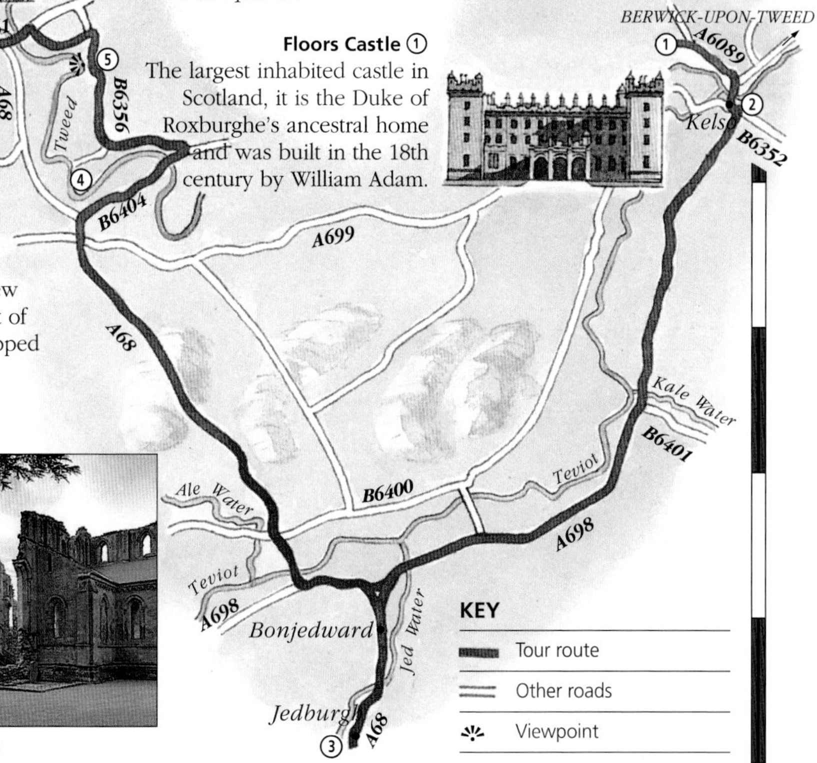

Floors Castle ①
The largest inhabited castle in Scotland, it is the Duke of Roxburghe's ancestral home and was built in the 18th century by William Adam.

Scott's View ⑤
This was Sir Walter Scott's favourite view of the Borders. Out of habit his horse stopped here during Scott's funeral procession.

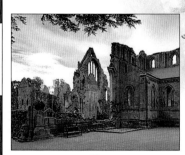

Dryburgh Abbey ④
Set on the banks of the Tweed, Dryburgh is considered the most evocative monastic ruin in Scotland. Sir Walter Scott is buried here.

TIPS FOR DRIVERS

Length: *32 miles (50 km).*
Stopping-off points: *There is a delightful walk northwards from Dryburgh Abbey to the footbridge over the River Tweed.*

KEY

▬▬	Tour route
═══	Other roads
☀	Viewpoint

0 kilometres	5
0 miles	3

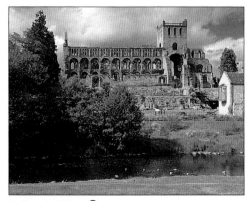

Jedburgh Abbey ③
Though established in 1138, fragments of 9th-century Celtic stonework survive from an earlier structure. A Visitors' Centre illustrates the lives of the Augustinian monks who once lived here.

Map labels: BERWICK-UPON-TWEED, GALASHIELS, Melrose, Kelso, Bonjedward, Jedburgh, A6089, A6091, A68, A699, A698, B6361, B6356, B6404, B6400, B6401, B6352, Kale Water, Teviot, Ale Water, Jed Water, Tweed

Edinburgh ⑯

With its striking medieval and Georgian districts, overlooked by the extinct volcano of Arthur's Seat and, to the northeast, Calton Hill, Edinburgh is widely regarded as one of Europe's most handsome capitals. The city is famous for the arts (it was once known as "the Athens of the North"), a pre-eminence reflected in its hosting every year of Britain's largest arts extravaganza, the Edinburgh Festival *(see p509)*. Its museums and galleries display the riches of many cultures.

Royal Scots soldiers from the castle

The doorway of the Georgian House, 7 Charlotte Square

Exploring Edinburgh

Edinburgh falls into two main sightseeing areas, divided by Princes Street, the city's most famous thoroughfare and commercial centre. The Old Town straddles the ridge between the castle and the Palace of Holyroodhouse, with most of the city's medieval history clustered in the alleys of the Grassmarket and Royal Mile areas. The New Town, to the north, evolved after 1767 when wealthy merchants expanded the city beyond its medieval walls. This district contains Britain's finest concentration of Georgian architecture.

🏛 National Gallery of Scotland

The Mound. *Tel 0131 624 6200.* ◯ *10am–5pm Fri–Wed, 10am–7pm Thu (extended during the festival).* 🖼 *for special exhibitions.* 🚻 🛗 *by appt.* www.nationalgalleries.org
One of Scotland's finest art galleries, the National Gallery of Scotland is worth visiting for its 15th- to 19th-century British and European paintings alone,

though plenty more can be found to delight the art-lover. Highlights among the Scottish works include portraits by Allan Ramsay and Henry Raeburn, such as his *Reverend Robert Walker Skating on Duddingston Loch* (c.1800). The Early German collection includes Gerard David's almost comic-strip treatment of the *Three Legends of Saint Nicholas* (c.1500). Works by Raphael, Titian and Tintoretto accompany southern European paintings such as Velázquez's *An Old Woman Cooking Eggs* (1620) and the entire room devoted to *The Seven Sacraments* (c.1640) by Nicholas Poussin.

The new £30-million Weston Link is an underground complex that connects the gallery with the Royal Scottish Academy. It contains a lecture theatre/cinema, shop, restaurant, café, and an IT and education room.

Raeburn's *Rev. Robert Walker Skating on Duddingston Loch*

🏰 Georgian House

(NTS) 7 Charlotte Sq. *Tel 0844 493 2118.* ◯ *Mar & Nov: 11am–3pm daily; Apr–Jun & Sep–Oct: 10am–5pm daily; Jul–Aug: 10am–7pm daily. (Last adm: half an hour before closing.)* ◯ *mid-Dec–mid-Jan.* 🖼 🛗 *limited.* www.nts.org.uk
In the heart of the New Town, Charlotte Square is a superb example of Georgian architecture, its north side, built in the 1790s, being a masterwork by the architect Robert Adam *(see pp28–9)*. The Georgian House at No. 7 has been furnished and repainted in its original 18th-century colours which provide a memorable introduction to the elegance of wealthy New Town life. In stark contrast, "below stairs" is the household staff's living quarters, demonstrating how Edinburgh's working class lived and worked.

The view from Duncan's Monument on Calton Hill, looking west towards the castle

🏛 Scottish National Gallery of Modern Art & Dean Gallery

Belford Rd. **Tel** 0131 624 6200. ○ 10am–5pm daily (7pm Thu). ♿ www. nationalgalleries.org

Housed in a 19th-century school to the northwest of the city centre, this gallery features most

Medieval chessmen, National Museum of Scotland

European and American 20th-century greats, from Vuillard and Picasso, to Magritte and Lichtenstein. Work by John Bellany can be found among the Scottish painters. Sculpture by Henry Moore is on display in the garden. The Dean Gallery shows a Dada and Surrealist collection.

Lichtenstein's In the Car, National Gallery of Modern Art

🏛 National Museum of Scotland

Chambers St. **Tel** 0131 225 7534. ○ 10am–5pm Mon–Sat (Tue to 8pm), noon–5pm Sun. ● 25 Dec. ♿ free. 🍴 www.nms.ac.uk

This purpose-built museum houses the Scottish Collections of the National Museums of Scotland. Exhibitions tell the story of Scotland, the land and its people, dating from its geological beginnings right up to the constitutionally exciting events of today.

Key exhibits include the famous medieval *Lewis Chessmen*; *Pictish Chains*, known as Scotland's earliest crown jewels, and the *Ellesmere* railway locomotive. There is also a new special exhibition gallery which houses fascinating temporary displays.

🏛 Scottish National Portrait Gallery

1 Queen St. **Tel** 0131 624 6200. ○ 10am–5pm daily (Thu to 7pm). ♿ by appointment. www.nationalgalleries.org

The National Portrait Gallery provides a unique visual history of Scotland told through the portraits of those who shared it, from Robert the Bruce *(see p482)* to Queen Anne. Memorabilia from many reigns include Mary, Queen of Scots' *(see p511)* jewellery and a silver travelling canteen abandoned by Bonnie Prince Charlie *(see p535)* at Culloden *(see p537)*. The upper gallery has portraits of famous Scots, including Robert Burns *(see p515)* by Alexander Nasmyth.

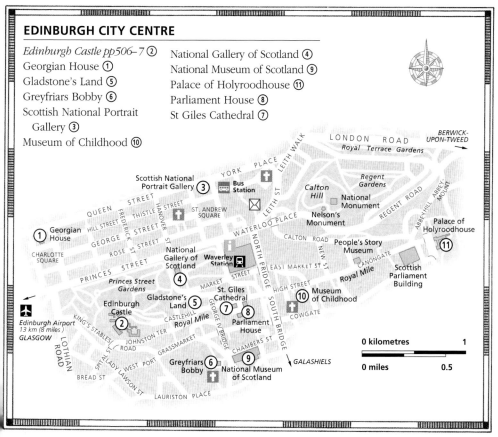

EDINBURGH CITY CENTRE

Edinburgh Castle

Beam support in the Great Hall

Standing upon the basalt core of an extinct volcano, Edinburgh Castle is an assemblage of buildings dating from the 12th to the 20th centuries, reflecting its changing role as fortress, royal palace, military garrison and state prison. Though there is evidence of Bronze Age occupation of the site, the original fortress was built by the 6th-century Northumbrian King Edwin, from whom the city takes its name. The castle was a favourite royal residence until the Union of Crowns *(see p483)* in 1603, after which the king resided in England. After the Union of Parliaments in 1707, the Scottish regalia were walled up in the Palace for over a hundred years. The castle is now the zealous possessor of the so-called Stone of Destiny, a relic of ancient Scottish kings which was seized by the English from Scone Palace, Perthshire and not returned until 1996.

Scottish Crown
On display in the palace, the Crown was restyled by James V of Scotland in 1540.

Military Prison

Governor's House
Complete with Flemish-style crow-stepped gables, this building was constructed for the governor in 1742. It can only be viewed from the outside only as it is still reserved for ceremonial use.

 Old Back Parade

Vaults
This French graffiti, dating from 1780, recalls the many prisoners who were held in the vaults during the wars with France in the 18th and 19th centuries.

MONS MEG

Positioned outside St Margaret's Chapel, the siege gun (or *bombard*) Mons Meg was made in Belgium in 1449 for the Duke of Burgundy, who gave it to his nephew, James II of Scotland. It was used by James against the Douglas family in their stronghold of Threave Castle *(see p515)* in 1455, and later by James IV against Norham Castle in England. After exploding during a salute to the Duke of York in 1682, it was kept in the Tower of London until it was returned to Edinburgh in 1829, at Sir Walter Scott's request.

STAR SIGHTS

★ Great Hall

★ Royal Palace

VISITORS' CHECKLIST

Castle Hill. ***Tel*** *0131 225 9846.* *9:30am–6pm daily (Oct–Mar: to 5pm). (Last adm: 45 mins before closing.)* *25, 26 Dec.* *book tickets online to avoid queuing.* **www**.edinburghcastle.gov.uk

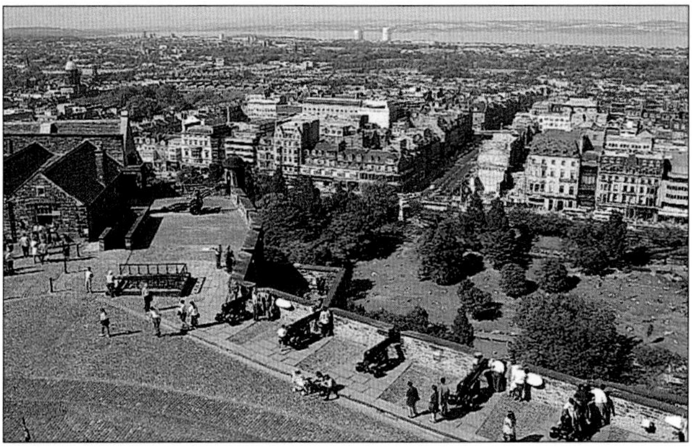

Argyle Battery
This fortified wall commands a spectacular view to the north beyond the city's Georgian district of New Town.

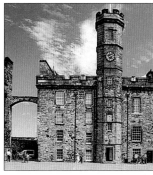

★ Royal Palace
Mary, Queen of Scots (see p511) *gave birth to James VI in this 15th-century palace, where the Scottish regalia are on display.*

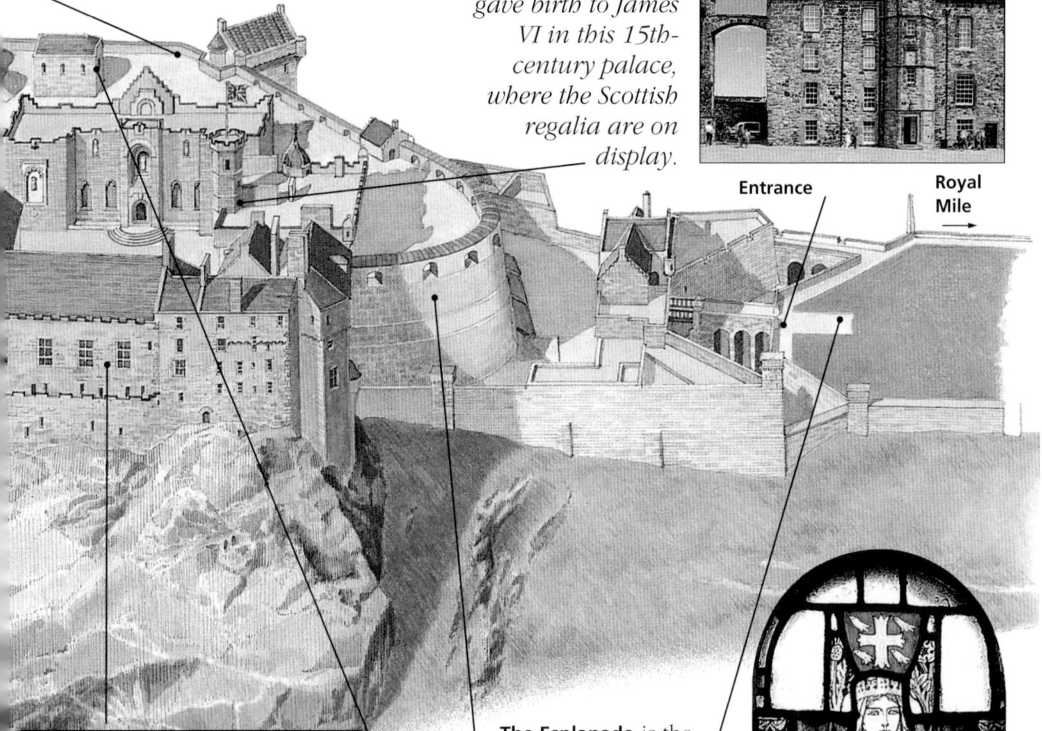

Entrance
Royal Mile

The Esplanade is the location of the Military Tattoo *(see p509).*

The Half Moon Battery was built in the 1570s as a platform for the artillery defending the northeastern wing of the castle.

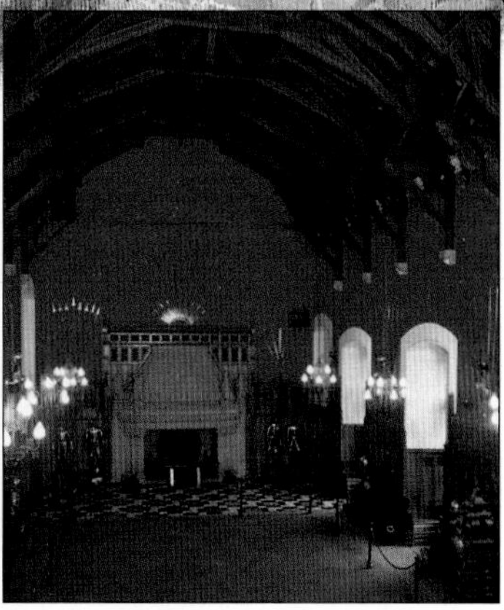

★ Great Hall
With its restored open-timber roof, the Hall dates from the 15th century and was the meeting place of the Scottish parliament until 1639.

St Margaret's Chapel
This stained-glass window depicts Malcolm III's saintly queen, to whom the chapel is dedicated. Probably built by her son, David I, in the early 12th century, the chapel is the castle's oldest existing building.

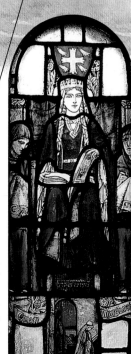

Exploring the Royal Mile: Castlehill to High Street

The Royal Mile is a stretch of four ancient streets (from Castlehill to Canongate) which formed the main thoroughfare of medieval Edinburgh, linking the castle to the Palace of Holyroodhouse. Confined by the city wall, the "Old Town" grew upwards, with some tenements climbing to 20 storeys. It is still possible, among the 66 alleys and closes off the main street, to sense the city's medieval past.

Eagle sign outside Gladstone's Land

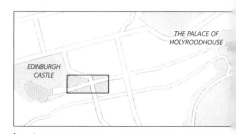

Locator map

Gladstone's Land is a preserved 17th-century merchant's house.

Scotch Whisky Heritage Centre introduces visitors to Scotland's national drink.

The Camera Obscura contains an observatory from which to view the city, plus optical illusions and giant kaleidoscopes.

Edinburgh Castle ←

CASTLE HILL

LAWNMARKET

Lady Stair's House
This 17th-century house is now a museum of the lives and works of Burns, Scott (see p512) and Stevenson.

The "Hub" (c.1840) has the city's highest spire.

🏛 Gladstone's Land
(NTS) 477B Lawnmarket. *Tel 0844 493 2120.* ◯ *Easter–Oct: 10am–5pm daily (Jul & Aug: to 7pm). (Last adm: 30 mins before closing.)* 📷 ♿
This 17th-century merchant's house provides a window on life in a typical Old Town house before overcrowding drove the rich to the Georgian New Town. "Lands", as they were known, were tall, narrow buildings erected on small plots of land. The six-storey Gladstone's Land was named after Thomas Gledstanes, the merchant who built it in 1617. The house still has the original arcade booths on the street front and a painted ceiling with fine Scandinavian floral designs. Though extravagantly furnished, it also contains items which are a reminder of the less salubrious side of the old city, such as wooden over-shoes which had to be worn in the dirty streets. A chest in the beautiful Painted Chamber is said to have been given by a Dutch sea captain to a Scottish merchant who saved him from a shipwreck. A similar house, Morocco Land, can be found on Canongate (see p511).

🏛 Parliament House
Parliament Sq, High St. *Tel 0131 225 2595.* ◯ *9am–5pm Mon–Fri.* ◯ *public hols.* ♿ *limited.*
This majestic, Italianate building was constructed in the 1630s for the Scottish parliament. Parliament House has been home to the Court of Session and the Supreme Court since the Union of Parliaments (see p483) in 1707. It is worth seeing, as much for the spectacle of its gowned and wigged advocates as for the stained-glass window in its Great Hall, commemorating the inauguration of the Court of Session by James V, in 1532.

The bedroom of Gladstone's Land

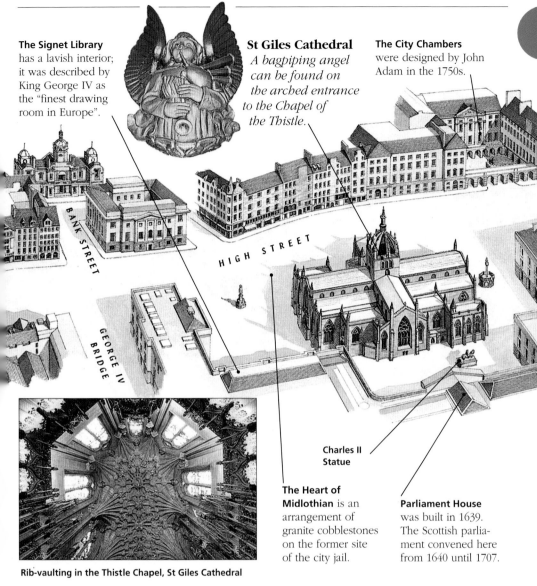

The Signet Library has a lavish interior; it was described by King George IV as the "finest drawing room in Europe".

St Giles Cathedral *A bagpiping angel can be found on the arched entrance to the Chapel of the Thistle.*

The City Chambers were designed by John Adam in the 1750s.

BANK STREET

HIGH STREET

GEORGE IV BRIDGE

Charles II Statue

The Heart of Midlothian is an arrangement of granite cobblestones on the former site of the city jail.

Parliament House was built in 1639. The Scottish parliament convened here from 1640 until 1707.

Rib-vaulting in the Thistle Chapel, St Giles Cathedral

🛈 St Giles Cathedral

Royal Mile. **Tel** *0131 225 9442.* ◯
May–Sep: 9am–7pm Mon–Fri, 9am–5pm Sat, 1–5pm Sun; Oct–Apr: 9am–5pm Mon–Sat, 1–5pm Sun. ◯ *1 Jan, 25 & 26 Dec.* 🈺 *donation appreciated.*
🖰 www.stgilescathedral.org.uk
Properly known as the High Kirk (church) of Edinburgh, it is ironic that St Giles is popularly known as a cathedral. Though it was twice the seat of a bishop in the 17th century, it was from here that John Knox *(see p483)* directed the Scottish Reformation with its emphasis on individual worship freed from the authority of bishops. A tablet marks the place where Jenny Geddes, a stallholder from a local market, scored a victory for the Covenanters *(see p483)* by hurling her stool at a preacher reading from an English prayer book in 1637.

The Gothic exterior is dominated by a 15th-century tower.

Inside, the impressive Thistle Chapel can be seen, with its elaborate rib-vaulted roof and carved heraldic canopies. The chapel honours the knights, past and present, of the Order of the Thistle. The carved royal pew in the Preston Aisle is used by the Queen when she stays in Edinburgh.

EDINBURGH FESTIVAL

Every year, for three weeks in late summer *(see p63)*, Edinburgh hosts one of the world's most important arts festivals, with every available space (from theatres to street corners) overflowing with performers. It has been held in Edinburgh since 1947 and brings together the best in international contemporary theatre, music, dance and opera. The alternative Festival Fringe balances the classic productions with a host of innovative performances. The most popular event is the Edinburgh Military Tattoo, held on the Castle Esplanade – a spectacle of Scottish infantry battalions marching to pipe bands. Also popular is the Edinburgh Book Festival and Edinburgh Film Festival (held in June).

Street performer from the Edinburgh Festival Fringe

Exploring the Royal Mile: High Street to Canongate

The second section of the Royal Mile passes two monuments to the Reformation: John Knox House and the Tron Kirk. The latter is named after a medieval *tron* (weighing beam) that stood nearby. The Canongate was once an independent district, owned by the canons of the Abbey of Holyrood, and sections of its south side have been restored. Beyond Morocco's Land, the road stretches for the final half-mile (800 m) to the Palace of Holyroodhouse.

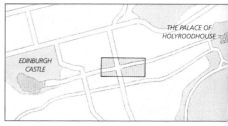

LOCATOR MAP

HIGH STREET

SOUTH BRIDGE STREET

The Mercat Cross marks the city centre. It was here that Bonnie Prince Charlie *(see p535)* was proclaimed king in 1745.

The Tron Kirk was built in 1630 for the Presbyterians who left St Giles Cathedral when it came under the Bishop of Edinburgh's control.

🏛 Museum of Childhood

42 High St. **Tel** *0131 529 4142.*
⬜ *10am–5pm Mon–Sat (& Sun pm during Festival).* ⬛ *25–27 Dec.*
♿ *limited.* **www**.cac.org.uk

This lovely museum is not merely a toy collection but a magical insight into childhood. Founded in 1955 by a city councillor, Patrick Murray (who claimed to enjoy eating children for breakfast), it was the first museum in the world to be devoted to the history and theme of childhood. The collection includes medicines, school books and prams as well as galleries full of old-fashioned toys. With its nickel-odeon, antique slot machines

An 1880 automaton of the Man on the Moon, Museum of Childhood

The entrance to the Palace of Holyroodhouse, seen from the west

and the general enthusiasm of visitors, this has been called the world's noisiest museum.

🏰 Palace of Holyroodhouse

East end of Royal Mile. **Tel** *0131 556 5100.* ⬜ *Apr–Oct: 9:30am–6pm; Nov–Mar: 9:30am–4:30pm daily.* ♿ ♿ *limited.* **www**.royalcollection.org.uk

Now the Queen's official Scottish residence, the Palace of Holyroodhouse is named after the "rood", or cross, which King David I is said to have seen between the antlers of a stag he was hunting here in 1128. The present palace was built in 1529 to accommodate James V *(see p501)* and his French wife, Mary of Guise, though it was remodelled in

the 1670s for Charles II. The Royal Apartments (including the Throne Room and Royal Dining Room) are used for investitures and banquets whenever the Queen visits the palace, though they are otherwise open to the public. A chamber in the James V tower is associated with the unhappy reign of Mary, Queen of Scots. It was here, in 1566, that she saw the murder of her trusted Italian secretary, David Rizzio, by her jealous husband, Lord Darnley. She had married Darnley a year earlier in Holyroodhouse chapel.

Bonnie Prince Charlie held court here in 1745 in the Jacobite *(see p537)* rising.

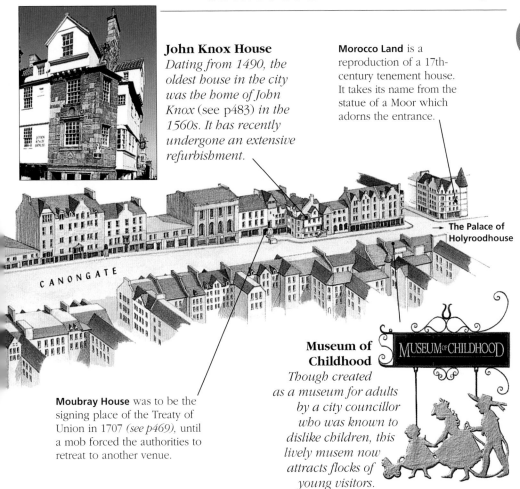

John Knox House
Dating from 1490, the oldest house in the city was the home of John Knox (see p483) in the 1560s. It has recently undergone an extensive refurbishment.

Morocco Land is a reproduction of a 17th-century tenement house. It takes its name from the statue of a Moor which adorns the entrance.

→ **The Palace of Holyroodhouse**

C A N O N G A T E

Moubray House was to be the signing place of the Treaty of Union in 1707 *(see p469)*, until a mob forced the authorities to retreat to another venue.

Museum of Childhood
Though created as a museum for adults by a city councillor who was known to dislike children, this lively musem now attracts flocks of young visitors.

MUSEUM OF CHILDHOOD

🏛 **National Museum of Scotland**

Chambers St. *Tel 0131 247 4219.*
⬜ *10am–5pm daily.* ⬤ *25 Dec.*
🔲 ♿ 🏷 🚻 www.nms.ac.uk
The National Museum first opened its doors in 1866. The Main Hall features a fine collection of Asian sculptures, including one of the Hindu Goddess Parvati, while European Art from 1200 to 1800 is on the first floor. On the second floor are rare scientific instruments, and geological specimens, and Eastern decorative arts are on the top floor. On the ground floor, the new science and technology gallery, Connect, is where Dolly the Sheep can be found.

Parvati, at the National Museum of Scotland

The museum will be partially closed until late summer 2011, while renovations take place.

🐕 **Greyfriars Bobby**
On an old drinking fountain near the gateway to Greyfriars Church stands the statue of a little Skye terrier. This commemorates the dog who, for 14 years, guarded the grave of his master, John Gray, who died in 1858. The people of Edinburgh fed him until his death in 1872. He was also granted citizenship to prevent him being destroyed as a stray.

MARY, QUEEN OF SCOTS (1542–87)
Born only days before the death of her father, James V, the young Queen Mary spent her childhood in France, after escaping Henry VIII's invasion of Scotland *(see p512)*. A devout Catholic, she married the French Dauphin, and made claims on the English throne. This alarmed Protestants throughout England and Scotland, and when she returned as a widow to Holyroodhouse, aged 18, she was harangued for her faith by John Knox *(see p483)*. In 1567 she was accused of murdering her second husband, Lord Darnley. Two months later, when she married the Earl of Bothwell (also implicated in the murder), rebellion ensued. She lost her crown and fled to England where she was held prisoner for 20 years, before being charged with treason and beheaded at Fotheringhay.

The ruins of Melrose Abbey, viewed from the southwest

Melrose Abbey ⓳

Abbey Street, Melrose, Scottish
Borders. **Tel** *01896 822562.* ◯
*9:30am–4:30pm daily (Apr–Sep: to
5:30pm). (Last adm: 30 mins before
closing.)* ● *1, 2 Jan, 25, 26 Dec.* 🈂
🚫 *ltd.* **www**.historic-scotland.gov.uk

The rose-pink ruins of this
beautiful Border abbey *(see
p503)* bear testimony to the
hazards of standing in the path
of successive English invasions.
Built by David I in 1136 for
Cistercian monks from Yorkshire, and also to replace a
7th-century monastery, Melrose
was repeatedly ransacked by
English armies, notably in
1322 and 1385. The final blow,
from which none of the
abbeys recovered, came in
1545 during Henry VIII's
destructive Scottish policy
known as the "Rough Woo-
ing". This resulted from the
failure of the Scots to ratify
a marriage treaty between
Henry VIII's son and the
infant Mary, Queen of Scots
(see p511). What remains of
the abbey are the outlines
of cloisters, the kitchen and
other monastic buildings and
the shell of the abbey church
with its soaring east window
and profusion of medieval
carvings. The rich decorations
of the south exterior wall
include a gargoyle shaped like
a pig playing the bagpipes.

An embalmed heart, found
here in 1920, is probably that
of Robert the Bruce *(see
p482),* who had decreed that

his heart be taken on a crusade to the Holy Land. It was
returned to Melrose after its
bearer, Sir James Douglas *(see
p515),* was killed in Spain.

Abbotsford House ⓴

Galashiels, Scottish Borders. **Tel**
01896 752043. 🚌 *from Galashiels.*
◯ *late Mar–late Oct: 9:30am–5pm
Mon–Sat, 11am–4pm Sun (except
Jun–Sep).* 🈂 🚫 *limited.* 🚫
www.scottsabbotsford.co.uk

Few houses bear the stamp
of their creator so intimately as
Abbotsford House, the home
of Sir Walter Scott for the last
20 years of his life. He bought
a farm here in 1811, known
as Clarteyhole ("dirty hole"
in Scots), though he soon
renamed it Abbotsford, after
the monks of Melrose Abbey
who used to cross the River
Tweed nearby. He later
demolished the house to
make way for the turreted
building we see today, funded
by the sales of his novels.

Scott's library contains more
than 9,000 rare books and his
collections of historic relics
reflect his passion for the
heroic past. An extensive
collection of arms and armour
includes Rob Roy's broad-
sword *(see p495).* Stuart
mementoes include a crucifix
that belonged to Mary, Queen
of Scots and a lock of Bonnie
Prince Charlie's *(see p535)*
hair. The small study in which
he wrote his *Waverley* novels
can be visited as can the
room, overlooking the river,
in which he died in 1832.

SIR WALTER SCOTT

Sir Walter Scott (1771–1832)
was born in Edinburgh and
trained as a lawyer. He is best
remembered as a major champion and literary figure of
Scotland, whose poems and
novels (most famously his
Waverley series) created
enduring images of a heroic
wilderness filled with the
romance of the clans. His
orchestration, in 1822, of the
state visit of George IV to
Edinburgh *(see p485)* was an
extravaganza of Highland culture that helped re-establish
tartan as the national dress of Scotland. He served as Clerk of
the Court in Edinburgh's Parliament House *(see p508)* and for
30 years was Sheriff of Selkirk in the Scottish Borders, which
he loved. He put the Trossachs *(see pp494–5)* firmly on the
map with the publication of the *Lady of the Lake* (1810). His
final years were spent writing to pay off a £114,000 debt following the failure of his publisher in 1827. He died with his
debts paid, and was buried at Dryburgh Abbey *(see p503).*

**The Great Hall at Abbotsford,
adorned with arms and armour**

Traquair House ㉑

Peebles, Scottish Borders. *Tel 01896 830 323.* from Peebles. Easter–May & Sep: noon–5:30pm; Jun–Aug: 10:30am–5pm; Oct: 11am–4pm; daily; Nov: noon–4pm Sat & Sun. limited. **www**.traquair.co.uk

As Scotland's oldest continuously inhabited house, Traquair has deep roots in Scottish religious and political history, stretching back over 900 years. Evolving from a fortified tower to a stout-walled 17th-century mansion *(see p487)*, the house was a Catholic Stuart stronghold for 500 years. Mary, Queen of Scots *(see p511)* was among the many monarchs to have stayed here and her bed is covered by a counterpane which she made. Family letters and engraved Jacobite *(see p537)* drinking glasses are among relics recalling the period of the Highland rebellions.

Mary, Queen of Scots' crucifix, Traquair House

After a vow made by the 5th Earl, Traquair's Bear Gates (the "Steekit Yetts"), which closed after Bonnie Prince Charlie's *(see p535)* visit in 1745, will not reopen until a Stuart reascends the throne.

A secret stairway leads to the Priest's Room which attests to the problems faced by Catholic families until Catholicism was legalized in 1829. Traquair House Ale is still produced in the 18th-century brewhouse.

Biggar ㉒

Clyde Valley. 2,000. High St (01899 221066).

This typical Lowland market town has a number of museums worth visiting. The **Gladstone Court Museum** boasts a reconstructed Victorian street complete with a milliner's, printer's and a village library, while the grimy days of the town's industrial past are recalled at the **Gasworks Museum**, with its collection of engines, gaslights and appliances. Established in 1839 and preserved in the 1970s, the Biggar Gasworks is the only remaining rural gasworks in Scotland.

Gladstone Court Museum
Northback Rd. *Tel 01899 221050.* Apr–Oct: 11am–4:30pm Mon–Sat, 2–4:30pm Sun.
Gasworks Museum
Gasworks Rd. *Tel 01899 221070.* Jun–Sep: 2–4:30pm daily.

Pentland Hills ㉓

The Lothians. Edinburgh, then bus. *Regional Park Headquarters, Biggar Rd, Edinburgh (0131 4453383).*

The Pentland Hills, stretching for 16 miles (26 km) southwest of Edinburgh, offer some of the best hill-walking country in the Lowlands. Leisurely walkers can saunter along the many signposted footpaths, while the more adventurous can take the chairlift at the Hillend dry ski slope to reach the higher ground leading to the 493 m (1,617 ft) hill of Allermuir. Even more ambitious is the classic scenic route along the ridge from Caerketton to West Kip.

To the east of the A703, in the lee of the Pentlands, stands the exquisite and ornate 15th-century **Rosslyn Chapel**. It was originally intended as a church, but after the death of its founder, William Sinclair, it was also used as a burial ground for his descendants. The delicately wreathed Apprentice Pillar recalls the legend of the apprentice carver who was killed by the master stonemason in a fit of jealousy at his pupil's superior skill.

Rosslyn Chapel
Roslin. *Tel 0131 4402159.* daily (Sun: pm only).

Details of the decorated vaulting in Rosslyn Chapel

The Classical 18th-century tenements of New Lanark on the banks of the Clyde

New Lanark ㉔

Clyde Valley. 185. Lanark.
Horsemarket, Ladyacre Rd
(01555 661661). Mon (Apr only).
www.newlanark.org

Situated by the falls of the
River Clyde, the village of
New Lanark was founded in
1785 by the industrial entre-
preneur David Dale. Ideally

DAVID LIVINGSTONE

Scotland's great missionary
doctor and explorer was
born in Blantyre where he
began working life as a
mill boy at the age of ten.
Livingstone (1813–73)
made three epic journeys
across Africa, from 1840,
promoting "commerce and
Christianity". He became
the first European to see
Victoria Falls and died in
1873 while searching for
the source of the Nile. He
is buried in Westminster
Abbey *(see pp92–3)*.

located for the working of its
water-driven mills, the village
had become Britain's largest
cotton producer by 1800.
Dale and his successor, Robert
Owen, were philanthropists
whose reforms proved that
commercial success need not
undermine the wellbeing of
the workforce. Now a museum,
New Lanark is a window on to
working life in the early 19th
century. The **New Millennium
Experience** provides a special-
effects ride through time, from
the life of a mill girl in 1820 to
the 23rd century.

Environs: 15 miles (24 km)
north, Blantyre has a memorial to the famous Scottish
explorer David Livingstone.

🏛 **New Millennium
Experience**
New Lanark Visitor Centre. *Tel* 01555
661345. 11am–5pm daily.
groups only, by appt – book ahead.

Glasgow ㉕

See pp516–21.

Sanquhar ㉖

Dumfries & Galloway. 2,500.
64 Whitesands, Dumfries
(01387 253862).

Now of chiefly historic
interest, the town of
Sanquhar was famous in the
history of the Covenanters

(see p483). In the 1680s, two
declarations opposing the rule
of bishops were pinned to the
Mercat Cross, the site of which
is now marked by a granite
obelisk. The first protest was
led by a local teacher, Richard
Cameron, whose followers
became the Cameronian regiment. The Georgian **Tolbooth**
was designed by William
Adam *(see p548)* in 1735 and
houses a local interest museum
and tourist centre. The Post
Office, opened in 1763, is the
oldest in Britain, predating
the mail coach service.

Drumlanrig Castle ㉗

Thornhill, Dumfries & Galloway.
Tel 01848 331555. Dumfries,
then bus. **Grounds** Apr–Oct:
11am–5pm daily. **Castle** Easter–
Aug: 11am–5pm daily.
www.buccleuch.com

Rising squarely from a
grassy platform, the
massive fortress-palace of
Drumlanrig *(see p487)* was
built from pink sandstone

**The Baroque front steps and
doorway of Drumlanrig Castle**

between 1679 and 1691 on the site of a 15th-century Douglas stronghold. A formidable multi-turreted exterior contains a priceless collection of art treasures such as paintings by Holbein and Rembrandt, as well as such Jacobite relics as Bonnie Prince Charlie's camp kettle and sash. The emblem of a crowned and winged heart, shown throughout the castle, recalls Sir James, the "Black Douglas", who bore Robert the Bruce's (see p482) heart while on crusade. After being mortally wounded he threw the heart at his enemies with the words "forward brave heart!"

The sturdy island fortress of Threave Castle on the Dee

Threave Castle ㉘

Castle Douglas, Dumfries & Galloway. *Tel* 07711 223101. 🚆 *Dumfries.* ◯ *mid-Mar–Sep: 9:30am–5:30pm daily; Oct: 9:30am–4:30pm. (Last boat leaves island 6pm.)* 🏷 **www**.historic-scotland.gov.uk

This menacing giant of a tower, a 14th-century Black Douglas (see above) stronghold standing on an island in the Dee, commands the most complete medieval riverside harbour in Scotland. Douglas's struggles against the early Stewart kings culminated in his surrender here after a two-month siege in 1455 – but only after James II had brought the cannon Mons Meg (see p506) to batter the castle. Threave was dismantled after Protestant Covenanters (see p483) defeated its Catholic defenders in

1640. Inside the tower, only the shell of the kitchen, great hall and domestic levels remains. Over the 15th-century doorway is the "gallows knob", a reminder of when the owners are said to have boasted that it never lacked its noose. Access to the castle is by small boat.

Whithorn ㉙

Dumfries & Galloway. 👥 *1,000.* 🚆 *Stranraer.* 🚌 ℹ *Dashwood Sq, Newton Stewart (01671 402431).* **www.**visitdumfriesandgalloway.co.uk

The earliest site of continuous Christian worship in Scotland, Whithorn (meaning white house) takes its name from the white chapel built here by St Ninian in 397. Though nothing remains of his chapel, a guided tour of the archaeological dig reveals evidence of Northumbrian, Viking and Scottish settlements ranging from the 5th to the 19th centuries. A visitors' centre, **The Whithorn Story**, provides information on the excavations and contains a collection of carved stones. One, dedicated to Latinus, dates to 450, making it Scotland's earliest Christian monument.

🏛 The Whithorn Story
The Whithorn Trust, 45–47 George St. *Tel* 01988 500508. ◯ *Apr–Oct: 10:30am–5pm daily.* 🏷 **www**.whithorn.com

Culzean Castle ㉚

See pp522–3.

Robert Burns surrounded by his creations, by an unknown artist

Burns Cottage ㉛

Burns National Heritage Park, Alloway, South Ayrshire. *Tel* 01292 443700. 🚆 *Ayr, then bus.* ◯ *Oct–Mar: 10am–5pm; Apr–Sep: 10am–5:30pm; daily.* ⬤ *25 & 26 Dec, 1 & 2 Jan.* 🏷 **www**.burnsheritagepark.com

Robert Burns (1759–96), Scotland's favourite poet, was born and spent his first seven years in this small thatched cottage in Alloway. Built by his father, the restored cottage still contains much of its original furniture. There is also a small museum next door displaying many of Burns's manuscripts along with early editions of his works. Much of his poem *Tam o' Shanter* (1790) is set in Alloway, which commemorates him with a huge monument on the outskirts of the village.

Burns became a celebrity following the publication in 1786 of the Kilmarnock Edition of his poems. Scots everywhere gather to celebrate Burns Night (see p65) on his birthday, 25 January.

SCOTTISH TEXTILES

Weaving in the Scottish Borders goes back to the Middle Ages, when monks from Flanders established a thriving woollen trade with the Continent. Cotton became an important source of wealth in the Clyde Valley during the 19th century, when handloom weaving was overtaken by power-driven mills. The popular Paisley patterns were based on Indian designs.

A colourful pattern from Paisley

Glasgow 25

St Mungo with the Glasgow symbols

Though its Celtic name, *Glas cu*, means "dear green place", Glasgow is more often associated with its industrial past, and once enjoyed the title of Second City of the Empire (after London). Glasgow's architectural standing, as Scotland's finest Victorian city, reflects its era of prosperity, when ironworks, cotton mills and shipbuilding were fuelled by Lanarkshire coal. The Science Centre sits on the Clyde's revitalized south bank, and Glasgow rivals Edinburgh *(see pp504–11)* in the arts, with galleries such as the Kelvingrove and the Burrell Collection *(see pp520–21)*.

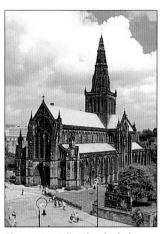

Glasgow's medieval cathedral viewed from the southwest

Exploring Glasgow

With some relics of its grimy industrial past and glossy new image, modern Glasgow is a city of contrasts. The deprived East End, with its busy weekend market, "the Barras", stands by the restored 18th-century Merchant City and Victorian George Square. The more affluent West End prospered in the 19th century as a retreat for wealthy merchants escaping the industrialized Clydeside, and it is here that restaurants, bars, parks and Glasgow University can be found. South Side, next to affluent Pollokshields, is Pollok Country Park, site of the Burrell Collection. An underground network and good bus and rail links provide easy travel around the city.

🛈 Glasgow Cathedral

2 Castle St. *Tel* 0141 5528198. ○ Apr–Sep: 9:30am–5:30pm Mon–Sat, 1–5:30pm Sun; Oct–Mar: 9:30am–4pm Mon–Sat, 1–4pm Sun. &

As one of the only cathedrals to escape destruction during the Scottish Reformation *(see pp482–3)* – by adapting itself to Protestant worship – this is a rare example of an almost complete 13th-century church. It was built on the site of a chapel founded by the city's patron saint, St Mungo, a 6th-century bishop of Strathclyde. According to legend, Mungo placed the body of a holy man named Fergus on a cart yoked to two wild bulls, telling them to take it to the place ordained by God. In the "dear green place" at which the bulls stopped he built his church. The cathedral is on two levels.

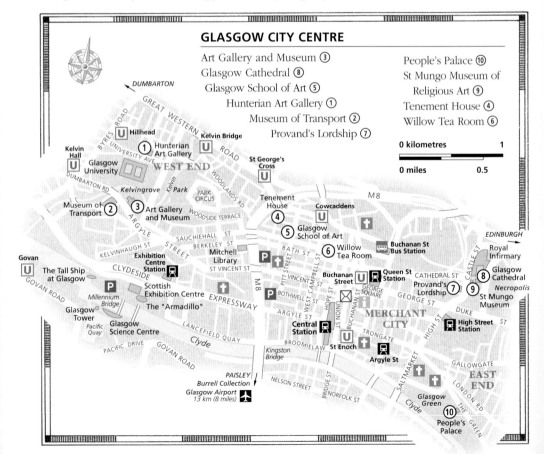

GLASGOW CITY CENTRE

Art Gallery and Museum ③
Glasgow Cathedral ⑧
Glasgow School of Art ⑤
Hunterian Art Gallery ①
Museum of Transport ②
Provand's Lordship ⑦

People's Palace ⑩
St Mungo Museum of Religious Art ⑨
Tenement House ④
Willow Tea Room ⑥

0 kilometres 1
0 miles 0.5

Dalí's *Christ of St John of the Cross* at the Kelvingrove Art Gallery *(see p519)*

Situated in the cathedral precinct, this museum is a world first. The main exhibition illustrates religious themes with superb artifacts, including a 19th-century dancing Shiva and an Islamic painting entitled the *Attributes of Divine Perfection* (1986) by Ahmed Moustafa. Other religious paintings on display include *Crucifixion VII* (1988) by Scottish artist Craigie Aitchison. An exhibition on religion in Glasgow throws light on the life of the missionary David Livingstone *(see p514)*. Outside you can visit Britain's only permanent Zen Buddhist garden.

The crypt contains the tomb of St Mungo, surrounded by an intricate forest of columns springing up to end in delicately carved rib-vaulting. The Blackadder Aisle, reputed to have been built over a cemetery blessed by St Ninian *(see p515)*, has a ceiling thick with decorative bosses.

🏛 St Mungo Museum of Religious Life and Art

2 Castle St. *Tel 0141 2761625.* ⬤ *10am–5pm daily (from 11am Fri & Sun).* ♿ 📷 *by appointment.* 🖥 🎫

VISITORS' CHECKLIST

City of Glasgow. 🏛 *580,000.*
✈ ⇄ *Argyle St (Glasgow Central).* 🚌 *Buchanan St.*
ℹ *11 George Square (0141 2044400).* 🎭 *Sat, Sun.*
www.seeglasgow.com

The preserved Edwardian kitchen of the Tenement House

🚉 Tenement House

(NTS) *145 Buccleuch St.* **Tel** *0141 3330183.* ⬤ *Mar–Oct: 1–5pm daily.* 📷 🎫 *by appt.* **www**.nts.org.uk

Less a museum than a time capsule, the Tenement House is an almost undisturbed record of life in a modest Glasgow flat in a tenement estate during the early 20th century. Glasgow owed much of its vitality and neighbourliness to tenement life, though many of these Victorian and Edwardian apartments were to earn a bad name for poverty and overcrowding, and many have now been pulled down. The Tenement House was first owned by Miss Agnes Toward who lived here from 1911 until 1965. It remained largely unaltered and, since Agnes threw very little away, it is now a treasure trove of social history. The parlour, previously used only on formal occasions, has afternoon tea laid out on a white lace cloth. The kitchen, with its coal-fired range and box bed, is filled with the tools of a vanished era such as a goffering iron for crisping waffles, a washboard and a stone hot-water bottle.

Agnes's lavender water and medicines are still in the bathroom, as though she had stepped out for a minute 70 years ago, and forgotten to return home.

The Kelvingrove Art Gallery and the Glasgow University buildings, viewed from the south

Glasgow's medieval house, Provand's Lordship

🏛 Museum of Transport
1 Bunhouse Rd. **Tel** *0141 2872720.*
⬤ *10am–5pm Mon–Thu, Sat;*
11am–5pm Fri, Sun. ♿ 🅿 📷
www.glasgowmuseums.com

Model ships and ranks of gleaming Scottish-built steam engines, cars and motorcycles recall the 19th and early 20th centuries, when Glasgow's supremacy in shipbuilding, trade and manufacturing made her the "second city" of the British Empire. Old Glasgow can be seen through fascinating footage of the town in the cinema and through a reconstruction of a 1938 street, with Art Deco shop fronts, a cinema and an Underground station. The museum will close in 2010 and reopen at a new location, on the banks of the Clyde, at Pointhouse Quay in Yorkhill, in spring 2011.

🏠 Provand's Lordship
3 Castle St. **Tel** *0141 5528819.* ⬤
10am–5pm daily (from 11am Fri & Sun). **www**.glasgowmuseums.com

Now a museum, Provand's Lordship was built as a canon's house in 1471, and is the city's oldest surviving house. Its low ceilings and austere wooden furnishings create a vivid impression of life in a wealthy 15th-century household. It is thought that Mary, Queen of Scots *(see p511)* may have stayed here in 1566 when she made a visit to see her cousin and husband, Lord Darnley.

🏠 Willow Tea Room
217 Sauchiehall St (also 97 Buchanan St). **Tel** *0141 332 0521.* ⬤ *9am–5pm Mon–Sat, 11am–4:15pm Sun.*
📷 **www**.willow tearooms.co.uk

This is the sole survivor of a series of delightful tea rooms created by Charles Rennie Mackintosh in 1904 for the celebrated restaurateur Miss Kate Cranston. Everything from the high-backed chairs to the tables and cutlery was his design. In particular, the 1904 Room de Luxe sparkles with silver furniture and flamboyant leaded glass work. The No. 97 Buchanan Street branch opened in 1997, and recreates Cranston's original Ingram Street Tea Rooms.

Mackintosh's interior of the Willow Tea Room

The Museum of Transport's reconstructed 1938 street, with Underground station

🏛 Glasgow Necropolis
Cathedral Sq. **Tel** *0141 2873961.*
⬤ *daily.* 🅿 ♿ *limited.*

Behind the cathedral, the reformer John Knox *(see p483)* surveys the city from his Doric pillar overlooking a Victorian cemetery. It is filled with crumbling monuments to the dead of Glasgow's wealthy merchant families.

CHARLES RENNIE MACKINTOSH

A Mackintosh floral design

Glasgow's most celebrated designer, Charles Rennie Mackintosh (1868–1928), entered Glasgow School of Art at 16. After his first big break with the Willow Tea Room, he became a leading figure in the Art Nouveau movement, developing a unique style that borrowed from Gothic and Scottish Baronial designs. He believed a building should be a fully integrated work of art, creating furniture and fittings that complemented the overall construction. Nowhere is this total design better seen than in the Glasgow School of Art, which he designed in 1896.

Unrecognized in his lifetime, Mackintosh's work is now widely imitated. Its characteristic straight lines and flowing detail are the hallmark of early 20th-century Glasgow style, in all fields of design from textiles to architecture.

People's Palace

Glasgow Green. **Tel** 0141 2760788.
◯ 10am–5pm Mon–Thu & Sat,
11am–5pm Fri & Sun. ⬤ 1 & 2 Jan,
25 & 26 Dec. ♿ ▢ ⬛
www.glasgowmuseums.com

This Victorian sandstone structure was built in 1898 as a cultural museum for the people of Glasgow's East End. It houses everything from temperance tracts to trade-union banners, suffragette posters to comedian Billy Connolly's banana-shaped boots, providing a social history of the city from the 12th century. A conservatory at the back contains an exotic winter garden.

⛫ Glasgow School of Art

167 Renfrew St. **Tel** 0141 3534500.
◯ by appointment only. ▨
◪ ♿ limited. **www**.gsa.ac.uk

Widely considered to be Charles Rennie Mackintosh's greatest architectural work, the Glasgow School of Art was built between 1897 and 1909 to a design he submitted in a competition. It was built in two periods due to financial constraints. The later, western wing displays a softer design than the more severe eastern half, built only a few years earlier and compared by a contemporary critic to a prison.

A student guide takes you through the building to the Furniture Gallery, Board Room and the Library, the latter a masterpiece of spatial composition. Each room is an exercise in contrasts between height, light and shade with innovative details echoing the architectural themes of the structure. How much of the school can be viewed depends on curricular requirements at the time of visiting.

⛫ Hunterian Art Gallery

82 Hillhead St. **Tel** 0141 3305431.
◯ 9:30am–5pm Mon–Sat. ⬤ 24
Dec–5 Jan & public hols. ⬛ ♿
limited. **www**.hunterian.gla.ac.uk

Built to house a number of paintings bequeathed to Glasgow University by ex-student and physician Dr William Hunter (1718–83), the Hunterian Art Gallery contains Scotland's largest print collection and works by major European artists stretching back to the 16th century. A

George Henry's Japanese Lady with a Fan (1894), Art Gallery and Museum

collection of work by Charles Mackintosh is supplemented by a complete reconstruction of No. 6 Florentine Terrace, where he lived from 1906 to 1914. A major collection of 19th- and 20th-century Scottish art includes work by William McTaggart (1835–1910), but the gallery's most famous collection is of work by the painter James McNeill Whistler (1834–1903).

Whistler's Sketch for Annabel Lee (c.1869), Hunterian Art Gallery

⛫ Kelvingrove Art Gallery and Museum

Argyle St, Kelvingrove. **Tel** 0141 276
9599. ◯ 10am–5pm Mon–Thu & Sat
(to 8pm Thu), 11am–5pm Fri & Sun.
⬤ 1 & 2 Jan, 25 & 26 Dec.
www.glasgowmuseums.com

The imposing red sandstone building that is Kelvingrove is a striking Glasgow landmark – even though it was supposedly built the wrong way round – and the gallery and museum is the most visited in Scotland. Having undergone a major (£27.9 million) refurbishment, the gallery and museum house an impressive array of art and artifacts. The outstanding collection has paintings of inestimable value, including works by Botticelli, Giorgione (*The Adulteress Brought Before Christ*), Rembrandt and Dalí (*Christ of St John of the Cross, see p517*). Its impressive representation of 17th-century Dutch and 19th-century French art is augmented by the home-grown talent of the Glasgow Boys and the Scottish Colourists.

The Georgian Pollok House, viewed from the south

Pollok House

(NTS) 2060 Pollokshaws Rd. *Tel* (0141) 616 6410. ◯ 10am–5pm daily. ● 1 & 2 Jan, 25 & 26 Dec. Apr–Oct only. **www**.nts.org.uk

Pollok House is Glasgow's finest 18th-century domestic building and contains one of Britain's best collections of Spanish paintings. The Neo-Classical central block was finished in 1750, the sobriety of its exterior contrasting with the exuberant plasterwork within. The Maxwells have lived at Pollok since the mid-13th century, but the male line ended with Sir John Maxwell, who added the grand entrance hall in the 1890s and designed most of the terraced gardens and parkland beyond.

Hanging above the family silver, porcelain, hand-painted Chinese wallpaper and Jacobean glass, the Stirling Maxwell collection is strong on British and Dutch schools, including William Blake's *Sir Geoffrey Chaucer and the Nine and Twenty Pilgrims* (1745) and William Hogarth's portrait of James Thomson, who wrote the words to *Rule Britannia*.

Spanish 16th- to 19th-century art predominates: El Greco's *Lady in a Fur Wrap* (1541) hangs in the library, while the drawing room contains works by Francisco de Goya and Esteban Murillo. In 1966 Anne Maxwell Macdonald gave the house and 146 ha (361 acres) of parkland to the City of Glasgow. The park provides the site for the city's fascinating Burrell Collection.

Glasgow: The Burrell Collection

Given to the city in 1944 by Sir William Burrell (1861–1958), a wealthy shipping owner, this internationally acclaimed collection is the jewel in Glasgow's crown, with objects of major importance in numerous fields of interest. The building was purpose-built in 1983. In the sun, the stained glass blazes with colour, while the shaded tapestries seem a part of the surrounding woodland.

Hutton Castle Drawing Room
This is a reconstruction of the Drawing Room at Burrell's own home – the 16th-century Hutton Castle, near Berwick-upon-Tweed. The Hall and Dining Room can also be seen nearby.

Bull's Head
Dating from the 7th century BC, this bronze head from Turkey was once part of a cauldron handle.

Figure of a Lohan
This sculpture of Buddha's disciple dates from the Ming Dynasty (1484).

Hornby Portal
This detail shows the arch's heraldic display. The 14th-century portal comes from Hornby Castle in Yorkshire.

Main entrance

STAR EXHIBITS

★ Stained Glass

★ Tapestries

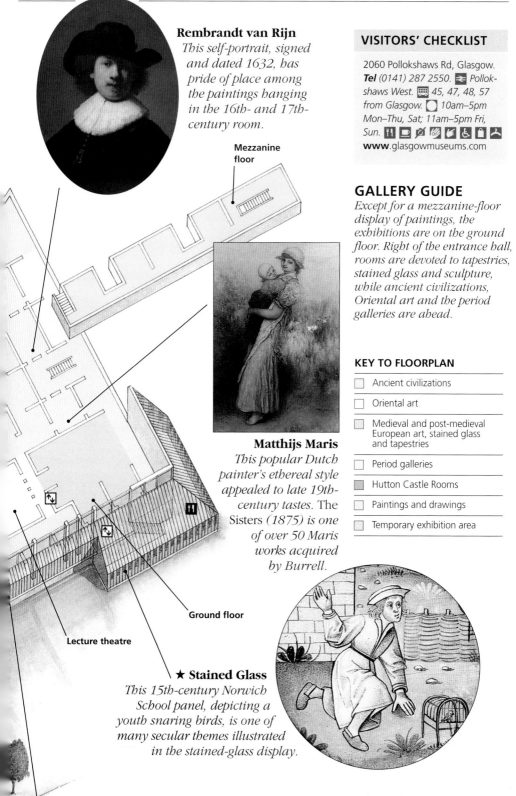

Rembrandt van Rijn
This self-portrait, signed and dated 1632, has pride of place among the paintings hanging in the 16th- and 17th-century room.

Mezzanine floor

Matthijs Maris
This popular Dutch painter's ethereal style appealed to late 19th-century tastes. The Sisters (1875) is one of over 50 Maris works acquired by Burrell.

Ground floor

Lecture theatre

★ Stained Glass
This 15th-century Norwich School panel, depicting a youth snaring birds, is one of many secular themes illustrated in the stained-glass display.

★ Tapestries
Scenes from the Life of the Virgin (c.1450), a Swiss work in wool and linen, is one of many tapestries on show.

VISITORS' CHECKLIST

2060 Pollokshaws Rd, Glasgow. *Tel* (0141) 287 2550. ⚊ Pollokshaws West. 🚌 45, 47, 48, 57 from Glasgow. ◯ 10am–5pm Mon–Thu, Sat; 11am–5pm Fri, Sun. 🍴 🛈 ♿ ⌖ 🖼 🎁 ♿ 🔒 🏛 ⬛
www.glasgowmuseums.com

GALLERY GUIDE
Except for a mezzanine-floor display of paintings, the exhibitions are on the ground floor. Right of the entrance hall, rooms are devoted to tapestries, stained glass and sculpture, while ancient civilizations, Oriental art and the period galleries are ahead.

KEY TO FLOORPLAN

☐	Ancient civilizations
☐	Oriental art
☐	Medieval and post-medieval European art, stained glass and tapestries
☐	Period galleries
▦	Hutton Castle Rooms
☐	Paintings and drawings
☐	Temporary exhibition area

Culzean Castle ⑳

Robert Adam by George Willison

Standing on a cliff's edge in an extensive parkland estate, the 16th-century keep of Culzean (pronounced Cullayn), home of the Earls of Cassillis, was remodelled between 1777 and 1792 by the Neo-Classical architect Robert Adam (see p28). Restored in the 1970s, it is now a major showcase of his later work. The grounds became Scotland's first public country park in 1969 and, with farming flourishing alongside ornamental gardens, they reflect both the leisure and everyday activities of a great country estate.

View of Culzean Castle (c.1815), by Nasmyth

Lord Cassillis' Rooms contain typical mid-18th-century furnishings, including a gentleman's wardrobe of the 1740s.

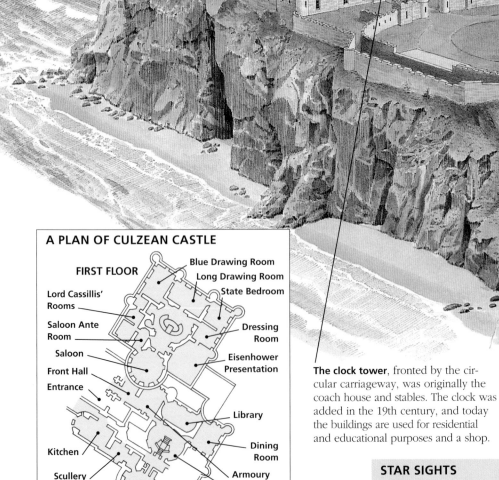

The clock tower, fronted by the circular carriageway, was originally the coach house and stables. The clock was added in the 19th century, and today the buildings are used for residential and educational purposes and a shop.

A PLAN OF CULZEAN CASTLE

FIRST FLOOR

- Blue Drawing Room
- Long Drawing Room
- State Bedroom
- Lord Cassillis' Rooms
- Saloon Ante Room
- Saloon
- Front Hall
- Entrance
- Dressing Room
- Eisenhower Presentation
- Kitchen
- Scullery
- Ailsa Exhibition
- Library
- Dining Room
- Armoury
- Oval Staircase

GROUND FLOOR

STAR SIGHTS

★ Saloon

★ Oval Staircase

Armoury
Displayed on the walls is the world's most important collection of flintlock pistols, used by the British Army and Militia between the 1730s and 1830s.

Fountain Court
This sunken garden is a good place to begin a tour of the grounds to the east.

The Eisenhower Presentation honours the general who was given the top floor of Culzean in gratitude for his role in World War II.

Carriageway

★ Saloon
With its restored 18th-century colour scheme and Louis XVI chairs, this elegant saloon perches on the cliff's edge 46 m (150 ft) above the Firth of Clyde. The carpet is a copy of the one designed by Adam.

★ Oval Staircase
Illuminated by an overarching skylight, the staircase, with its Ionic and Corinthian pillars, is considered one of Adam's finest achievements.

THE HIGHLANDS AND ISLANDS

ABERDEENSHIRE · MORAY · ARGYLL & BUTE · PERTH & KINROSS
SHETLAND · ORKNEY · WESTERN ISLES · HIGHLANDS · ANGUS

Most of the stock images of Scottishness – clans and tartans, whisky and porridge, bagpipes and heather – originate in the Highlands and enrich the popular picture of Scotland as a whole. But for many centuries the Gaelic-speaking, cattle-raising Highlanders had little in common with their southern neighbours.

Clues to the non-Celtic ancestors of the Highlanders lie scattered across the Highlands and Islands in the form of stone circles, brochs and cairns some over 5,000 years old. By the end of the 6th century, the Gaelic-speaking Celts had arrived from Ireland, along with St Columba who taught Christianity. Its fusion with Viking culture in the 8th and 9th centuries produced St Magnus Cathedral in the Orkney Isles.

For over 1,000 years, Celtic Highland society was founded on a clan system, built on family ties to create loyal groups dependent on a feudal chief.

However, the clans were systematically broken up by England after 1746, following the defeat of the Jacobite attempt on the British crown, led by Bonnie Prince Charlie *(see p521)*. A more romantic vision of the Highlands started in the early 19th century. Its creation was largely due to Sir Walter Scott, whose novels and poetry depicted the majesty and grandeur of a country previously considered merely poverty-stricken and barbaric. Another great popularizer was Queen Victoria, whose passion for Balmoral helped to establish the trend for acquiring Highland sporting estates. But behind the sentimentality lay harsh economic realities that drove generations of Highlanders to seek a new life overseas.

Today, over half the inhabitants of the Highlands and Islands still live in communities of less than 1,000. Oil and tourism have supplemented fishing and whisky as the main businesses and population figures are rising.

A wintry dawn over the Cairngorms, the home of Britain's only herd of reindeer

◁ The stunningly sited castle of Eilean Donan, Loch Duich in Glen Shiel

Exploring the Highlands and Islands

To the north and west of Stirling (the historic gateway to the Highlands) lie the magnificent mountains and glens, fretted coastlines and lonely isles that are the epitome of Scottish scenery. Inverness, the Highland capital, makes a good starting point for exploring Loch Ness and the Cairngorms, while Fort William holds the key to Ben Nevis. Inland from Aberdeen lie Royal Deeside and the Spey Valley whisky heartland. The romantic Hebrides can be reached by ferry from Oban or Ullapool.

0 kilometres 25

0 miles 25

Cape Wrath

Butt of Lewis · Port of Ness

Kinlochbervie

Barvas · North Tolsta

Standing Stones of Callanish · Portnaguran

Quinag 808m

Stornoway

Lechinver

Ledmo

Isle of Lewis

Hushinish · Lemreway

The Minch

Summer Isles

U

Tarbert

Inverewe Garden

A832

An 107

WESTER ISLES

Harris

Leverburgh

Newtonferry

4

Poolewe

S

4

North Uist

Lochmaddy

Uig · Staffin

WESTER ROSS

7

Torridon

A87

A890

Gramsdale

ISLAND OF SKYE

5

Portree

Lochcarron

Benbecula

Dunvegan

Kyle of Lochalsh

WESTERN ISLES

South Uist

Carbost

Sea of the Hebrides

Broadford

Cuillins

Morvich

A87

6 FIVE SISTE

The Saddle 1020m

Lochboisdale

Elgol

Ardvasar

Barra · Castlebay

Rhum

Mallaig

ROAD TO THE ISLES TOUR 2

A830

Mingulay

Eigg

Muck

Glenfinnan

Fort William

Inner Hebrides

Coll

Aringaur · Tobermory

GLENCOE

Tiree

Scarinish

Lochaline

A828

Staffa

27

Craignure

Torosay Castle

26 OBAN

Iona

ISLAND OF MULL

LOCH AWE 2

Fionnphort

INVERARAY CASTLE

AUCHINDRAIN MUSEUM 30

Colonsay

32

A816 31 CR GA

Lochgilp

Loch Fyn

JURA

Paps of Jura

Port Askaig · Craighouse

Tarbert

Port Charlotte

ISLAY

Gigha

A83

Loch

33

34

Port Ellen

Tayinloan

Carradale

KINTYRE

Isle o Arra

Campbeltown

Mull of Kintyre

Highland cattle grazing on the Isle of Skye

GETTING AROUND

There are no motorways in the region, though travel by car is made easy by a good system of A roads. Single-track roads predominate on the isles, which are served by a ferry network and a toll-free bridge to Skye. The rail link ends to the west at Kyle of Lochalsh and to the north at Wick and Thurso. There are regular flights from London to Inverness, Aberdeen and Wick.

JOHN
O'GROATS **3**

Thurso

Strathy

ess

Strathy

ope
m

A9

Wick

A882

Achavanich

Forsinard

A99

Latheron

Morven
705m

breck
961m

Kildonan

Helmsdale

Lairg

A9

Brora

Dunrobin Castle

Bonar
Bridge

8 DORNOCH

NORTH
SEA

Tain

Balintore

Cromarty

BLACK ISLE

A98

16 ELGIN

Lossiemouth

A95

A941

Keith

A96

Huntly

Rhynie

Newburgh

9

A9

10

14 FORT GEORGE

15 CAWDOR CASTLE

PHEFFER

RNESS **12**

A82

13 CULLODEN

Drumnadrochit

Grantown-on-Spey

Tomintoul

Don

A96

17 ABERDEEN

11 LOCH NESS

Aviemore

Cairn Gorm
1245m

Colnabaichin

Drum Castle

A93

t Augustus

A86

23

Ben Macdui
1309m

Kingussie

CAIRNGORMS

Balmoral

Ballater

Banchory

Stonehaven

hinnie

Braemar

**18 ROYAL
DEESIDE TOUR**

A90

A92

pian Mountains

A93

**BLAIR
CASTLE**

22

21 KILLIECRANKIE WALK

PITLOCHRY 20

Dundee

och
on

Aberfeldy

19 DUNKELD

en Lawers
1214m

um

Killin

Perth

A85

Stirling

A84

SHETLAND ISLANDS **1**

Yell

Unst

Fetlar

Mainland

Whalsay

Lerwick

Foula

Mousa Broch

Sumburgh

NORTH SEA

Fair Isle

Westray

Sanday

Maes
Howe

2 ORKNEY ISLANDS

Kirkwall

Mainland

Stromness

Hoy

0 kilometres   50

3 JOHN O' GROATS

0 miles   25

KEY

═══	Motorway
━━━	Major road
━━━	Secondary road
┄┄┄	Minor road
━━━	Scenic route
┅┅┅	Main railway
────	Minor railway
△	Summit

SIGHTS AT A GLANCE

**Colour-washed houses at the
harbour of Tobermory, Mull**

Shetland ❶

Shetland. 🏘 *22,000*. ✈ ⛴ *from Aberdeen and Stromness on mainland Orkney.* ℹ *Lerwick (08701 999440).* **www**.visitshetland.com

Lying six degrees south of the Arctic Circle, the rugged Shetland islands are Britain's most northerly region and were, with Orkney, part of the kingdom of Norway until 1469. In the main town of Lerwick, this Norse heritage is remembered during the ancient midwinter festival Up Helly Aa *(see p480),* in which costumed revellers set fire to a replica Viking longship. Also in the town, the **Shetland Museum** tells the story of a people dependent on the sea, right up to modern times with the discovery of North Sea oil and gas in the 1970s.

The Iron Age tower, **Mousa Broch**, can be visited on its isle by boat from Sandwick. There is more ancient history at Jarlshof where a museum explains the sprawling sea-front ruins which span 3,000 years.

A boat from Lerwick sails to the isle of Noss where grey seals bask beneath sandstone cliffs crowded with Shetland's seabirds – a spectacle best seen between May and June. Other wildlife includes otters and killer whales.

🏛 **Shetland Museum**
Hay's Dock, Lerwick. **Tel** *01595 694688.* ◯ *daily (pm only Sun).* **www**.shetland-museum.org.uk

Orkney ❷

Orkney. 🏘 *19,800*. ✈ ⛴ *from Gills Bay, Caithness; John o'Groats (May–Sep); Scrabster, Aberdeen.* ℹ *Broad St, Kirkwall (01856 872856).* **www**.visitorkney.com

The fertile isles of Orkney are remarkable for the wealth of prehistoric monuments which place them among Europe's most treasured archaeological sites. In the town of Kirkwall, the sandstone **St Magnus Cathedral** stands amid a charming core of narrow streets. Its many interesting tombs include that of its 12th-century patron saint.

THE SHETLAND SEABIRD ISLES

As seabirds spend most of their time away from land, nesting is a vulnerable period in their lives. The security provided by the inaccessible cliffs at such sites as Noss and Hermaness on Unst finds favour with thousands of migrant and local birds.

Puffin

Great Skua

Fulmar

Black Guillemot

Razorbills

Herring Gull

Nearby, the early 17th-century **Earl's Palace** is widely held to be one of Scotland's finest Renaissance buildings. To the west of Kirkwall lies Britain's most impressive chambered tomb, the cairn of **Maes Howe**. Dating from 2000 BC, the tomb has runic graffiti on its walls believed to have been left by Norsemen returning from the crusades in 1150.

Nearby, the great **Standing Stones of Stenness** may have been associated with Maes Howe rituals, though these still remain a mystery. Further west, on a bleak heath, stands the Bronze Age **Ring of Brodgar**.

Another archaeological treasure can be found in the Bay of Skail – the complete Stone Age village of **Skara Brae**. It was unearthed by a storm in 1850, after lying buried for 4,500 years. Further south, the

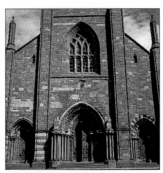

The Norman façade of the St Magnus Cathedral, Orkney

town of Stromness was a vital centre of Scotland's herring industry in the 18th century. Its story is told in the newly renovated local museum, while the **Pier Arts Centre** displays British and international art.

🏛 **Earl's Palace**
Palace Rd, Kirkwall. **Tel** *01856 871918.* ◯ *Apr–Sep: daily.* 🚫 ♿ *ltd.* **www**.historic-scotland.gov.uk

🏛 **Pier Arts Centre**
Victoria St, Stromness.
Tel *01856 850209.* ◯ *Mon–Sat.* **www**.pierartscentre.com

John o'Groats ❸

Highland. 🏘 *500*. ✈ ⛴ 🚌 *Wick* ⛴ *John o'Groats to Burwick, Orkney (May–Sep).* ℹ *John o'Groats (01955 611373).*

Some 876 miles (1,409 km) north from Land's End, Britain's most northeasterly mainland village faces Orkney, 8 miles (13 km) across the turbulent Pentland Firth. The village takes its name from a 15th-century Dutchman John de Groot, who, to avoid accusations of favouritism, is said to have built an octagonal house here with one door for each of his eight heirs. The spectacular cliffs and rock stacks of Duncansby Head lie a few miles further east.

Western Isles

Western Scotland ends with this remote chain of islands, made of some of the oldest rock on Earth. Almost treeless landscapes are divided by countless waterways, the western, windward coasts edged by miles of white sandy beaches. For centuries, the eastern shores, composed largely of peat bogs, have provided the islanders with fuel. Man has been here for 6,000 years, living off the sea and the thin turf, though such monuments as an abandoned Norwegian whaling station on Harris attest to the difficulties in commercializing the islanders' traditional skills. Gaelic, part of an enduring culture, is widely spoken.

The Black House Museum, a traditional croft on Lewis

The monumental Standing Stones of Callanish in northern Lewis

Lewis and Harris

Western Isles. 🏃 22,000. ✈ Stornoway. ⛴ Uig (Skye), Ullapool, Kyle of Lochalsh. 🛈 Stornoway, Lewis (01851 703088). **www.**visithebrides.com
Black House Museum. Tel 01851 710395. ◯ 9:30am–4pm daily (to 5:30pm in summer). 🚫 ♿ 🎥 🔓

Forming the largest landmass of the Western Isles, Lewis and Harris are a single island, though Gaelic dialects differ between the two areas. From **Stornoway**, with its bustling harbour and colourful house fronts, the ancient **Standing Stones of Callanish** are only 16 miles (26 km) to the west. Just off the road on the way to Callanish are the ruins of **Carloway Broch**, a Pictish *(see p482)* tower over 2,000 years old. The more recent past can be explored at Arnol's **Black House Museum** – a showcase of crofting life as it was until only 50 years ago.

South of the rolling peat moors of Lewis, a range of mountains marks the border with Harris, which one enters as one passes Aline Lodge at the head of Loch Seaforth. Only a little less spectacular than the "Munros" (peaks over 914 m; 3,000 ft) of the

mainland and the Isle of Skye *(see pp534–5)*, the mountains of Harris are a paradise for the hillwalker and, from their summits on a clear day, the distant Isle of St Kilda can be seen 50 miles (80 km) to the west.

The ferry port of Tarbert stands on a slim isthmus separating North and South Harris. Some local weavers of the famous Harris Tweed still follow the old tradition of using plants to make their dyes.

From the port of Leverburgh, close to the southern tip of Harris, a ferry can be taken to the isle of North Uist, where a causeway has been built to Berneray.

The Uists, Benbecula and Barra

Western Isles. 🏃 7,200. ✈ Barra, Benbecula. ⛴ Uig (Skye), Ullapool, Oban. 🚌 🚆 Oban, Mallaig, Kyle of Lochalsh. 🛈 Lochmaddy, North Uist (01876 500321); Lochboisdale, South Uist (01878 700286); Castlebay, Barra (01871 810336). **www.**visithebrides.com

After the dramatic scenery of Harris, the lower-lying, largely waterlogged southern isles may seem an anticlimax, though they nurture secrets well worth discovering. Long, white, sandy beaches fringe the Atlantic coast, edged with one of Scotland's natural treasures: the lime-rich soil known as *machair*. During the summer months, the soil is covered with wild flowers.

From **Lochmaddy**, North Uist's main village, the A867 crosses 3 miles (5 km) of causeway to Benbecula, the isle from which Flora MacDonald smuggled Bonnie Prince Charlie *(see p535)* to Skye. Another causeway leads to South Uist, with its golden beaches renowned as a National Scenic Area. From Lochboisdale, a ferry sails to the tiny isle of Barra. The ferry docks in Castlebay, affording an unforgettable view of **Kisimul Castle**, the ancestral stronghold of the MacNeils of Barra.

The remote and sandy shores of South Uist

The western side of the Five Sisters of Kintail, seen from above Loch Duich

Skye ❺

See pp534–5.

The Five Sisters ❻

Skye & Lochalsh. 🚂 *Kyle of Lochalsh.* 🚌 *Glenshiel.* 🛈 *Bayfield Road, Portree, Isle of Skye (01478 612137).* **www**.visithighlands.com

Dominating one of Scotland's most haunting regions, the awesome summits of the Five Sisters of Kintail rear into view at the northern end of Loch Cluanie as the A87 enters Glen Shiel. The **Visitor Centre** at Morvich offers ranger-led excursions in the summer. Further west, the road passes **Eilean Donan Castle**, connected by a bridge. A Jacobite *(see p537)* stronghold, it was destroyed in 1719 by English warships. In the 19th century it was restored and now contains Jacobite relics.

🏰 **Eilean Donan Castle**
Off A87, nr Dornie. **Tel** *01599 555202.* ◯ *Apr–Oct: 10am–5:30pm daily.* 🖾

Wester Ross ❼

Ross & Cromarty. 🚂 *Achnasheen, Strathcarron.* 🛈 *Visit Scotland (01445 712130).* **www**.visithighlands.com

Leaving Loch Carron to the south, the A890 suddenly enters the northern Highlands and the great wilderness of Wester Ross. The Torridon Estate includes some of the oldest mountains on Earth (Torridonian rock is over 600 million years old), and is home to red deer, wild cats and wild goats. Peregrine falcons and golden eagles nest in the towering sandstone mass of Liathach, above the village of Torridon with its breathtaking views over Applecross to Skye. The **Torridon Countryside Centre** provides guided walks in season and essential information on the natural history of the region.

To the north, the A832 cuts through the Beinn Eighe National Nature Reserve in which remnants of the ancient Caledonian pine forest still stand on the banks and isles of Loch Maree.

Along the coast, exotic gardens thrive in the warming currents of the Gulf Stream, most impressive being **Inverewe Garden** created in 1862 by Osgood Mackenzie (1842–1922). May and June are the months to see the display of

Typical Torridonian mountian scenery in the Wester Ross

rhododendrons and azaleas; July and August for the herbaceous borders.

🏛 **Torridon Countryside Centre**
(NTS) Torridon. **Tel** *0844 493 2229.* ◯ *Easter–Sep: 10am–6pm daily.* 🖾 🖿 **www**.nts.org.uk;

🌺 **Inverewe Garden**
(NTS) off A832, nr Poolewe. **Tel** *0844 493 2225.* ◯ *daily.* 🖾 🖿

Dornoch ❽

Sutherland. 🏘 *2,200.* 🚂 *Golspie, Tain.* 🛈 *The Square, Dornoch (01862 810916).* **www**.visithighlands.com

With its first-class golf course and extensive sandy beaches, **Dornoch** is a popular holiday resort, though it has retained a peaceful atmosphere. Now the parish church, the medieval cathedral was all but destroyed in a clan dispute in 1570; it was finally restored in the 1920s for its 700th anniversary. A stone at the beach end of River Street marks the place where Janet Horne, the last woman to be tried in Scotland for witchcraft, was executed in 1722.

Environs: Twelve miles (19 km) northeast of Dornoch is the stately Victorianized pile of **Dunrobin Castle**, magnificently situated in a great park with formal gardens overlooking the sea. Since the 13th century, this has been the seat of the Earls of Sutherland.

Many of its rooms are open to visitors. A steam-powered fire engine is among the miscellany of objects on display.

South of Dornoch stands the town of **Tain**. Though patronized by medieval kings as a place of pilgrimage, it became an administrative centre of the Highland Clearances. All is explained in the heritage centre, **Tain Through Time**.

♣ Dunrobin Castle
Nr Golspie. **Tel** 01408 633177.
◯ Mar–May, Sep & Oct: 10:30am–4:30pm daily (from noon Sun); Jun–Aug: 10:30am–5:30pm daily. ⚟

🏛 Tain Through Time
Tower St. **Tel** 01862 894089. ◯ Apr–Oct: 10am–5pm Mon–Sat. ⚟
♿ ⬛ www.tainmuseum.org.uk

The serene cathedral precinct in the town of Dornoch

Strathpeffer ❾

Ross & Cromarty. 🏔 1,400. ⇄ Dingwall, Inverness. 🚌 Inverness. 🛈 Visit Scotland (01463 731505; Easter–Oct). www.undiscoveredscotland.co.uk

Standing 5 miles (8 km) from the Falls of Rogie and to the east of the Northwest Highlands, the popular town of Strathpeffer still has the refined charm for which it was well known in Victorian times, when it flourished as a spa and health resort. The grand hotels, individually designed buildings and gracious layout of Strathpeffer recall the days when royalty from all over Europe used to flock to the chalybeate- and sulphur-laden springs, which were believed to help in the cure of tuberculosis, and in the treatment of rheumatism.

The shores of the Black Isle in the Moray Firth

The Black Isle ❿

Ross & Cromarty. ⇄ 🚌 Inverness.
🛈 Visit Scotland (01463 731505; Easter–Oct).

Though the drilling platforms in the Cromarty Firth are reminders of how oil has changed the local economy, the peninsula of the Black Isle is still largely composed of farmland and fishing villages. The town of **Cromarty** was an important port in the 18th century, with thriving rope and lace industries. Many of its merchant houses still stand; the museum in the **Cromarty Courthouse** provides heritage tours of the town. The **Hugh Miller Museum** is a museum to the theologian and geologist Hugh Miller (1802–56), who was born in the cottage; adjacent is the superb, new

Miller House, which has exhibitions on three floors. **Fortrose** boasts a ruined 14th-century cathedral, while a stone on Chanonry Point commemorates the Brahan Seer, a 17th-century prophet burnt alive in a tar barrel by the Countess of Seaforth after he foresaw her husband's infidelity. For local archaeology, visit **Groam House Museum** in Rosemarkie.

🏛 Cromarty Courthouse
Church St, Cromarty. **Tel** 01381 600 418. ◯ Mar–Oct: daily. ⚟

🏛 Hugh Miller Museum
(NTS) Church St, Cromarty. **Tel** 0844 493 2158. ◯ Easter–Sep: daily; Oct: Sun–Wed pm. ⚟ ♿ limited.

🏛 Groam House Museum
High St, Rosemarkie. **Tel** 01381 620 961. ◯ May–Sep: 10am–5pm daily (Sun pm); Oct–Apr: Sat & Sun (pm).

THE HIGHLAND CLEARANCES

During the heyday of the clan system (see p484), tenants paid their clan chiefs rent for their land in the form of military service. However, with the decline of the clan system after the Battle of Culloden (see p537) and the coming of sheep from the borders, landowners were able to command a financial rent their tenants were unable to afford and the land was bought up by Lowland and English farmers. In what became known as "the year of the sheep" (1792), thousands of tenants were evicted to make way for sheep. Many emigrated to Australia, America and Canada. Ruins of their crofts can still be seen in Sutherland and Wester Ross.

The Last of the Clan (1865) by Thomas Faed

Isle of Skye 36

Otter by the coast at Kylerhea

The largest of the Inner Hebrides, Skye can be reached by the bridge linking Kyle of Lochalsh and Kyleakin. A turbulent geological history has given the island some of Britain's most varied and dramatic scenery. From the rugged volcanic plateau of northern Skye to the ice-sculpted peaks of the Cuillins, the island is divided by numerous sea lochs, leaving the traveller never more than 8 km (5 miles) from the sea. North of the Dunvegan are small caves and white beaches, while Limestone grasslands predominate in the south, where the hillsides, home of sheep and cattle, are scattered with the ruins of crofts abandoned during the Clearances *(see p531)*. Historically, Skye is best known for its association with Bonnie Prince Charlie.

Skeabost has the ruins of a chapel which is associated with St Columba. Medieval tombstones can be found in the graveyard.

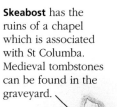

Grave of Flora MacDonald

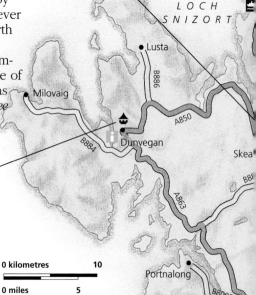

Dunvegan Castle

For over seven centuries, Dunvegan Castle has been the seat of the chiefs of the Clan MacLeod. It contains the Fairy Flag, a fabled piece of magic silk treasured for its protection in battle.

The Talisker Distillery produces one of the best Highland malts, often described as "the lava of the Cuillins".

Cuillins

Britain's finest mountain range is within walking distance of Sligachan, and in summer a boat sails from Elgol to the desolate inner sanctuary of Loch Coruisk. As he fled across the surrounding moorland, Bonnie Prince Charlie is said to have claimed: "Even the Devil shall not follow me here!"

KEY

ℹ	Tourist information
▬	Major road
▭	Minor road
—	Narrow lane
☼	Viewpoint

◁ **Dawn over the desolate tablelands of northern Skye, viewed from the Quiraing**

Quiraing

A series of landslides has exposed the roots of this volcanic plateau, revealing a fantastic terrain of spikes and towers. They are easily explored off the Uig to Staffin road.

Kilt Rock

The Storr

The erosion of this basalt plateau has created the Old Man of Storr, a monolith rising to 49 m (160 ft) by the Portree road.

Loch Coruisk

Luib has a beautiful thatched cottage, preserved as it was 100 years ago.

Bridge to mainland

Portree

With its colourful harbour, Portree (meaning "port of the king") is Skye's metropolis. It received its name after a visit by James V in 1540.

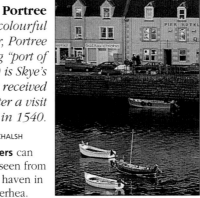

KYLE OF LOCHALSH

Otters can be seen from the haven in Kylerhea.

Armadale Castle Gardens and Museum of the Isles houses the Clan Donald visitor centre.

Kilchrist Church

This ruined pre-Reformation church's last service was held in 1843. It once served Skye's most populated areas, though the surrounding moors are now deserted.

BONNIE PRINCE CHARLIE

The last of the Stuart claimants to the Crown, Charles Edward Stuart (1720–88), came to Scotland from France in 1745 to win the throne. After marching as far as Derby, his army was driven back to Culloden where it was defeated. Hounded for five months through the Highlands, he escaped to Skye, disguised as the maidservant of a woman called Flora MacDonald, from Uist. From the mainland, he sailed to France in September 1746, and died in Rome. Flora was buried in 1790 at Kilmuir, on Skye, wrapped in a sheet taken from the bed of the "bonnie" (handsome) prince.

The prince, disguised as a maidservant

The ruins of Urquhart Castle on the western shore of Loch Ness

Loch Ness ⓫

Inverness. ⮀ 🚌 *Inverness*. ℹ️ *Castle Wynd, Inverness (01463 234353).* **www**.loch-ness-scotland.com

At 24 miles (39 km) long, one mile (1.5 km) at its widest and up to 305 m (1,000 ft) deep, **Loch Ness** fills the northern half of the Great Glen fault from Fort William to Inverness. It is joined to lochs Oich and Lochy by the 22-mile (35-km) Caledonian Canal,

---

THE LOCH NESS MONSTER

First sighted by St Columba in the 6th century, "Nessie" has attracted increasing attention since ambiguous photographs were taken in the 1930s. Though serious investigation is often undermined by hoaxers, sonar techniques continue to yield enigmatic results: plesiosaurs, giant eels and too much whisky are the most popular explanations. Nessie appears to have a close relative in the waters of Loch Morar *(see p546)*.

---

designed by Thomas Telford *(see p447)*. On the western shore, the A82 passes the ruins of the 16th-century **Urquhart Castle**, which was blown up by government supporters in 1692 to prevent it falling into Jacobite hands. A short distance west, **Loch Ness 2000 Exhibition Centre** offers a wealth of audio-visual information.

♟ **Urquhart Castle**
Nr Drumnadrochit.
Tel *01456 450551.*
◯ *9:30am–6pm daily (Oct–Easter: to 4:30pm). (Last adm: 45 mins before closing.)* 🖼️ 🍴 📷

🏛 **Loch Ness 2000 Exhibition Centre**
Drumnadrochit. **Tel** *01456 450573.*
◯ *daily, with longer opening hours in peak season and shorter opening hours in winter.* 🖼️ ♿ 🖥️ 📷

Inverness ⓬

Highland. 🏘 *60,000.* ⮀ 🚌
ℹ️ *Castle Wynd (0845 2255121).*
www.visithighlands.com

As the Highland capital, Inverness makes an ideal base from which to explore the surrounding countryside. The Victorian castle dominates the town centre, the oldest buildings of which are found in nearby Church Street. Today

the castle is used as law courts. The **Inverness Museum and Art Gallery** provides a good introduction to the history of the Highlands with exhibits including a lock of Bonnie Prince Charlie's *(see p535)* hair and a fine collection of Inverness silver. The **Scottish Kiltmaker Visitor Centre** explores the history and tradition of Scottish kilts as well as workshops, while those in search of tartans and knitwear should visit the **James Pringle Weavers of Inverness**. **Jacobite Cruises** run a variety of year-round cruises along the Caledonian Canal and on to Loch Ness. The unfolding scenery makes this a most pleasant and tranquil way to spend a sunny afternoon.

Kilt maker with royal Stuart tartan

🏛 **Museum and Art Gallery**
Castle Wynd. **Tel** *01463 237114.*
◯ *10am–5pm Mon–Sat.* ♿
www.invernessmuseum.com

🛍 **James Pringle Weavers of Inverness**
Holm Woollen Mill, Dores Rd.
Tel *01463 223311.* ◯ *daily.* ♿

🏛 **Scottish Kiltmaker Visitor Centre**
Huntly St. **Tel** *01463 222781.*
◯ *May–Sep: daily; Oct–Apr: Mon–Sat.* ● *1 Jan, 25 Dec.* 🖼️

Jacobite Cruises
Glenurquhart Road.
Tel *01463 233999.* ◯ *daily.*
🖼️ ♿ **www**.jacobite.co.uk

Culloden ⓭

(NTS) Inverness. ⇌ 🚌 *Inverness.*
www.nts.org.uk

A desolate stretch of moorland, Culloden looks much as it did on 16 April 1746, the date of the last battle to be fought on British soil *(see p483)*. Here the Jacobite cause, with Bonnie Prince Charlie's *(see p535)* leadership, finally perished under the onslaught of Hanoverian troops led by the Duke of Cumberland. All is explained in the excellent **NTS Visitor Centre**.

Environs: Signposted for a mile (1.5 km) or so east are the outstanding Neolithic burial sites, the **Clava Cairns**.

ℹ️ **NTS Visitor Centre**
On the B9006 east of Inverness.
***Tel** 01463 790607.* ⭘ *Apr–Sep: daily.* ⬤ *24–26 Dec, Jan.* 📷 ♿

Fort George ⓮

Inverness. ***Tel** 01667 460232.*
⇌ 🚌 *Inverness, Nairn.* ⭘ *Apr– Sep: 9:30am–6pm daily (to 4:30pm Oct–Mar).* ⬤ *25 & 26 Dec.* 📷 ♿
🖱️ **www.**historic-scotland.gov.uk

One of the finest works of European military architecture, Fort George stands on a windswept promontory jutting into the Moray Firth, ideally located to suppress the Highlanders. Completed in 1769, the fort was built after the Jacobite risings to discourage further rebellion in the Highlands and has remained a military garrison

THE JACOBITE MOVEMENT

James II, by Samuel Cooper (1609–72)

The first Jacobites (mainly Catholic Highlanders) were the supporters of James II of England (James VII of Scotland) who was deposed by the "Glorious Revolution" of 1688 *(see p53)*. With the Protestant William of Orange on the throne, the Jacobites' desire to restore the Stuart monarchy led to the uprisings of 1715 and 1745. The first, in support of James VIII, the "Old Pretender", ended at the Battle of Sheriffmuir (1715). The failure of the second uprising, with the defeat at Culloden, saw the end of Jacobite hopes and led to the end of the clan system and the suppression of Highland culture for over a century *(see p485)*.

The drawbridge on the eastern side of Cawdor Castle

ever since. The Fort houses the **Regimental Museum** of the Highlanders Regiment, and some of its barrack rooms reconstruct the conditions of the common soldiers stationed here more than 200 years ago. The **Grand Magazine** contains an outstanding collection of arms and military equipment. The battlements also make an excellent place from which to watch dolphins in the Moray Firth.

Cawdor Castle ⓯

On B9090 (off A96). ***Tel** 01667 404401.* ⇌ *Nairn, then bus.*
🚌 *from Inverness.* ⭘ *May–mid-Oct: 10am–5:30pm daily.* 📷 ♿ *gardens & ground floor only.* 🍴
www.cawdorcastle.com

With its turreted central tower, moat and drawbridge, Cawdor Castle is one of the most romantic stately homes in the Highlands. Though the castle is famed for being the 11th-century home of Shakespeare's *(see p322)* Macbeth and the scene of his murder of King Duncan, it is not historically proven that either came here.

An ancient holly tree preserved in the vaults is said to be the one under which, in 1372, Thane William's donkey, laden with gold, stopped for a rest during its master's search for a place to build a fortress. According to legend, this was how the site for the castle was chosen. Now, after 600 years of continuous occupation (it is still the home of the Thanes of Cawdor) the house is a treasury of family history, containing a number of rare tapestries and portraits by the 18th-century painters Joshua Reynolds (1723–92) and George Romney (1734–1802). Furniture in the Pink Bedroom and Woodcock Room includes work by Chippendale and Sheraton. In the Old Kitchen, the huge Victorian cooking range stands as a shrine to below-stairs drudgery. The grounds provide nature trails and a nine-hole golf course.

A contemporary picture, *The Battle of Culloden* (1746), by D Campbell

Elgin ⑯

Moray. 🏛 *21,000.* ⛴ 🚉
ℹ *17 High St, Moray (01343 542666).*

With its cobbled marketplace and crooked lanes, the popular holiday centre of Elgin still retains much of its medieval layout. The 13th-century **cathedral** ruins next to King Street are all that remain of one of Scotland's architectural triumphs, the design of its tiered windows reminiscent of the cathedral at St Andrews *(see p499).* Once known as the Lantern of the North, the cathedral was severely damaged in 1390 by the Wolf of Badenoch (the son of Robert II) in revenge for his excommunication by the Bishop of Moray. Worse damage came in 1576 when the Regent Moray ordered the stripping of its lead roofing. Among its remains is a Pictish cross-slab in the nave, and a basin in a corner where one of Elgin's benefactors,

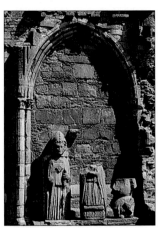

Details of the central tower of Elgin Cathedral

Andrew Anderson, was kept as a baby by his homeless mother. Next to the cathedral are the **Biblical Gardens** with all 110 plants mentioned in the Bible, while the **Elgin Museum** has anthropological displays and the **Moray Motor Museum** has over 40 vehicles.

🏛 **Elgin Museum**
1 High St. **Tel** *01343 543675.* ◯
Apr–Oct: Mon–Sat. 📷 ♿ *limited.*
🖥 www.elginmuseum.org.uk

🏛 **Moray Motor Museum**
Bridge St, Bishopmill. **Tel** *01343 541120.* ◯ *Easter–Oct: 11am–5pm daily.* 📷 ♿

Aberdeen ⑰

Scotland's third largest city and Europe's offshore oil capital, Aberdeen has prospered since the discovery of petroleum in the North Sea in 1970. The sea bed has now yielded over 100 oilfields. Widely known as the Granite City, its rugged outlines are softened by sumptuous year-round floral displays in its public parks and gardens, the Duthie Park Winter Gardens being one of the largest indoor gardens in Europe. The picturesque village of Footdee, which sits at the end of the city's 2-mile (3-km) beach, has good views back to the busy harbour.

The spires of Aberdeen, rising behind the city harbour

Exploring Aberdeen
The city centre flanks the mile-long (1.5 km) Union Street ending to the east at the Mercat Cross. The cross stands in Castlegate, the one-time site of the city castle. From here the cobbled Shiprow winds southwest and passes Provost Ross's House *(see p540)* on its way to the harbour with its fish market. A bus can be taken a mile (1.5 km) north of the centre to Old Aberdeen which, with its medieval streets and wynds, has the peaceful character of a separate village. Driving is restricted in some streets.

🏛 King's College
College Bounds, Old Aberdeen. *Tel 01224 272092.* **Chapel** ◯ *Opening times vary – phone to check.* ♿
King's College was founded in 1495 as the city's first university. The inter-denominational chapel (the only part of the college open to the public), in the past consecutively Catholic and Protestant, has a lantern tower rebuilt after a storm in 1633. Stained-glass windows by Douglas Strachan add a contemporary touch to the interior which contains a 1540 pulpit, later carved with heads of Stuart monarchs.

⛪ St Andrew's Cathedral
King St. **Tel** *01224 640290.*
◯ *May–Sep: 11am–4pm Tue–Fri.*
♿ 📷 *by appointment.*
The Mother Church of the Episcopal Communion in America, St Andrew's has a memorial to Samuel Seabury, the first Episcopalian bishop in the United States, who was consecrated in Aberdeen in 1784. Coats of arms adorn the ceiling above the north and south aisles, contrasting colourfully with the white walls and pillars. They represent the American States and local Jacobite *(see p537)* families.

The elegant lantern tower of the chapel at King's College

PROVOST SKENE'S HOUSE

Guestrow. *Tel 01224 641086.* ◯ *10am–5pm Mon–Sat, 1–4pm Sun (limited access to upper floors).* ● *25 & 26, 31 Dec–2 Jan.* **www**.aagm.co.uk

Once the home of Sir George Skene, a 17th-century provost (mayor) of Aberdeen, the house was built in 1545. Inside, period rooms span 200 years of design. The Duke of Cumberland stayed here before the Battle of Culloden *(see p537).*

VISITORS' CHECKLIST

City of Aberdeen. 203,500.
Guild St.
23 Union St (01224 288828).
www.aberdeen-grampian.com

The 18th-century Parlour, with its walnut harpsichord and covered chairs by the fire, was the informal room in which the family would have tea.

The Regency Room typifies early 19th-century elegance. A harp dating from 1820 stands by a Grecian-style sofa and a French writing table.

The Painted Gallery has one of Scotland's most important cycles of religious art. The panels are early 17th century, though the artist is unknown.

The 17th-century Great Hall contains heavy oak dining furniture. Provost Skene's wood-carved coat of arms hangs above the fireplace.

The Georgian Dining Room, with its Classical design, was the main formal room in the 16th century and still has its original flagstone floor.

Entrance

ABERDEEN CITY CENTRE

Aberdeen Art Gallery ①
St Andrew's Cathedral ⑤
Marischal College ④
Maritime Museum ⑦
Mercat Cross ⑥
Provost Skene's House ③
St Nicholas Kirk ②

INVERURIE
Aberdeen Airport
11 km (7 miles)

OLD ABERDEEN
PETERHEAD
FRASERBURGH

WEST NORTH ST

Provost Skene's House ③

Marischal College ④

St. Andrew's Cathedral ⑤

Aberdeen Art Gallery ①

His Majesty's Theatre
ROSEMOUNT VIADUCT
SCHOOLHILL
Belmont Picture House

Academy Shopping Centre

St Nicholas Kirk ②

Tolbooth

Mercat Cross ⑥

JUSTICE ST

Union Terrace Gdns.

Maritime Museum ⑦

TRINITY QUAY

REGENT QUAY

JAMES STREET

BRAEMAR BANCHORY

Harbour

Ferry Terminal

BLAIKIES QUAY

JAMESONS QUAY

BRIDGE STREET

DENBURN ROAD

GUILD STREET

Bus Station

Train Station

FISH MARKET

Fish Market

STONEHAVEN

0 metres 200

0 yards 200

🏛 Art Gallery

Schoolhill. **Tel** 01224 523700. ◯
10am–5pm Tue–Sat, 2–5pm Sun. ◉
25 Dec–2 Jan. ♿ www.aagm.co.uk

Housed in a Neo-Classical building, purpose-built in 1884, the Art Gallery has a wide range of exhibitions, with an emphasis on contemporary work. A fine collection of Aberdonian silver can be found among the decorative arts on the ground floor, and is the subject of a video presentation.
A permanent collection of 18th–20th-century fine art features such names as Toulouse-Lautrec, Reynolds and Zoffany. Several of the works were bequeathed in 1900 by a local granite merchant, Alex Macdonald. He commissioned many of the paintings in the Macdonald Room, which displays 92 self-portraits by British artists. Occasional poetry-readings, music recitals and films are on offer.

Aberdonian silver in the Art Gallery

⛪ St Nicholas Kirk

Union St. **Tel** 01224 643494.
◯ May–Sep: noon–4pm Mon–Fri & Sun, 1–3pm Sat. ♿

Founded in the 12th century, St Nicholas is Scotland's largest parish church. Though the present structure dates from 1752, many relics of earlier times can be seen inside.
After being damaged during the Reformation, the interior was divided into two. A chapel in the East Church contains iron rings used to secure witches in the 17th century, while in the West Church there are some embroidered panels attributed to one Mary Jameson (1597–1644).

🏛 Maritime Museum

Shiprow. **Tel** 01224 337700. ◯
10am–5pm Tue–Sat, noon–3pm Sun. ♿ 💻 📷 www.aagm.co.uk

Overlooking the harbour is Provost Ross's House, which dates back to 1593 and is one of the oldest residential buildings in the town. This museum traces the history of Aberdeen's seafaring tradition. Exhibitions include ship-wrecks, rescues, shipbuilding and the oil installations off Scotland's east coast.

⛪ St Machar's Cathedral

The Chanonry. **Tel** 01224 485988. ◯
9am–5pm daily (10am–4pm winter). ♿

Dominating Old Aberdeen, the 15th-century edifice of St Machar's is the oldest granite building in the city. The stonework of one arch even dates as far back as the 14th century. The impressive nave now serves as a parish church and its magnificent oak ceiling is adorned with the coats of arms of 48 popes, emperors and princes of Christendom.

Royal Deeside Tour ⑱

Since Queen Victoria's purchase of the Balmoral estate in 1852, Deeside has been best known as the summer home of the British Royal Family, though it has been associated with royalty since the time of Robert the Bruce (see p482). The route follows the Dee, formerly a prolific salmon river, through some magnificent Grampian scenery.

Muir of Dinnet Nature Reserve ④
An information centre on the A97 provides an excellent place from which to explore this beautiful mixed woodland area, formed by the retreating glaciers of the last Ice Age.

Balmoral ⑥
Bought by Queen Victoria for 30,000 guineas in 1852, after its owner choked to death on a fishbone, the castle was rebuilt in the Scottish Baronial style at Prince Albert's request.

Ballater ⑤
The old railway town of Ballater has royal warrants on many of its shop fronts. It grew as a 19th-century spa town, its waters reputedly providing a cure for tuberculosis.

Dunkeld ⑲

Perth & Kinross. 🚶 *2,500.* 🚉 *Birnam.*
🚌 ℹ️ *The Cross (01350 727688).*
www.visitdunkeld.com

Situated by the River Tay, this ancient and charming village was all but destroyed in the Battle of Dunkeld, a Jacobite *(see p537)* defeat, in 1689. The **Little Houses** lining Cathedral Street were the first to be rebuilt, and are fine examples of imaginative restoration. The ruins of the 14th-century **cathedral** enjoy an idyllic setting on shady lawns beside the Tay, against a backdrop of steep and wooded hills. The choir is used as the parish church and its north wall contains a Leper's Squint: a hole through which lepers could see the altar during mass. It was while on holiday in the Dunkeld country-side that Beatrix Potter *(see p367)* found the location for her Peter Rabbit stories.

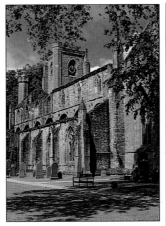

The ruins of Dunkeld Cathedral

Pitlochry ⑳

Perth & Kinross. 🚶 *2,900.* 🚉 🚌
ℹ️ *22 Atholl Rd (01796 472215).*
www.perthshire.co.uk

Surrounded by pine-forested hills, Pitlochry became famous after Queen Victoria *(see p56)* described it as one of the finest resorts in Europe. In early summer, salmon swim up the ladder built into the Power Station Dam, on their way to spawning grounds upriver. There is a viewing chamber here to see them. The **Power Station Visitor Centre** outlines the hydro-electric scheme that harnesses the waters of the River Tummel. The home of Bell's whisky, the **Blair Athol Distillery**, gives an insight into whisky making *(see p489)* and is open for tours. Scotland's famous **Festival Theatre** puts on a summer season when the programme changes daily.

ℹ️ **Power Station Visitor**
Centre Pitlochry. *Tel 01796 473152.*
⭘ *Apr–Oct: 10am–5:30pm Mon–Fri (Jul & Aug: daily).* 🎟️ 📷

🎭 **Festival Theatre**
Port-na-Craig. *Tel 01796 484626.*
⭘ *daily.* 🎟️ ♿ 📷

🥃 **Blair Athol Distillery**
Perth Rd. *Tel 01796 482003.* ⭘
Easter–Sep: Mon–Sat (& Sun pm Jun–Sep); Oct–Mar: Mon–Fri. ● *22 Dec–3 Jan.* 🎟️ ♿ limited. 📷 🛍️
www.discovering-distilleries.com

TIPS FOR DRIVERS

Length: *69 miles (111 km).*
Stopping-off points: *Crathes Castle café (May–Sep: daily); Station Restaurant, Ballater (food served all day).*

Drum Castle ①

This impressive 13th-century keep was granted by Robert the Bruce to his standard bearer in 1323, in gratitude for his services.

PETERHEAD

A96

ABERDEEN

A93

A956

Banchory ③

Local lavender is a popular attraction here. From the 18th-century Brig o' Feugh, salmon can be seen.

A980

A93

Crathes

① Peterculter

Dee

② Crathes

B9077

A90

STONEHAVEN

B974

Crathes Castle and Gardens ②

This is the family home of the Burnetts, who were made Royal Foresters of Drum by Robert the Bruce. Along with the title, he gave Alexander Burnett the ivory Horn of Leys which is still on display.

| 0 kilometres | 5 |
| 0 miles | 4 |

KEY

▰▰▰ Tour route

═══ Other roads

⋇ Viewpoint

Killiecrankie Walk ㉑

In an area famous for its scenery and historical connections, this circular walk offers typical Highland views. The route is fairly flat, though ringed by mountains, and follows the River Garry south to Loch Faskally, meandering through a wooded gorge, passing the Soldier's Leap and a Victorian viaduct. There are several ideal picnic spots along the way. Returning along the River Tummel, the walk crosses one of Queen Victoria's favourite Highland areas, before doubling back along the rivers to complete the circuit.

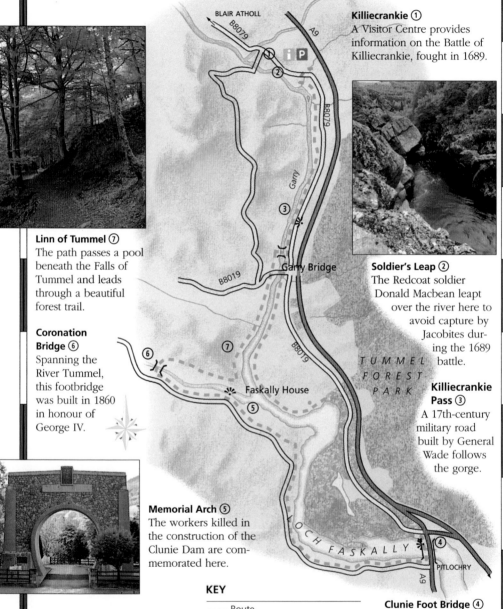

Killiecrankie ①
A Visitor Centre provides information on the Battle of Killiecrankie, fought in 1689.

Linn of Tummel ⑦
The path passes a pool beneath the Falls of Tummel and leads through a beautiful forest trail.

Coronation Bridge ⑥
Spanning the River Tummel, this footbridge was built in 1860 in honour of George IV.

Soldier's Leap ②
The Redcoat soldier Donald Macbean leapt over the river here to avoid capture by Jacobites during the 1689 battle.

Killiecrankie Pass ③
A 17th-century military road built by General Wade follows the gorge.

Memorial Arch ⑤
The workers killed in the construction of the Clunie Dam are commemorated here.

Clunie Foot Bridge ④
This bridge crosses the artificial Loch Faskally, created by the damming of the River Tummel for hydro-electric power in the 1950s.

BLAIR ATHOLL
B8079
A9
Garry
B8079
Garry Bridge
B8019
B8019
Faskally House
TUMMEL FOREST PARK
LOCH FASKALLY
PITLOCHRY
A9

KEY

▪ ▪	Route
▬▬	Major road
▭▭	B road
—	Minor road
☆	Viewpoint
P	Parking
ℹ	Visitor Centre

0 kilometres 1

0 miles 0.5

TIPS FOR WALKERS

Starting point: *NTS Visitor Centre Killiecrankie.* **Tel** *01796 473233.*
Getting there: *Bus from Pitlochry or Aberfeldy.*
Length: *10 miles (16 km).*
Difficulty: *Very easy.*

The Three Sisters, Glencoe, in late autumn

Blair Castle ㉒

Blair Atholl, Perthshire. *Tel 01796 481207.* ⊠ *Blair Atholl.* ◯ *Apr–Oct: 9:30am–4:30pm daily: Nov–Mar: Tue & Sat.* ⬤ *two weeks end Dec.* 🖼 ♿ *limited.* **www.**blair-castle.co.uk

This rambling, turreted castle has been altered so often in its 700-year history that it provides a unique insight into the history of Highland aristocratic life. The 18th-century wing, with its Victorian passages hung with antlers, has a display containing the gloves and pipe

of Bonnie Prince Charlie *(see p535)* who spent two days here gathering Jacobite *(see p537)* support. Family portraits cover 300 years and include paintings by such masters as Johann Zoffany and Sir Peter Lely. Sir Edwin Landseer's *Death of a Stag in Glen Tilt* (1850) was painted nearby.

In 1844 Queen Victoria visited the castle and conferred on its owners, the Dukes of Atholl, the distinction of being allowed to maintain a private army. The Atholl Highlanders still flourish.

THE MASSACRE OF GLENCOE

In 1692, the chief of the Glencoe MacDonalds was five days late in registering an oath of submission to William III, giving the government an excuse to root out a nest of Jacobite *(p537)* supporters. For ten days 130 soldiers, captained by Robert Campbell, were hospitably entertained by the unsuspecting MacDonalds. At dawn on 13 February, in a terrible breach of trust, the soldiers fell on their hosts, killing some 38 MacDonalds. Many more died in their wintry mountain hideouts. The massacre, unsurprisingly, became a political scandal, though there were to be no official reprimands for three years.

Detail of *The Massacre of Glencoe* by James Hamilton

The Cairngorms ㉓

See pp544–5.

Glencoe ㉔

Highland. ⊠ *Fort William.* 🚌 *Glencoe.* ℹ *Visit Scotland (01855 811866).* **www.**glencoe-scotland.net

Renowned for its awesome scenery and savage history, Glencoe was compared by Dickens to "a burial ground of a race of giants". The precipitous cliffs of Buachaille Etive Mor and the knife-edged ridge of Aonach Eagach (both over 900 m; 3,000 ft) present a formidable challenge even to experienced mountaineers.

Against a dark backdrop of craggy peaks and the tumbling River Coe, the Glen offers superb hill-walking in the summer. Stout footwear, waterproofs and attention to safety warnings are essential. Details of routes, ranging from the easy half-hour between the **NTS Visitor Centre** and Signal Rock (from which the signal was given to commence the massacre) to a stiff 6 mile (10 km) haul up the Devil's Staircase can be had from the Visitor Centre. Guided walks are offered in summer by the NTS Ranger service.

ℹ **NTS Visitor Centre** Glencoe. *Tel 01855 811307.* ◯ *daily.* 🖼 ♿ *ltd.* **www.**nts.org.uk

The Cairngorms ㉒

Wild Goat

Rising to a height of 1,309 m (4,296 ft), the Cairngorm mountains form the highest landmass in Britain. Cairn Gorm itself is the site of one of Britain's first ski centres. A weather station at the mountain's summit provides regular reports, essential in an area known for sudden changes of weather. Walkers should be sure to follow the mountain code without fail. The funicular railway that climbs Cairn Gorm affords superb views over the Spey Valley. Many estates in the valley have centres which introduce the visitor to Highland land use.

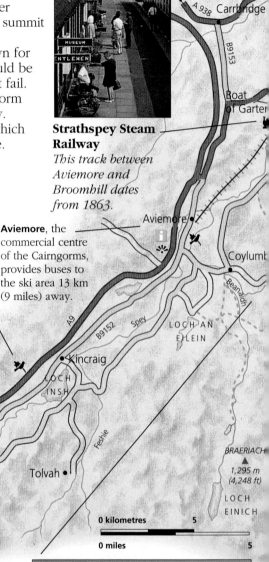

Strathspey Steam Railway
This track between Aviemore and Broomhill dates from 1863.

Aviemore, the commercial centre of the Cairngorms, provides buses to the ski area 13 km (9 miles) away.

Kincraig Highland Wildlife Park
Driving through this park, the visitor can see bison alongside wolves and wild boar. All of these animals were once common in the Highlands.

0 kilometres 5

0 miles 5

The Cairngorms by Aviemore

Rothiemurchus Estate
Highland cattle can be seen among many other creatures at Rothiemurchus. A visitor centre provides guided walks and illustrates life on a Highland estate.

Loch Garten Nature Reserve

Ospreys now thrive in this reserve in Abernethy Forest, which was established in 1959 to protect the first pair seen in Britain for 50 years.

GRANTOWN-ON-SPEY

Broomhill

A 95

Nethy Bridge

B970

E N

The **Cairngorm Reindeer Centre** provides walks in the hills among Britain's only herd of reindeer.

VISITORS' CHECKLIST

The Highlands. *Aviemore.*
King St, Kingussie (01540 661297). **Cairngorm Reindeer Centre**, *Loch Morlich. Tel 01479 861228.* ◯ *daily.* **Kincraig Highland Wildlife Park**. *Tel 01540 651270.* ◯ *daily (weather permitting).* **www**.highland wildlifepark.org **Rothiemurchus Visitor Centre**, *near Aviemore.* **Tel** *01479 812345.* ◯ *daily.* **Loch Garten Nature Reserve**. **Tel** *01479 831476.* ◯ *daily.* **Skiing Tel** *01479 861261.*

Skiing

From the Coire Cas car park, a funicular railway can be taken to the restaurant at the summit. There are 28 ski runs in all.

Nethy

H
CH

P

CAIRN GORM
▲
1,245 m
(4,084 ft)

BEN MACDHUI
▲
1,309 m
(4,296 ft)

CAIRNGORM

MOUNTAINS

Ben MacDhui is Britain's second highest peak, after Ben Nevis.

FLORA OF THE CAIRNGORMS

With mixed woodland at their base and the summits forming a sub-polar plateau, the Cairngorms present a huge variety of flora. Ancient Caledonian pines (once common in the area) survive in Abernethy Forest, while arctic flowers flourish in the heights.

The Cairngorm plateau holds little life except lichen (Britain's oldest plant), wood rush and cushions of moss campion, which is often completely covered with pink flowers.

Shady corries are important areas for alpine plants such as arctic mouse-ear, hare's foot sedge, mountain rock-cress and alpine speedwell.

Pinewoods occupy the higher slopes, revealing purple heather as they become sparser.

Mixed woodland covers the lower ground which is carpeted with heather and deergrass.

1,200 m (4000 ft)

1,000 m (3,300 ft)

800 m (2,600 ft)

600 m (2,000 ft)

400 m (1,300 ft)

200 m (650 ft)

0 m (0 ft)

An idealized section of the Cairngorm plateau

KEY

ℹ	Tourist information
▬	Major road
▭	Minor road
⋯	Narrow lane
- -	Footpath
☆	Viewpoint

Road to the Isles Tour ㉕

This scenic route goes past vast mountain-corridors, breathtaking beaches of white sand and tiny villages, to the town of Mallaig, one of the ferry ports for the isles of Skye, Rum and Eigg. As well as the stunning scenery, the area is steeped in Jacobite history *(see p537)*.

SKYE ⑦

⑥

A830

LOCH MORAR

Mallaig ⑦
The Road to the Isles ends at Mallaig, an active little fishing port with a very good harbour and one of the ferry links to Skye *(see pp534–5)*.

Arisaig

4830

⑤

LOCH NAN UAMH

ARDNISH

LOCH AILORT

LOCH EILT

Morar ⑥
The road continues through Morar, an area renowned for its white sands, and Loch Morar, rumoured to be the home of a 12-m (40-ft) monster known as Morag.

Prince's Cairn ⑤
Crossing the Ardnish Peninsula to Loch Nan Uamh, a cairn marks the spot from which Bonnie Prince Charlie finally left Scotland for France in 1746

TIPS FOR DRIVERS

Tour length: *45 miles (72 km).*
Stopping-off points: *Glenfinnan NTS Visitors' Centre (01397 722 250) explains the Jacobite risings and serves refreshments; the Old Library Lodge, Arisaig, has good Scottish food.*

Oban ㉖

Argyll & Bute. 8,500.
Argyll Sq (01631 563122).
www.oban.org.uk

Located on the Firth of Lorne and commanding a magnificent view of the Argyll coast, the bustling port of Oban is a popular destination for travellers on their way to Mull and the Western Isles *(see p529)*.

Dominating the skyline is McCaig's Tower, an unfinished Victorian imitation of the Colosseum in Rome. It is worth making the 10-minute climb from the town centre for the sea views alone. Attractions in the town include working centres for glass, pottery and whisky; the Oban distillery produces one of the country's finest malt whiskies *(see p489)*. The **Scottish Sealife Sanctuary** rescues injured and orphaned seals and has displays of underwater life. A busy harbour shelters car ferries going to Barra and South Uist, Mull, Tiree and Colonsay islands.

🏛 **Scottish Sealife Sanctuary**
Barcaldine. **Tel** 01631 720386.
◯ *daily.* ● *1 Jan, 25 Dec.*
www.sealsanctuary.co.uk

Mull ㉗

Argyll & Bute. 2,800. from Oban, Kilchoan, Lochaline. Main Street, Tobermory (01688 302182).

Most roads on this easily accessible Hebridean island follow the sharply indented rocky coastline, affording wonderful sea views. From Craignure, the Mull and West Highland Railway serves the baronial **Torosay Castle**. A pathway through its gardens is lined with statues, while inside, 19th-century furniture and paintings can be found. On a promontory to the east lies **Duart Castle**, home of the chief of Clan Maclean. Visitors can see the Banqueting Hall and State Rooms in the 13th-century keep. Its dungeons once held prisoners from a Spanish Armada galleon sunk by a Donald Maclean in 1588.

Looking out to sea across Tobermory Bay, Mull

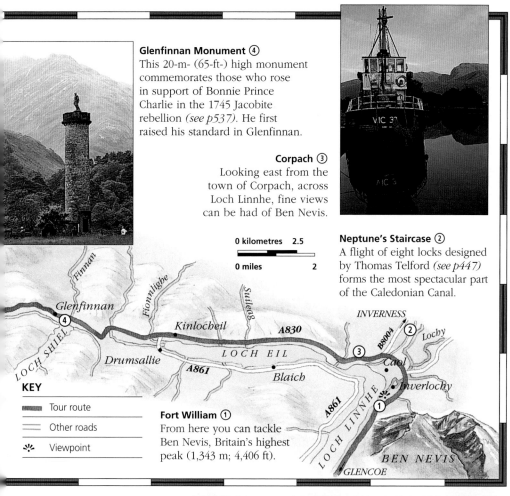

Glenfinnan Monument ④
This 20-m- (65-ft-) high monument commemorates those who rose in support of Bonnie Prince Charlie in the 1745 Jacobite rebellion *(see p537)*. He first raised his standard in Glenfinnan.

Corpach ③
Looking east from the town of Corpach, across Loch Linnhe, fine views can be had of Ben Nevis.

0 kilometres 2.5

0 miles 2

Neptune's Staircase ②
A flight of eight locks designed by Thomas Telford *(see p447)* forms the most spectacular part of the Caledonian Canal.

KEY

▬▬▬	Tour route
═══	Other roads
☀	Viewpoint

Fort William ①
From here you can tackle Ben Nevis, Britain's highest peak (1,343 m; 4,406 ft).

Environs: From Fionnphort, a ferry goes to **Iona**, where St Columba *(see p525)* began his mission in Scotland in 563. North of Iona, the Isle of Staffa should be visited for its magnificent **Fingal's Cave**.

⛫ **Torosay Castle**
Off A849, Nr Craignure. *Tel 01680 812421.* **Castle** ☐ *Easter–Oct: 10:30am–5pm daily.* **Gardens** ☐ *10am–5pm daily (dawn–dusk in winter).* 🖼 ♿ 🖥 🎫 *for groups.*

⛫ **Duart Castle**
Off A849, nr Craignure. *Tel 01680 812309.* ☐ *Apr–Oct: 10:30am–5:30pm daily.* 🖼

Loch Awe ㉘

Argyll & Bute. ⇄ 🚌 *Dalmally.* 🛈 *Inveraray (01499 302063).* **www**.loch-awe.com

One of the longest of Scotland's freshwater lochs, Loch Awe fills a 25-mile (40-km) glen in the southwestern Highlands. A short drive east of the village of Lochawe

The ruins of Kilchurn Castle on the shore of Loch Awe

leads to the lochside remains of **Kilchurn Castle**, abandoned after being struck by lightning in the 18th century. Dwarfing the castle is the huge bulk of Ben Cruachan, whose summit can be reached by the narrow Pass of Brander, in which Robert the Bruce *(see p482)* fought the Clan MacDougal in 1308. From the A85, a tunnel leads to the cavernous Cruachan Power Station.

Near the village of Taynuilt the preserved Lorn Furnace at Bonawe is a reminder of the iron-smelting industry that caused the destruction of much of the area's woodland in the 18th and 19th centuries.

Marked prehistoric cairns are found off the A816 between Kilmartin and Dunadd. The latter boasts a 6th-century hill fort from which the Stone of Destiny *(see p482)* originated.

Inveraray Castle ㉙

Inveraray, Argyll & Bute.
🚆 *Arrochar, then bus.* **Tel** *01499
302203.* ⬭ *Apr–Oct: 10am–
5:45pm Mon–Sat (Sun: pm only).*
🖼 ♿ limited. 🎫 ▣ 🛈
www.inveraray-castle.com

This multi-turreted mock
Gothic palace is the
family home of the powerful
Clan Campbell who have
been the Dukes of Argyll
since 1701. The castle was
built in 1745 by architects
Roger Morris and William
Adam on the ruins
of a 15th-century castle,
and the conical towers
added later, after a fire in
1877. Magnificent interiors,
designed by Robert Mylne
in the 1770s, form a backdrop to a huge collection
of Oriental and European
porcelain and Regency
furniture and portraits
by Ramsay, Gainsborough
and Raeburn. The Armoury
Hall features a display
of weaponry collected by
the Campbells to fight the
Jacobites *(see p537).*

The pinnacled, Gothic exterior of Inveraray Castle

Auchindrain Museum ㉚

Inveraray, Argyll & Bute.
Tel *01499 500235.* 🚌 *Inveraray,
then bus.* ⬭ *Apr–Oct: 10am–
5pm daily.* 🛈 🖼 ♿ limited.
www.auchindrain-museum.org.uk

The first open-air museum
in Scotland, Auchindrain
illuminates the working lives
of the kind of farming community that was typical of the
Highlands until the late 19th
century. Originally a township
of some 20 thatched buildings,
the site was communally
farmed by its tenants until
the last one retired in 1962.
Visitors can
wander through
the buildings,

many of which combine living
space, kitchen and cattle shed
under one roof. Some are
furnished with box beds and
old rush lamps. The homes of
Auchindrain are a fascinating
memorial to the time before
the transition from of subsis-
tence to commercial farming.

**An old hay turner at the
Auchindrain Museum**

Crarae Gardens ㉛

Crarae, Argyll & Bute. **Tel** *01546
886614 or NTS (01852 200366).*
🚌 *Inveraray, then bus.* ⬭ *9:30am–
sunset daily.* **Visitor Centre** ⬭ *Easter–
Sep 10am–5pm daily.* 🖼 ♿ limited.

Considered the most
beguiling of the gardens of
the West Highlands, the
Crarae Gardens were created
in the 1920s by Lady Grace
Campbell. She was the aunt
of explorer Reginald Farrer,
whose specimens from Tibet
were the beginnings of a
collection of exotic plants.
The gardens are nourished by
the warmth of the Gulf

Stream and the high rainfall.
Although there are many
unusual Himalayan rhodo-
dendrons flourishing here,
the gardens are also home
to exotic plants from various
countries including Tasmania,
New Zealand and the USA.
Plant collectors still contribute
to the gardens, which are
best seen in spring and early
summer against the blue
waters of Loch Fyne.

Jura ㉜

Argyll & Bute. 🚶 *200.* 🚢 *from
Kennacraig to Islay, then Islay to Jura.*
🛈 *Bowmore (01496 810254).*

Barren, mountainous and
overrun by red deer, the isle
of Jura has only one road
which connects the single
village of Craighouse to the
Islay ferry. Though walking is
restricted during the stalking
(deer hunting) season between August and October,
the island offers superb hill-
walking, especially on the
slopes of the three main peaks,
known as the Paps of Jura.
The tallest of these is Beinn
An Oir at 784 m (2571 ft). Beyond the northern tip of the isle
are the notorious whirlpools
of Corryvreckan. The novelist
George Orwell (who came to
the island to write his final
novel, *1984*) nearly lost his
life here in 1946 when he fell
into the water. A legend tells

Lagavulin distillery, producer of one Scotland's finest malts, on Islay

Mist crowning the Paps of Jura, seen at sunset across the Sound of Islay

of Prince Breackan who, to win the hand of a princess, tried to keep his boat anchored in the whirlpool for three days, held by ropes made of hemp, wool and maidens' hair. The Prince drowned when a single rope, containing the hair of a girl who had been untrue, finally broke.

Islay ㉝

Argyll & Bute. 🏘 3,500. ⛴ from Kennacraig. 🛈 The Square, Bowmore (0870 7200617). **www**.isle-of-islay.com

The most southerly of the Western Isles, Islay (pronounced 'Eyeluh') is the home of respected Highland single malt whiskies Lagavulin and Laphroaig. Most of the island's distilleries produce heavily peated malts with a distinctive tang of the sea. The Georgian village of Bowmore has the island's oldest distillery and a circular church designed to minimize the Devil's possible lurking-places. The **Museum of Islay Life** in Port Charlotte contains fascinating information on social and natural history. Seven miles (11 km) east of Port Ellen stands the Kildalton Cross. A block of local green stone adorned with Old Testament scenes, it is one of the most impressive 8th-

century Celtic crosses in Britain. Worth a visit for its archaeological and historical interest is the medieval stronghold of the Lords of the Isles, **Finlaggan**. Islay's beaches support a variety of bird life, some of which can be observed at the RSPB reserve at Gruinart.

🏛 **Museum of Islay Life**
Port Charlotte. **Tel** 01496 850358. ⭘ Easter–Oct: 10am–5pm Mon–Sat, 2–5pm Sun. 🈲 ♿

Kintyre ㉞

Argyll & Bute. 🏘 6,000. ✈ Oban. 🚌 Campbeltown. 🛈 MacKinnon House, The Pier, Campbeltown (01586 552056). **www**.kintyre.org

A long, narrow peninsula stretching far south of Glasgow, Kintyre has superb views across to the islands of Gigha, Islay and Jura. The 9 mile (14 km) Crinan Canal,

opened in 1801, is a delightful inland waterway, its 15 locks bustling with pleasure craft in the summer. The town of Tarbert (meaning "isthmus" in Gaelic) takes its name from the neck on which it stands, which is narrow enough to drag a boat across between Loch Fyne and West Loch Tarbert. This feat was first achieved by the Viking King Magnus Barfud who, in 1198, was granted by treaty as much land as he could sail around. Travelling south past Campbeltown, the B842 ends at the headland known as the Mull of Kintyre, which was made famous when former Beatle Paul McCartney commercialized a traditional pipe tune of the same name. Westward lies the isle of Rathlin, where Robert the Bruce *(see p482)* learned patience in his struggles against the English by watching a spider weaving a web in a cave.

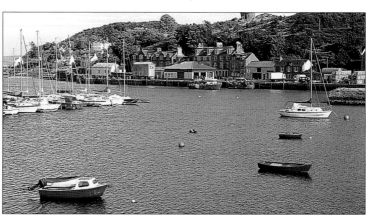

Fishing boats and yachts moored at Tarbert harbour, Kintyre

Index

Acknowledgments

Dorling Kindersley would like to thank the following people whose contributions and assistance have made the preparation of this book possible.

MAIN CONTRIBUTOR
Michael Leapman was born in London in 1938 and has been a professional journalist since he was 20. He has worked for most British national newspapers and now writes about travel and other subjects for several publications, among them *The Independent, Independent on Sunday, The Economist* and *Country Life.* He has written 11 books, including the award-winning *Companion Guide to New York* (1983, revised 1995) and *Eyewitness Travel Guide to London.* In 1989 he edited the widely praised *Book of London.*

ADDITIONAL CONTRIBUTORS
Paul Cleves, James Henderson, Lucy Juckes, John Lax, Marcus Ramshaw.

ADDITIONAL ILLUSTRATIONS
Christian Hook, Gilly Newman, Paul Weston.

DESIGN AND EDITORIAL
MANAGING EDITOR Georgina Matthews
SENIOR ART EDITOR Sally Ann Hibbard
DEPUTY EDITORIAL DIRECTOR Douglas Amrine
DEPUTY ART DIRECTOR Gaye Allen
PRODUCTION David Proffit
PICTURE RESEARCH Ellen Root, Rhiannon Furbear
DTP DESIGNER Ingrid Vienings
MAP CO-ORDINATORS Michael Ellis, David Pugh
RESEARCHER Pippa Leahy
Eliza Armstrong, Sam Atkinson, Moerida Belton, Lydia Baillie, Josie Barnard, Sonal Bhatt, Hilary Bird, Louise Boulton, Julie Bowles, Roger Bullen, Robert Butt, Chloe Carleton, Deborah Clapson, Elspeth Collier, Gary Cross, Cooling Brown Partnership, Guy Dimond, Nicola Erdpresser, Mariana Evmolpidou, Danny Farnham, Joy Fitzsimmons, Fay Franklin, Ed Freeman, Janice Fuscoe, Emily Griffin, Richard Hammond, Charlie Hawkings, Martin Hendry, Andrew Heritage, Annette Jacobs, Gail Jones, Steve Knowlden, Nic Kynaston, Esther Labi, Kathryn Lane, Pippa Leahy, Caroline Mead, James Mills Hicks, Rebecca Milner, Kate Molan, Elaine Monaghan, Mary Ormandy, Catherine Palmi, Marianne Petrou, Chez Picthall, Clare Pierotti, Andrea Powell, Mani Ramaswamy, Mark Rawley, Jake Reimann, Carolyn Ryden, David Roberts, Sands Publishing Solutions, Mary Scott, Meredith Smith, Alison Stace, Hugh Thompson, Simon Tuite, Conrad Van Dyk, Mary Villabona, Alice Wright.

ADDITIONAL PHOTOGRAPHY
Max Alexander, Peter Anderson, Apex Photo Agency: Stephen Bere, Deni Bown, June Buck, Simon Burt, Lucy Claxton, Michael Dent, Philip Dowell, Tim Draper, Mike Dunning, Chris Dyer, Andrew Einsiedel, Philip Enticknap, Jane Ewart, DK Studio/Steve Gorton, Frank Greenaway, Alison Harris, Stephen Hayward, John Heseltine, Ed Ironside, Dave King, Neil Mersh, Robert O'Dea, Ian O'Leary, Stephen Oliver, Vincent Oliver, Roger Phillips, Kim Sayer, Karl Shone, Chris Stevens, Jim Stevenson, Clive Streeter, Harry Taylor, Conrad Van Dyk, David Ward, Mathew Ward, Alan Williams, Stephen Wooster, Nick Wright, Colin Yeates.

PHOTOGRAPHIC AND ARTWORK REFERENCE
Christopher Woodward of the Building of Bath Museum, Franz Karl Freiherr von Linden, Gendall Designs, NRSC Air Photo Group, The Oxford Mail and Times, and Mark and Jane Rees.

PHOTOGRAPHY PERMISSIONS
DORLING KINDERSLEY would like to thank the following for their assistance and kind permission to photograph at their establishments: Banqueting House (Crown copyright by kind permission of Historic Royal Palaces); Cabinet War Rooms; Paul Highnam at English Heritage; Dean and Chapter Exeter Cathedral; Gatwick Airport Ltd; Heathrow Airport Ltd; Thomas Woods at Historic Scotland; Provost and Scholars Kings College; Cambridge; London Transport Museum; Madame Tussaud's; National Museums and Galleries of Wales (Museum of Welsh Life); Diana Lanham and Gayle Mault at the National Trust; Peter Reekie and Isla Roberts at the National Trust for Scotland; Provost Skene House; Saint Bartholmew the Great; Saint James's Church; London St Paul's Cathedral; Masters and Wardens of the Worshipful Company of Skinners; Provost and Chapter of Southwark Cathedral; HM Tower of London; Dean and Chapter of Westminster; Dean and Chapter of Worcetser Cathedral and all the other churches, museums, hotels, restaurants, shops, galleries and sights too numerous to thank individually.

PICTURE CREDITS
t = top; tl = top left; tlc = top left centre; tc = top centre; tr = top right; cla = centre left above; ca = centre above; cra = centre right above; cl = centre left; c = centre; cr = centre right; clb = centre left below; cb = centre below; crb = centre right below; bl = bottom left; b = bottom; bc = bottom centre; bcl = bottom centre left; br = bottom right; d = detail.

Works of art have been reproduced with the permission of the following copyright holders: © ADAGP, Paris and DACS, London 2006: 171t; © Alan Bowness, Hepworth Estate 277bl; © Fondazione Lucio Fontana 121tr; © The Estate of Patrick Heron/DACS, London 2006: 240cb; © D Hockney: 91tr, 411t; © Estate of Stanley Spencer/DACS, London 2006 235t; © Cy Twombly 121clb; © Angela Verren-Taunt/DACS, London 2006: 277br.

The work of Henry Moore, *Large Two Forms*, 1966, illustrated on page 413b *Recumbent Figure* 1938 illustrated on page 91c has been reproduced by permission of the Henry Moore Foundation.

The publisher would like to thank the following individuals, companies and picture libraries for permission to reproduce their photographs:

ABBOT HALL ART GALLERY AND MUSEUM, Kendal: 370b(d); ABERDEEN ART GALLERIES 540t; ABERDEEN AND GRAMPIAN TOURIST BOARD 479ca; ACTION PLUS: 67t; 480t; 434c; David Davies 67cr; Peter Tarry 66cla, 67bl; Printed by kind permission of MOHAMED AL FAYED: 97t; ALAMY IMAGES: Peter Adams Photography 11tr; Gina Calvi 373tl; Bertrand Collet 488cl; Nick Higham 375b; Angus Palmer 217b; Edward Parker 11br; Andrew Wiard 61crb; AMERICAN MUSEUM, Bath: 261tl; ANCIENT ART AND ARCHITECTURE COLLECTION: 42cb, 44ca, 44clb, 45ca, 45clb, 46bl, 46br, 48crb, 51ca, 232tl, 235br, 439t; THE ARCHIVE & BUSINESS RECORDS CENTRE, University of Glasgow: 483t; T & R ANNAN AND SONS: 516b(d); ASHMOLEAN MUSEUM, OXFORD: 47t. Barnaby's PICTURE LIBRARY: 60ca; BEAMISH OPEN AIR MUSEUM: 424c, 415b, 425ca, 425cb, 425b; BRIDGEMAN ART LIBRARY, LONDON AND NEW YORK: Agnew and Sons, London 323t; Museum of Antiquities, Newcastle upon Tyne 44tl; Apsley House, The Wellington Museum, London 30tl; Bibliotheque Nationale, Paris *Neville Book of Hours* 322t(d); Birgmingham City Museums and Gallery 319t; Bonham's, London, *Portrait of Lord Nelson with Santa Cruz Beyond,* Lemeul Francis Abbot 54cb(d); Bradford Art Galleries and Museums 49clb; City of Bristol Museums and Art Galleries 256c; British Library, London, *Pictures and Arms of English Kings and Knights* 4t(d), 39t(d), *The Kings of England from Brutus to Henry* 26bl(d), *Stowe manuscript* 40tl(d), *Liber Legum Antiquorum Regum* 46t(d), *Calendar Anglo-Saxon Miscellany* 46–7t(d), 46–7c(d), 46–7b(d), *Decrees of Kings of Anglo-Saxon and Norman England* 47clb, 49bl(d), *Portrait of Chaucer,* Thomas Occleve 49br(d), *Portrait of Shakespeare,* Droeshurt 51bl(d), *Historia Anglorum* 40bl(d), 236tl(d), *Chronicle of Peter of Langtoft* 285b(d), *Lives and Miracles* of St Cuthbert 419tl(d), 419cl(d), 419cr(d), *Lindisfarne Gospels* 419br(d), *Commendatio Lamentabilis intransitu Edward IV* 436b(d), *Histoire du Roy d'Angleterre Richard II* 438t(d), 537b; Christies, London 445t; Claydon House, Bucks, *Florence Nightingale*, Sir William Blake Richmond 162t; Department of Environment, London 48tr; City of Edinburgh Museums and Galleries, *Chief of Scottish Clan*, Eugene Deveria 484bl(d); Fitzwilliam Museum, University of Cambridge, *George IV as Prince Regent*, Richard Cosway 179cb, 212bl, *Flemish Book of Hours* 350tl(d); Giraudon/ Musee de la Tapisserie, with special authorization of the city of Bayeux 47b,181bl; Guildhall Library, Corporation of London, *The Great Fire*, Marcus Willemsznik 53bl(d), *Bubbler's Melody* 54br(d), *Triumph of Steam and Electricity*, The Illustrated London News 57t(d), *Great Exhibition, The transept from Dickenson's Comprehensive Pictures* 56–7, *A Balloon View of London as seen from Hampstead* 105c(d); Harrogate Museum and Art Gallery, North Yorkshire 388t; Holburne Museum and Crafts Study Centre, Bath 53t; Imperial War Museum, *London Field Marshall Montgomery*, J Worsley 31cbr(d); Kedleston Hall, Derbyshire 28br; King Street Galleries, London, *Bonnie Prince Charlie*, G Dupré 482tl; Lambeth Palace Library, London, *St Alban's Chronicle* 49t; Lever Brothers Ltd, Cheshire 349cra; Lincolnshire County Council, Usher Gallery, Lincoln, *Portrait of Mrs Fitzherbert after Richard Cosway* 179b; London Library, *The Barge Tower from Ackermann's World in miniature*, F Scoberl 55t; Manchester Art Gallery, UK, *Etruscan Vase Painters* 1871, Sir Lawrence Alma-Tadema 374b; Manchester City Art Galleries 373b; David Messum Gallery, London 447b; National Army Museum, London, *Bunker's Hill*, R Simkin 54ca; National Gallery, London, *Mrs Siddons the Actress*, Thomas Gainsborough 54t(d), 163ca; National Museet, Copenhagen 46ca; Phillips, the International Fine Art Auctioneers, *James I*, John the Elder Decritz 52b(d); Private Collections: 8–9, 30ca(d), 48–9, 55cla, 55bl, 56clb, Vanity Fair 57br, 163t, *Ellesmere Manuscript* 188b(d), *Armada: map of the Spanish and British Fleets*, Robert Adam 298t, 396t, 422b; Royal Geographical Society, London 163cb(d); Royal Holloway & Bedford New College, the *Princes Edward and Richard in the Tower*, Sir John Everett Millais 121b; Smith Art Gallery and Museum, Stirling 496b; Tate Gallery, London: 56crb, 237t; Thyssen-Bornemisza Collection, Lugo Casta, *King Henry VIII*, Hans Holbein the Younger 50b(d); Victoria and Albert Museum, London 28t(d), 56b, 97c, 204t, 351cr, 393b, *Miniature of Mary Queen of Scots*, by a follower of Francois Clouet 511br, 537t(d); Walker Art Gallery, Liverpool 378c; Westminster Abbey, London, *Henry VII Tomb effigy*, Pietro Torrigiano 30br(d), 40bc(d); The Trustees of the Weston Park Foundation, *Portrait of Richard III*, Italian School 49cla(d); Christopher Wood Gallery, London, *High Life Below Stairs*, Charles Hunt 29c(d); BFI LONDON IMAX CINEMA WATERLOO: Richard Holttum 153c; BRITISH LIBRARY BOARD: *Cotton Faustina BVII folio 85* 49cb, 109cl; © THE BRITISH MUSEUM: 42cr, 43cb, 73tl, 85c, 103, 106–7 all except 107t and 107bl; © THE BRONTE SOCIETY: 412 all; BURTON CONSTABLE FOUNDATION: Dr David Connell 350t. CADOGEN MANAGEMENT: 84b; CADW – Welsh Historic Monuments (Crown Copyright), 474t; CAMERA PRESS: Cecil Beaton 92bl; CARDIFF CITY COUNCIL: 472tr, 473t, 473c; CASTLE HOWARD ESTATE LTD: 399tl; COLIN DE CHAIRE: 197c; TRUSTEES OF THE CHATSWORTH SETTLEMENT: 334b, 335b; MUSEUM OF CHILDHOOD, Edinburgh: 510b; BRUCE COLEMAN LTD: 35br; Stephen Bond 294b; Jane Burton 35cra; Mark N. Boulton 35cl; Patrick Clement 34clb; Peter Evans 544tl; Paul van Gaalen 250tl; Sir Jeremy Grayson 35bl; Harald Lange 34bc; Gordon Langsbury 545t; George McCarthy 34t, 35bl, 242b, 285br; Paul Meitz 528clb; Dr. Eckart Pott 34bl, 528t; Hans Reinhard 34cb, 35tc, 294t, 494tl; Dr Frieder Sauer 534t; N Schwiatz 35clb; Kim Taylor 35tl, 528cra; Konrad Wothe 528ca; COLLECTIONS: Liz Stares 30tr, Yuri Lewinski 373tl; CORBIS: Bruce Burkhardt 295c; Ashley Cooper 12tr; Eurasia Press/ Steven Vidler 437br; Tim Graham 3br, 95bl; John Heseltine 111br; Angelo Hornak 117tc; Sygma/Sandro Vannini 11bl; JOE CORNISH: 403b; DOUG CORRANCE: 485b; JOHN CROOK: 171b; DESIGN MUSEUM: Amelia Webb 117bl; 1805 CLUB: 31t; 1853

Gallery, Bradford 411t; EMPICS LTD: Nigel French 66bl; Tony Marshall 66tl, 66c; ENGLISH HERITAGE: 126b, 208c, 208b, 209b, 248–9b, 263b, 350br, 351b, 394t, 419tr, 419c; Avebury Museum 42ca; Devizes Museum 42br, drawing by Frank Gardiner 423br; Salisbury Museum 42t, 42bl; Skyscan Balloon Photography 43t, 262b; 394t; 423bl; ENGLISH LIFE PUBLICATIONS LTD, Derby: 342tl, 342tr, 343t, 343b; ET ARCHIVE: 41tc, 41cr, 52cb, 53clb, 58crb, 162b; Bodleian Library, Oxford 48crb; British Library, London 48tl, 48ca; Devizes Museum 42cl, 43b, 262c; Garrick Club 436tl(d); Imperial War Museum, London 58clb(d), 59br; Labour Party Archives 60bc; London Museum 43cla; Magdalene College 50ca; National Maritime Museum, London 39b; Stoke Museum Staffordshire Polytechnic 41bc, 52tl; Victoria & Albert Museum, London 50t(d); MARY EVANS PICTURE LIBRARY: 9 inset, 40br, 41tl, 41cl, 41bl, 41br, 44bl, 44br, 46cb, 47cla, 51t, 51cb, 51br, 53crb, 54bl, 55br, 56tl, 58ca, 59ca, 59clb, 59crb, 79cb, 104t,105t, 157 inset, 162cb, 163b, 187c, 189c, 195b, 206c, 222bl, 228tl, 231c, 231bl, 231br, 234bl, 239 inset, 278t, 295 inset, 336b, 349t, 349cla, 420t, 447tl, 482b, 499b, 512bl, 514b, 515t, 535b. CHRIS FAIRCLOUGH: 295b, 352b; FALKIRK WHEEL: 507b; PAUL FELIX: 234c; FFOTOGRAFF © Charles Aithie: 435t; FISHBOURNE ROMAN VILLA: 45t; LOUIS FLOOD: 484br; FOREIGN AND BRITISH BIBLE SOCIETY: Cambridge University Library 435c; FOTOMAS INDEX: 105cra. GARDEN PICTURE LIBRARY: J S Sira 27crt; John Glover 27rb; Steven Wooster 26–27t; GETTY IMAGES: 61cr; Matthew Stockman 66crb; GLASGOW MUSEUMS: Burrell Collection 521ca, 520–1 all except 520tl; Art Gallery & Museum, Kelvingrove 519t, 531b, 543b(d); Saint Mungo Museum of Religious Life and Art 517tl; Museum of Transport 518cr; JOHN GLOVER: 62cr, 160cb, 205b; THE GORE HOTEL, London: 554c. SONIA HALLIDAY AND LAURA LUSHINGTON ARCHIVE: 409t; ROBERT HARDING PICTURE LIBRARY: 182t, 548t, 60cra; Jan Baldwin 287b; M H Black 288t; L Bond 337b; Michael Botham 36br; Nelly Boyd 374tl; Lesley Burridge 304tr; Martyn F Chillman 305bc; Philip Craven 103t, 200b, 324b; Nigel Francis 219b; Robert Francis 66–7; Paul Freestone 226b; Sylvain Gradadom 295tl; Brian Harrison 529b; Van der Hars 538t; Michael Jenner 45b, 529c; Norma Joseph 65b; Christopher Nicholson 253t; B O'Connor 37ca; Jenny Pate 161bc; Rainbird Collection 47crb; Roy Rainsford 37b, 168t, 298b, 338cr, 368t, 386t, 475b; Walter Rawling 25t; Hugh Routledge 2–3; Peter Scholey 299t; Michael Short 305br; James Strachen 384b; Julia K Thorne 486bl; Adina Tovy 61tl, 486br; Andy Williams 179t, 234br, 346c, 432t, 524; Adam Woolfitt 24t, 24c, 44tr, 45crb, 260b, 272, 287ca, 305bl, 439bl, 468tl, 544tr; HAREWOOD HOUSE: 410c; PAUL HARRIS: 36t, 62cl, 301bl(d), 338b, 367b; HARROGATE INTERNATIONAL CENTRE: 389b; HAYWARD GALLERY: Richard Haughton 273tl; Crown copyright is reproduced with the permission of the Controller of HMSO: 73br, 118bl, 118br, 119tl; CATHEDRAL CHURCH OF THE BLESSED VIRGIN MARY AND ST ETHELBERT IN HEREFORD: 316b; HERTFORDSHIRE COUNTY COUNCIL: Bob Norris 58–9; JOHN HESELTINE: 76t, 102, 107t, 108, 250tr, 250c, 469tl; HISTORIC ROYAL PALACES (Crown Copyright): 4crb, 118cla, 173, 235 all; HISTORIC SCOTLAND (Crown Copyright): 497c, 506tr, 506c, 5–7bl; PETER HOLLINGS: 348bl; NEIL HOLMES: 258b(d), 260c, 286t, 371b, 429tl, 429tr, 451b; ANGELO HORNAK LIBRARY: 406tl, 406bl, 406br, 409br; Reproduced by permission of the CLERK OF RECORDS, HOUSE OF LORDS: 483c; DAVID MARTIN HUGHES: 156–7, 164; HULTON-DEUTSCH COLLECTION: 26c, 26tr, 31cl, 31cr, 53cla, 54c, 56c, 57cb, 58tl 58tr, 58b, 59t, 60bl, 162ca, 169c, 233b, 300t, 348c, 349crb, 350bl, 377b, 397b, 398br, 437t, 495b, 522tl, 536b; HUNTERIAN ART GALLERY: 519b; Bernard Gerad 481t; HUTTON IN THE FOREST: Lady Inglewood 358t. David Gould 357b; Colin Molyneux 469bl; Trevor Wood 286b; Simon Wilkinson 180b; Terry Williams 112tc; IMAGES COLOUR LIBRARY: 34cla, 43c, 221b, 234t, 249t, 250bl, 251b, 336b, 338cl, 339t, 352c; Horizon/Robert Estall 438c; Landscape Only 37cb, 248, 365, 439br; IMPERIAL WAR MUSEUM NORTH: 375t; IRONBRIDGE MUSEUM: 317b. JARROLD PUBLISHERS: 212br, 229t(d), 304bl; MICHAEL JENNER: 304tl, 340b, 528b; JORVIK VIKING CENTRE, York: 405t. FRANK LANE PICTURE AGENCY: 400b(d); W Broadhurst 254b; Michael Callan 242crb; ANDREW LAWSON: 27c, 27cb, 244br, 245tl, 245tr, 245br; LEEDS CASTLE ENTERPRISES: 165b; LEIGHTON HOUSE, Royal Borough of Kensington: 122br; published by kind permission DEAN AND CHAPTER OF LINCOLN 340t, 341cb, 341bl; LINCOLNSHIRE COUNTY COUNCIL: USHER GALLERY, Lincoln: c 1820 by William Ilbery 341bl; LLANGOLEN INTERNATIONAL MUSICAL EISTEDDFOD 450c; LONDON AQUARIUM: 3c; LONDON FILM FESTIVAL: 62t; LONDON TRANSPORT MUSEUM: 84t; LONGLEAT HOUSE: 266t; THE LOWRY COLLECTION, Salford: *Coming From the Mill,* *1930,* L.S. Lowry 371tr. MADAME TUSSAUDS: 104b; MAGNA: 353b; MALDOM MILLENNIUM TRUST: 209t; MANSELL COLLECTION, London: 31clb, 40tr, 52ca, 55cb, 261tr, 323bl, 349clb, 402b; NICK MEERS: 22t, 238–9; ARCHIE MILES: 240ca; SIMON MILES: 352tr; MINACK THEATRE: Murray King 276b; MIRROR SYNDICATION INTERNATIONAL: 74b, 87b, 112; MUSEUM OF LONDON: 44crb, 113t; NATIONAL FISHING HERITAGE CENTRE, Grimsby: 403t; NATIONAL GALLERY, London: 73tr, 82–3 all; NATIONAL GALLERY OF SCOTLAND: *The Reverend Walker Skating on Duddington Loch,* Sir Henry Raeburn 504c(d); NATIONAL LIBRARY OF WALES: 436tr, 439c(d), 467b; NATIONAL MUSEUM OF FILM AND TELEVISION, Bradford: 411c; Board of Trustees of the NATIONAL MUSEUMS AND GALLERIES ON MERSEYSIDE: Liverpool Museum 379t; Maritime Museum 377t; Walker Art Gallery 346b, 378tl, 378tr, 378b, 379c; NATIONAL MUSEUMS OF SCOTLAND: 505t, 511bl; NATIONAL MUSEUM OF WALES: 436c; By courtesy of the NATIONAL PORTRAIT GALLERY, London: *First Earl of Essex,* Hans Peter Holbein 351t(d); NATIONAL TRUST MUSEUM, Crich: 339c; NATIONAL TRUST PHOTOGRAPHIC LIBRARY: *Bess of Hardwick (Elizabeth, Countess of Shrewsbury),* Anon 334tl(d); Mathew Antrobus 302br, 390cl, 391bl; Oliver Benn 29br, 278c, 293bl, 390b; John Bethell 279c, 279bl, 279br, 303t; Nick Carter 255b; Joe Cornish 456; Prudence Cumming 267c; Martin Dohrn 50crb; Andreas Von Einsidedel 29bl, 302cb, 303ca; Roy Fox 271t; Geoffry Frosh 289t; Jerry Harpur 244t, 244bl; Derek Harris 244clb, 267t; Nadia MacKenzie 28cl; Nick Meers 266b, 267b, 320b; Rob Motheson 292t; Ian Shaw 460t; Richard Surman 303br, 362b; Rupert Truman 303br, 379; Andy Tryner 302bl; Charlie Waite 391t; Jeremy Whitaker 303bc, 393t, 460b; Mike Williams 302ca, 391c; George Wright 244crb, 292c; NATIONAL TRUST FOR SCOTLAND: 478b, 500b, 501c, 508b, 522tr, 523tl, 523tr, 523br; Glyn Satterley 523bl; Lindsey Robertson 523bl; NATIONAL WATERWAYS MUSEUM AT GLOUCESTER: 301bc, 301br; NHPA: Martin Garwood 395ca; Daniel Heuclin 282la; NATURE PHOTOGRAPHERS: Andrew Cleave 242cla; E A James 35cla, 360t; Hugh Miles 421t; Owen Newman 35ca; William Paton 528crb; Paul Sterry 34crb, 34br, 35cb, 35crb, 234c, 255t, 387t, 528cla; Roger Tidman 197b; NETWORK PHOTOGRAPHERS: Laurie Sparham 480b; NEW SHAKESPEARE THEATRE CO: 153t; NORFOLK MUSEUMS SERVICE: Norwich Castle Museum 201b; OXFORD SCIENTIFIC FILMS: Okapia 282lb; 'PA' NEWS PHOTO LIBRARY: John Stillwell 61cr. PALACE THEATRE ARCHIVE: 152c; PHOTOS HORTICULTURAL: 161tlc, 161cra, 161cb, 161crb, 244ca, 245c; PLANET EARTH PICTURES: David Phillips 27crca; POPPERFOTO: 31br, 59bl, 60cb, 60br, 61bc, 86tl, 160tr, 203t, 284cl, 444b; AFP/ Eric Feferber 61br; SG Forester 67br; PORT MERION LTD: 454cr, 454tl; PRESS ASSOCIATION: Martin Keene 62b; PUBLIC RECORD OFFICE (Crown Copyright): 48b. ROB REICHENFELD: 174t, 175c, 175b, 300b; REUTERS: Ho New 61tr; REX FEATURES LTD: 31ca, 41tr, 60tl, 61lb, 236c, 237br; Barry Beattie 259cl; Peter Brooke 31bc; Nils Jorgensen 30c; Hazel Murray 61tl; Tess, Renn-Burrill Productions 269b; Brian Rasic 63t; Nick Rogers 61tr; Tim Rooke 64cr, 66tr; Sipa/Chesnot 31bl; Today 25c; Richard Young 60tl; REX FEATURES: Jonathon Player 294cla; THE RITZ, London: 81t; ROYAL ACADEMY OF ARTS, London: 84ca; Royal Collection © 1995 Her Majesty Queen Elizabeth II: *The Family of Henry VIII,* Anon 38(d), 85c, 86tr, 86bl, 87t, 236tr, 237tl(d), 237tr, 237bl, *George IV, in full Highland dress,* Sir David Wilkie 485t; David Cripps 87c; John Freeman 88br; ROYAL COLLEGE OF MUSIC, London: 96c; ROYAL PAVILION, ART GALLERY AND MUSEUMS, Brighton: 178c, 178bl, 178br, 179cl, 179cr; ROYAL BOTANIC GARDENS, Kew:74ca; ROYAL SHAKESPEARE THEATRE COMPANY: Donald Cooper 327c(d). ST. ALBAN'S MUSEUMS: Verulamium Museum 232b; ST. PAULS CATHEDRAL: Sampson Lloyd 114tr, 114cl, 114clb; SARTAJ BALTI HOUSE: Clare Carnegie 411b; SCOTTISH NATIONAL GALLERY OF MODERN ART: Roy Lichtenstein In the Car 507c; SCOTTISH NATIONAL PORTRAIT GALLERY: on loan from the collection of the Earl of Roseberry, *Execution of Charles I,* Unknown Artist 52–3; SIDMOUTH FOLK FESTIVAL: Derek Brooks 289b; SKYSCAN BALLOON PHOTO-GRAPHY: 262t; JOHN SNOCKEN: 27cr, 27ra; SOUTHBANK PRESS OFFICE: 154t; SPORTING PICTURES: 66cra, 66bc, 66br, 67cl, 358b; STILL MOVING PICTURES: Doug Corrance 548b; Wade Cooper 483b; Derek Laird 482c; Robert Lees 65t; STB 544br, 545c, Paisley Museum 515b, Paul Tomkins 529tr; SJ Whitehorn 495t; DAVID TARN: 389tl; Rex A.Butcher 81c; Richard Elliott 64b; Rob Talbot 353ca; David Woodfall 440; © TATE BRITAIN: 73bl, 91all; © TATE MODERN: 121tr, 121clb, 121bc; *Soft Drain Pipe – Blue (Cool) Version,* 1967 © Claes Oldenburg 121c; © TATE ST. IVES: 277cr, 277clb, 277br; ROB TALBOT: 353cb; TRANSPORT FOR LONDON: 378cl; TUILLE HOUSE MUSEUM, Carlisle: 358c; URBIS: 372c; courtesy of the Board of Trustees of the VICTORIA AND ALBERT MUSUEM, London: 72b, 98–99. CHARLIE WAITE: 549t; © WALES TOURIST BOARD: 433c, 434b, 438–9, 468br, 469tr, 469br; Roger Vitos 468tl, 468bl; THE WALLACE COLLECTION, London: 104cb; DAVID WARD: 525b, 543t; FREDERICK WARNE & CO: 367t(d); © WARWICK CASTLE: 323cra; Roger Vitos 468tl, 468bl; Courtesy of the Trustees of THE WEDGWOOD MUSEUM, Barlaston, Staffordshire, England: 311b; DEAN AND CHAPTER OF WESTMINSTER: 93bl; Tony Middleton 92bc; JEREMY WHITAKER: 228tr, 228c, 229b; WHITWORTH ART GALLERY, University of Manchester: courtesy of Granada Television Arts Foundation 374c; CHRISTOPHER WILSON: 404bl; WILTON HOUSE TRUST: 265b; WINCHESTER CATHEDRAL: 171t; WOBURN ABBEY – by kind permission of the Marquess of Tavistock and Trustees of the Bedford Estate: 50–1, 230t; TIMOTHY WOODCOCK PHOTOLIBRARY: 5b; Photo © WOODMAN-STERNE, Watford, UK: Jeremy Marks 114t, 115t. YORK CASTLE MUSEUM: 405cb; YORK CITY ART GALLERY: 407bl; DEAN & CHAPTER YORK MINSTER: 409cla, 409ca, 409cl; Peter Gibson 409cra, 409cr, 409cl; Jim Korshaw 406tr; Reproduced couresty of the YORKSHIRE MUSEUM: 408c; YORKSHIRE SCULPTURE PARK: Jerry Hardman Jones 413t. ZEFA: 64t, 154b, 263t, 269t, 486c; Bob Croxford 63cr; Weir 197t.

Front Endpaper: All special photography except ROBERT HARDING PICTURE LIBRARY/Andy Williams tl, Adam Woolfitt bl; DAVID MARTIN HUGHES brl; NATIONAL TRUST PHOTOGRAPHIC LIBRARY/ Joe Cornish clc; TONY STONE IMAGES/David Woodfall cl. Back Endpaper: All special photography except JOHN HESELTINE tl, br.

JACKET
Front – PHOTOLIBRARY: David Sellman. Back – CORBIS: Loop Images.

All other images © Dorling Kindersley. For further information see www.DKimages.com